EIGHTH EDITION

COGNITION
Theories and Applications

Stephen K. Reed
San Diego State University

WADSWORTH
CENGAGE Learning™

Australia • Brazil • Canada • Mexico • Singapore Spain • United Kingdom • United States

WADSWORTH
CENGAGE Learning™

Cognition: Theories and Applications, Eighth Edition

Stephen K. Reed

Senior Publisher: Linda Schreiber

Senior Acquisitions Editor: Jaime Perkins

Assistant Editor: Paige Leeds

Editorial Assistant: Philip Hovanessian

Associate Media Editor: Rachel Guzman

Marketing Manager: Elizabeth Rhoden

Marketing Assistant: Molly Felz

Marketing Communications Manager: Talia Wise

Project Management, Editorial Production: Pre-Press PMG

Creative Director: Rob Hugel

Art Director: Vernon Boes

Print Buyer: Karen Hunt

Permissions Editor: Bob Kauser

Production Service: Pre-Press PMG

Copy Editor: Pre-Press PMG

Cover Designer: Lisa Delgado

Cover Image: ©Guy Grenier/Masterfile

Compositor: Pre-Press PMG

For product information and technology assistance contact us at **Cengage Learning Academic Resource Center 1-800-423-0563**

For permission to use material from this text or product submit allrequests online at **www.cengage.com/permissions** Further permissions questions can be emailed to **permissionrequest@cengage.com**

Library of Congress Control Number: 2008942959

ISBN-13: 978-0-495-60230-9

ISBN-10: 0-495-60230-2

Wadsworth
10 Davis Drive
Belmont, CA 94002-3098
USA

Cengage Learning products are represented in Canada byNelson Education, Ltd.

For your course and learning solutions, visit **academic.cengage.com** Purchase any of our products at your local college store or at our preferred online store **www.ichapters.com**

Printed in the United States of America
1 2 3 4 5 6 7 8 9 12 11 10 09

To my parents,
Anita M. Reed and the memory of Kenneth D. Reed

BRIEF CONTENTS

CONTENTS

3 Attention   45

4 Short-Term Working Memory   73

PREFACE

COGNITION IN THE CONTEXT OF EVERYDAY LIFE

The most exciting development in the field of cognitive psychology is not a particular theory or experimental finding but a general trend. Cognitive psychologists have demonstrated an increasing interest in studying complex, real-world tasks and are making significant progress in understanding how people perform on these tasks. I hope that one result of this trend will be that undergraduates discover the direct relevance of cognitive psychology to many of their daily activities.

In this book I have attempted to place a greater emphasis on the application of cognitive psychology than is typically found in an undergraduate text. The study of reading, for example, is discussed in the chapters on pattern recognition, attention, language, and text comprehension. Efficient learning strategies are major topics in the chapters on long-term memory and visual imagery. The chapter on expertise and creativity shows how the study of problem solving is currently being extended to include the kinds of problems students encounter in their courses. The chapter on decision making includes a section on applications to jury decisions and to emergency situations.

To help students relate the study of cognition to popular articles they are likely to read, I have included many magazine and newspaper clippings on such contemporary topics as fading memories of the World Trade Center attack and biased decisions by jurors.

APPROACH OF THE BOOK

I use three criteria for selecting material. The first is whether the material makes an important contribution to cognitive psychology. The second is whether it is accessible to students. Will they understand it and find it interesting?

The third is whether it can be easily integrated with other material in the book. There must be a clear flow of ideas to tell a coherent story. Three major topics appear throughout the book:

1. Theoretical Work

Cognitive psychologists are interested in forming theories of how the mind works.

2. Research

Research is typically performed to evaluate previous theories or to propose new theories.

3. Cognitive Neuroscience

The study of the brain (cognitive neuroscience) provides additional information for evaluating theories. Examples of this approach include the discussion of brain structures and methodology (Chapter 1), neural network models (Chapter 2), the use of brain imaging to study conversations on cell phones (Chapter 3), the use of positron-emission tomography (PET) scans to show that storage and rehearsal of verbal information occur in different parts of the brain (Chapter 4), the proposal that different brain areas support implicit and explicit memory (Chapter 5), the effect of brain damage on disrupting verbal rehearsal (Chapter 6), the importance of brain studies to identify when we use visual imagery (Chapter 7), the effect of brain damage on memory loss (Chapter 8), and the localization of different language disorders in either Broca's area or Wernicke's area of the brain (Chapter 10). These studies provide students with a grounding in cognitive neuroscience that should help prepare them for a more specialized course.

ORGANIZATION OF THE BOOK

The 14 chapters in the book cover a wide range of topics, and instructors should be able to expand on whatever topics interest them. The book is divided into three parts: Information-Processing Stages, Representation and Organization of Knowledge, and Complex Cognitive Skills. Part One consists of an introductory chapter followed by chapters on pattern recognition, attention, short-term working memory, and long-term memory. The chapters describe what occurs during the different information-processing stages and how the stages interact. Part Two contains chapters on memory codes, visual images, categorization, and semantic organization. The first two chapters in this part describe qualitatively different memory codes, and the next two chapters discuss the organization of knowledge in long-term memory. Part Three consists of chapters on language, comprehension and memory for text, problem solving, expertise and creativity, and decision making. The discussion of these complex cognitive skills is often related to ideas presented earlier in the book.

The organization of a book on cognition should reflect what we actually know about cognition. Research suggests that a hierarchy is a particularly

partitioned into categories, which are further partitioned into smaller categories. Hierarchical organization seems to be particularly effective when the number of partitions varies from two to five. I deliberately selected such a structure for this book in the hope that the material would thereby be more accessible to students. In addition to the organization of chapters into three parts, the material in each chapter is organized into manageable sections and subsections. You should study the outline at the beginning of each chapter for an overview of the topics.

CHANGES IN THE EIGHTH EDITION

I have made changes in each of the 14 chapters. The chapter summaries in Chapter 1 now include applications. Chapter 2 has a new section on faces and a recent version of the interactive-activation model that incorporates neurological findings. Chapter 3 contains new material on training attentive skills in young drivers and cognitive neuroscience research that shows how cell phones diminish attention to driving. Chapter 4 now presents a more integrated discussion of Baddeley's working memory model, including its relation to LTM. The section on Control Processes in Chapter 5 is now labeled Metacognition and includes additional material on this topic.

Chapter 6 discusses neurological evidence for why people have enhanced confidence, but not accuracy, in recalling emotional events and how transfer-appropriate processing is related to metacomprehension. Chapter 7 has new material on enhanced vividness ratings of images by schizophrenics. Chapter 8 relates semantic dementia to Rosch's theory of hierarchical organization and to cognitive neuroscience. In Chapter 9 the perceptual symbols model is now a major section with expanded coverage. There is also a discussion of the brain regions involved in retrieval of autobiographical memories.

A new section on Embodied Cognition in Chapter 10 continues the discussion introduced in Chapter 9 to show how mental simulations support the comprehension of language. Chapter 11 has a new section on applications that includes text comprehension strategies and assessment. Chapter 12 shows how schema abstraction helps business consultants learn negotiation strategies. Chapter 13 includes updated material on the Cognitive Tutor and a graphics-oriented approach to learning. Chapter 14 contains recent material on adaptive heuristics and on how the want-should dilemma influences utilities.

Instructor's Manual with Test Bank on eBank (0-495-17152-2)

The Instructor's Manual with Test Bank contains chapter outlines, learning objectives, 40 multiple-choice, 10 true/false, 2 to 3 critical thinking, and 5 essay questions per chapter. The Electronic Transparencies and Interactive Demonstrations CD-ROM. Examview® (0-495-17153-0), a computerized testing package that allows teachers to see the test they are creating, is available to adopters of *Cognition: Theories and Applications*, Eighth Edition.

CogLab: An Optional Accompaniment to the Text

CogLab is a set of demonstrations of classic experiments and concepts from cognitive psychology. CogLab allows students to experience a variety of important experimental studies, which should help them to understand each experiment, the data, and the significance of the study. Essentially, the students participate in classic experiments as subjects—so they run the experiment, get an experimental result, and are able to export their data of results to a statistical package. CogLab comes in two different formats: a Web-based version and on CD-ROM. Each has a separate student manual that provides a write-up on the background of the experiment, basic questions about the experiment, advanced questions—and for some experiments, discussion questions—so you as the teacher may assign these questions. The instructor's manual that accompanies this book has a CogLab section that provides answers to questions from the CogLab student manual and also provides test questions on the CogLab experiments.

You will notice that at the end of appropriate chapters, there is a list of CogLab experiments related to material in that chapter. Turn to the endpapers at the front of this book for the Web address that allows you to see CogLab, **http://coglab.wadsworth.com**. You'll find ordering information in the front of the book, as well. CogLab online or on CD-ROM can be purchased at a nominal price, or it can be purchased at the higher, stand-alone price, which is comparable to that of study guides.

Electronic Transparencies and Interactive Demonstrations (0-495-17154-9)

These transparencies include figures and tables from the text, as well as more than 150 demonstrations in Microsoft® PowerPoint®.

Text Companion Website (0-4951-7151-4)

This robust website of rich teaching and learning resources includes chapter-by-chapter online tutorial quizzes, including a final exam, chapter-by-chapter weblinks, flashcards, and a glossary.

ACKNOWLEDGMENTS

I wrote the first edition of this book while spending a sabbatical year at the University of California at Berkeley. I am grateful to Case Western Reserve University and the Group in Science and Mathematics Education at Berkeley for providing financial support during that year. The Group in Science and Mathematics Education also furnished me with a stimulating environment, and the Institute of Human Learning provided an excellent library. Shortly after arriving at Berkeley, I had the good fortune to meet C. Deborah Laughton, a psychology editor at the time. She expressed confidence in the book long before it was deserved and, with the assistance of an excellent staff and first-rate reviewers, helped in the development of the text.

I am grateful to Jaime Perkins, Jared Sterzer, and all the others listed on page iv who have contributed to this Eighth Edition. I would also like to thank the following reviewers for their helpful suggestions on this edition: Tom Alley, Clemson University; Richard A. Block, Montana State University; Mary Jo Carnot, Chadron State College; Rajal Cohen, Pennsylvania State University; Mike Dillinger, San Jose State University; Julie Evey, University of Southern Indiana; Nancy Franklin, SUNY—Stony Brook; John Geiger, Cameron University; Gary Gillund, The College of Wooster; Lowell Groninger, University of Maryland—Baltimore County; Brenda Hannon, University of Texas—San Antonio; Laree Huntsman, San Jose State University; Bennett Schwartz, Florida International University; Greg Simpson, The University of Kansas; Ami L. Spears, Mercer University; Xiao Tian Wang, University of South Dakota; and Deanne Westerman, SUNY—Binghampton.

The comments of others are always welcome, and I would appreciate receiving suggestions from readers.

ABOUT THE AUTHOR

STEPHEN K. REED is currently professor of psychology and a member of the Center for Research in Mathematics and Science Education at San Diego State University. He has also taught at Florida Atlantic University (1980–1988) and at Case Western Reserve University (1971–1980). After receiving his BS in psychology from the University of Wisconsin in 1966 and his PhD in psychology from the University of California, Los Angeles, in 1970, Dr. Reed worked as an NIH postdoctoral fellow at the Laboratory of Experimental Psychology at the University of Sussex, Brighton, England. His research on problem solving, carried out in part through grants from NIMH, the National Science Foundation, and the Air Force Office of Scientific Research, has been extensively published in numerous journals, including *Cognition and Instruction*; *Cognitive Psychology*; *The Journal of Experimental Psychology: Learning, Memory, and Cognition*; and *Memory & Cognition*. He is the author of numerous articles and books, including *Psychological Processes in Pattern Recognition* (Academic Press, 1973), *Word Problems: Research and Curriculum Reform* (Erlbaum, 1999), and *Thinking Visually* (Taylor & Francis, in press).

COGNITION
Theories and Applications

1

Introduction

Cognitive psychology refers to all processes by which the sensory input is transformed, reduced, elaborated, stored, recovered, and used.
—Ulric Neisser (1967)

Cognition is usually defined simply as the acquisition of knowledge. However, both the acquisition and the use of knowledge involve many mental skills. If you glanced at the table of contents at the beginning of this book, you saw a list of some of these skills. Psychologists who study cognition are interested in pattern recognition, attention, memory, visual imagery, language, problem solving, and decision making.

cognitive psychology
The study of the mental operations that support people's acquisition and use of knowledge

The purpose of this book is to provide an overview of the field of **cognitive psychology**. The book summarizes experimental research in cognitive psychology, discusses the major theories in the field, and attempts to relate the research and theories to cognitive tasks that people encounter in their daily lives—for example, reading, driving, studying, judging advertising claims, evaluating legal testimony, solving problems in the classroom, and making medical decisions.

Neisser's definition of cognitive psychology quoted above reflects how psychologists study cognition. Let me repeat it for emphasis: "Cognitive psychology refers to all processes by which the sensory input is transformed, reduced, elaborated, stored, recovered, and used." This definition has several important implications. The reference to a sensory input implies that cognition begins with our contact with the external world.

Transformation of the sensory input means that our representation of the world is not just a passive registration of our physical surroundings but an active construction that can involve both reduction and elaboration. Reduction occurs when information is lost. That is, we can attend to only a small part of the physical stimulation that surrounds us, and only a small part of what we attend to can be remembered. Elaboration occurs when we add to the sensory input. For example, when you meet a friend, you may recall many shared experiences.

The storage and the recovery of information are of course what we call memory. The distinction between storage and recovery implies that the storage of information does not guarantee recovery. A good example of this distinction is the "tip of the tongue" phenomenon. Sometimes we can almost, but not quite, retrieve a word to express a particular thought or meaning. Our later recall of the word proves that the earlier failure was one of retrieval rather than one of storage. The word was stored in memory; it was simply hard to get it back out.

The last part of Neisser's definition is perhaps the most important. After information has been perceived, stored, and recovered, it must be put to good use—for example, to make decisions or to solve problems. We will learn more about problem solving and decision making in Part Three, after we review the progress that has been made in understanding perception and memory.

THE INFORMATION-PROCESSING APPROACH

human information processing The psychological approach that attempts to identify what occurs during the various stages (attention, perception, short-term memory) of processing information

The fact that cognitive psychology is often called **human information processing** reflects the predominant approach to the subject used by cognitive psychologists. The acquisition, storage, retrieval, and use of information comprise a number of separate stages, and the information processing approach attempts to identify what happens during these stages (Haber, 1969). This stage approach was influenced by the computer metaphor in which people enter, store, and retrieve data from a computer.

Figure 1.1 identifies the stages that researchers most commonly include in information-processing models. The stages are arranged in temporal order; however, because information flows in both directions, as indicated by the two-headed arrows, an earlier stage can be influenced by information in a later stage. For example, to recognize a pattern in the pattern-recognition stage, we need to store information about patterns in long-term memory.

A brief consideration of the model in Figure 1.1 provides a superficial account of the stages, each of which will be elaborated in later chapters. The **sensory store** provides brief storage for information in its original sensory form. Presumably, a sensory store exists for each of the senses, although the visual and auditory stores have been the most widely studied. The sensory store extends the amount of time that a person has to recognize a pattern. If a visual pattern is flashed on a screen for 5 msec (5 milliseconds, or 5/1000 of a second), the observer has more time than 5 msec to identify it if the visual information can be briefly maintained in a sensory store. Although the sensory store for vision lasts only approximately one-quarter of a second (250 msec), this is much longer than the 5-msec exposure.

sensory store The part of memory that holds unanalyzed sensory information for a fraction of a second, providing an opportunity for additional analysis following the physical termination of a stimulus

pattern recognition The stage of perception during which a stimulus is identified

The information in the sensory store is lost at the end of this time unless it can be identified during the **pattern recognition** stage. Most of the patterns we encounter are familiar, and recognition consists in identifying a pattern as a cat, the letter *a*, the word *ball*, and so on. When we recognize a familiar pattern, we are using information that we have previously stored in memory. If the description does not match a description of a familiar pattern, the observer may want to store the new description in memory if it is important.

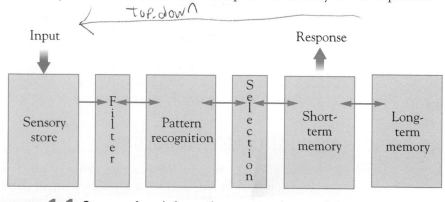

FIGURE **1.1** Stages of an information-processing model

The relation between pattern recognition and attention has been a topic of much debate. Some theorists have claimed that we can recognize only one pattern at a time. They argue that attention acts as a **filter** that determines which patterns will be recognized when many patterns arrive simultaneously. Other theorists have argued that simultaneous patterns can all be recognized but that only some of the recognized patterns will be remembered, whereas others are immediately forgotten. That is, this latter view states that attention selects the patterns that will be remembered. Because the most popular current view is that both theories are correct, depending on the circumstances, attention is represented in Figure 1.1 by both filter and **selection stages**. The filter limits the amount of information that can be recognized at one time, and the selection stage limits the amount of material that can be entered into memory.

Memory is represented in Figure 1.1 by short-term and long-term memory. We use **short-term memory (STM)**, for example, to remember a telephone number as we are dialing it. This form of memory is limited in both the amount of information it can hold (capacity) and the length of time it can hold the information (duration). Most adults can remember a seven-digit number, but they find it very difficult to remember a ten-digit number, such as an unfamiliar area code in addition to the telephone number. The limited duration of STM is illustrated by our quickly forgetting the number if we don't repeat it to ourselves by using verbal rehearsal. **Long-term memory (LTM)** has neither of the two limitations of STM. It has no limitations on the amount of information it can hold, and forgetting occurs relatively slowly, if at all.

My description of the flow of information from the sensory store to LTM is referred to as **bottom-up processing**. The name would be more descriptive if you mentally rotated Figure 1.1 90 degrees counterclockwise so that the sensory store is at the bottom of the figure and LTM is at the top. Remember that the two-headed arrows in Figure 1.1 imply that information can flow in either direction. The flow of information from LTM toward the sensory store is called **top-down processing**.

The distinction between top-down and bottom-up processing can be illustrated by attempting to recognize the word L̲ᴇᴛ̲T̲ᴇ̲ʀs. You are now using only bottom-up processing (sensory information) because the word appears out of context. Next, see if you can use the context of Figure 2.1 on page 19 to help you recognize the word. The verbal context allows you to use top-down processing based on knowledge stored in LTM regarding which words would best fit into the context of the sentence and paragraph. Hopefully, you found that this information allowed you to recognize a word that would be very difficult to recognize when taken out of context.

filter The part of attention in which some perceptual information is blocked (filtered) out and not recognized, while other information receives attention and is subsequently recognized

selection stage The stage that follows pattern recognition and determines which information a person will try to remember

short-term memory (STM) Memory that has limited capacity and that lasts only approximately 20 to 30 seconds in the absence of attending to its content

long-term memory (LTM) Memory that has no capacity limits and lasts from minutes to an entire lifetime

bottom-up processing The flow of information from the sensory store toward LTM

top-down processing The flow of information from LTM toward the sensory store

THE GROWTH OF COGNITIVE PSYCHOLOGY

It is difficult to pinpoint the exact beginning of any field of study, and cognitive psychologists would likely offer a wide variety of dates if asked when cognitive psychology began. James's *Principles of Psychology*, published in 1890, included chapters on attention, memory, imagery, and reasoning. Kohler's *The Mentality of Apes* (1925) investigated processes that occur in complex thinking. He and other Gestalt psychologists emphasized structural understanding—the ability to understand how all the parts of a problem fit together (the Gestalt). Bartlett's book *Remembering: A Study in Experimental and Social Psychology* (1932) contained a theory of memory for stories that is very consistent with current views. There are some other important articles or books that seemed modern but did not cause a major shift toward the way cognitive psychology is currently studied.

One book that had a major negative impact was Watson's *Behaviorism* (1924). The book's central theme was that psychologists should study only what they could directly observe in a person's behavior. Watson's argument lent support to a **stimulus-response (S-R)** approach, in which experimenters record how people respond to stimuli without attempting to discover the thought processes that cause the response. The S-R approach is consistent with Watson's view because the stimulus and the response are both observable. The problem with this approach is that it does not reveal exactly what the person does with the information presented in the stimulus.

By contrast, the information-processing approach seeks to identify how a person transforms information between the stimulus and the response. Psychologists who follow the latter approach seek to understand what occurs during each of the stages shown in Figure 1.1. Finding out what occurs during each of these stages is particularly important when a person has difficulty performing a task, because the psychologist can then try to identify which stage is the primary source of the difficulty.

Information Processing Gathers Momentum

The change from the S-R to the information-processing approach began to gather momentum in the middle-to-late 1950s, stimulated by the growing popularity of computers and computer programs that illustrated the different operations in information processing. Psychologists became interested in using the computer as an analog of how people process information and tried to identify how different stages of processing influence performance.

Broadbent (1958) proposed one of the first models based on an information-processing analysis—a filter model to account for performance on selective listening tasks. When subjects were asked to listen simultaneously to different messages played in each ear, they found it difficult. Broadbent proposed that many sensory inputs can simultaneously enter the sensory store, but only a single input can enter the pattern recognition stage. The filter model proposes that the listener can attend to only one message at a time; attention is controlled by the filter. Two simultaneous messages can both be recognized only if the unattended message passes through the filter before it decays from the sensory store. The filter model implies that a perceptual limitation prevents people from comprehending two messages spoken at the same time.

The year after Broadbent's filter model appeared, Sperling completed his doctoral dissertation at Harvard. In one of Sperling's tasks (1960), observers viewed a very brief exposure of an array of letters and were required to report all the letters in one of the rows of the display. The pitch of a tone signaled which row was to be reported. Sperling designed the procedure to determine whether perception or memory limited the number of letters people could

stimulus-response (S-R) The approach that emphasizes the association between a stimulus and a response, without identifying the mental operations that produced the response

report from the brief exposure. His analysis of this task resulted in an information-processing model that proposed how the sensory store, pattern recognition, and STM combined to influence performance on the task (Sperling, 1963). Both Broadbent's and Sperling's models had an important influence on subsequent information-processing theory, the former on models of auditory attention and the latter on visual recognition.

Higher Cognitive Processes

The information-processing analysis of perceptual tasks was accompanied in the late 1950s by a new approach to more complex tasks. The excitement of this new approach is described by Newell and Simon (1972). The development of digital computers after World War II led to active work in **artificial intelligence**, a field that attempts to program computers to perform intelligent tasks such as playing chess and constructing derivations in logic (Hogan, 1997). A seminar held at the RAND Corporation in the summer of 1958 aimed at showing social scientists how computer-simulation techniques could be applied to create models of human behavior. The RAND seminar had a major impact on integrating the work on computer simulation with other work on human information processing.

artificial intelligence The study of how to produce computer programs that can perform intellectually demanding tasks

One consequence of the RAND seminar was its influence on three psychologists who spent the 1958–1959 academic year at the Center for Advanced Study in the Behavioral Sciences at Stanford University. The three—George Miller, Eugene Galanter, and Karl Pribram—shared a common dissatisfaction with the then-predominant theoretical approach to psychology, which viewed human beings as bundles of S-R reflexes. Miller brought with him a large amount of material from the RAND seminar, and this material—along with other recent work in artificial intelligence, psychology, and linguistics—helped shape the view expressed in their book, *Plans and the Structure of Behavior* (Miller, Galanter, & Pribram, 1960).

plan A temporally ordered sequence of operations for carrying out some task

The authors argue that much of human behavior is planned. A **plan**, according to their formulation, consists of a list of instructions that can control the order in which a sequence of operations is to be performed. A plan is essentially the same as a program for a computer. Because the authors found it difficult to construct plans from S-R units, they proposed a new unit called TOTE, an abbreviation for Test-Operate-Test-Exit. A plan consists of a hierarchy of TOTE units. Consider a very simple plan for hammering a nail into a board. The goal is to make the head of the nail flush with the board. At the top of the hierarchy is a test to determine whether the goal has been accomplished. If the nail is flush, one can exit. If the nail sticks up, it is necessary to test the position of the hammer to determine which of two operations, lifting or striking, should be performed.

The ideas expressed by Miller, Galanter, and Pribram were influenced by earlier work in two areas outside psychology. The work of Newell, Shaw, and Simon (1958a) in the area of artificial intelligence identified strategies that people use to perform complex tasks such as playing chess. A second major influence came from the linguist Noam Chomsky, who argued that an S-R theory of language learning could not account for how people learn to comprehend and generate sentences (Chomsky, 1957). His alternative proposal—that people learn a system of rules (a grammar)—was consistent with Miller, Galanter, and Pribram's emphasis on planning.

Changing allegiance from a behavioral to a cognitive perspective required taking risks, as Miller (2003) points out in his personal account of the early years of the cognitive revolution. Miller (1951) wrote in the preface to his own book on language (*Language and Communication*) that the bias of the book was behavioristic. In 1951 he still hoped to gain scientific respectability by swearing allegiance to behaviorism. His later dissatisfaction with behaviorism resulted in the 1960 creation, with Jerome Bruner, of the Center for Cognitive Studies at Harvard. The cognitive emphasis at the Center reopened communication with distinguished psychologists abroad such as Sir Frederic Bartlett in Cambridge, England; Jean Piaget in Geneva, Switzerland; and A. R. Luria in Moscow, Russia. None of these three had been influenced by the behaviorism movement in the United States and therefore provided inspiration for the cognitive revolution.

COGNITION'S RELATION TO OTHER FIELDS

The ideas expressed by these theorists continue to be developed and refined. Neisser's *Cognitive Psychology* (1967) brought many of these ideas together into a single source; other books on cognition have followed. Cognitive psychology currently has widespread appeal among psychologists. Almost all psychologists studying perception, attention, learning, memory, language, reasoning, problem solving, and decision making refer to themselves as cognitive psychologists even though the methodology and theories vary widely across these topics. In addition, other disciplines, such as educational psychology (Gagne, 1985; Mayer, 1987) and social psychology (Devine, Hamilton, & Ostrom, 1994), have been greatly influenced by the cognitive approach.

The increasing prominence of cognitive psychology is documented in Figure 1.2. The data contrast four of the most influential and widely recognized schools within psychology: psychoanalysis, behaviorism, cognitive psychology, and neuroscience.

One of the measures of prominence, displayed in Figure 1.2, is the number of citations to journal articles in each of these fields. These citations were found in four "flagship" journals: *American Psychologist, Annual Review of Psychology, Psychological Bulletin*, and *Psychological Review*. These are widely read journals that represent the entire field of psychology. As is shown in Figure 1.2, citations of articles in cognitive psychology journals have greatly increased over the 20-year period from 1977 to 1996. Other measures, such as dissertation topics, also show the current prominence of cognitive psychology.

Cognitive psychology is also having an increasing impact on applied psychology (Hoffman & Deffenbacher, 1992; McDaniel, 2007). Much research funding is now directed toward applied projects, and many recent doctoral graduates are assuming positions in applied psychology. The increasing influence of cognitive theory is also evident in the emergence of journals such as *Applied Cognition* and the *Journal of Experimental Psychology: Applied*. I titled this book *Cognition: Theory and Applications* because I believe these applications are important. We will look at many applications throughout

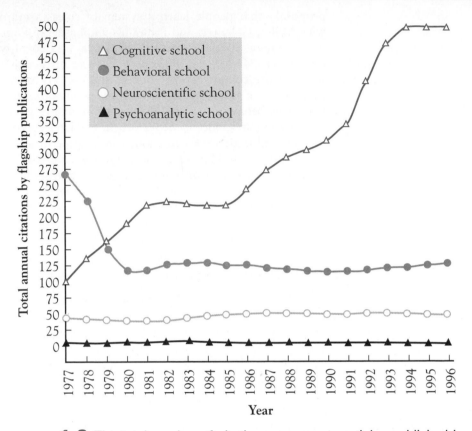

FIGURE **1.2** The total number of citations per year to articles published in cognitive, behavioral, psychoanalytic, and neuroscientific journals

Note: A smoothing function was used to transform the raw data.

Source: From "An empirical analysis of trends in psychology," by R. W. Robins, S. D. Gosling, and K. H. Craik, 1999, *American Psychologist*, 54, 117–128. Used with permission.

this book, including facilitating perceptual learning, improving the attention skills of young drivers, improving eyewitness recall, using memory strategies, applying categorization theories to clinical diagnosis, improving the readability of text, and using problem-solving strategies.

The influence of ideas does not move in only one direction. Other fields of study have also influenced cognitive psychology and led to a combined field of study called cognitive science, characterized by its own society, journal, and even major at some universities. **Cognitive science** is the study of intelligence in humans, computer programs, and abstract theories, with an emphasis on intelligent behavior as computation (Simon & Kaplan, 1989). It is also an attempt to unify views of thought developed by studies in psychology, linguistics, anthropology, philosophy, artificial intelligence, and the neurosciences (Hunt, 1989).

cognitive science The interdisciplinary attempt to study cognition through such fields as psychology, philosophy, artificial intelligence, neuroscience, linguistics, and anthropology

Unification is theoretically possible because some issues, such as knowledge representation, are important in all fields within cognitive science (Davis, Shrobe, & Szolovits, 1993; Stillings et al., 1995). For example, we will see in Chapter 9 that cognitive psychologists borrowed a concept from artificial intelligence (semantic networks) to describe how people organize ideas in LTM. Another concept borrowed from artificial intelligence (production systems) explains how we use rules to perform cognitive tasks. We will learn about production systems in Chapter 13.

An important field receiving increasing study since the changes shown in Figure 1.2 is **cognitive neuroscience**, which examines where cognitive operations occur in the brain. Figure 1.3 shows the four lobes of the cerebral cortex with their primary functions (Kalat, 2004). The primary visual cortex is located in the *occipital lobe*. A person who has damage to this area has normal pupillary reflexes and some eye movements, but no pattern perception or awareness of visual information. The *parietal lobe* is specialized for dealing with body information, including touch.

Common symptoms that follow from damage to this area include impairment to identify objects by touch and clumsiness on the side of the body opposite the damage. The *temporal lobe* is essential for understanding language and contributes to recognizing complex visual patterns such as faces. The *frontal lobe* receives sensations from all the sensory systems and contributes to planning motor movements. Damage to this area can also interfere with memory.

cognitive neuroscience The study of the relation between cognitive processes and brain activities

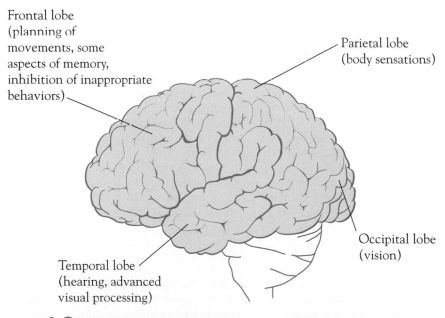

FIGURE **1.3** Some major subdivisions of the left hemisphere of the cerebral cortex, with a few of their primary functions

Source: Kalat, J. W. (2004). *Biological Psychology* (8th ed.). Belmont, CA: Wadsworth.

functional magnetic resonance imaging (fMRI) A diagnostic technique that uses magnetic fields and computerized images to locate mental operations in the brain

Advances in technology have made it possible to more precisely localize which parts of the brain are used to perform a variety of cognitive tasks. Imaging techniques, such as **functional magnetic resonance imaging (fMRI)** and **positron-emission tomography (PET)**, measure cerebral blood flow by sensing either a magnetic signal (fMRI) or low-level radiation (PET) to determine activity levels in various parts of the brain (Posner, DiGirolamo, & Fernandez-Duque, 1997). In the News 1.1 shows how such technology is greatly enhancing our understanding of cognitive problems.

positron-emission tomography (PET) A diagnostic technique that uses radioactive tracers to study brain activity by measuring the amount of blood flow in different parts of the brain

A limitation of spatial imaging techniques is that they do not provide the kind of precise temporal information that is important in analyzing many cognitive tasks in which fractions of a second are theoretically important. But recording electrical activity from the scalp does provide more precise temporal information. The use of these **event-related potentials (ERPs)** allows scientists to link mental operations recorded in reaction-time tasks to brain activity. By combining PET and ERP studies, it is possible to take advantage of the more precise spatial localization of imaging techniques and the more precise temporal resolution of electrical potentials (Posner & Rothbart, 1994).

event-related potential (ERP) A diagnostic technique that uses electrodes placed on the scalp to measure the duration of brain waves during mental tasks

---

IN THE NEWS **1.1**

From Brain Scan to Lesson Plan

Bridget Murray

Down in the basement of Haskins Laboratories, psychological researchers are starting to unravel a mystery that has long puzzled educators: What happens in the human brain as it wrestles with words?

Crowded around computer screens, scrolling through images that show the brain as it reads, the researchers are gaining insight into how we perform this crucial, yet complex, task. It's a science being repeated in labs everywhere, part of an explosion of imaging research on learning over the past decade.

While researchers at sites such as New Haven–based Haskins investigate reading, psychologists in Paris watch what happens in people's brains as they tackle math problems, and neuroscientists at Stanford University in California puzzle over

unusual brain patterns in people with attention-deficit/hyperactivity disorder (ADHD). Imaging is pinpointing what the brain does as people read, calculate, and estimate. It's also showing what goes wrong when people have difficulty with those tasks.

On the forefront of this work are the researchers at Haskins, whose labs are affiliated with Yale University and the University of Connecticut. They find that the brain of someone with dyslexia functions differently from a typical brain as it processes phonemes—the "c," "a," and "t" that come together to form "cat." Kenneth Pugh, PhD, is the experimental psychologist who heads the Haskins side of the research collaboration with Sally and Bennet Shaywitz, both doctors of

the nearby Yale University School of Medicine…

Imaging during specific learning tasks has potentially important implications for education, along with more basic imaging research being done on the role of memory, attention, emotion, and motivation in learning. Not only does it help with diagnosing and treating learning disabilities, but it may even change the way we teach all children, say cognitive experts, helping those slower to grasp reading or math to tap other, more efficient brain circuits.

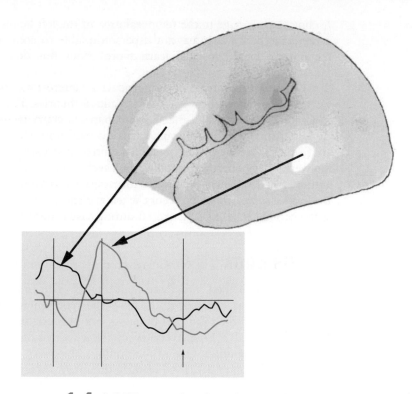

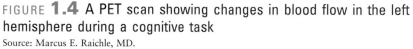

FIGURE **1.4** A PET scan showing changes in blood flow in the left hemisphere during a cognitive task

Source: Marcus E. Raichle, MD.

Figure 1.4 illustrates how the PET and ERP techniques can be combined to help us comprehend how people understand written words (Snyder, Abdullaev, Posner, & Raichle, 1995). The different shades of gray inside the outline of the left hemisphere show changes in blood flow when a person is asked to generate uses of visually presented nouns (such as *pound* for the word *hammer*), over and above the changes caused by simply reading aloud the same nouns. The lighter areas show the largest increases in blood flow, indicating that these areas of the brain are important for understanding the meaning of the words. Notice that these increases are particularly evident in the frontal and temporal areas of the left hemisphere.

The arrows in Figure 1.4 (also shown in color on the inside front cover) connect PET blood-flow changes with the ERP waveforms recorded at the nearest overlying electrode on the scalp. The activation in the frontal part of the left hemisphere leads the activation in the temporal part of the left hemisphere by several hundred milliseconds. An implication of these findings is that the earlier, frontal activation is important for encoding the meaning of individual words, and the later temporal activation may be more important for the integration of word meanings to obtain the overall meaning of phrases and sentences (Snyder et al., 1995). This hypothesis is consistent with the finding that damage to the temporal area of the left hemisphere often produces a language deficit that leaves the person unable to combine words to produce meaningful ideas. We will learn more about this deficit in Chapter 10 on language.

Cognitive neuroscience is particularly interesting to cognitive psychologists when it helps them evaluate cognitive theories. For instance, we will see in Chapter 7 that one of the classic debates in cognitive psychology is the role of visual imagery in cognition. How do we know when people are using visual imagery to perform a task? Cognitive neuroscience has been helpful in answering this question by allowing psychologists to study which part of the brain is active when people perform spatial reasoning tasks. Evidence for the use of visual imagery occurs when the same part of the brain is activated (the occipital lobe) as is activated during visual perception.

ORGANIZATION OF THIS BOOK

This book is divided into three major parts: The first discusses information-processing stages, the second discusses the representation and organization of knowledge, and the third part discusses complex cognitive skills. In this chapter I have presented a brief overview of the information-processing approach to the study of cognition. One of the primary objectives of that approach, as was illustrated in Figure 1.1, is to identify the major information-processing stages. Part One summarizes our knowledge of what occurs during each of these stages. Chapters 2 and 3, on pattern recognition and attention, are both concerned with perception. Theories of pattern recognition seek to specify how people recognize and store descriptions of patterns in memory. These theories also attempt to determine why performance limitations occur, such as when a person cannot report all the letters in an array of letters and why it is easier to perceive letters when they form a word. Theories of attention are needed to explain performance when too much perceptual information arrives at the same time. Experiments designed to measure how much is processed have led to theories about whether a particular stage causes the limitation or whether the tasks simply require too much mental effort to be performed at the same time. Applications include documenting the dangers of cell phones while driving and the successful training of attention skills in young drivers.

Chapters 4 and 5 are both concerned with memory, and they discuss STM and LTM, respectively. Short-term memory is a "working memory" that enables us to combine information retrieved from long-term memory with information that arrives from the environment. But the limited capacity and fast decay rate of STM make it necessary for us to enter into LTM any new information we want to remember over a long period. The chapter on LTM discusses the various strategies that we can use when learning new information, including verbal rehearsal. Applications include speed reading, the use of "chunking" to improve STM capacity, allocation of study time, and the role of LTM in eyewitness testimony.

The second part of the book is concerned with the representation and organization of knowledge in memory. Chapters 6 and 7 illustrate different kinds of memory codes because our ability to remember depends on the kind of memory code that is constructed. For example, memory codes that emphasize meaning are particularly effective. Memory codes can also be distinguished by whether they emphasize verbal information or visual information. The study of memory codes has important implications for how efficiently people can retrieve information from memory and perform spatial reasoning tasks.

Chapters 8 and 9 emphasize the organization of LTM. Chapter 8 is primarily theoretical; it examines how knowledge is organized into categories and how categories are organized into hierarchies The organization of knowledge in LTM can be studied by measuring how quickly people can make classification decisions. Chapter 9 examines how psychologists have used this and other techniques to study relations among concepts in semantic memory, the part of LTM that represents the meaning of words. Applications include the application of categorization strategies to clinical diagnosis and the study of knowledge loss during dementia.

The last part of the book contains five chapters on cognitive skills. The section begins with a discussion of language in Chapter 10. Language involves not only the meaning of individual words but the combination of words to form sentences that are grammatically correct and convey intended meanings. Chapter 11, on text comprehension, focuses on our ability to comprehend paragraphs rather than individual sentences. Psychologists have developed detailed models of how the organization of ideas in a text interacts with STM and LTM to determine what is remembered. Predicting the readability of text and documenting readers' strategies that improve comprehension are examples of applications.

Chapter 12, the first of two chapters on problem solving, shows how cognitive psychologists have studied this area. The chapter describes attempts to identify the skills needed to solve different kinds of problems, identify general strategies used, and examine the role of memory in problem solving. Chapter 13, on expertise and creativity, discusses how people use prior knowledge in reasoning and how they acquire expertise in solving "classroom" problems. The final section of this chapter describes recent theoretical and empirical approaches to the study of creativity. Examining the different problem-solving strategies and learning about experts may make you a better problem solver.

Chapter 14 discusses decision making. The study of decision making has shown that people often find it difficult to combine information in an optimal way when evaluating alternatives. The term *risky decision making* is used to describe situations in which there is uncertainty regarding possible outcomes. The study of how people make probability estimates, how they revise their estimates when they receive new information, and how they use their estimates to make decisions constitutes most of the research on risky decision making. Applications include the study of decisions aids and training as well as decisions made by groups such as jurists and fire fighters.

STUDY QUESTIONS

Although Chapter 1 is short, it is densely packed. It requires close attention because it provides a "road map" of where the book is going. Your learning journey will be easier if you know where you're headed and what landmarks to look for along the way.

1. Neisser's definition of cognitive psychology may not fit your notion of what this course would be about. If so, how does it differ?

2. Notice the assumptions of cognitive psychology. How does each jibe with what you imagine a person in the street would assume about the acquisition of knowledge?

3. What are the implications of the terms *information processing* and *stage model*, taken separately and together? Formulate a tentative idea of what is involved at each stage of processing mentioned.

4. The historical sketch may include many names that are new to you. Which ones are familiar? What do you know about them? Except for James and Watson, don't worry about the names of the other people now—but do explain the importance of their work for the development of cognitive psychology.

5. What are the higher cognitive processes? Why are they called "higher"? Think of an everyday example of each process and write it down. What did you have to consider in generating your examples?

6. If cognitive psychology is related to other fields, then some of the ideas in this book would appear in other courses. Have you already taken courses where some of these ideas have been discussed? If so, in what courses?

CogLab   The following experiment that relates to this chapter may be found at: http://coglab. wadsworth.com. Answer the questions in the CogLab Student Manual as required by your teacher for these experiments.

Brain Asymmetry

KEY TERMS

The page number in parentheses refers to where the term is discussed in the chapter.

artificial intelligence (6)

bottom-up processing (4)

cognitive neuroscience (9)

cognitive psychology (2)

cognitive science (8)

event-related potential (ERP) (10)

filter (4)

functional magnetic resonance imaging (fMRI) (10)

human information processing (3)

long-term memory (LTM) (4)

pattern recognition (3)

plan (6)

positron-emission tomography (PET) (10)

selection stage (4)

sensory store (3)

short-term memory (STM) (4)

stimulus-response (S-R) (5)

top-down processing (4)

RECOMMENDED READING

The first chapter in Eysenck and Keane (1990) provides a more elaborate account of the ideas expressed in this chapter. An early statement of the assumptions of the information-processing approach is given by Haber (1969). A more recent but advanced overview of information-processing models is described by Massaro and Cowan (1993). An interesting paper by Roediger (1980) discusses how people have used familiar analogies to help them understand memory. Roediger begins with Aristotle's and Plato's comparison of memory to a wax tablet and ends with the computer analogy that is currently emphasized. Readers interested in how other major theoretical approaches influenced the history of psychology should read Heidbreder (1961). The book contains chapters on prescientific psychology, the beginning of scientific psychology, the psychology of William James, functionalism, behaviorism, dynamic psychology, Gestalt psychology, and psychoanalysis. Gardner (1985) provides a very readable account of the evolution of cognitive psychology. Hoffman and Deffenbacher (1992) give a detailed account of the development of applied cognitive psychology. A special section in the journal *Psychonomic Bulletin & Review* (2007) contains articles on applications to education. The books *Foundations of Cognitive Science* (Posner, 1989), *Cognitive Science: An Introduction* (Stillings et al., 1995), and *How the Mind Works* (Pinker, 1997) provide introductions to the cognitive sciences. Articles on knowledge representation (Davis, Shrobe, & Szolovits, 1993) and cognitive neuroscience (Posner & Rothbart, 2005) provide more focused summaries.

2

Pattern Recognition

Describing Patterns
Template Theories
Feature Theories
IN THE NEWS 2.1 Why Do "They All
 Look Alike"?
Structural Theories

Information-Processing Stages
The Partial-Report Technique
Sperling's Model
Rumelhart's Model

Word Recognition
The Word Superiority Effect

A Model of the Word Superiority Effect
Neural Network Models

SUMMARY
STUDY QUESTIONS
COGLAB: *RECEPTIVE FIELDS; MULLER-LYER
ILLUSION; VISUAL SEARCH; PARTIAL
REPORT; WORD SUPERIORITY;
METACONTRAST MASKING*
KEY TERMS
RECOMMENDED READING

You are a creative genius. Your creative genius is so accomplished that it appears, to you and others, as effortless. Yet it far outstrips the most valiant efforts of today's fastest supercomputers. To invoke it you need only open your eyes.
—**Donald Hoffman (1998)**

The above quote is from the opening paragraph of Donald Hoffman's book *Visual Intelligence*. The quote describes our remarkable ability to recognize patterns, an ability that is still far from being duplicated by the world's fastest computers. It is difficult for us to appreciate this ability because it appears so effortless. Hopefully, you will appreciate it more after learning about the progress of cognitive scientists in discovering how we accomplish such a difficult task.

pattern recognition The stage of perception during which a stimulus is identified

The study of **pattern recognition** is primarily the study of how people identify the objects in their environment. Our ability to recognize patterns should seem impressive if we stop to consider how much variation there is in different examples of the same pattern. Each letter of the alphabet, for example, is one kind of pattern. Figure 2.1 shows various styles of handwriting. Obviously, not all people have the same style of writing, and some handwriting styles are much less legible than others. However, unless it is very illegible, we usually are successful in reading it—that is, in recognizing the words.

Our superiority over computers as pattern recognizers has the practical advantage that pattern recognition can serve as a test of whether a person or a computer program is trying to gain access to the Internet. If you have spent much time on the Internet you might have encountered a situation that required you to identify a distorted word before you were allowed to enter a site. The mangled word is easy for people to identify but difficult for computer search programs.

tachistoscope A box that presents visual stimuli at a specified duration and level of illumination

The ease and accuracy with which people can recognize patterns make it difficult to study this ability. It is not very interesting or revealing if someone easily identifies all of a variety of patterns. To make the task more difficult, psychologists often resort to using a **tachistoscope**—a device for presenting patterns very rapidly under controlled conditions. If the patterns are presented for only a few milliseconds, people start to make mistakes, and psychologists start to take notes about the kinds of mistakes they make.

A large part of the literature on pattern recognition is concerned with alternative ways of describing patterns. The first section of this chapter discusses three kinds of descriptions that represent different theories of pattern recognition. The second section is about information-processing models of visual pattern recognition. We will take a more detailed look at Sperling's research and how his results influenced later theories. The third section deals with word recognition and will give us the opportunity to consider some of the factors that influence reading.

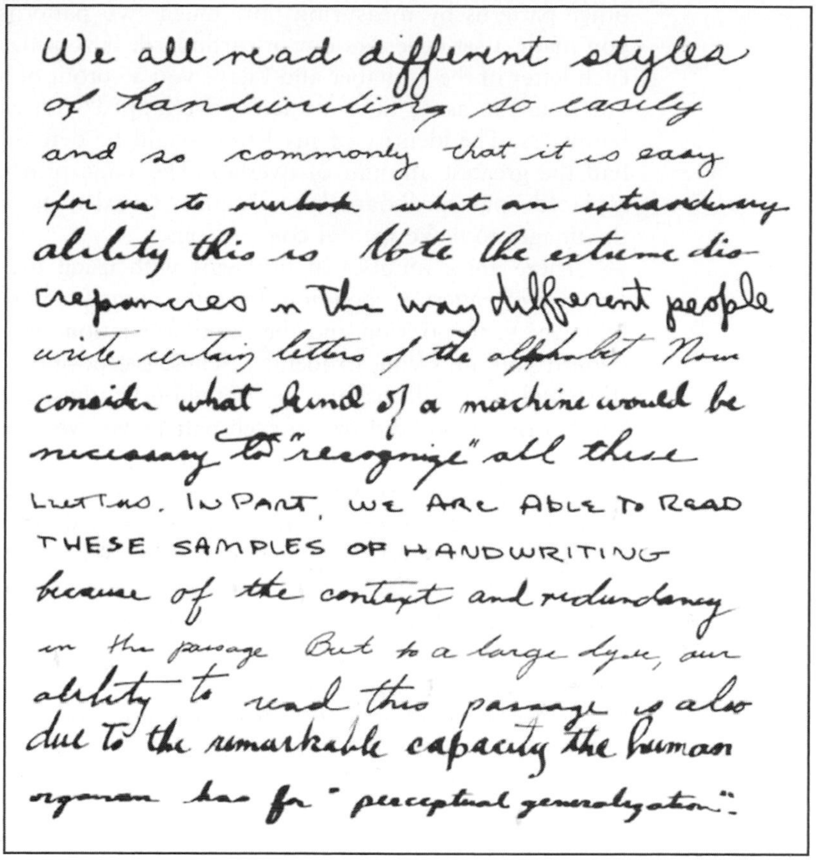

FIGURE **2.1** Variations in handwriting

Source: From *Man machine engineering*, by A. Chapanis. Copyright 1965 by Brooks/Cole, a division of Thomson Learning. Fax 800–730–2215.

DESCRIBING PATTERNS

Consider the following explanation of how we recognize patterns. Our long-term memory (LTM) contains descriptions of many kinds of patterns. When we see or hear a pattern, we form a description of it and compare the description against the descriptions stored in our LTM. We are able to recognize the pattern if its description closely matches one of the descriptions stored in LTM. Although this is a plausible explanation, it is rather vague. For example, what form do these descriptions take? Let us consider three explanations that have been suggested: (1) templates, (2) features, and (3) structural descriptions.

Template Theories

Template theories propose that patterns are really not "described" at all. Rather, **templates** are holistic, or unanalyzed, entities that we compare with

template An unanalyzed pattern that is matched against alternative patterns by using the degrees of overlap as a measure of similarity

other patterns by measuring how much two patterns overlap. Imagine that you made a set of letters out of cardboard. If you made a cutout to represent each letter of the alphabet and I gave you a cutout of a letter that I had made, you could measure how my letter overlapped with each of your letters—the templates. The identity of my letter would be determined by which template had the greatest amount of overlap. The same principle would apply if you replaced your cardboard letters with a visual image of each letter and used the images to make mental comparisons.

There are a number of problems with using the degree of overlap as a measure of pattern recognition. First, the comparison requires that the template be in the same position and the same orientation, and be the same size as the pattern you are trying to identify. Thus, the position, orientation, and size of the templates would have to be continuously adjusted to correspond to the position, orientation, and size of each pattern you wanted to recognize. A second problem is the great variability of patterns, as was illustrated in Figure 2.1. It would be difficult to construct a template for each letter that would produce a good match with all the different varieties of that letter. Third, a template theory doesn't reveal how two patterns differ. We could know from a template theory that the capital letters *P* and *R* are similar because one overlaps substantially with the other. But to know how the two letters differ, we have to be able to analyze or describe the letters. By contrast, the feature theory, considered in the next section, allows us to analyze patterns into their parts. A fourth problem is that a template theory does not allow for alternative descriptions of a pattern. The pattern in Figure 2.5 (page 27), for example, can be perceived as either a stingray or a full-blown sail, depending on which lines are grouped together. The structural theory, which we'll consider later, will allow us to specify the relations of parts of a pattern.

These weaknesses of the template theory make it very unpromising as a general theory of pattern recognition, and it is usually quickly dismissed. There are, however, some situations in which a template theory might provide a useful model. Remember from Chapter 1 that the **sensory store** briefly preserves sensory information to give the observer more time to recognize patterns. But how are the patterns preserved in the sensory store if they are unrecognized? One possibility is that the patterns can be represented as unanalyzed templates, which are analyzed into their features during the pattern recognition stage.

This interpretation of the sensory store is most clearly presented by Phillips (1974). Subjects in Phillips's experiment viewed patterns made by randomly filled cells in a square matrix. The first pattern was presented for 1 second and was followed after a variable interval by either an identical or a similar pattern. The subject's task was to decide, as quickly as possible, whether the two patterns were the same or different. In one-half of the trials, the second pattern occurred in exactly the same location as the first. Because the second pattern was exactly superimposed over the sensory image of the first pattern, it might be possible to use the sensory store to make a template match. In the other half of the trials, participants also responded whether the two patterns were the same or different, but the

sensory store The part of memory that holds unanalyzed sensory information for a fraction of a second, providing an opportunity for additional analysis following the physical termination of a stimulus

second pattern was moved horizontally by the width of one cell. The slight shift in position should prohibit a template match because the two patterns were not correctly aligned.

Figure 2.2 shows the results of Phillips's experiment. The **interstimulus interval**—the time separating the two patterns—was 20, 60, 100, 300, or 600 msec. When the two patterns were presented in identical locations (labeled "still" in Figure 2.2), accuracy declined as the interstimulus interval was lengthened. This finding suggests that the subjects were making use of a sensory store that was rapidly decaying. When the second pattern was moved, subjects could not use the sensory store to make a template match, and so accuracy was not influenced by the interval separating the patterns. Note that the use of the sensory store resulted in more accuracy when the interstimulus interval was less than 300 msec. This suggests that the sensory store lasts only approximately one-quarter of a second. When the separation was only 20 msec (the data points on the extreme left of the graph) and the patterns were presented in the same location, performance was almost perfect, even for the most complex pattern.

When the second pattern was moved, subjects had to rely on a description of the first pattern rather than on a sensory image. The description might be in the form of a visual image, but unlike a sensory image, in which the pattern still appears to be physically present, a visual image has to be retrieved from memory. Thus, the description was less accurate than the sensory image. Because comparing the descriptions of two patterns takes longer than making a template match, the speed of response was highly correlated with accuracy. The reaction-time results would look very much like the accuracy results in Figure 2.2 if we were to replace "Percentage correct" with "Speed of response." Reaction times were very fast for the "still" condition but became slower as the interstimulus interval was increased. Reaction times were slower for the "move" condition and were uninfluenced by the interstimulus interval. Both the accuracy and reaction-time results suggest that the sensory store can be used for a rapid template match if the two patterns are separated by less than 300 msec and are presented in the same location.

interstimulus interval
The amount of time between the end of a stimulus and the beginning of another stimulus

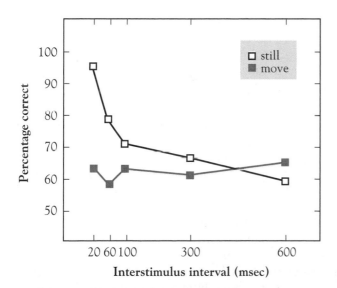

FIGURE **2.2** Percentage of correct responses for an 8 × 8 matrix as a function of interstimulus interval and movement

Source: From "On the distinction between sensory storage and short-term visual memory," by W. A. Phillips, 1974, *Perception and Psychophysics*, 16, 283–290. Copyright 1974 by the Psychonomic Society. Reprinted by permission.

Feature Theories

The success of the template theory in accounting for Phillips's results depends on matching the second pattern to a sensory image of the first pattern. The sensory image can be thought of as a kind of afterimage in which the pattern still appears to be physically present until the sensory store decays away. But it is questionable whether the sensory store plays an important role outside the laboratory; even if it did, the information would be quickly lost. As we usually cannot rely on the sensory store to match patterns, we must compare descriptions of patterns. **Feature theories** allow us to describe a pattern by listing its parts. For example, we might describe a friend as having long blond hair, a short nose, and bushy eyebrows.

Feature theories are convenient for describing perceptual learning, and one of the best discussions of feature theories is contained in Gibson's *Principles of Perceptual Learning and Development* (1969). Gibson's theory is that perceptual learning occurs through the discovery of features that *distinguish* one pattern from another. Part of the evidence for feature theories comes from recording the action potentials of individual cells in the visual cortex. By placing microelectrodes in the visual cortex of animals, Hubel and Wiesel (1962, 1963) discovered that cells respond to only certain kinds of stimuli, such as a line of a certain width, oriented at a correct angle, and located at the correct position in its visual field. Other cells are even concerned about the length of the line. In 1981 Hubel and Wiesel received a Nobel Prize for this work.

Although most pattern recognition theorists make use of the feature concept, it is often a challenging task to find a good set of features. Gibson (1969) proposed the following criteria as a basis for selecting a set of features for uppercase letters:

1. The features should be critical ones, present in some members of the set but not in others, so as to provide a contrast.
2. The identity of the features should remain unchanged under changes in brightness, size, and perspective.
3. The features should yield a unique pattern for each letter.
4. The number of proposed features should be reasonably small.

Gibson used these criteria, empirical data, and intuition to derive the set of features for uppercase letters shown in Figure 2.3. Note that the features consist primarily of different lines and curves but also include some global characteristics of the pattern, such as symmetry and closure.

A set of features is usually evaluated by determining how well it can predict **perceptual confusions** as confusable items should have many features in common. For example, Figure 2.3 reveals that the only difference in features for the letters *P* and *R* is the presence of a diagonal line for the letter *R*; therefore, the two should be highly confusable. The letters *R* and *O* differ in five features, and so they should seldom be confused.

One method for generating perceptual confusions is to ask an observer to identify letters that are presented very rapidly in a tachistoscope (Townsend, 1971). It is often difficult to discriminate physically similar letters under these conditions, and the errors provide a measure of perceived similarity. Holbrook (1975) compared two feature models to determine how successfully each could predict the pattern of errors found by Townsend. One was the Gibson model shown in Figure 2.3, and the other was a modification of the Gibson model proposed by Geyer and De Wald (1973). The major change in the modification was the specification of the number of features in a letter

feature theory A theory of pattern recognition that describes patterns in terms of their parts, or features

2 patterns mistakenly identified as each other.

perceptual confusion A measure of the frequency with which two patterns are mistakenly identified as each other

Features	A	E	F	H	I	L	T	K	M	N	V	W	X	Y	Z	B	C	D	G	J	O	P	R	Q	S	U
Straight																										
horizontal	●	●	●	●		●	●								●				●							
vertical		●	●	●	●	●	●	●	●	●				●		●		●				●	●			
diagonal /	●							●	●		●	●	●	●	●											
diagonal \	●							●	●	●	●	●	●		●								●			
Curve																										
closed																●		●			●	●	●	●	●	
open vertical																			●							●
open horizontal																	●		●	●					●	
Intersection	●	●	●	●			●	●		●			●			●						●	●	●		
Redundancy																										
cyclic change		●						●		●					●										●	
symmetry	●	●		●	●		●	●			●	●	●	●		●	●	●			●					●
Discontinuity																										
vertical	●		●	●	●		●	●	●	●	●											●	●			
horizontal		●	●			●	●								●											

FIGURE **2.3** A possible set of features for capital letters

Source: From *Principles of perceptual learning and development*, by E. Gibson, p. 88. Copyright 1969 by Prentice-Hall, Inc. Englewood Cliffs, NJ. Reprinted by permission.

(such as two vertical lines for the letter *H*) rather than simply listing whether that feature was present.

A comparison of the two models revealed that the feature set proposed by Geyer and De Wald was superior in predicting the confusion errors made both by adults (Townsend, 1971) and by 4-year-old children (Gibson et al., 1963). The prediction of both models improved when the features were optimally weighted to allow for the fact that some features are more important than others in accounting for confusions. Because the straight/curved distinction is particularly important, it should be emphasized more than the others.

Distinctive Features

Children learn to identify an object by being able to identify differences between it and other objects. For example, when first confronted with the letters *E* and *F*, the child might not be aware of how the two differ. Learning to make this discrimination depends on discovering that a low horizontal line is present in the letter *E* but not in the letter *F*. The low horizontal line is a **distinctive feature** for distinguishing between an *E* and an *F*; that is, it enables us to distinguish one pattern from the other.

distinctive feature A feature present in one pattern but absent in another, aiding one's discrimination of the two patterns

Perceptual learning can be facilitated by a learning procedure that high-lights distinctive features. An effective method for emphasizing a distinctive feature is to initially make it a different color from the rest of the pattern and then gradually change it back to the original color. Egeland (1975) used this procedure to teach prekindergarten children how to distinguish between the confusable letter pairs *R-P, Y-V, G-C, Q-O, M-N,* and *K-X.* One letter of each pair was presented at the top of a card with six letters below it, three of which matched the sample letter and three of which were the comparison letter. The children were asked to select those letters that exactly matched the sample letter.

One group of children received a training procedure in which the distinctive feature of the letter was initially highlighted in red—for example, the diagonal line of the *R* in the *R-P* discrimination. During the training session, the distinctive feature was gradually changed to black to match the rest of the letter. Another group of children viewed only black letters. They received feedback about which of their choices were correct, but they were not told about the distinctive features of the letters. Both groups were given two tests—one immediately after the training session and one a week later. The "distinctive features" group made significantly fewer errors on both tests, even though the features were not highlighted during the tests. They also made fewer errors during the training sessions.

Emphasizing the distinctive features produced two benefits. First, it enabled the children to learn the distinctive features so that they could continue to differentiate letters after the distinctive features were no longer highlighted. Second, it enabled them to learn the features without making many errors during the training session. The failure and frustration that many children experience in the early stages of reading (letter discrimination) can impair their interest in later classroom learning.

Faces

The contributions made by Eleanor Gibson and her colleagues focused on discrimination of letters and letter-like forms. Feature theories are very general, however, and can be used to represent many patterns including faces. If you describe a woman's face you would likely refer to features such as her nose, eyes, and mouth. The first two rows in Figure 2.4 illustrate variations in two types of facial features. Notice that mouths and ears are more complex than the lines and curves shown in Figure 2.3.

The pictures of the mouths and ears are examples of the kinds of features that are identified by artificial intelligence programs developed by Ullman (2007). Ullman discovered that more complex features such as mouths and ears (and taillights for cars) are particularly helpful for identifying objects. However, his computer programs can also identify low-level features such as the lines and curves shown in Figure 2.3. The low-level lines and curves are general for all patterns, but the more complex features such as mouths and taillights are specific for particular categories such as faces and cars. Low-level features are needed to distinguish among the different types of a complex feature, such as describing Angelina Jolie's mouth as a particular combination of curves.

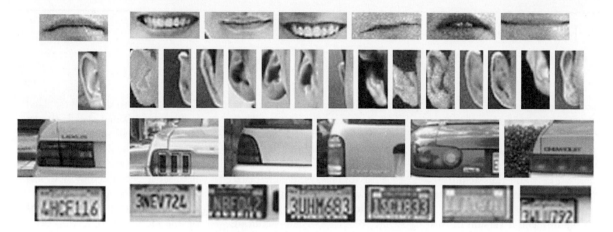

FIGURE **2.4** Examples of higher-level features in Ullman's pattern recognition programs

Source: From "Object recognition and segmentation by a fragment–based hierarchy," by S. Ullman, 2007, *Trends in the Cognitive Sciences, 11,* 58–64.

This distinction between different levels of description raises a practical issue in pattern recognition: At what level do we identify a pattern? Some levels are very general (a person's face), some are intermediate (an Asian face), and some are very specific (Angie Chen's face). Identifying faces within a category can be difficult when we emphasize features that allow us to distinguish *between* categories rather than *within* categories (Goldstone, Lippa, & Shiffrin, 2001; Goldstone & Steyvers, 2001). As indicated in In The News 2.1, we particularly have trouble distinguishing among faces of an ethnic category that is different from our own. Levin argues that this does *not* occur because we have more practice in identifying faces in our own race. Rather, it occurs because we simply don't try as hard to recognize people as individuals if they belong to other racial categories.

Research supports this explanation. Students are more accurate in recognizing faces of other races when informed in advance that people typically have trouble with this task and that they should therefore pay close attention to facial differences. White students who were given these instructions later showed no difference in their ability to recognize Black and white faces (Hugenberg, Miller, & Claypool, 2007). Students who did not receive these instructions showed the typical finding of lower recognition of faces belonging to another race. Racial differences in facial recognition can therefore be quickly eliminated through instructions.

Focusing on distinctive features might aid in distinguishing among faces, as it does in distinguishing among letters. To test this, Brennan (1985) used computer-generated **caricatures** that make distinctive features even more distinctive. For instance, if a person had large ears and a small nose, the caricature would have even larger ears and an even smaller nose than the accurate drawing. When students were shown line drawings of acquaintances, they

caricature An exaggeration of distinctive features to make a pattern more distinctive

IN THE NEWS **2.1**

Why Do "They All Look Alike"?

Siri Carpenter

People are notoriously awful at recognizing faces from other races. It's a human foible often explained by the notion that we have more experience looking at members of our own race and thus acquire "perceptual expertise" for characteristics of our own kind.

One influential version of this hypothesis argues that the so-called cross-race recognition deficit can be modeled by assuming that faces of other races are more psychologically similar than are faces of one's own race. But Daniel Levin, PhD, a cognitive psychologist at Kent State University, has been unsatisfied with that argument.

"The perceptual expertise position is pretty intuitive, and it makes sense," he says. "But I'm arguing that it's not really the case. The problem is not that we can't code the details of cross-race faces—it's that we don't."

Instead, he says, people place inordinate emphasis on race categories—whether someone is white, Black, or Asian—ignoring information that would help them recognize people as individuals. In recent research, Levin has shown that people can, in fact, perceive fine differences among faces of people from other races—as long as they're using those differences to make race classifications.

For example, Levin explains, "When a white person looks at another white person's nose, they're likely to think to themselves, 'That's John's nose.' When they look at a black person's nose, they're likely to think, 'That's a black nose.'"

The results are important, Levin maintains, because they help explain the long-standing question of why people are poor at recognizing the faces of people who belong to other racial groups. Such an understanding could be useful in a variety of settings, including training police and others in the justice system to identify faces more accurately.

Source: From "Why do 'they all look alike'?," by Siri Carpenter, *Monitor on Psychology*, December, 2000, 44. Copyright 2000 by the American Psychological Association. Reprinted by permission.

identified people faster when shown caricatures than when shown accurate line drawings (Rhodes, Brennan, & Carey, 1987). Making distinctive features more distinctive through exaggeration facilitated recognition.

Structural Theories

A limitation of feature theories is that descriptions of patterns often require that we specify how the features are joined together. Describing how features join together to create a structure is a guiding principle of Gestalt psychology. To Gestalt psychologists, a pattern is more than the sum of its parts. Relations among pattern features have been formalized by people working in the field of artificial intelligence who discovered that the interpretation of patterns usually depends on making explicit how the lines of a pattern are joined to other lines. I pointed out previously that a template theory would be unable to distinguish between the two interpretations of Figure 2.5. A feature theory would also have problems because, although it could identify the four sides as features, the features are identical for the two interpretations.

structural theory A theory that specifies how the features of a pattern are joined to other features of the pattern

Structural theories, however, emphasize the relations among the features; Clowes (1969) used Figure 2.5 as an example of why structural theories are often necessary to produce adequate descriptions of patterns. Perceiving the pattern as a stingray requires grouping adjacent lines: line *a* with line *d* (forming the head) and line *b* with line *c* (forming the tail). Perceiving the pattern

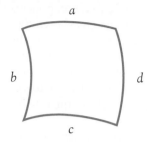

FIGURE **2.5** An ambiguous pattern, showing a stingray or a sail

Source: From "Transformational grammars and the organization of pictures," by M. Clowes, 1969, in A. Graselli (Ed.), *Automatic interpretation and the organization of pictures.* Copyright 1969 by Academic Press, Inc. Reprinted by permission.

as a sail requires grouping opposite lines: line *a* with line *c* (top and bottom) and line *b* with line *d* (the sides of the sail).

Structural theories build on feature theories. Before we can specify the relation among features, we have to specify the features. A structural theory allows for specification of how the features fit together. For example, the letter *H* consists of two vertical lines and a horizontal line. But we could make many different patterns from two vertical lines and a horizontal line. What is required is a precise specification of how the lines should be joined together—the letter *H* consists of two vertical lines connected at their midpoints by a horizontal line.

Moving from a two-dimensional world of letters to a three-dimensional world of objects creates additional challenges for identifying and describing the relations among features. Figure 2.6 illustrates the problem of identifying features by the relative difficulty of perceiving the three patterns as cubes (Kopfermann, 1930). The left pattern is the most difficult to perceive as a cube, and the pattern in the middle is the easiest. Try to guess why before reading further. (Hint: Think about the challenge of identifying features for each of the three examples.)

The theme of Hoffman's (1998) book on visual intelligence is that people follow rules in producing descriptions of patterns. The first of the many rules described in his book is to always interpret a straight line in an image as a straight line in three dimensions. Therefore, we perceive the long vertical line in the center of the right pattern in Figure 2.6 as a single line. However, it is necessary to split this line into two separate lines to form a cube because the lines belong to different surfaces. It is particularly difficult to see the figure on the left as a cube because you also need to split the two long diagonal lines into two shorter lines to avoid seeing the object as a flat pattern.

The pattern in the middle is easy to perceive as a cube, which you may have recognized as the famous Necker cube. The Necker cube is well known because your perception of the front and back surfaces of the cube changes as you view it (Long & Toppino, 2004). It is yet another example that a structural description can change when the features do not change!

Biederman's Component Model

Descriptions of three-dimensional objects would be fairly complicated if we had to describe each of the lines and curves in the object. For example, the cubes in Figure 2.6 each consist of 12 lines (which you may find easier to count in the left and right cubes after splitting the lines than in the reversing Necker cube). It would be easier to describe three-dimensional objects through simple volumes such as cubes, cylinders, edges, and cones than to describe all the features in these volumes.

Like the features of letters, these components can be combined in many different ways to produce a variety of objects. For

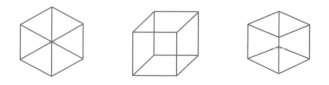

FIGURE **2.6** Perceiving cubes

Source: From *Visual intelligence*, by D. D. Hoffman. Copyright 1998 by W. W. Norton.

example, the mug and the pail in Figure 2.7 contain the same two components in a different arrangement. Research on searching for patterns has shown that both the components and the relations among the components determine the perceived similarity of patterns (Arguin & Saumier, 2004). For example, the briefcase and drawer in Figure 2.7 are similar because they share the same components. However, the briefcase is more similar to the pail than to the cup because of the *relation* between components—the handle is on top for both the briefcase and pail.

The advantage of being able to form many different arrangements from a few components is that we may need relatively few components to describe objects. Biederman (1985) has proposed that we need only approximately 35 simple volumes (which he called **geons**) to describe the objects in the world. If so, then pattern recognition consists mainly in describing the relations among this limited set of components, rather than in discriminating among hundreds of components.

One consequence of Biederman's argument is that deleting information about the relation of features should reduce people's ability to recognize patterns. To test this hypothesis, Biederman removed 65% of the contour from drawings of objects, such as the two cups shown in Figure 2.8. In the cup on the left, the contour was removed from the middles of the segments, allowing observers to see how the segments were related. In the cup on the right, the contour was removed from the vertices so observers would have difficulty recognizing how the segments were related. When drawings of different objects were presented for 100 msec, subjects correctly named 70% of the objects if the contours were deleted at midsegments. But if the contours were deleted at the vertices, subjects correctly named fewer than 50% of the objects (Biederman, 1985). As predicted, destroying relational information was particularly detrimental for object recognition.

These results show that the relations among features are important, but they do not directly show that features are grouped together to form larger components (geons). A later study (Biederman & Cooper, 1991) provided a direct test of this assumption and again used the contour-deletion method. This time, 50% of the contours were deleted to form a pair of complementary

geons Different three-dimensional shapes that combine to form three-dimensional patterns

↳ Different 3D shapes that combine in different ways to form different patterns.

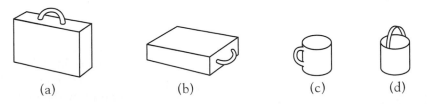

(a)   (b)   (c)   (d)

FIGURE **2.7** Different arrangements of the same components can produce different objects

Source: From "Human image understanding: Recent research and a theory," by I. Biederman, 1985, *Computer Vision, Graphics, and Image Processing, 32*, 29–73. Copyright 1985 by Academic Press. Reprinted by permission of Elsevier Science.

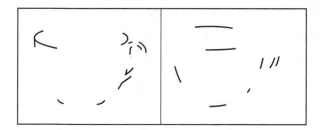

FIGURE **2.8** Illustration of 65% contour removal centered at either midsegments (left object) or vertices (right object)

Source: From "Human image understanding: Recent research and a theory," by I. Biederman, 1985, *Computer Vision, Graphics, and Image Processing*, *32*, 29–73. Copyright 1985 by Academic Press. Reprinted by permission of Elsevier Science.

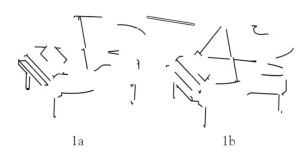

1a   1b

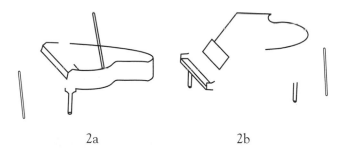

2a   2b

FIGURE **2.9** Examples of complementary images that show either the same geons (1a and 1b) or different geons (2a and 2b)

Source: From "Priming contour-deleted images: Evidence for intermediate representations in visual object recognition," by I. Biederman & E. E. Cooper, 1991, *Cognitive Psychology*, *23*, 393–419. Copyright 1991 by Academic Press. Reprinted by permission of Elsevier Science.

images. That is, contours missing from one image are present in its complementary image, as shown by the two pairs of examples in Figure 2.9. Notice that superimposing one complementary image over the other recreates the entire pattern.

The difference between the top and bottom complementary images in Figure 2.9 is that the geons are preserved in each complementary image for the top pair but are divided between the two complementary images for the bottom pair. For example, the contours and vertices of the uplifted cover of the piano are divided in the top pair but appear entirely in the right image in the bottom pair. Biederman and Cooper (1991) measured how quickly and how accurately participants could name the objects when they had already correctly named the complementary image. Based on their theory, they predicted that correctly naming "1a" should be particularly helpful for later naming "1b" because the same geons would be activated for "1a" and "1b." In contrast, correctly naming "2a" would be less helpful for later naming "2b" because different geons would be activated in "2a" and "2b." Both the response times and the accuracy levels supported their predictions. People were faster and more accurate when the complementary images had the same geons than when they had different geons. These findings support the theory that relations are important both for grouping features together into larger units (geons) and for showing the relation among geons to form more complex objects.

In conclusion, structural theories extend feature theories by specifying how the features are related. Sutherland (1968) was one of the first to argue that if we want to account for our very impressive pattern recognition capabilities, we will need the more powerful kind of descriptive language contained in a structural theory. The experiments in this section show that Sutherland was correct. We now look at how pattern recognition occurs over time.

INFORMATION-PROCESSING STAGES

The Partial-Report Technique

To understand how people perform on a pattern-recognition task, we have to identify what occurs during each of the information-processing stages discussed in Chapter 1. Sperling (1960) is responsible for the initial construction of an information-processing model of performance on a visual recognition task. Subjects in Sperling's task saw an array of letters presented for a brief period (usually 50 msec) in a tachistoscope and were asked to report all the letters they could remember from the display. Responses were highly accurate if the display contained fewer than five letters. But when the number of letters was increased, subjects never reported more than an average of 4.5 letters correctly, regardless of how many letters were in the display.

A general problem in constructing an information-processing model is to identify the cause of a performance limitation. Sperling was interested in measuring the number of letters that could be recognized during a brief exposure, but he was aware that the upper limit of 4.5 might be caused by an inability to remember more than that. In other words, subjects might have recognized most of the letters in the display but then forgot some before they could report what they had seen. Sperling therefore changed his procedure from a **whole-report procedure** (report all the letters) to a **partial-report procedure** (report only some of the letters).

In the most typical case, the display consisted of three rows, each containing four letters. Subjects would be unable to remember all 12 letters in a display, but they should be able to remember 4 letters. The partial-report procedure required that subjects report only one row. The pitch of a tone signaled which of the three rows to report: the top row for a high pitch, the middle row for a medium pitch, and the bottom row for a low pitch. The tone sounded just after the display disappeared, so that subjects would have to view the entire display and could not simply look at a single row (Figure 2.10). Use of the partial-report technique is based on the assumption that the number of letters reported from the cued row equals the average number of letters perceived in each of the rows since the subjects did not know in advance which row to look at. The results of this procedure showed that subjects could correctly report three of the four letters in a row, implying that they had recognized nine letters in the entire display.

Sperling's Model

It often happens that what is best remembered about a scientist's work is not what that person originally set out to investigate. Although Sperling designed the partial-report technique to reduce the memory requirements of his task and to obtain a "pure" measure of perception, his work is best remembered for the discovery of the importance of a visual sensory store. How did this come about? The estimate that subjects had perceived 9 letters was obtained when the tone occurred immediately after the termination of the 50-msec exposure. In this case, subjects could correctly report approximately

whole-report procedure A task that requires observers to report everything they see in a display of items

partial-report procedure A task in which observers are cued to report only certain items in a display of items

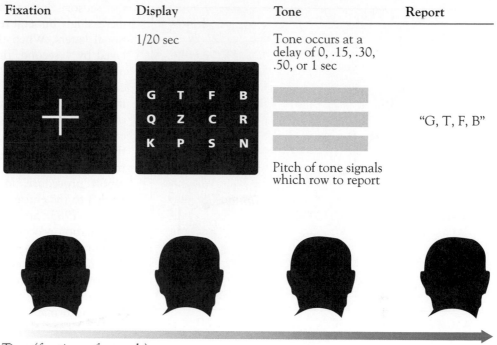

Fixation	Display	Tone	Report

Time (fractions of seconds)

FIGURE **2.10** Sperling's (1960) study of sensory memory. After the subjects had fixated on the cross, the letters were flashed on the screen just long enough to create a visual afterimage. High, medium, and low tones signaled which row of letters to report

Source: From "The information available in brief visual presentations," by G. Sperling, 1960, *Psychological Monographs*, 74 (Whole No. 498).

three-quarters of the letters, and three-quarters of 12 is 9. But when the tone was delayed until 1 sec after the display, performance declined to only 4.5 letters. That is, there was a gradual decline from 9 letters to 4.5 as the delay of the tone was increased from 0 to 1 second (Figure 2.11).

The most interesting thing about the number 4.5 is that it is exactly equal to the upper limit of performance on the whole-report task, as represented by the blue bar in Figure 2.11. The partial-report procedure has no advantage over the whole-report procedure if the tone is delayed by 1 second or more. To explain this gradual decline in performance, Sperling proposed that the subjects were using a visual sensory store to recognize letters in the cued row. When they heard the tone, they selectively attended to the cued row in the store and tried to identify the letters in that row. Their success in making use of the tone depended on the clarity of information in their sensory store. When the tone occurred immediately after termination of the stimulus, the clarity was sufficient for recognizing additional letters in the cued row. But as the clarity of

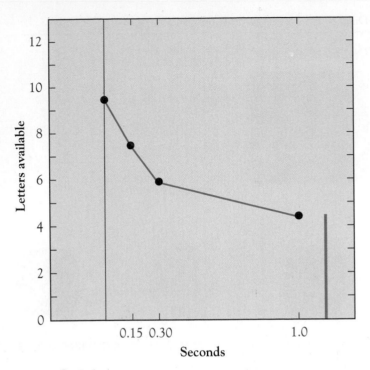

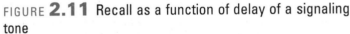

FIGURE **2.11** Recall as a function of delay of a signaling tone

Source: From "The information available in brief visual presentations," by G. Sperling, 1960, *Psychological Monographs, 74* (Whole No. 498).

visual information store (VIS) A sensory store that maintains visual information for approximately one-quarter of a second

rehearsal Repeating verbal information to keep it active in short-term memory or to transfer it into long-term memory

auditory information store In Sperling's model this store maintains verbal information in short-term memory through rehearsal

serial processing Carrying out one operation at a time, such as pronouncing one word at a time

the sensory image faded, it became increasingly difficult to recognize additional letters. When the tone was delayed by 1 second, the subjects could not use the sensory store at all to focus on the cued row, so their performance was determined by the number of letters they had recognized from the entire display that happened to be in that row. Their performance was therefore equivalent to the whole-report procedure, in which they attended to the entire display.

In 1963 Sperling proposed an information-processing model of performance on his visual report task. The model consisted of a visual information store, scanning, rehearsal, and an auditory information store. The **visual information store** is a sensory store that preserves information for a brief period lasting from a fraction of a second to a second. The decay rate depends on such factors as the intensity, contrast, and duration of the stimulus and also on whether exposure to the stimulus is followed by a second exposure. Visual masking occurs when a second exposure, consisting of a brightly lighted field or a different set of patterns, reduces the effectiveness of the visual information store.

For pattern recognition to occur, the information in the sensory store must be scanned. Sperling initially considered scanning to occur for one item at a time, as if each person had a sheet of cardboard with a hole in it just large enough for a single letter to appear.

The next two components of the model were **rehearsal** (saying the letters to oneself) and an **auditory information store** (remembering the names of the letters). To remember the items until recall, subjects usually reported rehearsing the items. Additional evidence for verbal rehearsal was found when recall errors often appeared in the form of auditory confusions—in other words, producing a letter that sounded like the correct letter. The advantage of the auditory store is that subvocalizing the names of the letters keeps them active in memory. Sperling's auditory store is part of short-term memory (STM), a topic we will consider later in the book.

Sperling revised his initial model in 1967. By this time, evidence had begun to accumulate suggesting that patterns were not scanned one at a time but were analyzed simultaneously. This distinction between performing one cognitive operation at a time (**serial processing**) and performing more than

parallel processing
Carrying out more than
one operation at a time,
such as looking at an art
exhibit and making
conversation

scan component The
attention component of
Sperling's model that de-
termines what is recog-
nized in the visual
information store

one cognitive operation at a time (**parallel processing**) is a fundamental distinction in cognitive psychology. Sperling therefore modified his idea of the
scan component to allow for pattern recognition to occur simultaneously
over the entire display, although the rate of recognition in a given location
depended on where the subject was focusing attention.

As I indicated in Chapter 1, this was one of the first models that attempted to indicate how various stages (sensory store, pattern recognition,
and STM) combined to influence performance on a visual processing task. It
contributed to the construction of the general model illustrated in Figure 1.1
and led to further development of more detailed models of how people recognize letters in visual displays (Rumelhart, 1970).

Rumelhart's Model

In 1970 Rumelhart proposed a detailed mathematical model of performance
on a wide range of information-processing tasks, including the whole-report
and partial-report procedures studied by Sperling. His model built on the key
assumptions of Sperling's model such as the importance of the visual information store and the use of a parallel scan to recognize patterns. But Rumelhart
was more specific in describing how pattern recognition occurs. He assumed
that recognition occurs by identification of the features of a pattern.

Feature recognition occurs simultaneously over the entire display, but it
takes time to recognize features; the more time the observer has, the more features the observer can recognize. Imagine that you are looking at the screen
of a tachistoscope, and the experimenter presents a brief exposure of the letters
F, R, and Z. If the exposure is very short, you might see only the vertical line
of the letter F, the curve of the letter R, and the diagonal line of the letter Z.
If forced to guess at this point, you would most likely use this information.
You might guess that the R was an R, P, or B because these letters have
curved segments at the top. If the exposure is a little longer, you will be able
to see more features, and it will be easier to guess or even recognize the entire
letter. Your success in identifying the letters will be determined then not only
by the length of the exposure but also by how quickly you can recognize the
features.

The rate of feature recognition in Rumelhart's model is influenced by
both the clarity of the information and the number of items in the display.
When the exposure terminates, the clarity declines as the visual information
store decays. The number of items in the display affects the rate of feature
recognition because the model assumes that people have a limited amount
of attention, which is divided across all items in the display. As the number
of items increases, the amount of attention that can be focused on each item
declines, and this slows the rate of recognizing that particular item.

The assumption that the rate of feature recognition depends on both the
number of items in the display and the clarity of the information is used by
Rumelhart to account for performance on Sperling's task. Rumelhart's model
proposed that people can report an average of only 4.5 letters in the whole-
report procedure because of a perceptual limitation rather than a memory
limitation. As the number of letters is increased to 12, people continue to try

to recognize all the letters simultaneously. But the rate of recognizing each letter slows as more letters are added to the display. Although there are more letters that could be recognized, the increase is compensated for by the lower probability of recognizing each letter.

Rumelhart's model assumed that in the partial-report procedure the observer tries to recognize letters over the entire display before hearing the tone. Then, on hearing the tone, the observer attends only to the cued row in the visual information store and tries to recognize additional letters in that particular row. The rate of recognition is faster because the observer now has to attend to only 4 letters rather than 12. But as the visual information store decays, not only is there less time to use it, but it also becomes harder to use because of decreasing clarity. Success in focusing on the cued row therefore depends very critically on the timing of the tone, as illustrated by Figure 2.11. Rumelhart's assumptions provided accurate quantitative predictions about performance not only on Sperling's tasks but also on a number of other tasks.

More recent studies have confirmed many of these assumptions, including the assumption that people switch from looking at the entire display to looking only at the cued row after they know which row to report (Gegenfurtner & Sperling, 1993). However, before receiving the cue, observers attend primarily to the middle row and therefore are more accurate when asked to report letters from this row.

You may have guessed by now that it is difficult to use the partial-report paradigm to answer Sperling's initial question about how many letters people perceive during a brief exposure. Observers begin by trying to perceive letters over the entire display with an emphasis on the middle row; they then hear a tone and decide where to shift their attention; and finally they try to recognize letters in only the cued row.

detection paradigm A procedure in which observers have to specify which of two possible target patterns is present in a display

A better procedure for answering this question, called the **detection paradigm**, was designed by Estes and Taylor (1966). This procedure requires that the observer report which one of two target letters is in a display of letters. For instance, the subject might be told that a display will contain either a *B* or an *F*, and the task is to report which letter is present. The memory requirements are minimal because the subject must report only a single letter. By using the percentage of trials on which the observer was right, and correcting for guessing, Estes and Taylor were able to calculate the average number of letters perceived on each trial. The detection procedure has also been analyzed by Rumelhart (1970) as a part of his general model—a model that provided an impressive account of performance on the visual information-processing tasks studied during the 1960s.

WORD RECOGNITION

The Word Superiority Effect

Much of the research on pattern recognition during the 1970s shifted away from how people recognize isolated letters to how people recognize letters in words. This research was stimulated by a finding that was labeled the *word superiority effect*. Reicher (1969), in his dissertation at the University of

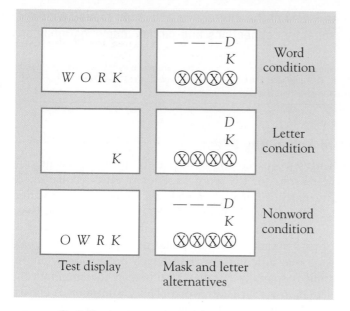

FIGURE **2.12** Example of the three experimental conditions in Reicher's (1969) experiment. The mask and response alternatives followed the test display. The task was to decide which of the two alternatives had appeared in the test position

Michigan, investigated a possible implication of the scan component in Sperling's 1967 model. If the observer tries to recognize all the letters in an array simultaneously, is it possible to recognize a four-letter unit in the same amount of time as it takes to recognize a single letter?

To answer this question, Reicher designed an experiment in which observers were shown a single letter, a four-letter word, or a four-letter nonword. The task was always to identify a single letter by selecting one of two alternatives. The exposure of the stimulus was immediately followed by a visual masking field with the two response alternatives directly above the critical letter. For example, one set of stimuli consisted of the word *WORK*, the letter *K*, and the nonword *OWRK*. The two alternatives in this case were the letters *D* and *K*, which were displayed above the critical *K* (Figure 2.12). Observers indicated whether they thought the letter in that position had been a *D* or a *K*.

This example illustrates several characteristics of Reicher's design. First, the four-letter word has the same letters as the four-letter nonword. Second, the position of the critical letter is the same for the word and the nonword. Third, both of the response alternatives make a word (WORD or WORK) for the word condition and a nonword for the nonword condition. Fourth, the memory requirements are minimized by requiring that subjects identify only a single letter, even when four letters are presented.

The results showed that subjects were significantly more accurate in identifying the critical letter when it was part of a word than when it was part of a nonword or when it was presented alone (the **word superiority effect**). Eight of the nine subjects did better on single words than on single letters. The one subject who reversed this trend was the only subject who said that she saw the words as four separate letters, which she made into words; the other subjects said that they experienced a word as a single word, not as four letters making up a word.

The word superiority effect is another example of top-down processing. We saw previously how our knowledge of what words would fit into a particular verbal context helped us recognize a word. The word superiority effect shows how our knowledge of words helps us to more rapidly recognize the letters within a word. Top-down processing, based on knowledge stored in LTM, can therefore aid pattern recognition in different ways.

A letter (critical letter) is easier to identify when part of a word than when alone.

word superiority effect
The finding that accuracy in recognizing a letter is higher when the letter is in a word than when it appears alone or is in a nonword

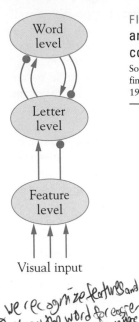

Visual input

we recognize features and
know the word because
identification for letters.

interactive activation model A theory that proposes that both feature knowledge and word knowledge combine to provide information about the identity of letters in a word

Show positive evidence for a certain letter

excitatory connection A positive association between concepts that belong together, as when a vertical line provides support for the possibility that a letter is a *K*

inhibitory connection A negative association between concepts that do not belong together, as when the presence of a vertical line provides negative evidence that a letter is a *C*

Show negative evidence for a letter.

FIGURE **2.13** The three levels of the interactive activation model, with arrows indicating the excitatory connections and circles indicating inhibitory connections

Source: From "An interactive-activation model of context effects in letter perception: Part 1. An account of basic findings," by J. L. McClelland & D. E. Rumelhart, 1981, *Psychological Review, 88,* 375–407, Fig. 2. Copyright 1981 by the American Psychological Association. Reprinted by permission.

A Model of the Word Superiority Effect

One of the great challenges for psychologists interested in word recognition has been to explain the reasons for the word superiority effect (Pollatsek & Rayner, 1989). A particularly influential model, the **interactive activation model** proposed by McClelland and Rumelhart (1981), contains several basic assumptions that build on the assumptions of Rumelhart's earlier model of letter recognition. The first assumption is that visual perception involves parallel processing. There are two different senses in which processing occurs in parallel. Visual processing is spatially parallel, resulting in the simultaneous processing of all four letters in a four-letter word. This assumption is consistent with Sperling's parallel scan and with Rumelhart's model of how people attempt to recognize an array of letters.

Visual processing is also parallel in the sense that recognition occurs simultaneously at three different levels of abstraction. The three levels—the feature level, the letter level, and the word level—are shown in Figure 2.13. A key assumption of the interactive activation model is that the three levels interact to determine what we perceive. Knowledge about the words of a language interacts with incoming feature information to provide evidence about which letters are in the word. This is illustrated by the arrows in Figure 2.13, which show that the letter level receives information from both the feature level and the word level.

There are two kinds of connections between levels: excitatory connections and inhibitory connections. **Excitatory connections** provide positive evidence, and **inhibitory connections** provide negative evidence about the identity of a letter or word. For example, a diagonal line provides positive evidence for the letter *K* (and all other letters that contain a diagonal line) and negative evidence for the letter *D* (and all other letters that do not contain a diagonal line). Excitatory and inhibitory connections also occur between the letter level and word level, depending on whether the letter is part of the word in the appropriate position. Recognizing that the first letter of a word is a *W* increases the activation level of all words that begin with a *W* and decreases the activation level of all other words.

The interactive activation model builds on the assumptions of Rumelhart's theory of letter recognition, discussed previously. Each feature in the display has some probability of being detected that varies with the visual quality of the display. Features that are detected increase the activation level of letters that contain the feature and decrease the activation level of those letters that do not contain the feature. The excitatory and inhibitory influences combine to determine the total activation of each letter. For instance, detecting a vertical and a diagonal line would strongly activate those letters (such as *K* and *R*) that contain both of these features.

Not all psychologists believe that the interactive activation model is correct. Massaro and Cohen (1991), in particular, have carefully compared the predictions of the interactive activation model with the predictions of a model that assumes that word and letter information combine independently, rather than interact. Unlike the interactive activation model, illustrated in Figure 2.13, their model does not have connections coming from the word level back down to the letter level. Information about words therefore does not directly influence the activation of letters. Massaro and Cohen's data suggest that assuming independent integration of information from letter and word levels may generate more accurate predictions than assuming that information at the word level interacts with information at the letter level.

A more recent critique of the interactive activation model was stimulated by an e-mail message that you may have seen. The message contained examples of phrases consisting of scrambled words that were remarkably easy to read. For example: Does the huamn mnid raed wrods as a wlohe? The examples demonstrated that a text composed of words whose inner letters were re-arranged could be read fairly easily. This finding presents a problem for any model, such as the interactive activation model, that assumes that all the letters of a word are in their correct order. It does not provide a problem for other models of word recognition that allow for more flexibility in how the letters are ordered (Grainger & Whitney, 2004).

I have devoted a considerable amount of space to discussing the interactive activation model, and you may be wondering if it is worth your time if some psychologists believe it is wrong. I have two responses. A general response is that there are very few (if any) theories in psychology that have gone unchallenged. Psychologists continually try to formulate better theories, and there is often considerable debate about which is the best theory. A more specific response is that the interactive activation model has had a tremendous impact on the formulation of psychological theories because it helped rekindle interest in neural network models of cognition. Although neural network models have been developed for many cognitive tasks, such as storing information in STM (Burgess & Hitch, 1992), selecting an analogous problem in problem solving (Holyoak & Thagard, 1989), and comprehending text (Kintsch, 1988), they have been most widely used to model pattern recognition. Let's now consider the general assumptions of this approach.

Neural Network Models

The interactive activation model was the first step for McClelland and Rumelhart in their development of neural network models of cognition. They referred to such models as **parallel distributed processing** (PDP) models because information is evaluated in parallel and is distributed throughout the network. A **neural network model** consists of a number of components (Rumelhart, Hinton, & McClelland, 1986), some of which we have already considered in the interactive activation model. These include:

1. A set of processing units called **nodes**. Nodes are represented by features, letters, and words in the interactive activation model. They can acquire different levels of activation.

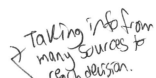

Taking info from many sources to reach decision.

parallel distributed processing (PDP) When information is simultaneously collected from different sources and combined to reach a decision

neural network model A theory in which concepts (nodes) are linked to other concepts through excitatory and inhibitory connections to approximate the behavior of neural networks in the brain

nodes The format for representing concepts in a semantic network

↳ A concept

2. A pattern of *connections* among nodes. Nodes are connected to one another by excitatory and inhibitory connections that differ in strength.

3. Activation rules for the nodes. **Activation rules** specify how a node combines its excitatory and inhibitory inputs with its current state of activation.

4. A state of *activation*. Nodes can be activated to various degrees. We become conscious of nodes that are activated above a threshold level of conscious awareness. For instance, we become consciously aware of the letter *K* in the word *WORK* when it receives enough excitatory influences from the feature and word levels.

5. *Output functions* of the nodes. The output functions relate activation levels to outputs—for example, what threshold has to be exceeded for conscious awareness.

6. A *learning rule*. Learning generally occurs by changing the weights of the excitatory and inhibitory connections between the nodes, and the learning rule specifies how to make these changes.

The last component—the learning component—is one of the most important features of a neural network model because it enables the network to improve its performance. An example would be a network model that learns to make better discriminations among letters by increasing the weights of the distinctive features—those features that are most helpful for making the discrimination.

By 1992 the neural network approach had resulted in thousands of research efforts and an industry that spends several hundred million dollars annually (Schneider & Graham, 1992). The excitement of this approach can be attributed to several reasons. First, many psychologists believe that neural network models more accurately portray how the brain works than other, more serial models of behavior. Second, adjusting the excitatory and inhibitory weights that link nodes allows a network to learn, and this may capture how people learn. Third, the models allow for a different kind of computing in which many weak constraints (such as evidence from both the feature and word levels) can be simultaneously considered.

Neural network models would be particularly attractive if their assumptions corresponded to the actual functioning of the brain. An example of such a model is the one developed by Huber and O'Reilly (2003) that builds on the assumptions of the interactive-activation model (McClelland & Rumelhart, 1981). Both models have a feature, letter, and word level, but there are two changes that make the Huber and O'Reilly model a closer approximation of neural activity. First, the connections in this model temporarily habituate, resulting in lower firing rates when viewing a stimulus for a longer time. Second, the inhibitory connections of this model are *within* levels (the lateral inhibition in Figure 2.14) rather than *between* levels, which produces masking effects and competition between alternative interpretations of the same stimulus.

Figure 2.15 illustrates a word recognition task in which a target word (SHADE) occurs for 50 msec, followed by a mask and test display. The test display requires identifying which of two words occurred—GUEST (the foil) or SHADE (the target). But the most important part of the experiment is the

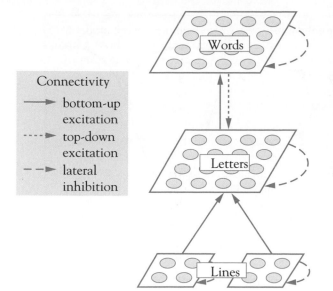

FIGURE **2.14** A neural network model developed by Huber and O'Reilly (2003)

Source: Based on Figure 3 from "Immediate priming and cognitive aftereffects," by D. E. Huber, 2008, *Journal of Experimental Psychology: General, 137,* 324–347. Copyright 2008 by the American Psychological Association. Reprinted by permission.

presentation of either the target word (target-primed) or foil word (foil-primed) at the beginning of each trial. It would seem intuitively obvious that presenting the target prime would increase correct identifications, and presenting the foil-prime would decrease correct identifications. The left panel of Figure 2.16, however, shows that the results are more complex and interesting than our intuitions.

Notice that relative effectiveness of the target-prime and foil-prime depends on the duration of the prime. At short durations of 150 msec or less, the target prime is more effective than the foil prime, but this effect reverses by 400 msec. The foil prime is particularly troublesome at a 50 msec duration because the perceiver sees two rapidly-presented 50-msec words and it is difficult to identify their order. Did GUEST or SHADE appear as the second word? Increasing the duration of the foil prime makes it easier to identify the target.

The puzzling aspect of the results is that increasing the duration of the target prime

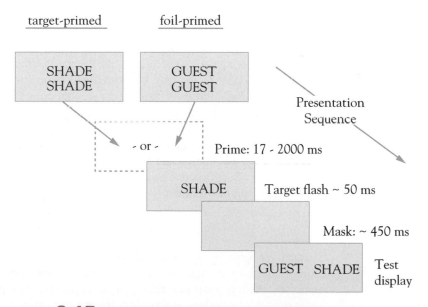

FIGURE **2.15** A methodology for priming word recognition

Source: Based on figure 1 from "Immediate priming and cognitive aftereffects," by D. E. Huber, 2008, *Journal of Experimental Psychology: General, 137,* 324–347.

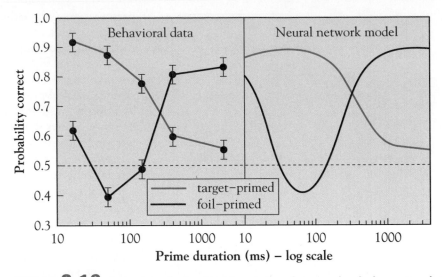

FIGURE **2.16** Actual and simulated results of a word-priming experiment shown in figure 2.15

Source: Based on figure 2 from "Immediate priming and cognitive aftereffects," by D. E. Huber, X. Tian, T. Curran, R. C. O'Reilly, & B. Woroch. (2008). *Journal of Experimental Psychology: Human Perception and Performance, 34,* 1389–1416.

has the opposite result. Why would having more time to look at the target prime make it more difficult to identify the target? The concept of habituation helps us answer this question. Viewing a word for longer durations creates neural habituation for that word, making the word more difficult to identify when it occurs again as the target. At the same time, this habituation makes other words easier to identify because they are no longer inhibited. This interplay between habituation of excitatory connections between levels and the inhibitory connections within levels in the Huber-O'Reilly model successfully predicts these findings, as shown by the right panel in Figure 2.16.

In conclusion, neural network models represent one approach to modeling cognition. Linking these models to discoveries in cognitive neuroscience (Huber et al., 2008) provides exciting opportunities for increasing our understanding of cognition and the brain.

SUMMARY

Pattern recognition is a skill that people perform very well. Three explanations of pattern recognition are template, feature, and structural theories. A template theory proposes that people compare two patterns by measuring their degree of overlap. A template theory has difficulty accounting for many aspects of pattern recognition, but it is a useful way of representing information in the sensory store before it is analyzed during the pattern recognition stage. The most common theories of pattern recognition assume that patterns are analyzed into features. Perceptual discrimination requires discovering those critical features that distinguish patterns. Structural theories state explicitly how the features of a pattern are joined together. They provide a more complete description of a pattern and are particularly useful for describing patterns consisting of intersecting lines.

Sperling's interest in the question of how many letters can be perceived during a brief tachistoscopic exposure resulted in the construction of information-processing models for visual tasks. Sperling proposed that information is preserved very briefly in a visual information store, where all the letters can be simultaneously analyzed. When a letter is recognized, its name can be verbally rehearsed and preserved in an auditory store (STM).

Rumelhart's model proposed that we recognize patterns by identifying their features. The rate of feature identification depends on both the clarity of items in the visual information store and the number of letters in a display. The model accounts for performance on Sperling's partial-report task by assuming that the observer focuses attention on the cued row as soon as the tone is heard. The probability of recognizing additional letters in the row depends on the clarity of the visual information store.

Recognition of letters in a word is influenced by perceptual information and the context of the letter. The finding that a letter can be recognized more easily when it is part of a word than when it is part of a nonword or is presented by itself has been called the word superiority effect. An influential model of the word superiority effect is the interactive activation model proposed by McClelland and Rumelhart. Its major assumption is that knowledge about the words of a language interacts with incoming feature information to provide evidence regarding which letters are in the word. This approach has continued under the general label of parallel distributed processing and is inspired by neural network models of the brain. Recent developments of neural network models use discoveries in cognitive neuroscience to evaluate their assumptions.

STUDY QUESTIONS

1. Some might claim there is no definite agreement of what a pattern is. Don't be daunted—write your own definition of *pattern*. Now look up *pattern* in a good dictionary.
   Does that help?

2. In what sense can pattern recognition be considered a skill? (To answer this question, you must have a usable definition of *skill*. What is yours?)

3. Distinguish among template, feature, and structure. What is each like, and how do the concepts differ?

4. What does Phillips's 1974 experiment tell us about the presumed characteristics of the sensory store? What is the difference between a sensory image and a visual image?

5. The text tells about an application of feature theory that helps children learn differences between similar letters. What is involved in the search for a "good" set of features—that is, how would you tell whether a suggested set of features is good?

6. Why are people better at discriminating among faces in their own ethnic group? How would the concept of "distinctive features" help them discriminate among faces in other ethnic groups?

7. How does structural theory go beyond feature theories? What evidence would you cite

to support its claim to be the best description of visual pattern recognition?

8. Why is Sperling's 1960s research still discussed in most introductory psychology texts?

9. How does a visual masking field work? What does it do? Why is this procedure essential to the study of the word superiority effect?

10. Neural network models represent a major theoretical approach in psychology but are difficult to summarize in simple terms. Explain the major assumptions of these models in your own words.

CogLab   The following experiment that relates to this chapter may be found at: http://coglab. wadsworth.com. Answer the questions in the CogLab Student Manual as required by your teacher for these experiments.

Receptive Fields

Muller-Lyer Illusion

Visual Search

Partial Report

Word Superiority

Metacontrast Masking

KEY TERMS

The page number in parentheses refers to where the term is discussed in the chapter.

activation rule (38)

auditory information store (32)

caricature (25)

detection paradigm (34)

distinctive feature (23)

excitatory connection (36)

Feature theory (22)

geons (28)

inhibitory connection (36)

interactive activation model (36)

interstimulus interval (21)

neural network model (37)

nodes (37)

parallel distributed processing (PDP) (37)

parallel processing (33)

partial-report procedure (30)

pattern recognition (18)

perceptual confusion (22)

rehearsal (32)

scan component (33)

sensory store (20)

serial processing (32)

structural theory (26)

tachistoscope (18)

template (19)

visual information store (VIS) (32)

whole-report procedure (30)

word superiority effect (35)

RECOMMENDED READING

Hoffman's (1998) book, *Visual Intelligence*, provides both a readable and scholarly analysis of how we construct descriptions of objects. Loftus, Shimamura, and Johnson (1985) describe characteristics of the visual information store. Fallshore and Schooler (1995) argue that verbally describing faces can lower later recognition because verbal descriptions ignore configural information. Other areas of research on pattern recognition include the recognition of speech (Poeppel & Monahan, 2008), faces (McKone, Kanwisher, & Duchaine, 2007; Palermo & Rhodes, 2007; Tarr & Cheng, 2003), scenes (Braun, 2003; Green & Hummel, 2004), maps (B. Tversky, 2005), and the teaching of reading (Rayner, Foorman, Perfetti, Psetsky, & Seidenberg, 2001). A collection of chapters explores analytic and holistic processes in object recognition (Peterson & Rhodes, 2003) and Bar (2007) discusses how the neurological components of these processes support prediction. Martindale's (1991) book, *Cognitive Psychology: A Neural-Network Approach*, and Pinker's (1997) *How the Mind Works* provide a very readable introduction to the influence of neural network, theories on cognitive theories.

3

Attention

Everyone knows what attention is. It is the taking possession by the mind, in clear and vivid form, of one out of what seem several simultaneously possible objects or trains of thought. Focalization, concentration of consciousness are of its essence.

—William James (1890)

selectivity The selective aspects of attention—we pay attention to some aspects of our environment and ignore other aspects

The preceding quote from William James's famous *The Principles of Psychology*, published in 1890, refers to two characteristics of attention that continue to be studied today—focalization and concentration. Focalization implies **selectivity**. We are usually bombarded by all kinds of perceptual stimuli and must decide which of these are of interest to us. The selective nature of attention is illustrated by the behavior of subjects in Sperling's partial-report task: When a cue signaled which row to report, subjects were able to attend selectively to the cued row and ignore the information in the other two rows.

The selective nature of perception is necessary to keep us from becoming overloaded with information. This is particularly true in large cities. According to Milgram (1970), a well-known social psychologist, in midtown Manhattan it is possible to encounter 220,000 people within a 10-minute radius of one's office. This kind of overload, Milgram argues, can affect our life on several levels, influencing role performance, the evolution of social norms, and cognitive functioning. Adaptive responses to information overload include spending less time on each input, disregarding low-priority inputs, or completely blocking off some sensory inputs.

bottleneck theory A theory that attempts to explain how people select information when some information-processing stage becomes overloaded with too much information

The first part of this chapter is concerned with theories that try to locate the stage at which this selection occurs. Do we block off the sensory input before it reaches the pattern recognition stage, or do we make the selection after recognition? Theories that attempt to answer this question are called **bottleneck theories** because they assume that selection is necessary whenever too much information reaches a bottleneck—a stage that cannot process all of it.

concentration Investing mental effort in one or more tasks

mental effort The amount of mental capacity required to perform a task

The second aspect of attention is **concentration**. Imagine that you are the first to arrive at a cocktail party, and you carry on a conversation with the hostess. As long as there are no other conversations in the room, it will require little concentration or mental effort to follow what your hostess is saying. If she were not speaking in your native language, however, comprehension would be less automatic and would require more **mental effort**. You would also have to concentrate more to follow what she was saying if you were surrounded by many other conversations. If you wanted to eavesdrop on one of the other conversations while you were listening to the hostess, still more concentration or mental effort would be required.

The amount of mental effort required to perform a task is also determined by differences in people. As shown in Figure 2 on the inside front cover, people who are at risk for developing Alzheimer disease (the top pair of brain scans) require more mental effort to perform a memory task than people who are not at risk (the middle pair of brain scans). Mental effort is determined by the amount of blood flow to different regions of the brain as measured by functional magnetic resonance imaging (fMRI). This discovery may lead to early detection of Alzheimer disease.

The next section of this chapter discusses **capacity theories** of attention, which try to determine how capacity or mental effort is allocated to different activities. Such theories propose that attention is limited in capacity, and when we try to attend to more than one event—studying while watching television, for instance—we pay the price of doing each less efficiently. Rumelhart's model, discussed in Chapter 2, is a theory that assumes a limited capacity. According to his model, feature recognition slows as the number of items increases because a limited amount of attention must be distributed over more patterns.

Before I talk about attention in my own course on cognitive psychology, I have the students try to listen to two verbal messages at once. Two volunteers come to the front of the class and read different passages from one of their books. The rest of the class usually find it very difficult to comprehend both of the messages simultaneously. It is easier to try to comprehend only one of the messages, but the difficulty of the task depends on physical characteristics such as pitch and separation. The difficulty increases as the pitch of the two speakers becomes more similar or the two speakers stand closer together. If you have the opportunity, try to participate in such a demonstration and observe some of these effects for yourself. It will give you a better understanding of the listener's task.

BOTTLENECK THEORIES

Broadbent's Filter Model

As you may recall, the discussion of information-processing models in Chapter 1 included a summary of Broadbent's (1958) filter model. That model could account for much of the data on attention that had been collected at that time. One example is an experiment in which enlisted men in England's Royal Navy listened to three pairs of digits (Broadbent, 1954). One member of each pair arrived at one ear at the same time that the other member of the pair arrived at the other ear. For example, if the sequence were 73-42-15, the subject would simultaneously hear 7 and 3, followed by 4 and 2, followed by 1 and 5. That is:

Left ear	Right ear
7	3
4	2
1	5

The pairs were separated by a half-second interval, and the subjects were asked to report the digits in whatever order they chose. They were able to report 65% of the lists correctly, and almost all the correct reports involved recalling all the digits presented to one ear, followed by all the digits presented to the other ear. In other words, if 741 had been presented to the left ear and 325 to the right ear, the subject would recall either in the order 741-325 or in the order 325-741.

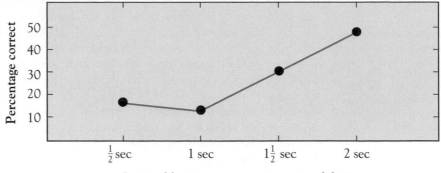

FIGURE **3.1** Recall of digit sequences as a function of the interval between pairs

Source: From "The role of auditory localization in attention and memory span," by D. E. Broadbent, 1954, *Journal of Experimental Psychology, 47*, 191–196. Copyright 1954 by the American Psychological Association. Reprinted by permission.

Another group of men was instructed to recall the digits in the actual order of their arrival: the first pair of digits, followed by the second pair, followed by the third pair. The time between successive pairs of digits varied from 1/2 to 2 seconds. Figure 3.1 shows the percentage of lists correctly recalled as a function of the interval between pairs. Performance was better at the longer intervals; nevertheless, it was much worse than when subjects could recall the digits heard in one ear and then the other ear.

To account for these findings, Broadbent (1957) used the **filter model**, which can be represented by the mechanical model shown in Figure 3.2. The mechanical model consists of a Y-shaped tube and a set of identifiable balls. The tube has a narrow stem that can accept only a single ball at a time (the **limited-capacity perceptual channel**), but upper branches (the *sensory store*) are wider and can accept more than one ball at a time. At the junction of the stem and branches is a hinged flap (the *filter*), which can swing back and forth to allow balls from either branch of the Y to enter the stem.

In this case the balls represent digits, and the two branches represent the two ears. Two balls are simultaneously dropped, one into each branch. The flap door would be set to one side to allow one of the balls to enter the stem, while the other ball would be held in a sensory store. If the observer wanted to report all the digits entering one ear, the flap would stay to one side until all three balls from one branch entered the stem. This is illustrated in Figure 3.2 for reporting the left ear first. The flap would then be shifted to the other side, allowing the three balls from the other branch to enter the stem. If the observer were forced to report the digits as they arrived, the flap would have to be shifted back and forth to allow balls to enter the stem in the order in which they arrived.

The model accounts for performance on Broadbent's (1954) task by assuming that it takes time to switch attention (represented by the flap, or filter)

filter model The proposition that a bottleneck occurs at the pattern recognition stage and that attention determines what information reaches the pattern recognition stage

limited-capacity perceptual channel The pattern recognition stage of Broadbent's model, which is protected by the filter (attention) from becoming overloaded with too much perceptual information

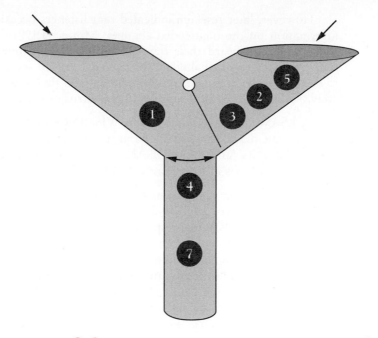

FIGURE **3.2** A mechanical model of attention

Source: From "A mechanical model for human attention and immediate memory," by D. E. Broadbent, 1957, *Psychological Review, 64,* 205–215. Copyright 1957 by the American Psychological Association. Reprinted by permission.

from ear to ear. If the interval separating the pairs of balls is too short, the flap will not have time to switch back and forth, and performance will deteriorate as it did when the interval was 1 second or less (see Figure 3.1). The easiest case should be when the listener can report all the digits entering one ear before reporting all the digits entering the other ear. In this case the listener can recognize all the digits entering one ear before recognizing the digits entering the other ear, and only a single shift of attention is required. But the shift has to occur *before* the information entering the unattended ear decays from the auditory sensory store. A limitation of the filter model is that the sensory store would have to last fairly long to operate as proposed; otherwise, the information would decay before it could be recognized.

Treisman's Attenuation Model

shadowing An experimental method that requires people to repeat the attended message out loud

A common experimental paradigm for testing Broadbent's assumption that the listener can recognize information on only one channel at a time is to present a different but continuous message to each ear and ask the listener to "**shadow**," or repeat aloud, one of the messages. Shadowing a message provides proof that the listener is following instructions and attending to the correct ear. The initial findings from shadowing experiments supported the filter model. As predicted, subjects were almost completely unaware of the content of the message played to the unattended ear (Cherry, 1953).

However, later research indicated that listeners occasionally could report information on the unattended channel. Moray (1959) discovered that subjects sometimes heard their own names on this channel. Treisman (1960) found that the **contextual effects** of language would sometimes cause subjects to report words on the unattended channel and therefore shadow inappropriately. Following are two examples of the intrusions that occurred:

contextual effect The influence of the surrounding context on the recognition of patterns

1.   ... I SAW THE GIRL / song was WISHING ...
    .... me that bird / JUMPING in the street ...
2.   ... SITTING AT A MAHOGANY / three POSSIBILITIES ...
    .... let us look at these / TABLE with her head ...

The first line in each example is the message that the listener was asked to shadow. The second line is the unattended message. The words in capital letters are the words actually spoken by the subjects. The intrusions from the unattended channel fit the semantic context better than the words on the attended channel. The contextual cues were not sufficient to cause subjects to change permanently to the unattended message in order to follow the meaning of the passage, but the results did raise some questions for the filter theory. If the filter completely blocks out the unattended message, how could subjects report hearing their names or shadow words on the unattended channel?

To answer this question, Treisman (1960) proposed a model consisting of two parts—a *selective filter* and a "dictionary." The filter distinguishes between two messages on the basis of their physical characteristics, such as location, intensity, or pitch. However, the filter in Treisman's model does not completely block out the unattended message but merely attenuates it, making it less likely to be heard. The recognition of a word occurs in the dictionary if the intensity or subjective loudness of the word exceeds its **threshold** (the minimum intensity needed for recognition). Thresholds have two important characteristics. First, they vary across words. Some words have permanently lower thresholds than others and thus are more easily recognized—for example, important words such as a person's own name and perhaps danger signals such as *fire*. Second, thresholds can be momentarily lowered by the listener's expectations. For instance, if the words *sitting at a mahogany* are heard, the threshold for the word *table* will be momentarily lowered, making recognition of that word more likely.

threshold The minimal amount of activation required to become consciously aware of a stimulus

The model proposed by Treisman was able to explain why usually very little is heard on the unattended channel, but occasionally some words are recognized. The **attenuation** of words on the unattended channel implies that they will be subjectively less loud than words on the attended channel. They will usually not be loud enough to exceed their threshold unless they have a very low threshold, or their threshold is momentarily lowered. Figure 3.3 shows a schematic representation of this effect. The height of the arrows represents the subjective loudness of the two messages, and the height of the thresholds represents the loudness that is necessary for recognition of the word. Because important words have permanently low thresholds, they can occasionally be heard on the unattended channel, as was found by Moray (1959). A word like *table* normally has a high threshold, but its threshold

attenuation A decrease in the perceived loudness of an unattended message

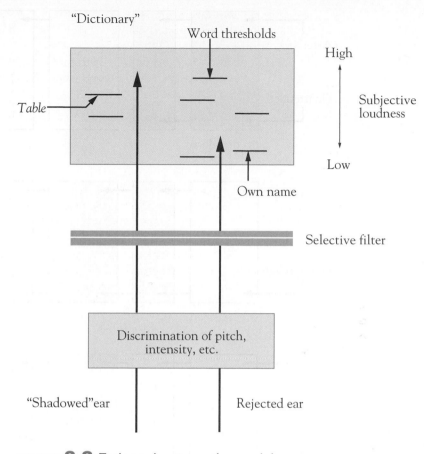

"Dictionary"

FIGURE **3.3** Treisman's attenuation model

Source: From "Contextual cues in selective listening," by A. M. Treisman, 1960, *Quarterly Journal of Experimental Psychology, 12,* 242–248. Copyright 1960 by the Experimental Psychology Society. Reprinted by permission.

can be momentarily lowered by expectations. This aspect of the model could account for Treisman's (1960) finding that words on the unattended channel were sometimes incorrectly shadowed if they better fit the context of the message on the attended channel.

The Deutsch-Norman Memory Selection Model

We have previously seen that a frequent problem in constructing information-processing models is identification of the stage at which a performance limitation occurs. Constructing models of attention is no exception. The models proposed by Broadbent and Treisman placed the bottleneck at the pattern recognition stage. However, according to the models proposed by Deutsch and Deutsch (1963) and Norman (1968), the bottleneck occurs *after* pattern recognition. The problem is not one of perception but one of selection into memory after perception occurs. Because selection occurs later, these models are often referred to as **late-selection models**.

late-selection model
Proposal that the bottleneck occurs when information is selected for memory

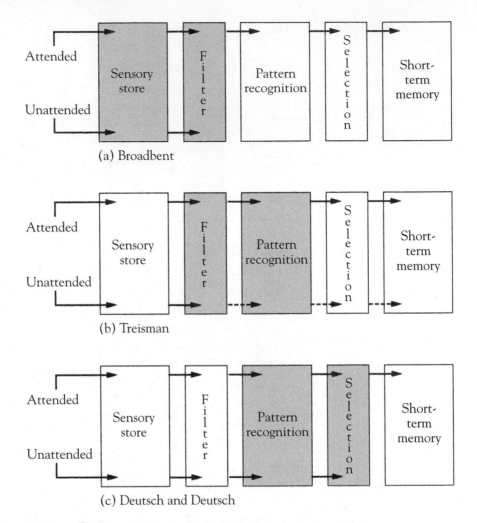

FIGURE 3.4 Comparison of three different models of attention. The blue stages show the most important components of each model (see text for explanation)

Let's apply a late-selection model to the task of listening to two different conversations (messages) in a shadowing experiment. The model assumes that words in both conversations are recognized but are quickly forgotten unless they are important. Words on the attended channel are important because people have to shadow them. Words on the unattended channel are usually unimportant because the listener is asked to attend to another channel. Although recognized, they are quickly forgotten unless they are important—a person's own name, for instance.

Figure 3.4 shows the differences in the models proposed by Broadbent, Treisman, and Deutsch and Deutsch. The two most important stages in Broadbent's model are the filter and the sensory store. Attention is represented by the filter that determines what information is recognized. An unattended message can be recognized in Broadbent's model only if attention switches to that message before it decays from the sensory store. The two most important stages in Treisman's model are the filter and pattern recognition stages. The filter attenuates the unattended message, with the implication that very few words are recognized on the unattended channel. Words in the unattended message are recognized only if their thresholds for pattern recognition are low enough to be exceeded by the attenuated message. The two most important stages in the Deutsch and Deutsch model are the pattern recognition and selection stages. Both messages are recognized, but only words selected into memory can be later recalled.

There have been many experimental attempts to evaluate the three models. Treisman attempted to determine the location of the bottleneck by asking participants to listen to a different list of words arriving in each ear and to tap whenever they heard an identical target word in either ear. In addition, they had to shadow (repeat out loud) all the words that arrived on the attended ear. She argued that the tapping response was so simple and immediate that people should do equally well in tapping to target words on the attended and unattended ears if the bottleneck occurred at the response-selection stage, but they should do much better in tapping to the target words in the attended ear if the bottleneck occurred at the perception stage. The participants detected the target word 87% of the time that it occurred in the attended ear and only 8% of the time that it occurred in the unattended ear (Treisman & Geffen, 1967), supporting the hypothesis that the bottleneck occurred at the perception stage.

However, Deutsch, Deutsch, and Lindsay (1967) did not accept these results as evidence against their theory. They argued that the shadowed words on the attended message are more important because they are shadowed, and this added importance increased the probability that they would elicit the tapping response. Furthermore, the fact that people occasionally report hearing their name or an expected word in the unattended message suggests that at least some words are heard on the unattended message.

CAPACITY THEORIES

The models proposed by Broadbent, Treisman, Deutsch, and Deutsch, and Norman stimulated many experiments and arguments regarding the location of the bottleneck. Some data seemed to support the assertion that the bottleneck was caused by the limitations of perception, whereas other data supported the assertion that the bottleneck occurred after perception (Johnston & Dark, 1986). The failure to agree on the location of the bottleneck has had two consequences.

First, it now seems reasonable to assume that the observer has some control over where the bottleneck occurs, depending on what is required in a particular task (Johnston & Heinz, 1978). However, as you can imagine, it would be more difficult to select information based on meaning than on pitch or location. This leads to the hypothesis that more mental effort (capacity) is required for late selection after pattern recognition than for early selection before pattern recognition.

Second, psychologists have become very interested in studying the capacity demands of different tasks. We will look first at the capacity model of attention proposed by Kahneman (1973) to see how a capacity model differs from a bottleneck model. Then we will review the theory proposed by Johnston and Heinz (1978) that suggests that attention is flexible. This theory is particularly interesting because it shows how a bottleneck theory can be related to a capacity theory.

Example of a Capacity Model

Capacity theories are concerned with the amount of mental effort required to perform a task. Kahneman's *Attention and Effort* (1973) helped to shift the emphasis from bottleneck theories to capacity theories. Kahneman argued that a capacity theory assumes there is a general limit on a person's capacity to perform mental work. His capacity model was designed to supplement, rather than to replace, the bottleneck models.

Both types of theories predict that simultaneous activities are likely to interfere with each other, but they attribute the interference to different causes. A bottleneck theory proposes that interference occurs because the same mechanism, such as speech recognition, is required to carry out two incompatible operations at the same time. A capacity model proposes that interference occurs when the demands of two activities exceed available capacity. Thus, a bottleneck model implies that the interference between tasks is specific and depends on the degree to which the tasks use the same mechanisms. A capacity model, in contrast, implies that the interference is nonspecific and depends on the total demands of the task.

A capacity model assumes that a person has considerable control over how this limited capacity can be allocated to different activities. For example, we can usually drive a car and carry on a conversation at the same time if both activities do not exceed our capacity for attending to two different tasks. But when heavy traffic begins to challenge our skills as a driver, it is better to concentrate only on driving and not try to divide our attention between the two activities.

allocation of capacity
When a limited amount of capacity is distributed to various tasks

A model of the **allocation of capacity** to mental activities is shown in Figure 3.5 Any kind of activity that requires attention would be represented in the model because all such activities compete for the limited capacity. Different mental activities require different amounts of attention; some tasks require little mental effort, and others require much effort. When the supply of attention does not meet the demands, the level of performance declines. An activity can fail entirely if there is not enough capacity to meet its demands or if attention is allocated to other activities.

arousal A physiological state that influences the distribution of mental capacity to various tasks

Kahneman's model assumes that the amount of capacity available varies with the level of **arousal**; more capacity is available when arousal is moderately high than when it is low. However, very high levels of arousal can interfere

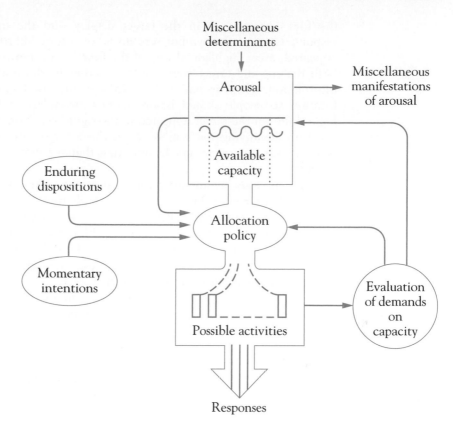

FIGURE **3.5** A capacity model for attention

Source: From Daniel Kahneman, *Attention and effort*, Copyright 1973, p. 10. Reprinted by permission of Prentice-Hall, Inc., Englewood Cliffs, NJ.

with performance. This assumption is consistent with Yerkes and Dodson's (1908) law that performance is best at intermediate levels of arousal.

The level of arousal can be controlled by feedback (evaluation) from the attempt to meet the demands of ongoing activities, provided that the total demands do not exceed the capacity limit. The choice of which activities to support is influenced by both enduring dispositions and momentary intentions. **Enduring dispositions** reflect the rules of involuntary attention. A novel event, an object in sudden motion, or the mention of our own name may automatically attract our attention. **Momentary intentions** reflect our specific goals or objectives at a particular time. We may want to listen to a lecturer or scan a crowd at an airport to recognize a friend.

The distinction between involuntary and voluntary attention raises the question of whether they interact. Folk, Remington, and Johnston (1992) report that they do interact; that involuntary attention can depend on voluntary attention. Look at the perceptual task in the upper half of Figure 3.6. Participants in this study were told that a symbol would appear in one of

enduring disposition An automatic influence where people direct their attention

momentary intention A conscious decision to allocate attention to certain tasks or aspects of the environment

the four outer boxes in the target display and the task was to rapidly respond whether the symbol was an × or an =. Shortly before the target appeared, a cue highlighted one of the four boxes. However, the location of both the cue and target were random so the cue did not provide any useful information. The cue had only a 25% chance of highlighting the correct location so people should ignore it. For example, the left box is cued in Figure 3.6 but the target appeared in the right box. Nonetheless, people were faster in identifying the symbol when the location was correctly cued than when it was incorrectly cued, indicating that the cue involuntarily captured attention.

The cue also involuntarily captured attention for the task shown in the lower half of Figure 3.6. In this case, both the target and cue are distinguished by the same color. People had to respond whether the color symbol in the target display was an × or an =. Notice that the color cue highlights the left box, but the color target occurs in the right box. However, the color cue also involuntarily captured attention even though it did not provide useful information about the location of the target.

The interaction between voluntary and involuntary attention is demonstrated by the finding that the cue was ignored when the cue displays in Figure 3.6 were interchanged. For example, if the top (noncolored) cue preceded the bottom (colored) target, the location of the cue had no effect on performance. In other words, involuntary attention to the cue depended on the voluntary attention to a specific feature of the target. If people were using color to select the target, the cue also had to be colored to attract attention. This finding indicates that not all stimuli automatically capture our attention—involuntary capture can depend on how we are directing our attention.

Capacity and Stage of Selection

Johnston and Heinz (1978) demonstrated the flexibility of attention and the interaction between a bottleneck and a capacity theory. They used selective listening tasks to develop their theory, so a bottleneck would be likely to occur. However, unlike the early bottleneck theories, their theory proposed that the listener has control over the location of the bottleneck. The location can vary along a continuum ranging from an early mode of selection—in other words,

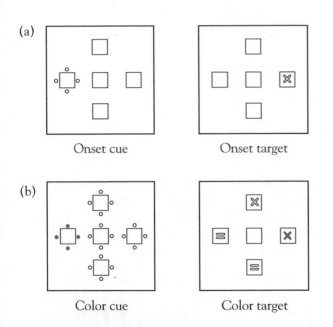

(a) Onset cue / Onset target

(b) Color cue / Color target

FIGURE **3.6** Example of a noncolored cue and target (a) and a colored cue and target (b).

Source: From "Involuntary covert orienting is contingent on attentional control settings," by C. L. Folk, R. W. Remington, & J. C. Johnston, 1992, *Journal of Experimental Psychology: Human Perception and Performance, 18,* 1030–1044. Copyright 1992 by the American Psychological Association. Reprinted by permission.

before recognition (as represented by Broadbent's theory)—to a late mode of selection—in other words, following a semantic analysis (as represented by Deutsch and Deutsch's theory). Johnston and Heinz call their theory a **multimode theory** because of its flexibility: The observer can adopt any mode of attention demanded by or best suited to a particular task.

Although a listener can attempt to understand the meaning of two simultaneous messages by adopting a late mode of selection, the use of a late mode is achieved at a cost. As the perceptual processing system shifts from an early to a late mode of selection, it collects more information about the secondary message, but this reduces the capacity to comprehend the primary message. The predicted result is that comprehension of the primary message will decline as the listener tries to process a secondary message more fully.

Johnston and Heinz tested these predictions in a series of five experiments. A common procedure for measuring the amount of capacity required to perform a task is to determine how quickly a person can respond to a **subsidiary task**. The main task in their research was a selective-listening task. A light signal occurred randomly throughout the listening task, and, as the subsidiary task, subjects were instructed to respond to it as quickly as possible by pushing a button. The experimenters assumed that the greater the portion of capacity allocated to selective listening, the less should be available for monitoring the signal light, causing longer reaction times.

One of the experiments used a paradigm in which subjects heard pairs of words presented simultaneously to both ears. Undergraduates at the University of Utah were asked to shadow words defined either by the pitch of a voice or by a semantic category. One set of stimuli used a male and a female voice, and the undergraduates were asked to shadow the words spoken by either the male or the female. These subjects could use an early, sensory mode of selection because the two messages were physically different. Another group of undergraduates heard two messages spoken by the same voice. One message consisted of words from a category, such as names of cities, and the other message consisted of words from a different category, such as names of occupations. Subjects were asked to report the words from one of the categories and ignore the words from the other category. These subjects had to use a late, semantic mode of selection because it was necessary to know the meaning of the words to categorize them.

The multimode theory predicts that more capacity is required to perform at a late mode of selection. Use of the semantic mode should therefore cause slower reaction times to the light signal and more errors on the selective-listening task. The theory also predicts that listening to two lists should require more capacity than listening to and shadowing one list, which should require more capacity than listening to no lists. Reaction times for the subsidiary task supported the predictions. The average time to respond to the light signal was 310 msec (millisecond) for no lists, 370 msec for one list, 433 msec for two lists that could be distinguished by using sensory cues (pitch), and 482 msec for two lists that could be distinguished by using only semantic cues (categories). These results were accompanied by

multimode theory A theory that proposes that people's intentions and the demands of the task determine the information-processing stage at which information is selected

subsidiary task A task that typically measures how quickly people can react to a target stimulus to evaluate the capacity demands of the primary task

different levels of performance on the shadowing task. The percentage of errors was 1.4 for a single list, 5.3 for the two lists that could be separated using sensory cues, and 20.5 for the two lists that could be separated using only semantic cues.

Johnston and Heinz interpreted the results as supporting their view that selective attention requires capacity and that the amount of capacity required increases from early to late modes of selection. The first assumption received support from the consistent finding across experiments that reaction times were slower when the listener had to listen to two lists rather than only one. The second assumption received support from the consistent finding that reaction times were slower when the listener had to attend on the basis of semantic cues rather than sensory cues. This latter finding, when combined with the performance results on the selective-listening task, suggests that a person can increase breadth of attention but only at a cost in capacity expenditure and selection accuracy.

After reviewing much of the research on visual and auditory attention, Pashler (1998) proposed a general model that is very similar to multimode theory. As shown in Figure 3.7, the model has both an early (filtering mechanism) and a late (semantic analysis) stage of selection. The filter can prevent stimuli, such as those represented by S3 in Figure 3.7, from being analyzed to a semantic level. For example, imagine that you are asked to report words spoken by a female voice (S1) and ignore words spoken by a male voice (S3). The difference in pitch enables you to block out the words

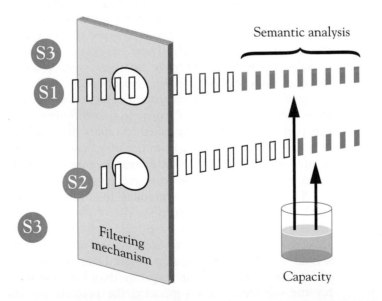

FIGURE **3.7** A model that incorporates both an early and a late stage of selection

Source: From *The psychology of attention*, by Harold Pashler, 1998, p. 227 (Cambridge, MA: MIT Press). Reprinted by permission.

spoken by the male, without analyzing their meaning. Now imagine that you must listen to pairs of simultaneously presented words spoken by the same voice. Your task is to report the name of a city (S1) and ignore the name of a profession (S2). It is now necessary to understand the meaning of both words to know which name is a city. The success of semantic analysis for those stimuli that pass the filter (S1 and S2) is determined by whether the analysis exceeds the available capacity, as in Kahneman's model. This appeared to be the case in Johnston and Heinz's results, which produced a rather high error rate when listeners had to recognize both words.

But there are two silver linings to this otherwise dark cloud. First, if attention is as flexible as suggested by the multimode theory, a person at least has the choice of how best to use it. Second, psychologists have demonstrated that, with sufficient practice, some tasks can become so automatic that they do not appear to require any of the precious capacity postulated by a capacity theory.

AUTOMATIC PROCESSING

The work of Johnston and Heinz and other cognitive psychologists has shown that tasks vary considerably in the amount of mental effort required to perform them. Some skills become so well practiced and routine that they require very minimal capacity. Psychologists have used the term **automatic processing** to refer to such skills. One characteristic of automatic processing is that it occurs without conscious awareness. Indeed, some theorists have argued that much of what we do is determined not by deliberate choices but by features of the environment that initiate mental processes that operate outside of consciousness (Bargh & Chartrand, 1999).

automatic processing
Performing mental operations that require very little mental effort

Acquisition of automatic processing is often an advantage. It allows us to perform routine activities without much concentration or mental effort. However, automatic processing can also be a disadvantage. We may put so little thought into what we are doing that we make a silly mistake or fail to remember what we did.

We begin by examining criteria that people can apply to determine whether they are using automatic processing. We then see how automatic processing is useful in performing complex tasks such as reading.

When Is a Skill Automatic?

Posner and Snyder (1975) have proposed three criteria to determine whether a skill is automatic. A skill is automatic if it (1) occurs without intention, (2) does not give rise to conscious awareness, and (3) does not interfere with other mental activities.

Learning to ride a bicycle is a familiar example that we can evaluate by using these criteria. Most of us have learned how to ride a bicycle, and perhaps we can still remember the early experience of wobbling back and forth for a few feet before stopping and having to start over. Balancing the bicycle initially required intention, conscious awareness of what we were trying to do, and mental effort that could interfere with our concentration on other activities. Once we learned how to balance, it became hard to imagine why we had had so much trouble initially. We could then ride a bicycle without consciously intending to balance, we had little conscious awareness of the movements we used to achieve balance, and we became more able to attend to the scenery or our thoughts because we no longer had to concentrate on balancing.

Another task that initially requires a lot of mental effort or capacity is reading a word. But, like riding a bicycle, reading a word eventually becomes a fairly automatic skill. In fact, it becomes so automatic that it is difficult to stop, even when reading would be a disadvantage. Consider a task in which you are shown words that are printed in red, green, or blue ink and your objective is simply to name the color of the ink. If the words are names of colors that cause a competing response (such as the word *red* printed in blue ink), it is better to avoid reading the words because it makes the task much harder. However, people cannot completely avoid reading the words, as is revealed by the fact that they perform the task more slowly when there are competing responses. This finding is called the **Stroop effect** after its discoverer (Stroop, 1935).

Stroop effect The finding that it takes longer to name the color of the ink a word is printed in when the word is the name of a competing color (for example, the word *red* printed in blue ink)

The Stroop effect provides a partial answer to the question asked by Posner and Snyder (1975) at the beginning of their article: To what extent are our conscious intentions and strategies in control of the way information is processed in our minds? The fact that people could not avoid reading words illustrates that we cannot always adapt our thought processes to the strategies required by the task. Because automatic processes occur without intention, they may occur even when they are a nuisance. Fortunately, automatic processes usually are advantageous and allow us to perform complex skills that would otherwise overload our limited capacity. Two of these skills are encoding information into memory and reading.

Automatic Encoding

You may be asked at the dinner table how your day went. You would find it fairly easy to recall the events that occurred even though you did not make a conscious effort to learn that information. It is likely that you automatically encoded that information into memory.

In 1979, Hasher and Zacks proposed a theory of *automatic encoding* that distinguished between two kinds of memory activities—those that require considerable effort, or capacity, and those that require very little or none. The former, or effortful processes, include various strategies to improve memory, such as visual imagery, elaboration, organization, and verbal rehearsal. The latter, or automatic processes, support **incidental learning**, when we are not consciously trying to learn. Hasher and Zacks proposed that we can automatically record frequency, spatial, and temporal information without consciously intending to keep track of this information.

incidental learning Learning that occurs when we do not make a conscious effort to learn

Frequency information is data that specifies how often different stimuli occur. An experimenter might vary the number of times people see different pictures during an experiment and then ask them to estimate how many times each picture appeared. *Spatial information* is data about where objects occur in the environment. The experimenter could present pictures in different locations and then ask people to recall the locations. *Temporal information* is data about when or for how long events occur. The experimenter might ask people about the relative recency or the relative duration of events that occurred during the experiment.

The claim that all three kinds of information can be automatically recorded in memory cannot be tested unless we specify the implications of automatic processing. Hasher and Zacks proposed five criteria that distinguish between automatic and effortful processing. Table 3.1 summarizes the criteria and their predicted effects. The predictions are:

1. *Intentional versus incidental learning.* Intentional learning occurs when we are deliberately trying to learn; incidental learning occurs when we are not. Incidental learning is as effective as intentional learning for automatic processes but is less effective for effortful processing. People have knowledge of frequency, spatial, and temporal information even when they are not trying to learn this information. (For example, we know that a word is more likely to begin with the letter *t* than with the letter *z* without trying to learn this information.)

2. *Effect of instructions and practice.* Instructions on how to perform a task and practice on the task should not affect automatic processes because they can already be carried out very efficiently. Both instructions and practice should, however, improve performance on effortful processes.

3. *Task interference.* Automatic processes should not interfere with each other because they require little or no capacity. Effortful processes require considerable capacity and should interfere with each other when they exceed the amount of available capacity.

4. *Depression or high arousal.* Emotional states such as depression or high arousal can reduce the effectiveness of effortful processes. Automatic processes should not be affected by emotional states.

TABLE **3.1**
Predicted effects for automatic and effortful processing

	Automatic Processing	Effortful Processing
Intentional versus incidental learning	No difference	Intentional better
Effect of instructions and practice	No effects	Both improve performance
Task interference	No interference	Interference
Depression or high arousal	No effects	Decreased performance
Developmental trends	None	Decreased performance in young children or elderly

5. *Developmental trends.* Automatic processes show little change with age. They are acquired early and do not decline in old age. Effortful processes show developmental changes; they are not performed as well by young children or the elderly.

If Hasher and Zacks (1979) are correct, then memory for frequency, temporal, and spatial information should not be affected by intentional versus incidental learning, practice, task interference, depression or high arousal, and developmental trends. The greatest amount of empirical support for these predictions has been for frequency information (Hasher & Zacks, 1984). Neither practice nor individual differences, including changes in development, have much influence on people's ability to judge the relative frequency of events. There is also considerable incidental learning of event frequencies. People were very good at judging the relative frequency of events, even when they did not know they would be tested on their knowledge of frequencies. The automatic encoding of this information is useful because knowledge of frequencies allows us to develop expectancies about the world. We will see specific examples of how people make use of this information in the chapters on categorization (Chapter 8) and decision making (Chapter 14).

Evidence for automatic encoding of spatial and temporal information has been more mixed and is influenced by such variables as the complexity of the task. Imagine that you are shown 20 drawings of common objects that occupy 20 of the cells in a 6 × 6 matrix. Later you see the same matrix, but the experimenter has switched the location of 10 of the objects. Could you identify the 10 objects that had not been moved?

If you had automatically encoded spatial location, this should be a relatively easy task, and it should not be influenced by the variables listed by Hasher and Zacks. But each of the variables investigated by Naveh-Benjamin (1988) influenced people's ability to identify which objects had not changed locations. Intentional learning was better than incidental learning, the simultaneous performance of another task disrupted spatial encoding, younger participants did better than older participants, and memory for locations improved with practice. Naveh-Benjamin argued that for fairly complex tasks, the criteria suggested by Hasher and Zacks might still hold but in a weaker sense. Those encoding processes showing less noticeable change as a function of age, practice, simultaneous processing, and incidental learning could be considered as more automatic than others.

An alternative theoretical approach is to argue that automatic processing is usually achieved only after extensive practice. The need for extensive practice is obvious for complex tasks, as is illustrated in "In the News" 3.1 on training quarterbacks. You may have had the experience that it was helpful to focus on the individual components of a skill when initially learning the skill, but difficult to focus on these components after they became integrated into a well-learned sequence. Indeed, research has confirmed this observation for athletic skills such as putting a golf ball or kicking a soccer ball (Beilock, Carr, MacMahon, & Starkes, 2002).

Automatic processing is also important for the acquisition of more familiar skills. In the next section, we consider the important role that automatic processing plays in reading.

IN THE NEWS **3.1**
Training Quarterbacks

Beth Azur

When a professional quarterback bungles a pass, spectators often question his vision or his brains. But human factors psychologists Arthur Fisk, PhD, and Neff Walker, PhD, view the quarterback's plight as "a classic visual search problem" and blame a lack of training, not a lack of smarts.

Capitalizing on skills-training research, the two Georgia Institute of Technology researchers have designed a computer-based training system to help quarterbacks choose the right receiver.... From previous work on skill acquisition, Fisk and Walker knew that to improve at a visual search task, people require thousands of practice trials. In support of this, the average age of the National Football League's (NFL)

best quarterbacks is 34, making it the only position where age—and presumably amount of practice—makes a difference ... "If you can automatize critical components of a critical skill, you can develop performance that is fast, error-resistant, and fluid," says Fisk. He and Walker wanted to design a training system that would give quarterbacks enough practice choosing the correct receiver to make each aspect of the process automatic.

The computer-based training system Fisk and Walker developed displays film clips of actual game and scrimmage plays on a large-screen, digitized video system. The video shows the playing field from a vantage point just behind the

quarterback, providing a view of all the offensive and defensive players. Giving a training quarterback a view similar to what he'd see on the field helps quarterbacks develop automatic responses to the visual stimuli they'll see during actual play—the look of the defense, the movement of players, explained Walker. Viewing plays from the sideline—where most teams shoot their video—helps players understand a play, but doesn't cultivate automatic responses to the images, he said.

Source: From "Solving a classic visual search problem," by Beth Azur, *APA Monitor*, July 1996, 20. Copyright 1996 by the American Psychological Association. Reprinted by permission.

Automatic Processing and Reading

One of the most demanding cognitive skills that face the young child is learning how to read. Learning to read requires many component skills, some of which we considered in the previous chapter. The child must analyze the features of letters, combine the features to identify the letters, convert the letters into sounds for pronouncing words, understand the meanings of individual words, and combine the meaning of the words to comprehend the text. According to a theory proposed by LaBerge and Samuels (1974), the ability to acquire complex, multicomponent skills such as reading depends on the capability of automatic processing.

Their criterion for deciding when a skill or subskill is automatic is that it can be completed while attention is directed elsewhere. The rationale behind this argument is that, unless at least some of the component skills can be completed without requiring capacity, the total demands of all the component skills will be simply too great for the individual to perform the task.

As we saw in the previous chapter, an initial component skill for successful reading is the ability to identify the features of a letter. The features must then be organized or combined to form a letter, a process that initially requires attention, according to LaBerge and Samuels. However, after sufficient practice in recognizing letters, the features can be combined automatically to form a letter, freeing some capacity for the other necessary component skills.

As an extension of their argument, words should require less capacity to recognize if we can recognize the word as a unit rather than as a string of individual letters. You may recall that almost all the people who participated in Reicher's (1969) experiment reported that they perceived a four-letter word as a unit rather than as four separate letters.

One consequence of perceiving a word as a unit is that it should cause us to attend less to the individual letters in the word. You can test your own ability to perceive individual letters in words by reading the following sentence. Read it once and then read it again, counting the *f*s.

FINISHED FILES ARE THE RESULT OF YEARS OF SCIENTIFIC STUDY COMBINED WITH THE EXPERIENCE OF MANY YEARS.

There are six *f*s in the sentence. If you counted fewer than six, please try again.

Most people find this a difficult task because they fail to detect the *f* in one of the words (*of*) even though it occurs three times in the sentence. One explanation of why we overlook this particular *f* is that it is pronounced like the letter *v*. Although this is a contributing factor, unitization also plays an important role (Schneider, Healy, & Gesi, 1991). Results obtained by Healy (1980) indicate that we often recognize frequently occurring words as units and therefore find it difficult to focus on their individual letters. Healy asked people to read a prose passage at normal reading speed but to circle the letter *t* whenever it occurred in the passage. She found that people were more likely to miss the letter when it occurred in common words than when it occurred in unusual words. In particular, they often missed the letter *t* in the word *the*, which is the most common word in the English language.

Healy's results are consistent with the theory advocated by LaBerge and Samuels. Because people encounter frequent words more often than unusual ones, they should be better able to recognize a frequent word as a unit. Less capacity should be required to recognize a frequent word because the reader does not have to pay as much attention to the individual letters. If less capacity is required to recognize a familiar word, the reader should have more capacity available for comprehending the meaning of the sentence.

APPLICATIONS

You should now have an appreciation for the importance of attention in performing many cognitive tasks, including those applied tasks discussed in "In the News" 3.1 and 3.2. The last part of this chapter discusses applications to driving. We will first look at how to improve selective attention in young drivers. We will then look at the controversial issue of whether the use of cell phones should be banned while driving.

Training Young Drivers

Perhaps the most important application for improving selective attention would be to assist young drivers. Per 100 million vehicle miles, a 16-year-old driver is almost eight times as likely to get into a fatal crash as a 45- to 64-year-old driver, and an 18-year-old driver is four times as likely. There is clearly a need for training programs that could provide needed experience.

A team of psychologists at the University of Massachusetts designed such a training program that requires less than an hour to complete on a personal computer (Pollatsek, Fisher, & Pradhan, 2006). The software requires dragging red circles to areas of the roadway that should be continually monitored and dragging yellow circles to areas that could contain relevant hidden information such as pedestrians emerging behind hedges. The training involved both coaching and review tests.

The team then used the University of Massachusetts driving simulator (Fisher et al., 2002) to evaluate the success of the training. The simulator uses a 1995 Saturn Sedan and a virtual world projected onto three screens surrounding the car, as shown in Figure 3.8. Participants control the vehicle in the same way that they would control a normal vehicle. A head-mounted eye tracker records where the drivers look as they navigate through the virtual world.

FIGURE 3.8 A driving simulator used to study attention to the (virtual) environment
Source: University of Massachusetts Driving Simulation Lab.

The investigators studied a group of novice 16- and 17-year-old drivers on the simulator to measure whether they would attend to critical areas. Those drivers who received the training program fixated the appropriate regions 58% of the time, whereas the untrained drivers fixated appropriately only 35% of the time. A follow-up experiment revealed that there was no decrement in the training when the test on the driving simulator was given three to five days after training. A field study in the Amherst, Massachusetts environment also showed that training transferred to real environments. The eye tracker revealed that trained drivers looked at critical areas 64% of the time, compared to 37% of the time for untrained drivers.

These findings show that even relatively brief training can enhance selective attention in inexperienced drivers. But, there remains a serious risk for both inexperienced and experienced drivers—the use of cell phones while driving.

Using Cell Phones

The driving test described in the previous section was used to measure the driver's attention to critical aspects of the environment. The results demonstrate that this is a challenging task for inexperienced drivers, even when they can focus solely on driving. However, driving requires divided attention to more than one event when the driver carries on a conversation while driving.

As you may already know, there has been increasing concern among state legislators regarding the use of cellular phones while driving. The use of cell phones has been dramatically increasing, and surveys indicate that 85% of cell phone owners use their phones at least occasionally while driving (Goodman, Tijerina, Bents, & Wierwille, 1999).

This concern is justified by accident reports. One study found that 24% of 699 individuals involved in accidents were using their cell phone within a 10-minute period preceding the accident (Redelmeier & Tibshirani, 1997). People who used cell phones while driving were four times as likely to be involved in an accident, an increase that is comparable to driving with a blood-alcohol level above the legal limit. It didn't matter whether they were holding the phone or using a hands-free device. This is an important finding because many legislatures assume that accidents would be reduced by using a cellular device that does not have to be held.

An experiment by Strayer and Johnston (2001) tested the hypothesis that conversing with someone on a cell phone while performing a simulated driving task would make it more difficult to perform the attentional demands of driving. The simulated driving task required participants to use a joystick to track a moving target on a computer display. At intervals ranging from 10 to 20 seconds, a red or green signal would appear on the display, and the instructions would indicate that participants should push a button for red signals. Participants either listened to a radio, carried on a conversation using a hand-held phone, or carried on a conversation using a hands-free phone while performing the task.

The two independent measures were the probability of missing the red signal and the reaction time to press the button when the red signal was detected.

Given the findings from accident reports that performance is not influenced by whether a handheld or a hands-free phone is used, these two conditions were combined and contrasted with performance while listening to the radio.

Figure 3.9 shows the results. The top figure indicates that participants missed 3% of the red signals when they did not talk on the phone or listen to the radio (single task) but missed 7% of the signals when talking on the phone (dual task). In contrast, listening to the radio did not interfere with detecting signals. The reaction-time data in the bottom figure also shows that using a cell phone significantly delayed reaction time to a detected signal, but listening to the radio did not delay reaction time.

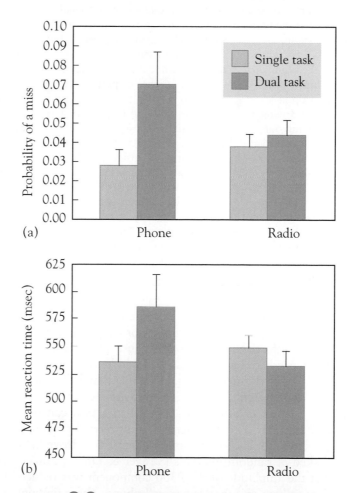

FIGURE **3.9** Probability of missing the simulated traffic signals (a) and reaction time to the simulated traffic signals (b) in single- and dual-task conditions

Source: From "Driven to distraction: Dual-task studies of simulated driving and conversing on a cellular telephone," by D. L. Strayer & W. A. Johnston, 2001, *Psychological Science, 12,* 462–466. Reprinted by permission of Blackwell Publishers.

IN THE NEWS **3.2**

Hands-Free Phones Still a Distraction

Marie McCullough

Listening on a cell phone, even with a headset and free hands, can make a driver as dangerous as a drunken one, a new study suggests.

Researchers have previously explored this territory, but Carnegie Mellon University scientists tried a new tack: They looked at the brain.

They used brain imaging to show that listening to a cell phone significantly reduces the brain activity that occurs during undistracted driving. This drop in brain function increased driving mistakes—such as weaving out of the lane or straying onto the road's shoulder.

Starting July 1, adult drivers in California will only be allowed to use hands-free phones while driving, while the ban extends to all cell phones, laptops or text-messaging devices for motorists younger than 18.

Scores of studies have shown that performing a mental task such as carrying on a conversation impairs driving performance, but the new research is the first to look at what is going on in the brain.

A cell-phone industry official said he could not comment on the study itself, having not seen it, but said it makes sense to reduce distractions while driving—whether dialing a number or putting on makeup.

In the study, to be published in the journal *Brain Research*, 29 drivers, ages 18 to 25, used a driving simulator while inside a sophisticated brain scanning machine, called functional MRI. They steered a car along an empty but winding two-lane highway at a fixed speed of 43 miles per hour.

Then, they repeated the simulation while listening to statements of general knowledge. After each statement, they had five seconds to say whether it was true or false.

The MRI measured second-by-second changes in activity in 20,000 brain locations. It showed that listening caused a 37 percent decrease in activity in the parietal lobe, which controls skills involved in driving. Activity also decreased in the occipital lobe, the center of visual information processing.

At the same time, listening increased activity in the area of the cortex linked to language.

Source: From "Hands-free Phones Still a Distraction," by Marie McCullough, *The San Diego Union-Tribune*, March 11, 2008. Copyright 2008 by MCT News Service. Reprinted by permission.

These results support the hypothesis that it is the *attentional* demands of using a cell phone that interfere with performance. Listening to a radio requires so little mental effort that it does not cause interference. Furthermore, the lack of difference between handheld and hands-free devices indicates that interference is caused by the mental demands rather than by having one less hand for driving.

More recent neurological research confirms these behavioral findings. The amount of attention allocated to a task can be measured by the amplitude of the P300 component of event-related potentials. Participants in a driving simulator such as the one in Figure 3.8 drove behind a simulated car that braked at random intervals (Strayer & Drews, 2007). Measurements showed that the amplitude of the P300 component was reduced by 50% when drivers were talking on a hands-free cell phone. These findings suggest the drivers did not encode the visual information as well when they were distracted by the conversation.

As indicated in "In the News" 3.2, fMRI research confirms that processing language decreases the amount of activity in the occipital lobe used to encode visual information. It also decreases activity in the parietal lobe, which controls other skills involved in driving. Beginning July 1, 2008, drivers younger than 18 years of age are not allowed to use hands-free cell phones in California. This should help reduce the accident rate of young drivers mentioned in the previous section. Unfortunately, drivers older than 18 years of age can still use hands-free phones, placing both them and their potential victims at risk.

SUMMARY

Two characteristics of attention are selectivity and mental effort. Selectivity is necessary to keep us from becoming overloaded with too much information. The initial theories developed within the information-processing approach proposed that selectivity occurred at a bottleneck—a stage that could process only one message at a time. Broadbent's filter theory specified that the bottleneck occurred at the perception or pattern recognition stage, and attention was represented by a filter that preceded this stage. Treisman modified the filter theory to allow for occasional recognition of words on an unattended channel. She proposed that the filter attenuated the unattended message but did not completely block it out. Important words or expected words could be recognized on the unattended channel if their thresholds were low enough to be exceeded by the attenuated message. Unlike Broadbent and Treisman, Deutsch and Deutsch suggested that the bottleneck occurs after perception and determines what is selected into memory. Norman further developed the latter theory and argued that the quality of the sensory information is combined with importance to determine what enters memory.

The results of many experiments on selective listening failed to agree on the location of the bottleneck. The effect was to shift emphasis to capacity theories of attention and to encourage a more flexible view of the stage at which selection occurs. Capacity theories emphasize the amount of mental effort that is required to perform tasks and are concerned with how effort is allocated to different activities. Capacity theory supplements bottleneck theory by proposing that the ability to perform simultaneous activities is limited when the activities require more mental effort than is available. The interaction between a capacity theory and a bottleneck theory is illustrated by results obtained by Johnston and Heinz. They effectively argue that a person has control over the stage at which selection occurs, but late modes of selection (following recognition) require more capacity than early modes. The attempt to comprehend two messages therefore results in a decline in accuracy on the primary message and slower responses to a subsidiary task designed to measure capacity.

Automatic processing occurs when a task requires very little capacity to perform. Posner and Snyder proposed three criteria to determine whether a skill is automatic: (1) It occurs without intention, (2) does not give rise to conscious awareness, and (3) does not interfere with other mental activities.

The work on selective attention has implications for performance outside the laboratory. LaBerge and Samuels suggested that the acquisition of complex, multicomponent skills such as reading depends on the ability to carry out some of the skills automatically, without attention. But ability to perform some components correctly does not necessarily mean that a person is ready to acquire new components if all the available capacity must be used to perform already learned components. Attention to critical parts of the environment while driving is increased by training young drivers but decreased by using cell phones.

STUDY QUESTIONS

More than usual, this chapter will necessitate learning several names—there is unfortunately no handier way to refer to the theories. Practice may foster automaticity.

1. Try to think of some common sayings or expressions that refer to attention. Do they relate to selectivity or mental effort (capacity)?

2. As you read, notice the paradigms or tasks used to study attention. Cognitive psychologists who attempt to deal with complex behaviors such as reading perform a task analysis to determine what component skills are required. Think of some everyday activities you engage in and try to identify how attention enters into the performance of each.

3. What is the essential difference between the filter models of Broadbent and of Treisman?

4. Because the Deutsch-Norman model is said to involve a stage after pattern recognition but before short-term memory, why is it called a "memory-selection model"? What are some examples of specific factors that would influence selection?

5. How persuasive do you find the explanation of the shift in interest from selection to the capacity aspect of attention?

6. It would be worthwhile to work through Kahneman's capacity model using a couple of the examples you generated in Question 2. How about shaving, or putting on makeup in different situations? Choose one and write it out.

7. How does one get a measure of capacity?

8. In what sense is Johnston and Heinz's multimode theory of attention interactive? What is the basis for their prediction that "more capacity is required to perform at a late mode of selection"? What task did they use to test this prediction?

9. Can you think of some skills that are automatic for you? What criteria did you use to decide?

10. Has the research convinced you that it is dangerous to talk on a cell phone while driving? Can you think of other real-world applications of either selection or capacity theories?

CogLab   The following experiments that relate to this chapter can be found at: http://coglab.wadsworth.com. Answer the questions in the CogLab Student Manual as required by your teacher for these experiments.

Attentional Blink

Simon Effect

Spatial Cueing

Stroop Task

KEY TERMS

The page number in parentheses refers to where the term is discussed in the chapter.

allocation of capacity 54

arousal 54

attenuation 50

automatic processing 59

bottleneck theories 46

capacity theories 47

concentration 46

contextual effects 50

enduring dispositions 55

filter model 48

incidental learning 60

late-selection models 51

limited-capacity perceptual channel 48

mental effort 46

momentary intentions 55

multimode theory 57

selectivity 46

shadow 49

stroop effect 60

subsidiary task 57

threshold 50

RECOMMENDED READING

Kahneman's *Attention and Effort* (1973) provides a comprehensive discussion of attention, in addition to presenting a capacity theory. More recent books include Cowan's (1995) *Attention and Memory: An Integrated Framework* and Pashler's (1998) *The Psychology of Attention*. Olivers (2007) discusses the time course of attention. Schneider and Shiffrin (1977; Shiffrin & Schneider, 1977) describe their research on the acquisition of automatic processing through extensive practice and present a general theoretical framework for integrating a large number of experimental findings. Bargh and Chartrand (1999) describe a theory for the pervasiveness of automatic processing in our daily lives. Theories of consciousness are contrasted (Atkinson, Thomas, & Cleeremans, 2000; Dijksterhuis & Nordgren, 2007) and the evolution of human consciousness is discussed by Donald (2001). Treisman's work (Treisman & Gelade, 1980; Treisman & Schmidt, 1982) on the importance of attention for integrating the features of a pattern is related to the theory proposed by LaBerge and Samuels (1974) and the discussion of "object-based" attention (Scholl, 2001). See Stanovich (1990) for an evaluation of LaBerge and Samuel's theory regarding the role of automaticity in reading. Thorough reviews of research on attention (Egeth & Yantis, 1997; Pashler, Johnston, & Ruthruff, 2001) appear frequently in the *Annual Review of Psychology*. Another thorough review (Lachter, Forster, & Ruthruff, 2004) found that "nonattended" stimuli may have been attended, supporting Broadbent's theory that attention is needed for identification.

4

Short-Term Working Memory

Forgetting
Rate of Forgetting
Decay versus Interference
Release from Proactive Interference

Capacity
The Magic Number 7
Individual Differences in Chunking

Memory Codes
Acoustic Codes and Rehearsal
Acoustic Codes in Reading

Recognition of Items in Short-Term Memory
Searching Short-Term Memory
Degraded Patterns

Working Memory
Baddeley's Working Memory Model
Baddeley's Revised Working Memory Model
Working Memory versus Short-Term and Long-Term Memory

SUMMARY

STUDY QUESTIONS

COGLAB: *BROWN-PETERSON; MEMORY SPAN; OPERATION SPAN; ABSOLUTE IDENTIFICATION; STERNBERG SEARCH*

KEY TERMS

RECOMMENDED READING

My problem is that I have been persecuted by an integer. For seven years this number has followed me around, has intruded in my most private data, and has assaulted me from the pages of our most public journals.
—**George A. Miller (1956)**

The preceding quotation is from the first paragraph of Miller's famous paper, "The Magical Number Seven, Plus or Minus Two: Some Limits on Our Capacity for Processing Information." Miller found that people are limited in the number of items they can keep active in memory and that this limited capacity influences their performance on a variety of tasks. The previous chapter, on attention, also dealt with a capacity limitation, but our concern there was with simultaneously arriving information. The capacity model of attention proposed that our ability to carry on several activities at the same time is restricted by the total amount of mental effort that is available for distributing to these activities.

The tasks in this chapter do not require that people recognize simultaneously arriving information. There is no perceptual overload, and there is enough time to recognize each item and enter it into short-term memory (STM). The problem is that STM can hold only a limited number of items, which has a profound effect on the many tasks that require using it. The implications of this limitation are evident throughout this book—not only in this chapter but also in later chapters on text comprehension, problem solving, and decision making.

Figure 4.1 shows a theory of memory proposed by Atkinson and Shiffrin (1968, 1971) that emphasizes the interaction among the sensory store, short-term memory, and long-term memory (LTM). We saw in Chapter 2 that the sensory store preserves information for a few hundred milliseconds; its characteristics were identified by Sperling (1960) for the storage of visual information.

Short-term memory, the second basic component of Atkinson and Shiffrin's system, is limited in both capacity and duration. Information is lost within 20 to 30 seconds if it is not rehearsed. Long-term memory is unlimited in capacity and holds information over a much longer interval, but it often takes a fair amount of effort to get information into it. The fact that STM is needed when we perform most cognitive tasks reflects its important role as a **working memory** that maintains and manipulates information. Figure 4.1 shows that STM can combine information from both the environment and LTM whenever a person tries to learn new information, make decisions, or solve problems. When you add the numbers in your checking account, you are receiving some information from the environment (the numbers in your account) and other information from LTM (the rules of addition). Getting a correct answer depends on using both sources of information appropriately.

The goal of this chapter is to summarize the major characteristics of STM. We begin by examining both the rate and the cause of forgetting. The emphasis will be on interference as the primary cause. The second section discusses the capacity of STM. After looking at Miller's (1956) insights about

working memory The use of short-term memory as a temporary store for information needed to accomplish a particular task

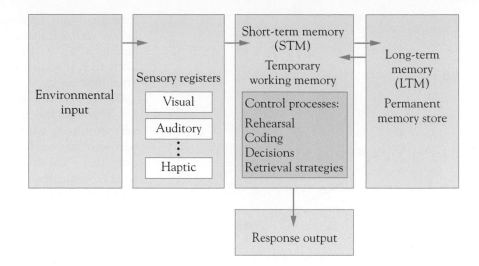

FIGURE **4.1** Flow of information through the memory system

Source: From "The control of short-term memory," by R. C. Atkinson & R. M. Shiffrin, 1971, *Scientific American, 225,* 82–90.

capacity, we will learn how the formation of groups of items in LTM can partly compensate for limited capacity. The third section deals with memory codes and emphasizes acoustic codes because they are used to maintain verbal information in STM, including information obtained from reading. The fourth section presents a model of how people recognize whether an item is in STM. In particular, we will consider how quickly people can examine the contents of their STM. A more complete model of STM as a working memory requires the storage of both visual and verbal codes in STM and the control of their use to maintain information. We will look at models of working memory in the final section.

FORGETTING

Rate of Forgetting

Information in STM is lost rapidly unless it is preserved through rehearsal. Peterson and Peterson (1959) at Indiana University established the rapid rate of forgetting from STM. They tested undergraduates on their ability to remember three consonants over a short retention interval. To prevent subjects from rehearsing the letters, Peterson and Peterson required them to count backwards by 3's, starting with a number that occurred after the consonants. For example, a subject might hear the letters *CHJ* followed by the number 506. She would then count backward until she saw a light, which was a signal for recalling the three consonants. The light went on 3, 6, 9, 12, 15, or 18 seconds after the subjects began counting.

Figure 4.2 shows the results of the experiment. The probability of a correct recall declined rapidly over the 18-second retention interval. The rapid

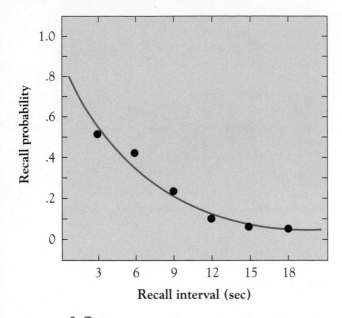

FIGURE 4.2 Correct recall as a function of recall interval

Source: From "Short-term retention of individual verbal items," by L. R. Peterson & M. J. Peterson, 1959, *Journal of Experimental Psychology, 58*, 193–198.

interference theory Proposal that forgetting occurs because other material interferes with the information in memory

decay theory Proposal that information is spontaneously lost over time, even when there is no interference from other material

forgetting rate implies that we must rehearse verbal information to keep it available in STM. It also shows why it is very likely that, if we are momentarily distracted after looking up a telephone number, we will have to look it up again before dialing.

This rapid rate of forgetting can be very frustrating when we are trying to learn new information, but it can also be beneficial. There are many occasions when we need to remember something only briefly. Think of all the phone numbers you have dialed. Most of these you dialed only once or twice and will never need again. If all these numbers were permanently stored in LTM, it could be very difficult to retrieve the few numbers that you constantly use.

Decay versus Interference

One question raised by Peterson and Peterson's findings is whether the loss of information from STM is caused by decay or by interference. Try to remember the consonants *RQW* over a short interval without thinking about them. Because it's difficult not to think about them if you have nothing else to do, subjects in memory experiments are asked to perform some other task. An **interference theory** proposes that memory for other material or the performance of another task interferes with memory and causes forgetting. A **decay theory** proposes that forgetting should still occur even if the subject is told not to do anything over the retention interval, as long as the subject does not rehearse the material.

The decay theory and interference theory make different predictions about whether the passage of time or the number of interfering items is the primary cause of forgetting. If memory simply decays over time, then the amount of recall should be determined by the length of the retention interval. If memory is disrupted by interference, then recall should be determined by the number of interfering items.

Waugh and Norman (1965) tested whether the loss of information from STM is caused mainly by decay or by interference. They presented lists of 16 single digits. The last digit in every list (a probe digit) occurred exactly once earlier in the list. The task was to report the digit that had followed the probe digit. For example, if the list were 5 1 9 6 3 5 1 4 2 8 6 2 7 3 9 4, the probe digit would be 4, and the correct answer (the test item) would be 2. For this particular example, there are 7 digits that occur after the test item. The number of interfering items is therefore 7. Waugh and Norman varied the number of interfering items by varying the location of the test digit in the list. There were many interfering items if the test item occurred early in the list and only a few if the test item occurred late in the list.

The experimenters also varied the rate of presentation to determine whether the probability of recalling the test digit would be influenced by the length of the retention interval. They presented the 16 digits in a list at a rate of either 1 digit or 4 digits per second. Decay theory predicts that performance should be better for the fast rate of presentation because there would be less time for the information to decay from memory. Figure 4.3 shows the results. The rate of presentation had very little effect on the probability of recalling the test digit. Consider the case in which there are 12 interfering items. The retention interval would be 12 seconds for the 1 per second rate and 3 seconds for the 4 per second rate. Memory is only slightly (and insignificantly) better for the shorter retention interval. In contrast, the number of interfering items has a dramatic effect on retention. The probability of recall declines rapidly as the number of interfering items increases.

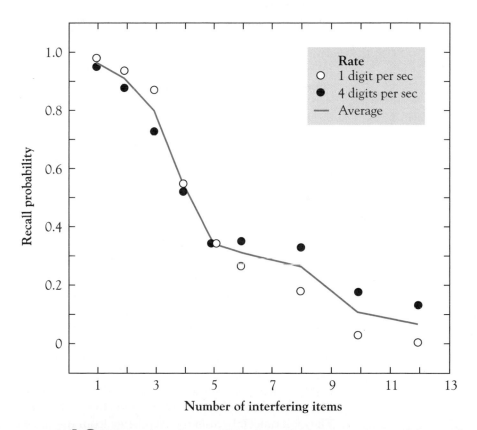

FIGURE **4.3** Effect of rate of presentation and number of interfering items on recall probability

Source: From "Primary memory," by N. C. Waugh & D. A. Norman, 1965, *Psychological Review*, 72, 89–104. Copyright 1965 by the American Psychological Association. Reprinted by permission.

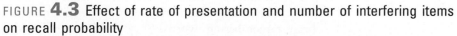

Waugh and Norman's findings support the contention that interference, rather than decay, is the primary cause of forgetting. Although some decay may occur (see Reitman, 1974), the amount of forgetting caused by decay is substantially less than the amount caused by interference. As Reitman and many others have shown, the extent of forgetting is determined not only by the number of interfering items but also by the degree of similarity between the interfering and test items. Increasing the similarity makes it harder to recall the test items.

The finding that interference is the chief cause of forgetting is good news. If information spontaneously decayed from memory, we would be unable to prevent its loss. If information is lost through interference, we can improve retention by structuring learning so as to minimize interference. A phenomenon called *release from proactive interference* illustrates how interference can be reduced by decreasing the similarity among items.

Release from Proactive Interference

retroactive interference Forgetting that occurs because of interference from material encountered after learning

proactive interference Forgetting that occurs because of interference from material encountered before learning

release from proactive interference Reducing proactive interference by having information be dissimilar from earlier material

Psychologists have distinguished between two kinds of interference—proactive interference and retroactive interference. **Retroactive interference** is caused by information that occurs after an event. The Waugh and Norman (1965) study demonstrated the effect of retroactive interference—the number of digits that followed the probe digit influenced how well it could be recalled. **Proactive interference**, in contrast, is caused by events that occurred before the event that someone attempts to recall.

Keppel and Underwood (1962) had previously demonstrated the effect of proactive interference in the Peterson and Peterson STM task. They found that people initially performed very well in recalling three consonants after a short retention interval, but their performance deteriorated over subsequent trials. The reason is that the consonants they had tried to remember during the initial trials began to interfere with their memory for consonants during the later trials. People found it increasingly difficult to distinguish between consonants that were presented on the current trial and consonants that had been presented on earlier trials.

Reduction of this interference is called the **release from proactive interference** (D. D. Wickens, Born, & Allen, 1963). The study by Wickens and his colleagues was the first of many studies to show that the recall of later items can be improved by making them distinctive from early items. Figure 4.4 shows a clear illustration of release from proactive interference. Students in this particular experiment were required to remember either three numbers or three common words over a 20-second interval, during which time they performed another task to keep from rehearsing. The control group received items from the same class (either numbers or words) on each of four trials. The interference effect is evident from the decline in performance over trials. The experimental group received items from the same class over the first three trials but on the fourth trial received items from the other class. If they had been remembering words, they now remembered three numbers; if they had been remembering numbers, they now remembered three words. The shift in categories caused a dramatic improvement in performance, as Figure 4.4

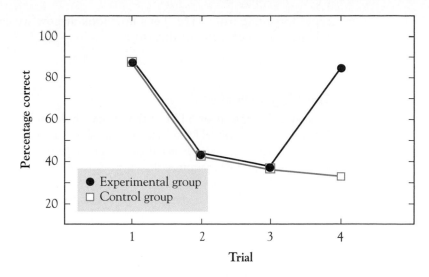

FIGURE **4.4** Release from proactive interference is demonstrated on trial 4 for the experimental group

Source: From "Characteristics of word encoding," by D. D. Wickens, in A. W. Melton & E. Martin (Eds.), *Coding processes in human memory.* Copyright 1972 by V. H. Winston & Sons. Reproduced with permission from Hemisphere Publishing Corporation, Washington, D.C.

illustrates. The interference effect was specific to the class of material being presented and was greatly reduced when the distinctive items occurred.

Release from proactive interference also occurs when people are asked to remember more complex events (Gunter, Clifford, & Berry, 1980). The events consisted of television news items that people heard while they viewed a videotape of the same events. People heard three items during each trial and attempted to recall them after a 1-minute delay. The control group received items from the same class (either politics or sports) over a series of four trials. The experimental group received items from the same class over the first three trials, but on the fourth trial they received items from the other class. If they had been recalling sports events, they now recalled political events, and vice versa. The results were very similar to the results shown in Figure 4.4. The proportion of correct responses declined for the control group over the four trials—87% on the first trial, 67% on the second, 55% on the third, and 43% on the fourth trial. The recall of the experimental group showed a similar decline over the first three trials but improved dramatically on the fourth trial, when they heard items from the different category. The experimental group recalled 82% of the items on the first trial, 67% on the second, 55% on the third, and 74% on the fourth.

The practical implications of these results are simply that, whenever possible, we should try to reduce interference by ordering material in an appropriate sequence. Items that are likely to interfere with each other should be studied at different times rather than during a single session. Reduction of interference through appropriate sequencing can partly compensate for the rapid forgetting from STM. Let's now look at how we can partly compensate for the limited capacity of this store.

CAPACITY

The Magic Number 7

A second limitation of STM is that it can hold only about seven items. The limited capacity of STM is demonstrated by a task that is often used as a measure of its capacity. It is called a *digit span* or, more generally, a *memory span task*. The task requires that a person recall a sequence of items in their correct order. **Memory span** is the longest sequence that a person can typically recall. An example of a memory span task follows. Read each row of letters once; then shut your eyes and try to recall these letters in the correct order.

T M F J R L B
H Q C N W Y P K V
S B M G X R D L T
J Z N Q K Y C

memory span The number of correct items that people can immediately recall from a sequence of items

If you are like most other adults, you could probably easily recall a string of seven letters (rows 1 and 4) but not a string of nine letters (rows 2 and 3). It was this number 7 that plagued Miller. The "magic number 7" kept appearing in two different kinds of studies: experiments on absolute judgment and those on memory span. In the **absolute judgment task**, an experimenter presents stimuli that vary along a sensory continuum, such as loudness. The experimenter selects different levels of loudness that are easy to discriminate and assigns a label to each. The labels are usually numbers that increase as the values on the continuum increase: If there were seven stimuli, the softest stimuli would be labeled 1, the loudest 7. The subject's task is to learn to identify each stimulus by assigning the correct label. The experimenter presents the stimuli in a random order and corrects mistakes by providing the correct answer.

absolute judgment task Identifying stimuli that vary along a single, sensory continuum

The experimenter is interested mainly in how many stimuli the subject can label correctly before the task becomes too difficult. The results vary depending on the sensory continuum, but Miller was impressed with the finding that the upper limit for a single dimension was usually around 7, plus or minus 2. The upper limit was about 5 for loudness, 6 for pitch, 5 for the size of squares, and 5 for brightness. The average across a wide variety of sensory tasks was 6.5, and most of the upper limits were between 5 and 9.

It is important to point out that these results were not caused by an inability to discriminate adjacent values of the stimuli. All the stimuli would be easy to discriminate if the subject had to judge which one of two adjacent stimuli was louder, larger, brighter, or higher in pitch. The limitation was caused by the inability to keep more than about seven sensory values available in STM because of its limited capacity. The results represent performance during the early stages of learning, before the different sensory stimuli are stored in LTM. With sufficient experience, the upper limits can be increased, as is illustrated by a musically sophisticated person who can accurately identify any one of 50 or 60 pitches. However, that person is using LTM, which is not limited in capacity.

The upper limit found in the absolute judgment experiments corresponds very well with the upper limit found in memory span tasks. Miller cited the results found by Hayes (1952), which indicated that the memory span ranged from five items for English words (*lake, jump, pen, road, sing*) to nine items for binary digits (0 0 1 0 1 1 1 0 1). The memory span for numbers or letters fell in about the middle of this range.

Miller's paper was important for drawing attention to how little the upper limit varies in performance on absolute judgment and memory span tasks. His paper was also important for suggesting that recoding the information to form chunks can help one overcome the limited capacity of STM. **Chunks** consist of individual items that have been learned and stored as a group in LTM. You can demonstrate for yourself how chunking can increase the number of letters that can be recalled from STM. Tell someone that you will read 12 letters to him and that you would like him to repeat them back in the correct order. Then read the 12 letters grouped in the following way: *FB-ITW-AC-IAIB-M*. Next read to another person the same 12 letters grouped in a different way: *FBI-TWA-CIA-IBM*. You will likely find that the second person can recall more letters (the groups are now familiar abbreviations). The first person has to recall 12 separate letters, but the second person can recall 4 chunks, each containing 3 letters. Miller argued that the capacity of STM should be measured in chunks rather than in individual items. The 12 letters should be easy for the second person to recall because they take up only 4 "slots" in STM rather than 12.

chunks A cluster of items that has been stored as a unit in long-term memory

Individual Differences in Chunking

Increasing evidence shows that a major determinant of individual differences in memory is how effectively people can group material into familiar chunks. The initial evidence for this conclusion came from the study of how chess players reproduce the pieces on a chessboard. The classic study of this task was begun by de Groot, a Dutch psychologist, during the 1940s and was later published in his book *Thought and Choice in Chess* (1965). The main conclusion of his study was that the difference in skill between chess masters and lesser players results more from differences in perception and memory than from differences in how they planned their moves.

Empirical support for de Groot's conclusion came from a series of clever experiments that required players of different abilities to reproduce a chessboard as it might appear 20 moves into a game (de Groot, 1966). Figure 4.5 shows two of the board configurations that were used in the study. The subjects were given 5 seconds to view the board. The pieces were then removed, and the subjects were asked to place the pieces back on the board to reproduce what they had just seen. When the subject was finished, the experimenter removed the pieces that were incorrectly placed and asked the subject to try again. The subjects continued to try to replace the incorrect pieces until they correctly reproduced the board or until 12 trials were completed.

The average performance of five master players and five weaker players is shown in Figure 4.6. The master players correctly reproduced approximately 90% of the pieces on their first attempt, compared with only 40% for the

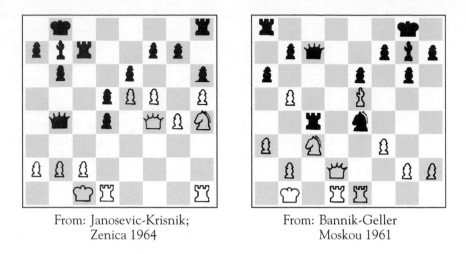

From: Janosevic-Krisnik;   From: Bannik-Geller
Zenica 1964   Moskou 1961

FIGURE **4.5** Examples of experimental positions used in the guessing and reproduction experiments

Source: From "Perception and memory versus thought: Some old ideas and recent findings," by A. D. de Groot, in B. Kleinmuntz (Ed.), *Problem solving: Research, method, and theory*. Copyright 1966 by John Wiley & Sons, Inc. Reprinted by permission.

weaker players. To determine whether the results were caused by the masters' ability simply to guess where the pieces should be located, de Groot chose other board configurations and asked the players to guess where the pieces were located, without ever seeing the board or receiving any clues. Figure 4.6 shows that the master players were only slightly better at guessing where the pieces were located. The weaker players, in fact, did about as well guessing as when they actually saw the board. De Groot argued that the master players depended on their ability to code the pieces into familiar groups. When the players viewed pieces that were placed randomly on the board, the master players no longer had an advantage over the weaker players, and the two groups performed about the same.

Chase and Simon (1973) extended de Groot's paradigm to identify the groups of pieces (chunks) that presumably produced the superior coding ability of master chess players. A master chess player, a class-A player, and a beginner were tested on de Groot's reproduction task. Chase and Simon assumed that pieces belonging to the same chunk would be placed on the board as a group. They measured the time between successive pieces and classified pauses greater than 2 seconds as indicating chunk boundaries. The latencies suggested that, for middle-game positions, the average number of chunks per trial was 7.7 for the master player, 5.7 for the class-A player, and 5.3 for the beginner; the number of pieces per chunk averaged 2.5, 2.1, and 1.9, respectively. There was some tendency for more skilled players to use more chunks, particularly for end-game positions, in which the average number of chunks per trial was 7.6, 6.4, and 4.2, respectively.

A simulation program (Memory-Aided Pattern Perceiver, or MAPP) of the chess reproduction task was developed by Simon and Gilmartin (1973)

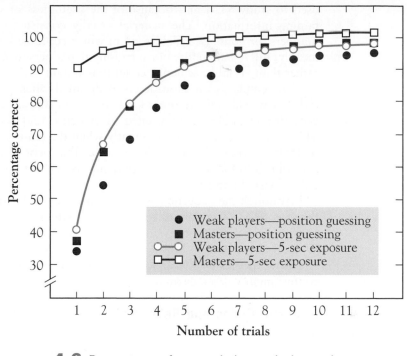

FIGURE **4.6** Percentage of correctly located chess pieces

Source: From "Perception and memory versus thought: Some old ideas and recent findings," by A. D. de Groot, in B. Kleinmuntz (Ed.), *Problem solving: Research, method, and theory.* Copyright 1966 by John Wiley & Sons, Inc. Reprinted by permission.

to gain further insight into the kinds of chunks stored in LTM. The memory of the program contained 572 chunks, with two to seven chess pieces in each. The simulation program was somewhat more effective than the class-A player in coding the configurations but less effective than the master player. There was, however, a substantial correlation between the pieces that MAPP remembered and those the master player remembered, even though the patterns stored by MAPP were selected independently of a detailed knowledge of the master's performance. Extrapolating from the performance of the simulation model, Simon and Gilmartin estimated that master players have between 10,000 and 100,000 chunks stored in LTM. Their estimate implies that there is no shortcut to becoming a chess master.

MEMORY CODES

acoustic code A memory code based on the sound of the stimulus

semantic code A memory code based on the meaning of the stimulus

Rapid forgetting rate and limited capacity are the two most important characteristics that distinguish STM from LTM. Psychologists once emphasized a third distinction based on differences in memory codes. They argued that **acoustic** (speech-based) **codes** are the predominant memory codes in STM, and **semantic** (meaning-based) **codes** are the predominant codes in LTM. The emphasis on acoustic codes occurred because of the nature of the material used to study STM and because of the usefulness of verbal rehearsal for retaining information. The material usually consisted of sequences of letters, numbers, or nonsense syllables, all of which could be labeled but were not very meaningful. It is therefore not surprising that a person would use acoustic codes rather than visual or semantic codes to maintain such information in STM.

The emphasis on acoustic codes declined when psychologists used material that would activate other kinds of codes. Release from proactive interference, for example, is often cited as evidence that semantic codes influence STM because recall improves greatly when the material changes to a different semantic category. There is also evidence that people can use visual images to maintain information in STM, particularly when trying to remember the details of visual patterns.

Although the acoustic code is no longer considered the only code that influences STM, it continues to be studied extensively. This code is important because verbal rehearsal is an effective way of retaining information in STM. We begin by looking at how acoustic codes are used to represent verbal rehearsal and how they can account for the errors that result from rehearsal (acoustic confusions). We then examine the importance of acoustic codes in reading.

Acoustic Codes and Rehearsal

Psychologists' interest in acoustic codes has been motivated by people's reliance on verbal rehearsal as a means of preserving information in STM. In fact, there is an interesting relation between memory span and verbal rehearsal. Recent evidence indicates that two separate verbal-processing rates influence a person's memory span (Cowan et al., 1998). One is the speed at which a person can pronounce the items on the list used to test the memory span. The other is the speed at which a person can retrieve the items from STM. Both rates determine how many items a person can keep active in STM.

Cowan and his colleagues discovered this finding in a developmental study in which students in the first, third, and fifth grades were asked to recall strings of digits. Pronunciation rates were measured by asking students to count from 1 to 10 as quickly as possible and by asking them to repeat short lists of digits as rapidly as possible. Retrieval rates were measured by timing the amount of time between digits as students attempted to recall the items during the memory span task. Notice that this measure is similar to the one used by Chase and Simon (1973) to determine chunk boundaries when players reproduced the chess board. The results indicated that both pronunciation rates and retrieval rates correlated with memory span but did not correlate with each other. In other words, students who had fast pronunciation rates tended to recall more than students who had slow pronunciation rates, and students who had fast retrieval rates tended to recall more than students who had slow retrieval rates. But students who had fast pronunciation rates did not necessarily have fast retrieval rates. The same pattern occurred in an experiment in which all the participants were college students.

Verbal rehearsal also occurs when visual patterns can be named. We saw in Chapter 2 that one of the early information-processing models provided for the translation of visual information into acoustic information so that people could verbally rehearse the names of the letters (Sperling, 1963). Evidence for this translation included Sperling's finding that subjects made acoustic confusions—errors that sounded like the correct response. The subsequent work of Conrad (1964) also established that acoustic confusions occur in STM. Conrad selected two groups of letters that had high within-group confusability but low between-group confusability: *BCPTV* and *FMNSX*. Conrad used a film projector to visually present six-letter sequences consisting of letters from both sets. After each sequence, subjects had to write the six letters in their correct order.

acoustic confusion An error that sounds like the correct answer

If acoustic confusions occur, an error would be more likely to involve substitution of a letter from the same group than substitution of a letter from a different group. Conrad found that 75% of the errors involved one of the other four letters belonging to the same acoustic group, and 25% of the errors involved one of the five letters in the other acoustic group. It is particularly easy for acoustic confusions to occur when all letters in a sequence sound alike. Try to recall the letters in each of the two following rows. You should find that the letters in the second row are easier to recall than the letters in the first row (Schweickert, Guentert, & Hersberger, 1990).

G Z D B P V C T
M J Y F H R K Q

The finding that acoustic confusions occur in an STM task shows that acoustic codes are important, but it does not reveal how the errors occur. One way of accounting for the errors is to use auditory components to represent the names of items. For example, the name of the letter *C* ("sē") has two components—namely, the *s* and *ē* sounds. The components—called **phonemes**—are the basic sounds of the English language.

phoneme Any of the basic sounds of a language that are combined to form speech

Some letters are represented by several phonemes because they can be pronounced in different ways. For example, the letter *a* is pronounced differently in the words *father, had, call*, and *take*; each pronunciation is represented by a different phoneme. The letter *e* has two pronunciations: the long-*e* sound in *heat* and the short-*e* sound in *head*. It is also possible for two letters to combine to form a phoneme—for example, *ch* and *th*.

It is convenient to use phonemes to account for acoustic confusions because words that sound alike usually have some phonemes in common. Let's look again at the two sets of letters in Conrad's experiment. The names of the letters in the set *FMNSX* (èf, èm, èn, ès, èx) have the same initial phoneme—the short-*e* sound—but their second phoneme differs. The letters in the set *BCPTV* (bē, sē, pē, tē, vē) all share a common phoneme—the long-*e* sound—but have different first phonemes.

The major assumption of a model proposed by Laughery (1969) is that each of the auditory components representing an item can be independently forgotten. In other words, if a name consists of two phonemes, a person might remember one phoneme but not the other. The model also assumes that the auditory components can be forgotten at different rates; the decay rates were determined from experimental results (Wickelgren, 1965).

Laughery makes the reasonable assumption that a person who cannot recall all the auditory components of a letter uses whatever is recalled to limit the number of possible responses. It is therefore easy for the model to account for acoustic confusions. Whenever only the $\bar{e}$ phoneme is recalled, the subject will guess one of the letters in the *BCPTV* set. If only the $\grave{e}$ phoneme is recalled, the subject will guess one of the letters in the *FMNSX* set. An incorrect guess in either case will result in an acoustic confusion.

Although acoustic confusions occasionally occur, it is usually advantageous to use verbal rehearsal when we want to maintain information in STM. Translation of visual material into an acoustic code is not limited to remembering strings of letters or digits. The most common example of converting visual material into acoustic codes occurs when we read.

Acoustic Codes in Reading

subvocalizing Silently speaking to oneself

Most of us read by **subvocalizing** (saying to ourselves) the words in the text. Although subvocalizing can help us remember what we read, it limits how fast we can read. Because covert speech is not much faster than overt speech, subvocalization limits reading speed to the rate of speaking; we could read faster if we didn't translate printed words into a speech-based code.

When I was a graduate student, I attempted to improve my reading rate by enrolling in a speed-reading course. A prerequisite for increasing my speed was that I learn to eliminate subvocalization. The trick is to go directly from the printed word to its meaning without covertly pronouncing the word. I was successful at increasing my reading rate while maintaining comprehension when the material was fairly simple. However, I found it quite difficult to read more complex or technical material without using subvocalization. I soon returned to my slower rate. I don't know how representative my experience was or what percentage of graduates from speed-reading courses successfully eliminate subvocalization. However, the experimental analysis of speech processing during reading has produced results that seem consistent with my own experience. The results suggest that, although we can comprehend the meaning of words without subvocalization, subvocalization is useful in facilitating the detailed recall of a text (Levy, 1978).

Levy attempted in her own experiments to suppress subvocalization by requiring that subjects repeatedly count from 1 to 10 as they read a short paragraph. They were told to count quickly and continuously in a soft voice while reading the sentences and to try to remember all the sentences in the paragraph. (You may want to try this as you read the paragraph in Table 4.1.) When they finished reading the paragraph, the subjects were shown one of the sentences in the paragraph or a slight variation and were asked to judge whether the test sentence was identical to the one presented earlier.

lexical alteration Substituting a word with similar meaning for one of the words in a sentence

semantic alteration Changing the order of words in a sentence to change the meaning of the sentence

Because the altered sentences were only slightly changed, the subjects had to remember the details to do well on this task. The first two sentences following the paragraph in Table 4.1 are examples of altered sentences. The **lexical alteration** changes a single word but preserves the meaning of the sentence—the word *mother* is changed to *woman* for the first paragraph and the word *child* to *youngster* for the second paragraph. The **semantic alteration** changes the meaning of the sentence by switching the order of two nouns—for the first paragraph, the order of *mother* and *physician*. The results of this study revealed that subjects performed more poorly when they had to count while

TABLE **4.1**
Examples of Lexical, Semantic, and Paraphrase Tests

An emergency

The hospital staff paged the busy doctor.

The solemn physician distressed the anxious mother.

The sobbing woman held her unconscious son.

A speeding truck had crossed the midline.

Her oncoming car was hit and damaged.

Her child had plunged through the windshield.

The medical team strove to save him.

The solemn physician distressed the anxious *woman*. (lexical)

The solemn *mother* distressed the anxious *physician*. (semantic)

The solemn *doctor upset* the anxious mother. (paraphrase—yes)

The solemn *officer helped* the anxious mother. (paraphrase—no)

Source: From "Speech processing during reading," by B. A. Levy, 1978, in A. M. Lesgold, J. W. Pellegrino, S. D. Fokkema, & R. Glaser (Eds.), *Cognitive psychology and instruction*, New York: Plenum. Copyright 1978 by Plenum Publishing Corporation. Reprinted by permission.

reading. They were not as accurate in identifying when changes occurred, regardless of whether there were lexical changes or semantic changes.

Suppressing subvocalization did not interfere with performance when the subjects listened to the sentence, however. The fact that counting while listening did not affect performance shows that suppression interfered specifically with reading, not with language comprehension in general. The difference between listening and reading is that the listener receives an acoustic code rather than a visual code. The fact that counting interfered only with recall following reading suggests that translating visual material into an acoustic code helps preserve detailed information in the text.

Although the acoustic code improved recall of detailed information, it was not necessary to preserve the gist of the paragraph (Levy, 1978). Support for this claim comes from a second experiment, in which subjects made paraphrase judgments. These subjects were not encouraged to maintain the exact wording of sentences because word changes occurred in all the test sentences. However, positive examples preserved the general meaning of an original sentence, and negative examples altered the meaning. In the **paraphrase** changes, unlike the semantic changes, the meaning was altered by replacing two words in the sentences rather than by changing the order of words (see Table 4.1). Therefore, less information was required to distinguish between positive and negative examples in the paraphrase task than to judge correctly in the lexical or semantic task. People could do well on the paraphrase if they remembered the general ideas expressed in the paragraph. Because the counting task did not interfere with performance, Levy concluded that acoustic coding was not required to remember the more important ideas.

paraphrase Using different words to express the same ideas in a sentence

Levy's findings are consistent with my own experiences in preventing subvocalization. When the material is relatively simple and detailed recall is not required, people can recall the major ideas without subvocalization. However, subvocalization did facilitate the detection of more subtle changes, such as changing the order of two words or replacing a word with a semantically similar word.

The studies on speech processing during reading suggest that, although subvocalization is not necessary for comprehension, it does facilitate retention of detailed or complex information. A popular explanation of these findings is that subvocalization makes it easier to retain words in STM until they can be integrated with other words in the sentence or paragraph (Conrad, 1972; Kleiman, 1975). We would be able to evaluate this suggestion more accurately if we had a better understanding of the role of STM in reading. Fortunately, considerable progress has been made understanding the psychological processes involved in text comprehension. Chapter 11 summarizes this progress and indicates how STM is used in reading.

RECOGNITION OF ITEMS IN SHORT-TERM MEMORY

Our discussion of STM up to this point has emphasized the recall of material, as shown in the experiments asking for recall of three consonants, a string of letters or digits, a chessboard, or a group of words after a short delay. Psychologists have also been interested in how people try to "recognize" whether a given item is contained in STM. Imagine that I show you four randomly chosen digits, perhaps 3, 8, 6, and 2. Then I show you a test digit and ask you to decide as quickly as possible whether the test digit was one of the four digits that I showed you previously. To perform this task you would need to store the initial set of digits in STM and then compare the test digit to the digits stored in STM to determine if there is a match.

Perhaps you can think of instances in which you have to carry out this kind of comparison. Such an instance occurs for me whenever I finish recording test scores for an exam. I always discover when I am finished that there are several students on my class list that don't have a test score. This usually means that they didn't take the test, but I am always concerned that they may have taken the test and I failed to record the score. I therefore place their names in my STM and again read the name on each test to see whether it matches one of the names in my STM. You may follow a similar procedure when you go shopping by comparing items on the shelves to the names of items you want to purchase and have stored in your STM. People are fairly accurate at performing this kind of task, so psychologists have focused on response time as a measure of performance. We now look at what determines response time and what this tells us about how we search STM.

Searching Short-Term Memory

The digit-example task that I just described was invented by S. Sternberg at Bell Laboratories to study how people encode a pattern and compare it with other patterns stored in STM. Sternberg first showed a sequence of digits

memory set A set of items in short-term memory that can be compared against a test item to determine if the test item is stored there

(the **memory set**), which the subject stored in STM. Then he presented a test digit, and the subject had to quickly decide whether the test digit was a member of the memory set. When S. Sternberg (1966) varied the size of the memory set from one to six digits, he discovered that the time required to make the decision increased as a linear function of the number of digits in STM. Whenever the size of the memory set was increased by one additional digit, the response time was lengthened by 38 msec. Sternberg proposed that the test digit was sequentially compared with each item stored in STM and that it required about 38 msec to make each comparison.

One important issue concerning the scanning process is whether it continues after a match is found. Imagine that I showed you the digits 5, 3, 7, and 1 and then gave you the test digit 3. Would you respond yes after matching the 3 in the memory set (a **self-terminating search**), or would you respond yes only after comparing the test digit with all digits in the memory set (an **exhaustive search**)? Most of us would probably say that we would respond yes as soon as we found a match. But Sternberg claimed that we scan the entire memory set before responding. This seems counterintuitive, so let's take a close look at the evidence.

self-terminating search A search that stops as soon as the test item is successfully matched to an item in the memory set

exhaustive search A search that continues until the test item is compared with all items in the memory set

Two aspects of Sternberg's data suggested that people were making an exhaustive search. First, response times for positive and negative responses were approximately the same. We would expect this finding if people always scanned the entire memory set. But if they responded as soon as they found a match, positive responses should be faster than negative responses because people would not always have to scan the entire memory set. Second, Sternberg found that response times were not influenced by the location of the matching digit in the memory set. We would expect this finding if people scanned the entire memory set, but not if they responded as soon as they found a match.

The trouble with an exhaustive search is that it would seem to be a very inefficient strategy to use. Why should comparisons continue once a match has been found? Sternberg's answer was that scanning occurs very rapidly but *checking* for a match takes considerably longer (S. Sternberg, 1967a). If we had to check for a match following each comparison, searching STM would be less efficient. But if we waited until after scanning the entire memory set to check whether a match occurred, we would have to perform the slower checking process only a single time.

Degraded Patterns

encode To create a visual or verbal code for a test item so it can be compared with the memory codes of items stored in short-term memory

In one of the early applications of this paradigm, S. Sternberg (1967b) varied the quality of the test digit in addition to the size of the memory set. The memory set consisted of one, two, or four digits, and the test digit was either intact or degraded to make it difficult to recognize. The degraded test digit looked like the degraded letters in Figure 5.7 (page 120). Sternberg suggested that two operations were needed to perform the task. First, the observer had to **encode** the test digit to compare it with other digits stored in STM. Then, the subject had to **scan** the memory set to determine whether any of the digits matched the test digit.

scan To sequentially compare a test item with items in short-term memory to determine if there's a match

Sternberg showed how it would be possible to determine whether a degraded pattern would influence the encoding time or the memory scan time.

slope A measure of how much response time changes for each unit of change along the *x*-axis (memory-set size)

The **slope** of the function relating reaction time (RT) to memory-set size indicates the amount of time needed to compare the test digit with a digit stored in STM; that is, it is the amount of additional time needed whenever another digit is added to the memory set. If a degraded digit slows the rate of comparison, the slope should increase. Figure 4.7a shows this prediction. Note that the more items in the memory set, the greater the difference in RT. The encoding of the test digit occurs only once, however, and should be independent of the number of items in the memory set. If the degraded digit lengthens the encoding time, the RT should increase by a constant amount (the additional time needed for encoding), which is independent of the number of items in the memory set. Figure 4.7b shows this prediction.

Figure 4.8 shows the results Sternberg actually obtained over two sessions. Degradation greatly affected the encoding time in both sessions. The data for degraded and intact digits form nearly parallel lines, similar to those shown in Figure 4.7b. The effect on the memory comparison time (as measured by differences in the slopes) was minimal. Degrading the test digit primarily affected the time needed to encode the pattern and had little effect on the time required to compare the test digit with other digits stored in STM. This finding implies that the visually degraded digit was not directly compared with the other digits because this would have slowed the comparisons. The longer encoding time suggests that the effect of degradation was compensated for during the encoding stage. The subject might have changed the degraded image into a normal image and matched the normal image against

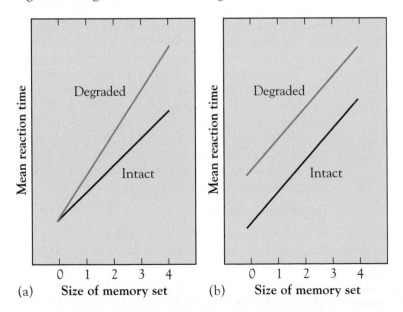

FIGURE **4.7** Predicted reaction-time functions if degrading affects the memory comparison time (a) or the encoding time (b)

Source: From "Two operations in character recognition: Some evidence from reaction time measurements," by S. Sternberg, 1967, *Perception & Psychophysics*, 2, 45–53. Copyright 1967 by the Psychonomic Society, Inc. Reprinted by permission.

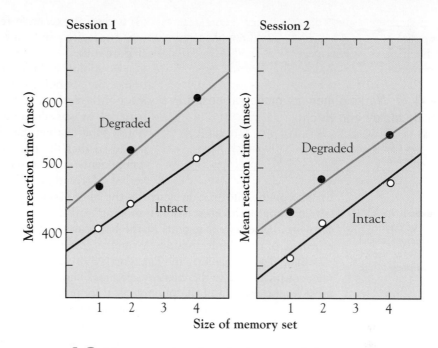

FIGURE **4.8** Mean reaction time for intact and degraded test stimuli

Source: From "Two operations in character recognition: Some evidence from reaction time measurements," by S. Sternberg, 1967, *Perception & Psychophysics*, 2, 45–53. Copyright 1967 by the Psychonomic Society, Inc. Reprinted by permission.

the visual images stored in STM. Or the subject might have named the test digit and compared it with the names of digits stored in STM. The latter explanation is particularly attractive because acoustic codes are usually used to maintain information in STM. It should take longer to name a degraded digit, and hence the encoding time would be slowed. However, once named, the degraded image would no longer be used, so the rate of comparison would be relatively unaffected.

WORKING MEMORY

phonological loop A component of Baddeley's working memory model that maintains and manipulates acoustic information

visuospatial sketchpad A component of Baddeley's working memory model that maintains and manipulates visual/spatial information

Baddeley's Working Memory Model

I mentioned at the beginning of this chapter that STM is often referred to as a working memory because of its use in numerous mental activities such as text comprehension, reasoning, and problem solving. More than 30 years ago Baddeley and Hitch (1974) began constructing a working memory model that is still evolving. In 1992 Baddeley (1992) gave the Bartlett Memorial Address at the University of Cambridge, which gave him the opportunity to evaluate what was then the current status of the model. The model consists of three components: (1) a **phonological loop** responsible for maintaining and manipulating speech-based information, (2) a **visuospatial sketchpad** responsible for maintaining and manipulating visual or spatial information, and

FIGURE **4.9** Working memory model proposed in 1974 by Baddeley and Hitch

Source: From "Is working memory still working?" by A. D. Baddeley, 2001, *American Psychologist*, 56, 849–864. Copyright 2001 by the American Psychological Association. Reprinted by permission.

central executive A component of Baddeley's working memory model that manages the use of working memory

(3) a **central executive** responsible for selecting strategies and integrating information (Figure 4.9).

Psychologists know most about the operation of the phonological loop, perhaps because most of the early research on STM used verbal material, as was illustrated in the previous sections of this chapter. Baddeley and others have proposed that the phonological loop has two components: a phonological store for holding verbal information and a rehearsal mechanism that keeps the information active in the phonological store. Evidence from research using positron-emission tomography (PET) supports this distinction by showing that different regions of the brain are responsible for the storage and rehearsal of verbal information (Awh et al., 1996).

Baddeley, Gathercole, and Papagno (1998) argue that the emphasis on studying acoustic coding in the memory span task should not obscure the fact that the most important role of the phonological loop is in learning how to pronounce new words. The phonological loop stores unfamiliar words until they are permanently learned and stored in LTM. We will see at the beginning of Chapter 6 how difficult it is to learn novel words if the phonological loop is damaged.

As psychologists began to include more visual or spatial material in their study of STM, it became apparent that not all material is translated into a speech-based code. Let's take another look at the task of reproducing a chessboard in which chess players group the pieces into familiar chunks. We might speculate that chunks are based more on visual/spatial information than on speech-based information. Certainly, de Groot (1966) believed that perception played an important role in distinguishing good chess players from weaker players. Therefore, we might need a component of working memory that can store visual/spatial information, such as the visuospatial sketchpad.

Baddeley (1992) reports a study on reproducing a chessboard that examined the relative contributions of the three components of his working memory model. As chess players of various abilities attempted to reproduce the board, they performed a secondary task that was designed to limit the use of a particular component. Levy's attempt to prevent subvocalization by asking people to count while reading is an example of this procedure. In fact, the experimenters used a similar procedure to prevent people from subvocalizing—that is, using the phonological loop component of Baddeley's model. To prevent the use of the visuospatial sketchpad, people were asked to tap a series of keys in a predetermined pattern. To prevent the use of the central executive, people were asked to produce a string of random letters at a rate of one letter per second. The rationale was that producing random letters requires people to make decisions about which letter to produce next, and this requirement will restrict their ability to make decisions about performing the primary task (how to code the chess pieces into memory).

The results of the study showed that suppressing speech had no effect on people's ability to reproduce a chessboard, but suppressing visual/spatial processing and requiring people to generate random letters caused a marked impairment in their ability to correctly place the pieces on the board. These findings suggest that verbal coding does not play an important role in this task, but both the visuospatial sketchpad and the central executive are needed to have good memory for the chess pieces (which is a visual task). Other research has confirmed that simply counting the number of pieces on the board, or making decisions about moves, is affected by secondary tasks that interfere with visual/ spatial processing but is unaffected by secondary tasks that prevent subvocalization (Saariluoma, 1992).

Although the results of both studies show that the visuospatial sketchpad is an important component in playing chess, Baddeley (1992) admits that its operation is still not well understood. One problem is that although it is clear that we can rehearse verbal information by subvocalization, it is not clear how we rehearse visual images. Another problem is that it may be difficult to separate maintaining visual information from maintaining spatial information. The secondary task of tapping keys in a set pattern primarily produces spatial interference because it is possible to tap the keys without looking at them. Research suggests that active spatial attention is required for maintaining visual/spatial information in STM, and this information is interfered with by any task (visual, auditory, perceptual, motor) that also makes demands on spatial attention (Smyth & Scholey, 1994).

Another component of Baddeley's model that requires further research is the central executive. This is the decision-making component of working memory, and it also played a role in reproducing the chessboard. A possible reason is that although chunking is important in this task, pieces on the board do not come "prepackaged" into chunks; the chess player has to decide how to partition the pieces to form chunks. The central executive also plays a predominant role when people have to reach conclusions in a logical-reasoning task (Gilhooly, Logie, Wetherick, & Wynn, 1993). A secondary task that interfered with the central executive (generating random numbers) significantly impaired logical reasoning, but tasks that interfered with subvocalization or visual/spatial processing did not impair logical reasoning.

In conclusion, Baddeley's working memory model shows that more is involved in using STM than simply maintaining and operating on phonological codes. However, assigning the task of controlling attention to the central executive has created a dilemma for the Baddeley and Hitch (1974) model because it leaves their model without a place for integrating visual and verbal information. If visual information is in the visuospatial sketchpad and verbal information is in the phonological loop, how can the visual and phonological codes be brought together? Answering this question forced Baddeley to revise his model.

Baddeley's Revised Working Memory Model

Imagine that you stop to ask for directions and someone gives you a verbal explanation of how to reach your destination. You may try to mentally form a visual map from the verbal directions to help you remember. Your ability to integrate visual and verbal information can also support more sophisticated forms of reasoning as we will discover in later chapters.

The placement of the central executive between the visuospatial sketchpad and the phonological loop in Figure 4.9 was no accident because Baddeley and Hitch initially thought that the central executive might function as a storage system where visual and verbal codes could be integrated. But the increasing emphasis on using the central executive to control attention has left their model with no way of explaining how we can combine information from different modalities. For this reason Baddeley (2000) proposed a revised model that contained a fourth component, the episodic buffer. The episodic buffer is a storage system that can integrate memory codes from different modalities. It explains how you could mentally form a visual map from verbal directions or how Feynman visually represented the conditions of a theorem as a funny ball.

Figure 4.10 shows Baddeley's revised model (Baddeley, 2000, 2001). The purpose of the new component, the episodic buffer, is to serve as a limited capacity store that can integrate information from both the visuospatial sketchpad and the phonological loop. It creates a **multimodal code** to form a model of the environment that can be manipulated to solve problems.

multimodal code An integration of memory codes such as combining visual and verbal codes

You may have noticed another change between the Baddeley and Hitch (1974) model shown in Figure 4.9 and Baddeley's (2000) revision shown in Figure 4.10. The inclusion of LTM in the revision represents the attempt to develop a greater understanding of the interaction of working memory with LTM. For example, Baddeley and Andrade (2000) found evidence for the use of the visuospatial sketchpad in working memory when participants were asked to form a novel visual image. However, when participants were asked to form an image of a familiar scene, such as a local market, LTM became more important. Vividness ratings of the images appeared to depend on the amount of available sensory information, whether based in STM or in LTM.

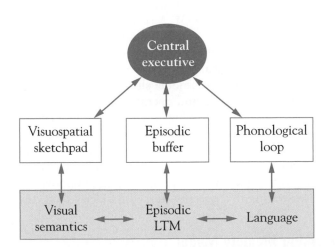

FIGURE **4.10** Baddeley's (2000) revised working memory model

Source: From "The episodic buffer: a new component of working memory," by A. D. Baddeley, *Trends in Cognitive Science, 4,* 417–423.

Working Memory versus Short-Term and Long-Term Memory

An important question raised by Baddeley's revised working memory model is, How is working memory related to STM and LTM? Psychologists now refer to "working memory" much more frequently than they refer to "short-term memory." Is "working memory" simply a new name for "short-term memory"—one that reflects our dynamic use of STM as we use it to carry out various cognitive tasks? Or is working memory different from STM, as proposed by Klapp, Marshburn, and Lester (1983)?

Although it is likely that this question will continue to be debated, one promising answer considers STM to be a component of working memory (Engle, Kane, & Tuholski, 1999; Engle & Oransky, 1999). The model proposed by Engle and his colleagues is shown in Figure 4.11 and was

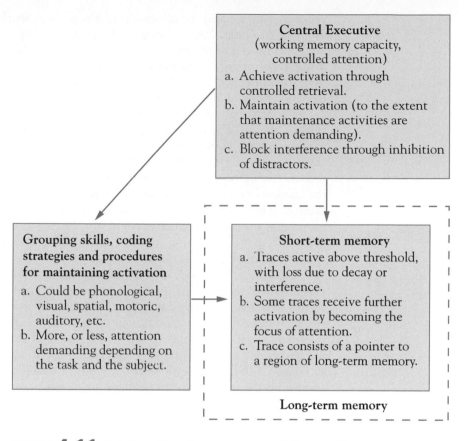

FIGURE **4.11** Relationship of components of the working memory system

Source: From "Individual differences in working memory capacity and what they tell us about controlled attention, general fluid intelligence, and functions of the prefrontal cortex," by R. W. Engle, M. J. Kane, & S. W. Tuholski, 1998, in A. Miyake & P. Shah (Eds.), *Models of working memory: Mechanism of active maintenance and executive control* (New York: Cambridge University Press). Reprinted by permission.

greatly influenced by the work of Cowan (1988, 1995). The model separates the central executive from STM and separately lists various control strategies such as grouping and coding strategies.

A critical feature of Engle's model is the prominent role that is given to the central executive and to controlled attention as the primary function of the central executive. Engle and Oransky (1999) proposed that individual differences in measures of working memory capacity reflect differences in controlled attention and that these differences will be reflected only in situations that either encourage or demand controlled attention. Controlled attention is necessary for actively maintaining task goals in working memory, scheduling actions, maintaining task information during distraction, and suppressing task-irrelevant information. For example, people with math anxiety waste working memory resources by attending to their own anxiety (Ashcraft & Krause, 2007).

This emphasis on controlled attention suggests that research should explore the relation between the capacity model of attention discussed in the previous chapter and the allocation of attention in working memory (Barrett, Tugdale, & Engle, 2004). Controlled attention is represented in the momentary intentions component of Kahneman's model (shown in Figure 3.5), and this control originates in the central executive component of working memory. Cowan's (1995) book *Attention and Memory: An Integrated Framework* was one of the first to make this important connection.

In contrast to the role of the central executive in controlling attention, the role of the STM component in Figure 4.10 is to maintain the activated-memory traces. These are typically phonological or visual codes and therefore correspond to the phonological loop and visuospatial sketchpad in Baddeley's model. According to Cowan (1995) and Engle, working memory consists of the contents of STM plus controlled attention as managed by the central executive. Their proposal is consistent with correlational research that has found that the central executive is not influenced by whether the task involves verbal or spatial reasoning, but storage in STM does depend on the verbal/spatial nature of the task (Kane et al., 2004).

The success of Baddeley's models in distinguishing between verbal and visual/spatial codes raises questions about other types of memory codes. As shown in Figure 4.11, we can remember events by using phonological, visual, spatial, motoric, auditory, and other types of codes. Representing all of these different modalities would require an explosion of components in Baddeley's model beyond the visuospatial sketchpad and phonological loop. According to Postle (2006), Baddeley's model (2000) is a victim of its own success. Demonstrating the importance of distinguishing between two memory codes also requires discriminating among many other types of memory codes.

Postle (2006) proposes that instead of adding more boxes to Figure 4.10, working memory should be viewed as directing attention to the many different kinds of memory codes stored in LTM. Working memory functions through the coordinated recruitment of brain systems that have evolved to accomplish sensory-, semantic-, and action-related functions. Neuroimaging studies have discovered different areas in the brain where such information is stored and will help psychologists better understand the relation between STM, working memory, and LTM depicted in Figures 4.10 and 4.11. We will learn more about these different types of memory codes in the chapters that follow.

SUMMARY

Short-term memory has several limitations that distinguish it from long-term memory. First of all, STM results in rapid forgetting. Items that are not actively rehearsed can be lost in 20 to 30 seconds. Evidence suggests that interference, rather than decay, is the primary cause of forgetting. Interference can result from items presented either before (proactive interference) or after (retroactive interference) the tested item. Release from proactive interference illustrates how the reduction of interference improves memory.

Another limitation of STM is its capacity. After reviewing a large number of findings on absolute judgment and memory span, Miller identified the capacity limitation as consisting of approximately seven chunks. A chunk is a group of items stored as a unit in LTM. For instance, the sequence *FBITWACIAIBM* is easy to recall when grouped as *FBI-TWA-CIA-IBM* because the 12 letters have been grouped as four chunks—as familiar abbreviations. De Groot argued that the superior ability of a master player to reproduce a chessboard is a result of the ability to group the pieces into familiar configurations. Using pauses as a measure of chunk boundaries, Chase and Simon concluded that master chess players have both more chunks and larger chunks stored in LTM than less experienced players.

Because verbal material is often used in studies of STM, emphasis has been placed on the importance of acoustic codes. Both the pronunciation rate and retrieval rate correlate significantly with verbal memory span. The use of verbal rehearsal to maintain information in STM is confirmed by acoustic confusions—errors that sound like the correct response. Laughery's simulation model accounts for acoustic confusions by assuming that acoustic codes consist of phonemes, which can be independently forgotten. Although we usually rely on an acoustic code when we read, we can remember the general ideas from our reading without subvocalizing. However, subvocalization improves our ability to recall details and complex material.

A recognition task consists of showing an item and asking the subject to verify whether the item is contained in a set of items stored in STM. The finding that the time required to make this decision increases as a linear function of the number of items stored in STM suggests that people search the items one at a time. Degrading the test item has relatively little effect on the rate of search, but it does lengthen the time needed to encode the test item before comparing it with the other items in STM.

Baddeley's working memory model provides a more complete account of STM by proposing a phonological loop for maintaining and manipulating acoustic information, a visuospatial sketchpad for maintaining and manipulating visual/spatial information, and a central executive for making decisions. His recent revision of the model added an episodic buffer to integrate different memory codes such as acoustic and visual codes. Cowan and Engle have distinguished between working memory and STM by proposing that STM is a component of working memory. The primary function of STM is to maintain the activated memory codes. The primary function of the central executive is to control attention, raising the possibility of a tighter link between capacity theories of attention and theories of working memory. Neuroimaging studies are revealing that directing attention to the many different kinds of codes stored in LTM is an essential role of working memory.

STUDY QUESTIONS

1. What is Miller's magic number? What is magical about it? Why is his 1956 paper famous?

2. The study by Peterson and Peterson is another "golden oldie." Why do you think it is still cited in virtually every introductory text? Why did they have their subjects count backward?

3. What different predictions do decay theory and interference theory make? How have these been tested?

4. What factors produce greater or lesser interference? Can you see how the findings on proactive and retroactive interference could be applied to your own study strategies?

5. Does your experience bear out the claim that chunking can partially overcome the limited capacity of STM? (Think of an area in which you are an expert rather than a novice.) Is there research evidence that chunking works?

6. A college student is ideally an expert reader. Do you believe that speed reading really exists? Write a sentence or two stating the reasons for your answer.

7. What is *acoustic coding?* Why is acoustic coding at issue in studies of reading comprehension? Does it help you remember what you read?

8. What is at issue in Sternberg's studies of recognition of items in STM? Why did he need to invent a paradigm to investigate the problem?

9. Describe Baddeley's revision of his working memory model, and why it was needed.

10. Why do some critics argue that Baddeley's model does not go far enough in proposing modality-specific memory systems? How would they modify his model?

CogLab   The following experiment that relates to this chapter may be found at: http://coglab. wadsworth.com. Answer the questions in the CogLab Student Manual as required by your teacher for these experiments.

Brown-Peterson
Memory Span
Operation Span
Absolute Identification
Sternberg Search

KEY TERMS

The page number in parentheses refers to where the term is discussed in the chapter.

absolute judgment task (80)

acoustic code (83)

acoustic confusions (85)

central executive (92)

Chunks (81)

decay theory (76)

encode (89)

exhaustive search (89)

interference theory (76)

lexical alteration (86)

memory set (89)

memory span (80)

multimodal code (94)

paraphrase (87)

phonemes (85)

phonological loop (91)

proactive interference (78)

release from proactive interference (78)

retroactive interference (78)

scan (89)

self-terminating search (89)

semantic alteration (86)

semantic code (83)

slope (90)

subvocalizing (86)

visuospatial sketchpad (91)

working memory (74)

RECOMMENDED READING

The chapters by Engle, Kane, and Tuholski (1999) and Engle and Oransky (1999) provide overviews of experimental and theoretical work on STM and working memory. Their general model has been successfully applied to individual differences in working memory (Barrett, Tugdale, & Engle, 2004) and to correlational analyses with other tasks (Kane et al., 2004). Gathercole (1997) contrasts four models of verbal STM, and Jonides (1995) discusses the role of working memory in thinking, including neurological evidence. A special section of the *Journal of Experimental Psychology: General* focuses on individual differences in working memory (Miyake, 2001). Research on math anxiety is a more recent example of this approach (Ashcraft & Krause, 2007). Baddeley's (2001) Distinguished Scientist

Address to the American Psychological Association presents an impressive list of studies that fit within his working memory model. Sweller's (2003) research has documented many instructional implications of a limited capacity working memory. Reviews of memory research frequently appear in the *Annual Review of Psychology* (for example, Roediger, 2008). There have been occasional critics of STM as a theoretical construct, such as Crowder (1982). Others have argued against the standard model of STM on the basis that retrieval is cue driven, much like LTM (Nairne, 2002) Neuroimaging studies are providing increasing support for this view (Postle, 2006) and for the use of similar processing in STM and LTM (Nee, Berman, More, & Jonides, 2008).

5

Long-Term Memory

With one singular exception, time's arrow is straight. Unidirectionality of time is one of nature's most fundamental laws.... The singular exception is provided by the human ability to remember past happenings. When one thinks today about what one did yesterday, time's arrow is bent into a loop.
—**Endel Tulving (2002)**

What would life be like if we did not have a normally functioning long-term memory (LTM)? The movie *Memento* provides an answer. The story is about a man who, because of a brutal attack on him and his wife, is unable to store new events in LTM. His life's ambition is to seek revenge on his attacker, and he attempts to function by taking Polaroid pictures of his world—his car, his motel, his friends, his enemies. Notes on the pictures and tattoos on his body serve as external memories of his present life. The movie's audience shares his difficulty as both the man and the audience use flashbacks to try to make sense of his life. I recommend this movie, but I had to watch it twice to piece together the story.

Although it is difficult for us to imagine the struggles of a person with a severely impaired memory, we all have envied someone with an extremely good memory and wished that we could improve our own memory. For students, this is particularly true at exam time. If only we could remember everything that we studied, we would do so much better. The need to remember the material after the exam may seem less pressing, but even in this case a good memory may be quite beneficial.

One question students often ask before I give my first cognition exam each semester regards the importance of remembering names. Students believe that names are particularly challenging to remember, and there is some evidence that this is correct. Students who completed a cognitive psychology course at the Open University in England were tested on their ability to recall names and general concepts following a retention interval that ranged from 3 to 125 months (Conway, Cohen, & Stanhope, 1991). The questions were fill-in-the-blank questions in which the missing name or concept was represented only by its initial letter. For example: *E_____ was an early German psychologist who studied the learning of nonsense syllables. In p_____ inhibition forgetting is caused by interference from prior learning.*

Figure 5.1 shows the results. Names were forgotten more rapidly than concepts over the initial 3 years, but between 3 and 10 years, recall leveled off at about the same level for both kinds of knowledge. Particularly encouraging is the finding that even after 10 years people were still recalling more than 25% of the material.

One of the best ways to remember material over a life span is simply to spend considerable time studying it (Bahrick & Hall, 1991). Students who took college-level mathematics courses at or above the level of calculus had excellent retention of high school algebra for nearly 50 years. The performance of students who did equally well in a high school algebra course, but took no college-level mathematics courses, declined to near chance levels

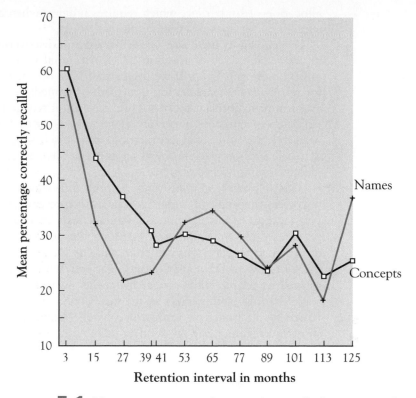

FIGURE **5.1** Mean percentage of correctly recalled names and concepts for different retention intervals

Source: From "On the very long-term retention of knowledge acquired through formal education: Twelve years of cognitive psychology," by M. A. Conway, G. Cohen, & N. Stanhope, 1991, *Journal of Experimental Psychology: General, 120,* 395–409. Copyright 1991 by the American Psychological Association. Reprinted by permission.

over the same period. Surprisingly, academic measures such as Scholastic Aptitude Test (SAT) scores and grades have little impact on retention (Bahrick & Hall, 1991; Semb & Ellis, 1994).

To retain information over a long time span, we have to get it out of short-term memory (STM) and enter it into a more permanent store called **long-term memory (LTM)**. This chapter summarizes some of the research on LTM—such as how we enter information into LTM and how it is tested. The first section of this chapter describes some ways in which information can be transferred from a temporary to a more permanent store. We start by considering the basic characteristics of LTM, including learning strategies. Much of what was known about this topic was summarized in an important paper by Atkinson and Shiffrin, published in 1968. The authors discussed several strategies that could facilitate learning, but they primarily studied verbal rehearsal. They assumed that each time an item was rehearsed, information about that item was entered into LTM. Another strategy that influences learning is the

long-term memory (LTM) Memory that has no capacity limits and lasts from minutes to an entire lifetime

allocation of study time, which requires judging when an item is learned well enough that it does not need additional study.

Psychologists have also been interested in discovering how people retrieve information after it is stored in LTM. An initial step is to decide whether the information is in LTM. If we decide that it is, our next step is to select a plan for retrieving the information if we cannot immediately recall it. Recalling relevant information is usually important, even in recognition tasks, because recognizing an event or a person as familiar is often insufficient—we usually need to know additional information. After discussing some theoretical aspects of recall and recognition, I will apply these ideas to eyewitness recall and the identification of suspects.

Recall and recognition tests are both direct tests of memory in which the instructions specifically refer to previously presented material, such as when you take an exam. In contrast, indirect tests of memory determine whether previously presented material helps people perform better on tasks that do not refer to the previous material, such as identifying degraded words when the words were previously shown. Patients with memory disorders often do as well as people with normal memories on indirect tests. We will examine some theories of this effect in the last section of this chapter, but first let us return to the basics, as represented by the Atkinson-Shiffrin model that was shown in Figure 4.1 (page 77).

THE ATKINSON-SHIFFRIN MODEL

Transferring Information from Short-Term Memory to Long-Term Memory

The theory proposed by Atkinson and Shiffrin (1968, 1971) emphasized the interaction between STM and LTM. They were particularly interested in how people could transfer information from STM to LTM. Long-term memory has two crucial advantages. First, as we have already seen, the rate of forgetting is much slower for LTM. Some psychologists have even suggested that information is never lost from LTM, although we lose the ability to retrieve it. Whether information is lost or impossible to recover may not be of much practical significance, but, if we knew that it was still in memory, we might hope to recover it eventually. Another difference between STM and LTM is that LTM is unlimited in its capacity. Although we saw in the previous chapter that there is a limit to the amount of information that we can maintain in STM, we will never reach the point where we cannot learn new information because LTM is filled.

Nevertheless, it is not always easy to enter new information into LTM. Atkinson and Shiffrin proposed several control processes that could be used in an attempt to learn new information. The **control processes** are strategies that a person uses to facilitate the acquisition of knowledge. They include the *acquisition strategies* of rehearsal, coding, and imaging.

Rehearsal is the repetition of information—either aloud or silently—over and over until it is learned.

control process A strategy that determines how information is processed

rehearsal Repeating verbal information to keep it active in short-term memory or to transfer it into long-term memory

coding Semantic elaboration of information to make it easier to remember

Coding attempts to place the information to be remembered in the context of additional, easily retrievable information, such as a mnemonic phrase or sentence. For example, many of us learned that the lines of a treble clef are E, G, B, D, F by remembering the sentence "Every good boy does fine."

imaging Creating visual images to make material easier to remember

Imaging involves creating visual images to remember verbal information. This is an old memory trick—it was even recommended by Cicero in ancient Rome for learning long lists or speeches.

The list could be further expanded, but rehearsal, coding, and imaging are three of the primary ways of learning. Because there are so many control processes to study, Atkinson and Shiffrin (1968) decided to focus their research on only one—verbal rehearsal.

Verbal Rehearsal and Learning

rote learning Learning by repetition rather than through understanding

Verbal rehearsal is usually considered a form of **rote learning** because it involves simply repeating information over and over until we think we have learned it. It can be useful when the material seems rather abstract, which makes it difficult to use strategies such as coding or imaging. The task designed by Atkinson and Shiffrin (1968) required the learning of abstract, meaningless material and therefore encouraged the use of rehearsal.

The undergraduates in the experiment tried to learn associations between a two-digit number (the stimulus) and a letter (the response). The paired associates included items such as 31-*Q*, 42-*B*, and 53-*A*. Each pair was shown for 3 seconds, followed by 3 seconds before the next trial. Interspersed throughout these study trials were test trials, in which only the two-digit number was presented, and the subject was asked to supply the letter that had accompanied it earlier. One of the variables in the experiment was the number of trials that occurred between the study and test trials. Some associates were tested on the very next trial and others after a delay that could last as long as 17 trials.

Atkinson and Shiffrin interpreted the data from this experiment by proposing a model in which verbal rehearsal was used to learn the associates. They assumed that the students maintained a fixed number of items in STM and that these items were rehearsed whenever the student was not viewing a new item or responding during a test trial. The effect of rehearsal was to transfer information about that item into LTM. The extent of learning depended on how long a particular pair was maintained in the rehearsal set. Atkinson and Shiffrin proposed that learning increased as a function of the number of trials over which the item was rehearsed. Once the item was no longer rehearsed, information about that particular item decreased as each succeeding item was presented for study. The predicted probability of a correct response therefore depended on both the number of trials in which the item was rehearsed and the number of intervening trials that occurred between the time the item left the rehearsal set and the test trial.

In this example, an item has been rehearsed but is not in STM at the time of the test. If the item has been rehearsed but is no longer in STM, the answer has to be retrieved from LTM. A second possibility is that the item is rehearsed and is still active in STM. A third possibility exists when an item is not rehearsed at all. Because the model assumes that only a limited number of items can be maintained in the rehearsal set, rehearsing a new item will be done at the expense of eliminating one of the items already in the set. Atkinson and Shiffrin proposed that an item that is not rehearsed can be responded to correctly only if it is tested on the trial immediately following its presentation.

Rehearsal and the Serial Position Effect

An easy way to test the proposal that verbal rehearsal results in learning is to ask someone to rehearse out loud. The experimenter can then count the times each item is rehearsed and determine whether the probability of recalling an item is related to the number of rehearsals. A task designed by Rundus (1971) was exactly of this type. He presented lists of 20 nouns to undergraduates at Stanford. The words were presented one at a time for a period of 5 seconds each. Rundus instructed the students to study by repeating aloud words on the list during each 5-second interval. They were free to rehearse any word they desired as long as their rehearsal filled the intervals. After presentation of the list, the students tried to recall the words in any order.

Figure 5.2 shows the results of the experiment. The probability of recalling a word depended on its position in the list. Words at the beginning and words at the end were easier to recall than words in the middle of the list. The U shape of the recall curve, which is called a **serial position effect**, is often obtained in recall experiments. The better recall of words at the beginning of the list is called a **primacy effect**, and the better recall of words at the end of the list is called a **recency effect**.

The curve showing the number of times each word was rehearsed illustrates that words at the beginning of the list were rehearsed more often than the other words. This is because there is time to rehearse several words between items on the list, and the initial items are the only ones available for rehearsal at the beginning. The relation between the rehearsal and recall curves reveals that the primacy effect can be explained by Atkinson and Shiffrin's theory. Because early words were rehearsed more often than the other words, they should have a higher probability of being retrieved from LTM. This explanation implies that the primacy effect should be eliminated if all the words on the list are rehearsed equally often. In fact, when subjects were instructed to rehearse each word equally often by rehearsing only the displayed word, the primacy effect disappeared (Fischler, Rundus, & Atkinson, 1970).

Although the number of rehearsals can predict the primacy effect, it does not predict the recency effect. People were very good at recalling the words at the end of the list even though they did not rehearse them any more than the words in the middle of the list. The recency effect is often explained by the proposal that the words at the end of the list are still in STM when a person begins the recall. The students in Rundus's experiment recalled the words immediately after the last item was presented; it is therefore reasonable to assume that the words they had just seen were still available in STM.

We learned from the Peterson and Peterson experiment discussed in Chapter 4 that information is rapidly lost from STM if people have to perform another task. If the recency effect is caused by retrieving the most recent

serial position effect
The ability to recall words at the beginning and end of a list better than words in the middle of the list

primacy effect The better recall of words at the beginning of a list

recency effect The better recall of words at the end of a list

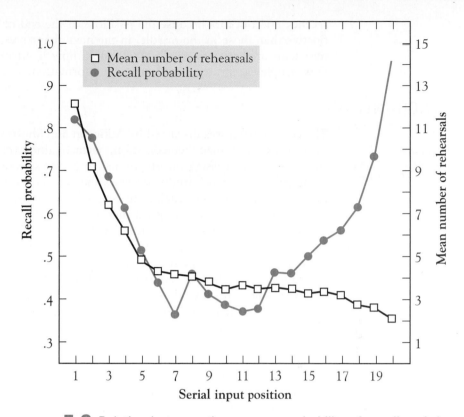

FIGURE **5.2** Relation between the average probability of recall and the average number of rehearsals as a function of a word's serial position

Source: From "Analysis of rehearsal processes in free recall," by D. Rundus, 1971, *Journal of Experimental Psychology, 89,* 63–77. Copyright 1971 by the American Psychological Association. Reprinted by permission.

items from STM, it should be eliminated if a person has to perform another task before recalling the items. Subjects in an experiment designed by Postman and Phillips (1965) had to perform an arithmetic task for 30 seconds before they tried to recall a list of words. The arithmetic task was successful in eliminating the recency effect, implying that the words at the end of the list had decayed from STM.

Another piece of evidence for the proposal that the primacy effect is caused by retrieval from LTM and the recency effect is caused by retrieval from STM comes from patients who suffer from amnesia. These people have difficulty in retrieving information from LTM but often have a normal STM as measured by the typical memory span test discussed in the previous chapter. This suggests that they should do much worse than control subjects on recalling the initial words on a list but should do as well as control subjects on recalling the most recent words on the list. In fact, these results were obtained (Baddeley & Warrington, 1970).

It is only fair to point out that there have been other explanations of the recency effect, reviewed by Greene (1986). One such explanation is that the recency effect occurs because the positions at the end of the list are more distinctive than those in the middle. In the next chapter we will see that distinctive items are easier to recall, but I would now like to return to the topic of how people use strategies to learn new information.

METACOGNITION

metacognition The selection of strategies for processing information

The control processes discussed by Atkinson and Shiffrin are part of a general area of research called metacognition. **Metacognition** refers to the selection of strategies for processing information such as the selection of study strategies to prepare for exams. Study strategies include such activities as determining the expectations of the teacher, managing time, interacting with the teacher and fellow students, selecting learning strategies, setting goals, and monitoring progress (Broekkamp & Van Hout-Wolters, 2007).

Students learn many of these strategies from their own experiences as indicated by a questionnaire that was given to 472 students enrolled in an introductory psychology course at UCLA. When asked "Would you say that you study the way that you do because a teacher (or teachers) taught you to study that way?," 80% of the students said "no" (Kornell & Bjork, 2007). However, there is merit in teaching these skills. As indicated in "In the News" 5.1, students who have learned effective study skills perform better on exams than students who have not learned these skills.

In the previous section, we examined a particular control process—verbal rehearsal—but this is only a single example of the kinds of strategies that we use to acquire and retrieve information. Figure 5.3 shows other examples of strategies that people use to learn material (Nelson & Narens, 1990).

Imagine that you have to learn the English translations of a list of German vocabulary words. First, you need to decide what kind of processing to use. Would you use rehearsal, coding, or imaging? If you could think of ways to make the material more meaningful (coding) or could easily generate visual images (imaging), you might want to use either of these more elaborative strategies rather than verbal rehearsal. Second, you need to decide how to allocate study time among the items (Nelson, Dunlosky, Graf, & Narens, 1994). You will probably need more time to learn the translation of *der Gipfel* than to learn the translation of *die Kamera*. Strategies such as selecting a good processing technique and allocating study time are concerned with the **acquisition of knowledge**—getting information into LTM. You next need to decide how to maintain the information that you learn. Periodic review minimizes forgetting (Pashler, Rohrer, Cepeda, & Carpenter, 2007), but students typically focus on whatever is due the soonest rather than develop periodic reviews of material they are trying to learn (Kornell & Bjork, 2007).

knowledge acquisition Storage of information in long-term memory

retrieval strategy A strategy for recalling information from long-term memory

Finally, you need to think of helpful retrieval strategies when you have difficulty recalling the appropriate translation. **Retrieval strategies** involve getting this information out of LTM by searching for the answer. As we see in Figure 5.3, most research on learning strategies has focused more on acquisition and retrieval than on retention. The next sections examine students' knowledge of strategies related to the acquisition, retention, and retrieval of information.

IN THE NEWS **5.1**

Teaching Students How to Learn

Bridget Murray

It's no secret that students learn best when they self-regulate—set their own academic goals, develop strategies to meet them, and reflect on their academic performance.

High-achieving students know what needs to be learned and how to learn it, educational psychology studies increasingly show. But while making those kinds of self-assessments may sound simple—and something most college students could do—many psychology professors find their students aren't self-aware enough to conduct them.

Some faculty believe they can help students develop these strategies through their teaching. Others, however, don't think it's their place to do so, pointing to the load of content they already must teach in one semester. Besides, some ask, isn't college too late to teach students how to learn?

Not according to self-regulation researchers Paul Pintrich, PhD,

cofounder of a "learning how to learn" course at the University of Michigan, and Barry Zimmerman, PhD, an educational psychology professor at the Graduate School and University Center at the City University of New York (CUNY)....

At the core of self-regulation are strategies to manage cognition, but motivation to use those strategies is also key, says Pintrich.

"You need the 'will' as well as the 'skill'," he says.

Researchers propose a variety of models for activating skill and will. Zimmerman has developed one of the best-known models and uses it to coach remedial students at CUNY. He says it's helpful to think of self-regulation in three phases:

- *Forethought*. Students set short-term, challenging but attainable academic goals. They estimate their ability—also called self-efficacy—to reach those goals.

- *Performance*. Students adopt "powerful" learning strategies, such as scheduling study time, using mnemonics, and outlining course content.

- *Self-reflection*. Students evaluate how effectively their strategies help them meet their academic goals and adjust strategies accordingly.

Studies show that such monitoring yields considerable payoffs. Zimmerman finds, for example, that when students set goals and monitor their self-efficacy they can boost their achievement potential by 30%, based on predictions from previous grades and scores on the Scholastic Aptitude Test.

Source: From "Teaching Students How to Learn," by Bridget Murray, *Monitor on Psychology*, June 2000, 62. Copyright 2000 by the American Psychological Association. Reprinted by permission.

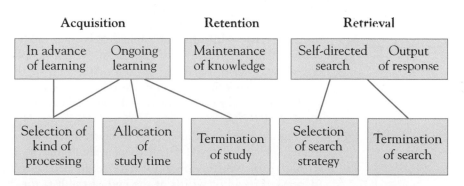

FIGURE 5.3 Examples of control strategies that influence the acquisition and retrieval of knowledge

Source: From "Metamemory: A theoretical framework and some new findings," by T. O. Nelson & L. Narens, in G. Bower (Ed.), *The psychology of learning and motivation*, Fig. 2. Copyright 1990 by Academic Press. Reprinted by permission of Elsevier Science.

Acquisition

Acquiring good acquisition strategies depends on our ability to judge how well we have learned the material. For example, determining which kind of processing is most effective requires that we recognize that we learned more from some strategies than from others. We saw that Atkinson and Shiffrin included three acquisition strategies in their model—rehearsal, coding, and imaging. They chose to study rehearsal, but is this the most effective one? As will be shown in the next two chapters, elaborative strategies such as coding and imaging are typically more successful than rehearsal.

Can people who do not know this research choose a good acquisition strategy by using their ability to judge that one strategy is more effective than another? A potential hurdle is that judgments of learning are often inaccurate if they are made shortly after studying an item because learning may only be temporary. We may be very confident that we have learned some material immediately after studying it, only to discover that we can't later recall it (Atkinson, 1972a, 1972b). For this reason, it is best to delay judgments of learning until we are more certain that learning is relatively permanent.

These points are nicely illustrated in a study by Dunlosky and Nelson (1994). They designed a paired associates task in which students studied half of the associates by using a rehearsal strategy and studied the remainder by using an imagery strategy. The imagery strategy was much more effective—it resulted in 59% correct recall, compared with only 25% correct recall for the rehearsal strategy. Students were more accurate in judging the differential effectiveness of the two strategies when they made delayed judgments (at least 30 seconds later) than when they made a judgment immediately after studying each item.

Accurate judgments of learning are useful not only for helping us select effective acquisition strategies but also for helping us determine which items need more study to later recall them. Dunlosky and Nelson found that delayed judgments also helped students identify which individual items they had learned. The problem with immediate judgments is that items are still in STM, making it difficult to predict how easy it will be to later retrieve the items.

Let's return to the serial position effect as an example of how our ability to easily retrieve information immediately after studying it can be a poor indicator of our ability to later retrieve it. When people begin recalling a word list, they typically recall the words at the end of the list first. These words are still available in STM and are therefore easy to recall. But people incorrectly believe that these words will also be easy to retrieve later (Benjamin & Bjork, 1996).

Figure 5.4 shows how serial position determines correct retrieval for both immediate and delayed recall (Benjamin & Bjork, 1996; Craik, 1970). The strong recency effect for immediate recall becomes a *negative* recency effect (depressed recall of words at the end of the list) for delayed recall. The recall of words from STM aided immediate recall but reduced delayed recall when it was necessary to rely on LTM. Benjamin and Bjork (1996) use these data to illustrate how **retrieval fluency** can be a misleading indicator of which items are best learned. Retrieval fluency—the ease with which an item can be

retrieval fluency The ease with which an item can be recalled

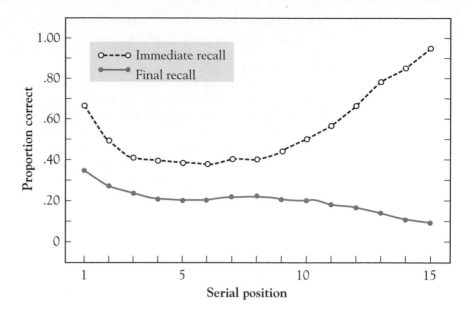

FIGURE **5.4** Effect of serial position on immediate and delayed recall

Source: From "The fate of primary items in free recall," by F. I. M. Craik, 1970, *Journal of Verbal Learning and Verbal Behavior*, *9*, 143–148. Copyright 1970 by Academic Press. Reprinted by permission of Elsevier Science.

recalled—failed to predict learning because those items that were easy to retrieve during immediate recall were difficult to retrieve during delayed recall.

Another aspect of acquisition shown in Figure 5.3 is allocation of study time. Recall the example of learning German vocabulary words referred to at the beginning of this section. If you were listening to a tape that presented the words in a predetermined order, you would have no choice of which words to study. But if you had a choice, you would likely spend more time on studying those words that you thought you hadn't learned.

A strategy that typically works well for students is to allocate more study time to the more difficult items. There is extensive evidence that students do, in fact, spend more time studying difficult items, with the exception of young students such as those in first grade (Son & Metcalfe, 2000). However, these studies provided students with ample time to study. Imagine that you were behind in your reading and had to prepare for an exam but did not have time to learn all the material. What would be the best strategy in this case? Son and Metcalfe (2000) found that under high time pressure people spent more time on the judged-easy items, whereas under lower time pressure they focused on the judged-difficult items.

Retention

A helpful framework for thinking about judgments of learning is to distinguish between how our experiences and our theoretical understandings influence these judgments (Koriat, Bjork, Sheffer, & Bar, 2004). Judgments based on retrieval fluency are influenced by our experiences. If we test ourselves and can easily retrieve the answer, we believe that we will easily retrieve the answer at some point later in time.

In contrast, theory-based judgments depend on our understanding of how different variables influence learning and retention. The students in Son and Metcalf's (2002) study realized that they would need to spend more time studying the more difficult items, and if they had only limited time, it would be better to focus on the easy items. However, students in Dunlosky and Nelson's (1994) experiment did not know that an imagery strategy is better than a rehearsal strategy. They were therefore more accurate in making delayed judgments of learning when their experiences were a more accurate predictor of learning.

The distinction between experience-based and theory-based judgments raises the issue of whether students know how the retention interval influences recall. Imagine that you have two final exams on Wednesday afternoon. You study for one exam on Tuesday and for the other exam on Wednesday morning. Would you spend more time studying on Tuesday because of the longer retention interval?

Koriat and his colleagues designed a series of experiments to investigate whether the retention interval would influence judgments of learning. Students studied a list of 60 paired associates and then took a test either immediately, one day later, or one week later. At the end of the learning session, they were asked either how many words they could (1) remember, (2) remember tomorrow, or (3) remember in one week, depending on whether their recall test was immediate, one day later, or one week later. Figure 5.5 shows that participants in each group estimated, on the average, that they could recall approximately 40% of the words. These findings are consistent with the retrieval fluency explanation in which students use their immediate experience to make judgments without considering how long they will have to remember the material. As expected by the experimenters, the retention interval did influence recall as shown by the performance of the three groups for each of the three retention intervals (Figure 5.5).

A possible reason why students did not consider that forgetting occurs over time is that each group was asked about only a particular retention interval. The design of Experiment 2 attempted to elicit theory-based predictions by asking a new group of participants to make predictions about the results obtained in Experiment 1. After receiving a detailed description of the Experiment 1 methodology, these students were asked to predict how many words on the average were recalled by each group after (1) 10 minutes, (2) a day, and (3) a week. These estimates were remarkably accurate, as shown in Figure 5.5. Students realized that forgetting would occur over time so estimated less recall as the retention interval increased. Their estimates were not biased by their experiences because they did not have to learn the words. Zhao and Linderholm (2008) argue that many metacognitive decisions are based on a combination of theory and experience. The challenge is to determine how different situations determine which receives the most emphasis.

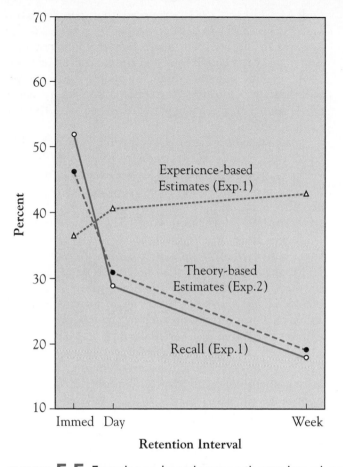

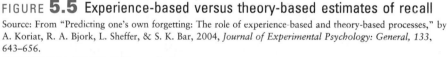

FIGURE **5.5** Experience-based versus theory-based estimates of recall

Source: From "Predicting one's own forgetting: The role of experience-based and theory-based processes," by A. Koriat, R. A. Bjork, L. Sheffer, & S. K. Bar, 2004, *Journal of Experimental Psychology: General, 133,* 643–656.

A benefit of taking a course on cognitive psychology is that you should be able to make more theory-based predictions. Unlike the students in Dunlosky and Nelson's (1994) experiment, you should be able to predict that you will have better recall if you use an imagery strategy than if you use a rehearsal strategy. You should also be able use STM for the immediate recall of words at the end of a list but realize that these words will need more study for delayed recall when you have to rely solely on LTM.

Retrieval

The third aspect of learning shown in Figure 5.3 is retrieval. Recovering information from LTM depends on getting it back out through the use of effective retrieval strategies. If asked a difficult question, you may have to initially decide whether you have the relevant information in memory. Glucksberg and McCloskey (1981) proposed that people first conduct a preliminary search of memory to decide whether they have stored any information that is relevant to the question. Most people would not find any relevant information if asked, "Did President Clinton use an electric toothbrush?" so they could quickly respond that they didn't know. If potentially relevant facts were retrieved, however (as could occur for a question such as "Is Kiev in the Ukraine?"), a person would then search LTM for confirming or disconfirming evidence.

After deciding that it is worthwhile to search LTM, you must decide how to conduct the search. Atkinson and Shiffrin (1968) proposed that people develop plans for searching LTM. For example, if asked to recall the names of all 50 states, you could organize your search by either alphabetic order or geographic location.

Recalling information from LTM sometimes occurs so rapidly that psychologists have little opportunity to study how people retrieve the information. However, occasionally retrieval succeeds only after a slow search of LTM, such as occurs in the **tip of the tongue** (TOT) phenomenon. A word is on the tip of your tongue when you know it is stored in LTM but are momentarily blocked from retrieving it. Successful retrieval is often helped by using partial information, such as the length of the word or its initial letter, to limit the search of LTM (R. Brown & McNeill, 1966).

tip of the tongue (TOT)
A retrieval state in which a person feels he or she knows the information but cannot immediately retrieve it

There are two general experimental methods for studying the TOT state. The laboratory approach requires bringing people into the laboratory and asking them to recall words that might elicit the TOT state. The diary approach requires that people keep detailed records of what happens when faced with memory blocks in their daily lives.

The first systematic laboratory study was conducted by R. Brown and D. McNeill (1966) who gave people definitions of infrequent words and asked them to try to recall the words. For example, "What is the name of the instrument that uses the position of the sun and stars to navigate?" Some of the words produced the TOT state; that is, people were unable to immediately think of the word but were confident that they would soon recall it. Successful retrieval was often helped by using partial information related to the spelling of the word, such as its length or its initial letter. When attempting to answer the previous question, people may recall that the word starts with the letter s and has two syllables (*sextant*).

Another study found similar results using pictures and verbal descriptions of entertainers (Read & Bruce, 1982). For example, the verbal description of Ray Bolger was "On Broadway he created the role of Charley in *Charley's Aunt*, but he is perhaps best remembered as the scarecrow in the Judy Garland movie *The Wizard of Oz.*" The most frequently reported strategy for recalling names was to make use of partial information, as reported initially by Brown and McNeill (1966). Partial information includes information about the length of a name or letters or sounds within a name (James & Burke, 2000).

Two other popular strategies were to generate plausible names and to use contextual information. The generation of plausible names was often guided by partial information to limit the search. Contextual information is information associated with the person, such as movie and television roles or ethnic origin. Only infrequently did subjects report that they spontaneously recalled the name without thinking about the target person. Successful retrievals therefore usually occurred as a result of a planned search of memory.

naturalistic study A study of the tip-of-the-tongue state in which people record these events as they occur outside the laboratory

In **naturalistic studies** of TOTs, subjects carry a diary to document TOT states as they occur. They are asked to record what information they could retrieve as they searched for the word and how the memory block was resolved. A review of this literature (A. S. Brown, 1991) reported a number of consistent findings. For example:

1. TOTs are reported to occur in daily life about once a week and to increase with age. Most are triggered by the names of personal acquaintances.
2. Words related both to the meaning and the spelling of the target word are retrieved, but spelling predominates. People can guess the first letter approximately 50% of the time.
3. Approximately one-half of the TOT states are resolved within 1 minute.

spontaneous retrieval A retrieval that occurs without making a conscious effort to recall information

The finding that the predominant retrieval strategy involves the partial recall of spelling information is consistent across both laboratory and naturalistic studies, but there are also some differences in the findings. Naturally occurring TOTs yield a moderate number (ranging from 17 to 41%) of **spontaneous retrievals** in which the word suddenly "pops into mind" without a conscious effort to retrieve it. In contrast, spontaneous retrievals seldom occur (5% or less) in laboratory studies. The greater occurrence of spontaneous retrievals in naturalistic studies makes sense because involuntary word retrieval, in general, typically occurs when a person is engaged in relatively automatic activities such as cleaning or doing dishes (Kvavilashvili & Mandler, 2003). In experimental studies of the TOT effect, participants are kept busy searching for particular words so there is little opportunity for spontaneous retrieval.

IMPROVING EYEWITNESS RECALL AND IDENTIFICATION

I have tried to mix both the theoretical and applied aspects of memory in this chapter. This theme continues in this section on the contributions of psychological research to improving eyewitness recall and identification. The impact of this research is clearly indicated from a survey published in the *American Psychologist* (Kassin, Tubb, Hosch, & Memon, 2001). The survey asked 64 psychologists about their courtroom experiences and opinions on 30 eyewitness topics. The questions asked them whether they (1) thought the evidence was reliable enough for psychologists to present it in testimony, (2) would be willing to testify in court on this topic, (3) based their opinion on published research, and (4) thought jurors believe this statement to be true as a matter of common sense.

Table 5.1 shows their responses to seven of these topics. The results show a wide range in the perceived reliability of the findings. Almost everyone

TABLE **5.1**

Experts' Agreement with Statements about Eyewitness Testimony (in Percentages)

Topic	Reliable?	Testify?	Research?	Common Sense?
1. Wording of questions	98	84	97	25
2. Mug-shot–induced bias	95	77	97	13
3. Hypnotic suggestibility	91	76	90	19
4. Accuracy-confidence	87	73	97	5
5. Hypnotic accuracy	45	34	89	55
6. Event violence	37	29	79	14
7. Long-term repression	22	20	87	79

Topics

1. An eyewitness's testimony can be affected by how the questions are worded.

2. Exposure to mug shots increases subsequent identification in a lineup.

3. Hypnosis increases suggestibility to leading and misleading questions.

4. Confidence is not a good predictor of identification accuracy.

5. Hypnosis increases the accuracy of reported memories.

6. Eyewitnesses have more difficulty remembering violent events.

7. Traumatic experiences can be repressed for many years and then recovered.

Source: From "On the 'general acceptance' of eyewitness testimony research," by S. M. Kassin, V. A. Tubb, H. M. Hosch, & A. Memon, 2001, *American Psychologist, 56*, 405–416. Copyright 2001 by the American Psychological Association. Reprinted by permission.

believed that the wording of questions can influence eyewitness testimony, but only 22% of the experts believed that traumatic experiences can be repressed for many years and then recovered. It is also clear that research findings often do not support perceived common sense. For example, the experts thought most jurors would expect that accuracy is related to the confidence level of the eyewitness although research has shown that confidence level is not a good predictor of accuracy (Busey & Loftus, 2008).

The following sections present some details of this research.

Improving Eyewitness Recall

One of the questions raised in Table 5.1 is whether hypnosis helps people accurately recall information. Fewer than half of the experts believed that it is helpful based on their knowledge of research. Although there have been many reports of cases in which hypnosis helped witnesses recall additional details about a crime, problems are associated with its use (M. E. Smith, 1983). A major concern is that encouragement by the hypnotist may induce witnesses to report inaccurately. For example, in one study 90% of the hypnotized witnesses tried to recall the number on a shirt in a simulated crime, compared with only 20% of the subjects in a control group (Buckhout, Eugenio, Licitra, Oliver, & Kramer, 1981). None of the witnesses was able to recall the number correctly. The possibility that recall may be inaccurate has caused the courts to question the reliability of recall during hypnosis.

Another problem with evaluating the effectiveness of hypnosis is that successful recall during hypnosis may not have been caused by the hypnosis. M. E. Smith (1983) identifies other possible causes, such as repeated testing and the reinstatement of context. As indicated by the findings of Read and Bruce (1982), repeated testing can cause additional recall. That is, improved recall attributed to hypnosis may simply result from the fact that witnesses are attempting a second or a third recall, which would have resulted in retrieval of more details without hypnosis. Or improved recall could result from some aspect of the procedure, such as encouraging witnesses to try to reinstate the context of the crime (Malpass & Devine, 1981).

To determine whether cognitive retrieval instructions are as effective as hypnosis, Geiselman, Fisher, MacKinnon, and Holland (1985) asked both hypnotized and nonhypnotized subjects to recall information about a simulated crime. Subjects saw a 4-minute film of a violent crime and were interviewed 2 days later by law-enforcement personnel.

The subjects were randomly assigned to one of three interview conditions. The standard interview followed questioning procedures that law-enforcement personnel would normally use. The hypnosis interview involved asking hypnotized subjects to restate what they remembered from the film. The **cognitive interview** involved the use of four memory-retrieval techniques that encouraged subjects to reinstate the context of the incident, report everything, recall the events in different orders, and recall the incidents from different perspectives.

cognitive interview The use of cognitively based retrieval techniques to improve recall

Both the cognitive and hypnosis procedures resulted in the recall of a significantly greater number of correct items of information than did the standard interview. The investigators attributed this finding to the memory-guidance techniques that are common to these two procedures. Although the cognitive interview did not result in better recall than the use of hypnosis, it is easier to learn and to administer.

The application of the cognitive-interview procedure to real crimes has also produced encouraging results (R. P. Fisher, Geiselman, & Amador, 1989). Seven experienced detectives in Dade County, Florida, were trained in the procedure. Both before and after training, the experimenters tape-recorded interviews with victims and witnesses of crimes. The detectives obtained 47% more information from the interviews following the training. In many cases there was more than one victim or witness, so it was possible to determine whether the obtained information was consistent across the people interviewed. A high rate of consistency suggested that the obtained information was accurate.

The positive results of this and other studies on interviewing procedures resulted in the U.S. Department of Justice releasing in 1999 the first national guide for collecting eyewitness evidence (Technical Working Group for Eyewitness Evidence, 1999). Psychological researchers participated in writing the guide and later wrote about their collaboration with the justice department (Wells et al., 2000). The analysis of police interviews revealed a number of avoidable errors including (a) asking too many closed-ended questions, (b) frequently interrupting the witness, and (c) asking questions in a predetermined, inflexible order. In contrast, the new recommended procedures are to conduct the interview at a slow pace and ask a few, primarily open-ended questions. Also recommended are the previously mentioned memory retrieval techniques such as reinstating the context and recalling events by using different retrieval pathways.

Eyewitness Identification

Psychologists have also made important contributions to assessing the accuracy of eyewitness identification. The major reason for establishing national guidelines for collecting eyewitness testimony was new DNA evidence that established that in some cases innocent people had been wrongly convicted. A review of these cases revealed that mistaken eyewitness identification was the primary evidence in 36 of the 40 convictions (Wells et al., 2000).

One source of mistakes is perceptual limitations. Viewing the suspect under low levels of illumination or from a distance makes it difficult to see facial details. Viewing an object from a distance is equivalent to blurring it by an amount that is determined by that distance. Figure 5.6 shows the difficulty of recognizing a mystery celebrity from 43, 172, and 450 feet (Busey & Loftus, 2008).

Other sources of error occur from introducing biases into the identification procedure. As indicated in Table 5.1, one of the most reliable findings according to experts is that looking at mug shots can make eyewitnesses more likely to identify a person as a suspect when later viewing a police lineup. Part of the problem in deciding whether we recognize someone or something is to recall the context in which a previous encounter might have occurred (G. Mandler, 1980; Humphreys & Bain, 1983). Mandler (1980) gives an example of a person who sees a familiar-looking person on a bus but is unsure why the person looks familiar. It is only after a suitable context is recalled—the person works in the supermarket—that recognition seems complete.

Eyewitness identification is a situation in which recalling the context of information is particularly important. Accurate identification depends not only on being able to recognize a face as someone familiar but also on recalling that the person was seen performing a crime rather than seen in a newspaper, on television, or in police mug shots. The possibility that the witness might be able to recognize a face without being able to recall the correct context was addressed by the U.S. Supreme Court in *Simmons v. United States* (390 U.S. 377, 1968) (cited in E. Brown, Deffenbacher, & Sturgill, 1977). The Court noted the potential biasing effect caused by showing a witness a single mug shot or by showing mug shots that emphasized a particular suspect. The ruling held that the biasing effects would be particularly misleading if the witness originally had only a brief glimpse of the suspect or saw the suspect under poor conditions (Buckhout, 1974).

The possible biasing effects that can occur during eyewitness identification were investigated in a study by Brown, Deffenbacher, and Sturgill (1977). Two

43 ft

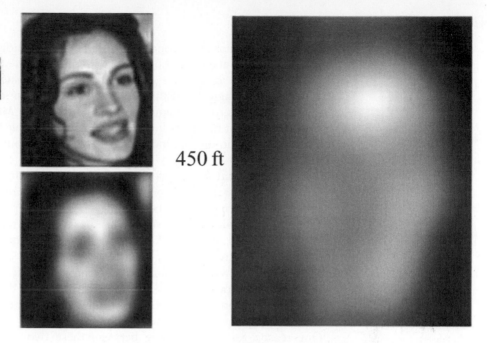

450 ft

172 ft

FIGURE **5.6** Illustration of how distance blurs facial details

Source: From "Cognitive science and the law." by T. Busey & G. Loftus, 2007, *TRENDS in the Cognitive Sciences, 11*, 111–117. Reprinted by permission.

males handed out the first midterm exam in the class; members of the class were not told that they would later be asked to identify the two individuals. Mug shots were shown 2 or 3 days after the exam, and a lineup occurred 4 or 5 days after the students viewed the mug shots. Presenting a mug shot of a person made it more likely that the person would be identified in the lineup as having passed out the exam.

The false identification occurred because the person identified looked very familiar as a result of having his picture included among the mug shots. However, as stated earlier, successful recognition often depends on the recall of a specific context in addition to a judgment of familiarity. Although these experiments do not pretend to duplicate what an actual witness is confronted with during a crime, they suggest that great care should be taken in what material is shown to a witness who must make the final identification of a suspected criminal.

Another example of possible biasing effects during a lineup is that the investigators' unintentional cues, such as body language or tone of voice, may reduce the reliability of eyewitness identification. The psychologists who served as advisors in writing the national guidelines argued strongly that the person who administers the lineup should not be aware of which person in the lineup is the suspect (Wells et al., 2000). This recommendation was not adopted but was identified as a procedural change for future exploration.

INDIRECT TESTS OF MEMORY

Traditional tests, such as recognition and recall, are not the only way to evaluate a person's memory. Look for a moment at the word fragment in Figure 5.7. Can you identify the word? People are more successful at identifying difficult word fragments if they are previously shown a list of words that includes the answers to the fragments (such as the word *METAL* for this example). The fact that the list is helpful suggests that people have a memory of some of the words on the list, indicating that this task could be used as a test for memory.

You may feel that this memory test is less direct than the recall and recognition tests discussed in the previous section. Recall and recognition tests are called **direct memory tests** because they refer to a particular event in a person's past. The directions ask people to recall or recognize events that occurred earlier and are therefore measures of **explicit memory**. In contrast, instructions for **indirect memory tests** refer only to the current task and do not refer to prior events (Richardson-Klavehn & Bjork, 1988). People performing the word-fragment task only have to identify the word, not judge whether they had previously seen the word during the experiment. Indirect tests are therefore measures of **implicit memory**.

One reason for distinguishing between these two types of tests is that what we learn about a person's memory depends on how we test it. This point was strikingly illustrated in a study by Warrington and Weiskrantz (1970) at the National Hospital in London. They compared patients with severe amnesia with control patients who were closely matched for age and intelligence. The comparison involved four tests of memory for word lists. The recall test required a verbal recall of the words. The recognition-memory test required a yes or no decision regarding whether a test word was on the list. The word-fragment test required the identification of a word fragment. The correct word appeared on the list, and the fragments were difficult to identify if subjects had not previously seen the list. The initial-letters test contained the first three letters of a word that had appeared on the list, and the subjects had to generate a word that began with those three letters.

The amnesic subjects did significantly worse than the controls on both the recognition and recall tests. However, they did not differ from the controls on the word-fragment or initial-letters tests. They were just as likely as the controls to successfully use the words that they had seen on the word list. The lack of difference on these two tests occurred even though the amnesic patients often did not remember that they had seen the word list and approached the tests as a kind of guessing game (Warrington & Weiskrantz, 1968). But the influence of the word list on their answers indicated that they still had a memory of many words on the list.

direct memory test A test that asks people to recall or recognize past events

explicit memory Memory evaluated by direct memory tests

indirect memory test A test that does not explicitly ask about past events but is influenced by memory of past events

implicit memory Memory evaluated by indirect memory tests

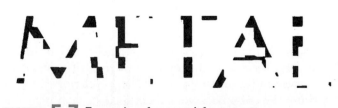

FIGURE **5.7** Example of a word fragment

Source: From "Amnesic syndrome: Consolidation or retrieval?" by E. K. Warrington & L. Weiskrantz, 1970, *Nature, 228,* 628–630. Copyright 1970 Macmillan Magazines Ltd. Reprinted by permission.

Processing Theories

Performance differences between direct and indirect tests of memory have encouraged many studies of how the tests differ (Table 5.2). One theoretical approach has emphasized the *different processing requirements* of the tests. An example of this approach (Jacoby & Dallas, 1981) builds on G. Mandler's (1980) two-process theory of **recognition memory**. According to this theory, recognition memory requires both a judgment of familiarity and an attempt to retrieve the context in which the item occurred. Jacoby and Dallas proposed that the familiarity component of this theory also applies to indirect tests that typically require perceptual identification. Prior experience with the material makes it more familiar and easier to identify in a perceptually difficult situation. However, the second basis for recognition memory—retrieval of when and where an item occurred—is not necessary to do well on indirect tests because such tests do not require memory for a particular context.

This formulation implies that changing the familiarity of the items should influence performance on tests of both recognition-memory and perceptual-identification. Jacoby and Dallas manipulated familiarity by presenting the study material either in the same modality (visual presentation) or in a different modality (auditory presentation) than the test material. As predicted, changing the modality made the test material less familiar and lowered performance on both the recognition-memory and perceptual-identification tasks.

In contrast, variables that help subjects determine in what context they saw a word should only enhance performance on recognition memory tasks. This prediction was tested by manipulating whether subjects read a list of words (such as *METAL*) or solved the words from anagrams (*EMTLA*). Prior research has shown that it is easier to remember which words occur in an experiment if subjects generate the words from anagrams rather than simply read them. As predicted, generating the words improved performance on a recognition-memory task but did not improve performance on a perceptual-identification task that did not require memory for the context of the presented words.

Jacoby and Dallas's explanation is an example of how direct and indirect measures of memory can be compared on the basis of what processes are

recognition memory
Deciding whether an item had previously occurred in a specified context

TABLE **5.2**
Differences between Direct and Indirect Memory Tests

	Direct Tests	Indirect Tests
Examples	Recall	Word fragment
	Recognition	Initial letters
Process theories	Conceptually driven	Data driven
	Retrieval strategies	Familiarity
Multimemory theories	Episodic memory	Procedural memory
Brain structure	Medial temporal lobe	Various locations

required to perform the task. Elaboration of the material through generating the words from anagrams helps people on recall and recognition tests, whereas increasing the familiarity of the material influences performance on recognition memory and perceptual-identification tasks.

A more general formulation of this approach claims that direct memory tests are primarily conceptually driven, and indirect tests of memory are primarily data driven (Schacter, 1987; Richardson-Klavehn & Bjork, 1988). **Conceptually driven processes** reflect subject-initiated activities such as elaborating and organizing information. Such processes help people on recall and recognition tests. **Data-driven processes** are initiated and guided by the perceptual information in the material, such as its familiarity. However, this distinction is not mutually exclusive. As we have just seen, recognition-memory tests are influenced by both kinds of processing, but data-driven processing is more predominant in indirect tests than in recognition-memory tests. Modality shifts therefore cause greater disruption in indirect tests such as word-fragment identification than in direct tests such as recognition memory (Schacter, 1987).

Multiple Memories

An alternative to arguing that memory tests measure different processes is to argue that memory tests measure different memories (Schacter, 1987). This view claims that LTM is not a single unitary system but consists of several different subsystems. It is important to recognize, however, that the argument for different memories does not necessarily imply that the argument for different processes is incorrect. Indeed, a leading proponent of different memory systems has argued that the two approaches are complementary (Tulving, 2002). Theorists can explain performance differences either by identifying different processes or by identifying different memories according to this view.

One major division of LTM into separate subsystems involves the distinction between episodic and semantic memory (Tulving, 1972, 1985, 2002). **Episodic memory** contains temporally dated recollections of personal experiences. It provides a record of what people have done; for example, I had chicken for dinner last night, received my PhD in 1970, and saw a particular person's face as I was looking at mug shots. **Semantic memory** contains general knowledge that is not associated with a particular time and context. For example, I know that a canary is a bird, Chicago is in Illinois, and the sum of 7 and 8 is 15. Episodic memory is therefore more autobiographical; it contains the kind of information I would record in a detailed diary. Semantic information is more general and contains the kind of information I would record in an encyclopedia.

According to this distinction, direct memory tests, which require recall or recognition of material that occurred earlier in the experiment, measure episodic memory. Subjects are asked to recall items (such as a list of words) from a particular time and place. Indirect memory tests, such as word identification or word completion, measure semantic memory. These tests depend only on our general knowledge of words and do not require that we associate the words with a particular time and place.

conceptually driven process A process that is influenced by a person's strategies

data-driven process A process that is influenced by the stimulus material

episodic memory Memory of specific events, including when and where they occurred

semantic memory Memory of general knowledge not associated with a particular context

The finding that patients with amnesia do much better on indirect tests than on direct tests has been used as evidence for the distinction between episodic and semantic memory. According to this argument, amnesia affects episodic memory but not semantic memory. However, critics of the episodic/semantic distinction argue that this explanation is less popular than the position that indirect tests differ from direct tests because they depend more on procedural memory (McKoon, Ratcliff, & Dell, 1986). **Procedural memory** is memory for actions, skills, and operations, whereas both episodic and semantic memory are concerned with factual information. Factual information seems more susceptible to forgetting than procedural information, as evidenced by amnesic patients who have difficulty recalling facts but do well at learning and retaining motor skills (Warrington & Weiskrantz, 1970).

procedural memory
Memory for actions, skills, and operations

Although I don't recall ever suffering from amnesia, I do recall an incident in which my procedural memory was left more intact than my memory for facts. I learned how to type in high school and did some typing in college, but I relied entirely on secretaries when I became a faculty member. When I later decided to try a word-processing program, I began by attempting to recall where the keys were on the keyboard but discovered that I could recall almost nothing. However, when I attempted to use the keyboard, I remembered how to correctly move my fingers. I remembered the correct procedure for typing even though I couldn't recall the location of the keys.

In summary, both process theories and multimemory theories offer suggestions for how direct tests of memory differ from indirect tests of memory (Roediger, 1990). Direct tests, such as recall and recognition, are conceptually driven and are influenced by subject-initiated strategies that facilitate retrieval, such as actively generating the items during the study phase. In contrast, indirect tests, such as the word-fragment and initial-letters tests, are data driven. They are influenced by the familiarity of the material, including changes in its modality. Direct tests measure episodic memory in which people recall information about particular events in their past. Indirect tests measure procedural memory in which people are not instructed to refer back to past events.

Brain Structures

The diminished performance of amnesic patients on direct memory tests and their relatively normal performance on indirect memory tests has led to the search for the biological foundations of memory (Knowlton & Foerde, 2008). Does damage to a specific part of the brain cause diminished performance in amnesic patients on tests of explicit memory, whereas other areas of the brain are responsible for performance on tests of implicit memory? Research by Larry Squire and his colleagues at the Veterans Affairs Medical Center in San Diego supports the idea that memory is not a single entity but consists of several separate entities that depend on different brain systems (Squire & Zola, 1996).

Figure 5.8 shows a taxonomy of systems in LTM, along with specific brain structures involved in each system (Squire & Knowlton, 1994). Research shows that amnesic patients' poor performance on tests of explicit memory is caused by damage to the hippocampal formation in the medial temporal lobe. In contrast, amnesic patients perform normally on a wide

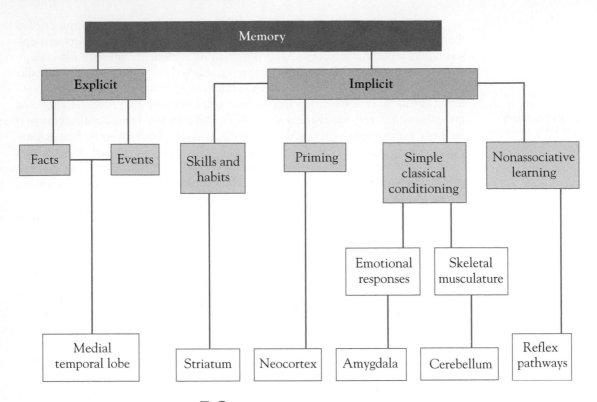

FIGURE **5.8** A taxonomy of long-term memory and associated brain structures

Source: Adapted from "Memory, hippocampus, and brain systems," by L. R. Squire & B. J. Knowlton, 1994, in M. Gazzaniga (Ed.), *The cognitive neurosciences* (Cambridge, MA: MIT Press). Reprinted by permission.

variety of tests that do not involve the medial temporal lobe. As shown in Figure 5.8, these tasks depend on a variety of brain systems that are intact in amnesia.

We began this section by contrasting amnesic patients' poor performance on recall and recognition tests with their good performance on a word-fragment test that depended on implicit memory for words (Warrington & Weiskrantz, 1970). The good performance on a word-fragment test is an example of priming. **Priming** refers to facilitation of the ability to detect or identify stimuli by using prior information. As shown in Figure 5.8, this is one type of implicit memory.

Another type of implicit memory is learned skills and procedures. We have seen that the multimemory theory claims that indirect tests measure procedural memory, and Squire and Knowlton's (1994) taxonomy is consistent with this claim. An example of a skill that depends on procedural memory is the improvement in reading speed that occurs when rereading the same passage. Musen, Shimamura, and Squire (1990) studied improvement in reading speed for both amnesic patients and those without amnesia and found that amnesic patients increased their speed as much as those without amnesia

priming Facilitation in the detection or recognition of a stimulus by using prior information

when rereading the passage. However, amnesic patients were markedly impaired in their ability to correctly answer multiple-choice questions about the content of the passage. Once again, there were no differences between groups for an indirect test of memory (improved reading skill) but large differences for a direct (multiple-choice) test of memory.

Other types of implicit memory are simple classical conditioning and reflex learning. These various types of implicit memory represent a variety of ways in which our experiences can lead to changes in our performance without any changes in conscious memory content (Squire & Zola, 1997). Performance changes as a result of experience, and therefore memory is involved, but these changes occur without an accompanying sense that memory is being consulted (Knowlton & Foerde, 2008). This, of course, is very different from direct memory tests where we are very aware that our memory is being evaluated.

SUMMARY

Learning can be represented as the transfer of information from STM to LTM. The decay rate for information in LTM is slow compared with the rapid decay rate from STM. Furthermore, LTM does not suffer from a capacity limitation; that is, it is not limited in the amount of information it can store. The distinction between STM and LTM, as well as the role of rehearsal in transferring information into LTM, was emphasized in a model proposed by Atkinson and Shiffrin. One of the findings that their model accounts for is the serial position effect: The better recall of words at the beginning of a list can be explained by their storage in LTM, and the better recall of words at the end of the list can be explained by their storage in STM.

In other situations it may be difficult to decide whether successfully retrieved new information came from STM or LTM. The ability to make this distinction is useful because the student should concentrate on items that are not yet stored in LTM. Deciding how much to study material can be based either on experiences such as retrieval fluency or on theoretical knowledge such as how the retention interval influences forgetting.

To retrieve information from LTM, we must initially decide whether the information is stored in LTM. The tip-of-the-tongue phenomenon occurs when a person knows information is stored in LTM but cannot immediately retrieve it. Strategies for searching LTM include using partial information such as word length or sounds, generating plausible names, and using contextual information associated with a name. The cognitive interview technique successfully instructs eyewitnesses how to carefully search memory to recall details about a crime. A recognition task differs from a recall task in that it tests judgment of whether an item was previously presented, usually within a specified context. Errors in eyewitness identification are increased by showing mug shots to a witness. The witness might falsely identify a person because of a failure to recall the context in which that person was previously seen.

Indirect tests of LTM typically determine whether memory for a list of words helps people identify word fragments or generate a word from initial letters. Patients with memory disorders usually perform better on these tests than on direct tests such as recognition or recall. Process theories attribute this difference to the conceptually driven nature of direct tests and the data-driven nature of indirect tests. In contrast, multimemory theories propose that direct tests evaluate episodic memory, whereas indirect tests evaluate procedural memory. Evidence from cognitive neuroscience supports the idea that there are different types of memory localized in different areas of the brain. Explicit memory, measured by direct tests, is localized in the hippocampal formation in the medial temporal lobe. Implicit memory, measured by indirect tests, is used for a variety of tasks (skill learning, priming, conditioning) that are supported by a variety of different brain structures.

STUDY QUESTIONS

1. Long-term memory (LTM) is what most of us mean when we speak of memory. What do we mean when we say a person has a "good memory"? What are the assumed characteristics of LTM?

2. As you think about your own attempts to learn new material, can you identify different instances in which you have used each of the metacognitive processes discussed in the book?

3. Notice that the task chosen for the study of verbal rehearsal was a "meaningless" task. Why was that desirable?

4. Do the assumptions of the Atkinson-Shiffrin model seem intuitively compelling to you? How well do the data fit the predictions generated by the model—for example, the primacy effect?

5. How can the recency effect be explained? How was the most popular theory tested?

6. Why did the participants in Koriat's Experiment 1 not show an awareness of retention interval, yet the participants in Experiment 2 made extremely accurate predictions of retention interval? How does this finding support the distinction between experience-based and theory-based predictions?

7. Be sure you understand the specific uses of the term *context* in studies of recognition and recall. Are recognition and recall different kinds of memory?

8. Were you surprised by any of the results of the application of recognition theory to eyewitness identification? Would you recommend any changes in criminal justice procedures on the basis of these experiments? Why or why not?

9. What techniques have been used to test memory indirectly? How do the tasks called for in direct and indirect tests differ?

10. One explanation of the differences shown in performance on direct and indirect tests points to differential processing demands. What sorts of empirical evidence lead to this view?

CogLab   The following experiments that relate to this chapter can be found at: http://coglab. wadsworth.com. Answer the questions in the CogLab Student Manual as required by your teacher for these experiments.

Serial Position
Remember/Know
Implicit Learning
False Memory

KEY TERMS

The page number in parentheses refers to where the term is discussed in the chapter.

coding (105)

cognitive interview (117)

conceptually driven process (122)

control process (104)

data-driven process (122)

direct memory test (120)

episodic memory (122)

explicit memory (120)

imaging (105)

implicit memory (120)

indirect memory test (120)

knowledge acquisition (108)

long-term memory (LTM) (103)

metacognition (108)

naturalistic study (115)

primacy effect (106)

priming (124)

procedural memory (123)

recency effect (106)

recognition memory (121)

rehearsal (104)

retrieval fluency (110)

retrieval strategy (108)

rote learning (105)

semantic memory (122)

serial position effect (106)

spontaneous retrieval (115)

tip of the tongue (TOT) (114)

RECOMMENDED READING

The general references on memory cited at the end of Chapter 4 discuss LTM as well as STM. Schacter (1989) summarizes the major assumptions and some of the research findings from four different approaches to studying memory: experimental cognitive psychology, neuropsychology, ecological psychology, and artificial intelligence. His book, *Searching for Memory: The Brain, the Mind, and the Past* (Schacter, 1996) is a readable but scholarly treatment of memory from a cognitive neuroscience approach. Edited books on metacognition include *Metacognition and Cognitive Neuropsychology* (Mazzoni & Nelson, 1998), *Applied Metacognition* (Perfect & Schwartz, 2002), and *Thinking and Seeing: Visual Metacognition in Adults and Children* (Levin, 2004). These are complemented by journal reviews of study strategies (Broekkamp & Van Hout-Wolters, 2007; Kornell & Bjork, 2007; Zhao & Linerholm, 2008). Bahrick (1979) studied very-long-term memory by asking alumni to recall various kinds of information (such as street and building names) about their college town. Ericsson and Kintsch (1995) argue for the concept of a long-term working memory. Estes (1997) discusses processes of memory loss, recovery, and distortion, and Wixted (2004) summarizes research on the neuroscience of forgetting. Berkerian and Dennett (1993) review the research literature on the cognitive-interview technique, and a book by Schwartz (2002) reviews the literature on tip-of-the-tongue states. Reviews of research on memory accuracy (Koriat, Goldsmith, & Pansky, 2000) and eyewitness testimony (Busey & Loftus, 2008; Lindberg, Keiffer, & Thomas, 2000) provide good overviews of these research areas. The distinction between direct and indirect tests of memory also attract considerable theoretical interest (Humphreys, Bain, & Pike, 1989; Roediger, 1990; Toth, Reingold, & Jacoby, 1994).

6

Memory Codes

It is abundantly clear that what determines the level of recall or recognition of a word event is not intention to learn, the amount of effort involved, the difficulty of the orienting task, the amount of time spent making judgments about the items, or even the amount of rehearsal the items receive; rather it is the qualitative nature of the task, the kind of operations carried out on the items, that determines retention.

—F. I. M. Craik and Endel Tulving (1975)

The preceding two chapters developed a theory of memory consisting of a short-term memory (STM) store and a long-term memory (LTM) store. This theory provides a beginning, but it leaves us with many questions. For example: Why are there many different decay rates in LTM? Does verbal rehearsal always cause learning? Are some memory codes better than others? How is memory organized? And what about visual knowledge?

In the next four chapters, I will try to provide some answers to these questions about the representation and organization of knowledge. Our immediate objective is to learn how memory codes differ and what the implications of these differences are for learning and retrieval. A **memory code** is the representation used to store an item in memory. Consider what memory codes might be involved if you were learning to associate pairs of words in a paired-associates task. If the words were presented visually, you might form a visual image of the words. You would also probably rehearse the words and create an acoustic (phonemic) code. If the words were meaningful, you might create meaningful associations to help you learn.

memory code The format (physical, phonemic, semantic) of information encoded into memory

The option of creating different memory codes is particularly advantageous when a memory deficit limits the kind of memory codes that a person can create. This is illustrated by a woman (P. V.) who had a selectively impaired **auditory-memory span**, being unable to repeat back auditory sequences longer than two or three words. To determine how this impairment would influence long-term learning, a group of psychologists varied the characteristics of a paired-associates task (Baddeley, Papagno, & Vallar, 1988). The most challenging task required P. V. to listen to eight pairs in which the stimuli were words and the responses were pronounceable nonwords, such as *svieti*. The dramatic results of this task are shown in Figure 6.1a. Most of the control subjects—matched with P. V. for age and education—had learned the list by ten trials, but P. V. failed to recall even a single item on any of the ten learning trials. Of course, the difficulty of this task might depend on the material—the auditory presentation made it difficult to use visual coding, and the nonword responses made it difficult to use semantic codes.

auditory-memory span Number of items recalled from short-term memory following an auditory presentation of the items

So, what would happen if P. V. were asked to learn eight visually presented word–nonword pairs? Figure 6.1b shows the answer. Her performance is still impaired but is markedly improved when compared with the auditory presentation. It looks like the possibility to visually encode the material partially compensates for her impaired auditory-memory span. But the big gain

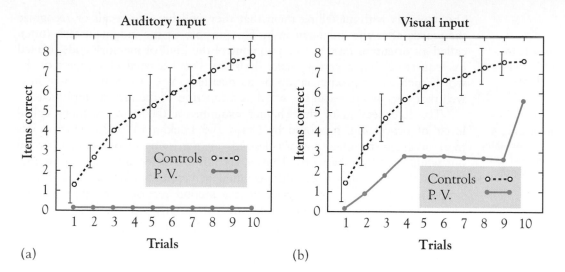

(a)

(b)

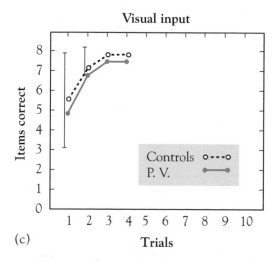

(c)

FIGURE **6.1** Comparison between P. V. and control subjects for learning
(a) auditory input of word-nonword pairs, (b) visual input of word-nonword pairs,
and (c) visual input of word pairs

Source: From "When long-term learning depends on short-term storage," by A. Baddeley, C. Papagno, & G. Vallar,
1988, *Journal of Memory and Language, 27,* 586–595. Copyright 1988 by Academic Press, Inc. Reprinted by permission
of Elsevier Science.

occurs when the material is meaningful, consisting of word–word pairs. The
opportunity to use meaningful associations between words (semantic codes)
resulted in a normal performance (Figure 6.1c).

When unimpaired people try to learn, they most likely form several kinds
of memory codes, and psychologists have little control over what people do.
So instead of asking people to learn, we often ask them to make judgments

about words without telling them that they will have to recall or recognize the words after the judgment task. The purpose of the judgment task (often called an **orienting task**) is to try to control the kind of memory code formed by requesting that a person make decisions about a particular aspect of the word, such as its pronunciation or its meaning. We can then examine how well that person can recall the word as a function of the aspect emphasized.

orienting task Instructions to focus on a particular aspect (physical, phonemic, semantic) of a stimulus

levels of processing A theory that proposes that "deeper" (semantic) levels of processing enhance memory

The first section of this chapter examines a theory of memory called **levels of processing**, proposed by Craik and Lockhart (1972), which holds that success in recalling a word depends on the kinds of operations carried out while encoding the word. That is, retention is determined by the characteristics that are emphasized during initial perception or rehearsal. Evidence supporting the theory is reviewed in the second section. The third section seeks to explain why semantic codes are particularly effective for increasing retention. The argument that memory for an event is improved by making the code more elaborate and distinctive is used to explain how coding influences retention. The final section considers the principle of encoding specificity, which states that the effectiveness of a retrieval cue depends on how well its characteristics correspond to the characteristics of the stored event.

THE LEVELS-OF-PROCESSING THEORY

Emphasis on Coding Strategies

The paper by Craik and Lockhart (1972) had three objectives: to examine the reasons for proposing multistore models, to question the adequacy of such models, and to propose an alternative framework in terms of levels of processing. We have already considered some of the major characteristics of the three memory stores (sensory store, STM, and LTM) in the previous chapters. Craik and Lockhart summarized the commonly accepted differences among these stores (Table 6.1).

The sensory store is preattentive in the sense that it occurs before perceptual recognition. Attention influences what observers recognize, as when they attend to a particular row of letters after hearing a tone. The sensory store provides a literal copy of the stimulus input but rapidly decays away. It isn't possible to use a control process or strategy to maintain the store, so information must be read out using pattern recognition to preserve it in a more permanent store.

To enter STM, the information must be attended to and described. It can be maintained in STM by continued attendance to it or by use of verbal rehearsal. Because verbal rehearsal is often used, the format is primarily phonemic, but it can also be visual or semantic. Short-term memory is limited by its small capacity and fast decay rate, but retrieval is easy because so few items have to be searched.

Information is entered into LTM mainly through verbal rehearsal. Long-term memory is largely semantic; that is, it is organized according to meaning. It has no known limits in capacity, and its contents, if lost at all, are lost through interference. The ability to retrieve information from LTM can last from minutes to years. Cues are very useful in retrieving information from

TABLE **6.1**
Commonly Accepted Differences Among the Three Stages of Verbal Memory

Feature	Sensory Store	Short-Term Memory	Long-Term Memory
Entry of information	Preattentive	Requires attention	Rehearsal
Maintenance of information	Not possible	Continued attention	Repetition
		Rehearsal	Organization
Format of information	Literal copy of input	Phonemic	Largely semantic
		Probably visual	Some auditory and visual
		Probably semantic	
Capacity	Large	Small	No known limit
Information loss	Decay	Displacement	Possibly no loss
		Possibly decay	Loss of accessibility or discriminability by interference
Trace duration	1/4–2 sec	Up to 30 sec	Minutes to years
Retrieval	Readout	Probably automatic	Retrieval cues
		Items in consciousness	Possibly search process
		Temporal/phonemic cues	

Source: From "Levels of processing: A framework for memory research," by F. I. M. Craik & R. S. Lockhart, 1972, *Journal of Verbal Learning and Verbal Behavior, 11*, 671–684. Copyright 1972 by Academic Press, Inc. Reprinted by permission of Elsevier Science.

LTM, as we will see later in this chapter, but retrieval may require a lengthy search and a considerable amount of time.

Although most psychologists had accepted the characterization of memory represented in Table 6.1, Craik and Lockhart believed that the evidence for a distinction between STM and LTM was not as clear as it should be. They argued, first, that the capacity of STM was really more variable than Miller's estimate of from five to nine chunks. For example, people can reproduce strings of up to 20 words if the words form a sentence. One might reasonably argue that the words in a sentence form chunks and that it should be easy to recall 20 words from STM if there are approximately 3 words in each chunk. But this argument requires objective evidence that such chunks exist. Second, although the format is mainly phonemic in STM and semantic in LTM, there is evidence for visual and semantic codes in STM (see Shulman, 1971) and for visual and phonemic codes in LTM. For example, we have seen that the limited capacity of STM is improved by chunking, and some chunks (such as *FBI*) are formed because they are meaningful. In addition, some LTM memory codes must be phonemic for us to remember how to pronounce words. Third, as we have already seen, decay rates vary considerably depending on the material being learned. Ideally, a single, fast rate of decay for STM and a single, slow rate of decay for LTM would provide the strongest evidence for a separate STM and LTM.

The distinction among the three memory stores summarized in Table 6.1 is therefore an idealized view of how the stores differ. Although there is much experimental support for this view, we must remember that most theories, including the theory that proposes three separate memory stores, are oversimplified. The part of the theory that seems the weakest to me is the variety of decay rates. Where do all these decay rates come from? The strength of the levels-of-processing theory is its attempt to answer this question.

The levels-of-processing theory proposes that there are different ways to code material and that some memory codes are better than others. Preliminary processing is concerned with the analysis of physical features such as lines, angles, brightness, pitch, and loudness. Later stages of analysis are concerned with pattern recognition and identification of meaning. After the stimulus is recognized, it may be further elaborated—a word, sight, or smell may trigger associations, images, or stories on the basis of the individual's past experience with that particular stimulus. The levels-of-processing theory claims that analysis proceeds through a series of sensory states to levels associated with pattern recognition to semantic-associative stages.

Each level of analysis results in a different memory code—but a memory code that varies in its decay rate. The memory code and its persistence are therefore both by-products of perceptual processing. When only the physical features of a stimulus have been analyzed, the memory code is fragile and quickly decays. When the stimulus has been identified and named, the memory code is stronger and can be represented by an intermediate decay rate. Memory is best when a person elaborates the meaning of the stimulus.

The levels-of-processing theory is a theory of how we analyze a stimulus and what memory codes result from different levels of analysis. Unlike the Atkinson-Shiffrin (1968) theory, it is not concerned with the structural components or stages of memory; the two theories can therefore coexist. Craik (1979) later stated that the point of most levels-of-processing studies has been to gain a fuller understanding of memory codes operating in LTM, not to deny the distinction between STM and LTM. When viewed from this perspective, the work on levels of processing extends rather than replaces a stage analysis by showing how control processes can influence the retention of material.

Implications for Verbal Rehearsal

We saw in the previous chapter that the Atkinson-Shiffrin model emphasized verbal rehearsal as a means of transferring information from STM to LTM. Because most of us have used this method to learn material, the role of rehearsal in learning seems intuitively attractive. But rehearsal does not automatically result in learning, according to Craik and Lockhart. The effectiveness of rehearsal, like that of other methods of study, depends on the level at which material is processed. The reason rehearsal often results in learning is that people usually attend to the meaning of the material during rehearsal.

Another issue raised by the Atkinson-Shiffrin formulation is what happens when rehearsal is *not* used for learning. Sometimes it is used to maintain information in STM, as when we dial a telephone number. Would rehearsal result in learning if people used it simply to maintain items in STM? Does rehearsal automatically result in learning, or are there different kinds of rehearsal, only some of which promote learning? To answer these questions, Craik and Watkins (1973) asked people to perform a fairly simple task. Students were told to listen to a series of word lists and, at the end of each list, to report the last word beginning with a particular letter. The experimenter told them the critical letter before each list and assumed that they would maintain a word starting with that letter in STM until they heard another word beginning with that letter or until the list ended. The task was quite easy, and students almost always gave the correct answer at the end of the list.

The purpose of the experiment was to vary the length of time a word would have to be maintained in STM. For example, if *g* were the critical letter and the list contained, in order, the words *daughter, oil, rifle, garden, grain, table, football, anchor*, and *giraffe*, the word *garden* would be immediately replaced by *grain*, which would eventually be replaced by *giraffe*. Because there are no intervening words between *garden* and *grain*, whereas there are three intervening words between *grain* and *giraffe, grain* would have to be maintained in STM for a longer time than *garden*. The word *grain* should therefore be rehearsed more often than *garden*. Craik and Watkins controlled the amount of time a word would have to be maintained in STM by varying the number of intervening (noncritical) words from 0 to 12. If **maintenance rehearsal** results in learning, the probability of recalling a word at the end of the experiment should be a function of the length of time it was maintained in STM.

After hearing 27 lists of words, the students were asked to recall as many words as they could from all the lists. Craik and Watkins found that the probability of recalling a word was independent of the length of time it was maintained in STM. To consider the two extreme cases, students recalled 12% of the words that were immediately replaced in STM by the next word on the list and 15% of the words that were maintained over 12 intervening words.

The small difference between 12% and 15% shows that rehearsal does not automatically cause learning. According to the levels-of-processing view of memory, the students did not try to form a lasting memory code because they thought they would have to remember the word for only a very short time. In particular, they did not emphasize the meaning of the words. A good analog might be reading the words in a book without thinking about what you are reading. You would be rehearsing the words in the sense that you would be covertly pronouncing them, but your thoughts might be on yesterday's football game or tonight's party. Suddenly you might realize that you can't remember what you just read because you weren't thinking about what it meant.

Another example of how thought processes influence what people remember comes from the study of how professional actors learn their lines. Analysis of recall protocols following the study of a six-page script revealed that actors learn their lines through an elaborative process that emphasizes how their character affects, or is affected by, the other characters in the script (Noice, 1991). When forced to learn their lines through rote rehearsal, they recalled significantly less than when studying by their usual, more elaborative

maintenance rehearsal
Rehearsal that keeps information active in short-term memory

process. Noice concludes that "actors are expert analyzers, not expert memorizers, and one result of this in-depth analysis is that by struggling to uncover the underlying meaning of each line, the actual words are also retained without much deliberate effort to commit them to memory" (Noice, 1991, p. 456).

Let's look now at additional evidence that the way material is processed determines what kind of memory code is formed, which in turn determines how well the material is remembered.

SUPPORTING EVIDENCE OF THE LEVELS-OF-PROCESSING THEORY

The Hyde-Jenkins Experiment

The influence of levels of processing on retention was nicely demonstrated in a study by Hyde and Jenkins (1969) at the University of Minnesota. Their results were published several years before Craik and Lockhart's theory and most likely influenced its development. Like most of the studies used later to test the levels-of-processing theory, Hyde and Jenkins's study used an incidental learning paradigm. In an **incidental learning task** people are given some material but are not told that they have to learn it. The experimenter then later gives them a recall or recognition test on the items presented during the experiment. In an intentional learning task, by contrast, the subjects are explicitly told to learn the material.

incidental learning task
A task that requires people to make judgments about stimuli without knowing that they will later be tested on their recall of the stimuli

The first experiment in Hyde and Jenkins's study compared seven groups of subjects, but we will consider only four to simplify the discussion. One of the four groups was given an intentional learning task in which the subjects were asked to try to remember 24 words. The words consisted of 12 pairs of **primary associates**—words that are highly associated. For example, the word *red* is highly associated with the word *green*, and *table* is highly associated with *chair*. The 24 words were presented in a random order, with the restriction that primary associates could not occur next to each other in the list. After the subjects in the "intentional" group had listened to a tape recording of the 24 words, they tried to recall as many as they could, in any order.

primary associates
Words that are strongly associated with each other, as typically measured by asking people to provide associations to words

The other three groups were incidental learning groups who were not informed that they should try to remember the words. They heard the same recording of 24 words but were asked to make a judgment about each item on the list. One group simply rated the words as pleasant or unpleasant, another group judged whether each word contained the letter *e*, and a third group estimated the number of letters in each word. The purpose of using three orienting tasks was to try to create different levels of processing. The first group would have to consider the meaning of the words. The latter two groups would have to consider the spelling of the words; the meaning of the words would be irrelevant to them. Because, according to the levels-of-processing theory, semantic processing should result in better recall than nonsemantic processing, the undergraduates who rated the pleasantness of the words should show better recall than those who considered the spelling of the words.

The results supported the prediction. The average number of words re-called was 16.3 for those students who rated pleasantness, 9.9 for those who estimated the number of letters, and 9.4 for those who judged the presence of the letter *e*. The most striking aspect of the results is that students in the pleasant-unpleasant group recalled virtually as many words as those who were told to try to learn the words (16.3 versus 16.1). In other words, inci-dental learning was as effective as intentional learning when the students con-sidered the meaning of the words.

We have been assuming, along with Hyde and Jenkins, that differences in recall among the three incidental groups were caused by the possibility that the students in the pleasant-unpleasant group were more likely to attend to the meaning of the words than the students in the other two groups. Do we have any direct evidence for this assumption? The fact that the list consisted of pairs of words that are semantically related provides a clue. Recognizing that words are related in meaning can make it easier to recall them. For example, the recall of *green* may remind a person that *red* was also on the list. One indication that people were attending to the meaning of the words would be if they recalled the primary associates together—*red* followed by *green* or vice versa.

clustering Percentage of occasions in which a word is followed by its primary associate during the free recall of words

Hyde and Jenkins defined the percentage of **clustering** as the number of associated pairs recalled together, divided by the total number of words re-called. The amount of clustering was 26% for the group that made judgments about the letter *e*, 31% for the group that estimated the number of letters, 64% for the group that was told to study the words, and 68% for the group that judged the pleasantness of the words. These results support the assump-tion that the groups differed in how much they used meaning to aid recall. Those groups that were the most sensitive to the meaning recalled the most words.

Structural, Phonemic, and Semantic Processing

Tests of the levels-of-processing theory have generally focused on three levels, in which the depth of processing increases from structural to phonemic to se-mantic coding. Table 6.2 shows examples of questions that were asked to

TABLE **6.2**
Typical Questions Used in Levels of Processing Studies

Level of Processing	Question	Yes	No
Structural	Is the word in capital letters?	*TABLE*	*table*
Phonemic	Does the word rhyme with *WEIGHT*?	*crate*	*MARKET*
Semantic	Would the word fit the sentence "He met a _____ in the street"?	*FRIEND*	*Cloud*

Source: From "Depth of processing and the retention of words in episodic memory," by F. I. M. Craik & E. Tulving, 1975, *Journal of Experimental Psychology: General, 104*, 268–294. Copyright 1975 by the American Psychological Association. Reprinted by permission.

structural coding A memory code that emphasizes the physical structure of the stimulus

phonemic coding A memory code that emphasizes the pronunciation of the stimulus

semantic coding A memory code based on the meaning of the stimulus

emphasize different levels of coding. The **structural coding** question asks whether the word is in capital letters. **Phonemic coding** is encouraged by asking whether a word rhymes with another word—the question emphasizes pronunciation. Questions about whether a word is a member of a certain category or whether it fits into a sentence encourage **semantic coding**—a person must evaluate the meaning to answer correctly.

In a series of experiments conducted by Craik and Tulving (1975), one of the questions preceded each brief exposure of a word. Participants were informed that the experiment concerned perception and speed of reaction. After a series of question-and-answer trials based on the kinds of questions shown in Table 6.2, the subject was unexpectedly given a retention test for the exposed words. Craik and Tulving expected that memory would vary systematically with depth of processing.

Figure 6.2 shows the results from one of Craik and Tulving's experiments that used a recognition test. When students were asked which words had been presented during the initial judgment task, they recognized the most words when they had initially judged whether the word fit into a sentence (semantic processing) and the fewest words when they had initially judged whether the letters were upper- or lowercase (structural processing). Recognition accuracy

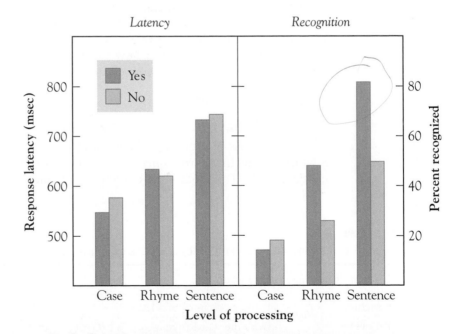

FIGURE **6.2** Initial decision time (response latency) and recognition performance for words as a function of the initial task

Source: From "Depth of processing and the retention of words in episodic memory," by F. I. M. Craik & E. Tulving, 1975, *Journal of Experimental Psychology: General, 104,* 268–294. Copyright 1975 by the American Psychological Association. Reprinted by permission.

was at an intermediate level when the students had been asked whether one word rhymed with another (phonemic processing). The findings supported the prediction that retention would increase as processing proceeded from the structural to the phonemic to the semantic level. The same pattern of results occurred when Craik and Tulving used a recall, rather than a recognition, test. Questions about a word's meaning resulted in better memory than those about a word's sound or the physical characteristics of its letters.

The left half of Figure 6.2 shows the average response time required to answer the three kinds of questions. The case questions could be answered most quickly, followed by the rhyme questions, followed by the sentence questions. Although the recognition results on the right can be predicted from the response times on the left, it is not always true that slower responses lead to better memory. It is possible to design a structural decision task that results in slow responses and poor retention.

Imagine that an experimenter shows you a card with a five-letter word such as *stoop* or *black*. Your task is to respond positively if the word consists of two consonants followed by two vowels followed by a consonant and negatively for any other sequence of consonants and vowels. As you might guess, your response times would be relatively slow. In fact, it takes about twice as long to make this kind of structural decision as to make a semantic decision about whether a word fits into a sentence. If good retention is caused by long response times, the structural processing should now result in better retention than the semantic processing. However, recognition is still much better after semantic processing, proving that the level of processing, not the time spent processing, is the best determinant of retention.

CRITICISMS AND MODIFICATIONS OF THE THEORY

Criticisms

The levels-of-processing theory has had a major impact on memory research—many investigators designed studies to explicitly test its implications; others found it a convenient framework in which to discuss their results. Because much of this research was quite supportive of the theory, it wasn't until about 5 years after the Craik and Lockhart paper that psychologists began to seriously question the usefulness of the theory (Baddeley, 1978; Eysenck, 1978; Nelson, 1977). One of the main criticisms was that it was too easy to account for differential rates of forgetting by appealing to the theory. An investigator might claim that differences in rates of forgetting were caused by differences in levels of processing, without measuring the levels of processing.

To avoid this criticism, it is necessary to be able to measure depth of processing independently of retention. The argument that depth increases from structural to phonemic to semantic processing appealed to most psychologists because it is consistent with the ordering of the information-processing stages shown in Figure 1.1 (page 3). Analyzing the physical structure of a pattern leads to retrieving its name, which in turn leads to considering its meaning by retrieving stored associations from LTM. One problem with this assumption is that, although this sequence provides a reasonable account of how information is analyzed, it is not a *necessary* sequence (Baddeley, 1978; Craik, 1979). Although Craik and Lockhart originally hoped that encoding time would provide an independent measure of depth of processing, we have seen that this measure has its limitations (Craik & Tulving, 1975).

Another difficulty with the concept of depth of processing is that, even if we had an objective ordering of the "depth" of different memory codes, it still would not tell us why some codes are more effective than others. Why are semantic codes better than phonemic codes and phonemic codes better than structural codes? Psychologists have suggested two possible answers. One is that memory codes differ in how elaborate they are, and more elaborate codes result in better memory. The other is that memory codes differ in distinctiveness, and more distinctive codes result in better memory.

Elaboration of Memory Codes

One explanation of how memory codes differ proposes that they differ in the number and types of elaborations stored in memory (J. R. Anderson & Reder, 1979). This view assumes that people store much more than simply the items presented to them—they also store additional associations that help them remember the items. Anderson and Reder have proposed that, although it is very easy to elaborate material at the semantic level, it is difficult to construct elaborations at the structural or phonemic level. Most of the associations we have are concerned with meaning rather than with the physical structure of letters, spelling, or pronunciation. Anderson and Reder suggest that the reason for this difference is that people usually try to remember the meaning of what they read rather than such details as what the letters looked like. As a consequence, people have learned to elaborate on the semantic content because doing so is generally more useful than elaborating on nonsemantic content.

One virtue of the elaboration hypothesis is that it provides a possible explanation of how differences can occur within a particular level of processing (Craik, 1979). Although the original levels-of-processing proposal predicted that semantic processing should be superior to nonsemantic processing, it could not account for differences in retention for two different semantic tasks. The elaboration hypothesis predicts that such differences should occur if the two tasks differ in the extent of semantic elaboration.

One method for increasing semantic elaboration is to provide a richer, more elaborate context. This approach is illustrated by one of the experiments in the Craik and Tulving (1975) study. The experiment tested for the recall of words after a semantic judgment task in which people determined whether a word would fit into a sentence frame. There were three levels of sentence complexity—simple, medium, and complex. For example:

Simple: She cooked the _____.

Medium: The ripe _____ tasted delicious.

Complex: The small lady angrily picked up the red _____.

After completing 60 judgments, subjects were asked to recall as many words as they could from the initial phase of the experiment. They were then shown the original sentence frames and asked to recall the word associated

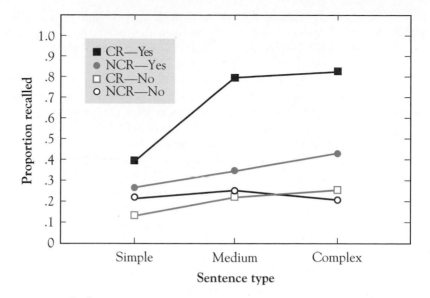

FIGURE **6.3** Proportion of words recalled as a function of sentence complexity: CR = cued recall; NCR = noncued recall

Source: From "Depth of processing and the retention of words in episodic memory," by F. I. M. Craik & E. Tulving, 1975, *Journal of Experimental Psychology: General, 104,* 268–294. Copyright 1975 by the American Psychological Association. Reprinted by permission.

noncued recall Recall that occurs without hints or cues provided by the experimenter

cued recall Recall that occurs with hints or cues, such as providing the questions asked during the judgment phase of a task

with each sentence. The first part of the recall task is called **noncued recall,** and the second part is called **cued recall** because students could use the sentence frames as retrieval cues. Figure 6.3 shows the proportion of words recalled as a function of sentence complexity. Sentence complexity had a significant effect on recalling words that did fit the sentence. This was true for both cued recall (CR—yes) and noncued recall (NCR—yes), although the effect was greater for cued recall. The effect of sentence complexity supported Craik and Tulving's hypothesis that more complex sentence frames would produce a more elaborate memory code and would improve recall.

The more elaborate code was ineffective, however, if the word did not fit the sentence. This finding suggests that the elaboration must be consistent with the meaning of the word to be effective. Even when elaboration is generally consistent with the meaning of a word, it can vary in effectiveness depending on how precisely it relates to the word's meaning. Imagine that you read the sentence "The fat man read the sign." Some time later someone shows you the same sentence with the word *fat* replaced by a blank and asks you to recall the missing word. If elaboration is effective, you might do better if you read an elaborated sentence such as

1. The fat man read the sign that was 2 feet high.
   or
2. The fat man read the sign warning about thin ice.

imprecise elaboration
Provision or generation of additional material unrelated to remembered material

precise elaboration Provision or generation of additional material closely related to remembered material

Although both sentences provide additional information, there is an important distinction between the two elaborations. The first is an **imprecise elaboration** because there is no apparent relation between the adjective *fat* and the height of the sign. The second is a **precise elaboration** because the degree of danger of thin ice depends on a person's weight.

Stein and Bransford (1979) tested the effectiveness of precise and imprecise elaboration by comparing four groups of students in an incidental learning task. Students in the control group read ten short sentences and were told that the purpose of the experiment was to measure sentence comprehensibility. The second and third groups of students were told the same thing. They read the same ten sentences elaborated by an additional phrase that was either precisely or imprecisely related to a target word in the sentence. A fourth group of students were told to generate their own elaborations so the experimenters could measure the probability that certain phrases would be generated. At the end of the experiment, everyone was shown the unelaborated sentences and asked to recall a missing target word.

Students in the control group recalled an average of 4.2 words, compared with 2.2 words for the imprecise elaboration group, 7.4 words for the precise elaboration group, and 5.8 words for the self-generation group. The results show that elaboration is not always effective in recall because imprecise elaboration actually caused a decline in performance relative to the control group. To be effective, the elaboration should clarify the significance or relevance of a concept (such as *fat man*) relative to the context (*thin ice*) in which it occurs.

self-generation Generation of items by participants in an experiment, rather than the provision of these items by the experimenter

The fact that recall following **self-generation** was intermediate between that for precise and imprecise elaboration suggests that the students' elaborations contained a mixture of the two types. Two judges therefore divided the subject-generated elaborations into two groups (precise and imprecise), depending on whether the information clarified the relevance of the target words in the sentence. Students were able to recall 91% of the target words in the cases where they had generated precise elaborations and 49% in the cases where they had generated imprecise elaborations.

A second experiment revealed that instructions were effective in encouraging subjects to generate precise elaborations. Subjects in the imprecise elaboration group were asked to elaborate with the question "What else might happen in this context?" Subjects in the precise elaboration group were prompted to elaborate with the question "Why might this man be engaged in this particular type of activity?" Students in the latter group recalled significantly more target words, indicating that elaboration is particularly effective when it is directed toward understanding the potential relevance of the information presented.

Distinctiveness of Memory Codes

distinctive item An item different in appearance or meaning from other items

Memory codes can differ in distinctiveness as well as in the extent of elaboration. To remember something, we would like to make it a **distinctive item**, one that really stands out from other items that could interfere with our memory. There are several different ways in which an item can be distinctive, and I will follow a classification proposed by Schmidt (1991) that distinguishes among four different kinds of distinctiveness.

One kind of distinctiveness is called **primary distinctiveness** in which distinctiveness is defined relative to the immediate context. Imagine that you are shown a list of common words and all the words are printed in red ink, except for one word that is printed in black ink. Later you are asked to recall the words on the list. Which word do you think you would have the best chance of recalling? The results of past research indicate that you would more likely recall the word in black ink than the words in red ink. Note that the word in black ink is distinctive only because the color differs from the color of other words on the list. In general, a common word in black ink is not particularly distinctive.

Release from proactive interference (discussed in Chapter 4) is an example of improving recall by making items distinct from other items in the immediate context. People recalled more items when the material changed from words to numbers or from numbers to words than when the material stayed the same. Recall also improved when the items changed from sports events to political events or from political events to sports events. All the changes made these items more distinct from the preceding items.

In contrast, **secondary distinctiveness** is defined relative to information in our LTM rather than to information in the immediate context. One example is a characteristic of a word's spelling. A word is **orthographically distinctive** if it has an unusual shape, as determined by the sequencing of short and tall letters in the word. Orthographically distinctive words include *lymph, khaki,* and *afghan.* Examples of orthographically common words are *leaky, kennel,* and *airway.* The first three words have unusual shapes, and the last three have more typical shapes. Notice that a shape is unusual (distinctive) relative to all other words stored in LTM, not just to words in the immediate context of the experiment.

When people are asked to recall a list of words, half of which are orthographically distinctive and half of which are orthographically common, they recall significantly more of the distinctive words (R. R. Hunt & Elliott, 1980). It is clear that the shape of the words, rather than some other factor, causes the results. When the same list is presented orally, rather than visually, there is no difference in recall. There is also no difference in recall when the words are typed in capital letters; people do not recall *LYMPH, KHAKI,* and *AFGHAN* any better than *LEAKY, KENNEL,* and *AIRWAY.* Apparently, the different heights of lowercase letters contribute to the effect because all letters are the same height when capitalized.

A third kind of distinctiveness is called **emotional distinctiveness** and is motivated by the finding that events that produce strong emotional responses are sometimes remembered well. These events include **flashbulb memories**— the vivid recollections that most people have of the circumstances surrounding their discovery of a shocking piece of news (R. Brown & Kulik, 1977). Events such as the assassination of President Kennedy or the explosion of the space shuttle *Challenger* (Winograd & Neisser, 1992) have been studied as examples of people's flashbulb memories. I don't remember how I first learned about the *Challenger*, but I'm certain my brother will never forget

primary distinctiveness
An item distinct from other items in the immediate context

secondary distinctiveness An item distinct from items stored in long-term memory

orthographic distinctiveness Lowercase words that have an unusual shape

emotional distinctiveness Items that produce an intense emotional reaction

flashbulb memory A memory of an important event that caused an emotional reaction

IN THE NEWS **6.1**

Memories May Not Be Clear Even with "Unforgettable" Events

Michele M. Melendez, Newhouse News Service

In crudely drawn signs on highway overpasses, in political speeches, in newspaper ads, and in casual conversation, the nation has uttered: "We will never forget."

But while Americans indeed may never forget the people killed in the terrorist attacks or their feelings of despair, memories of Sept. 11 will wither, psychologists say. People already are jumbling facts and creating their own senses of reality, preliminary research shows.

This occurred after other seemingly memorable events: the assassination of John F. Kennedy, the space shuttle *Challenger* explosion, and the Oklahoma City bombing. Experts say that often people can't distinguish their recollections, sometimes called "flashbulb memories," from what really happened.

Kathy Pezdek, a psychology professor at Claremont Graduate University in California, is studying the phenomenon among 700 people in California, Hawaii, and New York. "People were thinking (after Sept. 11), 'This is the most amazing thing that's ever happened, and I'll remember everything. I'll remember every detail'," she said. "Even now, this is kind of fading." Seven weeks after Sept. 11, Pezdek distributed a 22-question survey, asking for two kinds of recollections. One set of questions dealt with the details of the event: "Was the Pentagon struck before the first tower collapsed? … How much time passed between when the first tower was struck and when it collapsed?"

The other set explored firsthand experiences during Sept. 11—how the person found out about the attacks, what he or she was doing at the time.

Pezdek plans to revisit the participants in a year, in 3 years, and in 5 years to compare their responses.

So far, she has observed that New Yorkers, who experienced the attacks in real time, were not as clear on the sequence of events as people in Hawaii, where it is 5 hours earlier. By the time Hawaiians heard the news, the timeline and the terrorist involvement had been established.

On average, Pezdek said, study participants watched 14 hours of television news the week following Sept. 11, yet they are mixing up facts and condensing the timing of events.

Source: From "Memories may not be clear even with 'unforgettable' events," by Michele M. Melendez, *The San Diego Union-Tribune*, December 28, 2001. Reprinted by permission of Newhouse News Service.

his experience. He was driving in the direction of the Kennedy Space Center during a business trip to Orlando when he noticed that the vapor trail from the rocket's engine suddenly stopped. Suspecting that something had gone wrong, he turned on his car radio, which confirmed the failure of the launch.

Although Schmidt (1991) includes emotional distinctiveness in his taxonomy, he admits that it is not always clear which aspects of an emotional memory are enhanced or even whether the concept of "distinctiveness" provides an adequate explanation of the impact of emotion on memory. In addition, more recent evidence has questioned whether emotional events (flashbulb memories) are better remembered than ordinary events. For example, Weaver (1993) compared students' memory for an emotional event (the 1991 bombing of Iraq) and an ordinary event (a routine encounter with a roommate or friend). When their memory was tested both 3 months and 1 year later, Weaver found no difference in the accuracy of the two memories. He did find differences in confidence—students were more confident of the accuracy of their memory about the bombing, but their confidence was unwarranted. As indicated in "In the News" 6.1, even our memories of the terrorist attacks on the Pentagon and World Trade Towers soon began to fade.

Phelps and Sharot (2008) report on the neural mechanisms that mediate this feeling of confidence without an increase in accuracy. A part of the brain called the amygdala is responsible for the strong sense of recollection of emotional events. However, this recollection is based on only a few, central details. It is likely this strong memory for a few details produces the subjective sense of good recollection. In contrast, the encoding and retrieval of neutral events include more context. People's judgment of confidence therefore uses different information. For emotional events, the *quality* of memory for a few details may matter; for neutral events, the *quantity* of contextual details may be more important.

A fourth kind of distinctiveness is called **processing distinctiveness**. Processing distinctiveness depends on how we process the stimulus—it is therefore the result of the memory code that we create for an item rather than the characteristics of the item itself. For example, even if an item is not very distinctive, you may think of a distinctive way of remembering it. If it is distinctive, you may think of a way of processing it to make it even more distinctive. Elaboration is one possible strategy to make an item more distinctive, but the elaboration should emphasize characteristics that differentiate that item from other items (Eysenck, 1979).

processing distinctiveness Creation of a memory code that makes that memory distinct from other memories

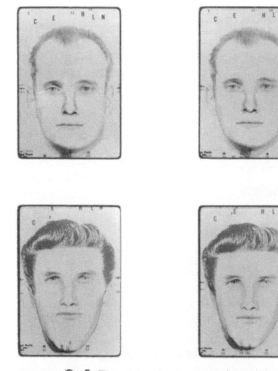

FIGURE **6.4** Two Identi-Kit faces (right) and their caricatures (left): top, high forehead; bottom, long chin

Source: From "Caricature and Face Recognition," by R. Mauro & M. Kubory, 1992, *Memory and Cognition, 20,* 440–443. Copyright 1992 Psychonomic Society. Reprinted by permission.

An example of processing distinctiveness is that people apparently remember faces as caricatures by exaggerating the distinctive features to make the faces even more distinct. When discussing distinctive features in Chapter 2, I gave an example of a study in which people more quickly identified line drawings of their friends when the line drawings were caricatures rather than accurate (Rhodes, Brennan, & Carey, 1987). Caricatures of unfamiliar faces are also better recognized in a standard recognition-memory test than the faces that were actually shown (Mauro & Kubovy, 1992). Undergraduates viewed 100 slides of faces constructed from an Identi-Kit, as illustrated by the two faces on the right in Figure 6.4. They later were shown 300 test faces and asked to indicate if each test face was exactly the same as one shown in the first series of slides. The test faces included some faces that were new, some faces that were old, and some faces that were caricatures of the old faces.

The caricatures are shown on the left side of Figure 6.4 and were created by making a distinctive feature even more distinct. The high forehead in the top face is made even higher, and the long chin of the bottom face is made even longer. The interesting finding is that the caricatures were recognized significantly better than the original (old) faces. This finding is consistent with the processing distinctiveness concept—people encoded the faces into memory in a manner that made each face even more distinct than the original face.

Because both processing distinctiveness and the levels-of-processing theory emphasize the importance of creating good memory codes, it is perhaps not surprising that some psychologists have proposed that the levels-of-processing effect is caused by differences in distinctiveness. To demonstrate that distinctiveness can account for the levels-of-processing effect, it would be necessary to show that semantic codes are more distinct than phonemic codes and that phonemic codes are more distinct than physical codes. Some research has already been directed toward the first comparison. Several psychologists (Moscovitch & Craik, 1976; Eysenck, 1979) have argued that semantic codes result in better retention than do phonemic codes because semantic codes are much more distinctive than phonemic codes. They base their argument on the fact that there is a relatively small number of phonemes; thus, phonemic codes necessarily overlap with each other, whereas the domain of possible meanings is essentially limitless.

The experimental study of elaboration and distinctiveness has modified the original conception of levels of processing (Craik, 1979). Some of the original ideas have survived, however. The central idea that there are qualitative differences in memory codes, that different orienting tasks can determine which codes are emphasized, and that memory codes differ in their decay rate remains a useful conception of memory. The major shift in emphasis has been the attempt to provide a theoretical basis for these findings by determining how structural, phonemic, and semantic codes can differ in distinctiveness and elaboration.

ENCODING SPECIFICITY AND RETRIEVAL

The Encoding Specificity Principle

The change in emphasis from "levels" to "elaboration" and "distinctiveness" was accompanied by another refinement in the theory. The original theory (Craik & Lockhart, 1972) had much to say about how words were coded but little to say about how they were retrieved. Yet we saw in the previous chapter that appropriate retrieval cues, such as encouraging eyewitnesses to reconstruct the context of the crime, can enhance recall. The usefulness of providing an appropriate context for facilitating retrieval is illustrated by the difference between positive and negative responses in Figure 6.2. Words that resulted in positive responses, because they either formed a rhyme or fit the context of a sentence, were recalled more often than words that resulted in negative responses.

We have also seen that the use of more complex, elaborate sentence frames facilitated recall for positive responses but not for negative responses (see Figure 6.3). This effect was particularly evident when the context was provided as a retrieval cue. Craik and Tulving (1975) interpreted this finding as support for their view that a more elaborate context is beneficial only when the test word is compatible with the context and forms an integrated unit. A complex sentence such as "The small lady angrily picked up the red _____" makes it easier to retrieve a positive response (*tomato*) but does not make it easier to retrieve a negative response (*walking*).

These results show that, under certain conditions, some retrieval cues are more effective than others. A general answer to the question of what makes a retrieval cue effective is provided by the **encoding specificity principle**, which has been stated as follows: "Specific encoding operations performed on what is perceived determine what is stored, and what is stored determines what retrieval cues are effective in providing access to what is stored" (Tulving & Thomson, 1973, p. 369).

Let's dissect this definition into two parts. The first part states that memory traces differ not only in their durability but also in the kind of information they contain. The second part states that the information that memory traces contain determines what kind of retrieval information should facilitate their recovery. The first part is essentially equivalent to the levels-of-processing framework; the second part forces us to take a closer look at retrieval. The second part implies that it is possible to hold constant the encoding conditions of an item and still observe large differences in its recall, depending on the retrieval conditions. The encoding and retrieval conditions can interact in the sense that a cue that is effective in one situation may or may not be effective in another.

The encoding specificity principle has usually been applied to studying how the retrieval cue relates to the memory code for the stimulus. However, the encoding and retrieval conditions can apply to a broader context such as the location in which learning occurred or even the mood of the learner. The study of **mood-dependent memory** tests the hypothesis that we are better able to recall information if our mood during retrieval matches our mood during learning. Although the evidence has generally been supportive of this hypothesis, the degree of support may depend on the particular paradigm used to test the hypothesis; for example, strongest support may come from situations in which people recall information that they generated themselves. A recent study found strong support for mood-dependent memory when people had to recall autobiographical events that they had generated several days earlier (Eich, Macaulay, & Ryan, 1994). Subjects who were in the same (pleasant or unpleasant) mood during both encoding and retrieval recalled significantly more events than people who were in different moods. Tests of the encoding specificity principle have generally focused on the material that people have to recall rather than on where learning occurred or on the mood of the learner. We will now look at this research.

Interaction between Encoding and Retrieval Operations

Let us consider how the encoding specificity principle applies when there are two different processing levels—semantic and phonemic. Imagine that you are in an experiment and have to answer yes or no to the question "Associated with sleet?" You then see the word *hail* and answer yes. After making a series of judgments about rhymes and associations, you are given one of the following retrieval cues:

1. Associated with *sleet*
2. Associated with *snow*
3. Rhymes with *bail*

encoding specificity principle A theory that states that the effectiveness of a retrieval cue depends on how well it relates to the initial encoding of an item

mood-dependent memory Memory that is improved when people are tested under conditions that re-create their mood when they learned the material

Which of the three retrieval cues do you think would be most helpful for retrieving the word *hail*?

You would probably agree that the first cue would be most effective because it is identical to the question asked during the encoding trials. But what about the second and third cues? The second cue is similar to the original context in that, like the initial question, it emphasizes semantic associations. The third cue, by contrast, emphasizes the phonemic code and is therefore different from the original context. The encoding specificity principle predicts that the original context is the best retrieval cue, a similar context is the next best cue, and a different context is the least effective cue. The results shown in Table 6.3 support this prediction (R. P. Fisher & Craik, 1977).

Now consider what might have happened if the word *hail* had been preceded by the question "Rhymes with pail?" The same principle applies. Reproducing the exact context is the best cue, and providing a different context—a semantic association in this case—is the worst cue (see Table 6.3). The interaction between encoding and retrieval is illustrated by the fact that the effectiveness of a retrieval cue depends on how a word was coded. When its semantic characteristics were emphasized, a semantic cue was more effective than a phonemic cue. When its phonemic characteristics were emphasized, a phonemic cue was more effective than a semantic cue. In other words, the specific encoding of an item determines which retrieval cues are most effective for gaining access to what is stored—the encoding specificity principle.

Another study (Hertel, Anooshian, & Ashbrook, 1986) found that people were unable to accurately predict the relative effectiveness of retrieval cues. Subjects rated the pleasantness of 40 words in a semantic-orienting task, predicted the number of words they could recall, and then tried to recall the words. One group received semantic retrieval cues, another group received phonemic retrieval cues, and a control group received no retrieval cues.

TABLE **6.3**

Proportions of Words Recalled as a Function of Similarity Between Encoding Context and Retrieval Cue

	Rhyme	Proportion	Associate	Proportion
Encoding context				
Example: *hail*	Rhymes with *pail*		Associated with *sleet*	
Retrieval context				
Identical	Rhymes with *pail*	0.24	Associated with *sleet*	0.54
Similar	Rhymes with *bail*	0.18	Associated with *snow*	0.36
Different	Associated with *sleet*	0.16	Rhymes with *bail*	0.22

Source: From "Interaction between encoding and retrieval operations in cued recall," by R. P. Fisher & F. I. M. Craik, 1977, *Journal of Experimental Psychology: Human Learning and Memory*, 3, 701–711. Copyright 1977 by the American Psychological Association. Reprinted by permission.

IN THE NEWS **6.2**
Remembering in Tongues

Siri Carpenter

Studies have long shown that people better recall events when their mood state or the environmental context in which information is presented—such as the specific location in which information was learned—matches that of when the memory is retrieved. In a novel extension of that research, experiments using Russian-English bilinguals have shown that a match between the language of encoding and the language of retrieval also yields enhanced memory effects.

The study, authored by psychologists Viorica Marian, PhD, of Northwestern University and Ulric Neisser, PhD, of Cornell University, was published in the September issue of APA's *Journal of Experimental Psychology: General* (Vol. 129, No. 3).

Marian's interest in language-dependent memory grew out of her own experience as a Romanian-English bilingual. "I would often

notice that when I would try to think of the name of someone or someplace in my home country while speaking English, I couldn't remember it," she recalls. "But then later, when I was speaking in Romanian, it would come to me."

To examine the role language plays in organizing memory, the researchers placed participants in interviews in both English and Russian, varying the order in which the two languages were used. An experimenter prompted participants with a series of words such as "summer," "neighbors," and "doctor," or the Russian translations of such words. They asked participants to describe an event from their lives that was brought to mind by each cue.

Participants recalled more English events than Russian events when they were interviewed in English and prompted with English words, the

researchers found. When participants were interviewed in Russian and prompted with Russian words, they accessed more Russian memories than English memories.

In a second experiment, Marian and Neisser discovered that the effect appeared to be driven not simply by the language of the prompt words, but by the general "language milieu" of the interview. Participants recalled more English events than Russian events when they were interviewed in English, even when the prompt words were in Russian. The reverse occurred for participants interviewed in Russian.

Source: From "Remembering in tongues," by Siri Carpenter, *Monitor on Psychology*, November 2000, 44–45. Copyright 2000 by the American Psychological Association. Reprinted with permission.

We would expect from Fisher and Craik's findings that the semantic retrieval cues would be more effective than phonemic cues—an expectation that was confirmed. Only those subjects who received semantic cues recalled significantly more words than the control group.

But the superiority of the semantic cues was not anticipated by subjects in the experiment, who predicted that the semantic and phonemic cues would be equally effective. The faulty predictions seemed to be based on overgeneralization from past experiences in which phonemic cues had been effective. For example, when our search has already been limited to a particular category, such as the names of songs, phonemic information is likely to be helpful. What subjects failed to realize was that the effectiveness of a retrieval cue depends on how the word was coded. The memory code, in this case, emphasized the semantic characteristics of the words.

A study of bilinguals illustrates how the encoding specificity theory can be applied to retrieving autobiographical knowledge. This study found that people tend to recall events from their lives that correspond to the language used in the interview. "In the News" 6.2 reports the details.

Transfer-Appropriate Processing

transfer-appropriate processing Encoding material in a manner related to how the material will be used later

A general implication of the encoding specificity principle is the use of **transfer-appropriate processing**, which emphasizes that the value of a particular learning strategy is relative to a particular goal. Transfer-appropriate processing implies that the effectiveness of learning can only be determined relative to the testing situation. For example, if the test emphasizes phonemic information and you had been concentrating on semantic information, you could be in trouble.

A situation from my own undergraduate education provides a good example of transfer-appropriate processing. I had taken three semesters of German in which there was very little emphasis on pronunciation, although we occasionally were asked to read aloud. I therefore did not attend very closely to the phonemic code but concentrated on the meaning of the passage so I could provide a correct translation. After three semesters I enrolled in a conversation course in which the emphasis was on correct pronunciation. I quickly learned how poorly I pronounced German words.

It is relatively rare, however, that we must emphasize the phonemic code because we are generally required to recall or recognize semantic information. Transfer-appropriate processing therefore usually means semantic processing. There are different ways to process material semantically, and knowledge of the test format should help you decide how to study. If the test is a multiple-choice test, it is likely that knowledge of details will be more useful than knowledge about the general organization of the material. If the test is an essay test, it is likely that careful organization of the material will be more useful than knowledge of many details.

Evidence supports these claims (Thomas & McDaniel, 2007). Students who were given a task that required them to focus on the details of the material did better on detailed than on conceptual questions. In contrast, students who were given a sentence-sorting task that encouraged relational processing of the material did better on conceptual than on detailed questions. Transfer-appropriate processing also influenced students' metacomphrehension predictions. Students accurately predicted how well they would do on the test when their study preparation matched the test format. However, they did not make accurate predictions when the their study preparation did not match the test format.

problem-oriented acquisition Encoding material in a manner that is helpful for its later use in solving problems

fact-oriented acquisition Encoding material in a manner that emphasizes factual knowledge without emphasizing its application

Another distinction between test questions is whether they emphasize factual recall or problem solving. Sometimes an instructor asks students to recall information; at other times students must apply the information to solve problems. The hypothesis about transfer-appropriate processing predicts that **problem-oriented acquisition** of the material is better than **fact-oriented acquisition** when people must solve problems.

Consider the following two problems:

- Uriah Fuller, the famous Israeli superpsychic, can tell you the score of any baseball game before the game starts. What is his secret?
- A man living in a small town in the United States married 20 different women in the same town. All are still living, and he has never divorced one of them. Yet he has broken no law. Can you explain?

Now imagine that you had rated a number of statements for general truthfulness earlier in an experiment. Among the statements were answers to the problems:

- Before it starts, the score of any baseball game is 0 to 0.
- A minister marries several people each week.

Somewhat surprisingly, receiving the answers in this incidental rating task was not very helpful for later solving the problems (Perfetto, Bransford, & Franks, 1983).

One interpretation of these findings is that people acquired the statements in a fact-oriented manner and therefore failed to perceive their relevance for the problem-solving task (L. T. Adams et al., 1988). Now suppose the statements were modified to encourage problem-oriented acquisition; would people be more likely to perceive their relevance? To induce problem-oriented processing, the experimenters changed the statement "A minister marries several people each week" to "It is possible to marry several people each week [pause] if one is a minister." The pause lasted approximately 2 seconds and gave people a brief chance to reflect on the problem-oriented content of the statement. There were corresponding changes for nine other statements that provided answers to problems. People who received problem-oriented statements later solved 56% of the problems, compared with 36% for people who received fact-oriented statements.

I want to conclude with a thought-provoking question: How are the two theoretical constructs, encoding specificity and transfer-appropriate processing, similar, and how are they different? I lectured about these constructs for quite a few years before asking myself this question. I encourage you to think about your own answer before reading mine.

My answer is illustrated in Figure 6.5. Both constructs are similar in that they emphasize that good performance depends on maximizing the similarity between the encoding and the retrieval of the material. They differ in whether the decision on how to do this is made at the encoding stage or the retrieval stage. In transfer-appropriate processing, the decision is made at the encoding stage. The retrieval conditions, such as a multiple-choice exam or an essay exam, are fixed, and you have to decide how to encode the material to prepare for the type of exam. In encoding specificity, the encoding has already

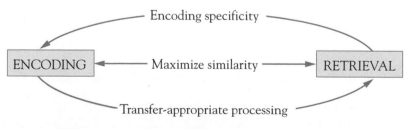

FIGURE **6.5** Comparison of encoding specificity with transfer-appropriate processing

occurred, and the decision requires finding effective retrieval cues to match the encoding. Transfer-appropriate processing therefore looks forward in time, from encoding to retrieval, whereas encoding specificity looks backward in time, from retrieval to encoding.

SUMMARY

The levels-of-processing theory proposes that how an item is encoded determines how long it can be remembered. Qualitatively different memory codes were established by asking people in an incidental learning task to make decisions about a word's physical structure, pronunciation, or meaning. When people are unexpectedly asked to recall the words, they recall the most words following semantic processing and the fewest words following structural processing. Further support for the theory comes from the finding that rehearsal does not necessarily result in learning, presumably because subjects do not attend to the meaning of words they want to keep active only in STM.

Although the levels-of-processing theory originally proposed that retention is determined by the depth of processing (with physical, phonemic, and semantic processing, respectively, representing increasing depth), the failure to find an independent measure of depth resulted in an increasing emphasis on the elaborateness and distinctiveness of memory codes. The elaboration hypothesis claims that it is easier to retrieve more elaborate codes and easier to provide associations at the semantic level. The distinctiveness hypothesis claims that it is easier to retrieve distinctive codes and that semantic codes are more distinctive than phonemic codes. Studies of elaborateness and distinctiveness using semantic material have found that increasing either one will improve recall. Making the semantic context more elaborate (by using complex sentences) or making words more distinctive (by shifting to a new semantic category) increases the number of words recalled.

The encoding specificity principle states that the effectiveness of a retrieval cue is determined by how well it corresponds to the characteristics of the memory trace. Although some studies have focused on the broader context of encoding, such as a person's mood during encoding and retrieval, most studies have focused on the encoding of the stimulus. When the memory trace emphasizes semantic characteristics, a semantic cue is the most effective; when the memory trace emphasizes phonemic information, a phonemic cue is most effective. The best retrieval cue is one that exactly duplicates the original context, and, for the cue to be at all effective, the item should fit the context. Transfer-appropriate processing suggests that people should create memory codes that will correspond to how they will eventually use the material, such as in a multiple-choice, essay, or problem-solving test.

STUDY QUESTIONS

This chapter and the next focus primarily on the representation of information. Representation implies that some sort of mental activity transforms physical stimuli into what are usually called *codes*. This reminds us that we construct reality— it is not somehow dropped into our heads like a slide into a projector. To understand the levels-of-processing approach, it is essential to appreciate what qualitative differences are. If you're not sure, look it up.

1. As you proceed, ask yourself whether the levels-of-processing theory (hereafter, LOP for short) necessarily conflicts with the STM–LTM separate store theory. (Remember, you don't have to take anybody's word for it.)
2. Because memory is at issue, what is the LOP rationale for using judgmental-orienting tasks rather than learning tasks?
3. Don't skip Table 6.1. Much information has been condensed in this valuable summary. Is the summary of STM and LTM consistent with what you read in the previous two chapters?
4. What were Craik and Lockhart's objections to the Atkinson-Shiffrin picture of the memory system represented in Figure 4.1? How persuasive do you find them to be?

5. Why is the assumption that the different memory traces vary in their decay rate essential to the LOP position?
6. If you had a friend who firmly believed that rehearsal automatically results in learning, which of Craik's studies would you describe to your friend? What makes it so conclusive at this point?
7. Why did Hyde and Jenkins (pre-LOP) use an incidental learning paradigm? How did their clever choice of materials allow inferences about what their subjects were doing?
8. To make sure you understand the distinctions, make up a new question, with new yes/no instances, for each of the levels of processing in Table 6.2. Write out your questions.
9. Why was it essential to basic LOP theory that one must be able to measure depth of processing independently of retention? How do the notions of elaboration and distinctiveness get around this problem?
10. What does it mean to say that there is an interaction between encoding and retrieval operations? Generate examples of different types of memory traces and retrieval cues and test your understanding by making predictions congruent with the encoding specificity principle.

CogLab   The following experiments that relate to this chapter can be found at: http://coglab. wadsworth.com. Answer the questions in the CogLab Student Manual as required by your teacher for these experiments.

Von Restorff Effect
Encoding Specificity

KEY TERMS

The page number in parentheses refers to where the term is discussed in the chapter.

auditory-memory span (130)

clustering (137)

cued recall (141)

distinctive item (142)

emotional distinctiveness (143)

encoding specificity principle (147)

fact-oriented acquisition (150)

flashbulb memory (143)

imprecise elaboration (142)

incidental learning task (136)

levels of processing (132)

maintenance
   rehearsal (135)

memory code (130)

mood-dependent memory (147)

noncued recall (141)

orienting task (132)

orthographically distinctiveness (143)

phonemic coding (138)

precise elaboration (142)

primary associates (136)

primary distinctiveness (143)

problem-oriented acquisition (150)

processing distinctiveness (145)

secondary distinctiveness (143)

self-generation (142)

semantic coding (138)

structural coding (138)

transfer-appropriate processing (150)

RECOMMENDED READING

A book edited by Cermak and Craik (1979) contains many excellent chapters on how the levels-of-processing concept evolved during the 1970s. Although elaborative rehearsal is clearly more effective than maintenance rehearsal, students are not always aware of this difference and may therefore not learn as much as they should (Shaughnessy, 1981). People can also improve their memories by paying more attention to the distinctiveness of items during the encoding and retrieval stages (Dodson, Koutstaal, & Schacter, 2000). Other applied areas that can be related to the concepts of levels of processing and encoding specificity are context-dependent memory of deep-sea divers, enhancement of face recognition, and attempts to understand certain aspects of amnesia and aphasia (Baddeley, 1982). A book edited by Winograd and Neisser (1992) contains chapters on affect and flashbulb memories. M. K. Johnson (1983) has proposed a memory model in which events can create multiple entries in a sensory, perceptual, and reflection system. The similarities—and differences—between her theory and the levels-of-processing theory are evident in her chapter. Lundeberg and Fox's (1991) review of the literature on test expectancy shows how the test format and our expectations about it influence our scores.

7

Visual Images

Mental imagery has long played a central role in psychologists' and philosophers' accounts of cognitive processes and the representation of knowledge in the mind. The construct of the image, however, has never been operationalized well enough to satisfy most psychologists, and so it is not surprising that imagery has disappeared periodically from the mainstream of Western psychology. Nevertheless, the concept has such magnetism that it has never stayed away for long, and it is currently enjoying remarkable popularity.
—**Stephen Kosslyn and James Pomerantz (1977)**

The discussion in the preceding chapters emphasized verbal knowledge. The stimuli studied usually consisted of items that could be easily assigned a verbal label, such as words, letters, digits, or even nonsense syllables. We might question, however, whether we assign verbal labels to everything we perceive. Some events can be hard to describe verbally, and others can simply be easier to remember as an image. Although images can exist for each of the sensory modalities, psychologists have been interested mainly in visual images. This chapter considers how visual images contribute to knowledge.

A distinction between verbal knowledge and visual or spatial knowledge is often made on intelligence tests. **Verbal knowledge** is usually measured by vocabulary questions or questions that test comprehension of written material. **Spatial knowledge** is usually measured by performance of such operations as mentally folding connected squares into a cube or mentally rotating an object to determine whether it matches another object. Although most tests place a much greater emphasis on verbal knowledge than on spatial knowledge, some specialized tests contain rather difficult questions on spatial transformations. One example is the Dental Admissions Test, used to help select applicants to dental schools. Because spatial skills are very useful in dentistry, the test includes some challenging problems on spatial relations. People would presumably answer the question illustrated in Figure 7.1 by forming a visual image of the object and rotating the image to align it with the openings.

The study of visual imagery has been one of the main contributions of cognitive psychology. However, psychologists ignored imagery for many years because of the influence of Watson's *Behaviorism* (1924), which was

verbal knowledge
Knowledge expressed in language

spatial knowledge
Knowledge of spatial relations that may be stored as images

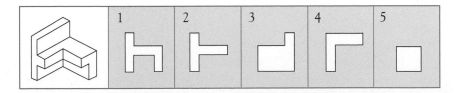

FIGURE **7.1** A sample question from the Dental Admissions Test. Students must select the opening through which the object at the far left could pass
Source: Reproduced with permission from the American Dental Association.

dedicated to wiping out the study of mental events. Watson argued that only behavior could be objectively studied, an argument that certainly had some merit but almost completely eliminated the study of mental processes such as visual imagery. It wasn't until the 1960s that psychologists once again began to try to understand the role of visual images in the acquisition of knowledge. Visual imagery is still difficult to study because it cannot be directly observed, but research over the past two decades has provided strong evidence that visual images are used in performing many tasks.

The first section of this chapter argues that forming visual images is an effective method for remembering information. However, formation of a visual image is much easier for concrete material than for abstract material, and we will examine the implications of this finding. For many centuries people have recognized the usefulness of imagery in aiding memory, and many mnemonic strategies are based on visual imagery. The second section presents some evidence that visual images are used in performing most spatial reasoning tasks. The results of the experiments would be difficult to explain if we believed that all knowledge was verbal. The final section shows that even visual images have limitations. Fortunately, their lack of detail usually doesn't restrict their usefulness.

VISUAL IMAGERY AND LEARNING

You may be able to recall times when you relied on visual imagery to learn material. When I moved to Cleveland some years ago to begin my academic career at Case Western Reserve University, my home telephone number was 283-9157. I decided to learn the number by verbal rehearsal. I wrote it down and rehearsed it several times before I was confident that I had learned it. After 2 days of unsuccessful practice, however, I decided to look for a different learning strategy.

My choice was influenced by the old "Sing Along with Mitch" routine, in which a bouncing ball appears over the words of a song. Where would the ball go if I pictured it bouncing over a sequence of numbers—1 2 3 4 5 6 7 8 9? If you try it for the sequence 283-9157, you will see that it has a rather nice pendulum motion, swinging back and forth and ending up in the middle. Once I discovered this relationship, I immediately learned the number, and I have been able to reconstruct it even though it ceased being my number quite a few years ago.

The use of visual imagery to learn material is a form of elaboration. Remember that Atkinson and Shiffrin (1986) proposed three methods for learning material: rehearsal, coding, and imaging. They used the term "coding" to refer to semantic elaboration. We saw in the previous chapter that semantic elaboration is very effective, but visual elaboration by forming visual images is also very effective as you will see in this chapter.

Memory for Pictures

One indication that visual imagery might provide an effective memory code is that people usually find it easier to recognize pictures than to recognize words. Shepard (1967) was one of the first to show that recognition accuracy for visual material is very high. Subjects in his experiment viewed 612 pictures at a self-paced rate and were later given a recognition-memory test on pairs of pictures. Each pair consisted of a picture they had previously seen and a novel picture. When they were tested 2 hours later, the participants were virtually perfect in identifying which member of the pair they had seen. Another group of participants, tested 1 week later, was still able to identify the correct picture in 87% of the pairs.

One reason they did so well is that the test was easy. The subjects could remember very little about a picture itself and still be able to tell which of two possibilities had been presented. But when the same test was repeated using words instead of pictures, recognition accuracy wasn't as high. Subjects tested immediately after seeing the words could identify which of two words had been presented in only 88% of the pairs (Shepard, 1967). Their performance was about the same as when pictures were tested after a week's delay.

An experiment by Standing (1973) provided further evidence that it is easier to remember pictures than words. One group of dedicated subjects viewed 10,000 pictures over a 5-day period. Immediately after the learning session on the fifth day, the participants were given a recognition-memory test similar to the one designed by Shepard. Standing estimated the number of items they must have retained in memory to reach the level of performance they attained on the test (taking into account the probability of guessing correctly). His estimate was that the participants must have remembered 6600 pictures. This estimate does not imply that the participants remembered all the details of a picture—but they did remember enough details to distinguish that picture from a novel picture.

Subjects in Standing's experiment were not shown 10,000 words for comparison, but other groups were shown 1000 words, 1000 ordinary pictures (such as a dog), or 1000 vivid pictures (such as a dog holding a pipe in its mouth). Two days later subjects were asked which of two possibilities had occurred in the experiment. Standing estimated that the participants had retained enough information about 880 vivid pictures, 770 ordinary pictures, and 615 words to make the correct choice without guessing. Demonstrating that recognition memory is better for pictures than for words replicates Shepard's results.

Paivio's Dual Coding Theory

The finding that we are good at remembering pictures suggests that we might improve our memory if we could form mental pictures (images). The work of Allan Paivio at the University of Western Ontario established that forming images does aid learning. After an extensive series of studies, Paivio (1969) argued that there were two major ways a person could elaborate on material in a learning experiment. One form of elaboration emphasizes verbal associations. A word such as *poetry* can result in many associations that could help you distinguish it from other words. You might think of different styles of poetry, particular poems, or experiences in an English class. We saw in the previous chapter that verbal associations helped people recall words in the Hyde and Jenkins (1969) experiment. People who considered the meaning of the words recalled primary associates together, because recalling one word reminded them of its associate.

The other form of elaboration is creation of a visual image to represent a word. If I asked you to remember the word *juggler,* you might form an image of a person juggling three balls. If I asked you to remember the word *truth*, however, you would probably have difficulty forming an image. The first word refers to a concrete object, the second to an abstract concept. It is easy to form an image to represent a concrete object but difficult to form an image for an abstract concept. Paivio (1969) argued that the **concrete-abstract dimension** is the most important determinant of ease in forming an image. At the concrete end of the continuum are pictures, because the picture itself can be remembered as a visual image, and the person doesn't have to create an image. Pictures often result in better memory than do concrete words, which usually result in better memory than abstract words.

If visual images and verbal associations are the two major forms of elaboration, is one more effective than the other? To answer this question, we have to know how easy it is to form either an image or a verbal association of a word. The **imagery potential** of words is usually measured by asking people to rate on a scale how easy it is to form an image for a given word. As we might expect, concrete words are rated high on imagery, and abstract words are rated low. The **association value** of a word is usually measured by asking people to give as many associations as they can over a 1-minute interval. Paivio and his colleagues have found that the imagery potential of words is a more reliable predictor of learning than the association potential of words. High-imagery words are easier to learn than low-imagery words, but high-association words are not necessarily easier to learn than low-association words (Paivio, 1969).

A study by Paivio, Smythe, and Yuille (1968) reveals the beneficial effect of imagery on learning. Students at the University of Western Ontario were asked to learn a list of paired associates consisting of 16 pairs of words. The words were equally divided between high-imagery (H) words, such as *juggler, dress, letter,* and *hotel*, and low-imagery (L) words, such as *effort, duty, quality*, and *necessity*. The list contained four pairs each that were high-high (H-H), high-low (H-L), low-high (L-H), and low-low (L-L), where the first term refers to the imagery value of the stimulus, and the second term refers to the imagery value of the response. Examples include *juggler-dress* (H-H), *letter-effort* (H-L), *duty-hotel* (L-H), and *quality-necessity* (L-L).

Figure 7.2 shows how well the students could recall the response when given the stimulus. The powerful effect of imagery is

concrete-abstract dimension Extent to which a concept can be represented by a picture

imagery potential Ease with which a concept can be imaged

association value The number of verbal associations generated for a concept

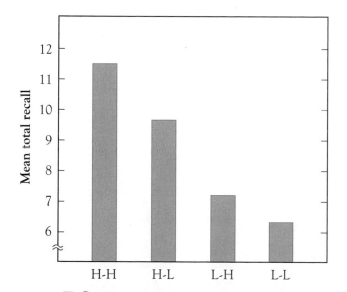

FIGURE **7.2** Mean total recall over four trials as a function of high (H) and low (L) imagery values

Source: From "Imagery versus meaningfulness of nouns in paired-associate learning," by A. Paivio, P. E. Smythe, & J. C. Yuille, 1968, *Canadian Journal of Psychology, 22,* 427–441. Copyright 1968 by the Canadian Psychological Association. Reprinted by permission.

quite evident. The H-H pairs resulted in the best recall and the L-L pairs the worst. When only one member of the pair had a high-imagery value, recall was better when that word was used as the stimulus (H-L). The fact that H-H pairs were easiest to learn is consistent with the previously mentioned finding that interactive pictures improve the recall of brand names. When images can be created for both members of a word pair, the images can be combined to form an interactive image. For example, one can associate the word *dress* with *juggler* by forming an image of a juggler wearing a dress.

It is interesting to note that high-imagery words were easier to recall than low-imagery words even though the learners were not told to use visual imagery. Perhaps the participants spontaneously generated images whenever they could. Support for this hypothesis was obtained in a questionnaire completed after the learning task. The students indicated, for each of the 16 pairs on the list, which one of five strategies they had used in trying to learn that pair. Their options were "none," "repetition" (rehearsal), "verbal" (a phrase or rhyme connecting two words), "imagery" (mental pictures that include the items), and "other." The "none" and "other" options were reported infrequently. The distribution of the other three responses depended on whether the pairs consisted of high- or low-imagery words (Figure 7.3). The reported use of imagery was highest for the H-H pairs and lowest for the L-L pairs. The striking resemblance between learning (see Figure 7.2) and the reported

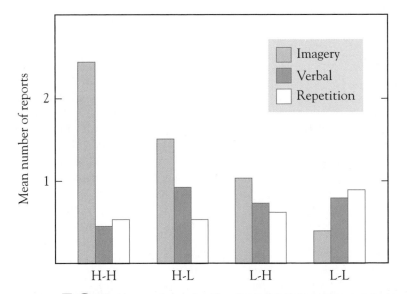

FIGURE **7.3** Mean number of pairs for which imagery, verbal, and repetition strategies were reported as a function of high (H) and low (L) imagery values

Source: From "Imagery versus meaningfulness of nouns in paired-associate learning," by A. Paivio, P. C. Smythe, & J. C. Yuille, 1968, *Canadian Journal of Psychology, 22,* 427–441. Copyright 1968 by the Canadian Psychological Association. Reprinted by permission.

use of imagery (see Figure 7.3) suggests that imagery is an effective learning strategy.

The reason images are effective, according to Paivio (1975), is that an image provides a second kind of memory code that is independent of the verbal code. Paivio's theory is called a **dual-coding theory** because it proposes two independent memory codes, either of which can result in recall. A person who has stored both the word *cat* and an image of a cat can remember the item if he or she retrieves either the image or the word. Evidence suggests that the two memory codes are independent in the sense that a person can forget one code without forgetting the other (Paivio, 1975). Having two memory codes to represent an item therefore provides a better chance of remembering that item than does having only a single code.

dual-coding theory
A theory that memory is improved when items can be represented by both verbal and visual memory codes

A criticism of dual-coding theory is that it works only in situations in which people focus on **relational information**, such as the associations between items in a paired-associates task (Marschark & Hunt, 1989). Subjects in Marschark and Hunt's experiment initially rated 12 concrete and 12 abstract word pairs in an orienting task. One group rated how easily the two words of each pair could be combined into an integrated unit. When they were later asked to recall the words, they recalled significantly more concrete than abstract words. Another group was told to ignore the fact that the words were presented in pairs and to rate the words individually on the ease with which each evoked a mental image. This group did not recall any more concrete words than abstract words, as would be expected from dual-coding theory. The emphasis on relational coding is also consistent with the finding that improving the recall of brand names depended on forming an *interactive* picture that combined the product and brand name (Lutz & Lutz, 1977). For example, showing people a picture of a man with a rocket strapped on his back carrying a package helped them remember the brand name Rocket Messenger Service. If Marschark and Hunt are correct—that relational processing is necessary to achieve the benefits of concreteness—then dual-coding theory has a restricted range of application. But the restricted range is still fairly large because many learning activities require that we learn associations between items such as associating a brand name with a product, a word in one language with a word in another language, or a name with a face. Because images facilitate recall in these situations, it is only natural that they should play a key role in suggestions for improving memory.

relational information
Information specifying how concepts are related

Comparison of Association-Learning Strategies

Every so often a book appears on how to improve memory. Such a book is usually written by a person who not only has practiced **mnemonic** (memory) **techniques** but can successfully apply them to demonstrate rather remarkable acts of recall. One example, *The Memory Book*, by Lorayne and Lucas (1974), was on the best-seller list for weeks.

mnemonic technique
A strategy that improves memory

Although memory books always discuss several techniques for improving memory, they usually emphasize visual imagery. The author presents a mnemonic strategy, in which imagery usually plays a key role, and claims that use of the strategy will improve recall. The claim, however, is seldom supported by experimental data. Is there proof that the proposed strategy works? Fortunately, supportive data exist in the psychology journals.

The results obtained by Paivio et al. (1968) suggested that visual imagery is a particularly good strategy to use when images can be generated to represent words. Their study, however, was not designed to teach people to use a particular strategy, unlike an experiment conducted by Bower and Winzenz (1970) in which people were asked to learn paired associates consisting of concrete nouns. Each participant was assigned to one of four groups given different instructions on how to learn the associations. Students in the *repetition condition* were asked to rehearse each pair silently. Students in the *sentence-reading condition* read aloud a sentence in which the two words of a pair were capitalized as the subject and object of the sentence. The experimenters told the members of this group to use the sentence to associate the two critical nouns. Students in the *sentence-generation condition* made up their own sentence to relate the two words in a sensible way. Students in the *imagery condition* formed a mental image that combined the two words in a vivid interaction. They were encouraged to make their image as elaborate or as bizarre as they wished.

After a single study trial on each of 30 word pairs, the students were given a recall test on 15 pairs and a recognition test on the other 15. Recognition of the correct response was easy, and all four study strategies resulted in a high level of performance. Recall of the correct response was more difficult, however, and here the differential effectiveness of the strategies was apparent. The average number of correct recalls was 5.6 for the repetition group, 8.2 for the sentence-reading group, 11.5 for the sentence-generation group, and 13.1 for the imagery group. The data dramatically illustrate that, although verbal rehearsal does result in some learning, it is less effective than the elaboration strategies. Comparison of the imagery and sentence-generation conditions shows that visual elaboration was more effective than semantic elaboration. But the fact that sentence generation was also an effective strategy suggests that this technique could be used when it is necessary to learn abstract words.

bizarre image A fantastic or unusual image

Although research has shown that the use of visual imagery is effective for learning associations, it has also shown that **bizarre images** are not always more effective than plausible images. Rather, the degree of interaction in the image is a better predictor of its effectiveness (Kroll, Schepeler, & Angin, 1986). Bizarre imagery is more effective than plausible imagery only in limited situations, such as when the greater distinctiveness of bizarre images can enhance memory (McDaniel & Einstein, 1986).

A specific application of the imagery strategy in paired-associates learning is learning to associate a name with a face. I would guess that just about everyone has had difficulty learning names at one time or another. Many authors of memory books can perform a very impressive demonstration in which they repeat back the names of all the members of an audience after hearing them only once. The method used by Lorayne involves first converting the name into a visual image and then linking the image to a prominent feature of the person's face. For example, if Mr. Gordon has a large nose, the image might be a garden (*garden* sounds like *Gordon*) growing out of his nose. Although the method may seem rather bizarre, it has experimental support. A group of British psychologists found that people who were taught this strategy learned significantly more names than a control group that was not taught the strategy (P. E. Morris, Jones, & Hampson, 1978). The learning task required associating a different name (randomly selected from a telephone directory) with each of 13 photographs of male adults. After a study period of 10 seconds for each item, the imagery group could correctly name 10 of the photographs, compared with 5 for the control group. The authors admit that the use of mnemonic strategies requires some effort, and not everyone will be willing to make that effort to learn names. However, their results should provide encouragement to those who wonder whether the effort will be worthwhile.

The Mnemonic Keyword Method and Vocabulary Learning

The use of imagery to remember names obviously depends on how easy it is to form an image from a name. Some names should be fairly easy, such as Smith (form an image of a blacksmith) or Green (form an image of the color). Other names, such as Gordon or Detterman, may require associating a concrete word with the name and then forming an image of the associated word. The associated word, called a **keyword**, should sound like the name that is being learned. The association of *garden* with *Gordon* is an example of the keyword method. *Garden* is a keyword that can be used to form an image. The words *debtor-man* might be a good keyword for Detterman if one formed an image of Mr. Detterman dressed in ragged clothes.

You may have some reservations at this point about the keyword method. It is certainly more complicated than simply forming an image because you have to remember not only the image but also the association between the keyword and the name to remember the original name correctly. Mr. Gordon might not appreciate being called Mr. Garden, and Mr. Detterman would certainly not like being called Mr. Debtorman.

Even though the **keyword method** requires two stages—learning the association between the name and the keyword and forming an image of the keyword—the method is still very effective. A striking demonstration of its effectiveness is illustrated in a study by Atkinson and Raugh (1975) on the acquisition of Russian vocabulary. The keyword method divides the study of a vocabulary word into two stages. The first stage is to associate the foreign word with an English word, the keyword, which sounds approximately like some part of the foreign word. The second stage is to form a mental image of the keyword interacting with the English translation. For example, the Russian word for *building* (*zdanie*) is pronounced somewhat like *zdawn-yeh*, with the emphasis on the first syllable. Using *dawn* as the keyword, one could imagine the pink light of dawn being reflected in the windows of a building.

Appropriate selection of keywords is an important aspect of this method. A good keyword should satisfy the following criteria: It should (1) sound as much as possible like a part of the foreign word, (2) be different from the

keyword A concrete word that sounds like an abstract word so that it can be substituted for the abstract word in an interactive image

keyword method A mnemonic strategy using keywords to improve paired-associates learning

other keywords, and (3) easily form an interactive image with the English translation. Table 7.1 shows a sample of 20 Russian words and their associated keywords. As an exercise in using the method, you can try to create an image linking the first pair of words.

Students in Atkinson and Raugh's study tried to learn the English translations of 120 Russian words over a 3-day period. The students were divided into two groups—the "keyword" group and a control group. Subjects in the keyword group were taught how to use the keyword method. After the pronunciation of each Russian word, they were shown both a keyword and the English translation. The instructions said that the students should try to picture an interactive image linking the keyword and the English translation or should generate a sentence incorporating both words if they could not form an image. The keywords were not shown to students in the control group, who were told to learn the translations in whatever manner they wished.

TABLE **7.1**
A Sample of 20 Russian Words with Related Keywords

Russian	Keyword	Translation
VNIMÁNIE	[pneumonia]	ATTENTION
DÉLO	[jello]	AFFAIR
ZÁPAD	[zap it]	WEST
STRANÁ	[straw man]	COUNTRY
TOLPÁ	[tell pa]	CROWD
LINKÓR	[Lincoln]	BATTLESHIP
ROT	[rut]	MOUTH
GORÁ	[garage]	MOUNTAIN
DURÁK	[two rocks]	FOOL
ÓSEN	[ocean]	AUTUMN
SÉVER	[saviour]	NORTH
DYM	[dim]	SMOKE
SELÓ	[seal law]	VILLAGE
GOLOVÁ	[Gulliver]	HEAD
USLÓVIE	[Yugoslavia]	CONDITION
DÉVUSHKA	[dear vooshka]	GIRL
TJÓTJA	[Churchill]	AUNT
PÓEZD	[poised]	TRAIN
KROVÁT	[cravat]	BED
CHELOVÉK	[chilly back]	PERSON

Source: From "An application of the mnemonic keyword method to the acquisition of a Russian vocabulary," by R. C. Atkinson & M. R. Raugh, 1975, *Journal of Experimental Psychology: Human Learning and Memory, 104*, 126–133.

The control group did not receive instructions on the use of keywords or mental imagery.

On the day after the three study sessions, students in both groups were tested on the entire 120-word vocabulary. Students in the keyword group provided the correct translations for 72% of the Russian words; students in the control group did so for 46% of the words. This difference is particularly impressive considering that Russian was selected as a special challenge to the keyword method because the pronunciation of most Russian words is quite different from English pronunciation. Because many people find Russian vocabulary harder to learn than the vocabularies of other foreign languages, it is valuable to have a method that can facilitate learning. Atkinson and Raugh planned to use the keyword method in a computerized vocabulary-learning program designed to supplement a college course in Russian. Students would be free to study the words in any way they wished but would have the option of requesting a keyword by pressing an appropriate button on the terminal.

EVIDENCE FOR IMAGES IN PERFORMING COGNITIVE TASKS

propositional theory A theory that all knowledge, including spatial knowledge, can be expressed in semantic-based propositions

Although psychologists have seldom questioned that images exist, some have questioned the usefulness of images as explanatory constructs. The most influential paper challenging the usefulness of images in psychological theories was written by Pylyshyn (1973). Pylyshyn argued that it was misleading to think of images as uninterpreted photographs, analogous to pictures in the head. He supported the alternative view that an image is much closer to being a description of a scene than a picture of it. The emphasis on the descriptive characteristics of images, rather than their sensory characteristics, is the central theme of a **propositional theory**.

Kosslyn and Pomerantz (1977) agreed with Pylyshyn that images are interpreted and organized, but they argued that we often process images in the same way that we process perceptual information. In response to Pylyshyn's paper, they summarized five experimental findings that they thought could be better explained on the basis of imagery than by nonsensory information. Two of the five findings were concerned with scanning visual images, a task studied by Kosslyn and his associates. We look first at one variable influencing scanning time—the effect of distance between objects. We then examine the other three findings, on visual matching, mental rotation, and selective interference.

Scanning Visual Images

visual scanning A shift of attention across a visual display or image

Many explanations of performance based on visual imagery assume that an image is a spatial representation analogous to the experience of seeing an object during visual perception. Furthermore, many of the operations that are used in analyzing visual patterns are also used to analyze visual images (Kosslyn & Pomerantz, 1977). One such operation is **visual scanning**. The analogy between pictures and images suggests that the time it takes to scan between two objects in an image should be a function of their distance from each other. Evidence obtained by Kosslyn, Ball, and Reiser (1978) supports this prediction.

FIGURE **7.4** A fictional map used to study the effect of distances on mental scanning time

Source: From "Visual images preserve metric spatial information: Evidence from studies of image scanning," by S. M. Kosslyn, T. M. Ball, & B. J. Reiser, 1978, *Journal of Experimental Psychology: Human Perception and Performance,* 4, 47–60. Copyright 1978 by the American Psychological Association. Reprinted by permission.

One of their experiments required that undergraduates at Johns Hopkins University learn the exact locations of the objects shown in Figure 7.4. The map was then removed, and the students were given a series of trials that began with the name of an object. The task required that they form a mental image of the entire map and focus on the named object. Subjects then heard the name of a second object and scanned the map in the way they had been instructed—by imagining a black speck moving in a straight line from the first object to the second. When they reached the second object, they pushed a button that stopped a clock. There are 21 possible distances among the 7 objects, and the longest distance is 9 times as great as the shortest distance. If distance determines the scanning time, as predicted, reaction time should be a linear function of the distance between two locations. Figure 7.5 shows how closely the prediction was supported.

These results suggest that we can mentally scan visual images in the same way that we can scan pictures. But an alternative view is that subjects in imagery tasks may be able to respond appropriately without actually using visual images (Intons-Peterson, 1983; Pylyshyn, 1981). According to this view, subjects may guess what the experimenter expects and respond so as to please the experimenter. A study by Mitchell and Richman (1980) showed that people can accurately predict how distance should influence scanning time. When the experimenters asked subjects to predict their scanning time for the different pairs of objects in Figure 7.4, predicted scanning times also increased as a linear function of distance. It is therefore possible that subjects did not actually mentally scan their visual images but simply waited longer before pushing the button as the distance increased between two objects.

This criticism can be avoided if the outcome of the experiment cannot be predicted. Reed, Hock, and Lockhead (1983) hypothesized that people may not be able to predict how the shape of patterns will influence their scanning time. For example, one of these researchers' patterns was a straight line, and another was a spiral. The rate at which people scanned a visual image of the pattern depended on its shape. An image of a straight line was scanned more quickly than an image of a spiral. However, people were unsuccessful in predicting how the different shapes would influence their scanning time. Because they couldn't predict the outcome of the experiment, their scanning times must have been produced by their actually scanning the different patterns rather than by their predictions.

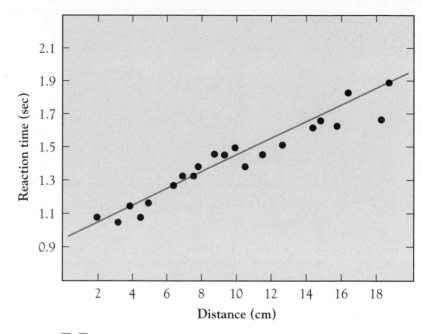

FIGURE **7.5** Scanning time between all pairs of locations
on the imaged map

Source: From "Visual images preserve metric spatial information: Evidence from studies of image scanning,"
by S. M. Kosslyn, T. M. Ball, & B. J. Reiser, 1978, *Journal of Experimental Psychology: Human Perception
and Performance, 4,* 47–60. Copyright 1978 by the American Psychological Association. Reprinted by
permission.

Although the data of some imagery experiments might have been generated without subjects' using imagery, it is highly unlikely that people could
perform many spatial tasks without using imagery. Finke (1980) cites specific
examples of tasks in which the expected outcome would not be obvious to
subjects, usually because they were doing the task for the first time. Let's
now consider some other tasks that allow us to distinguish between visual
and verbal memory codes.

Sequential versus Parallel Processing

One difference between information maintained in a visual image and information maintained as a verbal code is that a visual image makes it possible
to match information in parallel. When you look at the schematic faces in
Figure 7.6, you can perceive many features of the faces simultaneously. However, when you describe these same features verbally, you do not have access
to all the features at the same time because language is sequential. You would
have to decide the order in which to describe the features if you were to
describe someone's face over the phone.

The **parallel representation** of spatial information and the **sequential
representation** of verbal information influence how quickly a person can
determine whether a perceived pattern matches a memorized pattern. If the

parallel representation
Representation of knowl-
edge in which more than
one item at a time can be
processed

**sequential representa-
tion** Representation of
knowledge in which only
one item at a time can be
processed

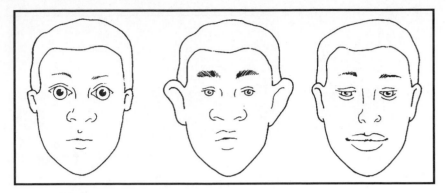

FIGURE **7.6** Three sample faces illustrating size differences
of feature values

Source: From "Representation and retrieval processes in short-term memory: Recognition and recall of faces,"
by E. E. Smith & G. D. Nielsen, 1970, *Journal of Experimental Psychology, 85,* 397–405. Copyright 1970 by
the American Psychological Association. Reprinted by permission.

memorized pattern is stored as a visual image, the match should occur
quickly and should be relatively uninfluenced by the number of features that
have to be matched. If a pattern is stored as a verbal description, the match
should occur more slowly and should be influenced by the number of features
that have to be compared.

Nielsen and Smith (1973) tested these predictions by showing students either
a picture of a schematic face or its verbal description. There were five features
of the face—ears, eyebrows, eyes, nose, and mouth—which varied in size.
Each feature could assume one of three values—large, medium, or small (see
Figure 7.6 for an example). After students studied either the description or
the picture for 4 seconds, the stimulus was removed. After a retention interval that lasted either 4 or 10 seconds, the experimenters presented a test
face, and the students had to decide whether it matched the face or description presented earlier.

To test the prediction that the number of features would influence reaction time only when people compared the test face with a verbal description,
Nielsen and Smith varied the number of relevant features from three to five.
The students knew that they could ignore the ears and eyebrows when there
were three relevant features because these features never changed, and they
could ignore the ears when there were four relevant features. But they had to
compare all five features when all five were relevant. Figure 7.7 shows the
amount of time needed to respond that either the initial face (FF task) or the
description (DF task) matched the test face. The data are from the 4-second
delay, but the same pattern of results occurred for the 10-second delay. The
response times indicate that matching was relatively fast and independent of
the number of relevant features only when the initial item was a visual
pattern.

The results imply that when a person can maintain a visual image of a
pattern in STM (short-term memory), a second visual pattern can be compared

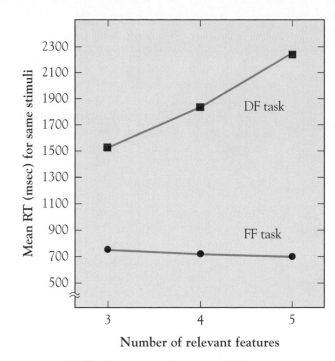

FIGURE **7.7** Mean reaction time (RT) for correct responses when stimuli were the same, as a function of the task and number of relevant features

Source: From "Imaginal and verbal representations in short-term recognition of visual forms," by G. D. Nielsen & E. E. Smith, 1973, *Journal of Experimental Psychology, 101,* 375–378. Copyright 1973 by the American Psychological Association. Reprinted by permission.

with it very quickly. It's almost as if the person were superimposing the two patterns and comparing all the features simultaneously. When the features are described verbally, a match requires sequentially retrieving information from the description, such as large ears, small eyebrows, small eyes, medium nose, and large mouth. Each feature on the list is individually compared with the corresponding feature on the test face. The response time therefore increases as a function of the number of relevant features on the list. The reaction-time functions for the DF task in Figure 7.7 may remind you of the reaction-time functions found in the S. Sternberg (1967b) memory-scanning task (Figure 4.8, page 91). The similarity is not surprising, because both tasks require that people sequentially scan a list of items in STM. Maintaining an image in the FF task avoids a list of separate items by combining the individual features on the list into a single integrated pattern. The efficiency with which this integrated pattern can be compared with other visual patterns is an important difference between a visual image and a verbal description.

Mental Transformations

Deciding whether two patterns match is considerably more difficult if they differ in orientation. The task shown in Figure 7.8 requires judging whether the two patterns in each pair are the same object (Shepard & Metzler, 1971). Pairs *a* and *b* are different orientations of the same pattern, but pair *c* consists of two different patterns. One method for determining whether two patterns are identical is to rotate one pattern mentally until it has the same orientation as the other pattern. When the patterns have the same orientation, it is easier to determine whether they match.

The pairs used by Shepard and Metzler differed in orientation from 0 degrees to 180 degrees in 20-degree steps. Half of the pairs could be rotated to match each other, and half were mirror images that did not match. Figure 7.9 shows that the time required to decide that two patterns were identical increased linearly with an increase in the number of degrees they differed in orientation, suggesting that the subjects were rotating a visual image of one of the forms until it had the same orientation as the other form. Self-reports were consistent with this interpretation—subjects reported that they imagined one object rotating until it had the same orientation as the other and that

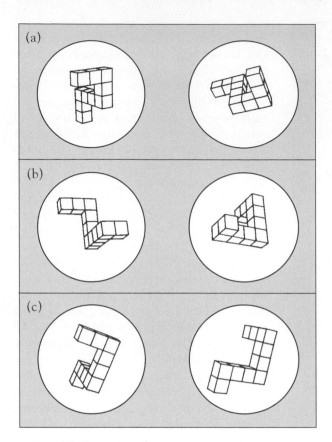

FIGURE **7.8** Examples of pairs of patterns differing in orientation

Source: From "Mental rotation of three-dimensional objects," by R. N. Shepard & J. Metzler, 1971, *Science, 171,* 701–703. Copyright 1971 by the American Association for the Advancement of Science. Reprinted by permission.

they could rotate an image only up to a certain speed without losing its structure. In addition, more recent neuroimaging studies provide evidence that mental rotation is a continuous transformation of spatial representations (Zacks, 2008).

The ability to mentally animate static pictures can also be useful for solving certain kinds of scientific reasoning problems (Hegarty, 2004). Look at the diagram of the pulley system in Figure 7.10 and try to determine whether the pulley on the left turns in a clockwise or a counterclockwise direction when the rope on the right side of the diagram is pulled. You probably tried to mentally animate the pulley system to answer the question. The mental animation creates a "causal chain" of events that begins with the first (right) pulley, precedes to the second (middle) pulley, and ends with the last (left) pulley. Hegarty (1992) hypothesized that people mentally animate the pulleys in the order of this causal chain to understand how the system works.

To test this hypothesis, she asked students to quickly respond "true" or "false" to a statement that appeared to the left of the diagram. Figure 7.10 shows two examples to illustrate that some of the (static) statements did not mention movement, whereas other (kinematic) statements did mention movement.

If people mentally animate the pulleys to evaluate the kinematic statements, then their response times should increase as the length of the causal chain increases. This is what Hegarty found. Students verified most quickly statements about the beginning pulley and verified least quickly statements about the end pulley. Verification errors also increased from the beginning pulley to the end pulley. In contrast, neither response times nor errors varied across pulleys for the evaluation of the static statements. The location of the pulleys was important only when the verification task required animation of the pulleys in a particular order.

Interference

We have seen in earlier discussions that a major cause of forgetting is interference. Research on release from proactive interference (D. D. Wickens, 1972) has demonstrated that interference can be reduced by shifting semantic categories. Interference can also be reduced by shifting between visual and verbal material, as shown in a study by Brooks (1968).

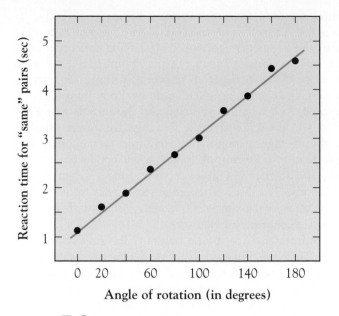

FIGURE **7.9** Reaction time to judge whether two patterns have the same three-dimensional shape

Source: From "Mental rotation of three-dimensional objects," by R. N. Shepard & J. Metzler, 1971, *Science, 171,* 701–703. Copyright 1971 by the American Association for the Advancement of Science. Reprinted by permission.

In the visual task in this study, subjects were shown a block diagram of a letter (Figure 7.11). The letter was then removed, and the subjects had to use their memory of the letter to respond yes to each corner that was on the extreme top or bottom and no to each corner that was in between. The correct answers for the example, starting at the asterisk at the lower left and proceeding in the direction of the arrow, are yes, yes, yes, no, no, no, no, no, no, yes.

The verbal task in Brooks's experiment required that people respond positively to each word in a sentence that was a noun. For example, people listened to the sentence "A bird in the hand is not in the bush" and then had to determine whether each word was a noun. The correct answers for the example are no, yes, no, no, yes, no, no, no, no, yes.

Brooks assumed that his subjects would rely on a verbal code to maintain the sentence in memory and a visual image to maintain the block diagram in memory. If his assumption is correct, it should be possible to *interfere selectively* with performance by using two different methods of

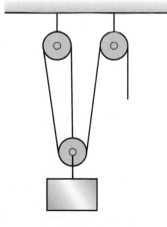

FIGURE **7.10** An example of a pulley system

Source: From "Mental animation: Inferring motion from static displays of mechanical systems," by M. Hegarty, 1992, *Journal of Experimental Psychology: Learning, Memory, and Cognition, 18,* 1084–1102. Reprinted by permission.

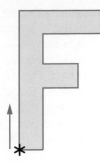

FIGURE **7.11**
Block diagram of a letter

Source: From "Spatial and verbal components of the act of recall," by L. R. Brooks, 1968, *Canadian Journal of Psychology, 22,* 349–368. Copyright 1968 by the Canadian Psychological Association. Reprinted by permission.

responding. One method required that the answers be given verbally, by overtly responding yes or no. A verbal response should cause a greater conflict when classifying the words of a sentence than when classifying the corners of a block diagram. Another method required that a subject point to a Y for each positive response and an N for each negative response, using a diagram in which the Y's and N's were arranged in crooked columns. Pointing to the correct letter therefore required close visual monitoring and should interfere more with the block task than with the sentence task. The selective nature of interference is revealed by the average response time required to complete each task. Classifying the words in a sentence took longer when people gave a verbal response; classifying the corners of a letter took longer when people pointed to the correct response. In other words, giving a verbal response interfered more with memory for verbal material (a sentence) than with memory for visual material (a block diagram) and vice versa.

The selective nature of interference within a modality has implications for the number of items that can be maintained in STM. When we reviewed the evidence on STM capacity in Chapter 4, we looked at research that presented items from the same modality, such as a string of letters in a memory span task or different levels of brightness in an absolute judgment task. What would happen if we designed a memory span task in which some items could be retained by using a verbal code and other items could be retained by using a visual code? According to Baddeley's (1992) working memory model, verbal information should be maintained in the articulatory loop, and visual information should be maintained in the visuospatial sketchpad (see pages 92–94). If such variety reduces interference, people should be able to recall more items.

An experiment by two Dutch psychologists (Sanders & Schroots, 1969) revealed that a person's memory span can in fact be increased by using material from two different modalities. One modality was the typical verbal modality, created by showing a string of consonants. The other modality was a visual or spatial modality, created by showing a random sequence of lights on a two-dimensional lightboard. In the second condition, subjects responded by pointing to the lights on the board in the correct order of their appearance.

The lack of interference between modalities suggests that people should be able to increase their memory span by storing the consonants as a verbal code and the light sequence as a visual code. Recall was in fact better when a sequence consisted of both visual and verbal items. For example, when people were asked to recall a string of 11 consonants, they correctly recalled an average of 5.4 items. When they were asked to recall a string of 6 consonants followed by a string of 5 spatial positions, they correctly recalled an average of 8.3 items. The improvement in recall was not caused by the possibility that spatial positions were easier to recall than consonants because previous research had shown that recalling spatial positions was actually more difficult. Rather, the findings were caused by the relative lack of interference between the visual and verbal codes. These results, along with those obtained by Brooks and many other psychologists, show that using two different modalities can reduce interference and improve performance.

This research illustrates how visual images can be used to improve performance on many cognitive tasks, including preserving the spatial relations among different parts of a picture, lowering reaction times for processing spatial information, and reducing interference between visual and verbal codes. These findings are strong evidence against the claim in propositional theory (Pylyshyn, 1973) that images are not necessary for building cognitive theories. We now look at an additional source of evidence about the use of visual imagery.

Evidence from Cognitive Neuroscience

In a 1995 chapter on visual imagery, Kosslyn (1995) divided the debate over mental imagery into three phases. The first phase was the argument over whether a propositional theory could represent all types of knowledge, making it unnecessary to propose a theory based on visual images. The beginning of this section (Evidence for Images in Performing Cognitive Tasks) raised that issue. The second phase was whether the demand characteristics of the task could explain the results of imagery experiments. As we have seen, that issue was initially raised by the critics of Kosslyn's visual-scanning experiments. But it was the third phase—evidence from cognitive neuroscience—that Kosslyn believed silenced the critics of the theoretical importance of visual images.

Farah (1988) was one of the first psychologists to gather together the evidence that would make a strong case for the use of imagery in performing many cognitive tasks. She argued that supporting evidence from neuropsychology could be grouped into two broad categories: results showing (1) that visual imagery uses the same brain areas as vision and (2) that selective damage to the brain impairs visual imagery in the same manner that it impairs vision.

Evidence that visual perception and visual imagery use the same areas of the brain comes from two different methods of measuring brain activity, based on either cerebral blood flow or electrophysiological activity. **Cerebral blood flow** provides a precise measure of brain activity, with increased blood flow indicating increased activity in that part of the brain. **Event-related potentials (ERPs)** measure electrical activity of the brain that is synchronized with (and presumably related to) the processing of a stimulus. Both measures indicate that many tasks in which we would expect visual imagery to be involved show increased activity in that part of the brain used for visual perception—the occipital lobes, which contain the primary and secondary visual cortex (Farah, 1988). See Figure 3 inside the front cover.

Roland and Friberg (1985) measured cerebral blood flow while subjects performed one of three cognitive tasks: mental arithmetic, memory-scanning of a musical jingle, or visually imaging a walk through one's neighborhood. They found increased activity in the visual cortex for the visual imagery task, but not for the mental arithmetic or the memory-scanning task. A similar finding occurred for a simpler imagery task (Goldenberg, Podreka, Steiner, & Willmes, 1987). Different groups of subjects listened to lists of concrete words under instructions to try to learn the words either by simply listening to them or by forming visual images to represent them. Recall was better for the imagery group, as would be expected from Paivio's dual-coding theory,

cerebral blood flow Measurement of blood flow to localize where cognitive operations occur in the brain

event-related potential (ERP) A diagnostic technique that uses electrodes placed on the scalp to measure the duration of brain waves during mental tasks

and there was more blood flow to the occipital lobes for the imagery group. There were also differences in the distribution of ERPs for concrete and abstract words, which is consistent with the dual-coding theory (Kounios & Holcomb, 1994).

Besides studying brain activation in normal people, psychologists have learned much about visual images by studying the behavior of people who have suffered brain damage (Farah, 1988). As one example, we have learned from patients with brain damage that there is a dissociation between knowing what an object is and knowing where the object is located. Damage to one part of the visual cortex results in an impairment of the ability to recognize visual stimuli, whereas damage to another part of the visual cortex results in an impairment of the ability to indicate the spatial location of visual stimuli. These preserved and impaired aspects of vision are similarly preserved and impaired in visual imagery (D. N. Levine, Warach, & Farah, 1985). A patient with object identification difficulties was unable to draw or describe the appearance of familiar objects from memory, despite being able to draw and describe in great detail the relative locations of landmarks in his neighborhood, cities in the United States, and furniture in his hospital room. A patient with object localization difficulties could not use his memory to perform well on the spatial localization tasks but could provide detailed descriptions of the appearance of a variety of objects.

Another very striking example of the parallel loss in visual perception and visual imagery comes from the study of **visual neglect**. Patients with right-parietal-lobe damage often fail to perceive stimuli presented in the left half of the visual field, and they have the same problem when viewing visual images. Two patients suffering from visual neglect were asked to imagine viewing a famous square in Milan, Italy, from a particular vantage point and to describe the view. Both patients failed to describe the landmarks that would have fallen on the left side of the scene. They were then asked to imagine the scene from a vantage point that was on the opposite side of the square. The left- and right-half of the visual scene was therefore reversed to see if the patients would now see landmarks they did not see in their previous imaging. And, indeed, the patients' descriptions now included landmarks that they had previously omitted and failed to include landmarks that they had previously described.

The major consequence of the neurological studies of imagery is that the results of these studies are having an increasing impact on the construction of cognitive models. This is particularly true for Kosslyn, a leader in the empirical and theoretical study of imagery. As described in his book *Image and the Brain: The Resolution of the Imagery Debate* (1994), Kosslyn's goal is to explain how each of a number of different subsystems interact to determine performance across various imagery tasks. His key assumption is that visual mental imagery shares processing subsystems with visual perception. For example, he proposed that an image is activated in the occipital lobe in a **visual buffer**. Because the visual buffer typically contains more information than can be processed, the **attention window** selects a region within the visual buffer for further detailed processing. That is, participants in Kosslyn, Ball,

visual neglect Failure to respond to visual stimulation on the side of the visual field that is opposite a brain lesion

visual buffer A component of Kosslyn's model in which a generated visual image is maintained in short-term memory

attention window The attended part of the visual buffer in Kosslyn's model

and Reiser's (1978) experiment could maintain the image of an island in the visual buffer and use the attention window to focus on a particular object on the island. The proposed operation of these and other subsystems is closely linked to both behavioral and neurological findings in Kosslyn's (1994) model. Although there are too many imagery operations for me to describe what they do and where they are located in the brain, readers who are interested in the cognitive neuroscience of imagery will find this an excellent starting point.

LIMITATIONS OF IMAGES

The emphasis throughout this chapter has been on the usefulness of visual images for learning and for performing many spatial reasoning tasks. Perhaps you find this surprising. If you are like me, you may feel that you cannot create very vivid images and perhaps even question whether you use any images at all. Let me give you a chance to form an image by asking: "Does the Star of David contain a parallelogram (a four-sided figure whose opposite sides are parallel)?" Try to form an image of the Star of David and examine it to answer the question. Many people have difficulty using images to identify the parts of a pattern, even after they have just seen the pattern (Reed & Johnsen, 1975). Because we have seen many results that show the usefulness of images, it is only fair to discuss a few limitations of images before leaving the topic.

Memory for Details

Our discussion so far has focused on the successful use of visual images. We learned that memory for pictures is better than memory for words and memory for concrete words is better than memory for abstract words. Both of these findings are related to the ease with which an image can be created to represent a concrete word or picture. We also saw how instructions to form interactive images facilitated the learning of people's names, vocabulary words, and lists of items. If images can do all this, in what ways are they limited?

One answer is that the tests that showed good memory for visual material were not very challenging. For example, the experiments by Shepard (1967) and Standing (1973) used a recognition-memory test in which a person decided which one of two pictures had occurred in the experiment. Although the results of these studies suggest that visual memory contains an abundance of information, in reality the results do not allow us to conclude how much information is stored. All we know is that people retained enough information to distinguish the "old" picture from the new one.

Nickerson and Adams (1979) investigated how completely and accurately people remember visual details by asking them to recognize a very common object, a U.S. penny. Figure 7.12 shows 15 drawings of a penny, only one of which is correct. If you can identify the correct choice, you did better than the majority of subjects in the experiment, who selected incorrectly. Although we have seen a penny many times, most of us have never learned its details,

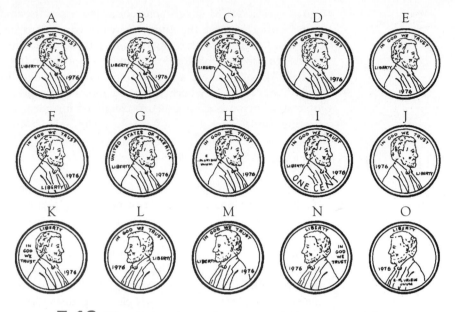

FIGURE **7.12** Fifteen drawings of a penny that were used in a recognition-memory test

Source: From "Long-term memory for a common object," by R. S. Nickerson & M. J. Adams, 1979, *Cognitive Psychology, 11,* 287–307. Copyright 1979 by Academic Press, Inc. Reprinted by permission of Elsevier Science.

probably because they are not very useful in everyday life. Attributes such as color and size allow us to distinguish quickly between a penny and other co-ins, making the learning of additional details unnecessary. If a new coin is in-troduced (such as the Susan B. Anthony dollar) that requires more attention to details to distinguish it from another coin, there is considerable resistance to its acceptance.

Evidence from imagery studies shows that people are quite selective in which details they maintain in their images. Let's begin with another demon-stration of your ability to manipulate a visual image. Form a visual image of the animal in Figure 7.13a. Now examine your image, without looking at the drawing in the book, and see if you can reinterpret the figure to perceive it as a different animal. Were you successful? If not, try to reinterpret the figure in the book. If your experience was similar to the students studied by Chambers and Reisberg (1985), you should have found it much easier to reinterpret the drawing in the book than to reinterpret your image of the drawing. In fact, in one of their studies they found that none of the 15 students in the experiment could reinterpret their image of the figure, but all 15 could reinterpret a drawing of the figure.

In a subsequent study Chambers and Reisberg (1992) examined why peo-ple had difficulty reinterpreting their image. They hypothesized that people maintain only the more important aspects of the image; in this case, the face of the animal (that is, the front side of the head). People who perceive the

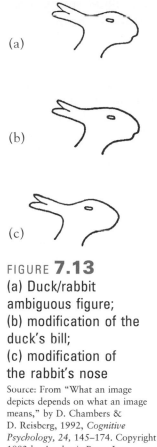

(a)

(b)

(c)

FIGURE **7.13**
(a) Duck/rabbit
ambiguous figure;
(b) modification of the
duck's bill;
(c) modification of
the rabbit's nose

Source: From "What an image
depicts depends on what an image
means," by D. Chambers &
D. Reisberg, 1992, *Cognitive
Psychology, 24,* 145–174. Copyright
1992 by Academic Press, Inc.
Reprinted by permission of Elsevier
Science.

pattern in Figure 7.13a as a duck should therefore have a detailed image of the left side of the pattern, and people who perceive the pattern as a rabbit should have a detailed image of the right side of the pattern. The results from a recognition-memory test confirmed this hypothesis. In one test people were asked to indicate whether they were shown pattern Figure 7.13a (the correct choice) or pattern Figure 7.13b, which changed the front part (the bill) of the duck's face. People who had perceived the pattern as a duck did significantly better than chance on this test, but people who had perceived the pattern as a rabbit performed at chance level. The opposite results occurred when the participants had to choose between the original pattern and a pattern that modified the front part (the nose) of the rabbit's face, shown in Figure 7.13c. People who had perceived the pattern as a duck now performed at a chance level, while people who had perceived the pattern as a rabbit performed significantly better than chance. People therefore have difficulty reinterpreting the pattern because they are missing those details that are important for the new interpretation.

The fact that we lose some of the details in our images is partly the result of our failing to maintain a detailed image once we have a verbal code. People are more successful in reinterpreting an image of the duck/rabbit ambiguous figure if they are discouraged from forming a verbal code during the initial encoding of the figure. Brandimonte and Gerbino (1993) had one group of subjects perform an articulatory suppression task (repeatedly say la-la-la) while viewing the ambiguous figure. These subjects were more successful in later reversing their image of the pattern than those subjects who did not have to perform an articulatory suppression task as they viewed the figure. The authors concluded that people are better at maintaining details in an image when forced to rely solely on the image.

Fortunately, images can be useful in many tasks even when we do not have a detailed memory of an object. For example, the retention of details is usually unnecessary when we use images to remember words. Your image of a penny would not have to be detailed or accurate to help you remember the word *penny*; it would only have to be detailed enough to allow you to recall the correct word when you retrieved your image. Experimental results have shown that people who were good at recalling the names of pictures they had seen 2 weeks earlier did not have more detailed images than people who could not recall as many names (Bahrick & Boucher, 1968).

For example, people who could recall that they had seen a cup did not necessarily remember many details of the cup in a recognition test similar to the one illustrated by Figure 7.12. The evidence suggested that people were using visual images to aid their recall, but it was necessary to remember only enough details about an object to recall its name. Visual images can therefore be incomplete if the task does not require memory for details.

Studies showing the limitations of visual images provide both good news and bad news. The bad news is that using visual images is not a universal solution for improving memory performance. The good news is that, even if people believe they have poor images, their images may still be sufficient for performing the many tasks that do not require great detail.

Reality Monitoring

If our images of objects or events were as accurate and detailed as the actual events, then our ability to distinguish between actual and imagined events would be impaired. People can remember information from two basic sources: external sources, derived from perception, and internal sources, derived from imagination or thought. The ability to distinguish between external and internal sources has been called **reality monitoring** by Johnson and Raye (1981).

reality monitoring
Discriminating between actual and imagined events

To study how well people can distinguish between actual and imagined events, Johnson, Raye, Wang, and Taylor (1979) showed subjects pictures of common objects. Subjects saw the picture of each object either two, five, or eight times and the name of each object either two, five, or eight times. They were instructed to generate an image of an object each time its name occurred. At the end of the session they received an unexpected test in which they had to estimate how often they had seen each of the pictures.

If people are very good at discriminating between seeing and imagining pictures, then their estimates of seeing should not be influenced by the number of times they imagined each picture. Note that, although the ability to form accurate images is an asset for performing most spatial tasks, good imagery would be a liability for this particular discrimination task. Because people with good imagery might find it hard to discriminate between what they imagined and what they saw, the experimenters also gave subjects an imagery test to measure their imagery ability.

Figure 7.14 shows the results. The left panel contains the average estimates of the good imagers, and the right panel contains the average estimates of the poor imagers. The labels 8, 5, and 2 on the lines that show the estimates refer to the number of times the pictures had been shown. Notice that subjects were quite good at estimating how many times they had seen each picture, even when they had to distinguish between seeing and imagining the pictures. But the image trials did influence their judgments—the estimates of presentation frequency increased as the number of image trials increased. A comparison of the left and right panels of Figure 7.14 reveals that the number of image trials had a greater effect on the good imagers than on the poor imagers.

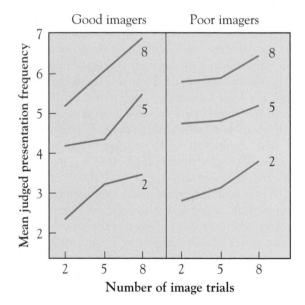

FIGURE **7.14** Judged presentation frequency of pictures as a function of the number of image trials. The number next to each line indicates whether a picture was presented two, five, or eight times

Source: From "Fact and fantasy: The roles of accuracy and variability in confusing imaginations with perceptual experience," by M. K. Johnson, C. L. Raye, A. Y. Wang, & T. T. Taylor, 1979, *Journal of Experimental Psychology: Human Learning and Memory, 5,* 229–240. Copyright 1979 by the American Psychological Association. Reprinted by permission.

As expected, people with good imagery distinguished less accurately between seeing and imagining.

Johnson and her colleagues' findings show that, although the number of image trials did influence subjects' judgments of presentation frequency, their judgments were nonetheless fairly accurate. In general, people are able to remember the origin of information (internal versus external) remarkably well. What kinds of cues help us make this distinction?

Johnson and Raye (1981) have proposed that several kinds of cues are helpful. First, there is *sensory information*. Perceptual events have more spatial detail than imagined events, although the amount of sensory information varies among individuals, as shown by the difference between good and poor imagers. Second, there is *contextual information*. Perceptual events occur in an external context that contains other information. We have seen in previous chapters that contextual information is important in recalling material, and it is also important in helping us distinguish whether an event was internally or externally generated.

A third cue for making this distinction is memory for the *cognitive operations* that are required to generate the image. If we can generate an image automatically without much conscious awareness, we will have poor memory of the cognitive operations used to generate the image. Dreams that occur during sleep are of this type. They often seem very real because we are not aware of generating them. In contrast, daydreams seem much less real because they are more influenced by our conscious control.

Breakdown of Reality Monitoring

Although people are normally fairly good at reality monitoring, there are cases where judging between reality and imagination breaks down. One aspect that has attracted much recent attention concerns whether a traumatic event, such as childhood sexual abuse, actually occurred or was imagined, perhaps because a therapist or other authoritative person suggested that it occurred. The importance of this topic resulted in an entire issue of the journal *Applied Cognitive Psychology* devoted to articles discussing it.

The lead article set the stage with these opening comments:

There is no doubt that many children are sexually abused, and that this is a tragedy. Furthermore, survivors of childhood sexual abuse often suffer long-lasting harm, and may be helped by competent therapists. Although cognitive researchers have differing views about the mechanisms underlying loss of memory (e.g., repression, dissociation, or normal forgetting; see E. F. Loftus, 1993; Singer, 1990), all would agree that it is possible that some adult survivors of childhood abuse would not remember the abusive events, and that memories might be recovered given appropriate cues. Thus we accept that some clients may recover accurate memories of childhood sexual abuse during careful, non-leading, non-suggestive therapies. But there is no doubt in our minds that extensive use of techniques such as hypnosis, dream interpretation, and guided imagery (which are advocated in some self-help books and by some clinical psychologists, psychiatrists, clinical social workers, therapists, and counselors) can create compelling illusory memories of childhood sexual abuse among people who were not abused. This too is a tragedy. (Lindsay & Read, 1994, pp. 281–282)

Lindsay and Read (1994) indicate that memory research has identified a number of factors that increase the possibility of creating false memories. These include long delays between the event and the attempt to remember, repeated suggestions that the event occurred, the perceived authority of the source of the suggestions, the perceived plausibility of the suggestions, mental rehearsal of the imagined event, and the use of hypnosis or guided imagery. Because some of these factors are necessarily part of therapy, practitioners need to be particularly concerned about the use of techniques that may increase the risk of creating illusory memories.

A study by Hyman and Pentland (1996) demonstrated that the repeated use of guided imagery significantly increases illusory memory of childhood events. They asked parents of college students to provide a description of early events that their daughter or son might be able to recall. Students were then asked if they could remember the events and supply some additional information during a series of three interviews. In addition to the true events from their past, one of the events was false. Each participant was told: You attended a wedding reception when you were 5 years old at which you spilled the punch bowl on the parents of the bride.

The experimenters compared an imagery condition with a control condition that differed in the advice given for aiding recall. When students in the imagery condition failed to recall information about either a true or a false event, they were instructed to imagine the event. When participants in the control condition failed to recall an event, they were required to quietly think about the event for 45 to 60 seconds. Events were categorized as recalled if the participant claimed to remember the event and provided additional information about what had occurred. By the end of the third interview, 12 of the 32 participants in the imagery condition falsely recalled the punch bowl incident, compared with 4 of 33 participants in the control condition.

Creating illusory memories can be especially damaging because there are no guaranteed techniques that experts can use to discriminate between real and false memories. Lindsay and Read argue that the overriding theme of their literature review is that illusory memories can look, feel, and sound like real memories and include the strong affect that accompanies real memories in case of childhood abuse. The experience of coming to believe that abusive events occurred would be tremendously traumatic regardless of whether the remembered event actually occurred.

hallucination An imagined event or image believed to be real

Another example of the breakdown in reality monitoring is the **hallucinations** of psychiatric patients. Available data suggest that hallucinations result from an impairment of skills in discrimination between real and imaginary events (Bentall, 1990). For example, a study in Wales found evidence that schizophrenics have enhanced imagery for all of the sensory modalities (Sack, van de Ven, Etschenberg, & Linden, 2005). The investigators gave a battery of tests to 50 schizophrenic patients and 50 age- and sex-matched healthy control participants. One of the tests was a standard questionnaire that measured the vividness of imagery on a seven-point scale ranging from "I perceive it perfectly clearly as if it were real" to "I think about it but I can not imagine it." The questionnaire contained 35 examples (the smell of leather, the meowing of a cat) that included seven sensory modalities. The schizophrenics gave significantly higher vividness ratings for all sensory images in comparison to the control group.

But it is important to recognize that hallucinators do not hallucinate random events. The content of the hallucinations is presumably related to the personalities and to the stresses of the patients so the correlation between the hallucination and imagery scales was low (Sack et al., 2005). Different kinds of hallucinations almost certainly reflect different causes of defective reality discrimination, and the challenge is to find which types of reality discrimination errors are linked to the different kinds of hallucinatory experiences (Bentall, 1990). Continuation of the theoretical and empirical work reported by Johnson and Raye should therefore provide a bridge between clinical and cognitive psychology in their study of imagery.

SUMMARY

The usefulness of visual images in learning is supported by research showing that people usually remember pictures better than concrete words and concrete words better than abstract ones. These results correspond to the fact that images are easiest to form from pictures and hardest to form from abstract words. Learning pairs of items is facilitated by forming an interactive image that combines the members of the pair. The dual-coding theory explains the usefulness of visual imagery in recall by proposing that a visual image provides an extra memory code that is independent of the verbal code. A person therefore has two chances to recall the item rather than only one.

The knowledge that visual imagery improves memory has existed for centuries and has resulted in the use of imagery in many mnemonic strategies. A study that compared four strategies—verbal rehearsal, sentence reading, sentence generation, and imagery—found that people who used the imagery strategy recalled the most words. However, the two sentence-elaboration strategies produced much better recall than simple rehearsal, suggesting that the former strategies could facilitate learning abstract words. Visual images can also be used to learn people's names and a foreign vocabulary, although it is often necessary to translate a name or foreign word into a similar-sounding concrete keyword first. An interactive image is then formed to link the keyword with a face or with the English translation of the foreign word.

A variety of evidence suggests that visual images are important to our ability to perform many spatial reasoning tasks. Visual images preserve the spatial relations among the objects of a scene or the features of a pattern. The time it takes to mentally scan between two objects in an image is therefore a function of the distance between them. Visual images also make it possible to compare all the features of two patterns simultaneously when we try to match a visual pattern with an image of another pattern. In contrast, features described verbally must be compared one at a time because of the sequential nature of language. When we are comparing two patterns that are in different orientations, a visual image makes it possible to rotate one of them mentally until the two patterns have the same orientation. The distinction between visual and verbal codes is also suggested by selective interference between the two codes. In addition, neurological studies provide evidence for when people use imagery. Electrophysiological and blood-flow measures of brain activity show that the same areas of the brain are used in visual perception and visual imagery. Studies of brain-damaged patients with visual deficits reveal that the same deficits occur during imagery tasks.

Although visual images are often helpful in many learning and spatial reasoning tasks, the images of most people seem to be limited in clarity and detail. An experiment that asked people to select the correct drawing of a penny from a set of similar alternatives found that most people made the wrong choice. The lack of memory for details is caused by focusing on only the most important details, but encouraging people to rely on images increases their ability to use them. Fortunately, detailed images are not always necessary. In fact, for images used to represent words in a memory task, it is only necessary to remember enough about the image to recall the word. An advantage of the lack of detailed sensory information in images is that it helps us distinguish between perceived and imagined events (reality monitoring). Research on reality monitoring should contribute to our understanding of hallucinations and illusory memories created through the suggestions of an authority figure.

STUDY QUESTIONS

1. The beginning quotation talks about the problem of operationalizing the construct of the image. Is the image construct any more difficult to observe directly than any other supposed mental event? Explain your answer.

2. What are the operations or processes that have been used to study images?

3. Critics pointed out that Kosslyn's mental scanning results could be explained by demand characteristics. Do you think Reed et al. succeeded in eliminating this possibility? How?

4. Be sure you know what parallel processing means. Why would it confer an advantage in matching tasks? In what sensory modalities besides vision is parallel processing possible?

5. Can you think of situations in which you found it helpful to transform or rearrange visual images to solve a problem?

6. How does Paivio explain the fact that using more than one code or modality usually improves learning? What is the best way to associate words and images? Words and words?

7. If formal mnemonic strategies produce such wonderful results, why don't more people use them more of the time? Do you use any of them at all?

8. What makes a keyword "good"? Take three words in a language you have studied, or some unfamiliar technical terms, and generate a list of good keywords for each. Write each word, keyword, and English translation.

9. Is there no limit to the usefulness of images to represent things in memory?

10. Explain why accurate imagery can occasionally be a liability.

CogLab   The following experiment that relates to this chapter can be found at: http://coglab. wadsworth.com. Answer the questions in the CogLab Student Manual as required by your teacher for this experiment.

Mental Rotation

KEY TERMS

The page number in parentheses refers to where the term is discussed in the chapter.

association value (159)

attention window (174)

bizarre image (162)

cerebral blood flow (173)

concrete-abstract dimension (159)

dual-coding theory (161)

event-related potential (ERP) (173)

hallucinations (180)

imagery potential (159)

keyword (163)

keyword method (163)

mnemonic techniques (161)

parallel representation (167)

propositional theory (165)

reality monitoring (178)

relational information (161)

sequential representation (167)

spatial knowledge (156)

verbal knowledge (156)

visual buffer (174)

visual neglect (174)

visual scanning (165)

RECOMMENDED READING

Paivio (1971) discusses the experimental work during the 1960s that helped restore imagery as a major topic in experimental psychology. Kosslyn (1983) provides a very readable introduction to the early research on creating and using images. His more recent book (Kosslyn, Thomson, & Ganis, 2006) shows how far we have come, although Pylyshyn (2003) remains a critic. Articles by Finke (1985) and Thomas (1999) discuss the representation of information in images and the relation between imagery and perception. Psychologists continue to study the practical implications of imagery, including its use as a mnemonic (Bellezza, 1987; Pressley, Levin, Hall, Miller, & Berry, 1980) and its role in the acquisition of spatial knowledge (Tversky, 2005), sports (Driskell, Copper, & Moran, 1994), and mechanical reasoning (Hegarty, 2004). In addition, research continues on issues related to the role of visual imagery in reality monitoring (M. K. Johnson, Hashtroudi, & Lindsay, 1993) and posttraumatic stress disorder (Kosslyn, 2005). Books on *Memory Distortion* (Schacter, 1995) and *Memory Distortions and Their Prevention* (Intons-Peterson & Best, 1998) discuss a variety of ways in which memory can become distorted (also see E. F. Loftus, 1997).

8

Categorization

Concept Identification
Discovering Rules and Attributes
Critique of the Concept Identification
  Paradigm

Natural Categories
Hierarchical Organization of Categories
Loss of Categorical Knowledge
Typicality and Family Resemblances
Person Perception

Categorizing Novel Patterns
Categorization Models
Evaluation of Categorization Models
Theory-Based Categorization

We begin with what seems to be a paradox. The world of experience of any normal man is composed of a tremendous array of discriminably different objects, events, people, impressions. But were we to utilize fully our capacity for registering the differences in things and to respond to each event encountered as unique, we would soon be overwhelmed by the complexity of our environment. The resolution of this seeming paradox— the existence of discrimination capacities which, if fully used, would make us slaves to the particular—is achieved by man's capacity to categorize. To categorize is to render discriminably different things equivalent, to group the objects and events around us into classes, and to respond to them in terms of their class membership rather than their uniqueness.
—**J. S. Bruner, J. J. Goodnow, and G. A. Austin (1956)**

This chapter and the next discuss ways in which people organize knowledge. One way to organize knowledge is to form categories. Categories consist of objects or events that we have grouped together because we feel they are somehow related. The ability to categorize enables us to interact with our environment without becoming overwhelmed by its complexity. Bruner, Goodnow, and Austin, in their influential book, *A Study of Thinking* (1956), listed five benefits of forming categories.

1. *Categorizing objects reduces the complexity of the environment.* Scientists have estimated that there are more than 7 million discriminable colors. If we responded to all of these as unique, we could spend our entire lifetime just trying to learn the names of colors. When we classify discriminably different objects as being equivalent, we respond to them in terms of their class membership rather than as unique items.

2. *Categorizing is the means by which objects of the world are identified.* We usually feel that we have recognized a pattern when we can classify it into a familiar category such as *dog, chair,* or the letter *A*.

3. *The third achievement is a consequence of the first two—the establishment of categories reduces the need for constant learning.* We do not have to be taught about novel objects if we can classify them; we can use our knowledge of items in the category to respond to the novel object.

4. *Categorizing allows us to decide what constitutes an appropriate action.* A person who eats wild mushrooms must be able to distinguish between poisonous and nonpoisonous varieties. Eating a poisonous variety is clearly not an appropriate action.

5. *Categorizing enables us to order and relate classes of objects and events.* Although classification is by itself a useful way to organize knowledge, classes can be further organized into subordinate and superordinate relations. The category *chair*, for example, has *high chair* as a subordinate class and *furniture* as a superordinate class. The three categories form a hierarchy in which *furniture* contains *chair* as a member and *chair* contains *high chair* as a member.

Psychologists have used several experimental procedures to study how people make classifications. The first section of this chapter describes a task called **concept identification** in which the experimenter selects a **logical rule** to define a concept, and the task requires discovering the rule through learning which patterns are examples of the concept.

One limitation of this approach is that many categories cannot be distinguished on the basis of a simple rule. We can usually distinguish a dog from a cat, but it is questionable whether we use a simple rule to make this distinction. The second section discusses some characteristics of natural, or real-world, categories and emphasizes how we use these characteristics to organize knowledge. To recognize objects and reduce the need for constant learning, we have to be able to classify novel objects into a familiar category. The final section discusses how people do this.

concept identification A task that requires deciding whether an item is an example of a concept, where concepts are typically defined by logical rules

logical rule A rule based on logical relations, such as conjunctive, disjunctive, conditional, and biconditional rules

CONCEPT IDENTIFICATION

Discovering Rules and Attributes

disjunctive rule A rule that uses the logical relation *or* to relate stimulus attributes, such as *small or square*

conjunctive rule A rule that uses the logical relation *and* to relate stimulus attributes, such as *small and square*

At the time Bruner, Goodnow, and Austin (1956) wrote *A Study of Thinking*, psychologists studied categorization by using the concept identification paradigm. The categories in concept identification tasks typically contain geometric patterns that vary along several dimensions—for example, shape, size, and color. The experimenter selects a rule to define the category and the task requires discovering this rule by learning which patterns belong to the category.

Consider the **disjunctive rule** "Patterns that are *large or a circle* are members of the category." A pattern that has either of these two attributes would belong to the category. All the large patterns and all the circles would therefore be members, as shown by a plus in Figure 8.1. The nonmembers are labeled with a minus.

Bruner and his colleagues proposed that people solve concept-identification problems by evaluating hypotheses. For example, you might initially hypothesize that a pattern has to be *small and square* (a **conjunctive rule**) to belong to the category. Both attributes have to be present to satisfy a conjunctive rule, so the only member would be a small square. However, you would have to abandon this hypothesis if you received contradictory information, such as learning that a small square was not a member of the category or that a large triangle was a member of the category (as shown in Figure 8.1). You would then have to formulate a new hypothesis that would be consistent with what you had learned in the experiment.

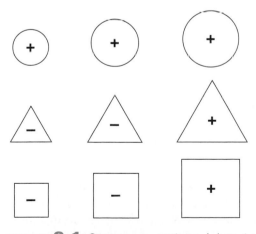

FIGURE **8.1** Category members (+) and nonmembers (–) for the disjunctive rule "large or a circle"

Concept identification tasks typically use many more stimuli than the ones shown in Figure 8.1 so discovering the correct rule can be very challenging. The difficulty is caused by the requirement to learn

rule learning A concept identification task in which people are told the relevant attributes (such as *small, square*) but have to discover the logical rule

attribute learning A concept identification task in which people are told the logical rule (such as conjunctive) but have to discover the relevant attributes

both the relevant rule (such as a disjunctive rule) and the relevant attributes (such as large, circle). One way to simplify the task would be to tell participants the relevant attributes. This task is called **rule learning** because people have to learn only the correct logical rule when they are told the relevant attributes (Haygood & Bourne, 1965). Rule-learning tasks allow researchers to study the relative difficulty of different rules, without having to be concerned about learning the relevant attributes (Bourne, 1970). A variation of this procedure—called **attribute learning**—is to tell people the rule and let them discover the appropriate attributes (Haygood & Bourne, 1965). By focusing on either rule learning or attribute learning, psychologists have learned how people formulate and evaluate hypotheses in concept identification tasks.

Critique of the Concept Identification Paradigm

Not all cognitive psychologists were satisfied with the concept-identification task; some criticized it as highly artificial and unrelated to the categorization tasks we usually encounter in the real world. This criticism does not mean that we cannot draw any analogy between the skills needed in concept identification tasks and skills needed in other tasks.

For example, to learn the correct rule in a concept identification task, subjects must evaluate a number of hypotheses. Our inability to evaluate a large number of hypotheses simultaneously is found not only in concept-identification tasks (M. Levine, 1966) but also in real-world tasks such as medical diagnosis (Elstein, Shulman, & Sprafka, 1978). Yet real-world tasks are often different enough from concept identification tasks that we must be very careful in making generalizations.

The predominant criticism of the concept-identification paradigm is that real-world categories, such as clothes, tools, and vehicles, are unlike the categories studied in the laboratory. This is not a new argument. The philosopher Wittgenstein (1953) argued that category members do not have to share identical attributes. Rather, they may have a family resemblance in which category members share some attributes with other members, but there are no or few attributes that are common to all members of the category.

A dramatic change in how psychologists viewed real-world categories had to wait until the 1970s, when Rosch and her students at the University of California, Berkeley, began to study the characteristics of natural categories (Rosch, 1973). One of the characteristics of concept identification tasks that bothered Rosch is that objects in natural categories often have **continuous dimensions** rather than the discrete dimensions studied in concept identification. Colors, for example, vary along a continuum in which red gradually becomes orange, and orange gradually becomes yellow. People might therefore consider a red object and an orange object as more likely to belong to the same category than a red object and a blue object. However, colors are treated as discrete dimensions in a rule-learning task in which red, orange, and blue are attributes that are considered to be equally different from each other.

continuous dimension An attribute that can take on any value along a dimension

hierarchically organized An organizing strategy in which larger categories are partitioned into smaller categories

Natural categories are also **hierarchically organized**—larger categories often contain smaller categories. Thus, clothing can be partitioned into smaller categories such as pants and shirt, and shirt can be partitioned into smaller categories such as dress shirt and sports shirt. The hierarchical organization of categories was not studied in concept identification tasks, even though it is now clear that it is extremely useful in helping us organize knowledge.

Another limitation of the concept identification paradigm is that it assumed that all members of a concept are equally good members. Consider the five examples in Figure 8.1 that satisfy the disjunctive rule *large or a circle*. All five positive instances are equally good members because they all satisfy the rule. In contrast, natural categories are not composed of equally good members. If we gave people different variations of the color *red*, they would agree that some variations were more representative of the color than others (a "good" red versus an "off" red).

Even mathematical categories that can be defined on the basis of rules contain examples that differ in the **typicality** of their members. For example, a rule can be used to determine whether a number is even or odd. People are therefore likely to agree that even numbers can be decided by definition (Malt, 1990). They also agree that it does not make sense to rate even numbers for degree of membership (Armstrong, Gleitman, & Gleitman, 1983). Nonetheless, people rate some even numbers (such as 4) as better examples of even numbers than others (such as 38). The better examples have fewer digits and do not contain any odd numbers.

Another example of where a rule fails to predict typicality ratings concerns the meaning of the word *water*. According to a scientific rule, water can be defined by its chemical composition as H_2O. If people use this rule, they should rate examples of water as more typical if they judge them to contain a higher percentage of H_2O (Malt, 1994). Table 8.1 shows examples of water that were judged for both typicality and percentage of H_2O. Drinking and tap water were rated most typical; followed by rain and tap water; then

typicality A measure of how well a category member represents that category

TABLE **8.1**
How Judged Percentage of H_2O Influences Typicality Judgments of Water

Typicality	Example	Percentage of H_2O
1	Drinking water	89
2	Tap water	88
	Rain water	91
	Water fountain water	89
3	Purified water	95
	Bottled water	92
	Ice water	90
4	Pure water	98
	Ocean water	79
	Soft tap water	90

Source: Based on "Water is not H_2O," by B. C. Malt, 1994, *Cognitive Psychology, 27,* 41–70. Reprinted by permission of Elsevier Science.

purified, bottled, and ice water; and finally pure, ocean, and soft tap water. Notice, however, that percentage of H_2O is not a good predictor of typicality. For example, pure, ocean, and soft tap water were rated as equally typical even though the estimated amount of H_2O ranged from 79% for ocean water to 98% for pure water.

The best examples—drinking and tap water—contain less judged H_2O than some of the other examples on the list. However, they are examples that play the most central role in our lives. This finding underscores an important point: Real-word categories and their examples are often organized according to how we use them, rather than by abstract rules (Malt, 1994; Ross, 1996).

NATURAL CATEGORIES

As we saw, one characteristic of real-world, or natural, categories is that they are hierarchical—some categories contain other categories. For example, the category *furniture* contains *chairs*, and the category *chairs* contains *living-room chairs*. Each of these levels contains a variety of objects, but the variety decreases as the category becomes smaller. There are many kinds of furniture (beds, sofas, tables, chairs), fewer kinds of chairs (living-room chairs, dining-room chairs, high chairs), and still fewer kinds of living-room chairs. The first part of this section looks at how the hierarchical organization of categories influences our behavior.

Another characteristic of natural categories is that some members seem to be better representatives of the category than others. We could all agree that chairs are furniture, but what about a piano? Shirts are certainly a good example of clothing, but what about a necklace? The second part of this section examines the implications of the fact that the members of categories are not all equally good members.

Hierarchical Organization of Categories

Rosch and her colleagues studied the hierarchical organization of categories by using the three levels shown in Table 8.2 (Rosch, Mervis, Gray, Johnsen, & Boyes-Braem, 1976). The largest categories are the **superordinate categories**, such as *musical instruments*. They contain the **basic-level categories** (such as *drum*), which in turn contain the **subordinate categories** (such as *bass drum*). The most important of the three levels, according to Rosch, is the basic level, because basic-level categories are the most differentiated from one another, and they are therefore the first categories we learn and the most important in language.

The differentiation of categories can be measured by determining how much the members of a category share attributes with one another but have different attributes than the members of other categories have. At the superordinate level, the difficulty is that members share few attributes. Examples of furniture—such as *table, lamp,* and *chair*—have few attributes in common. At the subordinate level, the difficulty is that the members share many attributes with members of similar subordinate categories. For example, a kitchen table has many of the same attributes as a dining-room table. The intermediate level of categorization—the basic level—avoids the two extremes. Members of a basic-level category, such as *chair*, not only share

superordinate category A large category at the top of a hierarchy, such as furniture, tools, and vehicles

basic-level category An intermediate category in the middle of a hierarchy, such as table, saw, and truck

subordinate category A small category at the bottom of a hierarchy, such as lamp table, jigsaw, and pickup truck

TABLE **8.2**
Examples of Subordinate, Basic, and Superordinate Categories

Superordinate	Basic Level	Subordinates	
Musical instruments	Guitar	Folk guitar	Classical guitar
	Piano	Grand piano	Upright piano
	Drum	Kettle drum	Bass drum
Fruit	Apple	Delicious apple	McIntosh apple
	Peach	Freestone peach	Cling peach
	Grapes	Concord grapes	Green seedless grapes
Tools	Hammer	Ball-peen hammer	Claw hammer
	Saw	Hack handsaw	Crosscutting handsaw
	Screwdriver	Phillips screwdriver	Regular screwdriver
Clothing	Pants	Levi's	Double-knit pants
	Socks	Knee socks	Ankle socks
	Shirt	Dress shirt	Knit shirt
Furniture	Table	Kitchen table	Dining-room table
	Lamp	Floor lamp	Desk lamp
	Chair	Kitchen chair	Living-room chair
Vehicles	Car	Sports car	Four-door sedan car
	Bus	City bus	Cross-country bus
	Truck	Pickup truck	Tractor trailer truck

Source: From "Basic objects in natural categories," by E. Rosch, C. B. Mervis, W. D. Gray, D. M. Johnsen, & P. Boyes Braem, 1976, *Cognitive Psychology, 8,* 382–440. Copyright 1976 by Academic Press, Inc. Reprinted by permission of Elsevier Science.

many attributes but also have attributes that differ from those of items in other basic-level categories, such as *lamp* and *table*.

Evidence for the differentiation of categories comes from a study in which people were asked to list the attributes of objects at different levels in the hierarchy (Rosch et al., 1976). Some people listed the attributes of superordinate objects (such as musical instruments, fruit, tools, clothing); others listed the attributes of basic-level objects (guitar, apple, hammer, pants); still others listed the attributes of subordinate objects (classical guitar, Mackintosh apple, claw hammer, Levi's).

The experimenters analyzed the data by identifying attributes that people seemed to agree were associated with the specified category. Table 8.3 shows the average number of shared attributes at each level in the hierarchy. The number of shared attributes increases from the superordinate to the subordinate level. The members of a superordinate category have very few attributes compared with those at the basic level. However, the increase in shared attributes from the basic level to the subordinate level is very small.

TABLE **8.3**
Number of Attributes in Common at Each Hierarchical Level

Category	Raw Tallies			Judge Amended Tallies		
	Super-ordinate	Basic Level	Sub-ordinate	Super-ordinate	Basic Level	Sub-ordinate
Musical instruments	1	6.0	8.5	1	8.3	8.7
Fruit	7	12.3	14.7	3	8.3	9.5
Tools	3	8.3	9.7	3	8.7	9.2
Clothing	3	10.0	12.0	2	8.3	9.7
Furniture	3	9.0	10.3	0	7.0	7.8
Vehicles	4	8.7	11.2	1	11.7	16.8

Source: From "Basic objects in natural categories," by E. Rosch, C. B. Mervis, W. D. Gray, D. M. Johnsen, & P. Boyes Braem, 1976, *Cognitive Psychology, 8,* 382–440. Copyright 1976 by Academic Press, Inc. Reprinted by permission of Elsevier Science.

Note: Raw tallies are attributes listed by subjects. These were modified if all seven judges thought another hierarchical level was more appropriate (judge amended columns).

The differences between levels can be illustrated by the three examples shown in Table 8.4. Only two attributes were listed for the superordinate category *clothing—you wear it* and *keeps you warm.* These same two attributes plus an additional six were listed for the basic-level category *pants.* Pants have *legs, buttons, belt loops, pockets,* and *two legs* and are made of *cloth.* One additional attribute was listed for the subordinate category *Levi's—blue—*and two additional attributes were listed for *double-knit pants—comfortable* and *stretchy.* Notice that, although the items in subordinate categories share slightly more attributes than those in basic-level categories, there is a considerable overlap of attributes for subordinate categories. Although Levi's and double-knit pants differ on a few attributes, they also share many attributes, which makes it easier to distinguish between pants and shirts than to distinguish between Levi's and double-knit pants.

Rosch tested her claim that categorization is fastest at the basic level, by asking people to verify the identity of an object at each of the three levels in the hierarchy. For example, before being shown a picture of a living-room chair, people given superordinate terms were asked whether the object was a piece of furniture, people given basic terms were asked whether the object was a chair, and people given subordinate terms were asked whether the object was a living-room chair. The fastest verification times occurred for the group that verified objects at the basic level (Rosch et al., 1976). Rosch proposed that people initially identify objects at the basic level and then classify them at the superordinate level, by making an inference (a chair is a piece of furniture), or classify them at the subordinate level, by looking for distinguishing features (in this case, features that distinguish a living-room chair from other chairs). But Rosch discussed the possibility that experts might be very quick in making subordinate classifications in their area of expertise.

TABLE **8.4**
Examples of Shared Attributes at Different Hierarchical Levels

Tools	Clothing	Furniture
Make things	You wear it	No attributes
Fix things	Keeps you warm	
Metal		**Chair**
	Pants	Legs
Saw	Legs	Seat
Handle	Buttons	Back
Teeth	Belt loops	Arms
Blade	Pockets	Comfortable
Sharp	Cloth	Four legs
Cuts	Two legs	Wood
Edge		Holds people—you
Wooden handle		sit on it
Cross-cutting handsaw	**Levi's**	**Kitchen chair**
Used in construction	Blue	No additional
Hack handsaw	**Double-knit pants**	**Living-room chair**
No additional	Comfortable	Large
	Stretchy	Soft
		Cushion

Source: From "Basic objects in natural categories," by E. Rosch, C. B. Mervis, W. D. Gray, D. M. Johnsen, & P. Boyes Braem, 1976, *Cognitive Psychology, 8,* 382–440. Copyright 1976 by Academic Press, Inc. Reprinted by permission of Elsevier Science.

For example, a furniture salesperson might be able to classify a living-room chair as a *living-room chair* as quickly as he or she could classify it as a *chair.* Subsequent work has confirmed this hypothesis (Tanaka & Taylor, 1991). Dog experts and bird experts, recruited from local organizations, were asked to identify colored pictures of dogs and birds at either the superordinate (*animal*), basic (*dog* or *bird*), or subordinate (such as *beagle* or *sparrow*) level.

The results replicated Rosch and her colleagues' (1976) findings when dog experts classified birds and bird experts classified dogs. Classification was fastest at the basic level. However, the results were different when dog experts classified dogs and bird experts classified birds. Their subordinate-level classifications were as fast as their basic-level classifications. The experts were so good at distinguishing between different kinds of dogs, or different kinds of birds, that they could identify the type of dog, or type of bird, as quickly as they could recognize that the picture was a dog or a bird.

Another characteristic of categories is particularly important for proto-type theories—the shape of objects within the category. The **prototype** of a category is usually defined as the "average" of the patterns in the category. It represents the central tendency of the category. But is it meaningful to talk about the average shape of real-world categories? The answer depends on which hierarchical level we are talking about.

prototype An item that typifies the members in a category and is used to represent the category

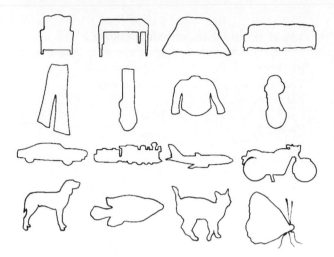

FIGURE **8.2** Examples of outlines of pictures representing basic-level categories. The pictures in each row belong to the same superordinate category.

Source: From "Basic objects in natural categories," by E. Rosch, C. B. Mervis, W. D. Gray, D. M. Johnsen, & P. Boyes Braem, 1976, *Cognitive Psychology*, *8*, 382–440. Copyright 1976 by Academic Press, Inc. Reprinted by permission of Elsevier Science.

The objects in Figure 8.2 represent basic-level categories, and the four objects in each row belong to the same superordinate category. Rosch and her colleagues found that people were not very good at identifying the average shape of two different basic-level objects belonging to the same superordinate category. For example, the average shape of a table and a chair together would look like neither a table nor a chair but something in between that would be difficult to identify. These results are not surprising if we try to think of what an "average" object would look like for superordinate categories such as *furniture, clothing, vehicles*, and *animals*. We can think of good examples of each category, but this is not the same as forming an average of all the examples.

The concept of an average example becomes meaningful if we think of objects from the same basic level. Although the average shape of furniture is unreasonable, the average shape of a chair is a more plausible concept. In fact, people were quite accurate in identifying the average shape of two objects from the same basic-level category—for example, the average of two chairs still looks reasonably like a chair, and the average of two shirts still looks reasonably like a shirt. Basic-level objects are sufficiently similar to each other that the average shape is identifiable. Creation of an average pattern to represent a category is therefore possible at the basic level (and at the subordinate level, where the shapes of objects in the same category are even more similar) but is not possible at the superordinate level.

Loss of Categorical Knowledge

Another source of evidence for how categories influence semantic knowledge is the selective loss of information during a progressive neurological condition called **semantic dementia**. Patients with semantic dementia gradually lose their knowledge about the meaning of words and objects while often retaining other cognitive abilities. Rogers and Patterson (2007) studied how the severity of this condition influences patients' ability to match words and pictures at each of the three hierarchical levels proposed by Rosch.

They examined eight patients who differed in their level of performance on the Word-Picture Matching Test. Rogers and Patterson then studied matching at different hierarchical levels by showing the patients a sequence of colored photographs with a single word printed above each. The experimenter read each word

semantic dementia Progressive deterioration of knowledge about words and objects

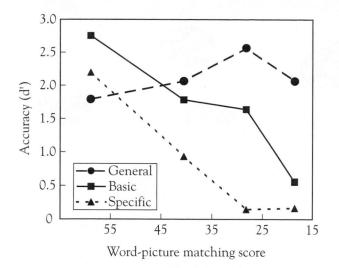

FIGURE **8.3** Word-picture matching accuracy as a function of the severity of semantic dementia

Source: From "Object categorization: Reversals and explanations of the basic-level advantage," by T. T. Rogers & K. Patterson, 2007, *Journal of Experimental Psychology: General*, 136, 451–469. Copyright 2007 by the American Psychological Association. Reprinted by permission.

aloud and asked whether the word matched the picture. The word described the picture at either the superordinate level (animal, vehicle), the basic level (dogs, birds, cars, and boats), or the subordinate level (Labrador, robin, ferry, BMW). Would matching be the best at the basic level, as would be predicted by Rosch's theory?

The answer depends on the severity of the dementia. Figure 8.3 shows the findings in which each point on the graph represents the average of two patients with similar scores on the Word-Picture Matching Test. Accuracy *was* highest for questions at the basic level for patients with mild dementia. But as expected, performance rapidly deteriorated for basic and subordinate categories in patients with lower test scores. The exception was that identification of objects at the superordinate level did not decline. The results show that although basic categories are easier to initially acquire, superordinate categories are easier to retain as semantic dementia worsens.

Rogers and Patterson (2007) used a neural network model (McClelland & Rogers, 2003) to explain why superordinate categories are better retained during dementia. We saw an early application of neural network theory (McClelland & Rumelhart, 1981) to the word superiority effect in Chapter 2. However, instead of connecting features, letters, and words, the network connects categories (robin, bird, animal) and attributes (red, sing, move). The theory assumes, as does Rosch, that categorical knowledge is represented by shared attributes at different hierarchical levels. These attributes are determined by the perceptual, motor, and language representations that are formed by our interaction with the environment and are stored in various parts of the brain. Figure 8.4 shows a network of different attributes that are used to classify pictures at different levels in the hierarchy. The node labeled "semantic representation" serves as a hub that creates a pattern of activation among the different attributes for each semantic concept.

The difficulty suffered by patients with semantic dementia is that when the anterior temporal cortex—the location of this hub—deteriorates, specific attributes in the semantic network become distorted while general properties remain more intact. Identifying a robin as a bird will therefore become more difficult than identifying a robin as an animal because general attributes such as eating are more intact than specific attributes such as having a beak. The loss of specific attributes will make categorization at the subordinate level even more difficult, as shown by its rapid decline in Figure 8.4 as semantic dementia becomes more severe.

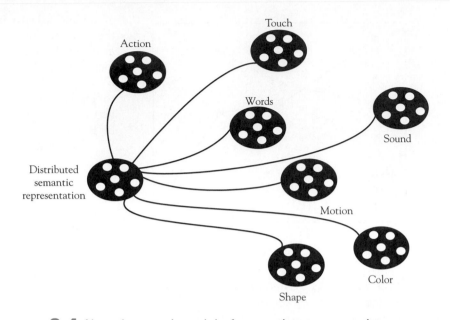

FIGURE **8.4** Neural network model of semantic representations

Source: From "Object categorization: Reversals and explanations of the basic-level advantage," by T. T. Rogers & K. Patterson, 2007, *Journal of Experimental Psychology: General*, 136, 451–469. Copyright 2007 by the American Psychological Association. Reprinted by permission.

Typicality and Family Resemblances

So far we have emphasized comparing categories at different levels of generality. We will now shift our emphasis to comparing members within a category. Psychologists use the term *typicality* to refer to differences in how well members of a category represent that category. For example, people agree that chairs, sofas, and tables are good examples of furniture; cars, trucks, and buses are good examples of vehicles; and oranges, apples, and bananas are good examples of fruit. Table 8.5 lists 20 members for each of 6 superordinate categories, ranked from the most typical to the least typical, based on people's ratings.

Although the rank order may seem fairly obvious to us, it isn't obvious why the order exists. Why is a car a good example and an elevator a poor example of a vehicle? Both can transport people and materials. Rosch and Mervis (1975) hypothesized that good members will share many attributes with other members of the category and few attributes with members of other categories. Notice that Rosch is applying the same hypothesis she used to compare superordinate, basic, and subordinate categories to compare the typicality of members within a category.

Rosch and Mervis tested their hypothesis by asking people to list the attributes of each of the category members shown in Table 8.5. For example, for a *bicycle*, people might list that it has two wheels, pedals, and handlebars; you ride on it; and it doesn't use fuel. To test the hypothesis that the good examples of categories should share many attributes with other members of the category,

TABLE **8.5**
Typicality of Members in Six Superordinate Categories

Item	Furniture	Vehicles	Fruit	Weapons	Vegetables	Clothing
			Category			
1	Chair	Car	Orange	Gun	Peas	Pants
2	Sofa	Truck	Apple	Knife	Carrots	Shirt
3	Table	Bus	Banana	Sword	String beans	Dress
4	Dresser	Motorcycle	Peach	Bomb	Spinach	Skirt
5	Desk	Train	Pear	Hand grenade	Broccoli	Jacket
6	Bed	Trolley car	Apricot	Spear	Asparagus	Coat
7	Bookcase	Bicycle	Plum	Cannon	Corn	Sweater
8	Footstool	Airplane	Grape	Bow and arrow	Cauliflower	Underpants
9	Lamp	Boat	Strawberry	Club	Brussels sprouts	Socks
10	Piano	Tractor	Grapefruit	Tank	Lettuce	Pajamas
11	Cushion	Cart	Pineapple	Tear gas	Beets	Bathing suit
12	Mirror	Wheelchair	Blueberry	Whip	Tomato	Shoes
13	Rug	Tank	Lemon	Ice pick	Lima beans	Vest
14	Radio	Raft	Watermelon	Fists	Eggplant	Tie
15	Stove	Sled	Honeydew	Rocket	Onion	Mittens
16	Clock	Horse	Pomegranate	Poison	Potato	Hat
17	Picture	Blimp	Date	Scissors	Yam	Apron
18	Closet	Skates	Coconut	Words	Mushroom	Purse
19	Vase	Wheelbarrow	Tomato	Foot	Pumpkin	Wristwatch
20	Telephone	Elevator	Olive	Screwdriver	Rice	Necklace

Source: From "Family resemblances: Studies in the internal structure of categories," by E. Rosch & C. B. Mervis, 1975, *Cognitive Psychology*, 7, 573–605. Copyright 1975 by Academic Press, Inc. Reprinted by permission of Elsevier Science.

family resemblance A measure of how frequently the attributes of a category member are shared by other members of the category

it is necessary to calculate a measure of **family resemblance** for each item by considering how many other members share each attribute of the item.

Let's take a specific example. Because a car has wheels as one of its attributes, we would count the vehicles that also have wheels. Because a car has a windshield, we would count the members that have a windshield. The numerical score for each attribute can vary from 1 to 20, depending on how many of the 20 members in Table 8.5 possess that attribute. The family resemblance score for each member is obtained by adding together the numerical scores of all attributes possessed by that member. If 14 members of the category have wheels and 11 have windshields, the family resemblance score would be 25 for a car if it had only those two attributes. The actual score is of course, much higher, because we also have to add the numerical scores for all the other attributes listed for a car. The results revealed that good representatives of a category had high family resemblance scores. The correlations between the two variables were between 0.84 (for *vegetable*) and 0.94 (for *weapon*) for the six superordinate categories listed in Table 8.5.

Another way of viewing these results is to compare how many attributes are shared by the five most typical and five least typical examples in each category. The five most typical vehicles are car, truck, bus, motorcycle, and train. The five share many attributes because they possess many common parts; the subjects in the experiment were able to identify 36 attributes that belonged to all five members. The five least typical examples are horse, blimp, skates, wheelbarrow, and elevator—subjects identified only two attributes that belong to all five of the least typical members (perhaps that they carry people and move). The results were similar for the other five superordinate categories.

The fact that typical members of categories tend to share attributes with other members is also true for basic-level categories. You may have noticed that the examples of the superordinate categories shown in Table 8.5 are basic-level categories. Rosch and Mervis (1975) selected six of these examples (car, truck, airplane, chair, table, lamp) to test the same hypothesis—that the most typical members of basic-level categories should share more attributes with other members than the least typical members. For each of the six categories, the experimenters selected 15 pictures, varying from good to poor examples. They then asked groups of undergraduates to rate how well each picture represented their idea of the category. As was found for the members of superordinate categories, there was a high correlation between the typicality of a member and the number of shared attributes.

Although family resemblance scores are useful for predicting the typicality of members in common taxonomic categories like those listed in Table 8.5, they are not useful in predicting typicality for **goal-derived categories** (Barsalou, 1985). Goal-derived categories consist of examples that satisfy a goal, such as "make people happy when you give a birthday present." According to subjects' ratings, good examples of birthday presents include clothing, a party, jewelry, dinner, a watch, a cake, and a card. Notice that these examples are dissimilar to one another and do not share many attributes. Barsalou calculated family resemblance scores for members of goal-derived categories and found that family resemblance scores did not predict the typicality of the examples.

The explanation for this finding is that members of goal-derived categories are selected on the basis of some underlying principle, rather than on the basis of shared attributes (Murphy & Medin, 1985). Thus, when we select weekend activities, we consider events that we enjoy; when we select things we would take from our home during a fire, we consider things that are valuable and irreplaceable, such as children and important papers. Although similarity of attributes determines how we form many categories and judge the typicality of category members, Murphy and Medin argue that we will need to learn more about underlying principles to have a more complete understanding of categorization.

goal-derived category A category whose members are selected to satisfy a specified goal

For goal-derived categories, an underlying principle is the extent to which members satisfy the goal. Barsalou (1991) has shown that goal-derived categories are organized around **ideals**, and the more typical members of the category are those members that best satisfy the goal. For the category *foods to eat on a weight-loss diet*, the ideal number of calories is zero, so the fewer calories a food has, the better it satisfies the goal of losing weight. Those of us who have attempted a weight-loss diet probably realize that we often like to satisfy more than one goal. We may therefore try to select foods that have minimal calories, maximal nutrition, and maximal taste to satisfy the multiple goals of losing weight, staying healthy, and enjoying food.

ideal An attribute value that relates to the goal of a goal-derived category

Person Perception

The structure of natural categories, such as hierarchical organization and typicality, is also relevant for how we classify people (Cantor & Mischel, 1979). An example of a superordinate category might be people who have a strong commitment to a particular belief or cause. This category can be subdivided into religious devotees and social activists. Religious devotees can be further classified according to their particular religions, and social activists can be classified according to their particular causes. Cantor and Mischel's work parallels that of Rosch and her colleagues, by examining such issues as the number of shared attributes at different levels in the person hierarchy.

As we saw at the beginning of this chapter, categorization allows us to create a manageable view of the world, but it also has disadvantages that can be particularly troublesome when the category members are people. We saw in Chapter 2 that people have difficulty in discriminating among faces within an ethnic category that differs from their own because they emphasize the category rather than individuals within the category. Exaggerating within-group similarity by creating **stereotypes** might not only result in erroneous assumptions about others but also make it more difficult for people to remember impressions that disconfirm their stereotypes (Cantor & Genero, 1986). In the process of organizing the world into social categories, people may perceive members of the same social category as remarkably similar and different from members of other social categories. Once having categorized a person, it is maladaptive to exaggerate the similarity among people in the category, discount disconfirming evidence, and focus on stereotypic examples of the category.

stereotype An attribute value believed to be representative of social categories

The need to distinguish among individuals is particularly important when the categories are created through clinical diagnosis. Examples of diagnostic categories include functional psychosis, paranoid schizophrenia, and affective disorder. Attributes associated with each of these categories are used in diagnosis. For example, attributes that characterize paranoid schizophrenia include delusions of persecution, hostility, suspicion, associative disturbance, delusions of grandeur, hallucinations, autism, affective disturbance, projection, and rigidity in coping with stress. Differences in typicality occur because more typical patients have most of the attributes associated with a particular diagnostic category, whereas less typical patients have only some of those attributes (Cantor, Smith, French, & Mezzich, 1980).

The diagnostic manual of the American Psychiatric Association distinguishes among different categories by listing a large number of features, some of which appear in more than one category (Cantor et al., 1980). This approach to classification has several implications. In contrast to the approach in which each category is defined by several unique features, the recommended approach allows treatment of the patient to take into account the overlap in symptoms across disorders. It also encourages clinicians to expect diversity among patients who have the same diagnosis and to react appropriately to individual differences. It should be noted, however, the clinical diagnosis is a complex task, and much thought and discussion occurs before each edition of the diagnostic manual (Widinger & Clark, 2000).

The variability among personality traits of people within a category is perhaps not surprising when we consider that even the traits of a single person can vary, depending on the situation. For example, judge which of the following traits describes you: (1) calm, (2) cruel, (3) friendly, (4) dishonest, and (5) polite. Next, try to recall an example in which you were rude.

You might reasonably speculate that if you decided that the trait *polite* applied to you, then this judgment would help you quickly retrieve specific occasions when you were polite. But an experiment by Klein, Cosmides, Tooby, and Chance (2002) found the opposite result! Judging personality traits helped people more quickly retrieve instances that were *inconsistent* with a self-described trait, such as recalling when they were rude if they judged themselves to be polite. The authors proposed that we place boundary conditions on self-described traits by thinking of examples when the trait does *not* apply. This leads to two different types of memory: an abstract semantic memory that consists of generalizations (I am usually honest) and a more specific episodic memory that constrains these generalizations (I once lied about a grade in my math course). The relative role of abstractions and particular examples is also important in theories of how people decide which category is the most appropriate one.

CATEGORIZING NOVEL PATTERNS

At the beginning of this chapter, we learned that one advantage of categories is that they enable us to recognize novel objects. A young child who encounters a new dog for the first time can use previous knowledge of dogs to recognize the new dog. Lacking this ability to classify novel objects, the child would have to be told the identity of every new object.

People are quite good at making perceptual classifications, and psychologists are naturally interested in how they do it. The characteristics of natural categories may provide a clue. One characteristic is that some category members are more prototypical, or better representatives, of the category than other members. People might therefore create a pattern, or prototype, that they feel is a very good representative of the category and use it to classify other patterns. A model based on this strategy is called a *prototype model*. Another characteristic of category members is that they share features, or attributes. People might therefore classify a novel pattern by determining how many of its feature values match the feature values of category patterns.

A model based on this strategy is called a *feature-frequency model*. Finally, people may simply remember the examples in a category and compare novel patterns to the examples. Because the examples are used directly, these kinds of models are called *exemplar models*. The next section discusses a categorization task to make these distinctions more concrete.

Categorization Models

The different categorization models can be illustrated by referring to the examples in Figure 8.4, taken from one of my experiments (Reed, 1972). If you were a subject in this experiment, I would first tell you that the upper row of faces represents one category (category 1) and the bottom row represents another category (category 2) (Figure 8.5). I would then ask you to study the two categories because you would have to classify novel faces as members of one of the two categories. Students in my experiments classified from 20 to 25 novel faces (faces that didn't match any of the faces shown in Figure 8.4). Figure 8.5 shows three novel faces.

The purpose of these experiments was to determine what kinds of strategies people use to classify pattern. I became interested in this question as a graduate student and decided to devote my dissertation to it. It seemed to me that people classify a pattern into a category because that pattern is similar to other patterns in the category.

One method of measuring similarity is simply to show people pairs of patterns and ask them to rate the similarity of the two patterns in each pair. The use of similarity to categorize patterns can be illustrated by considering a simple classification rule called the **nearest-neighbor rule**. The nearest-neighbor rule states that a person should classify a novel pattern by comparing

nearest-neighbor rule A classification strategy that selects the category containing an item most similar to the classified item

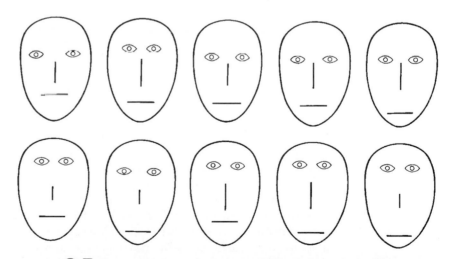

FIGURE **8.5** Example of a perceptual categorization task. The upper five faces represent category 1, and the lower five faces represent category 2

Source: From "Perceptual vs. conceptual categorization," by S. K. Reed & M. P. Friedman, 1973, *Memory & Cognition, 1,* 157–163. Copyright 1973 by the Psychonomic Society, Inc. Reprinted by permission.

it with all the patterns in each category to find the single category pattern most similar to the novel pattern. The novel pattern is then classified into the category that produces the best match.

The problem with the nearest-neighbor rule is that it requires a person to compare the test pattern with all category patterns but uses only a single pattern (the one most similar to the test pattern) as the basis for decision. If the most similar pattern is not very representative of its category, the decision could easily be wrong. For example, a young child who had a Pekingese dog as a pet might classify a long-haired cat as a dog because the cat looks more like the Pekingese than like other cats. The error would occur because, although a Pekingese is a dog, it is not a very good representative of the category.

average distance rule A classification strategy that selects the category containing items having the greatest average similarity to the classified item

A better rule, called the **average distance rule**, states that a person should compare the novel pattern with all the patterns in each category to determine the average similarity between the novel pattern and the patterns in each category. If the average similarity is greater for category 1 patterns, category 1 should be selected; otherwise, category 2 should be selected. The average distance rule has an advantage over the nearest-neighbor rule in that it uses all category patterns as the basis for the decision instead of only one pattern. It has the disadvantage that a person must compute average similarity in addition to comparing the novel pattern to all category patterns.

prototype rule A classification strategy that selects the category whose prototype is the most similar to the classified item

Both of these disadvantages are eliminated by the **prototype rule**. The prototype rule has the advantage that it doesn't require many comparisons to classify a pattern. Instead of comparing a novel pattern with every pattern in the category, a person has to compare a novel pattern with only a single pattern in each category—the pattern that is the best representative of that category. However, the prototype has to be created and is usually a pattern that is the average of all other patterns in the category. The prototype for either row of faces in Figure 8.5 is the pattern that is created by finding the average feature values of the five patterns in that category. It has the average forehead height, average eye separation, average nose length, and average mouth height. The middle pattern in Figure 8.6 is the prototype for the top row of faces, and the right pattern is the prototype for the bottom row of faces.

The prototype model proposes that the perceiver creates a prototype to represent each category and classifies a novel pattern by comparing it with the category prototypes, finding which prototype it most closely resembles, and selecting that category. For example, if the novel pattern is more similar to the category 1 prototype than to the prototype for any other category, it will be classified into category 1.

feature frequency rule A classification strategy that selects the category having the most feature matches with the classified item

The final model we will consider is different from the first three in that it uses features in making predictions. The **feature frequency rule** is concerned with matching features rather than measuring the similarity between patterns. It looks at the features of the novel pattern and compares how many times they exactly match features of the category patterns. Consider the face on the left shown in Figure 8.6. It has a large forehead, closely spaced eyes, a short nose, and a high mouth. Inspection of the two categories in Figure 8.5 reveals that four faces in category 1 have a large forehead, one has closely spaced

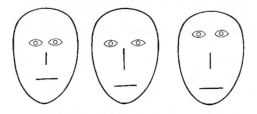

FIGURE **8.6** Examples of novel faces for Figure 8.4. The middle face is the category 1 prototype, and the face on the right is the category 2 prototype

Source: From "Pattern recognition and categorization," by S. K. Reed, 1972, *Cognitive Psychology, 3*, 382–407. Copyright 1972 by Academic Press, Inc. Reprinted by permission of Elsevier Science.

eyes, and one has a high mouth. Therefore the total number of feature matches with the novel face is six. By contrast, four faces in category 2 have closely spaced eyes, three have short noses, and two have high mouths. Because the number of matches is higher for category 2, the pattern should be classified into category 2, according to the feature frequency rule.

You may have noticed that each of the four models—nearest neighbor, average distance, prototype, and feature frequency—states how a pattern should be classified. Both the nearest-neighbor and average-distance models are examples of exemplar models because they propose that people compare patterns to the category examples. In contrast, the prototype model proposes that people compare patterns to abstracted prototypes, and the feature-frequency model proposes that people match features. Because the models use different information, they sometimes differ in their selection of categories. Therefore, the models could be used to make predictions about how people would classify the patterns. If the prototype model, for example, were more successful than the other models in predicting how people classified novel patterns, this would imply that they used a prototype strategy. The results of my studies did in fact support the prototype model.

The results do not prove that everyone used the prototype strategy, but they suggest that it was the predominant strategy used. This suggestion was confirmed by asking people which strategy of the four listed in Table 8.6 they had used. The majority selected the prototype strategy, and very few selected the two strategies that required comparing the novel patterns (projected faces) with all the category patterns. These particular results are from an experiment in which UCLA undergraduates had to classify novel patterns after learning the two categories shown in Figure 8.5. Comparing a novel pattern with all category patterns should be particularly difficult when the category patterns are stored in memory rather than physically present. However, the data supported the prototype model even when all the patterns were simultaneously present, as they are in Figure 8.4 (Reed, 1972).

My finding that the prototype model provided a good account of how people classified schematic faces does not imply that people will always use the prototype rule. One of the limitations of prototype models is that they are difficult to apply to patterns that cannot be represented along continuous dimensions. Schematic faces consist of features that vary along continuous dimensions, such as eye separation or mouth height, so it is possible to create an average pattern, or prototype, to represent the category.

Now imagine a task that requires classifying people into groups based on their age, education, and marital status. Hayes-Roth and Hayes-Roth (1977) designed such a task in which the age of a person was 30, 40, 50, or 60 years; the educational level was junior high, high school, trade school, or

TABLE **8.6**

Percentage of Subjects Who Reported Using Each Classification Strategy After Learning the Category Patterns

Strategy	Percentage
1. Prototype	
I formed an abstract image of what a face in Category 1 should look like and an abstract image of what a face in Category 2 should look like. I then compared the projected face with the two abstract images and chose the category that gave the closest match.	58
2. Nearest neighbor	
I compared the projected face with all the faces in the two categories, looking for a single face that best matched the projected face. I then chose the category in which that face appeared.	10
3. Feature frequency	
I looked at each feature on the projected face and compared how many times it exactly matched a feature in each of the two categories. I then chose the category that gave the highest number of matches.	28
4. Average distance	
I compared the projected face with each of the five faces in Category 1 and with each of the five faces in Category 2. I then chose the category in which the faces were more like the projected face, basing my decision on all faces in the two categories.	4

college; and the marital status was single, married, divorced, or widowed. Computing the average age in each group would be easy, but computing an average for education or marital status is more problematic. Hayes-Roth and Hayes-Roth found that a version of the feature-frequency model was a good predictor of how participants classified people. The feature-frequency model does not care whether a dimension is continuous. To classify a 30-year-old married person with a high school education, it simply counts how frequently these particular features appear in each of the groups.

Evaluation of Categorization Models

Theorists, of course, have continued to develop and evaluate categorization models. One general class of models that has received particular emphasis is called an **exemplar** theory. An exemplar theory proposes that people base their decisions on the examples in the category, rather than on information abstracted from the examples such as feature frequencies or a prototype. The nearest neighbor and the average-distance model in Table 8.6 are exemplar models because they assume that a test pattern is classified by comparing its similarity to the category examples.

The development of exemplar models has been greatly influenced by the one proposed by Medin and Schaffer (1978). They assume that people store examples of category patterns in memory and classify new patterns by comparing them with retrieved examples. The greater the similarity of the new

exemplar model Proposes that patterns are categorized by comparing their similarity to category examples

TABLE **8.7**
Examples of Coherent and Incoherent Category Exemplars

Coherent Exemplars	Incoherent Exemplars
Operates on surface of the water	Floats in the stratosphere
Works on absorbing spilled oil	Works on absorbing spilled oil
Coated with spongy material	Has a shovel
Operates on land	Operates on surface of the water
Works to gather harmful solids	Works to gather harmful solids
Has a shovel	Has an electrostatic filter
Floats in the stratosphere	Operates on land
Works to absorb dangerous gases	Works to absorb dangerous gases
Has an electrostatic filter	Coated with spongy material

pattern to an example stored in memory, the greater the probability that the example will be retrieved. But, unlike the nearest-neighbor and average-distance models, Medin and Schaffer's model uses combinations of features to measure similarity. In a test of how subjects would use symptoms to diagnose fictitious diseases, Medin and his colleagues found that subjects' decisions were influenced by feature combinations (Medin, Altom, Edelson, & Freko, 1982). For example, if someone has a cough and a temperature then the diagnosis of other patients who have *both* a cough and a temperature is particularly relevant information.

The most ambitious work on the development of exemplar models has been carried out by Nosofsky, whose goal is to explain all categorization effects by exemplar models (Nosofsky & Johansen, 2000). For example, Nosofsky (1991) had subjects learn the schematic faces shown in Figure 8.5 and found support for the view that they classified test faces by comparing them to the individual examples. His findings differ from mine (Reed, 1972) because a model based on memory for examples predicted better than a prototype model how subjects would classify the faces. However, the results were similar to mine in supporting the view that people emphasize those features that are most helpful in discriminating between categories when judging the similarity of two patterns. For example, the height of the eyes is a very helpful feature for discriminating between the two categories in Figure 8.5, but the height of the mouth conveys little information. The influence of differential attention to features in determining similarity has continued to be an important component of the exemplar models developed by Nosofsky (Nosofsky & Johansen, 2000).

Although Nosofsky has emphasized a single (exemplar) strategy in accounting for category learning, many other theorists have emphasized how the categorization task influences people's strategies (Ashby & Maddox,

2005; Hampton, 1997). One factor that influences whether people use a prototype or an exemplar classification rule is the amount of practice they have had in learning the category examples. Smith and Minda (1998) found that early learning results are more consistent with a prototype model because people have learned only the more prototypical patterns in the category. Eventually, however, they learn to correctly categorize all the examples in the category, which is more consistent with an exemplar model. Another influential factor is the number of examples in a category. Minda and Smith (2002) argue that exemplar models have been successful in categorization tasks that have only a small number of examples (typically five examples in one category and four in the other). This makes it possible to learn all the examples with enough practice.

Ashby and Maddox (2005) propose that recent evidence suggests that there are dramatic differences in the way people learn categories, depending on how the categories are constructed. Cognitive, neuropsychological, and neuroimaging results show that there are qualitative differences in people's strategies that are influenced by the task. Rule-based category learning depends on the frontal cortex and requires working memory and executive attention. Prototype distortion tasks that cannot be solved by rules, such as the schematic faces shown in 8.5, depend more on perceptual learning that uses the visual cortex. One implication of these findings is that different clinical populations can be selectively impaired in their ability to learn categories. For example, Parkinson's disease patients are normal in prototype distortion tasks but are profoundly impaired in rule-based categorization (Ashby, Alfonso-Reese, Tuken, & Waldron, 1998).

It is therefore not surprising that theorists have proposed a variety of classification strategies to describe how people categorize. It is likely that no single model will be sufficient to account for how people make classifications across a wide variety of situations. The best advice is that given by Hampton (1997) following his analysis of the strengths and weaknesses of the different models:

> There is a temptation for theorists to wish to apply their own approach to all conceptual representations. It is however most unlikely that all concepts are defined or represented in the same way. What is needed for the advance of the field is for a principled account to be given of the range of representational powers that people possess, and for a matching up of different kinds of representation with different conceptual domains. (pp. 105–106)

Theory-Based Categorization

One of the most important differences in categorization tasks is the extent to which people can use their previous knowledge as a basis for categorization. Most of the research has used rather artificial stimuli such as schematic faces. An advantage of these stimuli is that they enable investigators to evaluate how people use the similarity of patterns to make classifications. A disadvantage of this approach is that people might use different strategies when the stimuli are more meaningful. For example, they might use their theories about real-world categories if the task could be related to real-world categories.

I learned this lesson rather abruptly when my graduate advisor and I tested whether the categorization models that predicted the classification of schematic faces would also predict the classification of more meaningful stimuli (Reed & Friedman, 1973). The new categories consisted of the descriptions of five hypothetical people who lived in Suburb A and five hypothetical people who lived in Suburb B. The descriptions included a person's age, income, number of children, and years of education. The best predicting feature for these categories was *age*, and the worst predicting feature was *education*.

We asked people after categorizing novel patterns to rate how much they emphasized each of the four features and provide a reason. The results were more varied than we anticipated. For example, one student commented: "It seemed that in the two suburbs, Group A had mostly 40-year-olds and one 35. Group B, 30-year-olds and one 35 so I used age as my first attribute." This is what we expected to find. However, another student commented, "I emphasized education more because of a person's background and how it influences a community." This comment reveals that the student's ratings were influenced more by his theory of where people live than by membership in the categories that we provided. Approximately half of the students based their ratings on our categories and gave *age* the highest average rating. The rest based their ratings on their theories and gave *income* the highest average rating (Reed & Friedman, 1973).

This finding is consistent with Murphy and Medin's (1985) proposal that the importance of features depends on the role the features play in people's theories underlying the categories. For example, the students who used their prior knowledge to determine that *income* was the most important feature in our experiment likely believed that people's choice of neighborhoods is determined by how much they can afford to pay. The amount of income therefore would provide a causal explanation of the similarity among people in a particular suburb.

A more recent experiment (Ahn, Kim, Lassaline, & Dennis, 2000) directly tested Murphy and Medin's (1985) hypothesis that people emphasize features that provide causal explanations. Undergraduates at Yale were informed that members of a category tend to have three features; for example, blurred vision, headaches, and insomnia. They were further informed that blurred vision causes the headaches, and the headaches cause insomnia. They then rated the likelihood that an item belonged to the category if one of the features was missing. The results indicated that the judged likelihood of membership was low when the initial cause (blurred vision) was missing, higher when the intermediate cause (headache) was missing, and higher still when the terminal effect (insomnia) was missing. Identifying causes therefore is important in people's theories of categories. If the cause is missing, people think it is less likely that an item is a member of the category.

At a more general level, these findings suggest that it is not only the features, but the relation among the features that is important. Table 8.7 shows another example in which the relation among features determines category membership (Rehder & Ross, 2001). The coherent examples consist of features that tend to go together based on our prior knowledge. A device that operates on the surface of water, absorbs spilled oil, and is coated with spongy material is a plausible device. A device that floats in the stratosphere, absorbs spilled oil, and has a shovel seems to have the wrong combination of features. The results showed that learning to classify the coherent exemplars was easier than learning to classify the incoherent exemplars. Exemplars are coherent because they fit into our organized knowledge structures called *schemas*. We will learn about schemas in the next chapter.

SUMMARY

One way we organize knowledge is through categories and hierarchies made up of categories. Categories reduce the complexity of the environment and the need for constant learning and enable us to recognize objects, respond appropriately, and order and relate classes of events.

The concept identification paradigm is one approach to the study of categorization. People try to learn a logical rule by forming hypotheses and receiving feedback on positive and negative instances of the concept. *Rule learning* occurs when people know the relevant attributes and therefore only have to learn the rule. *Attribute learning* occurs when people know the rule but have to learn the relevant attributes.

Real-world, or natural, categories generally cannot be distinguished by a simple rule. They are frequently hierarchically organized—for example, double-knit pants are included in the category *pants*, and pants are included in the category *clothes*. Rosch has argued that most classifications are made at the intermediate or basic level—the most general level at which a prototype can be constructed and the level at which categories are most differentiated. However, information about superordinate categories is the most resistant to loss during semantic dementia. The members of natural categories vary in how well they represent the category. Oranges and apples are considered good examples of *fruit*; coconuts and olives are considered poor examples. The attributes of good members are shared with other members of the category, except for goal-derived categories in which the typicality of members is determined by how well they satisfy the goal. The concepts of hierarchical organization and category typicality also apply to person perception.

Two theories that assume people use abstracted information to classify novel patterns are the prototype model and the feature-frequency model. The prototype model proposes that people create patterns that best represent the categories and then classify novel patterns by comparing them with the category prototypes. The prototype is usually the central tendency of the category, formed by calculating the average of all patterns in the category. Prototype theories have been most successful in predicting how people will classify perceptual patterns consisting of feature values that vary continuously along a dimension. By contrast, the feature-frequency model proposes that people classify patterns by comparing how frequently their feature values match those of the category patterns and then selecting the category that results in the greatest number of feature matches. The feature frequency theory has been most successful in predicting how people classify patterns consisting of feature values that do not vary continuously along a dimension.

Exemplar theories propose that people remember specific examples rather than abstract information. The average-distance model and the nearest neighbor model are examples of exemplar models. More recent formulations of exemplar models include the helpful assumption that some features are emphasized more than others when judging the similarity of patterns. Exemplar models have been most successful when people have sufficient practice to learn small categories. Theory-based models propose that people use their knowledge of the world to classify patterns. Features that are causes of events are often emphasized in these situations. It is likely that no single theory will work for all situations; the challenge is therefore to show how different tasks influence people's classification strategies.

STUDY QUESTIONS

1. Bruner was one of the early group of U.S. psychologists who attempted study of the "higher mental processes." Among other things, he was interested in both education and creativity. Can you account for the fact that he and his colleagues chose to use such an apparently arid and mind-numbing procedure as concept identification in their research?

2. Much of the vocabulary here may be new, and it is certainly abstract. Don't panic. In concept identification, the task is something like the game of "Twenty Questions." The subject is shown patterns and is told that they *are* (positive) or *are not* (negative) instances of the to-be-identified concept. Rule learning and attribute learning are variants of what the subject must "guess." How do they differ?

3. Be sure you can give specific examples of the following terms and understand their relationship: *dimension, attribute, feature, category, subordinate, superordinate, hierarchy, conjunctive, disjunctive, continuous, discrete.*

4. What makes a basic category basic, according to Rosch? To put it another way, what are the characteristics of a basic category? How would you know whether a given category is basic or not?

5. How does expertise change people's ability to quickly identify objects at the different hierarchical levels? Do you have an area of expertise where you can make rapid identifications?

6. What makes an object a "good" member of a category? What is a family resemblance score? How do taxonomic and goal-derived categories differ?

7. For most of us, other people are the most important and interesting "objects" in our world. We say that each human being is unique, yet we constantly classify people. Is that good? Or bad? Or both? Why?

8. Can you recall specific instances in which your actions were inconsistent with your personality?

9. When we meet up with an object we have never encountered before, how do we decide what it is (to which class it belongs)? The prototype and feature-frequency models both attempt to answer this question. In your judgment, does either succeed?

10. Why do you think approximately half of the people used a theory-based rule to classify people into suburbs but no one seemed to use a theory-based rule to classify schematic faces?

CogLab The following experiments that relate to this chapter can be found at: http://coglab. wadsworth.com. Answer the questions in the CogLab Student Manual as required by your teacher for these experiments.

Prototypes

Categorical Perception: Identification

KEY TERMS

The page number in parentheses refers to where the term is discussed in the chapter.

attribute learning (188)

average distance rule (202)

basic-level category (190)

concept identification (187)

conjunctive rule (187)

continuous dimension (188)

disjunctive rule (187)

exemplar model (204)

family resemblance (197)

feature frequency rule (202)

goal-derived category (198)

hierarchically organized (188)

ideal (199)

logical rule (187)

nearest-neighbor rule (201)

prototype (193)

prototype rule (202)

rule learning (188)

semantic dementia (194)

stereotype (199)

subordinate category (190)

superordinate category (190)

typicality (189)

RECOMMENDED READING

Ashby and Maddox (2005), Medin and Rips (2005), and Rips (2001) provide overviews of the theoretical literature on categorization. Other reviews focus on different kinds of concepts (Medin, Lynch, & Solomon, 2000) and evolutionary advantages of different categorization strategies (Klein, Cosmides, Tooby, & Chance, 2002). Sloutsky (2003) discusses the role of similarity in the development of categorization. Mandler and Bauer (1988) argue that basic-level categories are not as developmentally important as Rosch's theory implies. Rogers and McClelland's (2004) book *Semantic Cognition: A Parallel Distributed Processing Approach* describes their neural network model. Other work on how semantic deficits influence categorization is described by Caramazza and Mahon (2003). The work of Ross (1996) focuses on how our use of examples influences our classification of them. Labeling categories, such as "chairs," can focus attention on the category rather than on the objects within the category (Lupyan, 2008). Fiske (1998) discusses the role of stereotyping in an extensive chapter on social categorization. Widinger (Widinger & Clark, 2000; Widiger & Trull, 1991) examines the role of categorization in clinical assessment. As implied by its title, *The Big Book of Concepts* (Murphy, 2003) presents a thorough overview of the categorization literature.

9

Semantic Organization

Organization and Recall
Recall of Hierarchical Information
Building Semantic Networks

Verification of Semantic Statements
The Hierarchical Network Model
The Feature Comparison Model
The Spreading Activation Model
IN THE NEWS 9.1 Study May Shed Light
   on Why False Memories Appear Real

Schema Theory
Bartlett's Schema Theory
Modern Schema Theory
Scripts: Representing Sequences of Events

The Perceptual Symbols Model
Semantic Verification
Autobiographical Memory
Resolution?

SUMMARY

STUDY QUESTIONS

COGLAB: *LEXICAL DECISION*

KEY TERMS

RECOMMENDED READING

A scientist must organize. One makes a science with facts in the same way that one makes a house with stones; but an accumulation of facts is no more a science than a pile of stones is a house.
—Henri Poincaré

The need to organize knowledge is universal—it applies as much to the arts and humanities as to the sciences. Imagine that you wrote every fact you ever learned on a separate card and someone shuffled all the cards and dropped them in a gigantic pile. Now imagine that someone asked you in which city the Declaration of Independence was signed and you had to retrieve the right card to answer the question. How would you find the card? Even worse, what if you had to write an essay on the Declaration of Independence? Because all the cards are mixed up, finding one card would provide no clues about the location of other cards on the same topic.

To retrieve related information from LTM (long-term memory), we must be able to organize our memory. Much of this organization is semantic—that is, it is based on the meaning of the information. Ericsson (1985) has argued that people who have exceptional memories are not genetically endowed with a superior memory. Rather, they have acquired very efficient encoding and retrieval skills through extensive practice. A particularly effective way to organize information is to form hierarchies. An illustration of how reorganizing information into a hierarchy can be very effective is Ericsson and Polson's (1988) analysis of how a waiter could recall up to 20 complete dinner orders without taking notes. We see other examples of how hierarchical organization facilitates recall in the first section of this chapter.

A popular procedure for studying the organization of semantic memory is to ask people to respond true or false to statements such as "A robin is a bird" or "A canary is a building." To answer the question "Is a robin a bird?" we have to consider the meaning of both *robin* and *bird*. We will see how the time needed to respond provides psychologists with a clue about the organization of semantic information in LTM. The second section of this chapter describes how psychologists have followed this approach to construct models of semantic memory. Two major classes of models are used. One model assumes that people compare the features of two categories to determine their relationship. For example, we could decide whether a robin is a bird by determining whether a robin possesses the features of a bird. This model is somewhat similar to the categorization models discussed in the previous chapter. The other model assumes that the relation between two categories is stored directly in memory in a **semantic network**, which consists of concepts joined to other concepts by links that specify the relation between them.

semantic network A theory proposing that semantic information is organized in long-term memory by linking concepts to related concepts

spreading activation A theoretical construct proposing that activation spreads from a concept in a semantic network to activate related concepts

The third section of this chapter illustrates how semantic networks can be applied to tasks that require the integration of ideas. A key assumption here is the idea of spreading activation. **Spreading activation** means that the activation of a concept can lead to the activation of related concepts as the activation spreads along the paths of the network. The number and organization of paths are therefore important variables in determining how rapidly people can retrieve information from LTM.

The fourth section discusses organized clusters of knowledge called *schemata*. When I briefly reviewed the history of cognitive psychology in Chapter 1, I mentioned that behaviorism had less of a hold on psychology in Europe than it did in the United States. Two psychologists in particular, Bartlett in England and Piaget in Switzerland, rejected the idea that knowledge consists of learning many stimulus-response associations in favor of the idea that knowledge consists of larger, schematic structures. These ideas eventually spread to the United States and have greatly influenced much of the research in cognitive psychology. We begin examining schema theories in this chapter and then apply them to theories of comprehension, reasoning, and problem solving in later chapters.

ORGANIZATION AND RECALL

We have seen examples in the previous chapter of how some information is hierarchically organized and how a hierarchical organization can influence our performance on cognitive tasks such as classifying visual patterns. Hierarchical organization can also influence performance by facilitating the recall of semantic information.

Recall of Hierarchical Information

One advantage of a well-organized memory is that it helps us retrieve information in a systematic way. I began this chapter by asking you to imagine that you had to retrieve information by searching a gigantic pile of cards. If the information on the cards was organized in some systematic way, this would be a manageable task. If the information was not systematically organized, the task would be very difficult, and your level of achievement would not be very impressive.

An experimental analog of this task was created to study the effects of hierarchical organization on recall (Bower, Clark, Winzenz, & Lesgold, 1969). The material consisted of conceptual hierarchies of words such as the one shown in Figure 9.1. Participants in the experiment saw four different hierarchies, each containing 28 words. One group of subjects, in the "organized" condition, studied the four hierarchies for approximately 1 minute each. They then tried to recall all 112 words in whatever order they wished. The study-and-recall trial was repeated three more times. The upper curve in Figure 9.2 shows how well this group performed—they recalled 73 words after the first study trial and all 112 words after three study trials.

Another group of subjects, in the "random" condition, saw the same 112 words inserted randomly in the four hierarchies. For example, if the four hierarchies consisted of plants, instruments, body parts, and minerals, each set of 28 words would contain words from all four hierarchies inserted randomly into a spatial tree like the one shown in Figure 9.1. The high level of performance of subjects in the organized condition is particularly impressive when compared with performance in the random condition. After four study trials

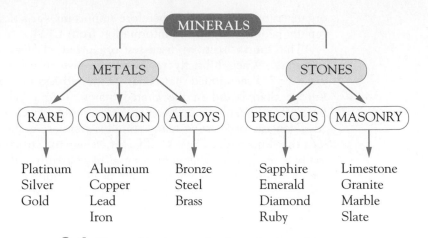

FIGURE **9.1** Hierarchical organization of minerals

Source: From "Organizational factors in memory," by G. H. Bower, 1970, *Cognitive Psychology, 1,* 18–46. Copyright 1970 by Academic Press, Inc. Reprinted by permission of Elsevier Science.

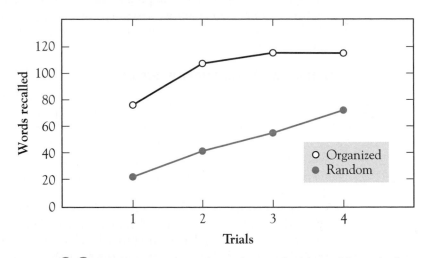

FIGURE **9.2** Average number of words recalled by subjects in "organized" and "random" conditions

Source: From "Organizational factors in memory," by G. H. Bower, 1970, *Cognitive Psychology, 1,* 18–46. Copyright 1970 by Academic Press, Inc. Reprinted by permission of Elsevier Science.

the random group was still recalling fewer words than the organized group recalled on the very first trial (see Figure 9.2).

Of course, the effects of organization are not limited to hierarchical organization. In another experiment Bower and colleagues (1969) presented people with associated words linked together. For example, the words *bread, mouse,* and *yellow* were linked to *cheese*; the words *cat* and *trap* were linked to *mouse*; and *sun* and *butterfly* were linked to *yellow*. When the associated words were linked together, people recalled many more words than when the same words were randomly linked together (for example, when *cat* and *bread* were linked to *yellow*). Semantic organization of the material improved recall, even though the organization did not consist of a hierarchy. The difference between the organized and random conditions was more striking for hierarchical organization, however, suggesting that hierarchical organization is particularly effective.

Hierarchical organization can also help people recall numerical information from STM as demonstrated by testing a single subject over a 1-year period (Chase & Ericsson, 1979). The subject began with a typical memory span of 7 digits, but after 1 year of practice, he could recall a string of 70 digits. Pauses in his recall indicated that he organized the digits into groups of three or four and never formed groups larger than five digits. Because the subject was a long-distance runner, he initially tried to encode many of the groups as running times. For example, he encoded 3492 as 3.492, a near-world-record time for running a mile. He also showed evidence of using hierarchical organization—he combined digits into larger groups that usually consisted of three smaller groups. After recalling the first three groups of four digits each, he would pause longer before recalling the next three groups of four digits each. One interesting finding is that the subject's ability to recall groups of digits didn't generalize to letters. When he was tested on recalling letters, his memory span immediately fell back to about six consonants.

Building Semantic Networks

The finding that organization aids recall raises the issue of how to teach people to improve their recall by using effective organizational strategies. One way to organize information is to construct a semantic network. Semantic networks show how concepts are related to each other. Networks are typically represented by diagrams in which the concepts are called **nodes** and the lines showing the relationship between two concepts are called **links**.

Figure 9.1, showing the hierarchical organization of minerals, is an example of a semantic network in which the links have not been labeled. The links in this diagram show only a single relation—that one mineral is a type of another mineral, which represents a larger category. Thus, bronze is a type of alloy, alloys are a type of metal, and metals are a type of mineral. This is a good start, but most knowledge is too complex to be represented by a single relation.

Figure 9.3 shows several different kinds of relations among concepts. Notice that this information is also hierarchical. There are two kinds of hierarchical relations, *part* (indicated by a "p") and *type* (indicated by a "t"). *Part* indicates that a concept in a lower node is part of a concept in a higher node. The discussion of wounds is divided into two parts: the types of wounds and the process of healing. *Type* indicates that a concept in a lower node is an example of a category in a higher node. Open and closed wounds are examples of different types of wounds. This categorical relation is the same one that relates the mineral concepts in Figure 9.1.

In addition, the information on wounds contains two nonhierarchical relations: *characteristics* (indicated by a "c") and *leads to* (represented by

nodes The format for representing concepts in a semantic network

links The format for representing relations in a semantic network

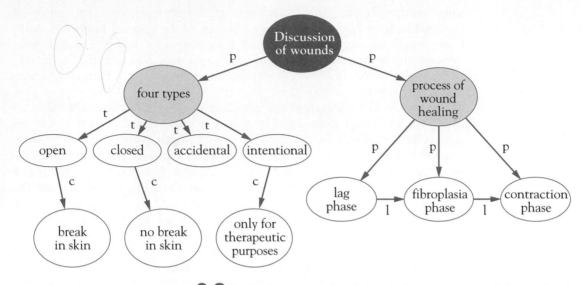

FIGURE **9.3** Part of a semantic network that represents information in a nursing text

Source: From "Evaluation of a hierarchical mapping technique as an aid to prose processing," by C. D. Holley, D. F. Dansereau, B. A. McDonald, J. C. Garland, & K. W. Collins, 1979, *Contemporary Educational Psychology, 4,* 227–237. Copyright 1979 by Academic Press, Inc.

an "l"). *Characteristics* are the features or properties of a concept. A characteristic of an open wound is that there is a break in the skin. The relation *leads to* specifies that one concept leads to or causes another concept. This relation is particularly useful for describing sequential processes, such as the three phases of healing.

The effectiveness of semantic networks has been extensively investigated at Texas Christian University. In a study described by Holley and Dansereau (1984), students received training on constructing semantic networks for material in their regular courses. These students and a control group of students then studied and were later tested on a 3000-word passage from a basic science textbook. Students who constructed semantic networks of this material did significantly better than the control group on short-answer and essay questions but did not do significantly better on multiple-choice questions.

This finding is consistent with the results mentioned at the end of Chapter 6 on transfer-appropriate processing. As you may recall, students who expected open questions did better on these questions than students who expected multiple-choice questions. Students who expected open questions apparently placed more emphasis on organizing their knowledge. Constructing semantic networks is a good method for organizing knowledge, as indicated by the resulting higher test scores on the open questions in the essay and short-answer tests.

To make the construction of semantic networks an effective learning strategy, we need more data on when they are effective, and we need good software to allow us to construct very large networks. The first of these needs is being addressed by continued research that forms the basis for the following guidelines (O'Donnell, Dansereau, & Hall, 2002):

- Begin with content that is extremely familiar to students so that they do not need to search for appropriate information.
- Use a number of well-constructed networks as initial examples.
- Include a discussion of the different types of links and the nature of the relationships among ideas.
- Ensure that students can recognize the corresponding relationships between information in the text and information in the networks.

The second need, effective computer software, allows the construction of very large networks that would be impractical on paper. An example is the SemNet® software, which allows users to construct very large semantic networks as a means of learning about and organizing their knowledge of a domain (Fisher, 2000). The largest network constructed to date consists of approximately 2500 concepts from an introductory biology course. The SemNet program allows the user to view a small piece of the network on the computer screen. If I wanted to review information about the nucleus of a cell, I would type *nucleus* to see its relation to other concepts. The computer would then display the part of the network in which *nucleus* was the central concept linked to related concepts.

VERIFICATION OF SEMANTIC STATEMENTS

feature comparison model A model proposing that items are categorized by matching the item's features to category features

hierarchical network model A model proposing that items are categorized by using the hierarchical relations specified in a semantic network

The first part of this chapter emphasized how effective organization, particularly hierarchical organization, increased the *amount* of information that we can retrieve from LTM. Hierarchical organization also influences the *time* required to retrieve information. A popular procedure for studying the organization of semantic knowledge is to ask people to quickly verify semantic statements. The experimenter might present a statement such as "A bird is an animal" and ask the subject to respond true or false as quickly as possible. The time it takes to respond to different kinds of statements provides some clues about the organization of semantic memory.

A number of theories have been proposed to account for these findings. We will begin by contrasting the hierarchical network model of Collins and Quillian (1969, 1970) and the feature comparison model of E. E. Smith, Shoben, and Rips (1974). The distinction between the two models can be summarized briefly with the aid of the diagram in Figure 9.4. The **feature comparison model** assumes that instances are classified by comparing the features, or attributes, of the two nouns representing the member and the category. To verify that a robin is a bird, a person would compare the features of *robin* with the features of *bird*. In contrast, the **hierarchical network model** assumes that category information is stored directly in memory by means of associations. The right half of Figure 9.4 shows that *robin* is associated with *bird* and *bird* is associated with *animal*. To make predictions, both theories require more specific assumptions. We will now examine the strengths and weaknesses of these assumptions.

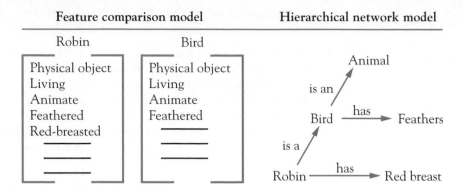

FIGURE **9.4** Distinction between the feature comparison model and the hierarchical network model

Source: From "Theories of semantic memory," by E. E. Smith, 1978, in *Handbook of Learning and Cognitive Processes*. Vol. 6, edited by W. K. Estes. Copyright 1978 by Lawrence Erlbaum Associates, Inc. Reprinted by permission.

The Hierarchical Network Model

Figure 9.5 shows how information is stored in the hierarchical network model. Each word in the network is stored with pointers (arrows) showing how it is related to other words in the network. By following the pointers, we know that *ostrich* and *canary* are examples of birds and that *bird* and *fish* are examples of animals. We also know that a canary, an ostrich, a shark, and a salmon are animals because the pointers connect these instances with the superordinate category *animal*.

The pointers also show how features are stored at different levels in the hierarchy. Features that are true of all animals—such as eating and breathing—are stored at the highest level. Features that apply to basic-level categories—such as that birds have wings, can fly, and have feathers—are stored at an intermediate level. Properties stored at the lowest level are true for that particular member but not for all members of the category. It is at this level that we know that a canary is yellow and can sing.

One advantage of this kind of network is that it provides an economical way to store information because the information does not have to be repeated at each of the three levels. It isn't necessary to specify that eating and breathing are features of birds, fish, canaries, ostriches, sharks, and salmon, because the network tells us that all are examples of *animals*, which eat and breathe. This economy of storage comes at a cost, however: retrieval of the fact that a canary eats requires two inferences—first, that a canary is a bird and, second, that a bird is an animal. In other words, it is necessary to go to the appropriate level in the hierarchy before retrieving the features stored at that level.

Although the network model was originally developed as an efficient means of storing information in a computer, it provides a number of interesting predictions if we use it as a model of human memory. Collins and Quillian (1969)

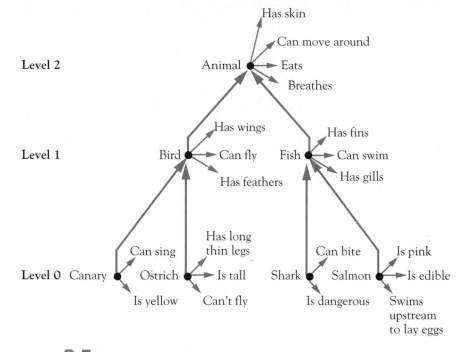

FIGURE **9.5** Example of a hierarchically organized memory structure

Source: From "Retrieval time From semantic memory," by A. M. Collins & M. R. Quillian, 1969, *Journal of Verbal Learning and Verbal Behavior, 8,* 240–248. Copyright 1969 by Academic Press, Inc. Reprinted by permission of Elsevier Science.

in fact used the model for that purpose by making two primary assumptions—that it takes time to move from one level in the hierarchy to another and that additional time is required if it is necessary to retrieve the features stored at one of the levels. Collins and Quillian tested the model by asking people to respond true or false as quickly as they could to sentences like "An elm is a plant" or "A spruce has branches." The first sentence is an example of a question about set relations—it asks whether one category is a member of another. The second question is a question about properties—it asks about the features of a category member.

The average reaction times to six kinds of true sentences are shown in Figure 9.6. A specific example illustrates the different points on the graph. The three lower points—the response times to questions about set relations—support the prediction that it takes time to move between levels in the network. To verify that "A canary is a canary" requires no change in level; "A canary is a bird" requires a one-level change; and "A canary is an animal" requires a two-level change. The graph shows that response times depend on the number of changes.

The upper three points show that it takes longer to respond to property questions. This finding is consistent with the assumption that response time should increase if it is necessary to retrieve the features stored at one of the

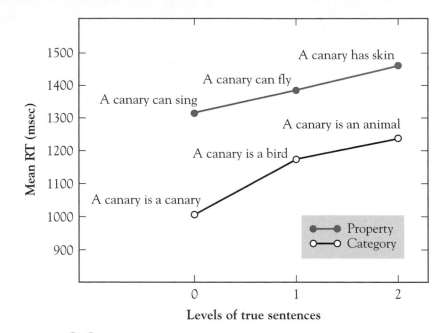

FIGURE **9.6** Reaction time (RT) to verify statements about properties and category membership

Source: From "Retrieval time from semantic memory," by A. M. Collins & M. R. Quillian, 1969, *Journal of Verbal Learning and Verbal Behavior, 8,* 240–248. Copyright 1969 by Academic Press, Inc. Reprinted by permission of Elsevier Science.

levels in the hierarchy. Furthermore, the level in the network where the properties are stored influences response times. The network model proposes that information about singing is stored at the lowest level, information about flying is stored at the intermediate level, and information about skin is stored at the highest level. The data support this assumption and suggest that this is how property information is stored in human memory.

Another interesting prediction based on the network model concerns facilitating retrieval from memory (Collins & Quillian, 1970). Facilitation occurs when the retrieval of information is made easier because the previous question required retrieval of similar information. For example, it should be easier to verify a property of a canary if the previous question was also about a canary. The network model, however, allows us to make a more specific prediction. Collins and Quillian proposed that the degree of facilitation should depend on whether one follows the same path in the network to answer the two questions. This concept can be illustrated by considering whether it would be easier to verify that "A canary is a bird" after "A canary can fly" or after "A canary can sing." The answer isn't intuitively obvious, but the network model predicts that "A canary can fly" should cause greater facilitation because the property *fly* is stored at the bird level, and *sing* is stored at the canary level. The same path is followed only when both questions require retrieving information from the bird level. The data were quite supportive of the prediction that the extent of semantic facilitation depends on using the same path as the previous question (Collins & Quillian, 1970).

The successful predictions of the reaction-time data in Figure 9.6 and the predictions about semantic facilitation are impressive accomplishments of the network model. There are two findings, however, that the model does not account for without additional assumptions. The first is that it is possible to find instances in which verification time is not a function of levels in the hierarchy. For example, it takes longer to verify that a chimpanzee is a primate than that a chimpanzee is an animal. The network model should predict the opposite because *primate*, like *bird* and *fish*, is at a lower level in the hierarchy than *animal*. The second finding is that the network model does not account for the **typicality effect**—the fact that more typical members of categories are easier to classify than less typical ones. It is easier to verify that a canary is a bird than that an ostrich is a bird. However, because both are one level from *bird*, as is illustrated in Figure 9.5, the model does not predict the differences in response time. The feature comparison model attempted to correct these deficiencies by offering an alternative formulation.

typicality effect The finding that the more typical members of a category are classified more quickly than the less typical category members

The Feature Comparison Model

The feature comparison model proposed by E. E. Smith and colleagues (1974) seeks to account for classification times in somewhat the same way that the prototype model accounts for classifications. This model assumes that the meaning of words can be represented in memory by a list of features and that classifications are made by comparing features rather than by examining links in a network (see Figure 9.4). The features can be used to define categories, but they vary in the extent to which they are associated with a category. Smith and colleagues considered the most essential features to be defining features and the remainder to be characteristic features. **Defining features** are features that an entity must have to be a member of a category, whereas **characteristic features** are usually possessed by category members but are not necessary. The defining features for birds might include being alive and having feathers and wings; the characteristic features might include being able to fly and being within a certain size range. Because the defining features are more essential, they should play a more important role in how people make classifications.

defining feature A feature that is necessary to be a member of that category

characteristic feature A feature that is usually present in members of that category, but is not necessary

The feature comparison model has two stages. The first stage compares all the features of two concepts to determine how similar one concept is to the other. For example, to determine whether a robin is a bird, we would compare the features of *robin* with the features of *bird*. If the comparison reveals that the two concepts are either very similar or very dissimilar, we can respond true or false immediately. The second stage is necessary when the degree of similarity is between the two extremes. The answer isn't obvious in this case, so the model proposes that we examine only the defining features to determine whether the example has the necessary features of the category. The distinction between the two stages corresponds to our experience that sometimes we make classifications very quickly on the basis of the close similarity between two concepts, and sometimes we make classifications more slowly after we evaluate the criteria for category membership.

Examples that are similar to the concept should usually be classified immediately, without consideration of their defining features during the second stage. The probability that the second stage is necessary increases as the similarity between the category concept and the example decreases. The model therefore predicts that the more typical members of a category (such as *robin, sparrow, blue jay*) should be classified more rapidly than the less typical members (*chicken, goose, duck*) because evaluating the defining features during the second stage slows the classification. E. E. Smith and colleagues (1974) found that people could in fact classify instances that are typical of the category faster than they could classify instances that are not typical of the category.

The reverse argument applies to false statements such as "A bat is a bird." High similarity between a negative example and a category concept makes it more difficult to reject the example. Because a bat and a bird share many features, it is difficult to reach a conclusion during the initial feature comparison stage. This increases the probability that a person will evaluate the defining features during the second stage. In contrast, two dissimilar noun pairs ("A pencil is a bird") share so few features that an immediate decision can be made during the first stage. The feature comparison model, unlike the hierarchical network model, provides an explanation of why some false statements are evaluated more quickly than others.

Another advantage of the feature comparison model is that, unlike the network model, it can account for the reversal of the category-size effect. The **category-size effect** refers to the fact that people are usually able to classify a member into a smaller category faster than into a larger category—for example, verifying that a collie is a dog more quickly than that a collie is an animal. The network model is consistent with the category-size effect because the smaller category (*dog*) requires fewer inferences than the larger category (*animal*). Because the smaller category is a part of the larger category, it appears lower in the hierarchy and will therefore be reached sooner. Some cases, however, violate the category-size effect because the classification times are faster for the larger category. For example, people were able to verify more quickly that Scotch is a drink than that Scotch is a liquor, even though *drink* is a larger category than *liquor*.

The feature comparison model can account for violations of the category-size effect because its predictions are based on similarity rather than category size. The reason it is usually easier to verify that an example belongs to a smaller category is that the similarity between the example and one's concept of the smaller category is greater than the similarity between the example and the larger category. However, there are exceptions to this rule. Sometimes—as E. E. Smith and coworkers showed—there is a greater similarity between the example and a larger category. The feature comparison model predicts that in this case people should be able to classify into the larger category more quickly than into the smaller category. Experimental results support this prediction (E. E. Smith et al., 1974). Although the feature comparison model accounts for both typicality and category-size effects, the model has

category-size effect The finding that members of smaller categories are classified more quickly than members of larger categories

some weaknesses. Let's now listen to what the critics have to say about its limitations.

Limitations of the feature comparison model

One of the problems with the feature comparison model, as one of its developers pointed out (E. E. Smith, 1978), is that it relies on similarity ratings to make most of its predictions. It's not very surprising that, if people rate an example as highly similar to their concept of a category, they will be fast to verify that it belongs to that category.

Presumably, these similarity judgments are made by comparing the features of the example and the category concept, but there is little direct support for this assumption. The predictions made by the feature comparison model are therefore rather weak predictions. Its principal asset is that the major alternative—the network model—does not make even these predictions unless it uses so many additional assumptions that it can predict almost anything.

A second criticism of the feature comparison model is its proposal that all our classifications require computations—that we use the features of concepts to compute their degree of similarity. Computation is an essential part of the categorization models discussed in the previous chapter, where the emphasis was on classifying novel patterns. But once we have learned to associate examples with categories, is it still necessary to use features to compare the similarity of two concepts? Couldn't we use the associations among concepts, as suggested by the proponents of the network model (Collins & Loftus, 1975)? If we have learned that a robin is a bird, it would seem easier to use this information directly rather than computing the similarity between *robin* and *bird*. What information is stored directly in memory and what is computed is a very important issue that is discussed by E. E. Smith (1978). The assumption that all verifications require computing similarity seems counterintuitive.

A third criticism of the feature comparison model is the argument against necessary, or defining, features (Collins & Loftus, 1975; McCloskey & Glucksberg, 1979; Rosch & Mervis, 1975). The feature comparison model avoids this criticism to some extent by proposing that features are more or less defining and that only the more defining features are evaluated during the second stage. This implies, however, that people can identify the more defining features of categories, and we have little direct support for this assumption. Rosch and Mervis's (1975) results in fact suggest the opposite—that the structure of categories is based not on defining features possessed by all members of the category but on a large number of features that are true of only some category members.

Although it may be difficult to specify defining features for some concepts, such as *fruit*, the distinction between characteristic and defining features may be helpful for explaining how children learn other concepts, such as *robber*. Consider the following two descriptions:

> This smelly, mean old man with a gun in his pocket came to your house one day and took your color television set because your parents didn't

want it anymore and told him that he could have it. Could he be a robber?

This very friendly and cheerful woman came up to you and gave you a hug, but then she disconnected your toilet bowl and took it away without permission and never returned it. Could she be a robber?

The first description contains characteristic features of a robber, but not the defining features. The second description contains the defining features of a robber, but not the characteristic features. A study of children in kindergarten, second, and fourth grades found that children become more sensitive to defining features as they grow older (Keil & Batterman, 1984). They become more likely to correctly respond that the mean old man is not a robber, but the friendly, cheerful woman is a robber.

One interpretation of this finding is that characteristic features are more salient and directly observable than defining features (T. P. McNamara & D. L. Miller, 1989). Characteristic features such as *mean* and *gun* are observable, whereas defining features such as *taking without permission* are more conceptual. Young children initially emphasize the directly observable features and have to learn to shift their emphasis to the more conceptual features.

In conclusion, the feature comparison model has some advantages over the hierarchical network model, but it also has some limitations. It is more promising for those concepts that we believe have defining features (Malt, 1990) and for those situations in which we use features to make a decision (Keil & Batterman, 1984; T. P. McNamara & D. L. Miller, 1989). A compromise is that at different times we use either direct associations—links in a semantic network—or features to evaluate a concept. This flexibility is part of the theory discussed in the next section.

The Spreading Activation Model

The preceding discussion reflected both the strengths and weaknesses of the hierarchical network model and the feature comparison model. Each provided an explanation for some aspects of the data but could not explain other aspects. In an attempt to account for a greater number of findings than either of these two models, Collins and Loftus borrowed assumptions from each of the models to build a model that had greater flexibility.

spreading activation model A model that accounts for response times by formulating assumptions about how activation spreads in a semantic network

Their **spreading activation model** (Collins & Loftus, 1975) is representative of semantic network models in its emphasis on concepts joined together by links that show relationships between concepts. Figure 9.7 shows how a part of human memory can be represented in a network that is somewhat analogous to the neural networks that were discussed in Chapters 2 and 8. A change from the hierarchical network model is that the length of each link represents the degree of semantic relatedness between two concepts. Thus, the concept *red* is closely related to other colors and less closely related to red objects. Notice that the model can now account for the typicality effect because the links represent different degrees of semantic relatedness. The shorter links reveal that the more typical examples *car* and *bus* are more closely related to *vehicle* than are *ambulance* and *fire engine*.

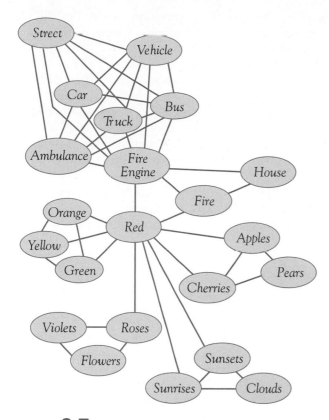

FIGURE **9.7** Example of a spreading activation model in which the length of each line (link) represents the degree of association between two concepts

Source: From "A spreading activation theory of semantic processing," by A. M. Collins & E. F. Loftus, 1975, *Psychological Review, 82,* 407–428. Copyright 1975 by the American Psychological Association. Reprinted by permission.

The spreading activation model assumes that, when a concept is processed, activation spreads out along the paths of a network, but its effectiveness is decreased as it travels outward. For example, presentation of the word red should strongly activate closely related concepts such as orange and fire and should cause less activation of concepts such as sunsets and roses. The model therefore predicts the typicality effect because more typical members will activate the superordinate category sooner than less typical members—for example, car and bus will activate vehicle sooner than fire engine or ambulance will.

The idea of activation spreading throughout a semantic network of interconnected concepts provides a clear picture of the semantic relations among concepts. It is easy to imagine activation decreasing in strength as it travels outward. The model also assumes that activation decreases over time or intervening activity. This assumption places a constraint on the amount of activation that can occur because the activation of a second concept will decrease the activation of the first concept.

Although the model provides a convenient metaphor, its success depends on how well it can account for experimental results. One such result is the effect of semantic priming. Recall that priming is the facilitation in the detection or recognition of a stimulus by using prior information. An example of priming can be found in the lexical decision task studied by Meyer and Schvaneveldt (1976), which required that people judge whether a string of letters formed a word. Some of the letters did (BUTTER), and some did not (NART). Each trial consisted of a pair of strings, and the second string was presented immediately after subjects made their decision about the first string. The most interesting results occurred when both strings were words. If the two words were semantically related, people were faster in verifying that the second string was a word than if the two words were unrelated. For example, people verified faster that the string BUTTER was a word when it was preceded by BREAD than when it was preceded by NURSE.

The spreading activation model can account for these results because it proposes that the presentation of a word activates related words. *BUTTER* will be activated by *BREAD* but will not be activated by *NURSE*. The activation of the word makes it easier to identify, resulting in faster response times.

One controversy regarding the spreading activation model (Ratcliff & McKoon, 1988) is whether activation spreads beyond a single node as predicted by the model. Although *BREAD* activates the word *BUTTER*, would it activate a word like *POPCORN* that is associated with *BUTTER*, but not with *BREAD*? According to the model, activation should spread from *BREAD* to *BUTTER* to *POPCORN*, but *POPCORN* should be less activated than *BUTTER* because activation decreases in strength as it spreads outward. Research supports the assumption that spreading activation facilitates identification of words that are two links away from the activated word, but the facilitation is weaker than for words directly linked to the activated word (T. P. McNamara, 1992).

Spreading activation also helps us explain how people can be extremely confident that they had heard a word that was never presented during an experiment (see "In the News" 9.1). After hearing a list of words that included *thread, pin, eye*, and *sewing*, they falsely recognized the word *needle*. The fascinating part of this study is the similarity of the brain activation between the primed word *needle* and the words they actually heard.

Limitations of the spreading activation model

An advantage of semantic network models is that they are extremely flexible. It is very easy to introduce many assumptions into a model to make it consistent with many kinds of data. For example, the spreading activation model also allows for the use of feature matching (as in the Feature Comparison model) to verify semantic relations. The price of this advantage, however, is that it is very hard to test the model. If a model becomes so flexible that it is consistent with almost any experimental finding, it loses its predictive power. A model has predictive power only if it predicts that certain events should not occur. One can then evaluate the model by determining which events do in fact occur.

The challenge for the developers of semantic network models is not only to take advantage of their flexibility but also to place some constraints on the models to make some interesting predictions. When a network model fails to make a correct prediction, the developers usually create additional assumptions to give the model greater flexibility. Consequently, the revised model usually succeeds where the original failed, but many psychologists find the revision less satisfactory. Collins and Loftus's (1975) revision of the hierarchical network model corrected the limitations of the former but sacrificed the precise predictions that made the hierarchical network model one of the more interesting semantic network theories.

Thus, their model has considerable flexibility, but predictions can be made only with difficulty. Critics of the model (for example, McCloskey & Glucksberg, 1979; E. E. Smith, 1978) have argued that, with so many assumptions, it is not surprising that the model accounts for many empirical findings. They find the model's main weaknesses to be both the number of assumptions made and the failure to make many clear-cut predictions based on it. In fact, the model was developed primarily to show how its assumptions are consistent with existing data rather than to make interesting new predictions.

IN THE NEWS 9.1

Study May Shed Light on Why False Memories Appear Real to People

False memories appear to come from the same place in the brain as real memories, but without critical sensory information, according to a neuroimaging study reported in the August 1996 issue of *Neuron*.

The study builds on earlier research by Rice University psychologists Henry Roediger, PhD, and Kathleen McDermott, PhD, reported in the July 1995 issue of the *Journal of Experimental Psychology: Learning, Memory and Cognition* (JEPLMC).

They found high levels of false recall and false recognition of words from previously studied word lists.

Roediger, now at Washington University, then teamed up with Harvard neuroscientist Daniel Schacter, PhD, and others to look at what the brain is doing during false recall. For the *Neuron* study, they used a similar word-list paradigm as in the JEPLMC experiment and added positron-emission tomography (PET) to measure brain activity during recall.

To measure true memories, they asked a group of 12 volunteers to remember a standard list of words read to them. They then heard another list of words and had to identify which words were on the first list. The researchers used PET to record what was happening in the brain during the memory phase.

To measure false memories, they did the same experiment but used word lists that prompt memories as established in Roediger's first study to prompt many false memories. For example, participants had to remember a list that included the words thread, pin, eye, and sewing. In the recall list they heard the word needle, which is so similar to the other words that it prompts false recognition.

PET scans taken while people tried to remember which words were on the lists revealed that an area in the hippocampus is active when people remembered words that truly were on a list and when they remembered words that hadn't been on a list. Indeed, the scans were virtually identical, said Roediger.

The difference showed up in another area of the brain—the left temporal parietal area—which processes speech and sounds. This makes sense because the true memory not only activated the word but also the sensory memory of hearing the word. Because the falsely recognized word was never actually heard, no such sensory information is activated.

This study adds to the evidence that it's easy to have a false recollection, said Roediger. But there's no indication that the visible neural difference between the two types of memory would be a lasting one. Sensory information attached to a real memory might fade, making it indistinguishable from a false memory.

What he finds most compelling is how similar the two memories are. "There's similar activation when an event didn't actually happen," he said. "That might be part of the reason why false memories seem so compelling and real."

Source: From "Study may shed light on why false memories appear real to people," appearing in the *APA Monitor*, August 1996. Copyright 1996 by the American Psychological Association. Reprinted by permission.

However, other theorists used the spreading activation theory to make interesting new predictions. Imagine that you learned three facts about someone named Marty: (1) Marty broke the bottle, (2) Marty didn't delay the trip, and (3) Marty cooked spaghetti. Later you had to quickly respond "yes" (Mary cooked spaghetti) or "no" (Marty played tennis) to a test sentence depending on whether you previously learned the fact. Anderson (1976) successfully predicted that learning more facts about a person would increase the time to verify any one of those facts. The basis for his prediction is that (1) each fact about a person is linked to that person in a semantic network and (2) spreading activation is divided among the links. Increasing the number of links therefore decreases the amount of spreading activation along each link, increasing the time it takes to verify the connection between the person and the fact.

Now imagine that instead you had learned that (1) Marty broke the bottle, (2) Marty didn't delay the trip, and (3) Marty christened the ship. Do you see how these three facts can be integrated around a common theme? The theme is that the ship launching was on schedule because the bottle broke during the christening. Reder and Anderson (1980) proposed that, in this case, the three facts are integrated around a subnode in the semantic network, allowing for the quick verification of any of the facts. The subnode creates a cluster of knowledge that facilitates retrieval. Specifying the organization of such clusters is the objective of schema theory.

SCHEMA THEORY

Semantic networks provide a convenient way of organizing knowledge, but the emphasis is on showing how two nodes are related, and not on showing how ideas are grouped together to form larger clusters of knowledge. The advantage of the subnode model is that it offers a way of forming larger clusters by grouping related ideas around subnodes. However, there is a much older and more fully developed theory for representing clusters of knowledge, called *schema theory*. A **schema** is a cluster of knowledge that represents a general procedure, object, percept, event, sequence of events, or social situation (Thorndyke, 1984). Schema theory refers to a collection of models presuming that we encode such knowledge clusters into memory and use them to comprehend and store our experiences.

schema A general knowledge structure that provides a framework for organizing clusters of knowledge

I mentioned during the brief historical overview in Chapter 1 that during the time period that U.S. psychologists were predominantly influenced by stimulus-response (S-R) theories, psychologists such as Bartlett in England and Piaget in Switzerland were arguing that behavior is influenced by large units of knowledge organized into schema. We will begin by looking at Bartlett's theory, as analyzed by Brewer and Nakamura (1984).

Bartlett's Schema Theory

The schema theory that Bartlett (1932) developed in his book *Remembering* has inspired many of the modern versions of schema theory. He defined a schema as an active organization of past experiences in which the mind abstracts a general cognitive structure to represent many particular instances of those experiences. Bartlett's book consists of an elaboration of schema theory and shows its application to experimental results that he had collected on memory for figures, pictures, and stories.

A fundamental assumption of Bartlett's schema theory is that all new information interacts with old information represented in the schema. This is illustrated by how people who did not share the cultural history of Indians recalled an Indian story that they had read called "The War of the Ghosts." Bartlett noticed that many of the errors people made in recall were more regular and conventional than the original material, suggesting that the material had been integrated with their prior knowledge structures.

Brewer and Nakamura (1984) point out that a number of fundamental differences exist between schema theory and the S-R approach to psychology. These include:

1. *Atomistic versus molar.* An S-R theory is atomistic and is based on small units of knowledge (a single stimulus). A schema is a much larger unit, showing how knowledge is combined into clusters.
2. *Associationistic versus nonassociationistic.* An S-R theory requires learning an association between a stimulus and a response. A schema provides a knowledge structure for interpreting and encoding aspects of a particular experience.
3. *Particularistic versus generic.* An S-R theory shows the association between a particular stimulus and a particular response. A schema is more general and represents a variety of particular instances, much as a prototype represents the particular instances of a category.
4. *Passive versus active.* The association between a stimulus and a response can be learned in a passive manner. Invoking a schema is a more active process in which a particular experience is matched to the schema that best fits that experience.

Bartlett's ideas had little theoretical impact during his lifetime. In the United States behaviorism and S-R psychology had a strong hold on theory construction. In England his theory was taken more seriously, but by the early 1970s even his own students thought the theory a failure. A dramatic turn of events occurred in 1975 when a number of prominent U.S. cognitive scientists argued that schema are needed to organize knowledge in artificial intelligence, cognitive psychology, linguistics, and motor performance. These theorists adopted the major assumptions of Bartlett's theory but were more specific about what these knowledge structures looked like. We now examine some of the contributions of these later theories.

Modern Schema Theory

Two of the strongest advocates for the importance of schema were Minsky (1975) for representing knowledge in artificial intelligence programs and Rumelhart (1980) for representing knowledge in cognitive psychology. Rumelhart argued that schema are the building blocks of cognition. According to Rumelhart, a schema theory is basically a theory about how knowledge is represented and about how that representation facilitates the use of knowledge in various ways. Schema are used to interpret sensory data, retrieve information from memory, organize action, and solve problems.

One of the main contributions from artificial intelligence has been that programming languages allow more detailed specification of schema organization than was possible in earlier formulations (Thorndyke, 1984). Although Bartlett emphasized that schema were organized, he was not always very specific about what the organization was. We now think of a schema as providing a skeleton structure, which can be filled out with the detailed properties of a particular instance.

Let's take a familiar routine for students: registering for courses. What kinds of knowledge would you like to have before signing up for a course? You would probably want to know what the prerequisites are, whether it meets some requirement, how many credits you will receive, when and where it meets, and perhaps who is teaching it. An advantage of having schematic knowledge is that we can sometimes rely on **default knowledge**—that is, likely values that enable us to make intelligent guesses in the absence of specific knowledge. For example, most lecture courses offer the same number of credits, so you could probably guess how many credits you would receive for a cognitive psychology course before looking it up. You might also have guessed that the prerequisite was introductory psychology and might even have guessed the name of the instructor if the same person usually teaches this course.

I indicated at the beginning of this section that a schema can represent a variety of knowledge structures: procedures, objects, percepts, events, sequences of events, or social situations. We have schemas for solving different kinds of problems, recognizing faces, going shopping for groceries, and forming social stereotypes. Schemas are particularly important for text comprehension and problem solving, and we will later examine their influence on these cognitive skills. For now, we want to examine the organization of a particular type of schematic structure—our knowledge about a sequence of events. This will enable us to move from this rather abstract overview to see how cognitive psychologists do research on schematic organization.

Scripts: Representing Sequences of Events

Part of our schematic knowledge is organized around routine activities—for example, going to a restaurant, visiting a dentist, changing a flat tire, or riding a bus. Schank and Abelson (1977) used the term **script** to refer to what we know about the sequence of events that make up such routine activities. For example, a restaurant script would specify what we know about going to a restaurant. At a very general level, a restaurant script consists of standard roles, props or objects, conditions, and results. The conditions for going to a restaurant are that a customer is hungry and is able to pay for the meal. The props are tables and chairs, a menu, food, a bill, and money or a credit card. Supporting actors include waiters or waitresses and sometimes other personnel such as bartenders or busboys. The results are that the customer has less money but is no longer hungry, whereas the owner has more money. Between the times that a customer enters and leaves, there is a fairly standard sequence of events that includes selecting a table, looking at the menu, ordering the food, eating, and paying the bill.

Because the sequence of events is quite standard, a natural way of organizing scripts is according to the temporal order in which the events occur. Imagine that you have a flat tire and need to put on the spare. Your memory might consist of an organized sequence of actions, beginning with what you do first and ending with what you do last. Alternatively, your memory might be organized according to the centrality or importance of the events, in which you think of the more important events before you think of the less important events. Figure 9.8 shows these two contrasting memory structures.

default knowledge Knowledge about the most likely values for the attributes of a schema

script Knowledge about what occurs during routine activities

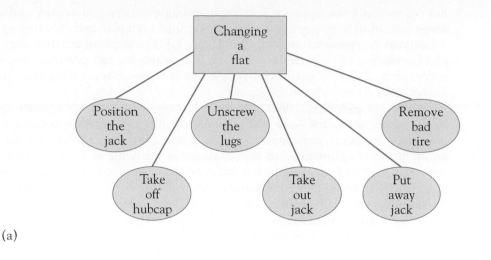

(a)

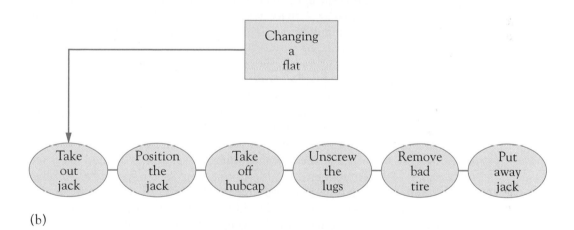

(b)

FIGURE **9.8** Two representations of a routine: (a) according to the centrality of component activities and (b) according to their sequential order

Source: From "Memory for routines," by J. A. Galambos & L. J. Rips, 1982, *Journal of Verbal Learning and Verbal Behavior, 21,* 260–281. Copyright 1982 by Academic Press. Reprinted by permission of Elsevier Science.

Figure 9.8a shows an organization in which some activities (such as removing the bad tire) are more central than others (such as putting away the jack). The more central activities are those that are particularly important in accomplishing the goal. If activities are organized according to their centrality, then people should be faster in verifying that the more central activities are included in a script. You may have noticed that the representation in Figure 9.8a is analogous to the semantic network proposed by Collins and Loftus (see Figure 9.7), but the shorter links represent a strong association between an activity and a script instead of a strong association between an exemplar and its category. An alternative representation, shown in Figure 9.11b, consists of activities organized according to their sequential order. If activities are reconstructed in the order in which they are performed, people should be faster in verifying that earlier activities are included in the script.

Galambos and Rips (1982) tested which theory was more appropriate by asking students to rank-order the activities of different scripts according to both their temporal order and their centrality. They then showed another group of subjects pairs of items that consisted of the name of a script (changing a flat) and an activity (take out jack). Students were asked to respond as quickly as possible whether the activity was included in the script. More central events were verified more quickly than less central events, but earlier events were not verified more quickly than later events. The results therefore supported the organization shown in Figure 9.8a.

However, this conclusion was challenged by Barsalou and Sewell (1985) who believed that the temporal order of events is very important in how people organize their experiences. They thought that the results would be different if they used a different experimental procedure. Instead of asking people to verify that a particular activity was part of a script, they gave people 20 seconds to name as many activities as they could that belonged to a particular script, such as doing the dishes. One group of subjects was asked "to generate actions from the most central action to the least central action," where centrality was defined in terms of the importance of the action. Another group of subjects was asked "to generate actions from the first action to the last action." The researchers hypothesized that if the events are temporally organized in memory, then it should be easier to name events in their temporal order than to name events in decreasing importance. Their findings supported this hypothesis. The average number of actions generated in 20 seconds was 8.17 when actions were listed in a temporal order and 6.10 when actions were listed according to importance. One interpretation of these conflicting findings is that both the centrality and the temporal order of events influence how we use our memory. The more central events provide the quickest access to a script, but the temporal order of events is useful for retrieving all the events that are in the script.

THE PERCEPTUAL SYMBOLS MODEL

Changing a flat tire is part of your knowledge about cars. Now let's look at your knowledge about a specific car. How would you respond if someone asked you to describe your own car? You would probably not mention that it has wheels, an engine, seats, and a steering wheel. This is also part of people's general (schematic) knowledge of cars. You would instead mention its specific features such as model, year, and color. But talking about your car might also evoke specific perceptual memories—the smell of a new car, the car's response when you turn the steering wheel, the clarity of the sound system, and the smoothness of the ride.

amodal Knowledge that is abstracted from sensory experiences

modal Knowledge is represented as sensory experiences

All the theories described thus far in this chapter are **amodal** because they do not directly represent the perceptual experiences encountered in learning about concepts. A dramatically different theoretical approach is the perceptual symbols system proposed by Barsalou (1999), in which perceptual experiences are directly stored in LTM. A perceptual symbols system is a **modal** approach because it stores sensory experiences such as audition, vision, taste, smell, and touch. Figure 9.9 shows the distinction between the previously discussed amodal approaches and the modal approach proposed by Barsalou (1999). Amodal systems represent perceptual information indirectly as a list of features or as a list of associations in a semantic network. In contrast, perceptual symbol systems retrieve information from LTM by reenacting or simulating perceptual experiences.

The strong neural basis of perceptual symbols reflects the important role that research by cognitive neuroscientists has played in shaping the model. The neural network model of semantic memory discussed in the previous chapter is one example. As shown in Figure 8.4, semantic concepts are represented by perceptual, motor, and linguistic information that is distributed across different areas of the brain. Behavioral data also support the perceptual symbols model. Let's look first at semantic verification tasks, which have provided a frequently used method for studying semantic memory.

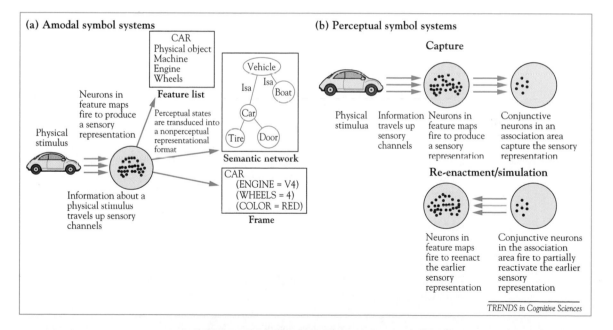

FIGURE **9.9** Representation of information in amodal symbol systems (a) and perceptual symbol systems (b)

Source: From "Grounding conceptual knowledge in modality-specific systems," by L. W. Barsalou, W. K. Simmons, A. K. Barbey, & C. D. Wilson, 2003, 7, 84–91 *Trends in Cognitive Sciences*.

Semantic Verification

A perceptual-based approach is helpful for explaining a number of semantic verification findings. You can participate in one of these tasks by judging whether the vertically aligned words in Table 9.1 are semantically related. Try to make your judgment for each of the pairs as quickly as you can. Zwaan and Yaxley (2003) proposed that if people use images to help them make the decision, the position of the words should influence response times. The results supported this prediction. When the vertical alignment of the words matched the alignment in our images (ATTIC above BASEMENT), students were significantly faster in verifying semantic relatedness than when the alignments mismatched (BASEMENT above ATTIC).

Another advantage of a modal theory is that it can account for slower response times when there is a shift from one modality to another. A study by Spence, Nicholls, and Driver (2000) required that participants quickly indicate whether a signal (either a light, a touch, or a tone) occurred on their left side or right side. They found that response times were slower when the previous signal was from a different modality than when it was from the same modality.

Pecher, Zeelenberg, and Barsalou (2003) therefore reasoned that if people simulate information, they should be slower when they have to shift modalities when verifying properties in a conceptual task. The task required the quick verification of properties that came from the six modalities shown in Table 9.2. People had to quickly respond "true" or "false" to statements such as a "BLENDER can be loud" and "CRANBERRIES can be tart." The statements shown in the first column of Table 9.2 are target items that were either preceded by statements from the same modality (column 2) or by statements from a different modality (column 3). The results confirmed the prediction that people would be slower in verifying properties when there was a shift in modality. People were slower, for example, in verifying that a "BLENDER can be loud" when it was preceded by "CRANBERRIES can be tart" then when it was preceded by "LEAVES can be rustling."

In a later study (van Dantzig, Pecher, Zeelenberg, & Barsalou, 2008), the investigators combined their conceptual verification task with the perceptual task used by Spence et al. (2000). Would the extra time required to switch modalities *within* a perceptual task or *within* a conceptual task also occur *between* a perceptual and a conceptual task? The perceptual symbols model suggests that it should take less time to verify a conceptual property when the statement was preceded by a perceptual judgment from the same modality.

TABLE **9.1**

Examples of Word Pairs from Zwaan and Yaxley's (2003) Semantic Relatedness Study

ATTIC	LAKE	SWAN	CANDLE	TAXI	NOSE
BASEMENT	BOAT	SINK	FLAME	PEACH	MOUTH

Source: "Spatial iconicity affects semantic relatedness judgments," by R. A. Zwaan & R. H. Yaxley, 2003, *Psychonomic Bulletin & Review*, 10, 954–958.

TABLE **9.2**

Examples of Modalities used in the Target and in the Preceding (Context) Trial

Modality	Target trial	Context trial	
		Same modality	Different modality
Audition	BLENDER-loud	LEAVES-rustling	CRANBERRIES-tart
Vision	BABY CLOTHES-pastel	HAIR-fair	TOAST-warm
Taste	CUCUMBER-bland	BUTTERMILK-sour	BIRD EGG-speckled
Smell	SOAP-perfumed	OLD BOOK-musty	TELEVISION-noisy
Touch	MARBLE-cool	PEANUT BUTTER-sticky	BED SPRINGS-squeaking
Motor	FAUCET-turned	ROCK-hurled	HIGHWAY SIGN-green

Source: "Verifying different-modality properties for concepts produces switching costs," by D. Pecher, R. Zeelenbreg, & L. W. Barsalou, 2003, *Psychological Science*, 14, 119–124.

The results supported the predictions. People were faster in verifying auditory (a bee buzzes), tactual (a coin is hard), and visual (an inner tube is black) statements after judging the location of a perceptual signal that was in the same modality as the conceptual statement.

Autobiographical Memory

autobiographical memory Memory about our personal experiences

A major assumption of the perceptual symbols model is that we reenact or simulate our experiences. This assumption would seem to be particularly relevant for **autobiographical memory**, which stores personal experiences. In fact, Rubin (2006) effectively argues that our autobiographical memories do not consist of abstract, homogenized information. Rather, they contain information from sensory, language, emotion, and other systems that process different kinds of information. Because, there are many memory systems that need to interact, memory becomes highly constructive, with the constructions guided by specific schemas associated with the different systems.

Autobiographical memory shares similarities with episodic memory discussed in Chapter 5. Like episodic memory, autobiographical memory has a context. Events in our lives occur at a particular place and time. However, Rubin proposes that there are also differences between the episodic tasks studied in the laboratory and the events that occur in our lives:

- Items in episodic memory usually do not tell a story. Our lives do.
- The retention interval for items in episodic memory is typically less than one hour. Autobiographical memories may last an entire lifetime.
- Autobiographical memories consist of many modalities. Laboratory tasks typically focus on a single modality.

- Episodic retrieval has minimal emotional involvement. Autobiographical retrieval may be emotional.

Research at Duke University has helped us better understand the neuropsychology of autobiographical memory. Figure 9.10 shows the major components of the brain that are involved in retrieval of our experiences. The prefrontal cortex (PFC) guides retrieval and monitors the feeling-of-rightness (FOR) regarding accuracy. Activation of visual imagery is prevalent in studies of autobiographical memory as revealed by greater activity in those areas of the brain that process visual images. Emotional memories are also prevalent as revealed by the greater activation of the amygdala.

So how do these different areas of the brain combine to aid retrieval? A group of Duke investigators answered this question by tracking the brain activity of 17 young adults as they retrieved autobiographical memories in response to 80 cue words (reported by Rubin, 2006). Participants indicated that they had retrieved a memory by pressing a button and then rated it for intensity of emotion and the extent to which they relived the experience.

Figure 9.11 shows when the maximum activity occurs for three brain areas shown in Figure 9.10. Maximum activity in the prefrontal cortex occurs at the time of the button press (0 sec) indicating the successful retrieval of a memory. Maximum activity in the hippocampus and amygdala occurred before the button press, suggesting that emotional content played an early role in retrieval before memories were well formed. Support for emotional content comes from the finding that activity in the amygdala correlated with the rated intensity of the emotion. In contrast, maximum activity in the visual cortex occurred after the button press and correlated with ratings of how much participants relived the experience.

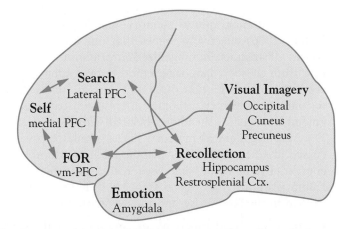

FIGURE **9.10** Brain regions involved in the retrieval of autobiographical memories

Source: From "Functional neuroimaging of autobiographical memory," by R. Cabeza & P. St. Jacques, 2007, *TRENDS in the Cognitive Sciences*, 11, 219–227.

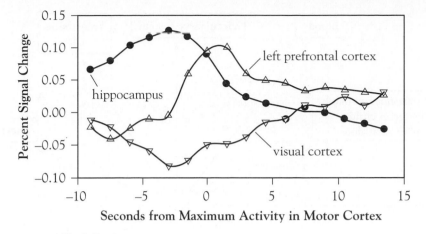

FIGURE **9.11** Temporal activation of brain regions during autobiographical retrieval

Source: From "The basic-systems model of episodic memory," by D. C. Rubin, 2006, *Perspectives in Psychological Science*, 1, 277–311.

Resolution?

This research on autobiographical memory is consistent with the perceptual-symbols view that our memories allow us to relive our experiences through simulations that have emotional and perceptual content. What does this mean for the many amodal theories that propose knowledge is stored more abstractly without perceptual and emotional content? A reasonable answer at this point in our understanding of memory is that some knowledge is stored in an amodal form and other knowledge is stored in a modal form that supports simulations.

For example, simulations would likely occur in temporal order. If you changed a flat tire by simulating how you did it previously, your recall would likely be based on the sequential representation in Figure 9.8b. However, the quicker verification of central events fits well with the assumptions of the spreading activation model in which more central events have shorter links (see Figure 9.8a).

In general, both amodal and modal theories have their merits. The perceptual symbols theory has been quite successful in predicting the outcome of semantic verification tasks that would be difficult to explain by amodal theories. However, it is not clear how perceptual simulations can be used to represent integrated knowledge that requires organizing hundreds of concepts. Organizing large bodies of knowledge is the strength of semantic network theories. As previously mentioned, students and faculty have used SemNet to construct semantic networks containing as many as 2500 concepts from an introductory biology course (Fisher et al., 1990).

The strength of the perceptual symbols theory for simulating particular cases and of semantic networks for organizing hundreds of cases can be combined in a hybrid system in which perceptual information is linked to concepts

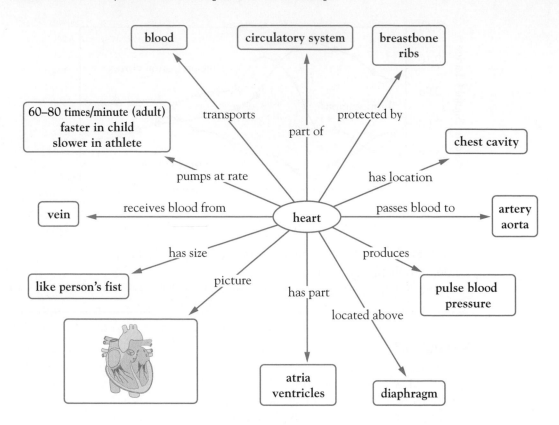

FIGURE **9.12** A semantic network with a linked picture

Source: From "Generating connections and learning in biology," by M. Gorodetsky & K. M. Fisher, 1996, in K. M. Fisher & M. R. Kibby (Eds.), *Knowledge acquisition, organization, and use in biology*, pp. 135–154. New York: Springer Verlag.

organized in a semantic network. Such a system is illustrated in Figure 9.12 in which a labeled diagram of a heart is one of the links in a semantic network (Gorodetsky & Fisher, 1996). Fisher (2000) provides other examples in which people have used SemNet to incorporate not only static pictures but also video and music into the network. This is not only a productive use of an educational tool, in my opinion, but a potential model of how human memory can represent both modal and amodal knowledge.

SUMMARY

Psychologists have studied semantic memory to learn how people use meaning to organize information in LTM. One effective way to organize material is to use hierarchical organization by partitioning a large category into smaller and smaller categories. Experiments have shown that people can learn hierarchical information quickly, but they have considerable difficulty learning the same information when it is presented randomly. Research on the learning of information in a text has found that creating a semantic network to represent the relations among concepts improves performance on essay and short-answer tests.

The hierarchical organization of categories influences the amount of time it takes to verify sentences about the members of categories. It usually takes less time to verify category membership at the basic level than at the superordinate level. For example, it is easier to verify that a canary is a bird than that a canary is an animal. The hierarchical network model predicts this result by assuming that semantic information is organized in a hierarchy and that it takes time to change levels in the hierarchy. The model also predicts that the time it takes to verify a property of an object will depend on the level in the hierarchy where the property is stored. This assumption implies that it should take longer to verify that a canary eats than that a canary can fly, because eating is stored at the animal level and flying is stored at the bird level. In contrast, the feature comparison model assumes that statements are verified by using features to compute the similarity of two concepts. When there is an intermediate amount of similarity, people must evaluate only the most necessary, or defining, features of the category. The feature comparison model correctly predicts that classification time depends more on similarity than on category size and also depends on whether the example is a typical member of its category. Critics of the feature comparison model question its reliance on ratings to make predictions, its failure to make direct use of learned associations in memory, and its somewhat artificial distinction between characteristic and defining features.

The hierarchical network model is an example of a semantic network model in which concepts are represented by nodes in a network and relations are represented by links joining the concepts. The spreading activation model was proposed to correct some limitations of the hierarchical network model. Its main assumption is that activation of a concept results in activation of related concepts spreading along the paths of the network. The typical increase in reaction time caused by increasing the number of unrelated facts can be avoided if the facts are well integrated.

The integration of knowledge into larger clusters is the primary assumption of schema theory. Emphasis on schematic structures began with the work of Bartlett and Piaget and started to have a major impact on cognitive science in the mid-1970s. In contrast to stimulus-response associations, schematic structures are molar, nonassociationistic, generic, and active. They provide a skeleton structure that can be filled out with the detailed properties of a particular instance, using default knowledge when information is missing. Scripts are one type of schema, consisting of sequences of events that make up routine activities. The temporal order of the events is useful for organizing recall, but the centrality of events determines how quickly people can access the script.

In contrast to the previous models, the perceptual symbols model assumes that verification of semantic statements occurs through mental simulations. Support for the model comes from findings that the time to judge whether two words are associated is faster if their vertical alignment is consistent with an image, and the time to verify properties is faster if two successive properties come from the same modality. Support also comes from brain imaging techniques that reveal autobiographical memory contains both sensory and emotional experiences. The model is successful in predicting judgments about individual events but perceptual simulations are difficult to organize into larger knowledge structures. Both amodal theories such as semantic networks and modal theories such as perceptual symbol systems therefore have different strengths.

STUDY QUESTIONS

Be prepared for some tough going in this chapter. Because much of it deals with alternative theories or models, the abstraction level is necessarily high. Consult the illustrations of specific examples early and often for visual aids.

1. What does semantic mean? Hierarchy?
2. What is the evidence that hierarchical organization allows one to recall more material and/or recall it faster? Are you impressed by the evidence?
3. Can you state the advantages and disadvantages of Collins and Quillian's network model?
4. Does the feature comparison model seem more useful to you? Or are you persuaded by its critics?
5. In what ways are the semantic network models more general than the two models already considered? Write your answer.
6. How does the spreading activation theory account for semantic priming and the typicality effect?

7. What do you make of the statement that "a model has predictive power only if it predicts that certain events should not occur. One can then evaluate the model by determining which events do in fact occur"?
8. Think of your memories that are (a) amodal, (b) modal. Are there any patterns that distinguish between the which ones are amodal and which ones are modal?
9. Are you convinced by the experiments supporting the perceptual symbols model or can you think of alternative explanations?
10. Think of an autobiographical memory of your own. Order the specific events according to their temporal order and their order of importance. How do you think each of these two characteristics would influence your recall?

CogLab   The following experiment that relates to this chapter can be found at: http://coglab. wadsworth.com. Answer the questions in the CogLab Student Manual as required by your teacher for this experiment.

Lexical Decision

KEY TERMS

The page number in parentheses refers to where the term is discussed in the chapter.

amodal (233)

autobiographical memory (235)

category-size effect (222)

characteristic features (221)

default knowledge (230)

defining features (221)

feature comparison model (217)

hierarchical network model (217)

links (215)

modal (233)

nodes (215)

schema (228)

script (230)

semantic network (212)

spreading activation (212)

spreading activation model (224)

typicality effect (221)

RECOMMENDED READING

The articles by Fisher (2000) and O'Donnell et al. (2002) are good overviews of the instructional uses of semantic networks. Chi and Ohlsson (2005) show how the growth and organization of knowledge can be represented in semantic networks. Chang (1986) evaluates alternative models of semantic memory. Ratcliff and McKoon (1988) and Neely and Keefe (1989) have each proposed alternative theories of priming to account for findings that are usually attributed to spreading activation. Hutchinson (2003) provides a detailed critique of alternative models of semantic priming. Discussions of the semantic feature approach to describe the meaning of concepts are provided by T. P. McNamara and D. L. Miller (1989) and Malt (1990). Markman and Dietrich (2000) argue that it is necessary to extend the classical view of representation to include perceptual simulations and Hesslow (2002) shows how simulations occur in the brain. Extensive evidence for perceptual simulations is discussed by Barsalou (2003). The organization of autobiographical memory continues to attract attention. S. J. Anderson and M. A. Conway (1993) report evidence for both centrality and temporal effects in autobiographical memory. Rubin (2006) provides an extensive overview of autobiographical memory from a perceptual systems perspective.

10

Language

Language comes so naturally to us that it is easy to forget what a strange and miraculous gift it is. We humans are fitted with a means of sharing our ideas, in all their unfathomable vastness.
—Steven Pinker (1999)

The discussion of semantic memory in the previous chapter emphasized associations among words. We are now ready to consider how words can be combined to form sentences. One possible theory is that this combination occurs by associations. We could argue that, just as *robin* is associated with *bird*, the words in a sentence can be associated with each other. The problem with this view of language is that there are so many ways words can be combined that we would have to learn an infinite number of associations to form sentences. An alternative theory is that we learn a **grammar**—a system of rules that is capable of producing sentences. Ideally, the rules of a grammar should generate all the sentences of a language without generating any strings of words that are not sentences.

This brings us to a definition of language. A **language** is a collection of symbols and rules for combining these symbols, which can be used to create an infinite variety of messages. This definition has three critical aspects. First, language is **symbolic**: We use spoken sounds and written words to represent and communicate about the world around us. The symbols are arbitrary—there is no built-in relation between the look or sound of the words and the objects they represent. Second, language is **generative**: A limited number of words can be combined in an endless variety of ways to generate an infinite number of sentences. Third, language is **structured**: By following grammatical rules, we can produce grammatical sentences.

Our goal as communicators is to express meaning as sound, but this does not occur in a single step. Instead, we can use an assembly line metaphor for constructing sentences from the modules that are shown in Figure 10.1 (Pinker, 1999). Notice that the speaker, represented at the bottom of the diagram, has beliefs and desires that she wishes to express through language. The listener, represented at the top of the diagram, listens to the sound patterns to understand the speaker. But for this to occur correctly, both the speaker and listener must be skilled at using the five modules shown in Figure 10.1. How we accomplish this is the topic of this chapter.

Let's begin with a specific example, shown in Figure 10.2. You have already learned in the previous two chapters about the usefulness of hierarchies so it may not surprise you that language is hierarchical. At the top of the hierarchy is a sentence that can be broken down into phrases based on the grammatical rules. The grammatical rules partition the sentence into a *noun phrase* ("The strangers") and a *verb phrase* ("talked to the players"). The phrases are composed of words, which can be partitioned into **morphemes**—the smallest units of meaning in a language. For spoken sentences, the morphemes can be further partitioned into *phonemes*—the basic sounds of a language.

The next section provides a brief overview of these three aspects of comprehending and producing sentences: grammar, meaning, and sound.

---

grammar A set of rules for producing correct sentences in a language

language A collection of symbols and rules for combining symbols, which can express an infinite variety of messages

symbolic The use of symbols, such as spoken or written words, to represent ideas

generative The capability to produce many different messages by combining symbols in different ways

structured The organization imposed on a language by its grammatical rules

morpheme The smallest unit of meaning in a language

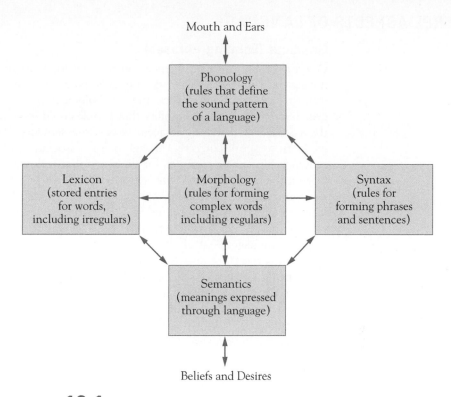

FIGURE **10.1** Components for producing sentences

Source: From *Words and rules: The ingredients of language*, by S. Pinker, p. 23. Copyright 1999 by Steven Pinker. Used by permission.

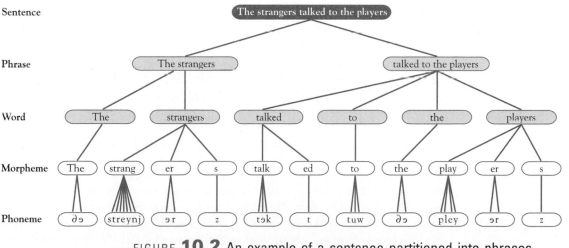

FIGURE **10.2** An example of a sentence partitioned into phrases, words, morphemes, and phonemes

Source: From *Child development: A topical approach*, by A. Clarke-Stewart, S. Friedman, & J. Koch, p. 417. Copyright 1985 by John Wiley & Sons. Reprinted by permission of John Wiley & Sons, Inc.

THREE ASPECTS OF LANGUAGE

Grammar (Forming Phrases)

One of the important influences on the development of cognitive psychology during the 1960s was the work of linguist Noam Chomsky. Prior to Chomsky's influence on psycholinguistics (the psychological study of language), psychologists had explored the possibility that people could learn a language by learning the associations between adjacent words in a sentence. According to this view, we learn to speak correctly through paired-associates learning—each word in a sentence serves as a stimulus for the word that follows it. In the sentence "The boy hit the ball," the word *the* is a stimulus for the word *boy*, and the word *boy* is a stimulus for the word *hit*. The speaker of a language would therefore have to learn which words could follow any other word in a sentence.

Chomsky (1957) argued that there are several problems with the association view of language. First of all, there are an infinite number of sentences in a language. It is therefore unreasonable to expect that people could learn a language by learning associations between all adjacent words. Consider simply a word like *the*. There are many, many words that could follow *the*, and a person might never learn all of them. When you consider all the possible words that can occur in a sentence and all the words that could possibly follow each word, you can see that this would be a very inefficient way to learn a language.

Another problem with the association view is that it does not account for the relations among nonadjacent words. For example, in the sentence "Anyone who says that is lying," the pronoun *anyone* is grammatically related to the verb *is lying*, but this relation is not revealed if we consider only the relation between adjacent words. The association view in fact ignores the hierarchical structure of sentences in proposing how people learn to speak grammatically correct sentences.

The hierarchical structure of sentences is revealed in the diagrams that you might have constructed in school. Many of us were taught how to break down a sentence into parts. We might begin by dividing a sentence into a noun phrase and a verb phrase, as shown in Figure 10.2, and then divide the noun phrase and verb phrase into smaller units that reveal the grammar of the sentence. After this brief overview, let's take a closer look at these grammatical rules and their relation to the hierarchy in Figure 10.2.

Meaning (Combining Words and Morphemes)

Although I have been emphasizing the grammatical aspects of language, a sentence that is grammatically correct isn't necessarily meaningful. Chomsky's famous example is the sentence "Colorless green ideas sleep furiously." Notice that this is a grammatically correct sentence even though it doesn't make sense. The opposite effect also occurs; we can make ourselves understood to a reasonable extent without producing grammatically correct sentences. I spent the summer before my junior year in college working in Germany with a student from Sweden. We managed to communicate with each other fairly well in German while violating many rules of German grammar.

This distinction between syntax (grammar) and semantics (meaning) is also evident in language disorders that are caused by brain damage (D. W. Carroll, 1986).

Broca's aphasia A language disorder attributed to damage in the frontal lobe of the brain

A disorder known as **Broca's aphasia** was discovered by and named after a French surgeon who noticed that some patients spoke in halting, ungrammatical speech following a stroke or accident (Broca, 1865). These patients were typically limited to expressing themselves by stringing together single words, as illustrated in the following excerpt from a patient who had come to the hospital for dental surgery:

> *Yes ... ah ... Monday er ... Dad and Peter H ..., and Dad ... er ... hospital ... and ah ... Wednesday ... Wednesday, nine o'clock ... and oh ... Thursday ... ten o'clock, ah doctors ... two ... an' doctors ... and er ... teeth ... yah.* (Goodglass & Geschwind, 1976, p. 408)

This inability to express grammatical relationships is typically found in individuals who have suffered damage to the frontal regions of the left hemisphere of the brain (an area called *Broca's area*, shown in Figure 10.3).

A few years after Broca's discovery, Carl Wernicke, another surgeon, discovered a different kind of aphasia (Wernicke, 1874), resulting from damage to the temporal lobe of the left hemisphere (see Figure 10.3). The speech associated with **Wernicke's aphasia** is more fluent and grammatical but doesn't convey much semantic content:

Wernicke's aphasia A language disorder attributed to damage in the temporal lobe of the brain

> *Well this is ... mother is away her working her work out o'here to get her better, but when she's looking in the other part. One their small tile into her time here. She's working another time because she's getting, too ...* (Goodglass & Geschwind, 1976, p. 410)

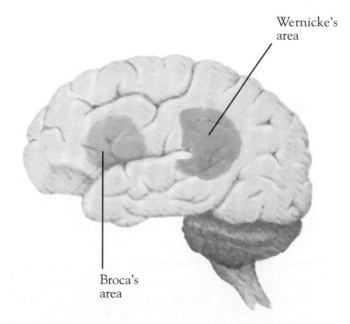

Wernicke's area

Broca's area

FIGURE **10.3** A view of the left hemisphere showing the location of two language centers in the brain

Source: From *Psychology: Themes and variations*, by Wayne Weiten. Copyright 1995, 1992, 1989 by Brooks/Cole Publishing Company, a division of Thomson Learning. Fax 800-730-2215.

This difficulty with the semantic content of words was confirmed by direct tests of semantic relations (Zurif, Caramazza, Meyerson, & Galvin, 1974). When given three words (such as *husband, mother, shark*) and asked to indicate which two were most similar, Wernicke's aphasics did poorly on the test, in contrast to Broca's aphasics.

More recent evidence based on neuroimaging studies indicates that understanding the meaning and grammar of sentences is more widely distributed throughout the brain than was indicated in the historic studies of Broca and Wernicke. Kaan and Swaab (2002) review this evidence and suggest that different parts of the brain are recruited for different aspects of syntactic processing. For example, they propose that the temporal lobe provides information about both semantic and syntactic information associated with incoming words. Although I have emphasized the distinction between semantic and syntactic processing, normal comprehension uses the meaning of words to indicate information about the grammatical form of the sentence. Later in the chapter we will see how the meaning of words provide clues about grammar.

We can represent the meaning of words by breaking them into morphemes, the smallest units of meaning. Morphemes include stem words, prefixes, and suffixes. The word *unfriendly* consists of the stem word *friend*, the prefix *un*, and the suffix *ly*. Notice that each of these morphemes produces a change in meaning. Adding *ly* to *friend* changes a noun into an adjective. Adding *un* to *friendly* changes the meaning of the adjective.

Other examples are shown in Figure 10.2. The word *strangers* consists of the stem word *strange* and the suffixes *er* and *s*. The first suffix (*er*) converts an adjective into a noun, and the second suffix (*s*) changes the noun from singular to plural. The verb *talked* contains the stem word *talk* and the suffix *ed*, which changes the tense of the verb. Each of these morphemes contributes to the meaning of the entire word.

One advantage of morphemes is that they allow us to generate novel words. A young child who did not know the plural of *stranger*, but knew that plurals are often formed by adding an *s* to the end of a noun, could generate the word *strangers*. If she did not know the past tense of *talk*, but knew that the past tense is often formed by adding *ed* to the end of a verb, she could generate the word *talked*. These rules do not always work (the plural of *deer* is not *deers* and the past tense of *speak* is not *speaked*), but children eventually learn the exceptions (Pinker, 1999).

Sound (Producing Phonemes)

The symbols of a language consist of both written and spoken words. However, as we saw in Chapter 4 when discussing acoustic coding in STM (short-term memory), written words are typically converted into spoken words through subvocalization. Thus, the acoustic aspects of language are important even when we encounter written words.

Before children can understand written sentences by learning to read, they must understand spoken sentences. The first step toward understanding spoken sentences is to be able to discriminate among the basic sounds (phonemes) of a language. This ability is excellent in newborns who are able to discriminate among phonemes in many different languages of the world (Kuhl, 1993). But infants also need to respond to similarity among sounds and to categorize sounds into the phonemic categories that make up their particular language. This presents the same pattern recognition problem that we discussed in Chapter 2, where we emphasized visual patterns. Just as there are variations in people's handwriting that can make visual pattern recognition difficult, there are variations in people's speech that can make speech recognition difficult.

We saw in Chapter 8 that a prototype theory of categorization argues that people classify patterns by comparing them to category prototypes. Work by Kuhl (1993) indicates that prototypes are important in speech recognition and that infants as young as 6 months old have formed prototypes to represent the phonemes in their language. Evidence for prototype formation comes from Kuhl's (1991) research demonstrating that the ability to discriminate sounds within a phonemic category (as if different people pronounced the long-*e* sound) is worse if the category prototype is involved in the discrimination. Adults and 6-month-old infants can more easily discriminate between two nonprototypical sounds than between a prototypical and a nonprototypical sound. Kuhl (1991) uses the metaphor of a "perceptual magnet" to describe the effect. The prototypic long-*e* sound draws similar long-*e* sounds closer to it, making these variations sound more like the prototype.

This magnet effect has several interesting implications. First, we might expect that infants become better at discriminating sounds as they grow older. Wrong—if the sounds belong to the same phonemic category. Forming prototypes of the various phonemes reduces discrimination within a phonemic category because variations of the prototype begin to sound more like the prototype. Notice, however, that this should make it easier to recognize the phonemes.

We might also expect that infants could better discriminate among familiar sounds in their own language than among unfamiliar sounds from a different language. Wrong again—if the sounds belong to the same phonemic category. For example, 6-month-old Swedish infants were better than U.S. infants at discriminating between a prototypic long-*e* sound and other long-*e* sounds, even though this was an unfamiliar sound to them (Kuhl, Williams, Lacerda, Stevens, & Lindblom, 1992). The reason is that the U.S. infants had formed a prototypic long-*e* sound and were therefore victims of the magnet effect, whereas the Swedish infants had not formed a prototypic long-*e* sound because this sound did not occur in their language. The opposite result occurred for a vowel that occurred in Swedish, but not in U.S. English. American infants were now better in discriminating variations of this vowel from the category prototype.

In conclusion, infants are born with the ability to discriminate among phonemes in many different languages but learn the prototypic speech sounds in their own language. Once the prototypic speech sounds are acquired, it becomes more difficult to discriminate between the prototype and variations of the prototype. In other words, variations of a phoneme caused by differences in pronunciation sound more alike. This makes us look bad on discrimination tests but presumably makes it easier to recognize speech because phonemes sound more like their category prototypes.

Evidence for Hierarchical Organization (Speech Errors)

The hierarchical diagram shown in Figure 10.2 is a convenient representation of the components in Figure 10.1, but is there evidence that people follow this hierarchical organization when producing sentences? The evidence comes from speech errors. As children grow older, they not only recognize speech but learn to produce speech of their own. However, children and even adults can make errors when speaking. Now that we have reviewed the grammatical, semantic, and phonemic aspects of sentences we can see how these three aspects of language can give rise to the kind of errors that occur when we produce spoken sentences. These speech errors, or **slips of the tongue**, are unintended deviations from a speech plan (Dell, 1986). Most of what we know about these slips comes from analyses of errors that were personally heard and noted by investigators. Although such methods may be subject to sampling biases, these collections of speech errors have so many irregularities that it is unlikely that there are systematic biases in the data.

The usefulness of the hierarchical organization shown in Figure 10.2 for representing speech errors is that the errors typically occur within but not across levels in the hierarchy (Dell, 1986). Errors can therefore be divided into *word errors, morpheme errors,* and *phoneme errors,* depending on the size of the linguistic unit involved in the error. Occurrence of errors within these linguistic units is most easily seen in **exchange errors** in which two linguistic units are substituted for each other in the sentence. That is, **word exchanges** are illustrated by the speaker saying "writing a mother to my letter" rather than "writing a letter to my mother." The exchanged words are typically members of the same syntactic category, demonstrating the constraints of grammar on speech. In this case, both *mother* and *letter* are nouns.

Morpheme exchanges are illustrated by the speaker saying "slicely thinned" rather than "thinly sliced." Morpheme errors also have categorical constraints; in this case the two stems *slice* and *thin* are interchanged while the suffixes *ly* and *ed* remain in their original position. Just as nouns are interchanged with other nouns or verbs interchanged with other verbs at the word level, stems are interchanged with other stems or suffixes interchanged with other suffixes at the morpheme level.

Phoneme exchanges are illustrated by the speaker saying "lork yibrary" for "York library." Once again, there are category constraints on the exchanges. In phoneme errors, initial consonants are exchanged with other initial consonants, final consonants are exchanged with other final consonants, and vowels are exchanged with other vowels.

The rest of this chapter focuses on the syntactic and semantic aspects of language. The next section provides a brief description of two kinds of grammatical rules—phrase-structure rules and transformation rules. This is followed

---

slip of the tongue A speech error

exchange error An error in which two linguistic units are substituted for each other during sentence production

word exchange An error in which two words are substituted for each other during sentence production

morpheme exchange An error in which two morphemes are substituted for each other during sentence production

phoneme exchange An error in which two phonemes are substituted for each other during sentence production

by a section that presents a general model of sentence comprehension. The comprehension of ambiguous sentences is a particularly interesting area of study because we must resolve the ambiguity to understand the sentences. The final section considers the distinction between asserted and implied statements. Findings on how well people can make this distinction offer some applications of research on the understanding of language, particularly in relation to the evaluation of courtroom testimony and advertising claims.

PSYCHOLOGY AND GRAMMAR

Phrase-Structure Grammar

We have seen that an alternative to representing language as a string of words is representing it as a rule system. For example, we saw in Figure 10.2 that we could divide the sentence into a noun phrase and a verb phrase. We could further subdivide the verb phrase "talked to the players" into the verb *talked* and the prepositional phrase *to the players*. The rules that we use to divide a sentence into its grammatical parts form a **phrase-structure grammar** because they reveal how we can partition a sentence into phrases consisting of groups of words.

phrase-structure grammar A set of rules for partitioning a sentence into its grammatical units

You should be familiar with phrase-structure rules if you have ever diagrammed a sentence. Let's look at the rules used in the sentence diagram in Figure 10.4. The first rule partitions the sentence (S) into a noun phrase (NP) followed by a verb phrase (VP). A second rule states that the noun phrase can be partitioned into a determiner (Det) followed by a noun. A determiner consists of the words *a*, *an*, and *the*. A third rule states that the verb phrase can be partitioned into a verb followed by a noun phrase, which is again broken down into a determiner and a noun. We can now produce sentences by substituting words for the determiners, nouns (such as *boy* and *ball*), and verbs (such as *hit*). For example:

The boy hit a ball.
The stick hit the boy.
A ball hit a ball.

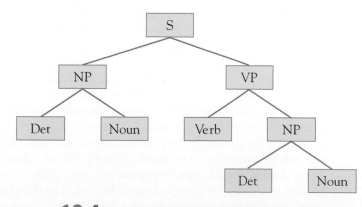

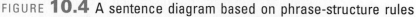

FIGURE **10.4** A sentence diagram based on phrase-structure rules

Although the number of sentences we can produce using this particular grammar is quite limited, the grammar illustrates how sentences can be produced through the application of rules. Creation of additional rules, such as including adjectives in a noun phrase, would allow us to generate a greater variety of sentences.

Transformational Grammar

Chomsky (1957) argued that one limitation of a phrase-structure grammar is that it does not reveal how a sentence can be modified to form a similar sentence. For example, how can we change (1) an active statement into a passive statement, (2) a positive statement into a negative statement, or (3) an assertion into a question? Given the sentence "The boy hit the ball," the first change produces "The ball was hit by the boy"; the second change produces "The boy did not hit the ball"; and the third change produces "Did the boy hit the ball?" The modification in each case *transforms* an entire sentence into a closely related sentence. Transformation rules therefore serve a different function than phrase-structure rules, which reveal the grammatical structure of a sentence. Chomsky, however, used phrase-structure rules in developing his transformational grammar because the transformations are based on the grammatical structure of a sentence.

Consider the transformation of "The boy hit the ball" into "The ball was hit by the boy." The transformation rule in this case is

$$NP1 + Verb + NP2 \rightarrow NP2 + was + Verb + by + NP1$$

The transformation changes the position of the two noun phrases and inserts additional words into the passive sentence. The passive sentence begins with the second noun phrase ("the ball") and ends with the first noun phrase ("the boy"). It is also necessary to add the words *was* and *by*. Notice that the transformation rule shows how a phrase-structure description of a passive sentence can be formed from a phrase-structure description of an active sentence.

transformational grammar A set of rules for transforming a sentence into a closely related sentence

The **transformational grammar** proposed by Chomsky in 1957 was an advance over a phrase-structure grammar because, in addition to revealing grammatical structure, it showed how sentences could be transformed. Chomsky was not entirely satisfied with the transformational grammar, however, and in 1965 he wrote a second book to correct some of its limitations. The changes that he made were concerned mainly with allowing meaning to play a more important role in the grammar.

ambiguous sentence A sentence that has more than one meaning

One reason for exploring the relation between grammar and meaning is that some sentences (called **ambiguous sentences**) have more than one meaning. Do the different meanings reflect different grammatical rules? The answer is that the alternative meanings of *some* ambiguous sentences reflect different phrase-structure rules. Consider the sentence "They are flying planes." One interpretation considers *flying* to be part of the verb phrase *are flying*, whereas the other interpretation considers *flying* to be an adjective in the noun phrase *flying planes*. In the first interpretation, *they* refers to someone who is flying planes; in the second interpretation, *they* refers to the planes. A phrase-structure grammar can make this distinction because each interpretation has a different derivation (Figure 10.5).

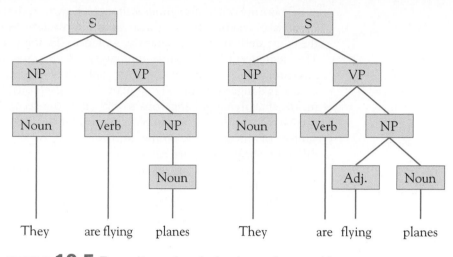

FIGURE **10.5** Two alternative derivations of an ambiguous sentence

Assigning a word to the appropriate phrase can have important consequences. As illustrated in "In the News" 10.1, the state of California had to spend considerable time and money to correct the misconception that the word "solely" referred to the phrase "in this state."

IN THE NEWS **10.1**

Wording on Driver's Licenses Costs State Almost $250,000

Ted Bell

SACRAMENTO—Nobody expected that the phrase "solely ... in this state" on driver's licenses would lead to the arrest and fining of California motorists by state troopers throughout the nation, at a cost to California taxpayers of almost $250,000.

But that is what has resulted from a bill designed to stop illegal immigrants from using easily obtained California driver's licenses to gain documents such as visas and work permits.

Under SB 946, sponsored by state Sen. Alfred Alquist, D-San Jose, all California driver's licenses issued after July 1 were printed to

include the following notice: "This license is issued solely as a license to drive a motor vehicle in this state; it does not establish eligibility for employment, voter registration or public benefits."

The problems arose when some law-enforcement agencies in other states interpreted the word "solely" to mean the licenses restrict the operation of a motor vehicle to California only—instead of a license just for operating a motor vehicle, said Department of Motor Vehicles spokesman Bill Madison....

The state agency then began mailing letters to anyone who had received a new license or renewal

since July. Each letter had a portion to be snipped off and kept with the license—with new language.

Subtracting the offensive "solely" and "in this state," the disclaimer reads: "This license is issued as a license to drive a motor vehicle; it does not establish eligibility for employment, voter registration or public benefits." Approximately 833,000 of the letters were mailed at a cost of $249,000, Madison said.

Source: From "Wording on driver's licenses costs state almost $250,000," by Ted Bell, *San Diego Tribune*, October 19, 1995.

There are other ambiguous sentences, however, that cannot be distinguished by phrase-structure rules because both interpretations of the sentence produce the same derivation. Consider the sentence "Flying planes can be dangerous." The sentence has the same ambiguity as the previous example. The two interpretations can be revealed by rephrasing the sentence as either "Flying planes is dangerous" or "Flying planes are dangerous." The first interpretation means that flying is dangerous to the pilot; the second means that the planes themselves are dangerous. In both interpretations, however, *flying planes* is the subject of the sentence, so the ambiguity cannot be resolved by appealing to different phrase-structure rules.

Chomsky (1965) proposed that, to resolve the ambiguity, it is necessary to postulate a level of analysis that directly represents the meaning of a sentence. He therefore modified the transformational grammar to consist of two levels: the **surface structure**, directly related to the sentence as it is heard, and the **deep structure**, directly related to the meaning of the sentence. The only way to resolve the ambiguity of a sentence such as "Flying planes can be dangerous" is to know which of the two deep levels is intended—flying is dangerous to the pilot or the planes themselves are dangerous.

The concepts Chomsky introduced had a major impact on the emerging field of psycholinguistics. Psychologists who were interested in language studied the implications of phrase structure and transformational grammars for theories of how people comprehend and remember sentences. One of the conclusions reached from these studies, and from Chomsky's (1965) analysis, is that it is difficult to study grammar without also studying meaning.

Words as Grammatical Clues

Studying the relation between meaning and grammar is important because producing a grammatical sentence does not guarantee the sentence will be meaningful. This point can be illustrated by adding another verb—*took*—to the rules shown in Figure 10.4. This addition allows us to produce new sentences like "The boy took the ball" and "The ball took the boy." Although both sentences are grammatical, the second sentence doesn't make much sense. The reason is that the verb *took* usually requires an animate subject—someone who is alive and therefore capable of taking something.

Chomsky (1965) tried to correct this deficiency by placing constraints on which words could be substituted into a sentence. Instead of treating all verbs the same, he argued that some verbs require animate subjects. This restriction is based on the meaning of words. Chomsky's analysis illustrates how the different components in Figure 10.1 can interact with each other. To express a meaningful idea (Semantics), the meaning of words in the Lexicon must be appropriately combined with grammatical rules (Syntax). Research by psycholinguists is helping us understand how the meaning of words provides hints as to which grammatical phrases will come next in a sentence.

There is increasing evidence that the meaning of words provide clues about grammatical structure (Carpenter, Miyake, & Just, 1995; MacDonald, Pearlmutter, & Seidenberg, 1994; Trueswell & Tanenhaus, 1994). For example, we use the distinction between animate and inanimate nouns to make

surface structure The structure of a spoken sentence

deep structure The underlying meaning of a sentence

guesses about the type of phrase that will follow the noun. This is illustrated by the difference between the following two sentences:

1.   The defendant examined by the lawyer turned out to be unreliable.
2.   The evidence examined by the lawyer turned out to be unreliable.

Eye movements indicate that readers slow down more in the first sentence than in the second sentence when they encounter the phrase *by the lawyer* (Trueswell & Tanenhaus, 1994). Try to apply Chomsky's analysis to figure out why before reading further.

The answer is that, in the first sentence, readers expect the word *examined* to be the main verb followed by a noun phrase, such as in the sentence "The defendant examined the jury." However, when they read *by the lawyer*, reading slows because their expectation turns out to be incorrect. But if the sentence begins with the inanimate noun *evidence*, our expectation that *examine* is the main verb becomes unlikely because we can't imagine how evidence can examine something.

In this case, the context—whether the sentence begins with an animate or an inanimate noun—influences how easily readers can comprehend the sentence. This example illustrates how a general characteristic of words—whether a noun is animate or inanimate—can serve as a clue for processing a sentence. However, even specific words (such as the verb *remembered*) provide clues about the grammatical structure of a sentence. Consider the following two sentences:

1.   John remembered my birthday.
2.   John remembered my birthday is coming.

In the first sentence, the word *remembered* is followed by the noun phrase *my birthday*. This sentence could be generated by a simple grammar, like the one shown in Figure 10.4. But the second sentence is more complex. Notice that *my birthday is coming* is another sentence, called a sentence complement. The word *remembered* is more often followed by a noun phrase than by a sentence complement. However, the word *claim* is more likely to be followed by a sentence complement ("Joan claimed the letter belonged to her") than by a noun phrase ("Joan claimed the letter"). Readers' knowledge of these frequency differences helps them process sentences by expecting syntactic structures that are likely to occur (Carpenter, Miyake, & Just, 1995; Trueswell, Tanenhaus, & Kello, 1993). We therefore expect a noun phrase after the word *remember* and a sentence complement after the word *claim*.

In summary, research has shown that the meaning of words conveys information about syntactic structures (Carpenter, Miyake, & Just, 1995; MacDonald, Pearlmutter, & Seidenberg, 1994; Trueswell & Tanenhaus, 1994). Notice that words provide clues because knowledge stored in one component of Figure 10.1 (the lexicon) can help us more quickly recognize the structure of another component (syntax). This interaction between components also occurs for semantics and the lexicon. In this case, recognizing and retrieving the meanings of words is the beneficiary of semantic knowledge, as illustrated in the next section.

USING SEMANTIC CONTEXT IN SENTENCE COMPREHENSION

Many words have more than one meaning but this usually does not confuse us because the context in which the word appears provides information about which meaning is appropriate (MacKay, 1966). For example, if a sentence begins with the statement *Although he was continually bothered by the cold*, we would be confused by whether the word *cold* referred to the temperature or to the person's state of health unless the context provided clues. Fortunately, the context usually does provides clues and we will now examine how people take advantage of them.

This discussion will be easier if we first consider Carpenter and Daneman's (1981) general model of the stages involved in sentence comprehension (see Figure 10.6)—stages that we learn more about in this section. The first stage ("fixate and encode the next word") involves pattern recognition. Although I discussed word recognition in the chapter on pattern recognition, I focused on the word superiority effect. We learned that a letter is easier to recognize in the context of a word than when it appears by itself. Similarly, a word is often easier to recognize when it appears in the context of a sentence than when it appears by itself.

The second stage involves retrieving the meaning(s) of the word. Although ambiguous words have more than one meaning, one of the meanings may occur much more frequently than the other. For the sentence "The port was a great success," you most likely associated the word *port* with ships. The less frequent meaning of *port*, a kind of drink, would be less strongly activated unless it were proceeded by a context that suggested this interpretation. Both meanings would be strongly activated in the sentence "When she finally served it to her guests, the port was a great success." The ship meaning would be strongly activated because it occurs more frequently, and the drink meaning would be strongly activated because it fits the context. By studying readers' eye movements while reading sentences with ambiguous words, Duffy, Morris, and Rayner (1988) concluded that the degree of activation of alternative meanings is influenced by prior context and by the frequency of the alternative meanings.

The selected meaning of the word is integrated with the prior context in the third stage of Carpenter and Daneman's model. If this

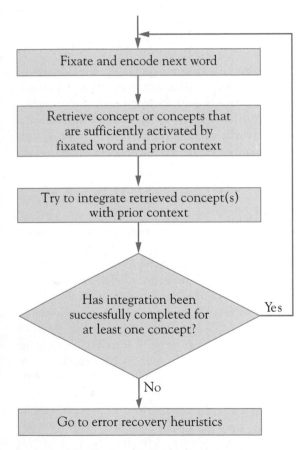

FIGURE **10.6** A flowchart showing the encoding, activation, integration, and error recovery stages of reading

Source: From "Lexical retrieval and error recovery in reading: A model based on eye fixations," by P. A. Carpenter & M. Daneman, 1981, *Journal of Verbal Learning and Verbal Behavior, 20*, 137–160. Copyright 1981 by Academic Press, Inc. Reprinted by permission of Elsevier Science.

integration is successful, the reader encodes the next word; otherwise, he or she tries to recover from the error by reinterpreting the word or the previous context. Let's now look in greater detail at what happens during each of these stages.

Semantic Context and Word Recognition

I mentioned that word recognition is often facilitated by the semantic context. We have all experienced difficulty in recognizing a word when reading illegible handwriting and having to rely on the surrounding words and sentences to help us identify the illegible word. An example of how context can influence word recognition is shown in Figure 10.7. The two sentences contain a physically identical word, yet we have little difficulty identifying the word as *went* in the upper sentence and as *event* in the lower sentence.

Although the effect of context is most obvious to us when we have to struggle to identify a word, it also influences recognition time when we identify words relatively quickly. Usually, context is helpful and facilitates faster word recognition, but it can also slow us down, as is illustrated in the following two sentences: (1) "John kept his gym clothes in a locker." (2) "John kept his gym clothes in a closet." The words *locker* and *closet* are both preceded by a suitable context, but the context creates a strong expectation for the word *locker*. Sentences that create a high expectation for a particular word are called **high-constraint sentences**.

high-constraint sentence A sentence that produces a high expectation for a particular word

Schwanenflugel and Shoben (1985) studied the effect of high-constraint sentences on the processing of expected words (*locker*) and unexpected words (*closet*) by using the **lexical decision task** that we discussed in the previous chapter. After reading either a high-constraint context or a neutral context, readers had to decide whether a string of letters was a word. The high-constraint context facilitated recognition of the expected word but interfered with recognition of the unexpected word. People were faster at deciding that *locker* was a word when they received the high-constraint context but were faster in deciding that *closet* was a word when they received the neutral context, consisting of a string of Xs.

lexical decision task A task that requires people to decide whether a string of letters is a word

The high-constraint sentence caused interference in the latter case because people were expecting a particular word, which did not occur. What would

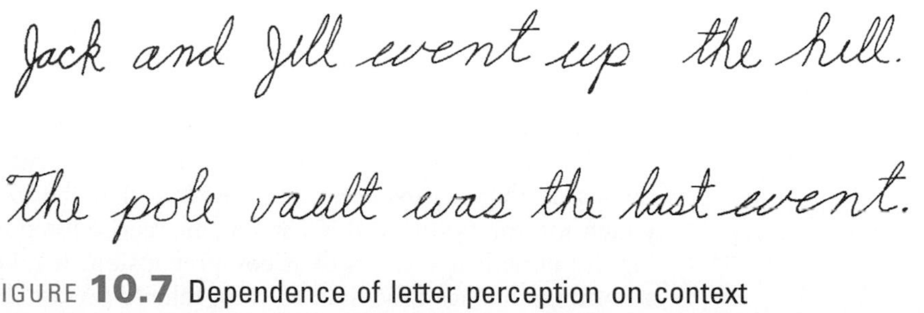

Jack and Jill event up the hill.

The pole vault was the last event.

FIGURE **10.7** Dependence of letter perception on context

Source: From "The role of semantics in speech understanding," by B. Nash-Webber, 1975, in *Representation and Understanding*, edited by D. G. Bobrow & A. Collins. Copyright 1975 by Academic Press. Reprinted by permission of Elsevier Science.

low-constraint sentence A sentence that produces an expectation for a broader range of words

happen if our expectations for a particular word were not as strong? Schwanenflugel and Shoben tried to answer this question by including **low-constraint sentences** in their study. The following two sentences are examples: (1) "The lady was a competent cook." (2) "The lady was a competent chef." The sentences are low-constraint because a lady could be competent in performing many different tasks. However, the first sentence contains an expected word, and the second sentence contains an unexpected word because a lady is more likely to be called a cook than a chef. The results of several experiments indicated that the low-constraint context caused facilitation for both the expected and unexpected words. In contrast to the high-constraint sentences, in which a large facilitation effect occurred for the expected word and a large interference effect occurred for the unexpected word, the low-constraint sentences caused a moderate amount of facilitation for both words.

The study by Schwanenflugel and Shoben (1985) shows that contexts may occasionally have negative, as well as positive, effects. A high-constraint context can slow lexical decisions for unexpected words. One caution, however, in evaluating such studies is the finding that contextual interference is affected by the research methodology used to study contextual effects. Another frequently used procedure, instead of lexical decision, is to measure how quickly subjects can name a word that follows a context. Studies that have used both procedures have revealed that interference effects are more likely to be found in lexical decision tasks than in naming tasks (Stanovich & West, 1983). An important challenge for cognitive psychologists is therefore to show how performance on such tasks as naming and lexical decision is related to the comprehension that occurs during normal reading (Seidenberg, Waters, Sanders, & Langer, 1984).

Semantic Context and Ambiguous Meanings

After readers or listeners identify words, they still must select the appropriate meaning if the word has multiple meanings. We have previously seen that psychologists like to study comprehension by including ambiguous words in their sentences. It is important to realize, however, that ambiguous sentences are not simply invented by psychologists to study language comprehension. They also frequently occur outside the laboratory, such as in newspaper headlines. Comprehending newspaper headlines is more challenging than comprehending ordinary sentences because space constraints sometimes make it necessary to delete helpful words. Examples of ambiguous headlines include "Teacher Strikes Idle Kids," "Pentagon Plans Swell Deficit," "Department Heads Store Clerk," and "Executive Secretaries Touch Typists." Each headline has more than one meaning. For example, the headline "Executive Secretaries Touch Typists" could mean that (1) executive secretaries are touch typists or that (2) executive secretaries touch the typists. Most people agree which interpretation of these statements is the intended meaning, but the ambiguity nonetheless slows their comprehension. It takes longer to comprehend an ambiguous headline than to comprehend one of the unambiguous interpretations (Perfetti, Beverly, Bell, Rodgers, & Faux, 1987).

The ambiguity of some newspaper headlines is particularly troublesome because we often lack a context to interpret the headline. The headline is the first sentence we read to find out what the article is about. The reason many potentially ambiguous sentences do not seem ambiguous is that the intended meaning is usually clear from the preceding sentences. If I say that I am bothered by the cold, the preceding sentences should reveal the intended meaning. We might therefore expect that a clarifying context should make it as easy to comprehend ambiguous sentences as unambiguous sentences. An experiment by Swinney and Hakes (1976) supports this hypothesis.

The subjects in their experiment performed two tasks simultaneously while they listened to pairs of sentences. One task asked them to judge how closely they felt the two sentences of each pair were related. This task required comprehension of the sentences. The second task required that they press a button as soon as they heard a word beginning with a specified sound (phoneme). The rationale of this experiment is that people should be slower in responding to the phoneme whenever they are having difficulty in comprehending the sentence. The following pair of sentences is a typical example:

> *Rumor had it that, for years, the government building had been plagued with problems. The man was not surprised when he found several "bugs" in the corner of his room.* (Swinney & Hakes, 1976, p. 686)

The target phoneme in this example occurs at the beginning of the word *corner*, shortly after the ambiguous word *bugs*. To determine whether the ambiguous word would delay comprehension and therefore detection of the phoneme, Swinney and Hakes compared performance on the ambiguous sentences with performance on unambiguous control sentences. The unambiguous version of the example contained the word *insects* in place of the word *bugs*. Swinney and Hakes found that subjects took significantly more time to detect the phoneme when it followed an ambiguous word than when it followed an unambiguous word.

However, sometimes the ambiguous word occurred in a context that made it clear which meaning of the word was intended. For example:

> *Rumor had it that, for years, the government building had been plagued with problems. The man was not surprised when he found several spiders, roaches, and other "bugs" in the corner of his room.* (Swinney & Hakes, 1976, p. 686)

When the context clarified the meaning of the ambiguous word, people could comprehend the ambiguous word *bug* as quickly as they could comprehend the unambiguous word *insect*. There was no longer any difference in response times to the target phoneme.

We could interpret these results by arguing that only a single meaning of the ambiguous word is activated when the context indicates the intended meaning. This argument has considerable intuitive appeal, but research results suggest that it is wrong. In the previous chapter we saw that when people are asked to decide whether a string of letters is a word, their decision is faster when a word is preceded by a semantically related word, such as *bread* preceded by *butter*. If people consider only a single meaning of an ambiguous word, a word such as *bug* should facilitate the recognition of either *ant* or *spy*, depending on which meaning is activated.

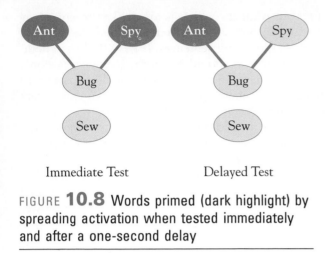

Immediate Test   Delayed Test

FIGURE **10.8** Words primed (dark highlight) by spreading activation when tested immediately and after a one-second delay

Swinney (1979) tested this prediction by replacing the phoneme-monitoring task with a lexical decision task. He explained to the subjects that a string of letters would appear on a screen as they listened to some sentences, and they were to decide as quickly as possible whether or not each letter string formed a word. He did not mention that some of the sentences and words were related. The letter string, which appeared on the screen immediately after subjects heard the ambiguous word, was contextually appropriate, contextually inappropriate, or unrelated to the meaning of the ambiguous word. A contextually appropriate word appearing on the screen, such as *ant*, was consistent with the meaning of the ambiguous word that was suggested by the context. A contextually inappropriate word, such as *spy*, was consistent with the meaning that was not suggested by the context. An unrelated word, such as *sew*, was consistent with neither of the two meanings.

If the context causes the activation of only a single meaning, it should be easier to recognize only the contextually appropriate word (*ant*). But if both meanings of the ambiguous word are activated, the contextually inappropriate word (*spy*) should also be easier to recognize than the unrelated word (*sew*). The results showed that when the visual test word immediately followed the ambiguous word, both the contextually appropriate and the contextually inappropriate words were easier to recognize than the unrelated words. But when the test word occurred four syllables (approximately 750–1000 msec) after the ambiguous word, recognition of only the contextually appropriate word was facilitated (Figure 10.8).

Swinney's findings suggest that more than one meaning of an ambiguous word is activated even when a prior context indicates which meaning is appropriate. If only one meaning of *bugs* were activated by the phrase "He found several spiders, roaches, and other bugs," it is not clear why it would be as easy to respond to *spy* as to *ant*. However, when the test word occurred four syllables after the ambiguous word, recognition of only the word *ant* was facilitated. It therefore appears that, although both meanings of an ambiguous word are momentarily activated, the context allows the listener to select the appropriate meaning quickly. Selection of the appropriate meaning occurred quickly enough to prevent interference in the phoneme-detection task. As you may recall, there was a slight delay between the ambiguous word and the target phoneme. This was sufficient time to resolve the ambiguity when there was an appropriate context. An appropriate context therefore seems to allow the listener to select the appropriate meaning of a word quickly rather than to prevent more than one meaning from being activated.

Individual Differences in Resolving Ambiguities

Some people are better at resolving ambiguities than others. In fact, the picture we have painted so far is for how good readers resolve ambiguities. The problem for less skilled readers is that they do not quickly resolve which of the activated meanings is the correct one (Gernsbacher, 1993). Like the good readers, both meanings of an ambiguous word are initially activated, but unlike the good readers, both meanings are still active 1 second after encountering the ambiguous word. Less skilled readers are simply less able to **suppress** the inappropriate meaning.

suppress Eliminating inappropriate meanings in a sentence

It would be simpler for everyone if only a single meaning (the correct one, of course) were initially activated. Although this might seem beneficial when the correct meaning is obvious, an advantage of activating multiple meanings is that the clarifying context occasionally does not occur until *after* the ambiguous word. In this case, it would be advantageous to try to keep both meanings active in STM until we gain enough information to select the appropriate one.

See if you can find the ambiguous word in the following partial sentence: "Since Ken really liked the boxer, he took a bus to the nearest...." If you found the ambiguous word, can you resolve the ambiguity by using the sentence context? The ambiguous word is *boxer*, and at this point we don't have enough information to know whether Ken is interested in a fighter or a dog. The remainder of the sentence resolves the ambiguity by informing us that Ken took the bus to the nearest pet store to buy the animal. Notice, however, that unlike the previous examples in which the clarifying context preceded the ambiguous word, in this case we had to read considerably more of the sentence following the ambiguous word before the meaning became clear.

People's ability to excel in these situations is influenced by the capacity of their working memory (Miyake, Just, & Carpenter, 1994). We saw in Chapter 4 that STM is often used as a working memory in which people both store and process material in STM. In this example we would like to keep active in working memory both interpretations of the word *boxer* until we later encounter information that would enable us to select the correct one. People who have a large **working memory capacity** are able to keep both interpretations active over a longer span than people who have a smaller working memory capacity. The latter group is able to maintain only the more likely (dominant) interpretation and therefore has difficulty resolving the ambiguity when the less likely interpretation proves to be the correct one.

working memory capacity The amount of information that can be kept active in working memory

Because the word *boxer* is more likely to refer to a fighter than to a dog, people with a small working memory capacity would have difficulty comprehending a sentence in which they later learned that the sentence was about a dog. In this case their integration would be unsuccessful, and they would have to use the **error recovery heuristics** in Figure 10.6. Examples include trying to reinterpret the inconsistent word, checking previous words that might have caused the difficulty, reading on for further information, and elaborating the apparent inconsistency to make it consistent (perhaps Ken was buying a dog at the pet store to give to the fighter).

error recovery heuristic A strategy for correcting comprehension errors

In conclusion, good readers are those readers who are able to initially keep active in working memory both interpretations of an ambiguous word and then quickly select the appropriate meaning as soon as they receive a clarifying context. We have seen two ways in which reading can be impaired.

Readers with limited working memory capacity are less able to maintain both meanings in working memory when the clarifying context occurs later, and less skilled readers are less able to quickly suppress the inappropriate meaning when they encounter the clarifying context.

Interpreting Phrases

The model proposed by Carpenter and Daneman (1981) in Figure 10.6 focuses on the encoding and integration of individual words. Research using the lexical decision task examined how prior context influences both the recognition of words (Schwanenflugel & Shoben, 1985) and the determination of the word's meaning (Swinney, 1979).

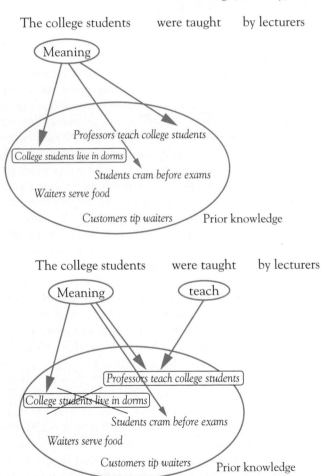

FIGURE **10.9** Interpretation of phrases for the sentence: The college students were taught by lecturers

Source: "Interpretation-based processing: a unified theory of semantic sentence comprehension," by R. Budiu & J. R. Anderson, 2004, *Cognitive Science*, 28, 1–44.

We can now look at a larger unit of analysis such as the noun phrases and verb phrases discussed in the section on grammar. Consider how you understand the sentence:

The college students were taught by lecturers.

One account is provided by the interpretation-based processing theory (Budiu & Anderson, 2004) that builds on the spreading activation assumptions that were discussed in the previous chapter.

The purpose of the interpretation-based processing theory is to produce syntactic and semantic representations of a sentence and relate the sentence to prior knowledge. For example, the noun phrase "the college students" activates in the reader propositions about college students such as the ones shown in Figure 10.9. College students (1) live in dorms, (2) are taught by professors, and (3) cram before exams. The proposition with the highest activation is selected for the initial interpretation (assume it is *college students live in dorms*).

However, this interpretation is not supported when the reader encounters the verb phrase "were taught." "Live" and "taught" are too dissimilar so there is little activation spreading from "taught" to "live." This results in the retrieval of the more promising proposition, *Professors teach college students*, as shown in the lower part of Figure 10.9. This interpretation is confirmed by the similarity of the meanings of "professors" and "lecturers." The theory therefore provides a plausible interpretation of the sentence by discarding invalid interpretations of phrases and making sure that all the interpretations are consistent. The activation of multiple implications of a phrase followed by the selection of the correct one is consistent with the activation of multiple meanings of an ambiguous word followed by the selection of the correct one.

Here's another example of connecting sentences to prior knowledge through spreading activation. Try answering the following question:

How many animals of each kind did Moses take on the ark?

If you answered none, you noticed the inconsistency. It was not Moses, but Noah, who took animals on the ark. Many people fail to notice these inconsistencies (Erickson & Mattson, 1981), which are called the Moses illusion in honor of the previous question. Reder and Kisbit (1991) designed a variation of this task in which participants knew they would encounter inconsistencies but were required to answer all questions as if there were no inconsistencies. The correct answer is therefore "two" for the Moses question, but we might expect longer responses when there is an inconsistency.

Budiu and Anderson (2004) hypothesized, based on the assumptions of the interpretation-based processing theory, that the time to answer inconsistent questions would depend on the degree of the distortion. Substituting "Moses" for "Noah" is a mild distortion because the concepts "Moses" and "Noah" are somewhat similar. Substituting "Adam" for "Noah" is a greater distortion because the two concepts are more dissimilar. It should be easier to answer questions in which there is less distortion because spreading activation requires less time to connect similar concepts. The results supported this hypothesis. It took longer to answer the questions as the sentences became more distorted. The interpretation-based processing theory is able to make many other successful predictions about how people interpret sentences but these examples should give you an idea of how the theory works.

EMBODIED COGNITION

embodied cognition
A theoretical framework in which perception and action have a central role in cognition

My discussion of language has proceeded along the same path as my initial discussion of semantic organization in Chapter 9. However, at the end of Chapter 9, I discussed the idea that perceptual simulations can help us make decisions about meaning. Judging that NOSE and MOUTH are related or that peanut butter is sticky seems to depend on forming an image of a face or simulating our interactions with peanut butter. The perceptual symbol systems (Barsalou, 1999) that are used to explain these findings fit into a more general theoretical framework called "embodied cognition." In contrast to more traditional views that perception and action are peripheral to cognition because they provide merely the input and output, **embodied cognition** proposes that perception and action are central to cognition (Gibbs, 2006; Wilson, 2002). Reenactment of memories through perceptual simulations is one example of this approach. Using simulations to comprehend language is another example.

Comprehension Through Simulations

Results obtained by Stanfield and Zwaan (2001) support the hypothesis that simulations help people comprehend the meaning of verbally described events. For example, reading that someone put a pencil in a drawer should evoke an image of a horizontal pencil, and reading that someone put a pencil in a cup should evoke an image of a vertical pencil. Stanfield and Zwan tested their hypothesis that visual simulations of verbal statements would include an object's orientation by asking students at Florida State University to quickly decide whether a pictured object had been mentioned in a sentence that they just read. You can obtain an approximate idea of this task by responding whether the object in Box 10.1 is mentioned in each of the three sentences. This demonstration is approximate because the test object did not appear until after participants read each sentence in Stanfield and Zwan's experiment.

According to the visual simulation hypothesis, the time to verify a mentioned object should depend on whether the picture matches the implied orientation in the sentence. The results supported the hypothesis, as illustrated by the distinction between the two sentences *She pounded the nail into the floor* versus *She pounded the nail into the wall*. The readers were faster in confirming a picture of a vertical nail following the first sentence (pounding a nail into the floor) and were faster in confirming a picture of a horizontal nail following the second sentence (pounding the nail into the wall).

The argument that visual simulations help us understand language is a particularly powerful one for supporting the importance of simulations. It says that understanding language itself rests on a foundation of visual thinking. I will therefore describe several more experimental paradigms that converge on the conclusion that visual simulations support our understanding of language.

One paradigm is based on the concept of visual occlusions. Horton and Rapp (2003) proposed that if visual simulations support comprehension, it should be more difficult to verify objects that disappear from sight. They illustrate an example from the classic story, *The Strange Case of Dr. Jekyll and Mr. Hyde*:

> As the cab drew up before the address indicated, the fog lifted a little and showed him a dingy street, a gin palace, a low French eating-house, a shop for the retail of penny numbers and two-penny salads, many ragged children huddled in the doorways, and many women of different nationalities passing out, key in hand, to have a morning glass; and the next moment the fog settled down again upon that part, as brown as umber, and cut him off from his blackguardly surroundings (Stevenson, 1895/1993, pp. 119–120).

BOX **10.1**   **Object Verification Task**

1. She pounded the nail into the floor.
2. She painted the fence with a brush.

3. She pounded the nail into the wall.

The story allows us to experience the surroundings through the eyes of a visitor to the home of Mr. Hyde. However, these surroundings became occluded (hidden) by the fog, as they often do in stories in which doors close, people leave rooms, or objects move in front of people. Horton and Rapp argued that if readers create images to understand narratives, the occluded objects should take longer to verify as having been mentioned in the story.

A typical story in their experiment described a patient named Marty, who was in the hospital recovering from surgery. The story described the details of his room, including a tall vase of flowers by his bedside. In the occluded version of the story, a nurse draws a curtain around Marty's bed to give him privacy during an examination. In the nonoccluded version, the nurse attaches a monitor to his bed to take his blood pressure. A visual simulation of the story should continue to show the flowers only in the second version. At the end of the story both groups were asked "Did Marty have a vase of flowers?" The time to answer a question was longer for occluded objects, supporting the visual simulation hypothesis.

My initial reaction to research on the verification of mentioned objects was that it provided convincing evidence for static images, but not for dynamic simulations that involve actions. Doesn't verifying that a nail or a vase of flowers was mentioned require only a static image of the object? Then it occurred to me that the results of both studies likely depend on the simulation of actions. The quicker verification of either a horizontal or a vertical nail depended on whether the nail was pounded into the floor or the wall. The slower verification of the occluded vase of flowers depended on the nurse closing the curtain.

Glenberg and Kaschak provided direct evidence that people mentally simulate such actions. In one of their experiments college students at the University of Wisconsin had to quickly judge whether a phrase, such as "open the drawer" or "boil the air," made sense. They had to move their hand either toward or away from their body to hit a response key. Participants were faster in responding when the response required an action in the same direction as the one implied in the phrase. For example, they were faster in responding by moving their hand toward their body when verifying the statement "open the drawer" and faster when moving their hand away from their body for the statement "close the drawer." These findings are consistent with a mental simulation of the action that requires moving your arm toward your body to open a drawer and away from your body to close a drawer.

Gestures as Simulated Actions

Mentally simulating phrases such as "pound the nail," "close the curtain," and "open the drawer" typically do not require performing an action unless required to press a response button in a psychology experiment. Although the mental simulation of actions during comprehension does not require overt actions, we occasionally do perform actions in the form of gestures when we speak. One advantage of mentally simulating actions during comprehension is that we could use these simulations as a basis for gestures. In other words, the same simulations could provide the foundation for both comprehending and producing language. This is exactly the claim made by Hostetter and Alibali (2008) in their gestures-as-simulated action (GSA) framework.

Figure 10.10 provides a schematic sketch of the framework. As proposed in embodied theories of cognition, the link between perception and action is central. The simulations that occur during language comprehension are based on both visual and motor images. Motor imagery activates premotor areas in the brain that have the potential to spread to motor areas and create gestures. The GSA framework proposes that there are three factors that determine whether a gesture occurs. The first is the strength of the simulated action. Some simulations involve only visual imagery. The word "beautiful" will likely invoke visual imagery, but not action imagery. The second factor is the

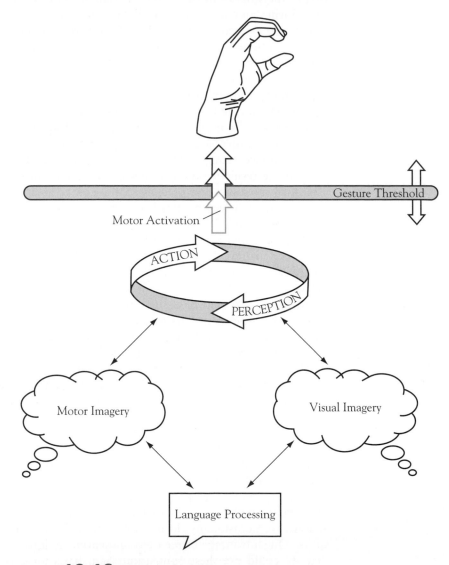

FIGURE **10.10** Gestures as simulated action framework

Source: From "Visible embodiment: Gestures as simulated action," by A. B. Hostetter & M. S. Alibali, 2008, *Psychonomic Bulletin & Review*, 15, 495–514.

height of the gesture threshold. You probably know some people who have a low threshold and use their hands frequently as they speak and others who have a high threshold and rarely gesture. The third factor is speech. Although both comprehending and producing language depend on simulations, gestures typically occur only when people produce language.

Gestures enable us to demonstrate concepts such as size that may be difficult to state verbally. They also facilitate reasoning as shown by the finding that gesturing *reduced* the cognitive demands on working memory when students explained mathematical solutions. Wagner, Nusbaum, and Goldin-Meadow (2004) asked college-age adults to factor quadratic equations on a white board and then explain their solutions. To determine the memory demands of the explanation task, the researchers gave the students supplementary information such as a random string of letters before their explanations. Students were later able to recall more supplementary items if they gestured while explaining their solution. The number of recalled items depended on the meaning of the gestures, with more items recalled when the gestures and verbal explanations conveyed the same meaning. Gesturing therefore reduced the memory demands of explaining the solution, particularly when the gestures and verbal explanation were compatible.

You may wonder why the gestures and verbal explanations would not be compatible. The answer is that people occasionally say one thing and do something else. Although this can at times be frustrating, it can also be revealing. The mismatch between information conveyed by gesture and by speech can provide useful diagnostic information, such as determining when students are considering alternative solutions as they reason about problems.

Consider a Piagetian task in which children are asked whether two jars contain the same amount of water. The height of the water is the same, but one jar has a larger diameter. Many children would reply that the amount of water is the same because the two heights are identical. Some children will give compatible gestures by pointing to the height of the water, but others will give incompatible gestures by showing an (unconscious) awareness of the different widths as they attempt to grasp the containers. It is those children whose gestures show an understanding that is not revealed in their verbal responses that are more likely to benefit from instruction. As pointed out by Goldin-Meadow and Wagner (2005), these children appear to have the correct knowledge at their fingertips.

In the next chapter, on text comprehension, we will continue to study language but at a larger unit of analysis. We will focus less on individual sentences and more on how information is combined across sentences. We will try to determine which variables influence people's ability to comprehend paragraphs and remember what they read.

SUMMARY

A language is a collection of symbols and rules for combining symbols that can generate an infinite variety of sentences. A sentence can be partitioned into grammatical phrases, words, morphemes, and phonemes. Morphemes are the smallest units of meaning and include stem words (friend), prefixes (un), and suffixes (ly). Phonemes are the basic sounds of a language. Newborns have the ability to discriminate among many different speech sounds but lose this ability as they learn to categorize sounds into the phonemic categories of their language. Errors in generating speech are consistent with the hierarchical organization of language. Exchange errors, in which two linguistic units are substituted for each other, occur at the same level in the hierarchy, producing either word exchanges, morpheme exchanges, or phoneme exchanges.

One of the major questions that have fascinated psychologists interested in language is how people learn to speak in grammatically correct sentences. An early view suggested that children learn to associate the adjacent words in a sentence. According to this view, each word serves as a stimulus for the word that follows it. There are several problems with this theory, the major one being that a person would have to learn an infinite number of associations. The alternative view is that a child learns a grammar consisting of rules for generating sentences. The transformational grammar proposed by Chomsky stimulated much research as psychologists investigated how well it could account for the results of language experiments. The grammar consisted of both phrase-structure rules for describing the parts of a sentence (such as noun phrase and verb phrase) and transformation rules for changing a sentence into a closely related sentence (such as an active sentence into a passive sentence). Specific words (such as the word *remember*) and general features of words (such as whether the sentence begins with an animate or inanimate noun) provide clues about the grammatical structure of a sentence.

A general model of sentence comprehension involves fixating and recognizing a word, retrieving conceptual meanings that are sufficiently activated by the word and the prior context, integrating one of these meanings with the prior context, testing to determine whether the integration is successful, and recovering from an error if unsuccessful. Psychologists have often used ambiguous sentences to study comprehension and have found that a clarifying semantic context allows the listener to quickly select the appropriate meaning of an ambiguous word, although both meanings have been activated. Individual differences in resolving ambiguities are caused by differences in the ability of readers to keep multiple meanings active in STM until encountering a clarifying context and then quickly suppressing the inappropriate meaning.

Embodied cognition emphasizes the important role of perception and action in cognition. Many different research paradigms have provided support for the claim that comprehension often occurs through mental simulations. Mentally simulating some phrases such as "pound the nail," "close the curtain," and "open the drawer" involves the simulation of actions. Although the simulation of actions during comprehension does not require overt actions, we occasionally do perform actions in the form of gestures when we speak. One advantage of mentally simulating actions during comprehension is that we could use these same simulations as a basis for gestures. In other words, the same simulations can provide the foundation for both comprehending and producing language. Gestures reduce demands on working memory and can reveal information that is not expressed verbally, such as consideration of alternative solutions.

STUDY QUESTIONS

By the time we are college students, we are such skilled users of language that we don't usually think about it at all. If you haven't thought about the "parts of speech" lately (or ever), you may need to look them up before you get into this chapter.

1. Make sure you understand the term *morpheme* by thinking of several stem words that you can change the meaning of by adding a prefix and a suffix.
2. What is a grammar? In what sense do all of us "know" English grammar?
3. What are the respective domains of phrase-structure grammar and transformational grammar? Or are the two fighting over the same turf?
4. Why are sentences yet another example of hierarchical organization? Do you think this is helpful?
5. Note the various experimental tasks that have been used to study language comprehension. Have you run into any of them before in this course?
6. Many of the words we use can take on separate meanings, but most of the time we don't experience ambiguity. Why, then, is it important to determine how we "disambiguate" words in a sentence?
7. It is intuitively obvious that context facilitates word interpretation, but how can it interfere with interpretation? How has the influence of context been studied experimentally?
8. What causes individual differences in resolving ambiguities? Can you think of an example in your life in which an ambiguity created a misunderstanding?
9. What is the relation between embodied cognition and the perceptual symbols theory discussed in Chapter 9?
10. Can you think of situations in which it would be difficult to mentally simulate ideas expressed in language?

CogLab   The following experiment that relates to this chapter can be found at: http://coglab.wadsworth.com. Answer the questions in the CogLab Student Manual as required by your teacher for this experiment.

Categorical Perception: Discrimination

KEY TERMS

The page number in parentheses refers to where the term is discussed in the chapter.

ambiguous sentence (252)
Broca's aphasia (247)
deep structure (254)
embodied cognition (263)
error recovery heuristic (261)
exchange error (250)
generative (244)
grammar (244)
high-constraint sentence (257)
language (244)
lexical decision task (257)
low-constraint sentence (258)
morpheme (244)

morpheme exchange (250)
phoneme exchange (250)
phrase-structure grammar (251)
slip of the tongue (250)
structured (244)
suppress (261)
surface structure (254)
symbolic (244)
transformational grammar (252)
Wernicke's aphasia (247)
word exchange (250)
working memory capacity (261)

RECOMMENDED READING

Steven Pinker's (1994) book, *The Language Instinct*, provides a very readable introduction to the many facets of language. An easy introduction to the early theoretical contributions of Chomsky is a book by Lyons (1970). Lasnik (2002) reviews Chomsky's more recent contributions to transformational-generative grammar, but the work is very technical. Keenan, MacWhinney, and Mayhew (1977) found that their colleagues often could remember the exact words of statements that had high emotional content, although usually only the general meaning of sentences was remembered (Sachs, 1967). Gernsbacher and Faust (1991) showed that the ability to quickly suppress inappropriate meanings is an important skill in a variety of comprehension tasks. Pickering and Garrod (2007) argue that people use language production to make predictions during comprehension. Chapters by Carpenter, Miyake, and Just (1995) and by McKoon and Ratcliff (1998) and Clifton and Duffy (2001) in the *Annual Review of Psychology* contain an overview of studies on language. Books by Gibbs (2006) and Reed (in press) discuss research on embodied cognition, including its application to language. Gleitman (2005) reviews research on language and thought.

11

Comprehension and Memory for Text

Reading furnishes the mind only with materials of knowledge; it is thinking that makes what we read ours.

—**John Locke (English philosopher)**

It can be difficult to single out any one cognitive skill as most important, but, if we had to make a choice, *comprehension* would be a prime contender for the honor. Much of what we learn depends on our ability to understand written material. Thus, the comprehension of written material has attracted considerable attention.

One method for studying the difficulty of comprehension is to measure reading speed. We have all adjusted our reading speed to meet the varying demands of comprehension. Consider how the content of the text influences reading speed. According to Gernsbacher's (1997) Structure Building Framework, understanding text involves three components: laying a foundation, mapping information onto the foundation, and shifting to build new structures. Research has demonstrated that people slow down when they read the first sentence of a paragraph because they are building a foundation for the ideas that follow. As long as subsequent ideas can be mapped onto this foundation, reading proceeds smoothly. However, when the topic, point of view, or location changes, readers must shift from building one structure to building another. Shifting to build a new structure requires increased comprehension time.

Another factor that influences reading speed is the familiarity of the material, and this depends on the knowledge of the reader. In Chapter 4, I mentioned my own struggles with comprehension after taking a speed-reading course. I was able to recall ideas after speed reading the simple stories that were used in the course, but I was unsuccessful in applying this technique to the material I read in graduate school. However, I could adjust my speed of reading as a function of the familiarity of the material. Some material was already familiar, and I could read this material more quickly. "In the News" 11.1 discusses research on speed reading and shows how we can adjust reading speed to maintain a high level of comprehension.

This introduction illustrates that two important components influence comprehension—the reader and the text. The three sections of this chapter emphasize the reader, the text, and the interaction between the reader and the text. The first section looks at how the reader's knowledge influences the comprehension and recall of ideas in a text. The second section is about how the organization of ideas in a text affects comprehension. The third section discusses a specific model of how comprehension occurs. In addition to its theoretical success, the model has increased our ability to measure and improve the readability of texts, as discussed in the final section.

PRIOR KNOWLEDGE OF THE READER

Effect on Comprehension

A central issue for psychologists interested in studying comprehension is specifying how people use their knowledge to understand new or abstract ideas

IN THE NEWS **11.1**

Speed-Reading Can Undermine Learning

Bridget Murray

Nearly every student who faces a week of heavy reading has heard the same advice from a professor: Don't read every word. Scan it. Read quickly. Ignore unimportant words. Focus on key concepts....

But can you really increase your reading speed from 300 words per minute (wpm)—the average for college students—to 1,000 wpm or more, and still understand the material as well? Certainly speed-reading gets you through more information, research suggests, but you'll likely absorb considerably less of it.

The strategy taught in speed-reading courses works best for people who are already familiar with the topics they're reading about, not for students trying to learn new information, says preeminent reading-speed researcher Ronald Carver, PhD, an educational psychologist at the University of Missouri–Kansas City.

The method helps when reviewing or checking for new information. But it's no way to absorb unfamiliar material, or to appreciate poetry or literature, Carver says....

Backing Carver's findings is a study by psychologists Marcel Just, PhD, and Patricia Carpenter, PhD, outlined in their book *The Psychology of Reading and Language Comprehension* (Allyn and Bacon, 1987). They compared the reading comprehension of 11 graduates of a speed-reading program with that of 25 college students, some of whom skimmed the material. Students read a difficult article on Mars geology and an easy article about John Colter, a 19th-century U.S. explorer. Both the skimmers and speed readers missed important details in both texts. Skipped words became unknown facts, Just says.

Reading is a lot like driving, Carver says. People's usual reading speed of between 200 and 300 wpm

is like a comfortable gear that works for most textual terrain. When the reading gets difficult, they shift gears to a lower reading speed that helps them understand more.

By comparison, skimming and speed-reading are overdrive gears that whisk knowledgeable readers to new information, he says.

"Speed-reading doesn't help you read more words, but it does help you to more actively apply what you already know," he says. For example, a geologist reading about rocks on Mars can skip the part about how they compare with Earth's rocks: She uses her own geological knowledge to make comparisons.

Source: From "Speed-reading can undermine learning," by Bridget Murray, *APA Monitor*, November 1997, 33. Copyright 1997 by the American Psychological Association. Reprinted by permission.

(Cook & Gueraud, 2005). The influence of prior knowledge on the comprehension and recall of ideas was dramatically illustrated in an early study by Bransford and Johnson (1973). They asked people to listen to a paragraph and try to comprehend and remember it. After listening to the paragraph, subjects rated how easy it was to comprehend and then tried to recall as many ideas as they could. You can get some feeling for the task by reading the following passage once and then trying to recall as much as you can.

If the balloons popped, the sound wouldn't be able to carry, since everything would be too far away from the correct floor. A closed window would also prevent the sound from carrying, since most buildings tend to be well insulated. Since the whole operation depends on a steady flow of electricity, a break in the middle of the wire would also cause problems. Of course, the fellow could shout, but the human voice is not loud enough to carry that far. An additional problem is that a string could break on the instrument. Then there could be no accompaniment to the message. It is clear that the best situation would involve less distance. Then there would be fewer potential problems. With face to face contact, the least number of things could go wrong. (p. 392)

Bransford and Johnson (1973) intentionally designed the passage to consist of abstract, unfamiliar statements. If you found it difficult to recall the ideas, your experience was similar to the experience of the people who participated in the experiment. They recalled only 3.6 ideas from a maximum of 14. The ideas can be made less abstract by showing people an appropriate context, as is illustrated in Figure 11.1. Does the picture help you recall any more ideas? Bransford and Johnson (1973) tested the effect of context by comparing a *no-context* group with two other groups. The *context-before* group saw the picture before they read the passage. They recalled an average of 8.0 ideas, a substantial improvement over the no-context group. The *context-after* group saw the picture immediately after reading the passage. They recalled only 3.6 ideas—the same number as the no-context group. The effect of context was useful, but only if people were aware of the context before reading the passage.

The results suggest that context does much more than simply provide hints about what might have occurred in the passage. If the picture provided useful retrieval cues, the people who saw the picture after reading the passage should have recalled more ideas than the group who didn't see the picture. Because recall was improved only when people saw the picture before reading the passage, the experiment suggests that the context improved comprehension, which in turn improved recall. People in the context-before group rated the passage as easy to comprehend, in contrast to the context-after group. When the abstract ideas were difficult to comprehend, they were quickly forgotten, and providing the context after the passage had no effect on recall.

The balloon passage is an example of a novel context because most of us have never encountered this particular situation. What would happen if readers saw a passage about a familiar event that could activate the kind of schematic structures that we discussed in Chapter 9? But even reading about a familiar event is helpful only when we can recognize it. Consider the following passage:

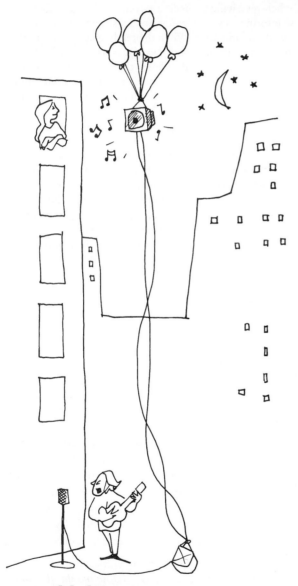

FIGURE **11.1** Appropriate context for the balloon passage

Source: From "Considerations of some problems of comprehension," by J. D. Bransford & M. K. Johnson, 1973, in *Visual Information Processing*, W. G. Chase (Ed.). Copyright 1973 by Academic Press, Inc. Reprinted by permission.

The procedure is actually quite simple. First you arrange things into different groups. Of course, *one pile may be sufficient depending on how much there is to do. If you have to go somewhere else due to lack of facilities, that is the next step; otherwise you are pretty well set. It is important not to overdo things. That is, it is better to do too few things at once than too many. In the short run this may not seem important, but complications can easily arise. A mistake can be expensive as well. At first the whole procedure will seem complicated. Soon, however, it will become just another facet of life. It is difficult to foresee any end to the necessity for this task in the immediate future, but then one never can tell. After the procedure is completed, one arranges the materials into different groups again. Then they can be put into their appropriate places. Eventually they will be used once more, and the whole cycle will then have to be repeated. However, that is part of life. (p. 400)**

The paragraph actually describes a very familiar procedure, but the ideas are presented so abstractly that the procedure is difficult to recognize. People who read the passage had as much trouble recalling ideas as the people who read the balloon passage—they recalled only 2.8 ideas from a maximum of 18. A different group of subjects, who were informed after reading the passage that it referred to washing clothes, didn't do any better; they recalled only 2.7 ideas. But subjects who were told before they read the passage that it described washing clothes recalled 5.8 ideas. The results are consistent with the results on the balloon passage and indicate that background knowledge isn't sufficient if people don't recognize the appropriate context. Although everyone is familiar with the procedure used to wash clothes, people didn't recognize the procedure because the passage was so abstract. Providing the appropriate context before the passage therefore increased both comprehension and recall, as it did for the balloon passage.

Effect on Retrieval

The failure of the context-after group to recall more ideas than the no context group was caused by the difficulty in comprehending material when there was not an obvious context. The results might have been different, however, if the material had been easier to understand as presented. Bransford and Johnson (1973) suggest that, if people initially understand a text and are then encouraged to think of the ideas in a new perspective, they might recall additional ideas that they failed to recall under the old perspective.

A study by R. C. Anderson and J. W. Pichert (1978) supports the hypothesis that a shift in perspective may result in the recall of additional ideas. The participants in their study read about two boys who played hooky from school. The story told that they went to one of the boys' homes because no one was there on Thursdays. It was a very nice home on attractive grounds, set back from the road. But because it was an older home, it had some defects—a leaky roof and a damp basement. The family was quite wealthy and owned a lot of valuable possessions, such as ten-speed bikes, a color television, and a rare coin collection. The entire story contained 72 ideas, which had previously been rated for their importance to a prospective burglar or to a

---

* From "Considerations of some problems of comprehension," by J. D. Bransford & M. K. Johnson, 1973, in *Visual information processing*, edited by W. G. Chase.

prospective home buyer. For example, a leaky roof and damp basement would be important to a home buyer, whereas valuable possessions and the fact that no one was usually home on Thursday would be important to a burglar.

The subjects read the story from one of the two perspectives and, after a short delay, were asked to write down as much of the exact story as they could remember. After another short delay they again attempted to recall ideas from the story. Half did so from the same **perspective** and half from a new perspective. The experimenters told the subjects in the same perspective condition that the purpose of the study was to determine whether people could remember things they thought they had forgotten if they were given a second chance. Subjects in the new-perspective condition were told that the purpose of the study was to determine whether people could remember things they thought they had forgotten if they were given a new perspective.

As might be expected, the perspective influenced the kind of information people recalled during the first recall period. The group that had the burglar perspective recalled more burglar information, and the group that had the home-buyer perspective recalled more home-buyer information. The results during the second recall attempt supported the hypothesis that a change in perspective can result in recall of additional information. The group that shifted perspectives recalled additional ideas that were important to the new perspective—7% more ideas in one experiment and 10% more in another. Their prior schematic knowledge about what would interest a home-buyer or a burglar aided their recall. For example, someone who shifted to the home-buyer perspective might now remember the leaky basement. In contrast, the group that did not shift perspective recalled slightly less information on its second attempt than on its first attempt.

Notice that these findings differ from the findings of Bransford and Johnson (1973) in that the shift to a new perspective aided the retrieval, rather than the comprehension, of ideas. Because the story was easy to comprehend, comprehension wasn't a problem; the problem was being able to recall all the ideas. Anderson and Pichert proposed three possible explanations for why changing perspectives aided recall. One possibility is that people simply guessed ideas that they didn't really remember but that were consistent with the new perspective. The chance of guessing correctly, however, is rather low. A second alternative is that people did not recall all they could remember because they thought it was not important to the original perspective. The instructions, however, were to recall all the information. The third possibility was the one favored by Anderson and Pichert because it was the most consistent with what the participants reported during interviews that followed their recall. Many subjects reported that the new perspective provided them with a plan for searching memory. They used their knowledge about what would interest a home buyer or a burglar to retrieve new information that was not suggested by the original perspective.

Effect on False Recognition and Recall

The previous studies support the idea that prior knowledge influences either the comprehension or the retrieval of information in a text. People who could

perspective A particular point of view

interpret abstract ideas as related to a serenade or to the washing of clothes had an advantage in comprehending and recalling the ideas. In addition, adopting a particular perspective enabled people to retrieve more concrete ideas than they had initially been able to comprehend.

Although background knowledge usually makes comprehension and recall easier, it can also be the source of errors. When we already know something about the given topic and then read more about it, we may have difficulty distinguishing between what we read and what we already know. This can create a problem if we are asked to recall the source of the information. Consider the following biographical passage:

> *Gerald Martin strove to undermine the existing government to satisfy his political ambitions. Many of the people of his country supported his efforts. Current political problems made it relatively easy for Martin to take over. Certain groups remained loyal to the old government and caused Martin trouble. He confronted these groups directly and so silenced them. He became a ruthless, uncontrollable dictator. The ultimate effect of his rule was the downfall of his country.* (Sulin & Dooling, 1974, p. 256)

People who read this passage should not associate it with their knowledge of famous people because Gerald Martin is a fictitious person. It would be easy, however, to modify the passage by changing the name of the dictator. In an experiment designed by Sulin and Dooling (1974), half the subjects read the Gerald Martin passage, and half the subjects read the same passage with the name changed to Adolf Hitler. Either 5 minutes or 1 week after reading the passage, the subjects were given a recognition-memory test consisting of seven sentences from the passage randomly mixed with seven sentences that were not in the passage. Subjects were asked to identify the sentences that occurred in the passage.

Four of the sentences not in the passage were completely unrelated (neutral), and the other three varied in their relatedness to the Hitler theme. The low-related sentence was "He was an intelligent man but had no sense of human kindness." The medium-related sentence was "He was obsessed by the desire to conquer the world." The high-related sentence was "He hated the Jews particularly and so persecuted them." Figure 11.2 shows the recognition of sentences for the two retention intervals. At the short retention interval, there were few false recognitions, and the results were uninfluenced by whether the passage was about a famous person (Hitler) or a fictitious person (Martin). After 1 week, however, it was more difficult for people who had read the Hitler passage to distinguish between what was in the passage and what they knew about Hitler. People were likely to recognize a sentence incorrectly as having occurred in the passage if it described Hitler. False recognitions also increased with the retention interval for people who read the Gerald Martin (fictitious) passage, but to a lesser degree.

Information can also be falsely recognized or recalled when it matches our knowledge of scripts. As we saw in Chapter 9, a script represents our memory for an organized sequence of events, such as what typically occurs during a crime. The false recall of such information can be a serious problem if members of a jury incorrectly remember events that they associate with a

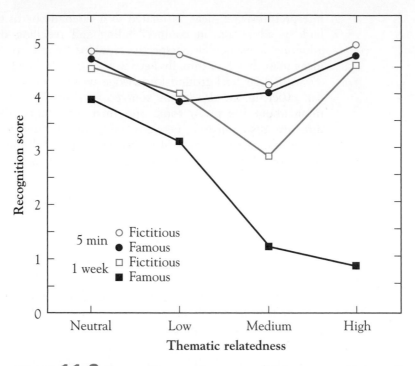

FIGURE **11.2** Recognition performance (high score = high performance) on new information as a function of main character, retention interval, and thematic relatedness

Source: From "Intrusion of a thematic idea in retention of prose," by R. A. Sulin & D. J. Dooling, 1974, *Journal of Experimental Psychology*, *103*, 255–262. Copyright 1974 by the American Psychological Association. Reprinted by permission.

crime but that did not actually occur in this case. Holst and Pezdek (1992) asked people to list all the events that occur in a typical robbery of a convenience store, a bank, and a mugging. Some of these events were then included in a tape-recorded transcript of a mock trial in which the prosecutor questions an eyewitness to a robbery. Four of the events associated with a robbery (act like a shopper, go to the cash register, demand money, threaten people) were stated by the eyewitness, but four other robbery events were unstated (case the store, pull out a gun, take the money, drive away in a getaway car).

The participants in the experiment then returned 1 week later and were asked to recall as many actions as they could from the witness's testimony. They recalled 31% of the stated events and falsely recalled 15% of the unstated events, indicating that their prior knowledge of what might occur in a robbery (such as pulling out a gun) influenced their recall. When misleading information was introduced by an attorney, the incorrect recall of unstated events increased to 25%. Thus, if an attorney implied that the robber had a gun, participants were more likely to recall that the robber had a gun even though they were instructed to recall only events mentioned by the eyewitness.

In conclusion, prior knowledge can influence the comprehension and recall of text in a variety of ways. Prior knowledge can make abstract ideas seem less abstract and easier to comprehend. It can also determine what we emphasize in a text and can provide a framework for recalling ideas. The price we pay for these benefits is that it may be more difficult to locate the source of our knowledge if what we read is integrated with what we know. In most cases the price is fairly small relative to the benefits, but it can have serious consequences in some instances.

ORGANIZATION OF TEXT

I mentioned at the beginning of this chapter that both the prior knowledge of the reader and the organization of ideas in the text influence comprehension. A large component of the research on text comprehension is concerned with reading stories that describe a sequence of events. To understand the story, we need to organize information at two levels (Graesser, Singer, & Trabasso, 1994). At one level we need to establish a **global coherence** about the main events that occur throughout the story. We need to keep track of what is happening to the major characters (Albrecht & O'Brien, 1993) and to the events related to achieving goals (Dopkins, Klin, & Myers, 1993). At a more detailed level we need to establish a **local coherence** about the most recent events in the story. We need to integrate the ideas that we are reading with the ideas that immediately preceded those ideas. Our ability to integrate ideas at both the local and global levels will be greatly influenced by how well the author has organized the text.

global coherence Integration of major ideas that occur throughout a text

local coherence Integration of ideas within an immediate context in a text

We begin by looking at the different parts of a story and the important role that goals play in organizing the major events in a story—global coherence. We then see how causal relations provide a means of organizing events around these goals. Finally, we look at how readers integrate the details of a story to establish local coherence by constructing a semantic network much like the semantic networks discussed in Chapter 9.

Story Structure

One characteristic of simple narrative stories is that the structure determines how the events in the story are organized. We can study this structure at a very general level by representing a story as consisting of a setting, a theme, a plot, and a resolution (Thorndyke, 1977). The **setting** describes time, location, and major characters. The **theme** provides the general focus of the story, often a goal that the main character is trying to achieve. The **plot** consists of a series of actions the main character takes to try and achieve the goal. Several subgoals or intermediate goals may have to be accomplished before the main goal is reached. The **resolution**—the final outcome of the story—often describes whether the main character was successful in achieving the goal.

setting The time and place in which narrative events occur

theme The main goals of characters in a narrative

plot The sequence of events related to achieving goals in a narrative

resolution The outcome of events in the plot

Thorndyke studied story structure by creating a story in which farmers on an island wanted to build a canal to water their crops. The first ten statements described the setting, which introduced the location and central characters. The next six statements established the theme and goal of building a canal across the island, followed by the plot. The last three statements described the final resolution, or outcome.

To evaluate how useful the goal structure of a story is in facilitating comprehension, Thorndyke modified the story to make the structure less apparent. One modification placed the theme at the end of the story, so people would not encounter the goal until after they had read the plot and the resolution. People read or heard the story only once, so, when they finally reached the information about the goal, they had to use it to interpret what they had previously read about the plot. A more extreme modification was to delete the goal statement entirely. People recalled less information when the goal statement occurred at the end of the story and still less information when the goal was deleted.

The importance that people place on goals is directly illustrated in a study on scripts. We saw in Chapter 9 that one facet of our organized knowledge is our knowledge of common activities (scripts). Bower, Black, and Turner (1979) performed one of the first investigations of how people's knowledge of such routine activities helps them understand and remember information in a text. The researchers first measured the extent to which people agree about the events that occur in standard activities such as going to a restaurant, attending a lecture, getting up in the morning, going grocery shopping, or visiting a doctor. They asked people to list approximately 20 actions or events that occur during each of these activities. Table 11.1 presents the lists in the order in which the events were usually mentioned. All events listed in Table 11.1 were mentioned by at least 25% of the subjects. The lists show that there is considerable agreement on the actions that occur during routine activities.

The typical events in a script provide a framework for comprehension but are themselves uninteresting because we already know about them. What is usually interesting is the occurrence of an event that is related to the script but unexpected. For example, a customer might need help translating a menu because it is in French, or the waiter might spill soup on the customer. Schank and Abelson (1977) refer to such events as **obstacles** because they interrupt the major goals of the script, such as ordering and eating in this case.

obstacle An event that delays or prevents the attainment of a goal

Bower and his colleagues (1979) hypothesized that such interruptions should be remembered better than the routine events in the scripts listed in Table 11.1. From the viewpoint of the reader, they are the only "point" of the story. The researchers also hypothesized that events irrelevant to the goals of the script should be remembered less well than the routine events in the script. For example, the type of print on the menu or the color of the waitress's hair is irrelevant to the goals of ordering and eating a meal.

Bower and his colleagues tested this hypothesis by asking subjects to read six script-based stories about making coffee, attending a lecture, getting up in the morning, attending a movie, visiting a doctor, and dining at a restaurant. After reading all six stories and then completing an intervening task for 10 minutes, subjects attempted to recall the stories in writing. The results supported the predictions—subjects recalled 53% of the interruptions, 38% of the script actions, and 32% of the irrelevant information. The interruptions either prevented or delayed the main character from accomplishing a goal, and this aspect of the story was well remembered.

TABLE **11.1**
Actions Associated with Different Events

Going to a Restaurant	Attending a Lecture	Getting Up	Grocery Shopping	Visiting a Doctor
Open door	ENTER DOOR	*Wake up*	ENTER STORE	*Enter office*
Enter	*Look for friends*	Turn off alarm	GET CART	CHECK IN WITH RECEPTIONIST
Give reservation name	FIND SEAT	Lie in bed	Take out list	SIT DOWN
Wait to be seated	SIT DOWN	Stretch	Look at list	Wait
Go to table	Settle belongings	GET UP	Go to first aisle	Look at other people
BE SEATED	TAKE OUT NOTEBOOK	Make bed	*Go up and down aisles*	READ MAGAZINE
Order drinks	*Look at other students*	Go to bathroom	PICK OUT ITEMS	*Name called*
Put napkins on lap	*Talk*	Use toilet	Compare prices	Follow nurse
LOOK AT MENU	Look at professor	*Take shower*	Put items in cart	*Enter exam room*
Discuss menu	LISTEN TO PROFESSOR	*Wash face*	Get meat	Undress
ORDER MEAL	TAKE NOTES	Shave	Look for items forgotten	*Sit on table*
Talk	CHECK TIME	DRESS	Talk to other shoppers	Talk to nurse
Drink water	Ask questions	Go to kitchen	Go to checkout counters	NURSE TESTS
Eat salad or soup	Change position in seat	Fix breakfast	*Find fastest line*	Wait
Meal arrives	Daydream	EAT BREAKFAST	WAIT IN LINE	Doctor enters
EAT FOOD	Look at other students	BRUSH TEETH	*Put food on belt*	Doctor greets
Finish meal	Take more notes	Read paper	Read magazines	Talk to doctor about problem
Order dessert	Close notebook	*Comb hair*	WATCH CASHIER RING UP	Doctor asks questions
Eat dessert	Gather belongings	Get books	PAY CASHIER	DOCTOR EXAMINES
Ask for bill	Stand up	Look in mirror	*Watch bag boy*	Get dressed
Bill arrives	Talk	Get coat	Cart bags out	Get medicine
PAY BILL	LEAVE	LEAVE HOUSE	Load bags into car	Make another appointment
Leave tip			LEAVE STORE	LEAVE OFFICE
Get coats				
LEAVE				

Source: From "Scripts in memory for text," by G. H. Bower, J. B. Black, & T. J. Turner, 1979, *Cognitive Psychology, 11*, 177–220. Copyright 1979 by Academic Press, Inc. Reprinted by permission of Elsevier Science.

Note: Items in all capital letters were mentioned by most subjects, items in italics by fewer subjects, and items in lowercase letters were mentioned by the fewest subjects.

Causal Connections

When a goal is included in a story, people use the goal to help themselves organize the actions described in the story. A character's attempts to achieve a goal result in the establishment of causal relations among many of the statements in a text. Work by Trabasso and his students at the University of Chicago (Trabasso & Sperry, 1985; Trabasso & van den Broek, 1985) indicates that it is these causal relations that underlie what a reader judges to be important in a text. A formal statement of a **causal relation** is that one event, *A*, is judged to be the cause of another event, *B*, if the absence of *A* implies the absence of *B*. In other words, you cannot accomplish your goal if someone eliminates the events that are necessary for achieving that goal. Consider the goal of walking into your house. You couldn't walk into your house unless you opened the door, which you couldn't do unless you unlocked the door, which you couldn't do unless you took out your keys. Thus, all three actions are causally related (necessary) for accomplishing the goal of walking into your house.

causal relation An event that results in the occurrence of another event

An important variable in determining the judged importance of statements in a story is the number of causal connections linked to the statement. In the previous example, walking into your house has three causal connections (taking out the keys, unlocking the door, and opening the door), and unlocking the door has one causal connection (taking out the keys). Trabasso and Sperry (1985) found that, when subjects rated the importance of events in stories, the judged importance of an action was directly related to the number of causal connections associated with that action. The number of causal connections was also important in determining what people could recall from a story and what they would include in a summary of the story (Trabasso & van den Broek, 1985).

In addition, causal connections determine how quickly people can retrieve text information. Trabasso and Wiley (2005) built a text comprehension model that they used to simulate other research findings including results obtained by McKoon and Ratcliff (1992). One of the experiments included a story about an assassin who attempts to kill the president using a rifle. Although the word "kill" describes the main goal and the word "rifle" describes a subordinate goal, the story had more causal connections to "rifle" than to "kill." The model therefore predicts that after reading the story, readers should be faster in verifying that the word "rifle" appeared in the story than the word "kill." The number of causal connections was a good predictor of verification times for this and other stories.

Trabasso and Wiley's (2005) findings are consistent with earlier results that adding casual connections to a story speeds up verification times. This is perhaps surprising because when we considered spreading activation models in Chapter 9, we learned that adding more links to a node in the network slows retrieval time unless the information could be integrated around a subnode (Reder & Anderson, 1980). What is remarkable about adding causal connections is that the added information actually speeded decisions about information in the text (Myers, O'Brien, Balota, & Toyofuku, 1984).

These psychologists followed the general procedure used by Reder and Anderson (1980) but, in a high-integration condition, used facts that were causally linked. The facts were presented in four pairs of stories. Each pair of stories shared a common theme—going to a baseball game, a restaurant, a saloon, or a racetrack.

Each story had three variations, as shown in Table 11.2 for the baseball pair. Notice that, although the Fan-3 condition contained three facts and the Fan-6 condition contained six facts, the two test sentences (marked by asterisks) were identical for each condition. For the high-integration condition, the two test sentences were preceded by statements that were causally related. For example, the banker had to wait in line *because* he found a crowd buying tickets, and he cheered loudly *because* his team scored. In the low-integration condition, the additional facts were not causally related to the test statements.

Myers and his colleagues found that students were usually faster in deciding whether test sentences were true or false if they had studied six highly

TABLE **11.2**
Sample Sentences Used in Integration Study

Fan 3	
The banker	The actor
arrived at the ball park.	went to the ball game.
waited in line.*	saw the start of the ball game.*
cheered loudly.*	went home early.*
Fan 6: High integration	
The banker	The actor
decided to see a baseball game.	had a ticket for a Red Sox game.
arrived at the ball park.	went to the ball game.
found a crowd buying tickets.	sat down as the umpire yelled play ball.
waited in line.*	saw the start of the game.*
entered to see his team score.	found the first few innings boring.
cheered loudly.*	went home early.*
Fan 6: Low integration	
The banker	The actor
decided to see a baseball game.	had a ticket for a Red Sox game.
arrived at the ball park.	went to the ball game.
bought a souvenir pennant.	bought a hot dog from a vendor.
waited in line.*	saw the start of the ball game.*
sat near the first-base dugout.	looked at his program.
cheered loudly.*	went home early.*

Source: From "Memory search without interference: The role of integration," by J. L. Myers, E. J. O'Brien, D. A. Balota, & M. L. Toyofuku, 1984, *Cognitive Psychology*, *16*, 217–242. Copyright 1984 by Academic Press, Inc. Reprinted by permission of Elsevier Science.

Note: The Fan-3 examples contain three facts, and the Fan-6 examples contain six facts. The test sentences are marked by asterisks.

integrated statements than if they had studied three statements. Providing the additional causal statements therefore facilitated memory retrieval. However, the fan effect usually occurred for the six low-integrated statements; that is, in the low-integration condition, students responded more slowly if they had learned six facts than if they had learned three.

The experiments that show the importance of goals and causal connections in texts demonstrate that both contribute to the global coherence of the text. However, readers also need to understand the details and establish local coherence by relating the ideas in a sentence to the immediately preceding ideas. Before considering a model of comprehension, we need to find out how the organization of ideas in a text determines how well readers can integrate these ideas. The answers to the following three questions generally determine the ease of integration.

1. Can a current idea be related to previously expressed ideas?
2. Are related ideas still available in working memory?
3. Is it necessary to make an inference to establish the relation?

Integration of Details

Establishing local coherence by integrating the details of a sentence is very challenging when the ideas in a sentence are not related to ideas expressed in previous sentences. An important determinant of comprehension difficulty is whether the ideas in a sentence were given in a previous sentence or whether they are new. The ease with which new ideas can be related to old ideas is illustrated by the two sequences of sentences in Table 11.3 (Kieras, 1978). The two examples contain the same seven sentences presented in a different order. The letter preceding each sentence indicates whether the information in the sentence is given (g) or new (n). The sentence is classified as *given* if it contains at least one noun that appeared in the preceding sentences. Example 1

TABLE **11.3**
Examples of Presentation Orders, Showing the Given (g) or New (n) Status of Each Sentence

Example 1	Example 2
n—The ants ate the jelly.	n—The kitchen was spotless.
g—The ants were hungry.	n—The table was wooden.
g—The ants were in the kitchen.	n—The ants were hungry.
g—The kitchen was spotless.	g—The ants were in the kitchen.
g—The jelly was grape.	n—The jelly was grape.
g—The jelly was on the table.	g—The jelly was on the table.
g—The table was wooden.	g—The ants ate the jelly.

Source: From "Good and bad structure in simple paragraphs: Effects on apparent theme, reading time, and recall," by D. E. Kieras, 1978, *Journal of Verbal Learning and Verbal Behavior, 17,* 13–28. Copyright 1978 by Academic Press, Inc. Reprinted by permission of Elsevier Science.

contains only one new sentence; all sentences but the first refer to information that preceded them. Example 2 contains four new sentences that do not refer to preceding information. Kieras predicted that the ideas in Example 1 should be easier to integrate and recall than the ideas in Example 2, and the results supported his prediction.

A second determinant of comprehension difficulty is whether the integration uses ideas that are active in working memory. You may have noticed that all but one of the given sentences in Example 1 repeat a noun from the immediately preceding sentence. The one exception, "The jelly was grape," repeats a noun (*jelly*) from a sentence that occurred four sentences earlier. This sentence may be more difficult to integrate with the preceding sentences because the given information may no longer be in working memory, a situation requiring a search of LTM (long-term memory) to retrieve the first sentence. Evidence in fact suggests that comprehension is influenced by whether the preceding relevant information is still active in STM or whether it must be retrieved from LTM (Lesgold, Roth, & Curtis, 1979).

The following sentences (from Lesgold et al., 1979) should be easy to integrate because the first sentence contains relevant information that should still be available in STM when the reader encounters the second sentence.

1. *A thick cloud of smoke hung over the forest. The forest was on fire.* (p. 294)

Now let's insert two sentences that change the topic and make it less likely that the information about the smoke over the forest is still in STM when the reader learns about the fire.

2. *A thick cloud of black smoke hung over the forest. Glancing to one side, Carol could see a bee flying around the back seat. Both of the kids were jumping around but made no attempt to free the insect. The forest was on fire.* (p. 295)

The inserted information is irrelevant to the fire in the forest and should make it more difficult to comprehend the final sentence than in case 1. Now consider the insertion of two sentences that are consistent with the initial topic.

3. *A thick cloud of smoke hung over the forest. The smoke was thick and black, and began to fill the clear sky. Up ahead Carol could see a ranger directing traffic to slow down. The forest was on fire.* (p. 295)

The two inserted sentences continue the initial topic, making it easier for the reader to keep active in STM information about the cloud of black smoke. Lesgold and his colleagues predicted that less time should be required to comprehend the final sentence in case 3 than in case 2. Their results supported their predictions.

inference The use of reasoning to establish relations in a text when the relations are not directly stated

A third determinant of comprehension difficulty is whether the ideas can be directly linked to each other or must be linked by making an **inference** (Haviland & Clark, 1974). This distinction can be illustrated by the following pairs of sentences:

1. *Ed was given an alligator for his birthday. The alligator was his favorite present.*

2. *Ed was given lots of things for his birthday. The alligator was his favorite present.*

In both cases the first sentence provides an appropriate context for the second sentence, but the first case makes it clear that Ed received an alligator for his birthday. The second requires an inference that one of the things Ed received was an alligator.

Participants in Haviland and Clark's experiment saw pairs of sentences in a tachistoscope. After reading the first sentence, they pressed a button to see the second sentence. When they thought they understood the second sentence, they pushed another button, which stopped a clock that measured how long the second sentence had been displayed. As predicted by Haviland and Clark, it took significantly less time to comprehend the second sentence when the same idea (such as an alligator) was mentioned in both sentences than when the relation between the two sentences had to be inferred.

In conclusion, a number of variables influence comprehension, according to these studies. All the variables reflect how easy it is to integrate what a person is reading with what that person has already read. One variable is whether the reader can relate newly acquired information to ideas that were already expressed in the text. Kieras's (1978) research indicated that it was easier to recall ideas in the text if the sentences referred to previous information than if they contained only new information. A second variable is whether previously expressed ideas are still active in STM or whether they must be retrieved from LTM. Comprehension is easier when related ideas are still active in STM (Glenberg et al., 1987; Lesgold et al., 1979). A third variable is whether newly acquired information can be related directly to previous information or whether the reader must infer the relation. Inferences slow comprehension (Haviland & Clark, 1974). A theory of comprehension should incorporate each of these three variables.

KINTSCH'S MODEL OF COMPREHENSION

The first two sections of this chapter reviewed research on two very important components of comprehension: the prior knowledge of the reader and the organization of ideas in the text. This final section describes psychologists' attempts to develop detailed models of text comprehension. Because text comprehension requires the integration of ideas in the text, a model of text comprehension requires assumptions about how this integration occurs.

Processing Assumptions

A model developed over nearly three decades by Kintsch (1979, 2005) at the University of Colorado has given us the most comprehensive theory of text comprehension. Because the model is fairly complex, I will give only a brief summary of its major assumptions, emphasizing those that are related to the previous studies. There are two inputs in the model, the reader and the text, both of which are necessary to understand comprehension. The knowledge and goals of the reader influence how the reader determines what is relevant,

proposition A meaningful idea that typically consists of several words

establishes expectations, and infers facts that are not directly stated in the text. The text itself is represented in the model by propositions. The **propositions** divide the text into meaningful units, which are then arranged in a network that is similar to the semantic networks discussed in Chapter 9.

The general characteristics of the model can be illustrated with a simple example (Kintsch, 1979). Consider the following text:

> The Swazi tribe was at war with a neighboring tribe because of a dispute over cattle. Among the warriors were two unmarried men, Kakra and his younger brother Gum. Kakra was killed in a battle. (p. 6)

The model specifies rules for dividing the text into propositions, but we are not concerned with the details of these rules. We consider word groups that correspond approximately to the underlying propositions. Figure 11.3 shows how the first sentence is divided into word groups and how the groups are related in a network. The proposition "was at war with" is the most important proposition, and the others are joined to it. An important parameter in the model is the number of propositions that can be kept active in STM. Because STM is limited in capacity, only a few propositions can be kept active; our example assumes that the capacity limit is three propositions, as indicated by the enclosed propositions in the figure. Propositions describing the plans and goals of the characters are particularly likely to be selected (Fletcher, 1986).

reinstatement search The search of long-term memory to place words in short-term memory where they can be used to integrate a text

Figure 11.4 shows the propositions of the second sentence and the propositions from the first sentence that are still active in STM. The reader first tries to connect the new propositions with the old ones in STM, but the words in the second sentence don't match any of the words in STM. The reader next determines whether the new propositions can be related to any propositions in LTM. Kintsch proposes that the search of LTM, which he calls a **reinstatement search**, is one of the factors that make a text difficult to read. If information in the text can be related to ideas that are still active in

Coherence analysis: Cycle I

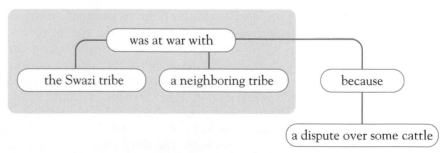

FIGURE **11.3** Analysis of the first sentence in the Swazi example

Source: From "On modeling comprehension," by W. Kintsch, 1979, *Educational Psychologist, 14*, 3–14. Copyright 1979 by Lawrence Erlbaum Associates, Inc. Reprinted by permission.

Coherence analysis: Cycle II

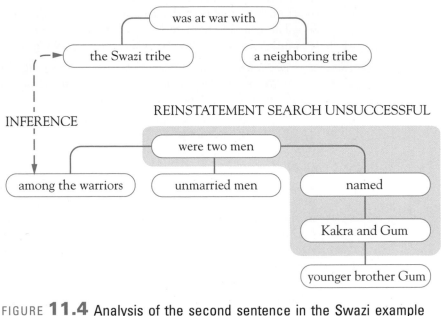

FIGURE **11.4** Analysis of the second sentence in the Swazi example

Source: From "On modeling comprehension," by W. Kintsch, 1979, *Educational Psychologist, 14*, 3–14. Copyright 1979 by Lawrence Erlbaum Associates, Inc. Reprinted by permission.

STM, comprehension is easier than if the reader must first search LTM to reinstate old information in STM so it can be integrated with the new information. This assumption is consistent with the findings of Lesgold and colleagues (1979) and of Glenberg and his colleagues (1987).

The reinstatement search also fails for the example because there are no concepts that are common to the first two sentences. The model must therefore construct a new network rather than add on to the old one. It may also make an inference at this point to interrelate the two networks. The inference is that the warriors mentioned in the second sentence were members of the Swazi tribe. This seems like a reasonable inference, but it is not stated directly. Kintsch's model assumes that inferences, like reinstatement searches, slow the reader and make comprehension more difficult. The evidence supports this assumption (e.g., Haviland & Clark, 1974).

The model once again selects three propositions from the second sentence to keep active in STM. Figure 11.4 shows that the three selected specify the names of the two men. The third sentence, "Kakra was killed in a battle," is easy to relate to previous information because information about Kakra is still available in STM. The new information can therefore be added directly to the network without having to search LTM or make an inference.

This example should give you an approximate idea of how the model works. The major theme of the model is that incoming information can be understood more easily when it can be integrated with information that the reader has already encountered. The easiest case is when the new information can be related to information that is still active in STM. If it cannot be related, a reinstatement search attempts to relate the new information to propositions stored in LTM. If the reinstatement search fails, a new network must be started, resulting in a memory for ideas that are not very well integrated. The result should be poorer recall, as was found by Kieras (1978) when the new sentences could not be related to previous sentences. Integration of ideas can sometimes be achieved by inference, but the need for inferences also contributes to the difficulty of the text.

The Construction-Integration Model

Kintsch (1988, 1998) further developed his theory by proposing that text comprehension occurs in two phases—a construction phase and an integration phase. During the construction phrase, words of the text are used to construct propositions that activate other words and propositions in LTM through spreading activation. These activated meanings are used to comprehend the sentence by selecting the appropriate meanings during the integration phrase. The proposed activation of many interpretations followed by the selection of the most appropriate ones is consistent with the research discussed in the previous chapter (Budiu & Anderson, 2004; Swinney, 1979).

Figure 11.5 illustrates that some of the activated meanings during the initial phase will need to be discarded as inappropriate. *Masked* can activate *Mardi gras*, and *gunman* can activate *cowboy*, in addition to the more appropriate meaning, *robber*. The ambiguous word *bank* initially activates both *river* and *money*, as we learned in the previous chapter from Swinney's (1979) research.

The integration phase assembles the meaning of the sentence from all the activated words and propositions. Many of these are inappropriate because

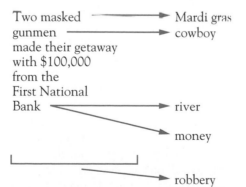

FIGURE **11.5** Some links between the words of a sentence and items in LTM

Source: *Comprehension: A paradigm for cognition*, by W. Kintsch, 1998, Cambridge, England: Cambridge University Press.

they do not fit the context. There are no other propositions in the sentence that indicate it describes Mardi gras participants or cowboys so these meanings are discarded in favor of more appropriate meanings. The sentence context is also used to discard inappropriate meanings of ambiguous words (such as *bank*). More recent research based on Swinney's (1979) lexical decision task indicates that it takes at least 350 msec to select the appropriate meaning of an ambiguous word and discard the inappropriate meaning (Kintsch, 1998, p. 228). It takes even longer (at least 750 msec at the end of the sentence) to identify the theme of the sentence as a robbery because identifying the theme requires determining the meaning of all the words in the sentence.

The construction-integration model demonstrates that comprehension is not immediate but occurs over time. It is a good example of the distinction between bottom-up and top-down processing that was introduced at the beginning of this book. The construction phase illustrates bottom-up processing (Kintsch, 2005). Words in the text activate related meanings without regard to context. The integration phase illustrates top-down processing. Context is now used to determine the appropriate meaning of the words (Long & Lea, 2005).

Incorporating Prior Knowledge

We began this chapter by looking at how a person's prior knowledge influences text comprehension. Can we "capture" this prior knowledge and incorporate it into Kintsch's model of comprehension? In his Distinguished Scientific Award address to the annual meeting of the American Psychological Association, Kintsch (1994) focused on the role that prior knowledge plays in learning from a text.

situation model Integration of prior knowledge and text information to construct an understanding of the situation described in a text

Our emphasis thus far has been on representing the semantic relations in the text through integrating the propositions in a semantic network. But there is another, deeper level of understanding that Kintsch calls a situation model. The **situation model** is constructed by combining prior knowledge and information in the text to produce a more elaborate understanding of the situation described in the text. Rather than treating language as information to analyze syntactically and semantically, language is now viewed as a set of processing instructions on how to construct a mental representation of the described situation (Zwaan & Radvansky, 1998). You used your prior knowledge to infer that the sentence in Figure 11.5 described a robbery. The use of prior knowledge becomes even more important to understand complex topics such as the circulation of blood.

Figure 11.6 shows an example for a two-sentence text fragment: "When a baby has a septal defect, the blood cannot get rid of enough carbon dioxide through the lungs. Therefore, it looks purple." The situation model in this case is represented as a diagram. It shows that, because of the septal defect, red blood carrying oxygen is mixed together with purple blood carrying carbon dioxide. Some of the purple blood is therefore recirculated back into the body without picking up oxygen in the lungs. Notice that much of the information in the situation model is derived from the reader's knowledge of the circulatory system, rather than derived directly from the text.

TEXT:
When a baby has a septal defect, the blood cannot get rid of enough carbon dioxide through the lungs. Therefore, it looks purple.

SITUATION MODEL:

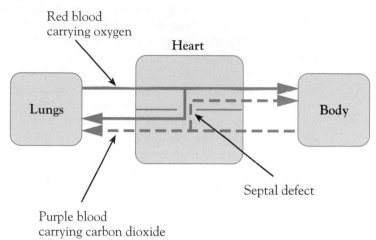

FIGURE **11.6** A diagrammatic situation model for the text fragment

Source: From "Text comprehension, memory, and learning," by W. Kintsch, 1994, *American Psychologist, 49,* 294–303. Copyright 1994 by the American Psychological Association. Reprinted by permission.

The deeper level of understanding represented by the situation model can also be represented in the semantic networks that we discussed previously. In this case the semantic network model would contain propositions that are derived both from the text and from the reader's prior knowledge. The propositions about the septal defect, color of the blood, and excess carbon dioxide come from the text, but other propositions such as the mixing of the blood depend on inferences based on prior knowledge.

APPLICATIONS

Predicting Readability

One attractive aspect of Kintsch's model is that it is complete enough to allow predictions about the ease of reading different kinds of text. Predicting readability is an important applied problem. The developers of educational materials want to be assured that their materials can be understood by the students who read them. A former professor of mine once wrote a chapter for *The Mind*, a book in one of the Time-Life series. His chapter required nine revisions before it satisfied the editors of Time-Life. Although he was a good writer and was familiar with the topic, he was inexperienced at writing for students in junior high school—the reading level selected for the series.

There have been many attempts to predict readability. According to Kintsch and Vipond (1979), the earliest formulas appeared in the 1920s.

readability formula A formula that uses variables such as word frequency and sentence length to predict the readability of text

There are now approximately 50 **readability formulas,** most containing word and sentence variables (unfamiliar words and long sentences generally make a text harder to read). What the formulas lack, however, is a good way of measuring text organization. If someone placed all the words in a sentence in a scrambled order, the sentence would be very difficult to comprehend, but the predictions of most formulas would be unchanged because they don't consider the order of words in a sentence or the order of sentences in a paragraph. The formulas are thus limited because they are not based on a theory of text comprehension.

The theory developed by Kintsch has already contributed to overcoming many of these limitations by providing an account of how the reader's information-processing capabilities interact with the organization of the text. Kintsch defined **readability** as the number of propositions recalled divided by the reading time. The measure takes into account both recall and reading time because it is easy to improve either measure at the expense of the other.

readability The number of recalled propositions divided by reading time

Kintsch used his model, along with more traditional measures, to predict the readability of paragraphs. The two best predictors of readability were word frequency and the number of reinstatement searches. The first measure is contained in most readability formulas. As we might expect, the use of common words, those that occur frequently in the language, improves comprehension. The second measure—the number of reinstatement searches—is calculated from Kintsch's model. Application of the model determines how often a person must search LTM to relate new information to previous information. A reinstatement search is required only when the new information cannot be related to the propositions in STM. Another theoretical measure that improves the readability predictions is the number of inferences that are required. An inference is required whenever a concept is not directly repeated—for example, when *war* was mentioned in the first sentence and *warriors* in the second sentence. Unfortunately, however, these newer theoretical constructs are difficult to measure, so readability is still primarily determined by such simple measures as word frequency and sentence length. This may change as technology becomes available to evaluate text based on the more complex measures that reflect semantic organization (Caccamise, Snyder, & Kintsch, 2008).

Although Kintsch found that the number of inferences influenced readability, they were less predictive than word frequency and the number of reinstatement searches. The required inferences were fairly easy, however, their influence might increase if they were more difficult.

More difficult inferences are often required for reading academic material as indicated in a study by Britton and Gulgoz (1991) that demonstrated how one can improve readability by rewriting academic material to reduce the need to make inferences. They used Kintsch's model to identify where inferences were required in a passage on the air war in North Vietnam. They found 40 such locations and then revised the text by inserting the inferences into the passage so readers would not have to make the inferences. For example, the information in parentheses was inserted into the original passage so the reader would not have to infer the relation between the title and the first sentence.

Air War in North (Vietnam)
By the Fall of 1964, Americans in both Saigon and Washington had begun to
focus on Hanoi (capital of North Vietnam) as the source of the continuing
problem in the South.

The insertion prevents an inference because the revision allows a direct link between the title and the first sentence. Both now contain the term *North Vietnam.*

Britton and Gulgoz used the same readability measure as Kintsch and found that their revised passage had a much higher readability score than the original. People who read the original version recalled 3.44 propositions per minute of reading time, and people who read the revision recalled 5.24 propositions per minute of reading time. The investigators suggested that writers typically do not include this additional material because their extensive knowledge about the topic makes the inferences easy for them.

Comprehension Strategies and Assessment

We have seen in this chapter that comprehension depends on both the reader and the text. Readability depends on the text; comprehension strategies depend on the reader. Although academic material requires more inferences than narratives, whether these inferences are made depends on a reader's goals. Some of the participants in a comprehension study by van den Broek and his colleagues were told to imagine they were studying for an essay exam. The other participants were told to imagine that they had come upon an article of interest while browsing through a magazine (van den Broek, Lorch, Linderholm, & Gustafson, 2001). The study-goal participants produced more inferences to establish the coherence of the text and had better memory for its content. The other students were less concerned with constructing a coherent representation but made more associative ("This reminds me of the movie *Apollo 13*") and evaluative ("How strange!") comments.

Table 11.4 lists nine effective comprehension strategies based on research (Block & Duffy, 2008). The strategies should interest you for two reasons. First, they should help you comprehend and learn material, and second, they provide an application of some of the main ideas expressed in Chapters 10 and 11.

The first strategy is to predict what will occur next based on an overview of the material. For example, you can study the outline provided at the beginning of each chapter in this text to learn its organization. The outline for this chapter informs you that the major sections are prior knowledge, organization of the text, Kintsch's model of comprehension, and applications. The subheadings provide additional information such as the prior knowledge of the reader influences comprehension, retrieval, and false recognition. You may also be able to make general predictions based on an evaluation of the text. For example, fiction contains a setting, theme, plot, and resolution, as indicated in the section on story structure.

Strategies 3 through 5 require close monitoring to maintain a high level of comprehension. The monitoring assures that local coherence is established for the immediate context. As indicated in Figure 10.9 in the previous chapter,

TABLE **11.4**
Recommended Comprehension Strategies

1. Predict. Size up text in advance by looking at title, text figures, sections, pictures, and captions.
2. Evaluate. Approach a fictional text expecting to note the setting, characters, and story structure.
3. Monitor. Activate comprehensions strategies to derive meaning from words, phrases, sentences, and text.
4. Question. Stop to reread and initiate comprehension processes when the meaning is unclear.
5. Fix-it. Look back and reread when necessary.
6. Image. Construct meanings expressed in the text by noticing and generating mental pictures.
7. Infer. Connect ideas in the text based on personal experiences and prior knowledge.
8. Synthesize. Combine sequence of details, unique types of information, and conclusions to make meaning.
9. Summarize. Find main ideas and draw conclusions.

Source: Based on "Research on teaching comprehension" by C. C. Block & G. G. Duffy, 2008, in *Comprehension Instruction: Research-Based Best Practices*, C. C. Block & S. R. Parris (Eds.), New York: Guilford Press.

monitoring requires selecting interpretations that are consistent with other words and phrases in the sentence. Rereading is necessary when the meaning is unclear and error-recovery heuristics (see Figure 10.6) are occasionally needed to successfully integrate the meaning of the individual words.

Strategies 6 and 7 are elaborative strategies that build on the material. We learned in Chapter 7 that imagery is an effective learning strategy because the image forms a second memory code. The dual coding theory formulated by Paivio (1971) has provided the theoretical basis for successful instruction that increased students' performance on standardized comprehension tests (Sadowski, 2008). The second elaboration strategy is to relate ideas in the text to prior knowledge. As we have seen in this chapter, prior knowledge is helpful for increasing comprehension (Bransford & Johnson, 1973), aiding retrieval (Anderson & Pichert, 1978), and building situation models (Kintsch, 1994).

The last two strategies are needed to see the big picture. Synthesizing information establishes global coherence, showing how all of the ideas in the passage fit together. Finally, summarizing the material involves finding the main ideas and reaching conclusions.

Research on comprehension strategies requires methods of assessing comprehension. A major limitation of current methods is their lack of ability to measure deep levels of comprehension at the level of the situation model (Caccamise et al., 2008). The quote from John Locke at the beginning of this chapter is as relevant today as it was in the seventeenth century: "Reading furnishes the mind only with materials of knowledge; it is thinking that makes what we read ours."

Essay questions are typically superior to multiple-choice questions for measuring deep levels of understanding, but they are difficult to grade. This is changing with advances in computer-based essay scoring (Landauer, McNamara, Dennis, & Kintsch, 2007) that is beginning to evaluate the semantic content of essays at the level of trained human graders. Computers are also beginning to help on the learning side of comprehension. A program called Interactive Strategy Training for Active Reading and Thinking or iSTART (McNamara, Levinstein, & Boonthum, 2004) teaches comprehension monitoring, paraphrasing, and constructing self-explanations, inferences, predictions, and elaborations. Caccamise and coworkers conclude their chapter by predicting that the classroom of the future will consist of computer-based tutors that combine strategy instruction with immediate feedback based on ongoing individual assessments that guide the learning process.

SUMMARY

Psychologists study comprehension by investigating how people's prior knowledge and information-processing characteristics interact with the organization of ideas in a text. The importance of prior knowledge is evident when people have to comprehend very abstract ideas. A meaningful context improves recall if the context is given before people read the abstract material. It is necessary to improve comprehension to improve recall. Recall of more concrete ideas may be improved by providing a context after people have read the text if the context causes a change in perspective. People's knowledge about everyday activities can be represented by scripts that describe the most common events associated with the activities. Scripts influence what a person emphasizes when reading a text. One disadvantage of prior knowledge is that it sometimes makes it hard to distinguish between recently read material and prior knowledge about the topic. Comprehension is determined not only by what a person already knows but also by the organization of ideas in a text. The global structure of narrative stories includes setting, theme, plot, and resolution. The theme provides the general focus of the story and often consists of a goal that the main character tries to achieve.

Comprehension is best when the theme precedes the plot; it deteriorates when the theme follows the plot and deteriorates even more when the theme is left out. Statements that have either a positive or a negative impact on the attainment of a goal are judged most important and are best remembered. Causal relations are also helpful in facilitating the quick retrieval of information. A model of text comprehension must account for how the reader attempts to relate the ideas in the text to ideas already read. Comprehension is easiest when the ideas can be related to ideas that are still available in STM. If no relations are found, the reader can search LTM to look for a relation. If no relations are found in LTM, the new material must be stored separately rather than integrated with old material. Relations can sometimes be found by making inferences, but inferences slow down comprehension compared with direct repetition of the same concepts.

A model of comprehension proposed by Kintsch has been quite successful in predicting and improving readability. The model can account for the organization of a text by considering how many LTM searches and inferences are required. Its parameters include the number of propositions that are processed at one time, the probability of storing a proposition in LTM, and the number of propositions that can be kept active in STM. Besides improving previous readability formulas, the model provides a theoretical framework for investigating how a person's information-processing characteristics interact with the organization of the text to influence comprehension. In particular, the prior knowledge of the reader determines the ease of making inferences and the subsequent success in recalling and using text information to solve problems.

STUDY QUESTIONS

1. What is a paraphrase? If a person can produce a paraphrase of something he or she has read, what does that tell us?

2. Why is the reader's prior knowledge of context especially important in trying to understand abstract ideas?

3. Anderson and Pichert list three possible explanations for the evidence that changing perspectives aids recall of a story. Can you think of any way to rule out those not favored by Anderson and Pichert?

4. How often does it make a difference if you can recall where you read something (the source of information)? Can you think of any real-life situation in which it could matter?

5. Using all the described components of scripts, write a brief script for a common activity not mentioned in the book. Did you have any trouble doing so, once you decided on the activity?

6. What sort of departures from a standard script are especially likely to be remembered? Think of weddings you attended, for example. Does what you remember most vividly agree with what Bower and others hypothesize would be the types of information recalled?

7. Consider the basic elements of story structure. Have you ever heard a young child retell a story? What is usually missing in young children's accounts that often make them difficult to follow?

8. The various studies on integration of ideas that led to Kintsch's model of comprehension used carefully contrived materials. What variables were the researchers attempting to manipulate? Did those variables actually influence text comprehension? Why or why not?

9. The exposition of Kintsch's model is necessarily abstract and therefore difficult to comprehend. Persevere in your reinstatement searches! See if you can use it to deal with a new example of text selected from another course. What factors are included in Kintsch's model? How does the *reader* enter into this model?

10. Why did Kintsch's definition of readability include two factors? What did he find to be the best predictors of readability? How would you use the ideas in his model to improve your writing?

KEY TERMS

The page number in parentheses refers to where the term is discussed in the chapter.

causal relation (282)

global coherence (279)

inference (285)

local coherence (279)

obstacles (280)

perspective (276)

plot (279)

proposition (287)

readability (292)

readability formula (292)

reinstatement search (287)

resolution (279)

setting (279)

situation model (290)

theme (279)

RECOMMENDED READING

Others have studied the effect of the reader's prior knowledge on learning information in a text (Chiesi, Spilich, & Voss, 1979; Vitali & Romance, 2007). Alba and Hasher (1983), Brewer and Nakamura (1984), and Graesser, Kassler, Kreuz, and McLain-Allen (1998) discuss the impact of schemata on comprehension and memory. Sharkey and Mitchell (1985) and Walker and Yekovich (1987) describe how scripts are used in reading. Zwaan and Radvansky (1998) organize the literature on situation models. More recent findings have begun to focus on perceptual components of situation models

(Finchler-Kiefer, 2001; Friedman & Miyake, 2000; Jahn, 2004, Paivio, 2008; Sadoski, 2008). Research on inferences (Graesser, Singer, & Trabasso, 1994) and causality (Keil, 2006) is summarized in review articles. The model developed by Kintsch and his associates is discussed in his book, *Comprehension: A Paradigm for Cognition* (Kintsch, 1998). *Reading Comprehension Strategies: Theories, Interventions, and Technologies* (McNamara, 2007) and a special issue of *Discourse Processes* (Vol. 29, Issues 2 & 3, 2005) contain articles by many leaders in the field.

12

Problem Solving

Solving a problem means finding a way out of a difficulty, a way around an obstacle, attaining an aim that was not immediately understandable. Solving problems is the specific achievement of intelligence, and intelligence is the specific gift of mankind: Solving problems can be regarded as the most characteristically human activity.

—**George Polya (1962)**

Humans are not the only creatures who can solve problems, yet identifying problem solving as the most characteristically human activity, as Polya has done in our chapter-opening quotation, emphasizes its importance in the development of civilization. This and the next chapter discuss problem solving and emphasize recent progress in our attempt to understand how people solve problems. This chapter establishes the basic components of a theory of problem solving.

The first section contains examples of different kinds of problems. Psychologists have been interested in the question: How general are problem-solving skills? At one extreme the answer is that the skills are very general, and a person who is good at solving one type of problem will also be very good at solving other types. At the other extreme is the claim that skills are very specific, and a person who is good at solving one type of problem may be poor at solving other types. The claim made in the first section falls between these two extremes. The proposed classification identifies three general kinds of problems on the basis of the skills required to solve them.

The second section describes the general characteristics of a theory of problem solving proposed by Newell and Simon (1972). The theory describes how problem solving is influenced by (1) people's information-processing capabilities as determined by STM (short-term memory) and LTM (long-term memory), (2) the structure of the problem and its effect on the search for a solution, and (3) the effectiveness of different strategies and sources of information. The third section discusses general strategies such as the use of subgoals, analogy, and diagrams.

The problems discussed in this chapter are mainly puzzles. You may wonder why psychologists are interested in puzzles—wouldn't it be more appropriate to study the kinds of problems people encounter in school or work? One reason for studying problems such as the anagram and series-completion problems shown in Table 12.1 is that they often appear on intelligence tests. If we want to understand what intelligence tests really measure, we must take a closer look at the specific skills required to answer the questions (Carpenter, Just, & Shell, 1990). Another reason is that, when studying puzzles, psychologists can be less concerned about differences in people's education; everyone should have more of an "equal chance" on puzzles than on problems taken from a textbook. However, psychologists have also become more interested in classroom problems, as we will see in the next chapter. Fortunately, most of the issues discussed in this chapter will still be relevant when we later discuss how prior knowledge and expertise influence problem solving.

CLASSIFYING PROBLEMS

Any attempt to improve problem-solving skills raises the question of what skills are needed for different kinds of problems. Students are taught how to solve statistics problems in a statistics class and chemistry problems in a chemistry class. Have they learned any general skills in a statistics class that can make them better problem solvers in a chemistry class, or do the problems in each class require a different set of skills? The question would be easier to answer if we could classify problems according to the skills needed to solve them.

Table 12.1 shows examples of problems that have been studied by psychologists. You will better understand this chapter if you try to solve these problems before reading further. When you have finished working on the problems, try to classify them according to the skills needed to solve them. We will examine one method of classification that proposes that the six problems can be divided into three categories.

The proposed classification is based on the general kinds of psychological skills and knowledge needed to solve different problems (Greeno, 1978). Greeno suggested that there are three types of problems: *arrangement, inducing structure*, and *transformation*. The classification does not imply that we will be able to classify every problem into one of the three categories. Rather, it provides three ideal types to determine whether a given problem requires primarily rearrangement, inducing structure, transformation, or some combination of the three skills. We now consider examples of each type, to see how the types differ.

Arrangement

arrangement problem A problem that requires rearranging its parts to satisfy a specified criterion

anagram A problem that requires rearranging a string of letters to form a word

Arrangement problems present some objects and require the problem solver to arrange them in a way that satisfies some criterion. The objects usually can be arranged in many different ways, but only one or a few of the arrangements form a solution. An excellent example is the rearrangement of the letters of an **anagram** to form a word, such as rearranging the letters *KEROJ* to spell *JOKER* and *RWAET* to spell *WATER*. Solving an arrangement problem often involves much trial and error, during which partial solutions are formed and evaluated. Greeno argued that the skills needed to solve arrangement problems include the following:

1. *Fluency in generating possibilities*. Flexibility is needed to generate many partial solutions and discard those that appear unpromising.
2. *Retrieval of solution patterns*. Ability to retrieve words from memory should be related to ability in solving anagrams.
3. *Knowledge of principles that constrain the search*. Knowing the relative frequency with which various letters occur together should help guide the search. Because the pair *JR* is an unlikely combination, for example, it should be avoided when forming partial solutions.

TABLE **12.1**

Examples of problems

A. Analogy

What word completes the analogy?

Merchant: Sell :: Customer:

Lawyer: Client :: Doctor:

B. String problem

Two strings hang from a ceiling but are too far apart to allow a person to hold one and walk to the other. On the floor are a book of matches, a screwdriver, and a few pieces of cotton. How could the strings be tied together?

C. Missionaries and cannibals

Five missionaries and five cannibals who have to cross a river find a boat, but the boat is so small that it can hold no more than three persons. If the missionaries on either bank of the river or in the boat are outnumbered at any time by cannibals, they will be eaten. Find the simplest schedule of crossings that will allow everyone to cross safely. At least one person must be in the boat at each crossing.

D. Water jar

You have an 8-gallon pail and a 5-gallon pail. How could you obtain 2 gallons of water?

E. Anagram

Rearrange the letters in each row to make an English word.

RWAET

KEROJ

F. Series completion

What number or letter continues each series?

1 2 8 3 4 6 5 6

A B M C D M

Gestalt psychologists were particularly interested in how people solve arrangement problems. Gestalt psychology, which began as the study of perception, emphasized the structure of patterns, and consequently it analyzed problem solving from this perspective. Many Gestalt tasks required the rearrangement of objects to find the correct relation among the parts.

A well-known example is the problem described by Kohler (1925) in his book *The Mentality of Apes*. Kohler hung some fruit from the top of a cage to investigate whether a chimpanzee or other ape could discover how to reach it. The cage contained several sticks and crates. The solution depended on finding a correct way to rearrange the objects—for example, standing on a crate and using a stick to knock down the fruit. According to the Gestalt analysis, solving the problem required the reorganization of the objects into a new structure.

Gestalt psychologists argued that discovering the correct organization usually occurred as a flash of insight. **Insight** is the sudden discovery of the correct solution following a period of incorrect attempts based primarily on trial and error. The metaphor of the solution suddenly becoming visible is perhaps not surprising, based on the Gestalt interest in perception. The term "insight" itself emphasizes its parallel with vision, as do expressions such as "a moment of illumination" or "seeing the light." However, the inability of a single metaphor to capture all facets of the concept suggests that we should remain open to alternative ways of viewing insight (Schooler, Fallshore, & Fiore, 1994).

The key factor distinguishing insight from other forms of discovery is the suddenness of the solution. In contrast to solutions that are achieved through careful planning or through a series of small steps, solutions based on insight seem to occur "in a flash." Evidence supports the argument that the correct arrangement of parts often occurs quite suddenly (Metcalfe, 1986a, 1986b). Metcalfe gave her subjects anagrams to solve, such as *ssoia, pmuoi,* and *ttnua.* They were asked to assess how close they were to solving the problem, on a scale from 1 to 10, during the course of solving the anagrams. Every 10 seconds, a tap occurred, and subjects recorded their ratings. The ratings remained very low until the discovery of the solution, implying that the correct answer suddenly appeared. In contrast, transformation problems are usually solved through an ordered sequence of correct steps in which people gradually progress toward the solution (Metcalfe, 1986b).

insight The sudden discovery of a solution following unsuccessful attempts to solve a problem

One factor that can make it difficult to find a solution to an arrangement problem occurs when a problem solver unnecessarily constrains the solution. According to this proposal, insight occurs when the problem solver removes the self-imposed constraint. You can test whether you place unnecessary constraints on the matchstick problems shown in Figure 12.1. The goal is to move a single stick to turn a false arithmetic statement into a true statement. The stick can not be discarded but can only change positions in the equation. Try to solve these problems before reading further.

An experiment confirmed the hypothesis that problems of type (a) would be the easiest, and problems of type (c) would be the most difficult (Knoblich, Ohlsson, Haider, & Rhenius, 1999). Type (a) problems are solved by moving a match stick in the Roman numerals, such as turning the number 4 into the number 6 to make the statement $6 = 3 + 3$. Problems of type (b) are solved by changing the arithmetic operations, such as moving a stick from the equals sign to the minus sign to make the

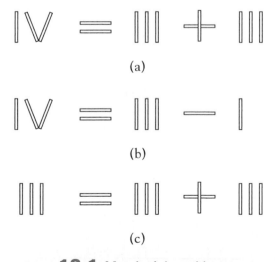

(a)

(b)

(c)

FIGURE **12.1** Matchstick problems

Source: From "Constraint relaxation and chunk decomposition in insight problem solving," by G. Knoblich, S. Ohlsson, H. Haider, & D. Rhenius, 1999, *Journal of Experimental Psychology: Learning, Memory and Cognition, 25,* 1534–1555. Copyright 1999 by the American Psychological Association.

functional fixedness
The tendency to use an
object in a typical way

statement $4 - 3 = 1$. Problems of type (c) create two equal signs, such as
$3 = 3 = 3$. Once people realize that they can modify and create new equal
signs, the three types of problems become equally easy.

Another factor that can make it difficult to find a correct arrangement is
functional fixedness—the tendency to perceive an object in terms of only its
most common use. The candle problem, studied by Duncker (1945), illustrates how functional fixedness can influence performance. The goal is to
place three small candles at eye level on a door. Among other objects on a
nearby table are a few tacks and three small boxes about the size of match-
boxes. In one condition the boxes were filled with candles, tacks, and
matches. In another condition the boxes were empty. The solution requires
tacking the boxes to the door so they can serve as platforms for the candles
(Figure 12.2). More subjects solved the problem when the boxes were empty
(Adamson, 1952; Duncker, 1945). The use of boxes as containers, rather
than as platforms, was emphasized when they contained objects, and so it
was more difficult to recognize their novel function.

The string problem in Table 12.1 requires finding a novel use for a tool.
The screwdriver is tied to one string to create a pendulum that can be swung
to the other string. One of the best examples of overcoming functional fixedness outside the laboratory is the attempt of prisoners to break out of jail.
Because tools are not readily available in prison, prisoners have to use items

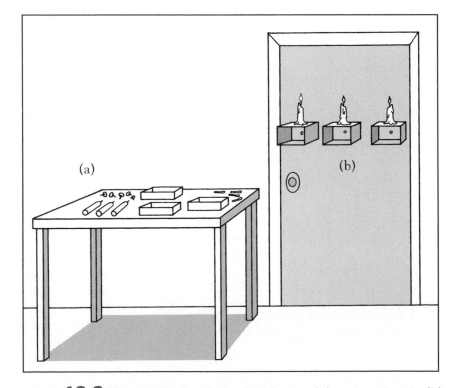

FIGURE **12.2** The candle problem—initial state (a) and goal state (b)

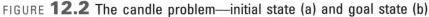

IN THE NEWS **12.1**

Pair of Crafty Inmates Melt Way Out of Jail

SALINAS (AP)—Two crafty inmates used a length of shower pipe, a sheet, and a wall socket to melt an unbreakable plastic window and escape from Monterey County's new jail, officials said Wednesday.

A sheriff's deputy said the pair escaped Tuesday night after using a makeshift cutting torch to reduce part of the cell window to mushy goo.

Lieutenant Ted Brown said the inmates wrapped a sheet around a piece of flattened shower pipe, wired the contraption and plugged it into a wall socket. The gizmo heated up and the inmates pressed it against the window until its edge had melted away, Brown said.

Then they snapped a leg off the cell bed, placed it into the newly burned hole, pried out the entire

window, and skipped to freedom, Brown said.

Source: From "Pair of crafty inmates melt way out of jail," appearing in the *Los Angeles Times*, January 6, 1978. Copyright 1978 by the Associated Press. Reprinted by permission of Associated Press Newsfeatures.

---

that are available. "In the News" 12.1 describes the ingenuity of two prisoners in finding novel uses for common objects.

Inducing Structure

inducing-structure problem A problem that requires finding a pattern among a fixed set of relations

series extrapolation A problem that requires finding a pattern among a sequence of items to continue the sequence in the same pattern

analogy problem A four-term problem that requires finding the answer that completes the relation: *A* is to *B* as *C* is to *D*

Arrangement problems require the rearrangement of objects to form a new relation among them. In **inducing structure problems,** by contrast, the relation is fixed and the problem is to discover it. Some objects are given, and the task is to discover how they are related. For example, in **series extrapolation**, problems consist of a series such as 1 2 8 3 4 6 5 6. The task is to find the next element of the series. Notice that there are two series in the example. One is the ascending series 1 2 3 4 5 6; the other is the descending series 8, 6, ... So the correct answer is 4. Similarly, the answer to the letter series in Table 12.1 is *E*.

Another example of inducing structure is **analogy problems** such as Merchant: Sell :: Customer: Buy. The instructions might indicate that the analogy should be labeled true or false, or the last word could be replaced by a blank, with instructions to fill in the word that best completes the analogy. Analogical reasoning is of particular interest because of its use in intelligence tests. The Miller Analogies Test, which was widely used for admission to graduate school, is composed exclusively of verbal analogies. Other ability tests, such as the Graduate Record Examination (GRE) and the Scholastic Aptitude Test (SAT), include analogies among the test items.

The psychological processes used in solving an analogy or a series-extrapolation problem involve identifying relations among the components and fitting the relations together in a pattern (Greeno, 1978). The importance of discovering relations among the terms of an analogy is illustrated in a model proposed by R. J. Sternberg (1977). There are four processes in Sternberg's model: encoding, inference, mapping, and application.

Consider the problem "Washington is to 1 as Lincoln is to 10 or 5." The task is to choose either 10 or 5 to complete the analogy. The *encoding process* identifies attributes of the words that could be important in establishing relations. The first term, *Washington*, might be identified as a president, a portrait on a $1 bill, or a war hero. The *inference process* establishes valid relations between the first two terms. Washington was the first president of the United States, and his portrait appears on a $1 bill—two possible relations between Washington and 1. The *mapping process* establishes relations between the first and third terms. Both Washington and Lincoln were presidents, and portraits of both appear on bills, so both possibilities remain as the basis for the analogy. The *application process* attempts to establish a relation between Lincoln and 10 or 5 that is analogous to the one between Washington and 1. Because Lincoln was the sixteenth president of the United States, neither answer fits the presidential relation. However, Lincoln's portrait appears on a $5 bill, so the choice of 5 is consistent with the currency relation. This example reveals the importance of discovering relations. Suppose we had considered only the presidential relation. If we did not know that Lincoln was the sixteenth president, we would be more likely to guess that he was the tenth president than the fifth, and so we would have chosen the wrong answer.

Sternberg measured how quickly students were able to answer different kinds of problems to estimate how much time was needed to complete each of the four processes—encoding, inference, mapping, and application. One goal of his research was to study how these times vary across individuals and to correlate the times with other measures of intellectual performance.

Sternberg and Gardner (1983) examined whether common components are involved in three different reasoning tasks that required inducing structure (series completion, analogy, and classification). They combined the three central reasoning components—inference, mapping, and application—to form a single reasoning variable, which correlated significantly across the different tasks. In other words, students who were rapid in reasoning in one kind of induction task were also rapid in reasoning during other induction tasks. The results indicate that some common skills are involved in inducing structure across different tasks, as implied by Greeno's (1978) taxonomy.

A particularly challenging test that requires the induction of abstract relations is the *Raven Progressive Matrices Test* (Raven, 1962). Each problem consists of a 3 × 3 matrix in which the bottom-right entry is missing. The instructions are to look across the rows and then down the columns to determine the rules that can be used to generate the missing pattern. You can try to solve one of these problems by determining which of the eight alternatives in Figure 12.3 is the missing pattern.

People initially try to match the rectangles, curves, and lines across rows, but exact matches do not exist. For example, the two curved vertical lines in the first row do not occur in the second and third rows. Number and shape are both relevant, however, because each row contains one, two, and three vertical shapes, representing each of the three shapes, and one, two, and three horizontal shapes, representing each of the three shapes. The missing number in the bottom row is three for the horizontal shape, and the missing horizontal shape is the open rectangles. The missing number is two for the

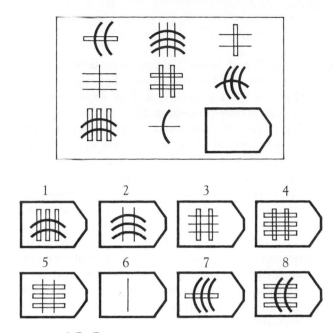

FIGURE **12.3** A test question based on Raven's Progressive Matrices Test

Source: From "What one intelligence test measures: A theoretical account of the processing in the Raven Progressive Matrices Test," by P. A. Carpenter, M. A. Just, & P. Shell, 1990, *Psychological Review, 97,* 404–431. Copyright 1990 by the American Psychological Association. Reprinted by permission.

transformation problem A problem that requires changing the initial state through a sequence of operations until it matches the goal state

means–end analysis A strategy that can be used to solve transformation problems by eliminating differences between the initial and goal states

vertical shape, and the missing vertical shape is the lines. The correct answer is 5. A high score on this test depends primarily on the ability to induce abstract relations and the ability to manage many comparisons in working memory (Carpenter et al., 1990).

Transformation

Transformation problems consist of an initial state, a goal state, and a sequence of operations for changing the initial state into the goal state. Transformation problems differ from problems of inducing structure and arrangement by providing the goal state rather than requiring solvers to produce it. An anagram problem requires finding the word that solves the anagram, and Duncker's candle problem requires finding the correct arrangement of parts that supports the candle. In contrast, a transformation problem such as the missionaries-and-cannibals problem provides the goal state.

The missionaries-and-cannibals problem requires transporting missionaries and cannibals across a river under the constraint that cannibals can never outnumber missionaries, in the boat or on either side of the river. In one version of this problem, the initial state consists of five missionaries, five cannibals, and a boat that can hold three persons, all starting on the left bank of the river. The goal state consists of the ten persons and the boat, all on the right bank of the river. The operations consist of moving from one to three persons in the boat back and forth across the river. The problem can be solved in 11 moves, but people usually require about 20 to 30 moves to reach a solution.

According to Greeno (1978), solving transformation problems primarily requires skills in planning based on a method called means–end analysis. Because a definite goal state is given in transformation problems, the problem solver can compare the current problem state with the goal state. **Means–end analysis** requires identifying differences that exist between the current state and the goal state and selecting operations that will reduce these differences.

The problems that we consider in the rest of this chapter are mostly transformation problems. This focus provides us the opportunity to study means–end analysis and alternative planning strategies. Much of what psychologists know about how people solve these problems is the result of the pioneering work of Newell and Simon at Carnegie Mellon University. We review the major aspects of their theory of human problem solving before looking at the applications of their ideas to particular problems.

NEWELL AND SIMON'S THEORY

Objectives and Method

The initial development of Newell and Simon's theory was described in a paper titled "Elements of a Theory of Human Problem Solving" (Newell, Shaw, & Simon, 1958b), which, as we saw earlier, had an important influence on the development of information-processing theory. The paper described the first 2 years of a project that involved programming a digital computer to solve problems. One objective of the project was in fact to consider how programming a computer could contribute to a theory of human problem solving. The first step was to use all available evidence about human problem solving to program processes resembling those used by humans. The second step was to collect detailed data on how humans solve the same problems as those solved by the computer. The program could then be modified to provide a closer approximation of human behavior. Once success was achieved in simulating performance on a particular task, the investigators could examine a broader range of tasks, attempting to use the same set of elementary information processes and program organization in all the **simulation programs**. A long-term goal would be to draw implications from the theories for improving human performance.

simulation program A computer program that attempts to reproduce the operations used by people to carry out various tasks

Why does the computer play a central role in theory construction? Simon and Newell's (1971) answer is that much of our thinking is not directly observable. The covert nature of thought can make it seem magical or mysterious, leading to vague theories that obscure more than they clarify. The advantage of computer programs is that terms such as *memory* and *strategy* can be defined in precisely stated instructions for a computer. Furthermore, the requirement that the programs must work—that is, must be able to solve the problem—provides a guarantee that no steps have been left unspecified. A successful program provides a **measure of sufficiency**—a test that the steps in the program are sufficient for solving the problem. However, a successful program does not guarantee that a person would solve the problem the same way; it is still necessary to make detailed observations on how people solve problems and modify the program to simulate their behavior.

measure of sufficiency A demonstration that the instructions in a computer program are capable of solving a problem

To obtain details about how people solve problems, Newell and Simon (1972) usually collected **verbal protocols** from their subjects. They told the subjects to report verbally everything they thought about as they worked on the problem. The verbal statements often provided enough details to build a computer simulation program that would solve the problem in the same way that people solved it.

verbal protocol A record of verbalized thought processes

The method of collecting verbal protocols and constructing a simulation program has not been widely adopted by other investigators, although the approach is slowly gaining more appeal. One deterrent is simply that this method requires a lot of work for the investigator. The investigator therefore usually studies only a few subjects and assumes that they are fairly typical in the way they solve problems. Another limitation is that the method yields many details, and it is not always clear how to summarize the results to emphasize what is most important. Failure to collect verbal protocols, however, can result in the loss of valuable information because a subject's behavior may reveal little about what he or she is thinking.

Although the particular method used by Newell and Simon has not been widely adopted, their theory of problem solving has been very influential in determining how psychologists think about human information processing in general and problem solving in particular. The theory provides a general framework for specifying how information-processing characteristics, the structure of the problem, and different sources of knowledge interact to influence behavior.

Theoretical Assumptions

An important component of Newell and Simon's theory is the identification of the basic characteristics of human information processing that influence problem solving. These characteristics are the same ones that we discussed in earlier chapters—performance on a problem-solving task is influenced by the capacity, storage time, and retrieval time of STM and LTM. The limited capacity of STM places a constraint on the number of sequential operations that can be carried out mentally. Although most people can multiply 17×8 without using paper and pencil, multiplying 17×58 is much more difficult because the number of required operations (multiplying 17×8 and 17×5, storing the products, aligning, and adding) can exceed the limit of STM. Long-term memory does not have these capacity limitations, but it takes time to enter new information into LTM. This can make it difficult to remember the steps that were used to solve a problem, causing us to repeat incorrect steps. Thus, both the limited capacity of STM and the time required to store new information in LTM can greatly influence the efficiency of a human problem solver (Atwood & Polson, 1976).

Simon and Newell's (1971) theory is concerned not only with the person but also with the task. The sequential nature of many problems raises the question of what options are available at each point in solving the problem. If many choices are available, but only a few of which lead to a solution, the problem can be very difficult. However, if one has a good plan for solving the problem and can therefore ignore unpromising paths, the number of unpromising paths will have little effect on performance.

Simon and Newell illustrate this point by referring to the problem DONALD + GERALD = ROBERT. The problem is to substitute a digit 0 to 9 for each of the ten letters to satisfy the constraint that the substitution obeys the rules of addition. The hint is $D = 5$. Therefore, $T = 0$, and a 1 has to be carried into the next column to the left. Although the number of possible choices is very large (there are 362,880 ways of assigning nine digits to nine letters), by following the rules of arithmetic and using accumulated information (such as that R must be odd), it is possible to explore relatively few promising choices. You can observe this for yourself by trying to solve the problem.

What is important, therefore, is not the number of incorrect paths but how effectively one can discover a plan that avoids the incorrect paths. To use Newell and Simon's analogy, we need not be concerned how large the haystack is if we can identify a small part of it in which we are quite sure to find the needle.

The problem itself determines the number of possible choices and paths that could be followed in searching for a solution (the **search space**), but the problem solver determines which of these to actually explore (the **problem space**). Among the sources of information that influence how a person constructs a problem space are the following:

search space The set of choices at each step in solving the problem as determined by the problem

problem space The set of choices evaluated at each step in solving a problem as determined by the problem solver

1. Task instructions that give a description of the problem and may contain helpful information
2. Previous experience with the same task or a nearly identical one
3. Previous experience with analogous tasks
4. Plans stored in LTM that generalize over a range of tasks
5. Information accumulated while solving a problem

Let's now take a closer look at how these sources of information influence problem solving. We will begin by showing how means–end analysis can be used to solve transformation problems.

Means–End Analysis

The use of means–end analysis is illustrated by a computer program called the General Problem Solver (Ernst & Newell, 1969). The program consists of general procedures that should apply across a variety of problems. A *general procedure* for solving transformation problems is to select operators that result in a problem state that is closer to the goal state. **Operators** are the allowed changes that can be made to solve the problem, such as moving missionaries and cannibals in the boat. Getting close to the goal is accomplished by trying to reduce the differences between the current problem state and the goal state.

operator An action that is selected to solve problems

To follow this procedure, the General Problem Solver (GPS) must be given the differences that exist between problem states and the operators that are capable of eliminating these differences. A **table of connections** combines these two sets of information by showing which differences can be eliminated by each of the operators. The particular operators and differences will of course vary across problems, but the general strategy of consulting a table of connections to determine which operators are useful for reducing differences should remain the same across problems.

table of connections A table that links differences between problem states with operators for eliminating those differences

In most cases the principles used to construct GPS form a reasonable model of how people attempt to solve transformation problems. In fact, GPS was specifically used as a model of human performance on a symbol transformation task studied by Newell and Simon (1972). The problems were similar to the kind of derivations that students encounter in an introductory logic course. Students were given some initial statements, a set of 12 transformation rules, and a goal statement. The task was to use the rules to transform the initial statements to produce the goal statement. Newell and Simon identified six differences that distinguish logic statements. The table of connections specified which of these differences could be changed by each of the 12 transformation rules.

For example, a student might be asked to prove that, if *A* implies *B* (*A* ⊂ *B*), then the absence of *B* implies the absence of *A* (–*B* ⊂ –*A*). Notice that there are two kinds of differences that distinguish the initial state (*A* ⊂ *B*) from the goal state (–*B* ⊂ –*A*). First, the two expressions differ in sign—there are negation signs before the *A* and the *B* in the goal state. Second, the positions of the *A* and the *B* have changed in the goal state. Students could use means–end analysis to solve this problem by applying transformation rules that changed either the sign or the position of the symbols. Newell and Simon (1972) asked their subjects to verbalize their strategies as they attempted to solve the symbol transformation problems. Students' solutions and verbal protocols revealed that many aspects of their thinking were similar to aspects of the means–end analysis used in the GPS.

GENERAL STRATEGIES

Means–end analysis is an example of a general strategy. A knowledge of general problem-solving strategies can be particularly useful because general strategies apply to many kinds of problems. For this reason, books such as Wickelgren's (1974) on how to solve problems emphasize general strategies such as forming subgoals or working backward.

Strategies such as using means–end analysis, forming subgoals, and working backward are called **heuristics** because they are often successful but do not guarantee success. In contrast, an **algorithm** is a procedure of steps that does guarantee a solution if one follows the steps correctly. The rules for multiplication constitute an algorithm because a correct answer is guaranteed if a person correctly follows the rules. We first consider three general heuristics—forming subgoals, using analogy, and constructing diagrams—and then evaluate both their potential usefulness and their limitations as general strategies.

heuristic A strategy that is often, but not always, helpful in solving problems

algorithm A set of rules that will solve a problem if correctly followed

Subgoals

subgoal A goal that solves part of the problem

A commonly suggested heuristic for solving problems is to divide the problem into parts—that is, to formulate subgoals. **Subgoals** are problem states intermediate between the initial state and the goal state; ideally, they are on the solution path. Some problems have fairly obvious subgoals, and research has shown that people take advantage of them. Consider the puzzle called the Tower of Hanoi (Figure 12.4). This puzzle consists of three pegs and a set of rings that vary in size. The initial state has all the rings stacked on peg A in order of decreasing size. The goal is to move the stack, one ring at a time, to peg C, under the constraint that a larger ring can never be placed on a smaller ring. A reasonable subgoal is to move the largest ring to peg C. But how does one begin to achieve this subgoal? The answer is not obvious, and people often make the wrong choice. But as they make other moves and come closer to achieving the subgoal, the correct moves become more obvious and errors decline (D. E. Egan & J. G. Greeno, 1974).

Using subgoals can make solving a problem easier because knowing that an intermediate problem state is on the solution path makes it possible to avoid searching many unpromising paths. Figure 12.5 shows a search space

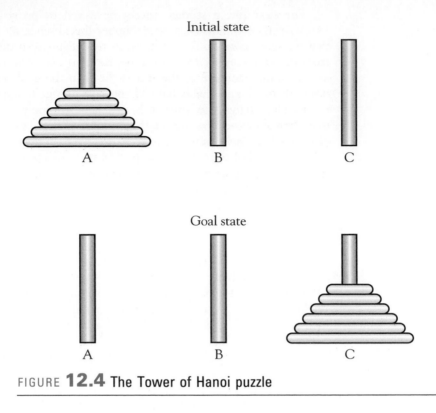

FIGURE **12.4** The Tower of Hanoi puzzle

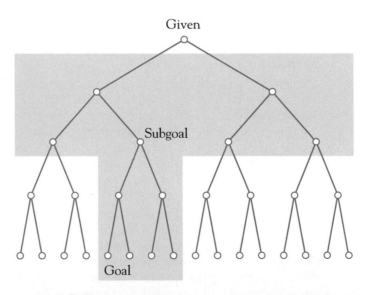

FIGURE **12.5** Search space. Knowledge of a subgoal limits search to the shaded area.

Source: From *How to solve problems*, by W.A. Wicklegren, Copyright 1974 by W. H. Freeman and Company.

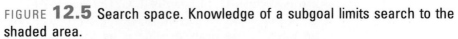

that contains 16 paths, each four steps in length. Only one path ends in the goal state. If the problem solver can generate a subgoal that can be reached in two steps, then she can reach the subgoal by searching only four paths, each two steps long. From the subgoal state there are another four paths, each two steps long. Formulating a subgoal reduces the search space from 16 four-step paths to a problem space consisting of 8 two-step paths represented by the shaded area in Figure 12.5. Instead of searching the entire search space, the problem solver needs to evaluate only those moves that are consistent with the generated subgoal.

Forming subgoals is often helpful, but it does not guarantee an easier solution. There are several limitations to keep in mind when using this method. First, it is not always obvious what are helpful intermediate problem states because some problems do not have obvious subgoals. Second, reaching a subgoal can create confusion about what to do next. Hayes (1966) found that giving people a subgoal helped them solve the part of the problem that came before the subgoal. However, some problems actually took longer to solve with a subgoal because it took a long time to figure out what to do after reaching the subgoal.

An example of a problem in which a subgoal improved performance is the missionaries-and-cannibals problem (described in Table 12.1) requiring the transportation of five missionaries and five cannibals across a river using a boat that can hold only three persons. One group of students, the control group, was simply asked to solve the problem. Another group, the "subgoal" group, was told that, to solve the problem, they would have to reach a state in which there were three cannibals across the river by themselves and without the boat. Students in the control group required an average of 30 moves to solve the problem, compared with an average of only 20 moves for students in the subgoal group (Simon & Reed, 1976).

To try to understand why the subgoal was so effective, Simon and I developed a simulation model of the way students in the two groups explored the search space. The goal of the model was to predict, for each of the possible legal moves, the average number of times students in each group would make that particular move. We thought students would follow a *means–end strategy* in which they would move as many people across the river as possible and bring as few back as possible. A model based on the means–end strategy was fairly successful in predicting their choices, but some of their moves did not follow this strategy.

Violations of the means–end strategy could be accounted for by proposing that people follow a *balance strategy*, which attempts to create equal numbers of missionaries and cannibals on each side of the river. The balance strategy makes it easy to avoid illegal moves because cannibals will never outnumber missionaries as long as the numbers of missionaries and cannibals are equal on both sides. The trouble with the balance strategy is that it tends to lead people away from the solution path and toward unpromising paths.

After analyzing the moves made by both groups, we proposed that the subgoal group was more likely to follow the means–end strategy, and the control group was more likely to follow the less effective balance strategy.

The fact that the subgoal—three cannibals and no missionaries—is an unbalanced state also makes it intuitively likely that students in the subgoal group would not persist in following the balance strategy.

As mentioned previously, one limitation of using the subgoal strategy is that it is not always obvious what constitutes a good subgoal. Educators can therefore help students by explicitly pointing out subgoals, as demonstrated by Catrambone (1995). Students were shown how to solve a probability problem that required finding total frequency as one of the subgoals. When this step was explicitly labeled as *Total Frequency*, students did better in transferring what they had learned to other probability problems that required finding the total frequency. The transfer problems required a different method for calculating total frequency, so it was insufficient to apply by rote the same steps shown in the example problem. Learning required understanding the example, and explicitly labeling a subgoal enhanced understanding.

Analogy

analogy Solving a problem by using a solution to a related problem

Analogy is another of the major heuristics for solving problems. **Analogy** requires that the problem solver use the solution of a similar problem to solve a current problem. Success in using analogy depends on both recognizing the similarity between the two problems and recalling the solution of the analogous problem. Because the recall of a solution is required, analogy depends more on LTM than do means–end analysis and subgoals.

One of the most famous studies of analogy involved a problem initially studied by Duncker (1945) labeled the tumor, or radiation, problem. The problem is to use radiation to destroy a tumor without destroying the healthy tissue that surrounds it. The dispersion solution requires dividing the rays so that they will have high intensity only when they converge on the tumor. Although this is a clever and practical solution ("In the News" 12.2), Duncker found that very few people solved the problem in this way.

Gick and Holyoak (1980) investigated whether more people would discover the dispersion solution if they were first exposed to an analogous solution. Their subjects read the attack-dispersion story before trying to solve the radiation problem. The attack-dispersion story described a solution to a

---

IN THE NEWS **12.2**

Radiation Beams Target Tumors, Bypass Healthy Tissue

LOS ANGELES (AP)—A treatment has been unveiled at the University of California Los Angeles that allows doctors to create beams of radiation that fit a tumor's dimension exactly, leaving other tissue unharmed, hospital officials said.

UCLA's Jonsson Cancer Center is the only U.S. facility to offer Novalis, a German-developed system that focuses thin rays of radiation through healthy tissue that unite on a brain tumor—like spokes meeting at the center of a wheel.

Each beam conforms to the dimensions of a patient's tumor—unlike conventional beam radiation—and leaves neighboring healthy tissue unharmed.

Source: From "Radiation beams target tumors, bypass healthy tissue," *San Diego Union Tribune*, October 2, 1998.

TABLE **12.2**

A Summary of the Attack Dispersion Story and of a Corresponding Solution to the Radiation Problem

Attack dispersion story

A fortress was located in the center of the country.

Many roads radiated out from the fortress.

A general wanted to capture the fortress with his army.

The general wanted to prevent mines on the roads from destroying his army and neighboring villages.

As a result the entire army could not attack the fortress along one road.

However, the entire army was needed to capture the fortress.

So an attack by one small group would not succeed.

The general therefore divided his army into several small groups.

He positioned the small groups at the heads of different roads.

The small groups simultaneously converged on the fortress.

In this way the army captured the fortress.

Radiation problem and dispersion solution*

A tumor was located in the interior of a patient's body.

A doctor wanted to destroy the tumor with rays.

The doctor wanted to prevent the rays from destroying the healthy tissue.

As a result the high intensity rays could not be applied to the tumor along one path.

However, high intensity rays were needed to destroy the tumor.

So applying one low intensity ray would not succeed.

The doctor therefore divided the rays into several low intensity rays.

He positioned the low intensity rays at multiple locations around the patient's body.

The low intensity rays simultaneously converged on the tumor.

In this way the rays destroyed the tumor.

Source: From "Analogical problem solving," by M. L. Gick & K. Holyoak, 1980, *Cognitive Psychology, 12,* 306–355. Copyright 1980 by Academic Press, Inc. Reprinted by permission of Elsevier Science.
*Italicized propositions summarize the target dispersion solution.

military problem in which the army had to be divided to converge on a fortress. Table 12.2 shows how the solution of this problem corresponds to the solution of the radiation problem. When the instructions indicated that the story might provide hints for solving the radiation problem, most people made use of the analogy. More than half of those who read the story included the dispersion solution among their proposed solutions, compared with only 8% of those who did not read the story. But when Gick and Holyoak omitted the hint to use the story, the number of dispersion solutions greatly decreased. Their findings thus demonstrated that people could generate an analogous solution when prompted but that they did not spontaneously recognize the similarity between the two problems.

People's inability to spontaneously notice the relation between analogous problems poses a challenge for psychologists to make analogies more obvious. One reason that analogies are often not obvious is that, although the analogy preserves relations among the concepts in a problem, the concepts themselves differ (Gentner, 1983). This point is illustrated in Table 12.3 for the military and radiation problems. Although the concepts (army and fortress; rays and tumor) differ in the two problems, the solutions preserve the

TABLE **12.3**
Correspondences among the Military Problem, the Radiation Problem, and the Convergence Schema

---

Military problem
Initial state

    Goal: Use army to capture fortress.

    Resources: Sufficiently large army.

    Constraint: Unable to send entire army along one road.

  Solution plan: Send small groups along multiple roads simultaneously.

  Outcome: Fortress captured by army.

Radiation problem
Initial state

    Goal: Use rays to destroy tumor.

    Resources: Sufficiently powerful rays.

    Constraint: Unable to administer high intensity rays from one direction.

  Solution plan: Administer low intensity rays from multiple directions simultaneously.

  Outcome: Tumor destroyed by rays.

Convergence schema
Initial state

    Goal: Use force to overcome a central target.

    Resources: Sufficiently great force.

    Constraints: Unable to apply full force along one path.

  Solution plan: Apply weak forces along multiple paths simultaneously.

  Outcome: Central target overcome by force.

Source: From "Schema induction and analogical transfer," by M. L. Gick & K. Holyoak, 1983, *Cognitive Psychology, 15*, 1–38. Copyright 1983 by Academic Press, Inc. Reprinted by permission of Elsevier Science.

relations of breaking up and converging. The similarity of the two solutions is represented at the bottom of the table by the convergence schema, in which the concepts are described more generally. The solutions to both problems require breaking up a large force so that weak forces can be simultaneously applied along multiple paths.

Gick and Holyoak (1983) discovered that people were likely to form this more general schema if they read and compared two analogous stories before trying to solve the radiation problem. For example, some students read the military story and a story about forming a circle around an oil fire to use many small hoses to spray foam on the fire. Students who described the relation between these two stories were much more likely to think of the convergence solution to the radiation problem than were students who read only a single analogous story. Creating the *convergence schema* requires that people compare two analogous stories, which makes them think about the solution in general terms. Reading the two analogous stories without comparing them is not very helpful (Catrambone & Holyoak, 1989).

These findings have been extended in various directions, as is illustrated in a study by Gentner, Loewenstein, Thompson, and Forbus (2008). The participants were management consultants who had approximately 15 years of work experience and were attending a negotiation-training program. The consultants studied two cases of a contingent contract that depended on an outcome of a future event. In one case, either a buyer in the United States or an Asian manufacturer would pay the cost of freight depending on whether a boat shipment arrived on time. In another case, the distribution of profit between two brothers from selling the family farm depended on whether the price of the main crop would rise or fall.

One group studied the two cases separately and after each case described the principle and likely success of the negotiation. Another group studied the two cases simultaneously and described their similarities. The comparison group formed a general schema that aided them in several different ways. They were more successful in describing the principles of a contingent contract than participants who did not compare the two cases. They were also more successful in recalling examples of contingent contracts from their own experiences. It is gratifying to see that the study of laboratory problems generalizes to important situations outside the laboratory.

The advantage of a general schema, whether for a puzzle or a negotiation strategy, is that it is easier for people to recognize how particular situations are similar to each other. But psychologists are still investigating the extent to which people create general schema, as opposed to recalling a particular problem (Ross, 1984) as a basis for analogy. After an extensive review of the literature on analogy, Reeves and Weisberg (1994) concluded that there is sufficient evidence to show that we use both specific problems and more abstract schemata in analogical reasoning. One promising theory is that we begin by using the solution of specific problems, but as we apply a specific solution to other problems, we begin to form more abstract schemata (Ross & Kennedy, 1990). We will see in the next chapter that forming these more abstract schemata is an important part of acquiring expertise.

Diagrams

Our final example of a general strategy for solving problems is the construction of diagrams. Diagrams can help us represent problems in a way that allows us to search efficiently for a solution. The importance of representation is illustrated by the fact that two problems with identical solutions but different story contents (**problem isomorphs**) can differ greatly in how easy they are to solve. One story can cause the solver to represent the problem in a way that leads to an easy solution, and another story can cause a representation that impedes finding the solution. Furthermore, a person who solves both of the problems might not recognize any similarity between them (Hayes & Simon, 1977).

J. M. Carroll, Thomas, and Malhotra (1980) studied the role of representation in design by creating two problem isomorphs. The *spatial version* involved designing a business office for seven employees. Each employee was to be assigned to a corridor a certain number of offices down from a central hallway containing a reception area at one end and accounting records at the other end. Subjects were told to try to assign compatible employees to the same corridor, assigning those with higher prestige nearer to the central hallway. A goal of the problem is to minimize the number of corridors.

Problems of this kind are usually easier to solve by using a diagram such as shown in Figure 12.6. The top of the diagram shows the central hallway connecting the reception and accounting areas. The columns represent corridors. Examples of constraints that are satisfied by the arrangement in

problem isomorphs
Problems that have different story contents but identical solutions

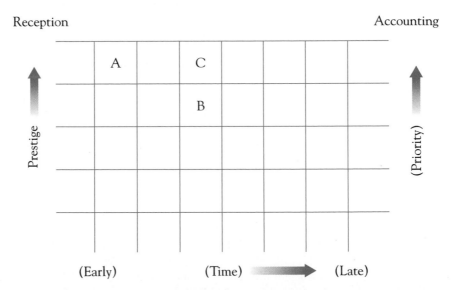

FIGURE **12.6** Graphic representation of a design problem. The labels in parentheses accompanied the temporal version

Source: From "Presentation and representation in design problem solving," by J. M. Carroll, J. C. Thomas, & A. Malhotra, 1980, *British Journal of Psychology, 71*, 143–153. Copyright 1980 by the British Psychological Society. Reprinted by permission.

Figure 12.6 are that A uses the accounting records less than C, B and C are compatible, and C has more prestige than B.

The *temporal version* of the isomorph had equivalent constraints, but the constraints were placed on a manufacturing process that consisted of seven stages. The columns in Figure 12.6 can now be used to represent work shifts rather than corridors. The horizontal dimension represents time, and the vertical dimension represents priority. Subjects were instructed to assign stages to the same work shift if the stages used the same resources. Some stages had to be assigned to earlier work shifts than others, and some stages had priority over others that belonged to the same work shift. Examples of constraints that are satisfied by the arrangement in Figure 12.6 are that stage A occurs before stage C, stages B and C use the same resources, and stage C has greater priority than stage B. Notice that distance from the accounting area in the spatial version corresponds to time in the temporal version, compatibility corresponds to use of the same resources, and prestige corresponds to priority.

Subjects who worked on the temporal version received 19 constraints that corresponded to the 19 constraints given to subjects who worked on the spatial version. Subjects were not instructed to use a diagram; they were able to select their own method for solving the problem. Performance was measured by how many constraints were satisfied in the design. The importance of representation is illustrated by the finding that subjects did significantly better on the spatial isomorph even though the two problems had equivalent constraints. Subjects given the spatial isomorph not only satisfied more of the constraints but completed their design faster. All 17 subjects in the spatial task used a sketch of the business office to formulate their design, but only 2 of the 18 subjects in the temporal task used a graphic representation.

To determine whether graphic representation made the problem easier for the spatial group, the experimenters conducted a second experiment, in which both groups were instructed to use the matrix shown in Figure 12.6. This time there were no significant differences between the two groups, either in performance scores or in solution times. The differences in the first experiment therefore appear to have been caused by the facilitating effects of a graphic representation of the problem. The usefulness of the graphic representation was obvious in the spatial task, and students spontaneously adopted it. It was not obvious in the temporal task. Performance on the two tasks became equivalent only when both groups were required to use a graphic representation.

An interesting question raised by these findings is whether students could use analogy to improve their performance on the temporal task if they had first worked on the spatial task. Spontaneous use of a graphic procedure to solve the spatial task might then transfer to the temporal task. If students recognized the analogy between the two tasks, the experimenter would not have to tell them to use the graphic procedure on the temporal task. Unfortunately, the initial research on this question indicates that the spontaneous transfer of general methods for solving problems is as difficult as the spontaneous transfer of specific solutions for solving problems.

Representational Transfer

Novick (1990) refers to the transfer of general methods for solving problems as representational transfer to distinguish it from the analogical transfer of specific solutions. In **analogical transfer** we were concerned with the transfer of a specific solution, such as using the solution of the military problem to solve the radiation problem. In **representational transfer** we are concerned with the transfer of a general method, such as using a *matrix diagram*, such as the one in Figure 12.6, to solve a transfer problem after being shown how to use it to solve an example problem.

Novick became interested in studying representational transfer after noticing that although many psychologists were studying the transfer of specific solutions, no one seemed to be studying the transfer of representations. Diagrammatic representations, in particular, help us represent the underlying structure of many problems. Because problem solvers often do not construct appropriate diagrams to represent problems, Novick and Hmelo (1994) examined whether students would transfer the use of an appropriate diagram from one problem to another problem that had a different solution but could be solved by using the same diagram.

Figure 12.7 shows three different kinds of diagrams. The first two should be familiar to you if you have read previous chapters in this book. A *network* consists of nodes joined by links. In the example problem, a couple had to plan a trip that involved visiting islands (nodes) joined by bridges (links). The test problem required figuring out which pairs of people (nodes) at a cocktail party shook hands (links) with each other. The example for the *hierarchy* was a categorization problem in which a mother was trying to group the words her young child knew into categories (zoo animals, farm animals, pets), like the semantic hierarchy shown in Figure 9.1 (page 214). The test problem involved representing different paths that a rat could take through a maze, such as the search space hierarchy shown in Figure 12.5. The example for the *part–whole representation* consisted of a set membership problem in which the solver had to determine the number of children who collected only rocks, the number who collected only shells, and the number who collected both. These problems can be represented by the **Venn diagram** shown in Figure 12.7. The test problem was a geometry problem in which the angles of two intersecting lines could be represented as either parts or wholes.

Novick and Hmelo (1994) compared students' ability to solve test problems under three conditions: Subjects did not previously see any examples in the control condition, saw a relevant example in the no-hint condition but were not told of its relevance, and saw and were informed about the relevant example in the hint condition. The complete lack of spontaneous transfer was shown by the lack of difference between the control and no-hint groups. When not informed that a previously studied example would be helpful, subjects did not change their representations and improve their performance.

The results for the hint group varied across the three representations. The network representation was the most successful. Students who were told to use the relevant example (bridge problem) were more likely to use a network representation to solve the handshake problem and were more successful.

analogical transfer Use of the same solution in solving two problems

representational transfer Use of the same format (such as a matrix) in solving two problems

Venn diagram A diagram that shows the set relations (such as overlap) among categories

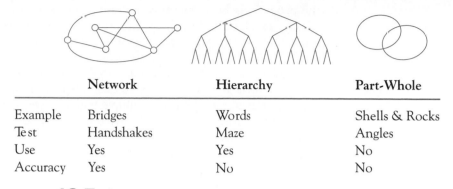

	Network	Hierarchy	Part-Whole
Example	Bridges	Words	Shells & Rocks
Test	Handshakes	Maze	Angles
Use	Yes	Yes	No
Accuracy	Yes	No	No

FIGURE **12.7** Representational transfer of network, hierarchical, and part–whole representations

Source: From "Transferring symbolic representations across nonisomorphic problems" by L. R. Novick & C. E. Hmelo, 1994, *Journal of Experimental Psychology: Learning, Memory, and Cognition, 20,* 1296–1321. Copyright 1994 by the American Psychological Association. Reprinted by permission.

The results were mixed for the hierarchical representation—more people used a hierarchy to solve the maze problem, but they were not more successful. A possible reason is that people who didn't draw a hierarchy typically drew the maze, and drawing the maze was as helpful as drawing a hierarchy to represent the maze. The part–whole problem was the least successful—neither the frequency of use nor the accuracy increased for solving the geometry problem. A limitation in this case is that students were not able to identify correspondences between the shells and rocks in the example problem and the angles in the geometry problem. Figure 12.7 summarizes these findings.

You may have noticed that there are some similarities between these initial results on representational transfer and the results on analogical transfer. Spontaneous transfer of either a specific solution or a more general method was poor because of the difficulty of noticing the similarity between two problems that had different physical descriptions, such as the attack-dispersion and radiation problems (Gick & Holyoak, 1983) or the bridges and handshake problems (Novick & Hmelo, 1994). Second, even when people are told to use an analogous problem, transfer of a particular solution depends on how easily people can find correspondences between objects in one problem and objects in the other problem (Gentner, 1983; Reed, 1993). This also limited transfer of the part–whole method from the shells-and-rocks problem to the geometry problem.

There is another potential similarity between analogical and representational transfer that is suggested by Gick and Holyoak's (1983) finding that spontaneous transfer is facilitated by representing solutions at an abstract level. For spatial diagrams, this requires understanding how the diagrams differ from each other in their representation of information. Novick and Hurley (2001) hypothesized 10 properties that could be used to distinguish between a matrix, network, and hierarchy to evaluate whether people use these properties when deciding which diagram to use in solving a problem. For example, one property is how one moves about a representation. In a matrix, such as the one in Figure 12.6, there are no links so it doesn't make sense to talk about moving along pathways. In a hierarchical model, such as shown in Figure 9.5 (page 219), there is only a single path from one node to another as illustrated by the path from *canary* to *bird* to *animal*. In a network model, such as shown in Figure 9.7 (page 225), there can be multiple paths between nodes. For example, there are multiple paths between *street* and *fire engine* by going either directly or through any one of five intermediary nodes. So one property that should influence the choice of which representation to use is whether no paths, one path, or multiple paths are needed to show the relations among the concepts.

Novick and Hurley (2001) tested their proposed properties by asking college students to select the type of diagram they thought would be most efficient for organizing information in each of 18 short scenarios and to justify their selected diagram. The results showed that students' justifications mentioned 9 of the 10 proposed properties, thus supporting Novick and Hurley's analysis.

In conclusion, the research on general strategies demonstrates that employing strategies such as subgoal formation, analogy, and construction of diagrams can be useful. However, the challenge is to know when and how to apply each of these strategies. Successful use of the strategies may therefore depend on having some amount of expertise in that problem-solving domain. In particular, many of the problems we encounter in the classroom require knowledge about that topic to solve them. Thus, both subject-matter knowledge and general strategies have to be learned if one is to become a proficient problem solver (Glaser, 1984). The next chapter is concerned with acquiring expertise for solving classroom problems and emphasizes the differences between novices and experts.

SUMMARY

Because there are many kinds of problems, constructing a theory of problem solving would be easier if we were able to classify problems according to the skills needed to solve them. One method of classification distinguishes among problems of arrangement, inducing structure, and transformation. Arrangement problems require the problem solver to arrange the elements of a problem in a way that satisfies some criterion. Anagrams are a good example because the letters have to be arranged to spell a word. In problems of inducing structure, some elements are given, and the task is to discover how the elements are related. Analogy and series-completion problems are examples. Transformation problems consist of an initial state, a goal state, and operations for changing the initial state into the goal state. Many puzzles are of this type, including the missionaries-and-cannibals and Tower of Hanoi.

Much of what psychologists know about how people solve problems is the result of the pioneering work of Newell and Simon. Their theory specifies how the basic characteristics of the human information processor, the search space, and different strategies affect problem solving. Performance on a task is influenced by the capacity, storage time, and retrieval time of STM and

LTM. It is also influenced by the search space, which determines the number of legal moves available at each point in solving the problem. Newell and Simon depended on computer simulation models and verbal protocols for testing and developing the many details of their theory.

Four general strategies for solving problems are means–end analysis, subgoals, analogy, and diagrams. These strategies are called heuristics because, although they are often useful, none guarantees a successful solution. The means–end strategy states that the problem solver should select operators that reduce the difference between the current problem state and the goal state. A table of connections shows which differences can be eliminated by each of the operators. Knowledge of subgoals is valuable because it reduces the size of the search space. A detailed simulation of how people solved the missionaries-and-cannibals problem revealed that a subgoal enabled them to avoid unpromising moves by selecting a better strategy than the one that is frequently used. The use of an analogous solution is often useful, but people may not notice a potential analogy. Diagrams can be beneficial in design tasks, but as is the case for analogy, it is not easy to spontaneously transfer a good representation from one problem to another.

STUDY QUESTIONS

1. Which problems did you find most difficult? Can you pinpoint the source of the difficulty? Which were the easiest for you? Can you say why? As your text asks, try to classify the six problems according to the skills needed to solve them.

2. What do most of the problems in your text have in common with items on standardized intelligence tests?

3. Why did Gestalt psychology tend to deal with problems that are classified as arrangement problems? Where does the "Aha!" phenomenon come in?

4. Children (and some adults) are fascinated by Robinson Crusoe–type adventures. Have you ever found yourself in a situation that required you to overcome functional fixedness? What did you do?

5. What characteristics of analogies place them in the class of induction problems? Make up an analogy of your own to demonstrate your understanding of Sternberg's model. Write out your analogy.

6. Can you think of some real-life problems that are clearly transformation problems? Does knowing the goal state make a problem easier?

7. How did Newell and Simon use the computer in building their theory of human problem solving? What advantages does it confer?

8. Is the problem space determined solely by the given task? How does the person enter into Newell and Simon's theory?

9. What parts do operators play in constructing a table of connections in the means–end analysis of a transformation problem? How would memory enter into the picture?

10. How good do you think people are at recognizing problem isomorphs? From your understanding of the research on generalized problem-solving strategies, would it do any good to teach such heuristics to all schoolchildren? Why or why not?

KEY TERMS

The page number in parentheses refers to where the term is discussed in the chapter.

algorithm (311)

anagram (301)

analogical transfer (320)

analogy (314)

analogy problems (305)

arrangement problems (301)

functional fixedness (304)

heuristics (311)

inducing-structure problems (305)

insight (303)

means–end analysis (307)

measure of sufficiency (308)

operators (310)

problem isomorphs (318)

problem space (310)

representational transfer (320)

search space (310)

series extrapolation (305)

simulation programs (308)

subgoals (311)

table of connections (310)

transformation problems (307)

venn diagram (320)

verbal protocols (308)

RECOMMENDED READING

A book by Robertson (2001) provides a very readable introduction to the field of problem solving. Simon (1983) discusses the distinction between search and reasoning. Ericsson and Simon (1980) critically analyze the role of verbal reports in constructing theories and argue that verbal reports can be very useful if they are treated like other kinds of data. Applications of work on problem solving have been used to teach critical thinking (Halpern, 1998) and help people plan the successful completion of projects (Taylor, Pham, Rivkin, & Armor, 1998). The classic work on the effect of set on problem solving was conducted by Luchins (1942) in a study using the water-jar problem. Information-processing models have been developed to account for performance on Duncker's candle problem (Weisberg & Suls, 1973), on insight problems (R. J. Sternberg & J. E. Davidson, 1994), and on geometric analogies (Mulholland, Pellegrino, & Glaser, 1980). Sharps and Wertheimer (2000) talk about the contributions of Gestalt psychology. The books by Vosniadou and Ortony (1989) and Detterman and Sternberg (1993) contain many chapters on the use of analogous solutions. In addition, Reeves and Weisberg (1994) have written a very thorough review of analogical transfer. Both structure-mapping (Chen, 2002; Gentner & Markman, 1997) and connectionist models (Hummel & Holyoak, 1997) have played important roles in theories of analogical reasoning. *The Cambridge Handbook of Thinking and Reasoning.* (Holyoak, & Morrison, 2005) is a good source for chapters that summarize various aspects of thinking. The chapters on problem solving (Novick & Bassok, 2005) and analogy (Holyoak, 2005) are particularly relevant to this chapter.

13

Expertise and Creativity

The secret to creativity is knowing how to hide your sources.
—**Albert Einstein**

One difference between a puzzle such as the missionaries-and-cannibals problem and a chemistry problem such as finding the concentration of a mixture is that we need considerable **domain-specific knowledge** to solve the latter problem. Domain-specific knowledge is knowledge about a particular subject matter. Most people could solve the standard version of the missionaries-and-cannibals problem (three missionaries, three cannibals) without previous experience on this problem, but few people could solve a mixture problem without previous classroom experience. This chapter is concerned with acquiring expertise through learning the domain-specific knowledge that enables us to excel in a particular academic area (Glaser, 1984; Polson & Jeffries, 1985).

In their article on expert performance, Ericsson and Charness (1994) contrast the two most dominant approaches to the study of expertise. The information-processing approach, emphasized in this book, attempts to explain exceptional performance in terms of the knowledge and skills acquired through experience. In contrast, the abilities approach focuses on the innate abilities of people that lead to exceptional performance in a particular domain. An example of this latter approach is illustrated in Howard Gardner's (1983) book *Frames of Mind: The Theory of Multiple Intelligences*. In this book Gardner argues that exceptional performance results from a close match between an individual's intelligence profile (such as having musical, linguistic, or spatial ability) and the demands of a particular task.

More recently, another major contributor to our knowledge of intelligence, Robert Sternberg, sought to provide a link between the literatures on human abilities and on expertise. Sternberg (1998) argued that human abilities are flexible rather than fixed. In fact, the main point (and title) of his article is that abilities reflect developing expertise. An important educational implication of this view is that abilities, like expertise, can be taught. One becomes an expert in the skills needed for success on ability tests in much the same ways that one becomes an expert in doing anything else—through a combination of genetic endowment and experience.

Among the characteristics of expertise that Sternberg considers important are the following:

- Having large, rich schemas containing a great amount of declarative knowledge about a given domain
- Spending proportionately more time determining how to represent problems before searching for a solution
- Developing sophisticated representations based on structural similarities among problems
- Having schemas that contain procedural knowledge about strategies for solving the problem
- Working forward from given information to implement procedures for finding problem unknowns

- Automatizing many sequences of steps within the solution procedures
- Carefully monitoring the problem-solving strategies

We will encounter many examples of these knowledge structures and strategies in this chapter. We first look at how experience influences performance on several reasoning tasks, including evaluating logical statements, classifying problems according to their mathematical structure, and designing experiments to test hypotheses. Experience also influences how people solve more complex transformation problems that require a sequence of steps. The second section discusses the transition from using general search procedures to using more domain-specific procedures as the problem solver acquires expertise. The third section explores the relation between becoming experts at solving fairly routine problems and generating creative solutions. Recent work in cognitive science suggests that a better understanding of expertise will also lead to a better understanding of creativity. Although creativity has been mostly neglected by cognitive psychologists as a research topic (Sternberg & Lubart, 1999), there are a few interesting studies that we can examine.

EXPERTISE AND REASONING

Logical Reasoning

Chapter 11 on text comprehension contained several examples of how the prior knowledge of the reader influences comprehension. A particularly striking example was the Bransford and Johnson (1973) study in which it was very difficult for readers to comprehend abstract ideas unless they could relate them to familiar experiences such as washing clothes. The same argument applies to reasoning and problem solving. A task that has abstract or unfamiliar content can be very difficult, compared with the same task with familiar content. This point is illustrated by varying the content of a logical reasoning task called the **four-card selection problem**.

four-card selection problem A reasoning task that requires deciding which of four cards should be turned over to evaluate a conditional rule

Imagine that you are shown four cards, each containing a *D*, a *K*, a 3, or a 7 (Figure 13.1). The experimenter tells you that each card has a letter on one side and a number on the other side and then asks which cards you would have to turn over to determine the truth of the sentence "Every card that has a *D* on one side has a 3 on the other side." Try to answer this question before reading further.

The experiment, known as the four-card selection problem, has been analyzed by Wason and Johnson-Laird (1972). It is an example of a conditional reasoning task. The correct answer is that you would have to turn over the cards containing a *D* and a 7. The selection of a *D* is fairly obvious—the rule would be false if the other side of the card did not contain a 3. The rule would also be false if you turned over the card containing the 7 and found a *D* on the other side. It is not necessary to turn over the card containing the 3, although this is a common mistake. The rule does not specify what should be on the opposite side of a 3; it only specifies what should be on the opposite side of a *D*. For example, finding a *K* on one side of the card and a 3 on the other side would not make the rule false.

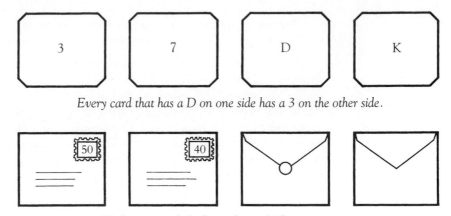

Every card that has a D on one side has a 3 on the other side.

If a letter is sealed, then it has a 50-lira stamp on it.

FIGURE **13.1** The four-card selection problem

Experiments using this task reveal that the implications of a conditional rule are not very clear to most people. The combined results of four experiments indicated that only 5 of 128 subjects correctly turned over only the two correct cards (Wason & Shapiro, 1971). The most popular choice was to turn over the two cards mentioned in the rule—the letter *D* and the number 3 for the above example.

Wason and Johnson-Laird (1972) argued that people make mistakes because they seek information that would verify the rule rather than information that would falsify it. Only the latter information is necessary. Turning over the card containing the 3 would verify the rule if a *D* were found on the other side, but it's not logically necessary to turn over this card because the rule does not specify what should be on the other side. It is necessary to turn over the 7, but people usually overlook this card because they are not seeking ways to disprove the rule.

Wason and Shapiro (1971) hypothesized that the poor performance in this task was caused in part by the abstract material. They predicted that using more realistic materials related to everyday knowledge would make the task significantly easier. The realistic rules were of the general form "Every time I go to Manchester I travel by car." The four cards contained two destinations (Manchester and Leeds) and two modes of transport (car and train). One side of the card specified the destination and the other side the transportation. Of 16 British subjects, 10 selected the two correct cards (Manchester and train) when realistic material was used, compared with only 2 of 16 subjects when abstract material was used.

A problem with even greater appeal as a realistic task is the letter-sorting task used by Johnson-Laird, Legrenzi, and Legrenzi (1972). The subjects were British, and at that time in Britain it cost more to send a sealed letter than an unsealed letter. Subjects in the realistic condition were asked to imagine that they worked at a post office, and their job was to make sure that the letters conformed to each of the following rules: (1) "If a letter is sealed, then it has a 50-lira stamp on it," and (2) "A letter is sealed only if it has a 50-lira stamp on it." Two letters were face down, revealing either a sealed or an unsealed envelope, and two letters were face up, revealing either a 40-lira or a 50-lira stamp (see Figure 13.1). Subjects in the symbolic condition were asked to test two abstract rules involving letters with an *A* or a *D* on one side and a 3 or a 5 on the other side. In the realistic condition 17 of the 24 subjects were correct on both rules, compared with none of the 24 subjects in the symbolic condition.

A question raised by these findings is why people improve when they are given realistic information. Do they become better reasoners, or do they recall specific experiences from memory that eliminate the need to reason? Research by Griggs and Cox (1982) initially suggested that the latter explanation is more appropriate. They tested undergraduates at the University of Florida on a variation of the letter task and found that students did as poorly on the realistic task as on the abstract task. Griggs and Cox proposed that the good performance reported by Johnson-Laird and his colleagues could be explained by their British subjects' personal knowledge about the postal rule and its counterexamples. The U.S. subjects, in contrast, lacked personal experience that they could retrieve from memory because U.S. rates are the same for sealed and unsealed letters.

memory-retrieval explanation The proposal that people solve reasoning problems about familiar situations by retrieving specific examples from their memory

To test the **memory-retrieval explanation** for the superiority of realistic materials, Griggs and Cox (1982) gave their subjects a rule that was familiar: "If a person is drinking beer, then the person must be over 19 years of age." This rule was the law in the state of Florida when the study was conducted. Furthermore, 76% of the subjects later reported that they had personally violated the rule more than once, and 97% of the subjects could remember specific instances of someone other than themselves violating the drinking-age rule. When given the four cards that read DRINKING A BEER, DRINKING A COKE, 16 YEARS OF AGE, and 22 YEARS OF AGE, 29 of 40 subjects made the correct selection for detecting violations of the drinking-age rule (DRINKING A BEER, 16 YEARS OF AGE), whereas none of the 40 subjects did so for the abstract version of the task ("If a card has an *A* on one side, then it has a 3 on the other side").

pragmatic reasoning schemata Organized knowledge structures used to evaluate practical situations such as seeking permission or fulfilling an obligation

A more recent view, however, is more encouraging about our reasoning abilities than the memory-retrieval explanation proposed by Griggs and Cox. According to this view, we possess **pragmatic reasoning schemata** that are general knowledge structures that enable us to reason about a variety of situations that can be interpreted by the schemata (Cheng, Holyoak, Nisbett, & Oliver, 1986).

permission schema Knowledge that taking an action (such as entering a country) requires fulfilling a prerequisite (such as being inoculated)

Two examples of pragmatic reasoning schemata are the **permission schema** and the **obligation schema**. The students did well on the drinking-age rule not only because of their personal familiarity with drinking but also because they had a more general understanding of permission. Permission requires that a condition be satisfied (being old enough) before some action (drinking beer) may be taken. According to this hypothesis, people should also do well in evaluating permission statements about situations that are unfamiliar to them.

obligation schema Knowledge that taking an action (such as paying a pension) is required if a prerequisite (such as retirement) is fulfilled

Imagine that you are hired to enforce the rule "If a passenger wishes to enter the country, then he or she must have had an inoculation against cholera."

You are shown the four cards PASSENGER A WISHES TO ENTER THE COUNTRY, PASSENGER B DOES NOT WISH TO ENTER THE COUNTRY, PASSENGER C HAS BEEN INOCULATED, PASSENGER D HAS NOT BEEN INOCULATED. Which cards would you have to turn over to obtain more information to enforce the rule?

People should also do well in reasoning about situations that involve obligation, such as "If any urithium miner gets lung cancer, then the company will pay the miner a sickness pension." An obligation requires that some action (paying a sickness pension) must be taken if some condition (having lung cancer) is satisfied. Research supports the hypothesis that people do much better in evaluating conditional statements about permission and obligation than in evaluating conditional statements about arbitrary relations (Cheng et al., 1986). By the way, the answer to the question in the previous paragraph is that it is necessary to find out more information about passengers A and D by turning over the cards.

Analogical Reasoning

We would ideally like students to perceive how unfamiliar tasks are related to familiar tasks. They could then apply their prior knowledge to solve unfamiliar problems. Unfortunately, as discussed in the previous chapter, people find it difficult to spontaneously notice an analogy between two problems (Gick & Holyoak, 1980; Reed, Ernst, & Banerji, 1974).

Difficulty in noticing an analogy can occur even when students are very familiar with the analogous problem. One of the experiments on reasoning about the postal regulation was designed to determine if the high level of performance on the postal rule would transfer to the abstract rule (Johnson-Laird et al., 1972). Each subject had two trials with the familiar rule and two trials with the abstract rule. Consistent with the previous results, 22 of the 24 British subjects in this experiment made at least one correct selection with the familiar rule. However, even though they made their selections for the abstract rule immediately afterward, there was no significant transfer from the familiar to the unfamiliar material. Only 7 of the 24 subjects made at least one correct selection for the abstract material.

Johnson-Laird (1989) proposed two reasons for why there was no transfer from the familiar to the unfamiliar task. First, as mentioned in the previous chapter, people often fail to notice analogies because the problems have very different content. To notice the analogy between the rules "If a letter is sealed, then it has a 50-lira stamp" and "If a letter has an *A* on one side, then it has a 2 on the other side," it is necessary to see the correspondence between *has an A* and *is sealed* and the correspondence between *has a 2* and *has a 50-lira stamp*. Second, even the abstract version of the task may seem easy to people, so they answer quickly without searching for an analogy.

The failure to spontaneously notice a useful analogy is discouraging from an instructional perspective, but—as they become better problem solvers and more expert about a particular subject matter—people become more capable of perceiving how problems are related even when they have different content. That is, they become better at classifying problems based on their solutions

TABLE **13.1**
A Word Problem and Related Problems

Word problem	A farmer is counting the hens and rabbits in his barnyard. He counts a total of 50 heads and 140 feet. How many hens and how many rabbits does the farmer have?
Related structure	Bill has a collection of 20 coins that consists entirely of dimes and quarters. If the collection is worth $4.10, how many of each kind of coin are in the collection?
Related content	A farmer is counting the hens and rabbits in his barnyard. He counts six coops with four hens in each, two coops with three hens in each, five cages with six rabbits in each, and three cages with four rabbits in each. How many hens and how many rabbits does the farmer have?

Source: From "Recall of mathematical problem information: Solving related problems," by E. A. Silver, 1981, *Journal for Research in Mathematics Education*, 12, 54–64. Copyright 1981 by the National Council of Teachers of Mathematics. Reprinted by permission.

and are less influenced by the specific story content. A study by Silver (1981) was one of the first to demonstrate this finding.

Silver asked seventh-grade students to form groups of problems that were "mathematically related" and to explain the basis for categorizing them. He used 16 problems that could be represented by a 4×4 matrix. The four problems in each horizontal row were mathematically related, and the same mathematical procedure could be used to solve each. The four problems in each vertical column described a similar story content but required different procedures to solve them. (The first two problems in Table 13.1 are mathematically related because the same procedure is used to solve each. The third problem has the same story content as the first but requires a different mathematical procedure.)

Although Silver asked his students to classify mathematically related problems, students who had difficulty perceiving the mathematical structure of the problems might use story content as a basis of classification. Students were asked to solve 12 of the problems after they made their classification to determine whether there was any relation between the ability to classify and the ability to solve problems. Silver classified the students as good, average, or poor problem solvers on the basis of the number of problems they solved.

The results indicated that the better problem solvers formed categories on the basis of mathematical structure, and the poorer problem solvers formed categories on the basis of story content. The good problem solvers formed an average of 3.1 categories based on mathematical structure, compared with 1.8 categories for the average problem solvers, and 0.4 category for the poor problem solvers. The opposite trend occurred for story content. The poor problem solvers formed an average of 2.3 categories based on story content, compared with 0.6 category for the average problem solvers, and 0.1 category for the good problem solvers.

Similar results were obtained when students were asked to recall information about story problems. Good problem solvers were able to recall information about mathematical structure. Poor problem solvers rarely recalled this information, even when the solutions were discussed prior to their recall. However, they could often remember details about the story content and were sometimes better than the good problem solvers at recalling these details. The results suggest that an important source of individual differences in mathematical problem solving is the ability to categorize problems initially according to the mathematical procedure needed to solve them.

Differences in ability to categorize problems according to their mathematical structure also distinguish novices from experts in more advanced courses. Chi, Glaser, and Rees (1982) asked eight novices and eight experts to sort 24 physics problems into categories based on similarity of solutions. The novices were undergraduates who had recently completed a physics course. The experts were advanced doctoral degree students from the physics department. Each group formed approximately the same number of categories, but the problems in the categories differed for the two groups.

Novices tended to categorize problems on the basis of common objects, such as spring problems and inclined-plane problems. Experts tended to categorize problems on the basis of physics principles that could be applied to solve them, such as the conservation-of-energy law or Newton's second law ($F = MA$). Thus, just as in Silver's (1981) experiment with seventh-grade students, the better problem solvers were more sensitive to the formal structure of the problem.

Scientific Reasoning

Scientists also engage in analogical reasoning. Dunbar and Blanchette (2001) videotaped leading molecular biologists and immunologists during laboratory meetings to study their reasoning in generating hypotheses, designing experiments, fixing problems, and explaining findings. The results showed that the scientists typically used between 3 and 15 analogies during a 1-hour meeting. Almost all of the analogies came from biology, although many were based on a different organism than the one being studied. For example, if a gene in clams and a gene in a malaria-producing parasite had a similar genetic sequence, the biologists might hypothesize that the genetic sequence has the same function in both organisms.

As you probably already know, the design and interpretation of experiments is also important in psychology. You can expect to acquire two kinds of expertise that will be helpful if you pursue a research career in psychology. One is knowledge about good experimental design that should help you design experiments for a wide variety of topics in psychology. The other is knowledge about the specific hypothesis being tested. For example, psychologists who study memory should be able to design better experiments on memory than psychologists who study interpersonal relations.

To evaluate these different types of expertise, Schunn and Anderson (1999) compared the capabilities of three groups of participants to design an experiment on memory. One group consisted of cognitive psychology faculty who had done much of their research on memory, another group consisted of social and developmental faculty who had done very little research on memory, and the third group consisted of undergraduates from a variety of backgrounds.

The task was to design an experiment to test two alternative hypotheses of the spacing effect: It is better to wait awhile between study trials than it is to mass the study trials too closely in time. One hypothesis is that spaced practice creates a greater variety of contexts so at least one of the study contexts should be similar to the text context. As we saw in Chapter 6 on memory codes, similarity between the study and test contexts can be beneficial. Another hypothesis is that people don't create a very good memory code when study trials are massed together because they don't have to remember the information for very long. We also saw in Chapter 6 that some memory codes last longer than others.

The participants designed experiments by using a computer interface that allowed them to vary three study variables (number of repetitions, amount of time between repetitions, and change of context on repetitions) and three test variables (type of test, delay of test, and text context). The faculty and undergraduates were evaluated on both domain-general skills that are useful for designing psychology experiments and domain-specific skills that are useful for designing memory experiments. General skills included designing experiments that would distinguish between alternative theories and keeping experiments simple by not varying variables irrelevant to the hypotheses. Specific skills included choosing useful values for the variables and including variables that would likely interact with each other.

Figure 13.2 shows the results for the domain experts (memory researchers), task experts (social/developmental researchers), and the (high-ability and mid-ability) undergraduates. For the domain-specific skills, the memory researchers did significantly better than the other three groups, which did not differ. Even undergraduates did as well as the social/developmental faculty in designing experiments for those aspects of the task that required some expertise in the field of memory. However, the social/developmental faculty did significantly better than the undergraduates and as well as the memory researchers on domain-general skills. The undergraduates usually did not refer to the theories in designing or interpreting the experiments, an important lesson to keep in mind in your next laboratory class.

ACQUIRING EXPERTISE

The preceding studies showed how prior knowledge influenced performance on several different kinds of reasoning tasks, including evaluating logical statements, classifying problems according to their mathematical structure, and designing experiments. Prior knowledge also influences how people solve more complex transformation problems, which require constructing a sequence of steps to solve the problem. Early models of problem solving (Newell & Simon, 1972) emphasized general search procedures that used heuristics such as means–end analysis to guide the search. More recent models indicate that, with practice, students can learn specific solutions that replace the less efficient

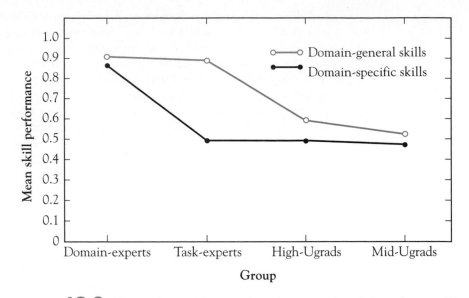

FIGURE **13.2** Effect of expertise on domain-general and domain-specific skills in designing and interpreting experiments

Source: From "The general/specificity of expertise in scientific reasoning," C. D. Schunn & J. R. Anderson, 1999, *Cognitive Science*, 23, 337–370. Copyright 1999 by the Cognitive Science Society. Reprinted by permission.

general heuristics (Gick, 1986). This distinction between applying a learned solution and searching for the solution is illustrated in Figure 13.3.

Search versus Implementation

Figure 13.3 shows three major stages in solving a problem (Gick, 1986). The problem solver first attempts to construct a representation of the problem by connecting it to prior knowledge. Certain features of the problem may activate a schema for solving the problem if the problem solver does find a connection with prior knowledge. As we saw in Chapter 9, a *schema* is an organized cluster of knowledge, and in this case it is a cluster of knowledge for a particular problem type. It contains information about the typical problem goals, constraints, and solution procedures for that kind of problem. If schema activation occurs during the construction of a problem representation, the solver can proceed directly to the third stage and implement the solution. There is very little need to search for a solution because the appropriate solution procedures are activated by recognizing the particular problem type.

I have become very proficient at recognizing many types of algebra word problems because I study these problems in my research. When I see an algebra word problem, I usually quickly recognize it as a familiar type and can immediately construct an equation to solve it. But every so often I find an unfamiliar problem that I have to spend some time thinking about before I can solve it. This requires that I search for a solution, which is the second stage in Figure 13.3.

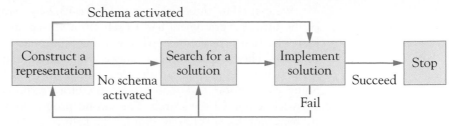

FIGURE **13.3** Schematic diagram of the problem-solving process

Source: From "Problem-solving strategies," by M. L. Gick, 1986, *Educational Psychologist*, 21, 99–120, Fig. 1. Copyright by Lawrence Erlbaum Associates, Inc. Reprinted by permission.

general strategy A strategy (heuristic) that applies in many situations but does not always result in a solution

Searching for a solution requires the use of **general strategies** such as the ones I discussed in the previous chapter. One strategy is means–end analysis, in which the problem solver attempts to reduce differences between the current problem state and the goal state. A second general strategy is to search for an analogous problem that might provide a useful solution. A third general strategy is planning the solution by breaking down the problem into subgoals.

Gick (1986) emphasizes, however, that general strategies can require some specific knowledge about a problem to be successful. For example, planning implies that the problem solver is looking ahead and is not simply taking one step at a time. This of course is usually not possible the first time a person encounters a problem. Planning has not been emphasized in much of the research on puzzles because people usually do not have detailed knowledge about how to solve a particular puzzle. Successful models of puzzle solving have therefore been based on general strategies such as means–end analysis (Atwood & Polson, 1976; Simon & Reed, 1976).

A good example of a task that can be accomplished more efficiently through planning is the writing of computer programs (Atwood, Polson, Jeffries, & Ramsey, 1978). The subjects in this experiment were three experienced computer programmers who differed in their knowledge about an assigned task. The task was to write a program that would accept as input the text of a book and would produce as output a list of specified index terms and page numbers on which each term appeared. The results showed that the subjects differed in the extent to which they followed a planning procedure. The protocols of the three subjects showed fairly clear differences in the overall quality, completeness, and organization of their knowledge. The knowledge of one subject was sufficiently developed to allow for the construction of a plan for producing the index. The knowledge of the second subject was less well developed, and, as a result, backtracking was necessary to correct deficiencies in the design. The knowledge of the third subject was developed to such an extent that this subject was able to retrieve most of the design directly from memory and therefore required less planning than the other two subjects. These findings suggest that planning is most likely to be carried out by someone who has enough knowledge to approach the task systematically but is unable to retrieve the solution directly from memory.

We can relate these findings to Figure 13.3 by comparing how much each of the three programmers had to rely on a search strategy to solve the problem. The first programmer, who used planning, had partial knowledge about the task. The task activated a schema about designing a book index, but the schema knowledge was not detailed enough to produce a complete solution. Some exploration and search were therefore required in which the partial knowledge guided the search. The second programmer did the task primarily by searching for a solution without the help of a plan. The third programmer could solve the problem by simply implementing the solution from detailed schema knowledge about solving this particular kind of problem.

Learning a Solution

The transition from following a general strategy to applying a specific solution is particularly evident from the study of how people solve physics problems. The problems require calculating the value of an unknown variable by using several equations. Table 13.2 shows an example. Before reading further, determine how you would use the equations shown below the problem to calculate the distance the pile driver fell.

Research on how problem solvers solved these problems reveals that novices are more likely to use a general search strategy based on means–end analysis, whereas experts are more likely to **work forward** by referring to the equations in the order that they are actually needed (Larkin, McDermott, Simon, & Simon, 1980). Because the goal is to find the value of the unknown variable, the means–end strategy searches for an equation that contains the unknown variable. The unknown is *distance* in the example problem, so the novice would attempt to use Equation 1 to calculate distance by multiplying rate by time. The value for time (3.7 seconds) is stated in the problem, but the value for rate is not stated (30.4 meters per second is the final rate). The novice would then search for an equation that allows calculation of rate. This value is calculated from Equation 2 and then substituted into Equation 1 to solve the problem.

Notice that the novice referred to the equations in the reverse order of how they were actually used. He first referred to Equation 1 because it contained the unknown variable, but he had to calculate a value in Equation 2

work forward Selecting relevant information to solve a problem in the order that it should be used in the solution

TABLE **13.2**
A Motion Problem

Problem

A pile driver takes 3.7 sec to fall onto a pile. It hits the pile at 30.4 m/sec. How high was the pile driver raised?

Equations

1. Distance = rate × time
2. Rate = 0.5 × final rate
3. Final rate = acceleration × time

before solving Equation 1. In contrast, an expert refers to the equations in the order in which they are needed. An expert would go immediately to Equation 2, calculate rate, and then substitute the value into Equation 1. The expert has learned the correct sequence of steps and doesn't have to search for the solution. Searching for a solution should become more time-consuming as the number of equations increases. For example, if the example problem gave the rate of acceleration rather than the final velocity, it would be necessary to use all three equations.

Research has shown that students switch from a means–end to a working-forward strategy as they become more experienced in solving problems. Sweller, Mawer, and Ward (1983) gave students a series of 25 motion problems like the one in Table 13.2. The average number of solutions based on a means–end strategy significantly declined from 3.9 for the first 5 problems to 2.2 for the last 5 problems.

Sweller has argued that, although the means–end strategy is an efficient one for obtaining the goal, it is an inefficient strategy for learning the sequence of steps required to solve the problem. By eliminating differences between the current state and the goal state, the problem solver may rapidly obtain the goal but fail to remember the sequence of steps used. Remembering the steps is difficult because the learner's attention is focused on reducing differences, not on learning steps. Furthermore, reducing differences requires a relatively large amount of cognitive capacity (as we saw in the previous chapter), which is consequently unavailable for learning the solution (Sweller, 1988).

A remedy for encouraging students to learn the correct sequence of steps is to omit the goal by asking them to solve for as many variables as they can, rather than solving for a particular variable. If students were asked to use Equations 1 and 2 in Table 13.2 to solve for as many variables as they could, they would first solve for rate in Equation 2 and then substitute this value into Equation 1 to solve for distance. This approach encourages students to use a working-forward strategy and eliminates the capacity demands of the means–end strategy that make it difficult to learn the correct sequence of steps.

A study of 20 high school students demonstrated the success of this approach (Sweller et al., 1983). Ten of the students were assigned to a goal condition ("Find the distance"), and ten students were assigned to a *nongoal* condition ("Calculate as many variables as you can"). After practicing on solving problems, the students solved two test problems that had a specific goal. Nine of the ten students in the nongoal group solved the test problems by working forward, but only one of the ten students in the goal group solved the problems by working forward. The working-forward strategy helped the nongoal students reduce their search by taking significantly fewer steps in solving the test problems.

Combining Theory and Instruction

Sweller's study demonstrates that psychological theory regarding the capacity demands of the means–end strategy was useful in modifying instruction to improve problem solving. But the most systematic effort to use cognitive theory to improve instruction is the work of John Anderson and his colleagues at Carnegie Mellon University (Anderson, Boyle, & Reiser, 1985; Ritter, Anderson, Koedinger, & Corbett, 2007). Their work has focused on the design of intelligent tutoring systems for teaching algebra, high school geometry, and the LISP programming language. The systems are based on the learning principles of ACT* (pronounced "A-C-T star").

ACT* consists of a set of assumptions about both declarative knowledge and procedural knowledge. The assumptions about **declarative knowledge** emphasize the representation and organization of factual information. The assumptions about **procedural knowledge** emphasize how we use this knowledge to carry out various tasks. The procedural assumptions of the theory are particularly relevant for tutoring cognitive skills.

The procedural component of the theory consists of a set of rules (usually called **production rules**) that specify which actions should be performed under a particular set of conditions. A production rule therefore consists of two parts—a condition part and an action part. The action is carried out whenever the condition is satisfied. An example of a production rule is the following:

IF the goal is to generate the plural of a noun,

THEN add an s to the noun.

Notice that the condition specifies a goal, and the action specifies a potential way to achieve the goal.

Production rules provided the basis for constructing a computer tutor that instructs students in how to program in the programming language LISP. The major theoretical assumptions underlying the construction of the LISP tutor include the following (J. R. Anderson, 1990):

1. *Production rules.* A skill such as programming can be decomposed into a set of production rules.
2. *Skill complexity.* Hundreds of production rules are required to learn a complex skill. This assumption is consistent with the domain-specific view of knowledge.
3. *Hierarchical goal organization.* All productions are organized by a hierarchical goal structure. The condition part of the production therefore specifies a goal, as illustrated above for generating the plural of a noun.
4. *Declarative origins of knowledge.* All knowledge begins in some declarative representation, typically acquired from instruction or example. Before people practice solving problems, they are instructed in how to solve problems.
5. *Compilation of procedural knowledge.* Solving problems requires more than being told about how to solve problems. We have to convert this declarative knowledge into efficient procedures for solving specific problems.

The LISP tutor consists of 1200 production rules that model student performances on programming problems. It covers all the basic concepts of LISP during a full-semester, self-paced course at Carnegie Mellon University. It is quite successful; students who worked on problems with the LISP tutor generally received one letter grade higher on exams than students who had not worked with the tutor.

declarative knowledge Knowledge about factual information

procedural knowledge Knowledge that relates actions to goals

production rule A conditional rule that specifies the prerequisite condition for carrying out an action

Both the theory and tutors (Cognitive Tutors) have continued to evolve. The most extensive application of the Cognitive Tutors has been to mathematics classes, and by 2007 data had been collected from more than 7000 students in pre-algebra classes (Ritter et al., 2007). The curriculum includes both a text and software so students can divide their time between the classroom (typically three days a week) and computer lab (typically two days a week). As is the case for all applications of the Cognitive Tutor, instruction consists of focusing on those procedures that require additional practice by presenting problems that require those procedures.

In contrast to the Cognitive Tutor's emphasis on learning procedures, the Animation Tutor emphasizes the viewing and manipulation of perceptual icons to help students learn mathematics (Reed, 2005). The theoretical basis for the Animation Tutor is the embodied cognition framework discussed in Chapter 11 in which perception and action are important components of cognition (Gibbs, 2006; Reed, in press). Figure 13.4 shows a perceptual portrayal of an interest problem in which balances and interest are represented by stacks of money. In the action portrayal, students construct the total interest on the right side of the equals sign by dragging the interest from the two stacks on the left side of the equals sign. The designers of the Cognitive and Animation tutors are currently collaborating on a research project to explore the effectiveness of combining the procedural and perceptual approaches.

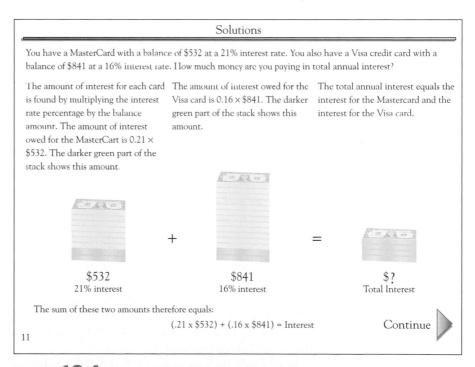

Solutions

You have a MasterCard with a balance of $532 at a 21% interest rate. You also have a Visa credit card with a balance of $841 at a 16% interest rate. How much money are you paying in total annual interest?

The amount of interest for each card is found by multiplying the interest rate percentage by the balance amount. The amount of interest owed for the MasterCart is 0.21 × $532. The darker green part of the stack shows this amount.

The amount of interest owed for the Visa card is 0.16 × $841. The darker green part of the stack shows this amount.

The total annual interest equals the interest for the Mastercard and the interest for the Visa card.

$532
21% interest

+

$841
16% interest

=

$?
Total Interest

The sum of these two amounts therefore equals:

$$(.21 \times \$532) + (.16 \times \$841) = \text{Interest}$$

Continue ▷

11

FIGURE **13.4** A perceptual portrayal of an interest problem in the Animation Tutor

CREATIVITY

creativity Creating a
novel and useful product
or solution

Expertise implies that people are good problem solvers in their area of expertise but doesn't necessarily imply that they are creative. We think of creative problem solvers as being better than simply good problem solvers. **Creativity** implies that the solutions are not only correct but also novel and useful. We might even hold a special reverence for creative solutions, believing that they are produced by a mysterious process that requires the ability of a genius to produce them. However, work by cognitive scientists suggests that creativity may be less mysterious than we expected. In fact, two books even suggest that we can apply what we already know about expertise to explain creativity.

One book, *Creativity: Beyond the Myth of Genius*, by Weisberg (1993) argues that although the effects of creative ideas are extraordinary, the thought processes that produce them are not:

> *Many creative products are indeed extraordinary. They are rare; they are sometimes the result of a lifetime of hard work; they can answer questions that have perplexed people for centuries; they can have far-ranging influence, beyond even the expectations of their creators. It is often assumed that if a creative product has extraordinary effects, it must have come about in extraordinary ways, but that does not necessarily follow. The creative achievement can be extraordinary because of the effect it produces, rather than because of the way in which it was brought about.* (p. 10)

Weisberg's "myth of genius" view is based, in part, on his analysis of creative individuals, whose discoveries he felt could be explained by their use of ordinary thought processes. Ordinary thinking goes beyond past achievements, but it does so by slowly accumulating new pieces of information. There are no sudden leaps or unconscious illuminations. Weisberg uses case studies to illustrate that Watson and Crick's discovery of the structure of DNA, the Wright brothers' invention of the airplane, and Picasso's development of a new style of painting occurred through incremental processes that built on previous work. In addition, the quote at the beginning of this chapter—"The secret to creativity is knowing how to hide your sources"—indicates that even Einstein attributed part of his success to the work of others.

I have mixed feelings about Weisberg's view because of my admiration for highly creative individuals. Certainly, Einstein went way beyond his "sources" to give us a new understanding of the universe. Many other highly creative people, such as Frank Lloyd Wright and Dr. Seuss, seem to have had a special genius. Perhaps the resolution of the conflict between a great admiration for creative works and the desire to explain their production is contained in the preface to Boden's (2004) book, *The Creative Mind: Myths and Mechanisms*. Boden agrees that creativity is not mysterious and can be explained by the computational concepts of artificial intelligence. But providing explanations, says Boden, should allow us to appreciate the richness of creative thought better than before—even if our sense of mystery is dispelled, our sense of wonder should not be.

In addition to Weisberg's (1993) autobiographical approach and Boden's (2004) computational approach, a neurological approach also suggests continuities between creativity and expert thinking. Dietrich's (2004) cognitive neuroscience analysis assumes that the neural circuits that process information to yield noncreative combinations of information are the same ones that generate creative or novel combinations of that information. In both cases the prefrontal cortex, which comprises approximately one-half of the frontal lobe in humans (Figure 1.3, p. 9), is needed to combine information that has been processed in other parts of the brain. Creativity requires cognitive abilities such as the effective control of working memory, sustained attention, cognitive flexibility, and judgment of appropriateness, that are typically ascribed to the prefrontal cortex.

The Constraining Effects of Examples

Although Weisberg (1993) believes that creative discoveries can often be explained by ordinary thought processes, he admits that highly creative individuals may be exceptional in some respects. Creative individuals are not only experts in their domain but also are highly motivated. In addition, they often take paths of inquiry that others ignore, take intellectual risks, and persevere in the face of obstacles (R. J. Sternberg & T. L. Lubart, 1996). In contrast to the biographical studies of creativity, laboratory studies have typically studied college students' performance on tasks that do not require much expertise. Although this may limit generalization to the creative thinking of experts, the findings are nonetheless interesting.

The design of these experimental studies are extensions of previous research paradigms in cognitive psychology, modified to emphasize the novelty of the creations. Take the case of using examples. Examples are important in problem solving—they provide the source of analogies in analogical problem solving and are an important source for learning production rules in ACT*. They also can be the source of creative ideas, but there is a subtle difference in how we use examples to solve routine problems and how we use examples to produce creative solutions. When we search for an analogous problem to solve a routine problem, we try to maximize the similarity between the example and test problem to minimize the differences in the two solutions. When we use an example to produce something creative, we want to make changes in the example to produce a novel product or solution.

If we are not careful, examples can have a constraining effect on creativity. This is illustrated in a task in which people were given the following instructions:

> Imagine a planet just like Earth existing somewhere in the universe. It is currently uninhabited. Your task is to design new creatures to inhabit the planet. Within the allotted 20 minutes draw as many new and different creatures of your own creative design as you are able. Duplication of creatures now extinct or living on the planet Earth are not permitted. Provide both a side view and front view of each creature. (S. M. Smith, Ward, & Schumacher, 1993, p. 839)

One group was then shown the three examples in Figure 13.5 before beginning the task. Their work was compared with that of a control group that received the same instructions without the examples. Would the examples be

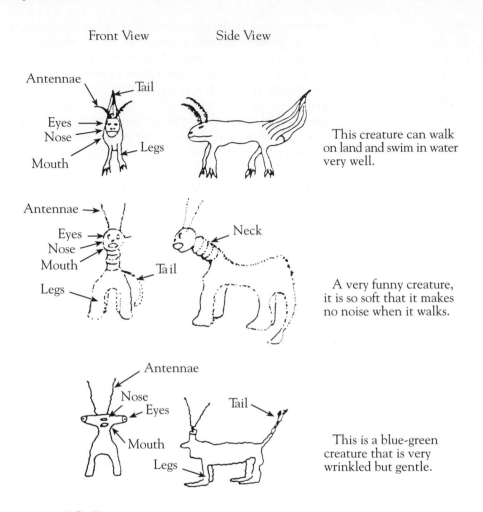

Front View   Side View

This creature can walk on land and swim in water very well.

A very funny creature, it is so soft that it makes no noise when it walks.

This is a blue-green creature that is very wrinkled but gentle.

FIGURE **13.5** Example creatures, along with their labels and descriptions

Source: S. M. Smith, T. B. Ward, & J. S. Schumacher, 1993, *Memory & Cognition*, 21, 837–845. Copyright 1993 by the Psychonomic Society, Inc. Reprinted by permission.

helpful, as typically found in many studies, or would they stifle creativity by causing the participants to produce "novel" animals that closely resembled the examples? Unfortunately, the examples constrained the productions. The examples group was significantly more likely to draw creatures that had four legs, antennae, and a tail, like those shown in the examples. The same results occurred when participants were instructed to create novel toys. Instructions to create products that differed from the examples had little effect—people were still constrained by the examples.

In another study, students were told: "We showed you these examples in order to help you think about creating your own original creatures and to get your creative juices flowing. However, we do not want you to copy any aspect of the examples" (Marsh, Landau, & Hicks, 1996, p. 671). These instructions worked fairly well for students who drew animals immediately after reading the instructions, but copying aspects of the examples was significantly higher for participants who drew the animals after a 1-day delay. One interpretation of these findings is related to Marsh and Bower's (1993) concept of **inadvertent plagiarism**: Memory for the examples was sufficiently activated to cause copying but insufficiently activated to cause realization of the copying.

inadvertent plagiarism
Unintentionally copying someone else's ideas

I experienced a possible case of inadvertent plagiarism when I worked on the fourth edition of this book. This chapter was originally titled "Classroom Problem Solving" in the first three editions of the book. When I added research on creativity in the fourth edition, I decided I needed a new title and selected the current title "Expertise and Creativity." One advantage of the new title was that I couldn't recall any other cognitive psychology textbooks that had a chapter on this topic. So you can imagine my surprise when I discovered a chapter in an older book (Medin & Ross, 1992) labeled "Expertise and Creativity."

Inventing Products Through Imagery

Another case of a novel research program on creativity that grew out of previous paradigms in cognitive psychology is the work of Finke (1990). Finke has been one of the main contributors to a theory of visual imagery, and he used his expertise in this area to extend imagery paradigms to the study of creativity. Writings by Shepard (1988) and others had indicated that many famous scientific discoveries depended on visual imagery. For example, Einstein reported that his thought experiments relied on imagery. Imagining the consequences of traveling at the speed of light helped him formulate his special theory of relativity. Faraday claimed to have visualized force lines from electric and magnetic fields, leading to the modern theory of electromagnetic fields. Kekule reported that his discovery of the molecular structure of benzene occurred after he imagined a snake coiled in a circle.

Finke (1990) extended previous studies on the visual synthesis of artificial patterns (such as those by Palmer, 1977) to determine whether people could visually combine basic parts to create useful and novel products. The object parts consisted of such basic forms as a sphere, half sphere, cube, cone, cylinder, rectangular block, wire, tube, bracket, flat square, hook, wheels, ring, and handle (somewhat like the geons in Biederman's [1985] theory of pattern recognition that was discussed in Chapter 2). After either the experimenter or the subject selected three parts, the subjects were instructed to close their eyes and imagine combining the parts to make a practical object or device. They had to use all three parts but could vary their size, position, and orientation. The created object had to belong to one of eight categories: furniture, personal items, transportation, scientific instruments, appliances, tools or utensils, weapons, and toys or games.

Judges then scored the created objects on a 5-point scale for practicality and for originality. Strict criteria were used—the average rating for practicality had to be at least 4.5 to be classified as practical, and the average rating

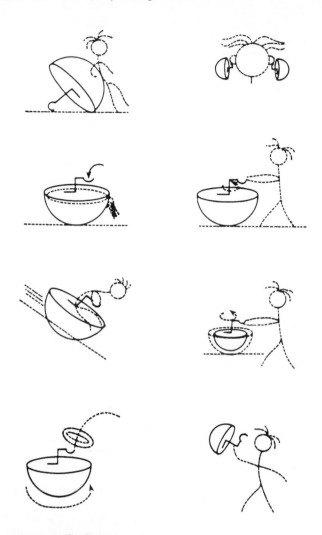

FIGURE **13.6** Multiple interpretations of a single preinventive form (assembled from a half sphere, bracket, and hook). The interpretations are lawn lounger (furniture), earrings (personal items), water weigher (scientific instruments), portable agitator (appliances), water sled (transportation), rotating masher (utensils), ring spinner (toys), and slasher basher (weapons).

Source: From *Creative imagery: Discoveries and inventions in visualization*, by R. A. Finke, Fig. 7.24. Copyright © 1990 by Lawrence Erlbaum Associates, Inc. Reprinted by permission.

for originality had to be at least 4.0 to be classified as original. In one condition, subjects were allowed to select their own parts but were told the category of their invention (such as appliances). In another condition, they were allowed to invent an object that belonged to any one of the eight categories but were told which parts to use (such as half sphere, wheels, and hook). In the most restrictive condition, they were told both the parts to use and the category of their invention (use a half sphere, wheels, and a hook to make an appliance). Although the number of inventions scored as practical was approximately the same across the three conditions, the most restrictive condition resulted in the highest number of creative inventions, judged to be both practical and original. The more restrictive the task, the more difficult it was to think of an object that satisfied all the criteria and was like existing objects.

There is, however, an even more restrictive condition than assigning both the parts and category. In another experiment, people were again given the parts but didn't find out about the category until *after* they had assembled their object. Finke (1990) refers to these objects as **preinventive forms** because their use cannot be identified until after the object is constructed. Figure 13.6 shows how a preinventive form that was assembled from a half sphere, bracket, and hook could be used for each of the eight categories. The results demonstrated that this was the most successful condition of all for generating creative inventions.

The Geneplore Model

Even in the less constraining conditions, however, many subjects reported that they

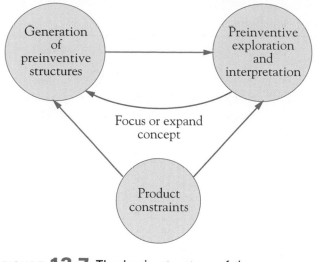

FIGURE 13.7 The basic structure of the Geneplore (generation-exploration) model

Source: From *Creative cognition: Theory, research, and applications,* by R. A. Finke, T. B. Ward, & S. M. Smith. Copyright 1992 by MIT Press. Reprinted by permission.

preinventive form
Creating an object before determining its use

generation strategy A strategy for producing preinventive forms

exploration strategy A strategy for determining how to use a preinventive form

preferred to initially use a **generation strategy** in which they imagined interesting combinations of parts, followed by an **exploration strategy** in which they figured out how to use the invented object. Finke, Ward, and Smith (1992) describe these two phases in their Geneplore (generation-exploration) mode l shown in Figure 13.7.

In the initial phase, the inventor forms preinventive structures that are then explored and interpreted during the second phase. The preinventive structures are the precursors to the final, creative product and would be generated, regenerated, and modified throughout the cycle of invention. Finke et al. (1992) recommend that people should place greater emphasis on generating preinventive structures and then later think of possible uses. Notice that this is contrary to the usual order in which we begin with a particular use in mind—a wallet that fits in a shirt pocket or a garment that allows us to change clothes at the beach—and then try to invent something to accomplish our goal. There is an interesting analogy here between the recommended strategy and the no-goal condition of Sweller and colleagues' (1983) research in which people benefited from an initial goal-free exploratory phase.

I must admit, however, that I was initially skeptical about the Geneplore model. It didn't seem likely to me that designers assemble forms without having a particular goal in mind. Wouldn't they at least have a category in mind such as furniture, appliances, or transportation? I believe that designers typically begin with a general goal (such as design a car), but they can expand on that goal in creative ways by elaborating on their design structures. The Geneplore model could therefore apply to discoveries in this more constrained situation.

Jerry Hirshberg (1998) describes such a discovery in his book *The Creative Priority.* As director of Nissan Design America, he studied the drawings of a car created by one of his designers. He noticed that the upper rear quadrant of the car (including the rear window and trunk lid) was set off by an unusually thick line. The thick line separating this part of the car suggested to him that a vehicle could be decomposed into a set of interlocking panels that could be removed and replaced with other panels for diverse uses.

The designers went back to work to further develop this idea while the engineers studied product constraints such as possible problems with hinges, structural reinforcements, and sealing. The various stages of the Geneplore model apply to the production of the Pulsar NX, the world's first production

TABLE **13.3**
A Dual Process Theory of Reasoning

	Associative System	Rule-Based System
Principle of operation	Similarity	Symbol manipulation
Source of knowledge	Personal experience	Language and culture
Relations	Associations	Causal and logical
Nature of processing	Reproductive	Productive
	Automatic	Strategic
Functions	Intuition	Deliberation
	Creativity	Formal analysis
	Visual recognition	Verification
	Associative memory	Strategic memory

Source: "Two systems of reasoning," by S. A. Sloman, 2002, in T. Gilovich, D. Griffin & D. Kahneman (Eds.), *Heuristics and biases: The psychology of intuitive judgment* (pp. 379–396). Cambridge: Cambridge University Press.

modular car. The preinventive structure in this case is a standard car, exploration of this structure leads to a modular car, and engineering constraints influence the final design. Such creativity is obviously a highly regarded attribute. Hopefully, cognitive models will lead to methods to stimulate it.

Associative versus Rule-Based Reasoning

This chapter and the previous one on problem solving discussed a variety of skills and strategies that can be used to solve different problems. It may be helpful to think about this research within the context of two forms of reasoning proposed by Sloman (2002). Table 13.3 lists the differences between reasoning that is based on associations and reasoning that is based on rules.

Associative reasoning uses associations such as the ones represented in the semantic networks of Chapter 9. Many of these associations are learned through personal experiences rather than through cultural institutions such as schools. In contrast, causal and logical rules support strategic reasoning. The correct application of a rule is often determined by the relations among symbols rather than by the meaning of the symbols (Sloman, 2002). For example, you can apply rules to solve for x in the equation $11 + x = 14$ without knowing the meaning of x.

A problem with using the distinctions shown in Table 13.3 is that it is not always easy to determine whether performance is based on associations or on rules. Sloman (2002) proposes that the task itself does not dictate whether reasoning is association- or rule-based, and that many tasks require both forms of reasoning. Nonetheless, some tasks are better candidates for rule-based reasoning, and other tasks are better candidates for associative reasoning. For example, the abstract version of the four-card selection problem (every card that has a D on one side has a 3 on the other side) is a good example of a task that requires rule-based reasoning. The familiar version of this task studied by Griggs and Cox (1982)—If a person is drinking beer, then the person must be over 19 years of age—is a good example of a task that could be solved by using associative reasoning. Students could use their personal experiences to solve the familiar version.

You may have already noticed that creativity is listed as part of the associative system in Table 13.3. This is consistent with Dietrich's (2004) argument that *spontaneous* insightful thinking often involves associative, unconscious thinking that does not originate in the prefrontal cortex. Examples of this kind of thinking are Newton's conception of gravity after watching a falling apple, Einstein's conceptualization of relativity while imagining riding on a beam of light, and Kekule's discovery of the structure of benzene while dreaming. However, there is another side to creativity that reflects the rule-based component of creative thinking. In contrast to spontaneous thinking, Dietrich (2004) states that *deliberative* thinking does originate in the prefrontal cortex. Examples of deliberative thinking include Watson and Crick's methodical work that determined the structure of DNA and Edison's systematic approach to inventing. Finke (1996) also argues for two forms of reasoning (unstructured and ordered) that have parallels to associative and rule-based thinking. Unstructured creativity is produced by thinkers who are generally impulsive, reactive, spontaneous, playful, and metaphorical. Unstructured thinking is associative and produces ideas that are strikingly original. In contrast, ordered thinking is organized and controlled. The creative thinking of ordered thinkers is often highly structured and connected to previous ideas and concepts. Structured thinking involves (rule-based) deliberation and verification that is helpful in judging the practicality of ideas.

Both unstructured and ordered thinking are important in creativity. Unstructured thinking produces creative ideas that are often excessively fanciful. Ordered thinking tends to be realistic, but unimaginative. Sloman's (2002) argument that many tasks involve both associative and rule-based thinking likely applies to those tasks that require creative thinking. As pointed out by Finke (1996, p. 391):

> *Creativity is neither fully controlled and structured nor completely unplanned and unstructured. Creative ideas, concepts, and images can result either from the intentional workings of the human mind or from its spontaneous, intuitive qualities.*

SUMMARY

Our ability to reason and solve problems is influenced by the familiarity of the material. For example, correctly evaluating the implications of a logical rule depends on whether the semantic content of the rule is abstract ("If a card has a *D* on one side, then it has a 3 on the other side") or familiar ("If a person is drinking beer, then the person must be over 19 years of age"). Answers are more accurate for familiar content than for unfamiliar content, and showing students how an unfamiliar task is isomorphic to a familiar task can vastly improve performance on the unfamiliar task. As students acquire expertise, they become better at identifying the formal structure of problems and are less influenced by story content.

Acquiring expertise also results in a change in strategies for how students solve transformation problems. Novices rely on general search strategies such as means–end analysis to search for equations to solve physics problems. In contrast, experts use a working-forward strategy because they have learned the correct order for using equations. Using means–end analysis can interfere with learning a correct sequence of operations because of the cognitive demands of applying a means–end strategy. Requesting that students solve for a variety of unknown variables, rather than for a specific unknown variable, prevents them from using means–end analysis and facilitates learning the correct sequence of operations. However, the most comprehensive program of using cognitive theory to improve instruction involves applying the learning principles of ACT* to assist students in learning to program in LISP and to solve geometry and algebra problems.

The early results are now in on a cognitive theory of creativity. They suggest that creativity may not be all that mysterious and that it may simply be good problem solving. A big difference, however, between standard solutions and creative solutions is that creative solutions are novel. This means that our solutions must not be constrained by previous examples. Mental imagery has played an important role in some creative discoveries and is now being analyzed by asking people to create products by mentally synthesizing parts. Limiting the parts that people can use and the categories of their inventions makes the task more difficult, but the product is more likely to be novel. The successive generation and exploration phases of developing ideas is captured in the Geneplore model. Both associations and rules are helpful.

STUDY QUESTIONS

1. Where do you stand on the issue of how much time should be allotted to teaching problem-solving strategies versus subject-matter instruction? Do you think your academic life would have been more productive if you had had a course in reasoning and problem solving? What's the research on this question?

2. Much of the existing experimental evidence on logical reasoning makes most of us out to be pretty "dim bulbs." Is that a fair characterization, or is there some other plausible explanation for the miserable showing?

3. The chapter on semantic organization (Chapter 9) listed various characteristics of schemata. Do the permission and obligation schemata proposed by Cheng and her colleagues have these characteristics?

4. Reasoning can sometimes be improved by making a connection between an unfamiliar problem and a familiar one. Think of some unfamiliar domain that you were better able to understand by using an analogy to a familiar domain. Explain your reasoning.

5. Apply Gick's (1986) schematization of the problem-solving process, shown in Figure 13.3, to predict your own performance in these circumstances: Choose two specific content domains in which you have widely different degrees of expertise and make up a test question for each. How would you proceed in your attempt to solve each problem?

6. How does working forward differ from means–end analysis? Which strategy depends on schema activation?

7. From its earliest beginnings, U.S. psychological science has exhibited a penchant for studying "the mind in use." Can you make a case for ACT* fitting into this tradition, broadly conceived? Try your hand at the most basic level of application by writing a production rule or two for a grammar to be programmed into a computer tutor for English.

8. Weisberg claims that creativity can be explained by current theories of problem solving. What relation do you see between creativity and theories of problem solving?

9. Why do you think that creativity was stimulated by telling people the functional category of their invented object *after* they had assembled it? Is this result related to the finding that familiar examples can constrain our ability to invent novel examples?

10. What does associative, spontaneous, and unstructured thinking have in common? What does rule-based, deliberative, and ordered thinking have in common?

CogLab The following experiment that relates to this chapter can be found at: http://coglab.wadsworth.com. Answer the questions in the CogLab Student Manual as required by your teacher for this experiment.

Wason Selection Task

KEY TERMS

The page number in parentheses refers to where the term is discussed in the chapter.

creativity (340)

declarative knowledge (338)

domain-specific knowledge (326)

exploration strategy (345)

four-card selection problem (327)

general strategy (335)

generation strategy (345)

inadvertent plagiarism (343)

memory-retrieval explanation (329)

obligation schema (329)

permission schema (329)

pragmatic reasoning schemata (329)

preinventive form (345)

procedural knowledge (338)

production rule (338)

work forward (336)

RECOMMENDED READING

Galotti (1989) contrasts formal reasoning with everyday reasoning, and Kuhn (1989) reviews research on scientific reasoning. The differences between experts and novices has been a popular topic of investigation in areas such as physics (Larkin, McDermott, Simon, & Simon, 1980), computer programming (Adelson, 1984), electronic warfare (Randel, Pugh, & Reed, 1996), and memory recall (Vincente & Wang, 1998). J. R. Anderson and C. D. Schunn (2000) discuss the instructional implications of the ACT-R learning theory, and Halpern (1998) shows how to teach critical thinking for transfer across domains. Books by Roskos-Ewoldsen, Intons-Peterson, and Anderson (1993) and Finke (1990) elaborate on the role of visual imagery. The book *Explaining Creativity* (Sawyer, 2006) gives an introductory overview of this topic. See Buchanan (2001) for a very readable article on the contributions of artificial intelligence to creativity and the book *Creativity Across Domains: Faces of the Muse* (Kaufman & Baer, 2005) for chapters on its manifestation in different areas. *The Handbook of Creativity* (Sternberg, 1999) contains chapters on many facets of creativity, *Scientific and Technological Thinking* (Gorman, Tweney, Gooding, & Kincannon, 2005) includes material on creativity, and *The Creative Priority* (Hirshberg, 1998) discusses building design environments that foster creativity. The diverse approaches to studying creativity are reviewed by Runco (2004), and the educational implications are discussed by Plucker, Beghetto, and Dow (2004). Dual process theories of reasoning continue to be explored by theorists (Evans, 2003; Osman, 2004; Smith & DeCoster, 2000).

14

Decision Making

I cannot, for want of sufficient premises, advise you what to determine, but if you please I will tell you how.... My way is to divide half a sheet of paper by a line into two columns; writing over one Pro, and over the other Con. Then, doing three or four days' consideration, I put down under the different heads short hints of the different motives, that at different times occur to me for or against the measure. When I have thus got them all together in one view, I endeavor to estimate the respective weights ... [to] find at length where the balance lies....
—**Benjamin Franklin (1772/1887)**

Every day we make many decisions. Most of these are relatively unimportant—what to eat for breakfast, for example. Others—such as selecting a car, a home, or a job—are more important. Making decisions is often difficult because each alternative usually has many aspects, and very seldom does the best alternative excel over all others.

The first section of this chapter describes models of how people select from a set of alternatives. Examples include selecting a dinner from a menu, a home, or a car. These models do not consider probabilities because they assume that a person knows the values of relevant dimensions, such as price, gas mileage, and optional equipment in the case of buying a car. The following sections are concerned with examples of risky decision making—those in which the decision maker must consider probabilities. We first examine how people make probability estimates, including ways they revise their estimates when they receive new information. We then consider how people use the estimates to make decisions.

normative model A model that describes what people should do

descriptive model A model that describes what people actually do

The study of decision making has been influenced by both normative and descriptive models. **Normative models** specify what a person should do. They often provide a standard for comparing how closely actual decisions match normative decisions. **Descriptive models** seek to describe how people actually arrive at decisions. The relation between normative and descriptive models is a theme that occurs throughout the discussion of decision making. The final section of the chapter discusses decision aids, as well as jury and action-based decision making as examples of complex skills. The discussion illustrates how psychological models can be used to describe each of these skills, and how different models are needed for different situations.

MAKING CHOICES

Compensatory Models

One reason decisions can be difficult is that alternatives usually have many attributes. If one of the attributes is not very attractive, the decision maker must decide whether to eliminate that alternative or continue to consider it because its other attributes may be very attractive. For example, a person might buy a car with low gas mileage because of the smooth ride and spaciousness of a large car. Decision-making models that allow attractive attributes to

compensatory model A strategy that allows positive attributes to compensate for negative ones

additive model A strategy that adds attribute values to assign a score to each alternative

compensate for unattractive ones are called **compensatory models**. The advice by Benjamin Franklin quoted at the beginning of this chapter is consistent with a compensatory model because Franklin combined the pros and cons of each option.

An **additive model** is a kind of compensatory model. An additive model combines the attractive and unattractive attributes to arrive at a total score for each alternative. Consider the case of John Smith. John has lived in a college dormitory for 3 consecutive years. It is now his senior year, and he feels that it is time to enjoy the greater freedom that an apartment can offer. He has found two rather attractive apartments and must select one. John decides to follow Ben Franklin's advice and systematically lists the advantages and disadvantages of each. First, he lists the attributes that will influence his decision, and then he rates each on a scale that ranges from –3 (a very negative impression) to +3 (a very positive impression). Here are his ratings:

	Apartment A	Apartment B
Rent	+1	+2
Noise level	−2	+3
Distance to campus	+3	−1
Cleanliness	+2	+2
	+4	+6

The sums of the ratings for the various attributes of the two apartments reveal that John's best choice is to select apartment B, which is rated higher.

There are two ways of modifying the summation rule that could change the results. First, the four attributes were equally weighted in the example. If some attributes are more important to John than others, he will want to emphasize these attributes when making his decision. For example, he might want to emphasize distance from campus if he lives in a cold climate and has to walk to classes. If this variable is twice as important as the others, he could multiply his ratings of distance by 2 to give this dimension greater emphasis. The sum of the ratings would then be +7 for apartment A and +5 for apartment B. Second, adding the ratings of the four attributes does not account for how the attributes might interact. Although apartment A is very noisy, it is so close to campus that the library would be a convenient place to study. The high noise level is therefore not as detrimental as it would be if the apartment were the only convenient place for studying. The low rating for noise level should perhaps be modified to take into account the interaction between that dimension and distance to campus.

additive–difference model A strategy that compares two alternatives by adding the difference in their values for each attribute

A model that is very similar to the additive model is called the **additive–difference model**. This model compares two alternatives by totaling the differences between their values on each attribute. The values on each attribute are shown in the following. The third column shows the value obtained by subtracting the second column from the first.

	Apartment A	*Apartment B*	*Difference*
Rent	+1	+2	−1
Noise level	−2	+3	−5
Distance to campus	+3	−1	+4
Cleanliness	+2	+2	+0
	+4	+6	−2

The sum of the differences is −2, which implies that apartment A is 2 units less attractive than apartment B. The additive model implies the same conclusion—the sum of the ratings for apartment A is 2 less than the sum of the ratings for apartment B. Although the additive and the additive–difference models result in the same conclusion, the search for information is different. The additive model evaluates all attributes of one alternative before considering the next alternative. The additive–difference model compares the two alternatives attribute by attribute. If there are more than two alternatives, a given alternative is compared with the best of the preceding alternatives.

Both the additive and the additive–difference models describe a good procedure for evaluating alternatives. Both evaluate alternatives on all their attributes and allow attractive values to compensate for unattractive values. Although Ben Franklin's advice is good, we may question how often we follow it. The examples show that the additive model provides a systematic procedure for making decisions, but are we really this systematic in making decisions? How often do we take the time to make the kind of calculations required by the models? Perhaps some other model might better describe how we actually make choices. The alternative to a compensatory model is a **noncompensatory model**, in which unattractive attributes result in eliminating alternatives.

Noncompensatory Models

If we do not calculate, how do we make decisions? A. Tversky (1972) has proposed that we make choices by gradually eliminating less attractive alternatives. His theory is called **elimination by aspects** because it assumes that the elimination is based on the sequential evaluation of the attributes, or aspects, of the alternatives. If the attribute of an alternative does not satisfy some minimum criterion, that alternative is eliminated from the set of choices.

Consider Ms. Green, who is looking for a used car. If Ms. Green has only $9000 to spend, she may first eliminate from her set of possible choices those cars that cost more than $9000. She may also be interested in gas economy and eliminate cars that cannot travel at least 25 miles on a gallon of gas. By continuing to select attributes and rejecting those that do not satisfy some minimum criterion, she will gradually eliminate alternatives until there is only a single car remaining that satisfies all her criteria.

The final choice, based on this procedure, depends on the order in which the attributes are evaluated. If the price of the car is one of the last attributes Ms. Green evaluates, she might have eliminated all cars costing less than $9000 early in her decision process—an undesirable situation if she has only $9000 to spend. The model therefore proposes that the attributes differ in

noncompensatory model A strategy that rejects alternatives that have negative attributes without considering their positive attributes

elimination by aspects A strategy that evaluates one attribute at a time and rejects those alternatives whose attribute values fail to satisfy a minimum criterion

importance, and the probability of selecting an attribute for evaluation depends on its importance. If price is a very important attribute, it has a high probability of being selected early in the sequence.

The elimination-by-aspects model has the advantage that it does not require any calculations. The decision maker simply selects an attribute according to some probability that depends on the importance of that attribute. She then determines whether an alternative satisfies a minimum criterion for that attribute and eliminates those alternatives that do not meet the criterion.

The **conjunctive model**—a variant of elimination by aspects—requires that all the attributes of an alternative satisfy minimum criteria before that alternative can be selected. It differs from elimination by aspects by proposing that people finish evaluating one alternative before considering another. The first alternative that satisfies all the minimum criteria is selected. The conjunctive model is an example of what Simon (1957) has called a **satisficing search**. Simon argued that limited capability to evaluate many alternatives often prevents people from selecting the best alternative. Instead, they are willing to settle for a good alternative—that is, one that satisfies all the minimum criteria. Other constraints, such as limits in time or availability, may also influence us to choose a good alternative rather than wait for the best alternative. For example, we may simply become tired of looking at apartments, or an apartment we liked may be rented by the time we return, so we will choose an available alternative rather than continue searching for a better one.

Selecting a Strategy

The four models we have looked at differ with respect to how people search for information. Payne (1976) took advantage of this difference in designing a procedure for finding out which strategies people use. He presented information describing the attributes of apartments, such as rent, cleanliness, noise level, and distance from campus. The information describing each apartment was printed on the back of a card, which had to be turned over to reveal its value (Figure 14.1). Subjects were allowed to turn over as many cards as they needed to make their decision. The order in which they turned over the cards should reveal how they searched for information. Payne gathered additional evidence about how they arrived at a decision by asking them to think aloud as they evaluated the information on the cards.

conjunctive model A strategy that evaluates one alternative at a time and rejects it if the value of one of its attributes fails to satisfy a minimum criterion

satisficing search A strategy that follows the conjunctive model and therefore selects the first alternative that satisfies the minimum criterion for each attribute

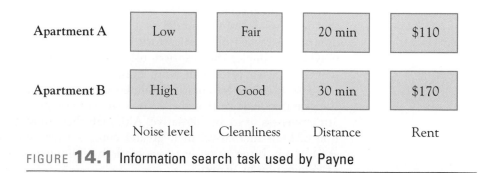

	Noise level	Cleanliness	Distance	Rent
Apartment A	Low	Fair	20 min	$110
Apartment B	High	Good	30 min	$170

FIGURE **14.1** Information search task used by Payne

Payne did not expect that everyone would follow the same strategy in searching for information. His expectations were influenced by work on problem solving that showed how individuals adapted their strategies to the demands of the task. An important characteristic of people's problem-solving strategies is that they attempt to keep the demands of the task within a limited capacity. Payne argued that the strategies used by decision makers should also be adaptive to the information-processing demands of the task. One implication of this view is that the decision maker might change strategies as the demands of the task change.

Payne's results supported his expectations. Students were given a variety of tasks that differed in both the number of alternatives (2, 4, 8, or 12 apartments) and the number of dimensions (4, 8, or 12 attributes). The principal finding was that the students changed strategies as the number of alternatives decreased. The search strategies and verbal protocols revealed that, when asked to evaluate many alternatives, the subjects reduced the complexity of the task by using the conjunctive or elimination-by-aspects procedure to eliminate some of the alternatives quickly. When only a few alternatives remained in the choice set, the subjects might then use one of the cognitively demanding procedures—such as the additive or additive–difference strategy—to make the final evaluation and choice.

The following excerpt from a protocol illustrates the use of the elimination-by-aspects model to reduce the number of alternatives:

I'm going to look at landlord attitude. In H it's fair. In D it's poor. In B it's fair, and in A it's good. In L the attitude is poor. In K it's poor. In J it's good, and in I it's poor…. So, that's important to me…. So, I'm not going to live any place where it's poor. (Payne, 1976, p. 379)

The subject never again examined alternatives D, I, K, and L.

Contrast that protocol with this excerpt illustrating the use of the additive–difference model to compare two alternatives:

O.K., we have an A and a B. First look at the rent for both of them. The rent for A is $170 and the rent for B is $140. $170 is a little steep, but it might have a low noise level. So we'll check A's noise level. A's noise level is low. We'll go to B's noise level. It's high. Gee, I can't really very well study with a lot of noise. So I'll ask myself the question, is it worth spending that extra $30 a month for, to be able to study in my apartment. (Payne, 1976, p. 378)

The two protocols reveal how a low value on a dimension results in elimination of an alternative in the elimination-by-aspects model. However, when the additive–difference model is used, an alternative scoring low on one dimension might still be selected if it scores high on other dimensions; in the previous example, the decision requires determining whether a lower rent will compensate for a high noise level.

The additive and additive–difference strategies are cognitively demanding because they require that the decision maker compute values to represent the attractiveness of each alternative. Although they allow for the careful evaluation of each alternative, their greater complexity may result in decisions that are not any better than decisions made by following a simpler strategy, such as elimination by aspects.

One way to compare the effectiveness of the different strategies is to train several groups of people to make decisions by following a particular strategy and then evaluate the quality of their decisions. Paquette and Kida (1988) used this approach to compare the relative effectiveness of the additive, additive–difference, elimination-by-aspects, and mixed strategies. The mixed strategy, based on Payne's finding that people switch strategies, initially used the elimination-by-aspects strategy followed by the additive strategy when the number of alternatives was reduced to three.

The subjects were 48 professionals who had experience at evaluating a firm's financial characteristics. They were given financial data on firms and had to select the one with the highest bond rating by following the strategy taught to them during the training session. The experimenters could then evaluate the accuracy of the selections because they knew the bond rating of each firm. They found no significant differences in the accuracy of the four strategies, but the simpler elimination-by-aspects strategy required significantly less time to make a decision than the more demanding additive and additive–difference strategies. For this particular task the elimination-by-aspects strategy was a highly efficient one.

ESTIMATING PROBABILITIES

We turn now to a somewhat more complex problem: making decisions under conditions of uncertainty. There was some amount of uncertainty in the previous examples. Although the location of an apartment is not likely to change, the noise level can change as the neighbors change. **Uncertainty** is a major factor in the examples discussed in the rest of the chapter and requires that people estimate the probability that a certain event will occur because they do not know which event will occur.

uncertainty Lacking knowledge about which events will occur

Kahneman and Tversky (1972, 1973; A. Tversky & D. Kahneman, 1973) have shown that probability estimates are based on *heuristics* that sometimes yield reasonable estimates but often do not. Two of these heuristics are availability and representativeness. Before reading further, answer the questions in Table 14.1 to determine how you might use these heuristics.

TABLE **14.1**
Questions About Subjective Probabilities

1. How many cities that begin with the letter *F* do you think you can recall? Give your estimate before you start recalling examples.
2. Are there more words in the English language that start with the letter *K* or that have a *K* as their third letter?
3. Which is the more likely cause of death—breast cancer or diabetes?
4. If a family has three boys (B) and three girls (G), which sequence of births is more likely—B B B G G G or B G G G B G B?
5. Are you more likely to find 60 boys in a random sample of 100 children or 600 boys in a random sample of 1000 children?

Availability

The **availability heuristic** proposes that we evaluate the probability of an event by judging the ease with which relevant instances come to mind (A. Tversky & D. Kahneman, 1973). For example, we may assess the divorce rate in a community by recalling divorces among our acquaintances. When availability is highly correlated with actual frequency, estimates should be accurate. But other factors besides actual frequency can influence availability and cause systematic biases in which people consistently underestimate probabilities for some problems and consistently overestimate probabilities for other problems.

In the first experiment conducted by A. Tversky and D. Kahneman (1973), subjects were shown nine letters, which were to be used to construct words. They were given 7 seconds to estimate the number of words they believed they could produce in 2 minutes. The average number of words actually constructed varied from 1.3 (for the letters *XUZONLCJM*) to 22.4 (for *TAPCERHOBO*). The correlation between the estimates and the number of words produced over 16 problems was 0.96.

In another experiment subjects were asked to estimate the number of instances they could recall from a category in 2 minutes. The average number of instances recalled varied from 4.1 (city names beginning with the letter *F*) to 23.7 (four-legged animals). The correlation between estimation and word production was 0.93 over 16 categories. The high correlation between estimation and production revealed that subjects were quite accurate in estimating the relative availability of instances in the different conditions.

Some instances, however, might be difficult to retrieve from memory even though they occur frequently. The availability hypothesis would predict that frequency should be underestimated in this case. Suppose you sample a word at random from an English text. Is it more likely that the word starts with a *K* or that *K* is its third letter? The availability hypothesis proposes that people try to answer this question by judging how easy it is to think of examples in each category. Because it is easier to think of words that begin with a certain letter, people should be biased toward responding that more words start with the letter *K* than have a *K* in the third position. The median estimated ratio for each of five letters was that there were twice as many words in which that letter was the first letter, rather than the third letter, in the word. The estimates were obtained despite the fact that all five letters are actually more frequent in the third position.

Slovic, Fischhoff, and Lichtenstein (1976) have used the availability hypothesis to account for how people estimated the relative probability of 41 causes of death—including diseases, accidents, homicide, suicide, and natural hazards—that were combined into 106 pairs. A large sample of college students judged which member of the pair was the more likely cause of death; Table 14.2 shows how often they were correct as a function of the relative frequency of the two events. Examination of the events most seriously misjudged provided indirect support for the hypothesis that availability, particularly as influenced by the media, biases probability estimates.

The frequencies of accidents, cancer, botulism, and tornadoes—all of which receive heavy media coverage—were greatly overestimated. Asthma

TABLE **14.2**
Judgments of Relative Frequency for Selected Pairs of Lethal Events

Less Likely	More Likely	True Ratio*	Percentage of Correct Discrimination
Asthma	Firearm accident	1.20	80
Breast cancer	Diabetes	1.25	23
Lung cancer	Stomach cancer	1.25	25
Leukemia	Emphysema	1.49	47
Stroke	All cancer	1.57	83
All accidents	Stroke	1.85	20
Pregnancy	Appendicitis	2.00	17
Tuberculosis	Fire and flames	2.00	81
Emphysema	All accidents	5.19	88
Polio	Tornado	5.30	71
Drowning	Suicide	9.60	70
All accidents	All diseases	15.50	57
Diabetes	Heart disease	18.90	97
Tornado	Asthma	20.90	42
Syphilis	Homicide	46.00	86
Botulism	Lightning	52.00	37
Flood	Homicide	92.00	91
Syphilis	Diabetes	95.00	64
Botulism	Asthma	920.00	59
Excess cold	All cancer	982.00	95
Botulism	Emphysema	10,600.00	86

*1.20 means 1.20:1, and so on.

Source: From "Cognitive processes and societal risk taking," by P. Slovic, B. Fischhoff, & S. Lichtenstein, 1976, in *Cognition and social behavior*, J. S. Carroll & J. W. Payne (Eds.). Copyright 1976 by Lawrence Erlbaum Associates, Inc. Reprinted by permission.

and diabetes, which receive less media coverage, were underestimated. Similarly, the spectacular event of fire—which often takes many victims and receives much media coverage—was perceived as considerably more frequent than the less spectacular event of drowning, even though they are about equally frequent causes of death.

A more selective effect of availability on probability estimates is illustrated by research on how our mood influences estimates. Emotions can have a substantial impact on the kind of information that people retrieve from LTM (long-term memory). A happy mood makes it more likely that we will recall positive events, and a sad mood makes it more likely that we will recall negative events (Blaney, 1986). The greater availability of positive events in memory should increase our estimates that more positive events will occur in the future, and the greater availability of negative events in memory should increase our estimates that negative events will occur.

Wright and Bower (1992) tested these hypotheses by inducing a happy mood or a sad mood in their subjects through hypnosis. The subjects then estimated the probability of occurrence of 24 events, some of them positive events ("I will win an important honor or award during the next year") and some of them negative events ("I will be seriously injured within the next 5 years"). The results were consistent with the prediction of the availability hypothesis. The mean estimate of a positive event occurring was 0.52 for people in a happy mood and 0.38 for people in a sad mood. The mean estimate of a negative event occurring was 0.52 for people in a sad mood and 0.37 for people in a happy mood. Notice that these results present a challenge for therapists: It may be necessary to change someone's sad mood before convincing them that the future will be brighter.

Representativeness

Representativeness is another heuristic that we use to make probability judgments. You may have used this heuristic to answer Question 4 in Table 14.1. The question asks "If a family has three boys (B) and three girls (G), which sequence of births is more likely—B B B G G G or B G G B G B?" Subjects in a study by Kahneman and Tversky (1972) estimated that the sequence of boy–girl births in the order B G G B G B was significantly more likely than the order B B B G G G, even though the two sequences are equally probable. Three boys followed by three girls appeared too orderly to have been generated by a random process.

The bias toward selecting the unorderly sequence as more probable can be explained by the representativeness heuristic (Kahneman & Tversky, 1972). Questions about probabilities typically have the general form: (1) What is the probability that object A belongs to class B? or (2) What is the probability that process B will generate event A? People frequently answer such questions by evaluating the degree to which A is **representative** of B—that is, the degree to which A resembles B. When A is very similar to B, the probability that A originates from B is judged to be high. When A is not very similar to B, the probability that A originated from B is judged to be low.

representative The extent to which an event is typical of a larger class of events

We expect that the birth order of boys and girls should form a random pattern. A major characteristic of apparent randomness is the absence of any systematic patterns. The representativeness heuristic therefore predicts that people should judge orderly events as having low probability if they believe the events were generated by a random process. Although there are many sequences of boys and girls that are unorderly, a particular unorderly sequence (such as B G G B G B) is as difficult to obtain as a particular orderly sequence (such as B B B G G G).

One problem with basing decisions solely on representativeness is that the decisions ignore other relevant information, such as *sample size*. For example, finding 600 boys in a sample of 1000 babies was judged as likely as finding 60 boys in a sample of 100 babies, even though the latter event is much more likely. Because the similarity between the obtained proportion (0.6) and the expected proportion (0.5) is the same in both cases, people do not see any difference between them. However, statisticians tell us that it is easier to obtain a discrepancy for small samples than for large samples.

Another situation in which the representativeness heuristic can cause faulty estimates is when we ignore probabilities entirely by basing our decision only on the similarity between an instance and a concept (Kahneman & Tversky, 1973). Imagine that a team of psychologists has administered personality tests to 30 engineers and 70 lawyers. I then randomly choose the following description from the 100 available descriptions:

Jack is a 45-year-old man. He is married and has four children. He is generally conservative, careful, and ambitious. He shows no interest in political and social issues and spends most of his free time on his many hobbies, which include home carpentry, sailing, and mathematical puzzles. The probability that Jack is one of the 30 engineers in the sample of 100 is _____ %.

Imagine now that you have the same description but were told that 70 of the 100 descriptions came from engineers. "What is the probability that Jack is one of the 70 engineers in the sample of 100?" The average estimate was identical for both questions. People estimated the probability of Jack's being an engineer as 0.9, which reflected that the personality description matched their concept of an engineer more closely than their concept of a lawyer. But notice that there was a difference between the two cases—in the first case there were 30 engineers in the sample of 100, and in the second case there were 70 engineers in the sample of 100. The probability that Jack is an engineer is influenced both by the number of engineers in the sample (called the **prior probability**) and by the personality description. We should use the personality description to revise the prior probabilities, rather than entirely ignore the prior probabilities.

prior probability The probability that an event will occur before obtaining additional evidence regarding its occurrence

I mentioned in Chapter 12 on problem solving that heuristics are often useful but do not guarantee success. Similarly, the availability and representativeness heuristics can mislead us if we do not consider relevant information such as how the media may influence the availability heuristic and how prior probabilities and sample size should influence the representativeness heuristic. We can learn to give more accurate estimates if we learn what variables should influence our estimates.

COMBINING PROBABILITIES AND VALUES

Estimating probabilities accurately is an important decision-making skill, but it is not sufficient for making good decisions. Consider a situation in which U.S. oil interests in the Middle East are threatened. The response to this situation will depend in part on the probability that the threat is a real one. But the response also depends on the perceived consequences of various courses of action that the government might take. For example, one response might be to increase U.S. military forces in the Middle East. This course of action, like other alternative actions, has both advantages and disadvantages. It is therefore necessary to assess both the probability of events and the consequences of various actions when making decisions.

When we considered the different choice models in the first section of this chapter, we assigned values to the different dimensions of each alternative in the choice set. It is also necessary to assign values in risky decision making, but in addition we have to combine the values of the different outcomes with the probabilities that they will occur. A normative procedure for combining probabilities and values is called **expected value**. This section describes the expected value model and then shows how psychologists have modified the model to make it more descriptive of how people make risky decisions.

expected value The average value, as determined by combining the value of events with their probability of occurrence

Expected Value

Like other normative models, expected value provides a standard of reference against which psychologists can compare how people make decisions. Psychologists have usually made this comparison by designing rather simple gambling situations in which they can inform people about probabilities (of winning and losing) and values (amount won or lost). The expected value is the average amount of money people can expect to win or lose each time they decide to gamble. Let's see how it is calculated.

Expected value is calculated by multiplying the value of each possible outcome by its probability and adding the products. Its use can be illustrated by a simple game. I'm going to offer you the opportunity to play the game, and you must decide whether it would be to your advantage to play. I'm going to roll a fair die. If a 6 appears, you win $5. If any of the other five numbers appear, you win nothing. It costs $1 every time you play. Should you participate?

Expected value allows you to estimate the average amount of money you can expect to win or lose on every roll of the die. You can calculate this amount if you know the probability of a win, $P(W)$; the amount of a win, $V(W)$; the probability of a loss, $P(L)$; and the amount of a loss, $V(L)$. Substituting these amounts into the equation below yields

$$\text{Expected value} = P(W) \times V(W) + P(L) \times V(L)$$
$$= \frac{1}{6} \times \$4 + \frac{5}{6} \times -\$1$$
$$= -\$\frac{1}{6}$$

The probability of a win is 1/6 and the amount of a win is $4 ($5 minus the $1 entry fee). The probability of a loss is 5/6 and the value of a loss is $1. The expected value of this game is –$1/6, implying that you would lose an average of approximately 17¢ every time you played the game. A decision based on a normative model should be to play the game for a positive expected value and not to play the game for a negative expected value.

A problem with using expected value as a descriptive model is that it does not always predict behavior. Gambling casinos are usually crowded with people playing games that have negative expected values. People also buy insurance despite its negative expected value. Because insurance companies pay out less money in claims than they collect in premiums, a purchaser of insurance can expect to lose money. And yet the purchase of insurance can be justified on the basis that it provides protection against a large financial setback.

Expected Utility

Two changes were made in the concept of expected value to make it more descriptive of actual behavior (Payne, 1973). The first change replaced the value of an outcome by its utility. **Utility** is the subjective value of an outcome, or what the outcome is actually worth to an individual. If people enjoy gambling, the act of gambling has utility over and above the money that is won or lost. If you enjoy winning money and don't mind losing money, then you could formulate a positive expected utility for the game I described earlier. If the utility of a win—$U(W)$—is $6 to reflect the joy of winning rather than $4, and the utility of a loss—$U(L)$—remains at $1, the expected utility would be positive rather than negative.

utility Subjective value as determined by the decision maker

$$\text{Expected utility} = P(W) \times U(W) + P(L) \times U(L)$$
$$= \frac{1}{6} \times \$6 + \frac{5}{6} \times -\$1$$
$$= \$\frac{1}{6}$$

The expected-utility model could also explain why people buy insurance if they are more concerned about losing a substantial amount of money at one time than about paying out the much smaller premiums each year.

Another reason why utilities or subjective values are important is that how much we value an object is influenced by how we obtained it. For example, you may have received gifts that you value more for the expressed sentiment than for the gift itself. We also value objects more if we feel we deserve them. In one experiment, students in an executive education class were given mugs that had a retail value of $6. Half of the students were informed that they were randomly selected to receive a mug; the other half were told that they received a mug because of their performance on a graded exercise. All students were then given the opportunity to trade the mug for money and were asked to indicate the amount of money they would want for the exchange. The average requested amount was $6.35 for the group who believed they earned the mug and $4.71 for the group who believed they received the mug by chance (Lowenstein & Issacharoff, 1994).

An important aspect of utility that we all struggle with is whether to select an option that we *want* to do or the option that we *should* do. The *want* option typically provides immediate benefits and the *should* option provides long-term benefits (Milkman, Rogers, & Bazerman, 2008). Eating pizza provides immediate gratification, but eating a salad contributes to a more healthy lifestyle.

Khan and Dhar (2006) found that people's resolution of the want-should dilemma depends on how they resolved related decisions. People who have recently selected the *should* option now feel entitled to select the *want* option. Participants in their study were more likely to report that they would spend a tax rebate on expensive designer sunglasses (the *want* choice) than less-expensive sunglasses (the *should* choice) if they had just imagined donating $100 of their tax rebate to charity. They also found that participants who had agreed to help a foreign student understand a lecture decided to donate less to charity than participants who had not been asked to help the student.

Subjective Expected Utility

subjective probability
An estimated probability as determined by the decision maker

A second change in the expected-value model was to make it more descriptive by replacing probabilities with **subjective probabilities**. When decision makers don't know the actual probabilities, they must use subjective probabilities, or what they think the actual probabilities are. As we learned in the previous section, subjective probabilities often differ from actual probabilities as a result of possible biases introduced by using the availability and representativeness heuristics. Such findings indicate that we should be more accurate in predicting people's decisions if we used their subjective probabilities rather than the actual probabilities.

subjective expected utility A variation of expected value that uses utilities and subjective probabilities instead of values and probabilities

Subjective expected utility is calculated the same way as expected value, but the actual probabilities are replaced by subjective probabilities (*SP*), and the values are replaced by utilities. The subjective probability of each outcome is multiplied by its utility, and the products are added.

$$\text{Subjective expected utility} = SP(W) \times U(W) + SP(L) \times U(L)$$

By replacing probabilities with subjective probabilities and values with utilities, the subjective expected-utility model bases its predictions on subjective information. Therefore, it should be more accurate than the expected-value model in predicting people's decisions.

Here is an example of a decision that cannot be predicted by expected value: Would you rather win $900 or have a 90% chance of winning $1,000? Answer this question before answering the next one. Would you rather lose $900 or have a 90% chance of losing $1,000?

You may have noticed that the expected value is the same for both choices in the first question (1.00 × $900 = $900 and 0.90 × $1000 = $900). Expected value theory would therefore predict that people should be evenly divided in their selection of the two alternatives. However, most people prefer a sure gain of $900 over the chance to gamble for $1,000. Expected value is also the same for both choices in the second question (1.00 × –$900 = –$900 and 0.90 × –$1000 = –$900). But most people now prefer the gamble because it provides them with a small (0.10) probability of not losing any money.

loss aversion Reaction to losses is more intense than reactions to corresponding gains

Kahneman and Tversky (1979) incorporated these kinds of decisions into a general theory called *prospect theory*. One of its assumptions (called **loss aversion**) is that people's reaction to losses is more intense than their reaction to corresponding gains. In other words, losing $900 produces more negative affect than winning $900 produces positive affect. People therefore try to avoid the certain loss of $900, even if it means gambling for a 90% chance of losing $1,000.

Kahneman (2003) reports that he and Tversky deliberately chose a meaningless name (prospect theory) to give their theory a distinctive label in case it ever became well known. It did become well known and had a tremendous influence on economics. Kahneman's 2003 article in the *American Psychologist* describes how prospect theory influenced economic thinking—an impact that resulted in his reception of a Nobel prize in economics (Amos Tversky died prematurely).

RISK DIMENSIONS

The theoretical evolution from expected value to subjective expected utility is an example of how a normative model (expected value) was transformed to make it more descriptive. Discovering how people thought about risk made it easier to make accurate predictions about their choices. Like the expected value model, however, subjective expected utility assumes that people place an equal emphasis on its four components—$U(W)$, $SP(W)$, $U(L)$, and $SP(L)$. People are likely influenced by the probability of winning, the amount of a win, the probability of losing, and the amount of a loss, but they might not place equal emphasis on these four **risk dimensions**. This has resulted in attempts to determine whether some risk dimensions are perceived as more important than others.

risk dimension A component of a gamble such as the probability of winning or the amount of a loss

Importance of Risk Dimensions

Slovic and Lichtenstein (1968) tested the hypothesis that people will be more influenced by some dimensions than others. They had subjects evaluate the attractiveness of gambles, using a special type of gamble illustrated in Figure 14.2. A duplex gamble requires that the subject spin two spinners. The first spinner determines whether he will win money, and the second spinner determines whether he will lose money. The gamble shown in Figure 14.2 has four possible outcomes: win $1 and lose $4 (a net loss of $3), win $1 and lose nothing, win nothing and lose nothing, or win nothing and lose $4. Slovic and Lichtenstein used **duplex gambles** to change the probability of winning and the probability of losing independently. This is not possible in a standard gamble (represented by only one spinner) because the probability of winning is equal to 1 minus the probability of losing. It is not possible to determine whether people are more influenced by the probability of winning or the probability of losing if the two probabilities cannot be varied independently.

duplex gamble A gamble in which the probability of winning is assigned independently of the probability of losing

Slovic and Lichtenstein used two methods to evaluate the attractiveness of gambles. One method used a simple rating scale that varied from +5 (strong preference for not playing) to −5 (strong preference for playing). The second method required that subjects indicate the largest amount of money they would be willing to pay the experimenter to play the gamble (for attractive gambles) or to not have to play the gamble (for unattractive gambles). In both cases Slovic and Lichtenstein correlated the judged attractiveness of the gambles with the four risk dimensions. The correlations should be approximately equal if people were placing an equal emphasis on all four dimensions. The results indicated that there was a large difference in the correlations. A person's highest correlation was, on the average, twice the size of the lowest correlation. The responses of many people were determined by one or two risk dimensions and were unresponsive to changes in the values of the less important dimensions.

People's preference for some risk dimensions over others has practical consequences, as illustrated in "In the News" 14.1. The California Lottery was able to increase lagging

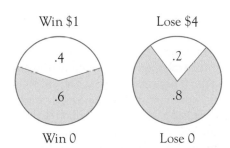

FIGURE **14.2** Example of a duplex gamble where $P(W) = 0.4$, $V(W) = 1, $P(L) = 0.2$, and $V(L) = 4

Source: From "Relative importance of probabilities and payoffs in risk taking," by P. Slovic & S. Lichtenstein, 1968, *Journal of Experimental Psychology Monograph*, 78 (3, Pt. 2). Copyright 1968 by the American Psychological Association. Reprinted by permission.

IN THE NEWS **14.1**

Lottery Fans Drawn to Bigger Prizes

Ready to dream again?

Because it is happening again. The SuperLotto Plus jackpot is mushrooming to dreamy levels— tonight's drawing is for $85 million—just a month after it reached a record $193 million.

The California Lottery's move to tweak the game in the summer of 2000—making it tougher to win so that jackpots would bulge—is having the desired effect and then some.

People want bigger jackpots, the Lottery said.

And they are getting them.

Of course, there's a catch: A very, very, very lucky few are enjoying the extravagant riches.

Before the adjustments—which saw odds go to 41 million to one from 18 million to one—there were complaints that the payouts were too small. Hence people weren't as likely to throw down a buck or two

for a shot at winning a measly few million. Sales had gone flat.

"The game was losing its luster," said Norma Minas, a California Lottery spokeswoman. "After a certain amount of time it needs refreshing."

Source: From "Lottery fans drawn to bigger prizes," by Michael Stetz, *The San Diego Union-Tribune*, March 20, 2002. Reprinted by permission.

ticket sales by *lowering* the probability of winning. But this didn't matter because it increased the amount won, which was what ticket purchases were emphasizing. The California example is part of a national trend, according to the article. Other state lotteries have also increased their jackpots by lowering the probability of winning.

Decision Frames

The previous research has shown that people regard some risk dimensions as more important than others. It is also possible to influence people's focus on different risk dimensions by emphasizing a particular dimension when describing the situation. In other words, the situation can be "framed" in different ways, and this framing determines how people perceive the situation. Tversky and Kahneman (1981) use the term **decision frame** to refer to the decision maker's conception of the decision-making situation.

decision frame Decision maker's conception of the decision-making situation

The following example shows how the formulation of the problem influences the frame adopted by the decision maker (Dunegan, 1993). The subjects were 128 members of an international company that develops high-technology engineering systems. The subjects read a scenario in which a project team was requesting an additional $100,000 for a project begun several months before. Everyone read the same scenario except for the last sentence. The last sentence for half of the participants read "Of the projects undertaken by this team, 30 of the last 50 have been successful" (a positive frame). The other half read "Of the projects undertaken by this team, 20 of the last 50 have been unsuccessful" (a negative frame). Notice that the probability of successfully completing a project is 0.6 for both cases, but the positive frame mentions the 60% success rate, and the negative frame mentions the 40% failure rate. People given the positive frame allocated significantly more money to the project than people given the negative frame.

The selection of a decision frame has important implications outside the laboratory. Although a medical treatment that results in a 75% survival rate is logically equivalent to one that results in a 25% death rate, McKenzie (2003) has argued that the choice of frames can convey information so there is a practical difference in whether a speaker selects a positive frame or a negative frame. Emphasis on a 75% survival rate is appropriate if the 75% survival represents an increase in the survival rate over an older treatment because a patient might now want to seriously consider the new treatment. In other situations, emphasis on the 25% death rate might be more appropriate such as when discussing risky surgery. Elderly men with prostate cancer could be discouraged from seeking an operation if the cancer is slow to spread, and the operation is risky. Emphasizing the death rate in this situation might convince a patient that it is better to avoid surgery. Research shows that both speakers and listeners are sensitive to the choice of frames because of the information contained in the frames (McKenzie, 2003).

Perceived Risk

An advantage of looking at how risk dimensions influence decisions is that it may tell us how people perceive risk. For example, perceived risk may depend on how much money could be lost, as suggested by Slovic and Lichtenstein's (1968) finding that people emphasized this dimension when they determined how much money they would bid to play a gamble.

Expected value tells us the average amount of money we can expect from a gamble but does not tell us the amount of perceived risk. This is illustrated by a question that I ask my class. I ask them to choose between two hypothetical gambles. In the first case, I flip a fair coin, and they win $1 if it lands heads and lose $1 if it lands tails. In the second case, I flip a fair coin, and they win $100 if it lands heads and lose $100 if it lands tails. Because the probabilities of winning and losing are identical, and the amounts won and lost are identical, the expected value is zero for both gambles. If you played either gamble many times, you would expect to go home with the same amount of money you had at the beginning.

A few students choose to gamble for $100, but the vast majority chooses to gamble for $1. Expected value cannot explain this result because both gambles have the same expected value. But the $100 gamble is considered more risky because it has a greater variance—there is a much greater difference between the value of a win and the value of a loss. And the outcome of my class experiment is consistent with the finding that most people do not like to take risks (E. U. Weber, 1998).

But a few people did prefer the $100 gamble, and this raises the question of whether risk taking is a stable personality trait. You probably know some people who like to take risks and others who are very conservative. However, E. U. Weber's (1998) review of the experimental evidence shows that most people, regardless of gender or culture, do not like to take perceived risks. When people make choices that are considered risky, it is usually because they do not *perceive* the choice as risky. For example, a cross-cultural study of students at major universities in the People's Republic of China, Germany,

Poland, and the United States found that the Chinese respondents were more likely than the others to show preferences for risky financial options (E. U. Weber & C. Hsee, 1998). However, these apparent differences in risk preference were caused primarily by cultural differences in the perception of risk rather than by cultural differences in attitude toward risk. The Chinese respondents, like the others, did not like to take risks; however, they did not perceive the risky choices to be particularly risky.

Weber and Hsee conclude by examining practical applications of these findings. An interesting implication is that it may be easier to reach bargaining solutions when different countries are involved than when negotiations take place among different groups in the same country. If international traders and cross-cultural negotiators were aware of differences in risk perception among different cultures, they could restructure options in a way to take advantage of these differences. In the next, concluding section we look at other applications of research on decision making.

APPLICATIONS

Our emphasis so far has been on examining decision making within simple but well-controlled laboratory experiments. Cognitive psychologists of course hope their theories have some relevance to the real world, and decision making is no exception. In this concluding section, we look at how some of these ideas are being applied to more complex situations. The first application looks at how converting probabilities into frequencies can help people understand a medical diagnosis. The second application is concerned with jury decision making. The third application analyzes what people do in situations in which they must make a series of rapid decisions, such as in fighting a fire or a battle. Each of these applications draws on different theoretical ideas, illustrating the flexibility in theorizing that is needed to model decision making in different situations.

Decision Aids and Training

decision aid A tool for helping people make better decisions

One of the first issues that you might consider when thinking about applications of decision models to real-world decision making is whether there are **decision aids** (Kleinmuntz, 1990) that would help you make a better decision. We have already encountered a number of instances in which people's decisions overlooked important information. For example, in Kahneman and Tversky's (1973) experiment, people ignored the prior probability when deciding whether Jack is an engineer. They based their decision solely on the evidence contained in a biographical description.

Bayes' theorem A normative procedure for revising a probability by combining a prior probability with evidence

There is a normative model called **Bayes' theorem** that enables people to combine a prior probability with new evidence to calculate a revised probability. If one knew the formula and had a calculator, it would not be too difficult to use this method. But without either, it would be surprising if people's probability estimates closely matched the normative estimates calculated from Bayes' theorem.

Because of the cognitive demands of complex decision making, providing decision aids can help people make better decisions. Consider the following problem investigated by Gigerenzer and Hoffrage (1995):

The probability of breast cancer is 1% for a woman at age 40 who participates in routine screening. If a woman has breast cancer, the probability is 80% that she will get a positive mammography. If a woman does not have breast cancer, the probability is 9.6% that she will get a positive mammography. A woman in this age group had a positive mammography in a routine screening. What is the probability that she actually has breast cancer?

The right half of Figure 14.3 shows how to solve this problem by using the formula for Bayes' theorem. The formula uses the data (D) of a positive mammography to evaluate the hypothesis (H) that the woman has breast cancer. The prior probability of having breast cancer, p(H), is 0.01. The probability of a positive mammography for a woman who has breast cancer,

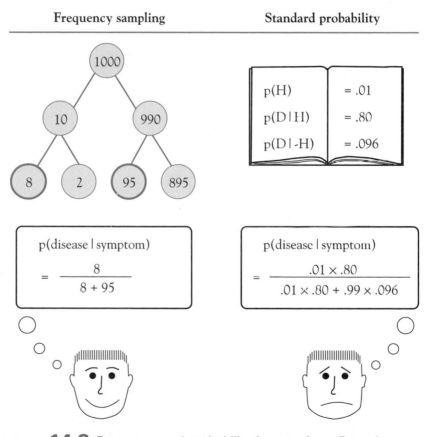

FIGURE **14.3** Frequency and probability formats for a Bayesian inference problem

Source: From "How to improve Bayesian reasoning without instruction: Frequency formats," by G. Gigerenzer & U. Hoffrage, 1995, *Psychological Review*, 102, 684–704.

p(D|H), is 0.80. And the probability of a positive mammography for a woman who does not have breast cancer, p(D|-H), is 0.096. The equation at the bottom shows how to calculate the probability that the patient has breast cancer by combining the prior probability and new data. The sad face illustrates that this is hard!

The left half of Figure 14.3 represents the same problem expressed in frequencies rather than in probabilities. The frequencies show that in a group of 1000 women at age 40 we can expect 10 women to have breast cancer. Of these 10 women, 8 test positive on a mammography exam. Of the 990 women who do not have breast cancer, 95 test positive on a mammography exam. The smiling face indicates that the probability that the patient has breast cancer is now much simpler to calculate. One simply divides the frequency of positive test results for women who have cancer (8) by the total number of positive test results (8 + 95). This gives the same answer as the more complex formula on the right.

Gigerenzer and Hoffrage (1995) found that when problems were expressed in frequency formats, rather than in probability formats, people provided more accurate estimates (they were not given formulas to solve the problems). In the frequency format, students were given frequencies in the problem and gave their answer in frequencies. Cosmides and Tooby (1996) also found that people did much better in using frequencies than in using probabilities and argued that the ability to encode and use frequencies is important from an evolutionary perspective.

Gigerenzer and Hoffrage concluded their article by considering the practical consequences of these findings. Instead of teaching people to use a complex formula such as Bayes' theorem, they suggest teaching people to translate probabilities into frequencies. For example, in the mammography problem, the probability of 0.01 can be represented as 10 women in 1000, and the probability of 0.80 can be represented as 8 of these 10 women, as was done in Figure 14.3. Reasoning with frequencies should then be easier than reasoning with the initially specified probabilities. This has been confirmed in subsequent research that has demonstrated that reasoning with frequencies was both relatively easy to learn and remember (Sedlmeier & Gigerenzer, 2001).

Jury Decision Making

Jury decision making differs from the previous examples in the length of time required to make a decision. Jurists may hear days or even weeks of testimony before deliberating on the case. Not surprisingly, the models that we have considered so far do not readily apply to this situation. Fortunately, however, we can use some familiar theoretical ideas to help us understand jury decisions. These ideas come from Chapter 11 on text comprehension.

Nancy Pennington and Reid Hastie (Hastie & Pennington, 2000; Pennington & Hastie, 1991) have proposed a story model of jury decision making because they believe that story construction is the central cognitive process in this task. Their story model has three components: (1) evidence evaluation through story construction, (2) representation of the decision alternatives by verdict categories, and (3) reaching a decision through classification of the story into the best-fitting verdict category. Figure 14.4 shows these components.

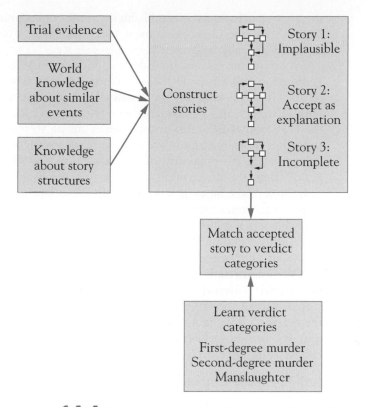

FIGURE **14.4** The story model for juror decision making

Source: Adapted from "Explaining the evidence: Tests of the story model for juror decision making," by N. Pennington & R. Hastie, *Journal of Personality and Social Psychology*, 62, 189–206. Copyright 1992 by the American Psychological Association. Reprinted by permission.

Constructing a story is difficult because there is typically a massive amount of evidence that is presented in a jumbled temporal sequence. Witnesses and exhibits convey pieces of the puzzle, but not in the order that the events occurred. Nevertheless, there are some striking similarities between Pennington and Hastie's story model and the research on text comprehension described in Chapter 11.

One similarity is the role of prior knowledge. Prior knowledge influences both how well readers comprehend a story and how people judge the plausibility of a constructed story. An example is the dramatic differences between White and African American reactions to the verdict in the O. J. Simpson murder trial (Hastie & Pennington, 2000). African Americans have a much larger memory store of beliefs and experiences that support the plausibility of stories of police misconduct and bigotry. This background makes it easy to believe a story in which a white police officer manufactured and implanted incriminating evidence.

Another similarity between comprehending stories and judging their plausibility is that knowledge about story structures influences both of these situations. Initiating events, goals, actions, and consequences are important aspects of story structure, as is establishing causal connections. As is illustrated in Figure 14.4, the jurist often must judge which of several different stories is the most plausible explanation of the evidence.

A dramatic finding provides supporting evidence for the story model. Pennington and Hastie (1988) simulated a trial in which mock jurors listened to 50 statements made by the prosecution and 50 statements made by the defense. One set of 50 statements was presented in the order of occurrence at the trial (witnesses order) and the other set of 50 statements was rearranged to form a coherent story in the order that events might have actually happened (story order). The majority of the mock jurists (78%) judged the defendant guilty when the prosecution evidence was presented in the story order, but only 31% of the mock jurists judged the defendant guilty when the defense evidence was presented in a story order. A story was presumably judged more plausible when it did not have to be constructed from a scrambled order.

Another finding that can be interpreted as supporting the story model is shown in "In the News" 14.2. This study found that mock jurors are biased in their interpretation of new evidence to make it consistent with whatever verdict they currently favor (Carlson & Russo, 2001). New evidence is distorted toward the currently leading verdict to make it more compatible with the currently dominant story. Notice that this is another misuse of Bayes' theorem. By distorting evidence to make it consistent, people are placing too much emphasis on prior probabilities and not enough emphasis on the new evidence.

Action-Based Decision Making

The previous example of jury decision making involved a situation in which jurists had the luxury of time. They could carefully examine the evidence,

---

IN THE NEWS **14.2**

Most Jurors Unwittingly Deliver Biased Verdicts

Jurors may be highly susceptible to issuing unfair verdicts due to "predecisional distortion," the tendency to view each new piece of evidence with a bias toward the part that the juror favors, according to a study at Cornell University.

"Biased interpretation of evidence by mock jurors," by Kurt A. Carlson and J. Edward Russo, PhD, of Cornell's Johnson Graduate School of Management, raises concerns about conventional pretrial instructions to jurors and advocates alternative pretrial procedures.

In their study, Carlson and Russo evaluated the effect of jurors'

personal beliefs on verdicts by using two sample groups: one of university students and another of potential jurors, ages 40 to 45. All participants viewed a video explaining the importance of refraining from making decisions before all of the evidence was presented. Participants were then given affidavits, case backgrounds, and opening arguments and asked to assess whether the plaintiff or defendant benefited from each.

The researchers found that 75 percent of students and 85 percent of potential jurors exhibited predecisional distortion: The typical participant evaluated new evidence

as too supportive of whichever party was leading in his or her mind when the new evidence was encountered.

Predecisional distortion builds on story theory, which states that people have a need to view a coherent world: thus jurors will create narratives based on their own experiences to make the facts of a case understandable to themselves.

Source: From "Most jurors unwittingly deliver biased verdicts, new study suggests," by R. Ballie, *Monitor on Psychology*, September 2001, 13. Copyright 2001 by the American Psychological Association. Reprinted by permission.

discuss its implications, and deliver their verdict after hours or even days of deliberation. But what about decisions made by physicians in emergency rooms or commanders in the heat of battle? Time is no longer a luxury, and decisions have to be made quickly before lives are lost.

Here's another scenario that requires a series of rapid decisions (Orasanu & Connolly, 1993). A fire-fighting crew arrives at a four-story apartment building, the scene of a reported fire. The commander sends his crew into the first and second stories to extinguish the fire, but they report that the fire has spread beyond the second floor. Observing smoke pouring from the eaves, the commander calls for a second unit. He also orders his crew to stop trying to extinguish the fire and to search the building for people trapped inside.

This scenario comes from the first chapter of a book called *Decision Making in Action: Models and Methods* (Klein, Orasanu, Calderwood, & Zsambok, 1993). The central argument of the book is that the traditional models and methods for studying decision making are not very helpful in explaining what people do in these kinds of emergency situations. The reason is that the traditional approach has focused on only one particular type of decision making—the **decision event**. The decision event consists of a situation in which the decision maker evaluates a fixed set of alternatives according to stable criteria and differentially weights and combines these criteria to select the best alternative. Most of the tasks that we previously considered, such as selecting the best apartment, are good examples of a decision event.

In contrast, emergency situations have a number of characteristics that distinguish them from the more traditional tasks that we have already considered. For example:

1. Emergency situations typically involve *ill-structured problems* in which the decision maker has to do significant work to generate hypotheses about what is happening. The fire commander knew almost nothing about the extent of the fire when he arrived at the scene.
2. Decision making occurs within an *uncertain, dynamic environment*. Information about what is happening is often incomplete, ambiguous, and/or of poor quality. The environment may also change quickly, as when a small fire suddenly becomes a large fire.
3. There may be *shifting or competing goals*. Goals in the previous scenario would include saving the building, the occupants, and the crew. These goals can shift as the fire grows, from saving the building to saving the occupants to saving the crew.
4. Responses to emergency situations require reacting to a sequence of events rather than to a single event. This creates *action–feedback loops* in which the decision maker has to react to the consequences of each action before determining the next action.
5. There is often considerable *time pressure*. Lack of time will typically produce less complicated reasoning strategies and perhaps high levels of personal stress.
6. There are *high stakes*. One obviously wants to avoid mistakes in life-threatening situations.

decision event Making a single decision, rather than a sequence of decisions, in a changing situation

7. Often there are *multiple players*. Although there is usually a single person in charge, the leader interacts with others to solve the problem.
8. *Organizational goals* guide the decision making. Unlike the personal life decisions that we all face, medical and fire-fighting personnel are guided by rules set by others in the organizations.

recognition-primed decision (RPD) A decision that is quickly made following recognition of a situation

One of best-known models of how people make decisions in these situations is the **recognition-primed decision (RPD)** model proposed by Klein (1993). The starting premise is that people who make decisions in these situations are typically very experienced. They are therefore capable of responding more quickly than the less experienced subjects tested in laboratory studies. There is of course a parallel here to the novice–expert difference that we saw in the previous two chapters on problem solving.

Klein initially formulated the RPD model after interviewing how fire ground commanders made choices. Rather than evaluate many alternatives, they reported that they used their prior experience to immediately generate and modify plans in reaction to the changing situation. The model is called a *recognition-primed* model because of the emphasis it places on situation assessment and recognition of what is occurring. Once the problem is recognized, experienced decision makers can usually identify an acceptable course of action as the first one they consider, rather than having to consider multiple options.

Notice that there are several reasons why this is a plausible strategy in these circumstances. First, expertise allows the decision maker to avoid considering many alternatives that would have a low probability of working. Second, there is not enough time to allow for a thorough consideration of many options. Third, Klein proposes, as did Simon many years earlier, that decision makers usually try to find a *satisfactory* course of action, not the best alternative. This allows them to respond more quickly than if they had to select the best strategy.

Sources of Power

Earlier in this chapter we reviewed some research by Payne (1976) that indicated that decision makers adapt their strategies to the demands of the task, selecting a simpler strategy when task complexity increased. The continuation of this work was summarized in a book called *The Adaptive Decision Maker* (Payne, Bettman, & Johnson, 1993) in which the authors argue that decision makers are guided by the dual goals of maximizing accuracy and minimizing effort, causing them to emphasize different strategies in different situations.

The concept of the adaptive decision maker has continued, particularly in the work of Gigerenzer (2006, 2008) and his colleagues at the Max Planck Institute for Human Development in Berlin, Germany. They use the metaphor of an adaptive toolbox that contains a variety of heuristics that can be effectively used in different situations. We have already encountered examples of heuristics such as availability and representativeness in the work of Kahneman and Tversky. Much of the research in the Kahneman and Tversky tradition has demonstrated the limitations of heuristics. In contrast, Gigerenzer and his colleagues have shown how simple heuristics can be quite effective, such as the use of frequencies shown in Figure 14.3.

Another example is the recognition heuristic that helped some people answer the question "Which city has more inhabitants: San Diego or San Antonio?" One hundred percent of Germans answered correctly (San Diego), compared to 62% of Americans (Goldstein & Gigerenzer, 2002). So why did the Germans appear more knowledgeable? Goldstein and Gigerenzer proposed that many Germans could use the recognition heuristic: If you recognize one city, but not the other, infer that it has the larger population. Americans could not use this heuristic because they likely knew the names of both cities.

The recognition heuristic applies in only limited situations, but other heuristics in the adaptive tool box are quite general, such as imitate the majority (Boyd & Richerson, 2005). I find this heuristic to be helpful when I am in unfamiliar locations. For example, when I needed to take the Metro from a western suburb of Chicago into the city, I found the correct track by watching where others were standing. I also knew where to stand on the platform by joining one of the lines. Imitating the majority, however, is probably not the best advice for situations in which you want to excel. Imitating the successful (Boyd & Richerson, 2005) would be more promising.

In his book *Sources of Power: How People Make Decisions*, Klein (1998) discusses the different strategies used by experts. Successful execution of these strategies depends on the development of a variety of skills that Klein refers to as sources of power. Figure 14.5 illustrates these different skills, including

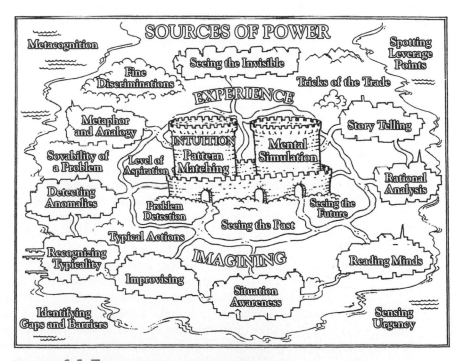

FIGURE **14.5** Sources of cognitive power

Source: From G. Klein, *Sources of Power: How People Make Decisions*, Cambridge, MA: MIT Press, 1998, figure 17.1.

some that were discussed in this chapter and some that were discussed in other chapters. I conclude with this figure because I hope that you have achieved two benefits from reading this book. First, I hope that you now have a better theoretical understanding of cognition. Second, I hope that you use what you have learned as sources of power to become a more skilled learner, problem solver, and decision maker.

SUMMARY

Making decisions usually requires evaluating at least two alternatives that differ on a number of attributes. Selecting an alternative requires the decision maker to combine this information to form an overall evaluation for each alternative. The study of how people search for information provides evidence about decision strategies.

Four of the more popular decision models can be differentiated by whether people compare the alternatives attribute by attribute or alternative by alternative and whether the decision is a compensatory or noncompensatory one. In the elimination-by-aspects model, alternatives are compared by attributes, and the decision is noncompensatory. The conjunctive model is similar but considers only one alternative at a time; the first alternative that satisfies the minimum criteria for each attribute is selected. The additive and additive–difference models are both compensatory because they allow for positive attributes to compensate for negative attributes. The additive model assigns a numerical score to each attribute and sums the scores to determine the relative attractiveness of each alternative. The additive–difference model compares alternatives attribute by attribute and determines the difference between the scores on each attribute; the sum of the differences determines which alternative is more attractive.

Research on how people select a decision strategy has shown that the choice of a strategy depends on task characteristics. People were likely to use a noncompensatory strategy such as elimination by aspects when there were many alternatives and a compensatory strategy such as the additive model when there were few alternatives. Although compensatory strategies are more thorough than noncompensatory strategies, they are more difficult to use. A study of how effectively professionals could select a firm with the highest bond rating found that elimination by aspects was the most efficient strategy. It produced the same level of accuracy as the additive and additive–difference strategies, but by quicker decisions.

Risky decision making refers to decisions that are concerned with uncertainty—for example, evaluating the potential dangers of a nuclear reactor, buying insurance, and diagnosing medical problems. To make good decisions, it is necessary to make accurate estimates of probabilities. Probability estimates are often based on heuristics, which sometimes yield reasonable estimates but often do not. Two heuristics are availability and representativeness. The availability heuristic proposes that we evaluate the probability of an event by judging the ease with which instances can be recalled. The representativeness heuristic states that the probability of an event is estimated by evaluating how similar it is to the essential properties of its population.

Expected value is a normative procedure for making decisions. Expected value is calculated by multiplying the value of events by their probability of occurring and summing the products. Subjective expected utility is a modified version of this procedure in which subjective values (utilities) replace values, and subjective probabilities replace probabilities. The expected-value model can be further modified by allowing for the possibility that people can emphasize some components of the model more than others.

Applications of decision making include the use of decision aids or training to help people make better decisions. Combining prior probabilities with evidence can be improved by substituting frequencies for the probabilities required in Bayes' theorem. Jury decision making requires combining many sources of evidence that are presented in a scrambled order. A story model accounts for findings of how jurists integrate this evidence. However, the slow, deliberate approach of jurists is not possible in emergency situations. In action-based decision making, it is necessary to quickly carry out a sequence of actions rather than make a single decision. The recognition-primed decision (RPD) model proposes that the decision maker quickly assesses the situation, uses his or her expertise to evaluate a single course of action, and evaluates fairly immediate feedback to determine whether that action is working.

STUDY QUESTIONS

1. What is the distinction between normative and descriptive models? What is the usefulness of each?
2. Try to think of some real-life choices you have made. For example, in choosing which college to attend, did you use a compensatory or noncompensatory model? Did you use the same procedure for all the decisions that you recalled?
3. Assuming that a search for information is involved, Payne devised a rather clever procedure for studying choice making. How did it work, and what did he find?
4. Where is the "risk" in risky decision making—as contrasted with other decision making?
5. If probabilities of events or outcomes of actions are unknown, how do people go about estimating the likelihood of occurrence? Are we very good at doing so?
6. What is the relation between sample size and the accuracy of the estimates of probability of events in the population from which the sample was drawn?
7. Why do you suppose so few people seem to calculate subjective expected utility, let alone expected value? Would lotteries stay in business if they did?
8. Can you think of specific examples of how your mood may have influenced your probability estimates? Think of an experiment that you could design to explore how mood might influence decision making in additional ways.
9. Can you think of important decisions for which you would like decision aids or training to improve your ability to make good decisions?
10. What are some of the differences between making decisions in emergency situations and making decisions when there is no time pressure?

CogLab The following experiments that relate to this chapter can be found at: http://coglab. wadsworth.com. Answer the questions in the CogLab Student Manual as required by your teacher for these experiments.

Typical Reasoning

Risky Decisions/Monty Hall

KEY TERMS

The page number in parentheses refers to where the term is discussed in the chapter.

additive model (353)

additive–difference model (353)

availability heuristic (358)

Bayes' theorem (368)

compensatory models (353)

conjunctive model (355)

decision aids (368)

decision event (373)

decision frame (366)

descriptive models (352)

duplex gambles (365)

elimination by aspects (354)

expected value (362)

loss aversion (364)

noncompensatory models (354)

normative model (352)

prior probability (361)

recognition-primed decision (RPD) (374)

representative (360)

risk dimensions (365)

satisficing search (355)

subjective expected utility (364)

subjective probabilities (364)

uncertainty (357)

utility (363)

RECOMMENDED READING

Review articles by Payne, Bettman, and Johnson (1992), Dawes (1997), Mellers, Schwartz, and Cooke (1998), Hastie (2001), and Shafir and LeBoeuf (2002, LeBoeuf & Shafir, 2005) summarize research on decision making. Frish and Clemen (1994) provide a critical overview of models based on expected value. Slovic (1997) makes an interesting distinction between risk analysis and decision analysis. *Decision Making in Action: Models and Methods*, edited by Klein, Orasanu, Calderwood, & Zsambok (1993), contains chapters on making multiple, action-based decisions during a brief time period. Two books provide an interesting contrast in approaches to decision making. *Rational Choice in an Uncertain World* (Hastie & Dawes, 2001) discusses a deliberative approach to judgment and decision making, whereas *Educating Intuition* (Hogarth, 2001) focuses on judgments and decisions that involve little or no conscious deliberation. The edited book, *Heuristics and Biases: The Psychology of Intuitive Judgment* (Gilovich & Kahneman, 2002), contains chapters on a wide variety of topics including affect (Slovic, Finucane, Peters, & MacGregor, 2002) and individual differences (Stanovich & West, 2002). Another edited book, *Emerging Perspectives on Judgment and Decision Research* (Schneider & Shanteau, 2003), also contains many valuable chapters including a summary chapter by Doherty (2003) that is particularly interesting.

GLOSSARY

absolute judgment task Identifying stimuli that vary along a single, sensory continuum

acoustic code A memory code based on the sound of the stimulus

acoustic confusion An error that sounds like the correct answer

activation rule A rule that determines how inhibitory and excitatory connections combine to determine the total activation of a concept

additive model A strategy that adds attribute values to assign a score to each alternative

additive–difference model A strategy that compares two alternatives by adding the difference in their values for each attribute

algorithm A set of rules that will solve a problem if correctly followed

allocation of capacity When a limited amount of capacity is distributed to various tasks

ambiguous sentence A sentence that has more than one meaning

amodal Knowledge that is abstracted from sensory experiences

anagram A problem that requires rearranging a string of letters to form a word

analogical transfer Use of the same solution in solving two problems

analogy problem A four-term problem that requires finding the answer that completes the relation: *A* is to *B* as *C* is to *D*

analogy Solving a problem by using a solution to a related problem

arousal A physiological state that influences the distribution of mental capacity to various tasks

arrangement problem A problem that requires rearranging its parts to satisfy a specified criterion

artificial intelligence The study of how to produce computer programs that can perform intellectually demanding tasks

association value The number of verbal associations generated for a concept

attention window The attended part of the visual buffer in Kosslyn's model

attenuation A decrease in the perceived loudness of an unattended message

attribute learning A concept identification task in which people are told the logical rule (such as conjunctive) but have to discover the relevant attributes

auditory information store In Sperling's model this store maintains verbal information in short-term memory through rehearsal

auditory-memory span Number of items recalled from short-term memory following an auditory presentation of the items

autobiographical memory Memory about our personal experiences

automatic processing Performing mental operations that require very little mental effort

availability heuristic Estimating probability by the ease with which examples can be recalled

average distance rule A classification strategy that selects the category containing items having the greatest average similarity to the classified item

basic-level category An intermediate category in the middle of a hierarchy, such as table, saw, and truck

Bayes' theorem A normative procedure for revising a probability by combining a prior probability with evidence

bizarre image A fantastic or unusual image

bottleneck theory A theory that attempts to explain how people select information when some information-processing stage becomes overloaded with too much information

bottom-up processing The flow of information from the sensory store toward LTM

Broca's aphasia A language disorder attributed to damage in the frontal lobe of the brain

capacity theory A theory that proposes that we have a limited amount of mental effort to distribute across tasks, so there are limitations on the number of tasks we can perform at the same time

caricature An exaggeration of distinctive features to make a pattern more distinctive

category-size effect The finding that members of smaller categories are classified more quickly than members of larger categories

causal relation An event that results in the occurrence of another event

central executive A component of Baddeley's working memory model that manages the use of working memory

cerebral blood flow Measurement of blood flow to localize where cognitive operations occur in the brain

characteristic feature A feature that is usually present in members of that category, but is not necessary

chunks A cluster of items that has been stored as a unit in long-term memory

clustering Percentage of occasions in which a word is followed by its primary associate during the free recall of words

coding Semantic elaboration of information to make it easier to remember

cognitive interview The use of cognitively based retrieval techniques to improve recall

cognitive neuroscience The study of the relation between cognitive processes and brain activities

cognitive psychology The study of the mental operations that support people's acquisition and use of knowledge

cognitive science The interdisciplinary attempt to study cognition through such fields as psychology, philosophy, artificial intelligence, neuroscience, linguistics, and anthropology

compensatory model A strategy that allows positive attributes to compensate for negative ones

concentration Investing mental effort in one or more tasks

concept identification A task that requires deciding whether an item is an example of a concept, where concepts are typically defined by logical rules

conceptually driven process A process that is influenced by a person's strategies

concrete-abstract dimension Extent to which a concept can be represented by a picture

conjunctive model A strategy that evaluates one alternative at a time and rejects it if the value of one of its attributes fails to satisfy a minimum criterion

conjunctive rule A rule that uses the logical relation *and* to relate stimulus attributes, such as *small and square*

contextual effect The influence of the surrounding context on the recognition of patterns

continuous dimension An attribute that can take on any value along a dimension

control process A strategy that determines how information is processed

creativity Creating a novel and useful product or solution

cued recall Recall that occurs with hints or cues, such as providing the questions asked during the judgment phase of a task

data-driven process A process that is influenced by the stimulus material

decay theory Proposal that information is spontaneously lost over time, even when there is no interference from other material

decision aid A tool for helping people make better decisions

decision event Making a single decision, rather than a sequence of decisions, in a changing situation

decision frame Decision maker's conception of the decision-making situation

declarative knowledge Knowledge about factual information

deep structure The underlying meaning of a sentence

default knowledge Knowledge about the most likely values for the attributes of a schema

defining feature A feature that is necessary to be a member of that category

descriptive model A model that describes what people actually do

detection paradigm A procedure in which observers have to specify which of two possible target patterns is present in a display

direct memory test A test that asks people to recall or recognize past events

disjunctive rule A rule that uses the logical relation *or* to relate stimulus attributes, such as *small or square*

distinctive feature A feature present in one pattern but absent in another, aiding one's discrimination of the two patterns

distinctive item An item different in appearance or meaning from other items

domain-specific knowledge Knowledge about a specific subject, such as chess or physics

dual-coding theory A theory that memory is improved when items can be represented by both verbal and visual memory codes

duplex gamble A gamble in which the probability of winning is assigned independently of the probability of losing

elimination by aspects A strategy that evaluates one attribute at a time and rejects those alternatives whose attribute values fail to satisfy a minimum criterion

embodied cognition A theoretical framework in which perception and action have a central role in cognition

emotional distinctiveness Items that produce an intense emotional reaction

encode To create a visual or verbal code for a test item so it can be compared with the memory codes of items stored in short-term memory

encoding specificity principle A theory that states that the effectiveness of a retrieval cue depends on how well it relates to the initial encoding of an item

enduring disposition An automatic influence where people direct their attention

episodic memory Memory of specific events, including when and where they occurred

error recovery heuristic A strategy for correcting comprehension errors

event-related potential (ERP) A diagnostic technique that uses electrodes placed on the scalp to measure the duration of brain waves during mental tasks

exchange error An error in which two linguistic units are substituted for each other during sentence production

excitatory connection A positive association between concepts that belong together, as when a vertical line provides support for the possibility that a letter is a K

exemplar model Proposes that patterns are categorized by comparing their similarity to category examples

exhaustive search A search that continues until the test item is compared with all items in the memory set

expected value The average value, as determined by combining the value of events with their probability of occurrence

explicit memory Memory evaluated by direct memory tests

exploration strategy A strategy for determining how to use a preinventive form

fact-oriented acquisition Encoding material in a manner that emphasizes factual knowledge without emphasizing its application

family resemblance A measure of how frequently the attributes of a category member are shared by other members of the category

feature comparison model A model proposing that items are categorized by matching the item's features to category features

feature frequency rule A classification strategy that selects the category having the most feature matches with the classified item

feature theory A theory of pattern recognition that describes patterns in terms of their parts, or features

filter model The proposition that a bottleneck occurs at the pattern recognition stage and that attention determines what information reaches the pattern recognition stage

filter The part of attention in which some perceptual information is blocked (filtered) out and not recognized, while other information receives attention and is subsequently recognized

flashbulb memory A memory of an important event that caused an emotional reaction

four-card selection problem A reasoning task that requires deciding which of four cards should be turned over to evaluate a conditional rule

functional fixedness The tendency to use an object in a typical way

functional magnetic resonance imaging (fMRI) A diagnostic technique that uses magnetic fields and computerized images to locate mental operations in the brain

general strategy A strategy (heuristic) that applies in many situations but does not always result in a solution

generation strategy A strategy for producing preinventive forms

generative The capability to produce many different messages by combining symbols in different ways

geons Different threedimensional shapes that combine to form threedimensional patterns

global coherence Integration of major ideas that occur throughout a text

goal-derived category A category whose members are selected to satisfy a specified goal

grammar A set of rules for producing correct sentences in a language

hallucination An imagined event or image believed to be real

heuristic A strategy that is often, but not always, helpful in solving problems

hierarchical network model A model proposing that items are categorized by using the hierarchical relations specified in a semantic network

hierarchically organized An organizing strategy in which larger categories are partitioned into smaller categories

high-constraint sentence A sentence that produces a high expectation for a particular word

human information processing The psychological approach that attempts to identify what occurs during the various stages (attention, perception, short-term memory) of processing information

ideal An attribute value that relates to the goal of a goal-derived category

imagery potential Ease with which a concept can be imaged

imaging Creating visual images to make material easier to remember

implicit memory Memory evaluated by indirect memory tests

imprecise elaboration Provision or generation of additional material unrelated to remembered material

inadvertent plagiarism Unintentionally copying someone else's ideas

incidental learning Learning that occurs when we do not make a conscious effort to learn

incidental learning task A task that requires people to make judgments about stimuli without knowing that they will later be tested on their recall of the stimuli

indirect memory test A test that does not explicitly ask about past events but is influenced by memory of past events

inducing-structure problem A problem that requires finding a pattern among a fixed set of relations

inference The use of reasoning to establish relations in a text when the relations are not directly stated

inhibitory connection A negative association between concepts that do not belong together, as when the presence of a vertical line provides negative evidence that a letter is a C

insight The sudden discovery of a solution following unsuccessful attempts to solve a problem

interactive activation model A theory that proposes that both feature knowledge and word knowledge combine to provide information about the identity of letters in a word

interference theory Proposal that forgetting occurs because other material interferes with the information in memory

interstimulus interval The amount of time between the end of a stimulus and the beginning of another stimulus

keyword A concrete word that sounds like an abstract word so that it can be substituted for the abstract word in an interactive image

keyword method A mnemonic strategy using keywords to improve paired-associates learning

knowledge acquisition Storage of information in long-term memory

language A collection of symbols and rules for combining symbols, which can express an infinite variety of messages

late-selection model Proposal that the bottleneck occurs when information is selected for memory

levels of processing A theory that proposes that "deeper" (semantic) levels of processing enhance memory

lexical alteration Substituting a word with similar meaning for one of the words in a sentence

lexical decision task A task that requires people to decide whether a string of letters is a word

limited-capacity perceptual channel The pattern recognition stage of Broadbent's model, which is protected by the filter (attention) from becoming overloaded with too much perceptual information

links The format for representing relations in a semantic network

local coherence Integration of ideas within an immediate context in a text

logical rule A rule based on logical relations, such as conjunctive, disjunctive, conditional, and bi-conditional rules

long-term memory (LTM) Memory that has no capacity limits and lasts from minutes to an entire lifetime

loss aversion Reaction to losses is more intense than reactions to corresponding gains

low-constraint sentence A sentence that produces an expectation for a broader range of words

maintenance rehearsal Rehearsal that keeps information active in short-term memory

means–end analysis A strategy that can be used to solve transformation problems by eliminating differences between the initial and goal states

measure of sufficiency A demonstration that the instructions in a computer program are capable of solving a problem

memory code The format (physical, phonemic, semantic) of information encoded into memory

memory set A set of items in short-term memory that can be compared against a test item to determine if the test item is stored there

memory span The number of correct items that people can immediately recall from a sequence of items

memory-retrieval explanation The proposal that people solve reasoning problems about familiar situations by retrieving specific examples from their memory

mental effort The amount of mental capacity required to perform a task

metacognition The selection of strategies for processing information

mnemonic technique A strategy that improves memory

modal Knowledge is represented as sensory experiences

momentary intention A conscious decision to allocate attention to certain tasks or aspects of the environment

mood-dependent memory Memory that is improved when people are tested under conditions that re-create their mood when they learned the material

morpheme The smallest unit of meaning in a language

morpheme exchange An error in which two morphemes are substituted for each other during sentence production

multimodal code An integration of memory codes such as combining visual and verbal codes

multimode theory A theory that proposes that people's intentions and the demands of the task determine the information-processing stage at which information is selected

naturalistic study A study of the tip-of-the-tongue state in which people record these events as they occur outside the laboratory

nearest-neighbor rule A classification strategy that selects the category containing an item most similar to the classified item

neural network model A theory in which concepts (nodes) are linked to other concepts through excitatory and inhibitory connections

nodes The format for representing concepts in a semantic network

noncompensatory model A strategy that rejects alternatives that have negative attributes without considering their positive attributes

noncued recall Recall that occurs without hints or cues provided by the experimenter

normative model A model that describes what people should do

obligation schema Knowledge that taking an action (such as paying a pension) is required if a prerequisite (such as retirement) is fulfilled

obstacle An event that delays or prevents the attainment of a goal

operator An action that is selected to solve problems

orienting task Instructions to focus on a particular aspect (physical, phonemic, semantic) of a stimulus

orthographic distinctiveness Lowercase words that have an unusual shape

parallel distributed processing (PDP) When information is simultaneously collected from different sources and combined to reach a decision

parallel processing Carrying out more than one operation at a time, such as looking at an art exhibit and making conversation

parallel representation Representation of knowledge in which more than one item at a time can be processed

paraphrase Using different words to express the same ideas in a sentence

partial-report procedure A task in which observers are cued to report only certain items in a display of items

pattern recognition The stage of perception during which a stimulus is identified

perceptual confusion A measure of the frequency with which two patterns are mistakenly identified as each other

permission schema Knowledge that taking an action (such as entering a country) requires fulfilling a prerequisite (such as being inoculated)

perspective A particular point of view

phoneme Any of the basic sounds of a language that are combined to form speech

phoneme exchange An error in which two phonemes are substituted for each other during sentence production

phonemic coding A memory code that emphasizes the pronunciation of the stimulus

phonological loop A component of Baddeley's working memory model that maintains and manipulates acoustic information

phrase-structure grammar A set of rules for partitioning a sentence into its grammatical units

plan A temporally ordered sequence of operations for carrying out some task

plot The sequence of events related to achieving goals in a narrative

positron-emission tomography (PET) A diagnostic technique that uses radioactive tracers to study brain activity by measuring the amount of blood flow in different parts of the brain

pragmatic reasoning schemata Organized knowledge structures used to evaluate practical situations such as seeking permission or fulfilling an obligation

precise elaboration Provision or generation of additional material closely related to remembered material

preinventive form Creating an object before determining its use

primacy effect The better recall of words at the beginning of a list

primary associates Words that are strongly associated with each other, as typically measured by asking people to provide associations to words

primary distinctiveness An item distinct from other items in the immediate context

priming Facilitation in the detection or recognition of a stimulus by using prior information

prior probability The probability that an event will occur before obtaining additional evidence regarding its occurrence

proactive interference Forgetting that occurs because of interference from material encountered before learning

problem isomorphs Problems that have different story contents but identical solutions

problem space The set of choices evaluated at each step in solving a problem as determined by the problem solver

problem-oriented acquisition Encoding material in a manner that is helpful for its later use in solving problems

procedural knowledge Knowledge that relates actions to goals

procedural memory Memory for actions, skills, and operations

processing distinctiveness Creation of a memory code that makes that memory distinct from other memories

production rule A conditional rule that specifies the prerequisite condition for carrying out an action

proposition A meaningful idea that typically consists of several words

propositional theory A theory that all knowledge, including spatial knowledge, can be expressed in semantic-based propositions

prototype An item that typifies the members in a category and is used to represent the category

prototype rule A classification strategy that selects the category whose prototype is the most similar to the classified item

readability formula A formula that uses variables such as word frequency and sentence length to predict the readability of text

readability The number of recalled propositions divided by reading time

reality monitoring Discriminating between actual and imagined events

recency effect The better recall of words at the end of a list

recognition memory Deciding whether an item had previously occurred in a specified context

recognition-primed decision (RPD) A decision that is quickly made following recognition of a situation

rehearsal Repeating verbal information to keep it active in short-term memory or to transfer it into long-term memory

reinstatement search The search of long-term memory to place words in short-term memory where they can be used to integrate a text

relational information Information specifying how concepts are related

release from proactive interference Reducing proactive interference by having information be dissimilar from earlier material

representational transfer Use of the same format (such as a matrix) in solving two problems

representative The extent to which an event is typical of a larger class of events

resolution The outcome of events in the plot

retrieval fluency The ease with which an item can be recalled

retrieval strategy A strategy for recalling information from long-term memory

retroactive interference Forgetting that occurs because of interference from material encountered after learning

risk dimension A component of a gamble such as the probability of winning or the amount of a loss

rote learning Learning by repetition rather than through understanding

rule learning A concept identification task in which people are told the relevant attributes (such as *small*, *square*) but have to discover the logical rule

satisficing search A strategy that follows the conjunctive model and therefore selects the first alternative that satisfies the minimum criterion for each attribute

scan component The attention component of Sperling's model that determines what is recognized in the visual information store

scan To sequentially compare a test item with items in short-term memory to determine if there's a match

schema A general knowledge structure that provides a framework for organizing clusters of knowledge

script Knowledge about what occurs during routine activities

search space The set of choices at each step in solving the problem as determined by the problem

secondary distinctiveness An item distinct from items stored in long-term memory

selection stage The stage that follows pattern recognition and determines which information a person will try to remember

selectivity The selective aspects of attention—we pay attention to some aspects of our environment and ignore other aspects

self-generation Generation of items by participants in an experiment, rather than the provision of these items by the experimenter

self-terminating search A search that stops as soon as the test item is successfully matched to an item in the memory set

semantic alteration Changing the order of words in a sentence to change the meaning of the sentence

semantic code A memory code based on the meaning of the stimulus

semantic dementia progressive deterioration of knowledge about words and objects

semantic memory Memory of general knowledge not associated with a particular context

semantic network A theory proposing that semantic information is organized in long-term memory by linking concepts to related concepts

sensory store The part of memory that holds unanalyzed sensory information for a fraction of a second, providing an opportunity for additional analysis following the physical termination of a stimulus

sequential representation Representation of knowledge in which only one item at a time can be processed

serial position effect The ability to recall words at the beginning and end of a list better than words in the middle of the list

serial processing Carrying out one operation at a time, such as pronouncing one word at a time

series extrapolation A problem that requires finding a pattern among a sequence of items to continue the sequence in the same pattern

setting The time and place in which narrative events occur

shadowing An experimental method that requires people to repeat the attended message out loud

short-term memory (STM) Memory that has limited capacity and that lasts only approximately 20 to 30 seconds in the absence of attending to its content

simulation program A computer program that attempts to reproduce the operations used by people to carry out various tasks

situation model Integration of prior knowledge and text information to construct an understanding of the situation described in a text

slip of the tongue A speech error

slope A measure of how much response time changes for each unit of change along the x-axis (memory-set size)

spatial knowledge Knowledge of spatial relations that may be stored as images

spontaneous retrieval A retrieval that occurs without making a conscious effort to recall information

spreading activation A theoretical construct proposing that activation spreads from a concept in a semantic network to activate related concepts

spreading activation model A model that accounts for response times by formulating assumptions about how activation spreads in a semantic network

stereotype An attribute value believed to be representative of social categories

stimulus-response (S-R) The approach that emphasizes the association between a stimulus and a response, without identifying the mental operations that produced the response

Stroop effect The finding that it takes longer to name the color of the ink a word is printed in when the word is the name of a competing color (for example, the word *red* printed in blue ink)

structural coding A memory code that emphasizes the physical structure of the stimulus

structural theory A theory that specifies how the features of a pattern are joined to other features of the pattern

structured The organization imposed on a language by its grammatical rules

subgoal A goal that solves part of the problem

subjective expected utility A variation of expected value that uses utilities and subjective probabilities instead of values and probabilities

subjective probability An estimated probability as determined by the decision maker

subordinate category A small category at the bottom of a hierarchy, such as lamp table, jigsaw, and pickup truck

subsidiary task A task that typically measures how quickly people can react to a target stimulus to evaluate the capacity demands of the primary task

subvocalizing Silently speaking to oneself

superordinate category A large category at the top of a hierarchy, such as furniture, tools, and vehicles

suppress Eliminating inappropriate meanings in a sentence

surface structure The structure of a spoken sentence

symbolic The use of symbols, such as spoken or written words, to represent ideas

table of connections A table that links differences between problem states with operators for eliminating those differences

tachistoscope A box that presents visual stimuli at a specified duration and level of illumination

template An unanalyzed pattern that is matched against alternative patterns by using the degrees of overlap as a measure of similarity

theme The main goals of characters in a narrative

threshold The minimal amount of activation required to become consciously aware of a stimulus

tip of the tongue (TOT) A retrieval state in which a person feels he or she knows the information but cannot immediately retrieve it to approximate the behavior of neural networks in the brain

top-down processing The flow of information from LTM toward the sensory store

transfer-appropriate processing Encoding material in a manner related to how the material will be used later

transformation problem A problem that requires changing the initial state through a sequence of operations until it matches the goal state

transformational grammar A set of rules for transforming a sentence into a closely related sentence

typicality A measure of how well a category member represents that category

typicality effect The finding that the more typical members of a category are classified more quickly than the less typical category members

uncertainty Lacking knowledge about which events will occur

utility Subjective value as determined by the decision maker

Venn diagram A diagram that shows the set relations (such as overlap) among categories

verbal knowledge Knowledge expressed in language

verbal protocol A record of verbalized thought processes

visual buffer A component of Kosslyn's model in which a generated visual image is maintained in short-term memory

visual information store (VIS) A sensory store that maintains visual information for approximately one-quarter of a second

visual neglect Failure to respond to visual stimulation on the side of the visual field that is opposite a brain lesion

visual scanning A shift of attention across a visual display or image

visuospatial sketchpad A component of Baddeley's working memory model that maintains and manipulates visual/spatial information

Wernicke's aphasia A language disorder attributed to damage in the temporal lobe of the brain

whole-report procedure A task that requires observers to report everything they see in a display of items

word exchange An error in which two words are substituted for each other during sentence production

word superiority effect The finding that accuracy in recognizing a letter is higher when the letter is in a word than when it appears alone or is in a nonword

work forward selecting relevant information to solve a problem in the order that it should be used in the solution

working memory capacity The amount of information that can be kept active in working memory

working memory The use of short-term memory as a temporary store for information needed to accomplish a particular task

REFERENCES

Adams, L. T., Kasserman, J. E., Yearwood, A. A., Perfetto, G. A., Bransford, J. D., & Franks, J. J. (1988). Memory access: The effects of fact-oriented versus problem-oriented acquisition. *Memory & Cognition*, 16, 167–175.

Adamson, R. E. (1952). Functional fixedness as related to problem solving: A repetition of three experiments. *Journal of Experimental Psychology, 44*, 288–291.

Adelson, B. (1984). When novices surpass experts: The difficulty of a task may increase with expertise. *Journal of Experimental Psychology: Learning, Memory, and Cognition, 10*, 483–495.

Ahn, W. K., Kim, N. S., Lassaline, M. E., & Dennis, M. J. (2000). Causal status as a determinant of feature centrality. *Cognitive Psychology, 41*, 361–416.

Albrecht, J. E., & O'Brien, E. J. (1993). Updating a mental model: Maintaining both local and global coherence. *Journal of Experimental Psychology: Learning, Memory, and Cognition, 19*, 1061–1070.

Anderson, J. R. (1976). *Language, memory, and thought*. Hillsdale, NJ: Erlbaum.

Anderson, J. R. (1982). Acquisition of cognitive skill. *Psychological Review, 89*, 369–406.

Anderson, J. R. (1983). *The architecture of cognition*. Cambridge, MA: Harvard University Press.

Anderson, J. R. (1990). Analysis of student performance with the LISP tutor. In N. Frederiksen, R. Glaser, A. Lesgold, & M. Shafto (Eds.), *Diagnostic monitoring of skill and knowledge acquisition* (pp. 27–50). Hillsdale, NJ: Erlbaum.

Anderson, J. R., & Reder, L. M. (1979). An elaborative processing explanation of depth of processing. In L. S. Cermak & F. I. M. Craik (Eds.), *Levels of processing in human memory*. Hillsdale, NJ: Erlbaum.

Anderson, J. R., & Schunn, C. D. (2000). Implications of the ACT-R learning theory: No magic bullets. In R. Glaser (Ed.), *Advances in instructional psychology* (Vol. 5). Mahwah, NJ: Erlbaum.

Anderson, J. R., Boyle, C. F., & Reiser, B. J. (1985). Intelligent tutoring systems. *Science, 228*, 456–462.

Anderson, J. R., Corbett, A. T., Koedinger, K. R., & Pelletier, R. (1995). Cognitive tutors: Lessons learned. *Journal of the Learning Sciences, 4*, 167–207.

Anderson, R. C., & Pichert, J. W. (1978). Recall of previously unrecallable information following a shift in perspective. *Journal of Verbal Learning and Verbal Behavior, 17*, 1–12.

Anderson, R. E. (1984). Did I do it or did I only imagine doing it? *Journal of Experimental Psychology: General, 113*, 594–613.

Anderson, S. J., & Conway, M. A. (1993). Investigating the structure of autobiographical memories. *Journal of Experimental Psychology: Learning, Memory, and Cognition, 19*, 1178–1196.

Anderson, S. J., & Conway, M. A. (1997). Representations of autobiographical memories. In M. A. Conway (Ed.), *Cognitive models of memory*. Cambridge, MA: MIT Press.

Arguin, M., & Saumier, D. (2004). Independent processing of parts and of their spatial organization in complex visual objects. *Psychological Science, 15*, 629–633.

Armstrong, S. L., Gleitman, L. R., & Gleitman, H. (1983). What some concepts might not be. *Cognition, 13*, 263–308.

Ashby, F. G., & Maddox, W. T. (2005). Human category learning. *Annual Review of Psychology, 56*, 149–178.

Ashby, F. G., Alfonso-Reese, L. A., Turken, A. U., & Waldron, E. M. (1998). A neuropsychological theory of multiple systems in category learning. *Psychological Review, 105*, 442–481.

Ashcraft, M. H., & Krause, J. A. (2007). Working memory, math performance, and math anxiety. *Psychonomic Bulletin & Review, 14*, 243–248.

Atkinson, A. P., Thomas, M. S. C., & Cleeremans, A. (2000). Consciousness: mapping the theoretical landscape. *TRENDS in Cognitive Sciences, 7*, 84–91.

Atkinson, R. C. (1972a). Ingredients for a theory of instruction. *American Psychologist, 27,* 921–931.

Atkinson, R. C. (1972b). Optimizing the learning of a second-language vocabulary. *Journal of Experimental Psychology, 96,* 124–129.

Atkinson, R. C., & Raugh, M. R. (1975). An application of the mnemonic keyword method to the acquisition of a Russian vocabulary. *Journal of Experimental Psychology: Human Learning and Memory, 104,* 126–133.

Atkinson, R. C., & Shiffrin, R. M. (1968). Human memory: A proposed system and its control processes. In K. W. Spence & J. T. Spence (Eds.), *The psychology of learning and motivation* (Vol. 2, pp. 89–195). Orlando, FL: Academic Press.

Atkinson, R. C., & Shiffrin, R. M. (1971). The control of short-term memory. *Scientific American, 225,* 82–90.

Awh, E., Jonides, J., Smith, E. E., Schumacher, E. H., Koeppe, R. A., & Katz, S. (1996). Dissociation of storage and rehearsal in verbal working memory: Evidence from PET. *Psychological Science, 7,* 25–31.

Baddeley, A. D. (1978). The trouble with "levels": A reexamination of Craik and Lockhart's framework for memory research. *Psychological Review, 85,* 139–152.

Baddeley, A. D. (1982). Domains of recollection. *Psychological Review, 89,* 708–729.

Baddeley, A. D. (1992). Is working memory working? The fifteenth Bartlett lecture. *Quarterly Journal of Experimental Psychology, 44A,* 1–31.

Baddeley, A. D. (2000). The episodic buffer: A new component of working memory? *Trends in Cognitive Sciences, 4,* 417–423.

Baddeley, A. D. (2001). Is working memory still working? *American Psychologist, 56,* 851–864.

Baddeley, A. D., & Andrade, J. (2000). Working memory and the vividness of imagery. *Journal of Experimental Psychology: General, 129,* 126–145.

Baddeley, A. D., & Hitch, G. (1974). Working memory. In G. H. Bower (Ed.), *The psychology of learning and motivation* (Vol. 8, pp. 17–90). Orlando, FL: Academic Press.

Baddeley, A. D., & Warrington, E. K. (1970). Amnesia and the distinction between long- and short-term memory. *Journal of Verbal Learning and Verbal Behavior, 9,* 176–189.

Baddeley, A. D., Gathercole, S., & Papagno, C. (1998). The phonological loop as a language learning device. *Psychological Review, 105,* 158–173.

Baddeley, A. D., Papagno, C., & Vallar, G. (1988). When long-term learning depends on short-term storage. *Journal of Memory and Language, 27,* 586–595.

Bahrick, H. P. (1979). Maintenance of knowledge: Questions about memory we forgot to ask. *Journal of Experimental Psychology: General, 108,* 296–308.

Bahrick, H. P., & Boucher, B. (1968). Retention of visual and verbal codes of the same stimuli. *Journal of Experimental Psychology, 78,* 417–422.

Bahrick, H. P., & Hall, L. K. (1991). Lifetime maintenance of high school mathematics content. *Journal of Experimental Psychology: General, 120,* 20–33.

Bar, M. (2007). The proactive brain: using analogies and associations to generate predictions. *TRENDS in the Cognitive Sciences, 11,* 280–289.

Bargh, J. A., & Chartrand, T. L. (1999). The unbearable automaticity of being. *American Psychologist, 54,* 462–479.

Barrett, L. F., Tugade, M. M., & Engle, R. W. (2004). Individual differences in working memory capacity and dual-process theories of the mind. *Psychonomic Bulletin, 130,* 553–573.

Barsalou, L. W. (1985). Ideals, central tendency, and frequency of instantiation as determinants of graded structure in categories. *Journal of Experimental Psychology: Learning, Memory, and Cognition, 11,* 629–654.

Barsalou, L. W. (1991). Deriving categories to achieve goals. In G. H. Bower (Ed.), *The psychology of learning and motivation* (Vol. 27, pp. 1–64). San Diego: Academic Press.

Barsalou, L. W. (1999). Perceptual symbol systems. *Behavioral and Brain Sciences, 22,* 557–660.

Barsalou, L. W. (2003). Situated simulation in the human conceptual system. *Language and Cognitive Processes, 18,* 513–562.

Barsalou, L. W., & Sewell, D. R. (1985). Contrasting the representation of scripts and categories. *Journal of Memory and Language, 24,* 646–665.

Barsalou, L. W., Simmons, W. K., Barbey, A. K., & Wilson, C. D. (2003). Grounding conceptual knowledge in modality-specific systems. *TRENDS in Cognitive Sciences, 7,* 84–91.

Bartlett, F. C. (1932). *Remembering: A study in experimental and social psychology.* New York: Macmillan.

Beilock, S. L., Carr, T. H., MacMahon, C., & Starkes, J. L. (2002). When paying attention becomes counterproductive: Impact of divided versus skill-focused attention on novice and experienced performance of sensorimotor skills. *Journal of Experimental Psychology: Applied, 8,* 6–16.

Bellezza, F. S. (1987). Mnemonic devices and memory schemas. In M. A. McDaniel & M. Pressley (Eds.), *Imagery and related mnemonic processes.* New York: Springer-Verlag.

Benjamin, A. S., & Bjork, R. A. (1996). Retrieval fluency as a metacognitive index. In L. M. Reder (Ed.), *Implicit memory and metacognition* (pp. 309–338). Mahwah, NJ: Erlbaum.

Bentall, R. P. (1990). The illusion of reality: A review and integration of psychological research on hallucinations. *Psychological Bulletin, 107,* 82–95.

Biederman, I. (1985). Human image understanding: Recent research and a theory. *Computer Vision, Graphics, and Image Processing, 32,* 29–73.

Biederman, I., & Cooper, E. E. (1991). Priming contour-deleted images: Evidence for intermediate representations in visual object recognition. *Cognitive Psychology, 23,* 393–419.

Block, C. C., & Duffy, G. G. (2008). Research on teaching comprehension. In C. C. Block & S. R. Parris (Eds.), *Comprehension Instruction: Research-based best practices* (pp. 19–37). New York: Guilford Press.

Boden, M. A. (2004). *The creative mind. Myths and mechanisms* (2nd ed). New York: Routledge.

Bourne, L. E., Jr. (1970). Knowing and using concepts. *Psychological Review, 77,* 546–556.

Bourne, L. E., Jr., Ekstrand, B. R., Lovallo, W. R., Kellogg, R. T., Hiew, C. C., & Yaroush, R. A. (1976). Frequency analysis of attribute identification. *Journal of Experimental Psychology: General, 105,* 294–312.

Bower, G. H. (1970). Organizational factors in memory. *Cognitive Psychology, 1,* 18–46.

Bower, G. H., & Winzenz, D. (1970). Comparison of associative learning strategies. *Psychonomic Science, 20,* 119–120.

Bower, G. H., Black, J. B., & Turner, T. J. (1979). Scripts in memory for text. *Cognitive Psychology, 11,* 177–220.

Bower, G. H., Clark, M., Winzenz, D., & Lesgold, A. (1969). Hierarchical retrieval schemes in recall of categorized word lists. *Journal of Verbal Learning and Verbal Behavior, 8,* 323–343.

Boyd, R., & Richerson, P. J. (2005). *The origin and evolution of cultures.* New York: Oxford University Press.

Brandimonte, M. A., & Gerbino, W. (1993). Mental image reversal and verbal recoding: When ducks become rabbits. *Memory & Cognition, 21,* 23–33.

Bransford, J. D., & Johnson, M. K. (1973). Considerations of some problems of comprehension. In W. G. Chase (Ed.), *Visual information processing.* Orlando, FL: Academic Press.

Brennan, S. E. (1985). The caricature generator. *Leonardo, 18,* 170–178.

Brewer, W. F., & Dupree, D. A. (1983). Use of plan schemata in the recall and recognition of goal-directed actions. *Journal of Experimental Psychology: Learning, Memory, and Cognition, 9,* 117–129.

Brewer, W. F., & Nakamura, G. V. (1984). The nature and function of schemas. In R. S. Wyer & T. K. Srull (Eds.), *Handbook of social cognition.* Hillsdale, NJ: Erlbaum.

Britton, B. K., & Graesser, A. C. (Eds.). (1996). *Models of understanding text.* Mahwah, NJ: Erlbaum.

Britton, B. K., & Gulgoz, S. (1991). Using Kintsch's computational model to improve instructional text: Effects of repairing inference calls on recall and cognitive structures. *Journal of Educational Psychology, 83,* 329–345.

Britton, B. K., Van Dusen, L., Glynn, S. M., & Hemphill, D. (1990). The impact of inferences on instructional text. In A. C. Graesser & G. H. Bower (Eds.), *Inferences and text comprehension.* San Diego: Academic Press.

Broadbent, D. E. (1954). The role of auditory localization in attention and memory span. *Journal of Experimental Psychology, 47,* 191–196.

Broadbent, D. E. (1957). A mechanical model for human attention and immediate memory. *Psychological Review, 64,* 205–215.

Broadbent, D. E. (1958). *Perception and communication.* London: Pergamon Press.

Broca, P. (1865). Sur le siege de la faculté du langage articulé. *Bulletin de la Société d'Anthropologie, 6,* 377.

Broekkamp, H., & Van Hout-Wolters, B. H. A. M. (2007). Students' adaptation of study strategies when preparing for classroom tests. *Educational Psychology Review, 19,* 401–428.

Brooks, L. R. (1968). Spatial and verbal components of the act of recall. *Canadian Journal of Psychology, 22,* 349–368.

Brown, A. S. (1991). A review of the tip-of-the-tongue experience. *Psychological Bulletin, 109,* 204–223.

Brown, E., Deffenbacher, K., & Sturgill, W. (1977). Memory for faces and the circumstances of encounter. *Journal of Applied Psychology, 62,* 311–318.

Brown, R., & Kulik, J. (1977). Flashbulb memories. *Cognition, 5,* 73–99.

Brown, R., & McNeill, D. (1966). The "tip-of-the tongue" phenomenon. *Journal of Verbal Learning and Verbal Behavior, 5,* 325–337.

Bruner, J. S., Goodnow, J. J., & Austin, G. A. (1956). *A study of thinking.* New York: Wiley.

Buchanan, B. G. (2001). Creativity at the metalevel. *AI Magazine, 22,* 13–28.

Buckhout, R. (1974). Eyewitness testimony. *Scientific American, 231,* 23–31.

Buckhout, R., Eugenio, P., Licitra, T., Oliver, L., & Kramer, T. H. (1981). Memory, hypnosis, and evidence: Research on eyewitnesses. *Social Action and the Law, 7,* 67–72.

Budiu, R., & Anderson, J. R. (2004). Interpretation based processing: A unified theory of semantic sentence comprehension. *Cognitive Science, 28,* 1–44.

Burgess, N., & Hitch, G. J. (1992). Toward a network model of the articulatory loop. *Journal of Memory and Language, 31,* 429–460.

Burke, D. M., & Light, L. L. (1981). Memory and aging: The role of retrieval processes. *Psychological Bulletin, 90,* 513–546.

Bussey, T. A., & Loftus, G. R. (2007). Cognitive science and the law. *TRENDS in the Cognitive Sciences, 11,* 111–117.

Cabeza, R., & St. Jacques, P. (2007). Functional neuroimaging of autobiographical memory. *TRENDS in the Cognitive Sciences, 11,* 219–227.

Caccamise, D., Snyder, L., & Kintsch, E. (2008). Constructivist theory and the situation model. In C. C. Block & S. R. Parris (Eds.), *Comprehension Instruction: Research-based best practices* (pp. 80–97). New York: Guilford Press.

Cantor, N., & Genero, N. (1986). Psychiatric diagnosis and natural categorization: A close analogy. In T. Milton & G. Klerman (Eds.), *Contemporary directions in psychopathology: Toward the DSM-IV.* New York: Guilford.

Cantor, N., & Mischel, W. (1979). Prototypes in person perception. In L. Berkowitz (Ed.), *Advances in experimental social psychology* (Vol. 12). Orlando, FL: Academic Press.

Cantor, N., Smith, E. E., French, R., & Mezzich, J. (1980). Psychiatric diagnosis as prototype categorization. *Journal of Abnormal Psychology, 89,* 181–193.

Caramazza, A., & Mahon, B. Z. (2003). The organization of conceptual knowledge: Evidence from category-specific semantic deficits. *TRENDS in Cognitive Sciences, 7,* 354–361.

Caramazza, A., & Shelton, J. R. (1998). Domain specific knowledge systems in the brain.

Carlson, K. A., & Russo, J. E. (2001). Biased interpretation of evidence by mock jurors. *Journal of Experimental Psychology: Applied, 7,* 91–103.

Carpenter, P. A., & Daneman, M. (1981). Lexical retrieval and error recovery in reading: A model based on eye fixations. *Journal of Verbal Learning and Verbal Behavior, 20,* 137–160.

Carpenter, P. A., Just, M. A., & Shell, P. (1990). What one intelligence test measures: A theoretical account of the processing in the Raven Progressive Matrices Test. *Psychological Review, 97,* 404–431.

Carpenter, P. A, Miyake, A., & Just, M. A. (1995). Language comprehension: Sentence and discourse processing. *Annual Review of Psychology, 46,* 91–120.

Carroll, D. W. (1986). *Psychology of language.* Pacific Grove, CA: Brooks/Cole.

Carroll, J. M., Thomas, J. C., & Malhotra, A. (1980). Presentation and representation in design problem solving. *British Journal of Psychology, 71,* 143–153.

Catrambone, R. (1995). Aiding subgoal learning: Effects on transfer. *Journal of Educational Psychology, 87,* 5–17.

Catrambone, R., & Holyoak, K. J. (1989). Overcoming contextual limitations on problem-solving transfer. *Journal of Experimental Psychology: Learning, Memory, and Cognition, 15,* 1147–1156.

Cermak, L. S., & Craik, F. I. M. (Eds.). (1979). *Levels of processing in human memory.* Hillsdale, NJ: Erlbaum.

Chambers, D., & Reisberg, D. (1985). Can mental images be ambiguous? *Journal of Experimental Psychology: Human Perception and Performance, 11,* 317–328.

Chambers, D., & Reisberg, D. (1992). What an image depicts depends on what an image means. *Cognitive Psychology, 24,* 145–174.

Chang, T. M. (1986). Semantic memory: Facts and models. *Psychological Bulletin, 99,* 199–220.

Chapanis, A. (1965). *Man machine engineering.* Pacific Grove, CA: Brooks/Cole.

Chase, W. G., & Ericsson, K. A. (1979, November). A mnemonic system for digit span: One year later. Paper presented at the 20th annual meeting of the Psychonomic Society, Phoenix, AZ.

Chase, W. G., & Simon, H. A. (1973). Perception in chess. *Cognitive Psychology, 4,* 55–81.

Chen, Z. (2002). Analogical problem solving: A hierarchical analysis of procedural similarity. *Journal of Experimental Psychology: Learning, Memory and Cognition, 28,* 81–98.

Chen, W., Kato, T., Shu, X. H., Ogawa, S., Tank, D. W., & Ugurbil, K. (1998). Human primary visual cortex and lateral geniculate nucleus activation during visual imagery. *Neuroreport, 9,* 3669–3674.

Cheng, P. W., Holyoak, K. J., Nisbett, R. E., & Oliver, L. M. (1986). Pragmatic versus syntactic approaches to training deductive reasoning. *Cognitive Psychology, 18,* 293–328.

Cherry, C. (1953). Some experiments on the recognition of speech with one and with two ears. *Journal of the Acoustical Society of America, 25,* 975–979.

Chi, M. T. H., Ohsson, S. (2005). Complex declarative learning. In K. J. Holyoak & R. G. Morrison (Eds.), *The Cambridge handbook of thinking and reasoning* (pp. 371–400). New York: Cambridge University Press.

Chiesi, H. L., Spilich, G. J., & Voss, J. F. (1979). Acquisition of domain-related information in relation to high and low domain knowledge. *Journal of Verbal Learning and Verbal Behavior, 18,* 257–273.

Chomsky, N. (1957). *Syntactic structures.* The Hague: Mouton.

Chomsky, N. (1965). *Aspects of the theory of syntax.* Cambridge, MA: MIT Press.

Clifton, C., & Duffy, S. A. (2001). Sentence and text comprehension: Roles of linguistic structure. *Annual Review of Psychology, 52,* 167–196.

Clowes, M. (1969). Transformational grammars and the organization of pictures. In A. Graselli (Ed.), *Automatic interpretation and the organization of pictures.* Orlando, FL: Academic Press.

Collins, A. M., & Loftus, E. F. (1975). A spreading activation theory of semantic processing. *Psychological Review, 82,* 407–428.

Collins, A. M., & Quillian, M. R. (1969). Retrieval time from semantic memory. *Journal of Verbal Learning and Verbal Behavior, 8,* 240–248.

Collins, A. M., & Quillian, M. R. (1970). Facilitating retrieval from semantic memory: The effect of repeating part of an inference. *Acta Psychologica, 33,* 304–314.

Conrad, R. (1964). Acoustic confusions in immediate memory. *British Journal of Psychology, 55,* 75–84.

Conrad, R. (1972). Speech and reading. In J. F. Kavanagh & I. G. Mattingly (Eds.), *Language by ear and by eye: The relationships between speech and reading.* Cambridge, MA: MIT Press.

Conway, M.A., Cohen, G., & Stanhope, N. (1991). On the very long-term retention of knowledge acquired through formal education: Twelve years of cognitive psychology. *Journal of Experimental Psychology: General, 120,* 395–409.

Cook, A. E., & Gueraud, S. (2005). What have we been missing? The role of general world knowledge in discourse processing. *Discourse Processes, 39,* 265–278.

Cook, A. E., Gueraud, S., Was, C. A., & O'Brien, E. J. (2007). Foregrounding effects during reading, revisited. *Discourse Processes, 44,* 91–111.

Cosmides, L., & Tooby, J. (1996). Are humans good intuitive statisticians after all? Rethinking some conclusions from the literature on judgment under uncertainty. *Cognition, 58,* 1–73.

Cowan, N. (1988). Evolving conceptions of memory storage, selective attention, and their mutual constraints within the human information processing system. *Psychological Bulletin, 104,* 163–191.

Cowan, N. (1995). *Attention and memory: An integrated framework.* Oxford: Oxford University Press.

Cowan, N., Wood, N. L., Wood, P. K., Keller, T. A., Nugent, L. D., & Keller, C. V. (1998). Two separate verbal processing rates contributing to short-term memory span. *Journal of Experimental Psychology: General, 127,* 141–160.

Craik, F. I. M. (1970). The fate of primary memory items in free recall. *Journal of Verbal Learning and Verbal Behavior, 9,* 143–148.

Craik, F. I. M. (1979). Levels of processing: Overview and closing comments. In L. S. Cermak & F. I. M. Craik (Eds.), *Levels of processing in human memory.* Hillsdale, NJ: Erlbaum.

Craik, F. I. M., & Lockhart, R. S. (1972). Levels of processing: A framework for memory research. *Journal of Verbal Learning and Verbal Behavior, 11,* 671–684.

Craik, F. I. M., & Rabinowitz, J. C. (1983). Age differences in the acquisition and use of verbal information: A tutorial review. In H. Bouma & D. G. Bowwhuis (Eds.), *Attention and performance X.* Hillsdale, NJ: Erlbaum.

Craik, F. I. M., & Tulving, E. (1975). Depth of processing and the retention of words in episodic memory. *Journal of Experimental Psychology: General, 104,* 268–294.

Craik, F. I. M., & Watkins, M. J. (1973). The role of rehearsal in short-term memory. *Journal of Verbal Learning and Verbal Behavior, 12,* 599–607.

Davis, R., Shrobe, H., & Szolovits, P. (1993). What is a knowledge representation? *AI Magazine, 14,* 17–33.

Dawes, R. B. (1997). Behavioral decision making and judgment. In D. T. Gilbert, S. T. Fiske, & G. Lindzey (Eds.), *The handbook of social psychology* (Vol. 1, pp. 497–548). Boston: McGraw-Hill.

de Groot, A. D. (1965). *Thought and choice in chess.* The Hague: Mouton.

de Groot, A. D. (1966). Perception and memory versus thought: Some old ideas and recent findings. In B. Kleinmuntz (Ed.), *Problem solving: Research, method, and theory.* New York: Wiley.

Dell, G. S. (1986). A spreading activation theory of sentence production. *Psychological Review, 93,* 283–321.

Detterman, D. K., & Sternberg, R. J. (Eds.). (1993). *Transfer on trial: Intelligence, cognition, and instruction.* Norwood, NJ: Ablex.

Deutsch, J. A., & Deutsch, D. (1963). Attention: Some theoretical considerations. *Psychological Review, 70,* 80–90.

Deutsch, J. A., Deutsch, D., & Lindsay, P. (1967). Comments on "Selective attention: Stimulus or response." *Quarterly Journal of Experimental Psychology, 19,* 362–367.

Devine, P. G., Hamilton, D. L., & Ostrom, T. M. (1994). *Social cognition: Impact on social psychology.* San Diego: Academic Press.

Dietrich, A. (2004). The cognitive neuroscience of creativity. *Psychonomic Bulletin and Review, 11,* 1011–1026.

Dijksterhuis, A., & Nordgren, L. F. (2006). A theory of unconscious thought. *Perspectives in Psychological Science, 1,* 95–109.

Dodson, C. S., Koutstaal, W., & Schacter, D. L. (2000). Escape from illusion: Reducing false memories. *TRENDS in Cognitive Sciences, 4,* 391–397.

Doherty, M. E. (2003). Optimists, pessimists, and realists. In S. L. Schneider & J. Shanteau, *Emerging perspectives on Judgment and Decision Research* (pp. 643–679). Cambridge: Cambridge University press.

Donald, M. (2001). *A mind so rare: The evolution of human consciousness.* New York: Norton.

Dopkins, S., Klin, C., & Myers, J. L. (1993). Accessibility of information about goals during the processing of narrative texts. *Journal of Experimental Psychology: Learning, Memory, and Cognition, 19,* 70–80.

Driskell, J. E., Copper, C., & Moran, A. (1994). Does mental practice enhance performance? *Journal of Applied Psychology, 79,* 481–492.

Duffy, S. A., Morris, R. K., & Rayner, K. (1988). Lexical ambiguity and fixation times in reading. *Journal of Memory and Language, 27,* 429–446.

Dunbar, K., & Blanchette, I. (2001). The in vivo in vitro approach to cognition: The case of analogy. *TRENDS in Cognitive Sciences, 5,* 334–339.

Duncker, K. (1945). On problem solving. *Psychological Monographs, 58* (5, Whole No. 270).

Dunegan, K. J. (1993). Framing, cognitive modes, and image theory: Toward an understanding of a glass half full. *Journal of Applied Psychology, 78,* 491–503.

Dunlosky, J., & Nelson, T. O. (1994). Does the sensitivity of judgments of learning (JOLs) to the effects of various study activities depend on when the JOLs occur? *Journal of Memory and Language, 33,* 545–565.

Egeland, B. (1975). Effects of errorless training on teaching children to discriminate letters of the alphabet. *Journal of Applied Psychology, 60,* 533–536.

Egeth, H. E., & Yantis, S. (1997). Visual attention: Control, representation, and time course. *Annual Review of Psychology, 48,* 269–297.

Eich, E., Macaulay, D., & Ryan, L. (1994). Mood dependent memory for events of the personal past. *Journal of Experimental Psychology: General, 123,* 201–215.

Elstein, A. S., Shulman, L. S., & Sprafka, S. A. (1978). *Medical problem solving.* Cambridge, MA: Harvard University Press.

Engle, R. W., & Oransky, N. (1999). The evolution from short-term to working memory: Multistore to dynamic models of temporary storage. In R. Sternberg (Ed.), *The nature of cognition.* Cambridge, MA: MIT Press.

Engle, R. W., Kane, M. J., & Tuholski, S. W. (1999). Individual differences in working memory capacity and what they tell us about controlled attention, general fluid intelligence, and functions of the prefrontal cortex. In A. Miyake & P. Shah (Eds.), *Models of working memory: Mechanism of active maintenance and executive control.* New York: Cambridge University Press.

Erickson, T., & Mattson, M. (1981). From words to meaning: A semantic illusion. *Journal of Verbal Learning and Verbal Behavior, 20,* 540–552.

Ericsson, K. A. (1985). Memory skill. *Canadian Journal of Psychology, 39,* 188–231.

Ericsson, K. A., & Charness, N. (1994). Expert performance: Its structure and acquisition. *American Psychologist, 49,* 725–747.

Ericsson, K. A., & Kintsch, W. (1995). Long-term working memory. *Psychological Review, 102,* 211–245.

Ericsson, K. A., & Polson, P. G. (1988). An experimental analysis of the mechanisms of a memory skill. *Journal of Experimental Psychology: Learning, Memory, and Cognition, 14,* 305–316.

Ericsson, K. A., & Simon, H. A. (1980). Verbal reports as data. *Psychological Review, 87,* 215–251.

Ernst, G. W., & Newell, A. (1969). *GPS: A case study in generality and problem solving.* Orlando, FL: Academic Press.

Estes, W. K. (1997). Processes of memory loss, recovery, and distortion. *Psychological Review, 104,* 148–169.

Estes, W. K., & Taylor, H. A. (1966). Visual detection in relation to display size and redundancy of critical elements. *Perception & Psychophysics, 1,* 9–16.

Evans, J. S. B. T. (2003). In two minds: Dual process accounts of reasoning. *TRENDS in Cognitive Sciences, 7,* 454–459.

Eysenck, M. W. (1978). Levels of processing: A critique. *British Journal of Psychology, 69,* 157–169.

Eysenck, M. W. (1979). Depth, elaboration, and distinctiveness. In L. S. Cermak & F. I. M. Craik (Eds.), *Levels of processing in human memory.* Hillsdale, NJ: Erlbaum.

Eysenck, M. W., & Keane, M. T. (1990). *Cognitive psychology: A student's handbook.* Hove, England: Erlbaum.

Fallshore, M., & Schooler, J. W. (1995). Verbal vulnerability of perceptual expertise. *Journal of Experimental Psychology: Learning, Memory, and Cognition, 21,* 1608–1623.

Farah, M. J. (1988). Is visual imagery really visual? Overlooked evidence from neuropsychology. *Psychological Review, 95,* 307–317.

Fincher-Kiefler, R. (2001). Perceptual components of situation models. *Memory & Cognition, 29,* 336–343.

Finke, R. A. (1980). Levels of equivalence in imagery and perception. *Psychological Review, 87,* 113–132.

Finke, R. A. (1985). Theories relating mental imagery to perception. *Psychological Bulletin, 98,* 236–259.

Finke, R. A. (1990). *Creative imagery: Discoveries and inventions in visualization.* Hillsdale, NJ: Erlbaum.

Finke, R. A. (1996). Imagery, creativity and emergent structures. *Consciousness and Cognition, 5,* 381–393.

Finke, R. A., Ward, T. B., & Smith, S. M. (1992). *Creative cognition: Theory, research, and applications.* Cambridge, MA: MIT Press.

Fischhoff, B., & Bar-Hillel, M. (1984). Focusing techniques: A shortcut to improving probability judgments? *Organizational Behavior and Human Performance, 34,* 175–194.

Fischler, I., Rundus, D., & Atkinson, R. C. (1970). Effects of overt rehearsal processes on free recall. *Psychonomic Science, 19,* 249–250.

Fisher, D., Laurie, N. Glaser, R., Comerney, K., Pollatsek, A., Duffy, S., & Brock, J. (2002). The use of a fixed-base driving simulator to evaluate the effects of experience and PC-based risk awareness training on drivers' decisions. *Human Factors, 44,* 287–302.

Fisher, K. M. (2000). SemNet® Semantic Networking. In K. M. Fisher, J. H. Wandersee, & D. E. Moody (Eds.), *Mapping biology knowledge.* Dordrecht: Kluwer Academic.

Fisher, K. M., Wandersee, J. H., & Moody, D. E. (Eds.). (2000). *Mapping biology knowledge.* Dordrecht: Kluwer Academic.

Fisher, R. P., Geiselman, R. E., & Amador, M. (1989). Field test of the cognitive interview: Enhancing the recollection of actual victims and witnesses of crime. *Journal of Applied Psychology, 74,* 722–727.

Fisher, R. P., & Craik, F. I. M. (1977). Interaction between encoding and retrieval operations in cued recall. *Journal of Experimental Psychology: Human Learning and Memory, 3,* 701–711.

Fisk, S. T. (1998). Stereotyping, prejudice, and discrimination. In D. T. Gilbert, S. T. Fiske, & G. Lindsey (Eds.), *The handbook of social psychology* (4th ed.) (pp. 357–411). New York: McGraw-Hill.

Fletcher, C. R. (1986). Strategies for the allocation of short-term memory during comprehension. *Journal of Memory and Language, 25,* 43–58.

Folk, C. L., Remington, R. W., & Johnston, J. C. (1992). Involuntary covert orienting is contingent on attentional control settings. *Journal of Experimental Psychology: Human Perception and Performance, 18,* 1030–1044.

Franklin, B. (1887). *Complete works* (Vol. 4, J. Bigelow, Ed.). New York: Putnam.

Friedman, N. P., & Miyake, A. (2000). Differential roles for visuospatial and verbal working memory in situation model construction. *Journal of Experimental Psychology: General, 129,* 61–83.

Frish, D., & Clemen, R. T. (1994). Beyond expected utility: Rethinking decision research. *Psychological Bulletin, 116,* 46–54.

Gagne, E. (1985). *The cognitive psychology of school learning.* Boston: Little, Brown.

Galambos, J. A., & Rips, L. J. (1982). Memory for routines. *Journal of Verbal Learning and Verbal Behavior, 21,* 260–281.

Galotti, K. (1989). Approaches to studying formal and everyday reasoning. *Psychological Bulletin, 105,* 331–351.

Gardner, H. (1983). *Frames of mind: The theory of multiple intelligences.* New York: Basic Books.

Gardner, H. (1985). *The mind's new science: A history of the cognitive revolution.* New York: Basic Books.

Garner, W. R. (1974). *The processing of information and structure.* Hillsdale, NJ: Erlbaum.

Gathercole, S. E. (1997). Models of verbal short-term memory. In M. A. Conway (Ed.), *Cognitive models of memory.* Cambridge, MA: MIT Press.

Gegenfurtner, K. R., & Sperling, G. (1993). Information transfer in iconic memory experiments. *Journal of Experimental Psychology: Human Perception and Performance, 19,* 845–866.

Geiselman, R. E., Fisher, R. P., MacKinnon, D. P., & Holland, H. L. (1985). Eyewitness memory enhancement in the police interview: Cognitive retrieval mnemonics versus hypnosis. *Journal of Applied Psychology, 70,* 401–412.

Gentner, D. (1983). Structure-mapping: A theoretical framework for analogy. *Cognitive Science, 7,* 155–170.

Gentner, D., & Markman, A. B. (1997). Structure mapping in analogy and similarity. *American Psychologist, 52,* 45–56.

Gentner, D., Lowenstein, J., Thompson, L., & Forbus, K. D. (2008). Reviving inert knowledge: Analogical encoding supports relational retrieval of past events. Unpublished manuscript.

Gernsbacher, M. A. (1993). Less skilled readers have less efficient suppression mechanisms. *Psychological Science, 4,* 294–298.

Gernsbacher, M. A. (1997). Two decades of structure building. *Discourse Processes, 23,* 265–304.

Gernsbacher, M. A., & Faust, M. E. (1991). The mechanism of suppression: A component of general comprehension skill. *Journal of Experimental Psychology: Learning, Memory and Cognition, 17,* 245–262.

Geyer, L. H., & De Wald, C. G. (1973). Feature lists and confusion matrices. *Perception & Psychophysics, 14,* 479–482.

Gibbs, R. W. (2006). *Embodiment and Cognitive Science.* New York: Cambridge University Press.

Gibson, E. J. (1969). *Principles of perceptual learning and development.* Englewood Cliffs, NJ: Prentice-Hall.

Gick, M. L. (1986). Problem-solving strategies. *Educational Psychologist, 21,* 99–120.

Gick, M. L., & Holyoak, K. J. (1980). Analogical problem solving. *Cognitive Psychology, 12,* 306–355.

Gick, M. L., & Holyoak, K. J. (1983). Schema induction and analogical transfer. *Cognitive Psychology, 15,* 1–38.

Gigerenzer, G. (2008). Why heuristics work. *Perspectives in Psychological Science, 3,* 20–29.

Gigerenzer, G., & Hoffrage, U. (1995). How to improve Bayesian reasoning without instruction: Frequency formats. *Psychological Review, 102,* 684–704.

Gilhooly, R. H., Logie, R. H., Wetherick, N. E., & Wynn, V. (1993). Working memory and strategies in syllogistic-reasoning tasks. *Memory & Cognition, 21,* 115–124.

Gilovich, T., Griffin, D., & Kahneman, D. (Eds.). (2002). *Heuristics and biases: The psychology of intuitive judgment.* Cambridge: Cambridge University Press.

Gleitman, L. (2005). Langauge and thought. In K. J. Holyoak & R. G. Morrison (Eds.), *The Cambridge handbook of thinking and reasoning* (pp. 633–662). New York: Cambridge University Press.

Glenberg, A. M., & Kaschak, M. P. (2002). Grounding language in action. *Psychonomic Bulletin & Review, 9,* 558–565.

Glucksberg, S., & McCloskey, M. (1981). Decisions about ignorance: Knowing that you don't know. *Journal of Experimental Psychology: Human Learning and Memory, 7,* 311–325.

Goldenberg, G., Podreka, I., Steiner, M., & Willmes, K. (1987). Patterns of regional cerebral blood flow related to memorizing of high and low imagery words: An emission computer tomography study. *Neuropsychologia, 25,* 473–486.

Goldin-Meadow, S., & Wagner, S. M. (2005). How our hands help us learn. *TRENDS in Cognitive Sciences, 9,* 234–241.

Goldstein, D. G., & Gigerenzer, G. (2002). Models of ecological rationality: The recognition heuristic. *Psychological Review, 109,* 75–90.

Goldstone, R. L., & Steyvers, M. (2001). The sensitization and differentiation of dimensions during category learning. *Journal of Experimental Psychology: General, 130,* 116–139.

Goldstone, R. L., Lippa, Y., & Shiffrin, R. M. (2001). Altering object representations through category learning. *Cognition, 78,* 27–43.

Goodman, M. J., Tijerina, L., Bents, F. D., & Wierwille, W. W. (1999). Using cellular phones in vehicles: Safe or unsafe? *Transportation Human Factors, 1,* 3–42.

Gopher, D., & Kahneman, D. (1971). Individual differences in attention and the prediction of flight criteria. *Perceptual and Motor Skills, 33,* 1335–1342.

Gorodetsky, M., & Fisher, K. M. (1996). Generating connections and learning in biology. In K. M. Fisher & M. R. Kibby (Eds.), *Knowledge acquisition, organization, and use in biology* (pp. 135–154). New York: Springer Verlag.

Graesser, A. C., Kassler, M. A., Kreuz, R. J., & McLain-Allen, B. (1998). Verification of statements about story worlds that deviate from normal conceptions of time: What is true about *Einstein's Dreams? Cognitive Psychology, 35,* 246–301.

Graesser, A. C., Singer, M., & Trabasso, T. (1994). Constructing inferences during narrative text comprehension. *Psychological Review, 101,* 371–395.

Grandin, T., & Johnson, C. (2005). *Animals in translation.* Orlando, FL: Harcourt.

Grainger, J., & Whitney, C. (2004). Does the huamn mnid raed wrods as a wlohe? *TRENDS in Cognitive Sciences, 8,* 58–59.

Green, C., & Hummel, J. E. (2004). Relational perception and cognition: Implications for cognitive architecture and the perceptual-cognitive interface. In B. H. Ross (Ed.), *The psychology of learning and motivation* (Vol. 44, pp. 201–226). San Diego, CA: Academic Press.

Greene, R. L. (1986). Sources of recency effects in free recall. *Psychological Bulletin, 99,* 221–228.

Greeno, J. G. (1978). Natures of problem solving abilities. In W. K. Estes (Ed.), *Handbook of learning and cognitive processes* (Vol. 5). Hillsdale, NJ: Erlbaum.

Griggs, R. A., & Cox, J. R. (1982). The elusive thematic-materials effect in Wason's selection task. *British Journal of Psychology, 73,* 407–420.

Gunter, B., Clifford, B. R., & Berry, C. (1980). Release from proactive interference with television news items: Evidence for encoding dimensions within televised news. *Journal of Experimental Psychology: Human Learning and Memory, 6,* 216–223.

Haber, R. N. (1969). Introduction. In R. N. Haber (Ed.), *Information processing approaches to visual perception.* New York: Holt, Rinehart & Winston.

Halpern, D. F. (1998). Teaching critical thinking for transfer across domains. *American Psychologist, 53,* 449–455.

Hampton, J. A. (1997). Psychological representation of concepts. In M. A. Conway (Ed.), *Cognitive models of memory* (pp. 81–110). Cambridge, MA: MIT Press.

Hasher, L., & Zacks, R. T. (1979). Automatic and effortful processes in memory. *Journal of Experimental Psychology: General, 108,* 356–388.

Hasher, L., & Zacks, R. T. (1984). Automatic processing of fundamental information: The case of frequency of occurrence. *American Psychologist, 39,* 1372–1388.

Hastie, R. (2001). Problems for judgment and decision making. *Annual Review of Psychology, 52,* 653–683.

Hastie, R., & Dawes, R. M. (2001). *Rational choice in an uncertain world.* Thousand Oaks, CA: Sage.

Hastie, R., & Pennington, N. (2000). Explanation based decision making. In T. Connolly, H. R. Arkes, & K. R. Hammond (Eds.), *Judgment and decision making: An interdisciplinary reader* (2nd ed.) (pp. 212–228). Cambridge, England: Cambridge University Press.

Hayes, J. R. (1952). Memory span for several vocabularies as a function of vocabulary size. *Quarterly Progress Report, Acoustics Laboratory, Massachusetts Institute of Technology.*

Hayes, J. R. (1966). Memory, goals, and problem solving. In B. Kleinmuntz (Ed.), *Problem solving: Research, method, and theory.* New York: Wiley.

Hayes, J. R., & Simon, H. A. (1977). Psychological differences among problem isomorphs. In N. J. Castellan, D. B. Pisoni, & G. R. Potts (Eds.), *Cognitive theory* (Vol. 2). Hillsdale, NJ: Erlbaum.

Hayes-Roth, B., & Hayes-Roth, F. (1977). Concept learning and the recognition and classification of examples. *Journal of Verbal Learning and Verbal Behavior, 16,* 321–338.

Haygood, R. C., & Bourne, L. E., Jr. (1965). Attribute and rule learning aspects of conceptual behavior. *Psychological Review, 72,* 175–195.

Healy, A. F. (1980). Proofreading errors on the word "The": New evidence on reading units. *Journal of Experimental Psychology: Human Perception and Performance, 6,* 45–57.

Hegarty, M. (1992). Mental animation: Inferring motion from static displays of mechanical systems. *Journal of Experimental Psychology: Learning, Memory, and Cognition, 18,* 1084–1102.

Hegarty, M. (2004). Mechanical reasoning by mental simulation. *TRENDS in the Cognitive Sciences, 8,* 280–285.

Heidbreder, E. (1961). *Seven psychologies.* New York: Appleton-Century-Crofts.

Hertel, P. T., Anooshian, L. J., & Ashbrook, P. (1986). The accuracy of beliefs about retrieval cues. *Memory & Cognition, 14,* 265–269.

Hesslow, G. (2002). Conscious thought as simulation of behavior and perception. *TRENDS in Cognitive Sciences, 6,* 242–247.

Hirshberg, J. (1998). *The creative priority.* New York: HarperCollins.

Hoffman, D. D. (1998). *Visual intelligence.* New York: Norton.

Hoffman, R. R., & Deffenbacher, K. A. (1992). A brief history of applied cognitive psychology. *Applied Cognitive Psychology, 6,* 1–48.

Hogan, J. P. (1997). *Mind matters: Exploring the world of artificial intelligence.* New York: Random House.

Hogarth, R. M. (2001). *Educating intuition.* Chicago: University of Chicago Press.

Holley, C. D., & Dansereau, D. F. (1984). Networking: The technique and the empirical evidence. In C. D. Holley & D. F. Dansereau (Eds.), *Spatial learning strategies.* New York: Academic Press.

Holley, C. D., Dansereau, D. F., McDonald, B. A., Garland, J. C., & Collins, K. W. (1979). Evaluation of a hierarchical mapping technique as an aid to prose processing. *Contemporary Educational Psychology, 4,* 227–237.

Holst, V. F., & Pezdek, K. (1992). Scripts for typical crimes and their effects on memory for eyewitness testimony. *Applied Cognitive Psychology, 6,* 573–587.

Holyoak, K. J. (2005). Analogy. In K. J. Holyoak & R. G. Morrison (Eds.), *The Cambridge handbook of thinking and reasoning* (pp. 117–142). New York: Cambridge University Press.

Holyoak, K. J., & Morrison, R. G. (Eds.) (2005). *The Cambridge handbook of thinking and reasoning.* New York: Cambridge University Press.

Holyoak, K. J., & Thagard, P. (1989). Analogical mapping by constraint satisfaction. *Cognitive Science, 13,* 295–355.

Horton, W. S., & Rapp, D. N. (2003). Out of sight, out of mind: Occlusion and the accessibility of information in narrative comprehension. *Psychonomic Bulletin & Review, 10,* 104–110.

Hostetter, A. B., & Alibali, M. W. (2008). Visible embodiment: Gestures as simulated action. *Psychonomic Bulletin & Review, 15,* 495–514.

Hubel, D. H., & Wiesel, T. N. (1962). Receptive fields, binocular interaction, and functional architecture in the cat's visual cortex. *Journal of Physiology, 160,* 106–154.

Hubel, D. H., & Wiesel, T. N. (1963). Receptive fields of cells in the striate cortex of very young visually inexperienced kittens. *Journal of Neurophysiology, 26,* 994–1002.

Huber, D. E. (2008). Immediate priming and cognitive after effects. *Journal of Experimental Psychology: General, 137,* 324–347.

Huber, D. E., & O'Reilly, R. C. (2003). Persistence and accommodation in short-term priming and other perceptual paradigms: Temporal segregation through synaptic depression. *Cognitive Science: A Multidisciplinary Journal, 27,* 403–430.

Huber, D. E., Tian, X., Curran, T., O'Reilly, R. C., & Woroch, B. (2008). The dynamics of integration and separation: ERP, MEG, and neural network studies of immediate repetition effects. *Journal of Experimental Psychology: Human Perception and Performance, 34,* 1389–1436.

Hugenberg, K., Miller, J., & Claypool, H. M. (2007). Categorization and individuation in the cross-race recognition deficit: Toward a solution to an insidious problem. *Journal of Experimental Social Psychology, 43,* 334–340.

Hummel, J. E., & Holyoak, K. J. (1997). Distributed representations of structure: A theory of analogical access and mapping. *Psychological Review, 104,* 427–466.

Humphreys, M. S., & Bain, J. D. (1983). Recognition memory: A cue and information analysis. *Memory & Cognition, 11,* 583–600.

Humphreys, M. S., Bain, J. D., & Pike, R. (1989). Different ways to cue a coherent memory system: A theory for episodic, semantic, and procedural tasks. *Psychological Review, 96,* 208–233.

Hunt, E., Pellegrino, J. W., & Yee, P. L. (1989). Individual differences in attention. In G. H. Bower (Ed.), *The psychology of learning and motivation* (Vol. 24, pp. 285–310). Orlando, FL: Academic Press.

Hunt, R. R., & Elliott, J. M. (1980). The role of nonsemantic information in memory: Orthographic distinctiveness effects on retention. *Journal of Experimental Psychology: General, 109,* 49–74.

Hutchison, K. A. (2003). Is semantic priming due to association strength or feature overlap? A microanalytic review. *Psychonomic Bulletin & Review, 10,* 785–813.

Hyde, T. S., & Jenkins, J. J. (1969). The differential effects of incidental tasks on the organization of recall of a list of highly associated words. *Journal of Experimental Psychology, 82,* 472–481.

Hyman, I. E., & Pentland, J. (1996). The role of mental imagery in the creation of false childhood memories. *Journal of Memory and Language, 35,* 101–117.

Intons-Peterson, M. J. (1983). Imagery paradigms: How vulnerable are they to experimenter's expectations? *Journal of Experimental Psychology: Human Perception and Performance, 9,* 394–412.

Intons-Peterson, M. J., & Best, D. L. (Eds.) (1998). *Memory distortions and their prevention.* Mahwah, NJ: Erlbaum.

Jacoby, L. L., & Dallas, M. (1981). On the relationship between autobiographical memory and perceptual learning. *Journal of Experimental Psychology: General, 110,* 306–340.

Jahn, G. (2004). Three turtles in danger: Spontaneous construction of causally relevant spatial situation models. *Journal of Experimental Psychology: Learning, Memory, & Cognition, 30,* 969–987.

James, L. E., & Burke, D. M. (2000). Phonological priming effects on word retrieval and tip-of-tongue experiences in young and older adults. *Journal of Experimental Psychology: Learning, Memory, and Cognition, 26,* 1378–1391.

James, W. (1890). *The principles of psychology* (2 vols.). New York: Holt.

Johnson, M. K. (1983). A multiple-entry, modular memory system. In G. H. Bower (Ed.), *The psychology of learning and motivation* (Vol. 17). Orlando, FL: Academic Press.

Johnson, M. K., & Raye, C. L. (1981). Reality monitoring. *Psychological Review, 88,* 67–85.

Johnson, M. K., Hashtroudi, S., & Lindsay, D. H. (1993). Source monitoring. *Psychological Bulletin, 114,* 3–28.

Johnson, M. K., Raye, C. L., Wang, A. Y., & Taylor, T. T. (1979). Fact and fantasy: The roles of accuracy and variability in confusing imaginations with perceptual experiences. *Journal of Experimental Psychology: Human Learning and Memory, 5,* 229–240.

Johnson, S. (1967). Hierarchical clustering schemes. *Psychometrika, 32,* 241–254.

Johnson-Laird, P. N. (1989). Analogy and the exercise of creativity. In S. Vosniadou & A. Ortony (Eds.), *Similarity and analogical reasoning.* Cambridge, England: Cambridge University Press.

Johnson-Laird, P. N., Legrenzi, P., & Legrenzi, M. S. (1972). Reasoning and a sense of reality. *British Journal of Psychology, 63,* 395–400.

Johnston, W. A., & Dark, V. J. (1986). Selective attention. *Annual Review of Psychology, 37,* 43–75.

Johnston, W. A., & Heinz, S. P. (1978). Flexibility and capacity demands of attention. *Journal of Experimental Psychology: General, 107,* 420–435.

Jonides, J. (1995). Working memory and thinking. In E. E. Smith & D. N. Osherson (Eds.), *An invitation to cognitive science* (Vol. 3, pp. 215–264). Cambridge, MA: MIT Press.

Just, M. A., & Carpenter, P. A. (1980). A theory of reading: From eye fixations to comprehension. *Psychological Review, 87,* 329–354.

Just, M. A., & Carpenter, P. A. (1987). *The psychology of reading and language comprehension.* Newton, MA: Allyn & Bacon.

Kahn, U., & Dhar, R. (2006). The licensing effect in consumer choice. *Journal of Marketing Research, 43,* 259–266.

Kahneman, D. (1973). *Attention and effort.* Englewood Cliffs, NJ: Prentice-Hall.

Kahneman, D. (2003). Experiences of collaborative research. *American Psychologist, 58,* 723–730.

Kahneman, D., & Tversky, A. (1972). Subjective probability: A judgment of representativeness. *Cognitive Psychology, 3,* 430–454.

Kahneman, D., & Tversky, A. (1973). On the psychology of prediction. *Psychological Review, 80,* 237–251.

Kahneman, D., & Tversky, A. (1979). Prospect theory: An analysis of decisions under risk. *Econometrica, 47,* 263–291.

Kahneman, D., & Tversky, A. (1984). Choices, values, and frames. *American Psychologist, 39,* 341–350.

Kahneman, D., Ben-Ishai, R., & Lotan, M. (1973). Relation of a test of attention to road accidents. *Journal of Applied Psychology, 58,* 113–115.

Kalat, J. W. (2004). *Biological Psychology* (8th ed.). Belmont, CA: Wadsworth.

Kane, M. J., Hambrick, D. Z., Tuholski, S. W., Wilhelm, O., Payne, T. W., & Engle, R. W. (2004). The generality of working memory capacity: A latent-variable approach to verbal and visuospatial memory span and reasoning. *Journal of Experimental Psychology: General, 133,* 189–217.

Kanizsa, G. (1979). *Organization in vision: Essays on Gestalt perception.* New York: Praeger.

Kassin, S. M., Tubb, V. A., Hosch, H. M., & Memon, A. (2001). On the "general acceptance" of eyewitness testimony research. *American Psychologist, 56,* 405–416.

Kaufman, J. C., & Baer, J. (Eds.) (2005). *Creativity across domains: faces of the muse.* Mahwah, NJ: Erlbaum.

Keenan, J. M., MacWhinney, B., & Mayhew, D. (1977). Pragmatics in memory: A study of natural conversation. *Journal of Verbal Learning and Verbal Behavior, 16,* 549–560.

Keil, F. C. (2006). Explanation and understanding. *Annual Review of Psychology, 57,* 227–254.

Keil, F. C., & Batterman, N. (1984). A characteristicto- defining shift in the development of word meaning. *Journal of Verbal Learning and Verbal Behavior, 23,* 221–226.

Keppel, G., & Underwood, B. (1962). Proactive inhibition in short-term retention of single items. *Journal of Verbal Learning and Verbal Behavior, 1,* 153–161.

Kieras, D. E. (1978). Good and bad structure in simple paragraphs: Effects on apparent theme, reading time, and recall. *Journal of Verbal Learning and Verbal Behavior, 17,* 13–28.

Kintsch, W. (1979). On modeling comprehension. *Educational Psychologist, 14,* 3–14.

Kintsch, W. (1988). The use of knowledge in discourse processing: A construction-integration model. *Psychological Review, 95,* 163–182.

Kintsch, W. (1994). Text comprehension, memory, and learning. *American Psychologist, 49,* 294–303.

Kintsch, W. (1998). *Comprehension: A paradigm for cognition.* Cambridge, England: Cambridge University Press.

Kintsch, W. (2005). An overview of top-down and bottom-up effects in comprehension: The CI perspective. *Discourse Processes, 39,* 125–128.

Kintsch, W., & Van Dijk, T. A. (1978). Toward a model of text comprehension and production. *Psychological Review, 85,* 363–394.

Kintsch, W., & Vipond, D. (1979). Reading comprehension and readability in educational practice and psychological theory. In L. G. Nilsson (Ed.), *Perspectives on memory research.* Hillsdale, NJ: Erlbaum.

Klapp, S. T., Marshburn, E. A., & Lester, P. T. (1983). Short-term memory does not involve the "working memory" of information processing: The demise of a common assumption.

Journal of Experimental Psychology: General, 112, 204–264.

Kleiman, G. M. (1975). Speech recoding in reading. *Journal of Verbal Learning and Verbal Behavior, 14,* 323–339.

Klein, G. (1998). *Sources of power: How people make decisions.* Cambridge, MA: The MIT Press.

Klein, G. A. (1993). A recognition-primed (RPD) model of rapid decision making. In G. A. Klein, J. Orasanu, R. Calderwood, & C. E. Zsambok (Eds.), *Decision making in action: Models and methods.* Norwood, NJ: Ablex.

Klein, G. A., Orasanu, J., Calderwood, R., & Zsambok, C. E. (Eds.). (1993). *Decision making in action: Models and methods.* Norwood, NJ: Ablex.

Klein, S. B., Cosmides, L., Tooby, J., & Chance, S. (2002). Decisions and the evolution of memory: Multiple systems, multiple functions. *Psychological Review, 109,* 306–329.

Kleinmuntz, B. (1990). Why we still use our heads instead of formulas: Toward an integrative approach. *Psychological Bulletin, 107,* 296–310.

Knoblich, G., Ohlsson, S., Haider, H., & Rhenius, D. (1999). Constraint relaxation and chunk decomposition in insight problem solving. *Journal of Experimental Psychology: Learning, Memory and Cognition, 25,* 1534–1555.

Knowlton, B. J., & Foerde, K. (2008). Neural representations of nondeclarative memories. *Current Directions in Psychological Science, 17,* 107–111.

Kohler, W. (1925). *The mentality of apes.* New York: Harcourt.

Kopfermann, H. (1930). Psychologische Untersuchunen uber die Wirkung zweidimensionaler Darstellungen Korperlicher Gehilde. *Psychologische Forschung, 13,* 293–364.

Koriat, A., Bjork, R. A., Sheffer, L., & Bar, S. K. (2004). Predicting one's own forgetting: The role of experience-based and theory-based processes. *Journal of Experimental Psychology: General, 133,* 643–656.

Koriat, A., Goldsmith, M., & Pansky, A. (2000). Toward a psychology of memory accuracy. *Annual Review of Psychology, 51,* 481–537.

Kornell, N., & Bjork, R. A. (2007). The promise and perils of self-regulated study. *Psychonomic Bulletin & Review, 14,* 219–224.

Kosslyn, S. M. (1975). Information representation in visual images. *Cognitive Psychology, 7,* 341–370.

Kosslyn, S. M. (1983). *Ghosts in the mind's machine: Creating and using images in the brain.* New York: Norton.

Kosslyn, S. M. (1994). *Image and brain: The resolution of the imagery debate.* Cambridge, MA: MIT Press.

Kosslyn, S. M. (2005). Reflective thinking and mental imagery: A perspective on the development of posttraumatic stress disorder. *Development and Psychopathology, 17,* 851–863.

Kosslyn, S. M., & Pomerantz, J. R. (1977). Imagery, propositions, and the form of internal representations. *Cognitive Psychology, 9,* 52–76.

Kosslyn, S. M., Ball, T. M., & Reiser, B. J. (1978). Visual images preserve metric spatial information: Evidence from studies of image scanning. *Journal of Experimental Psychology: Human Perception and Performance, 4,* 47–60.

Kosslyn, S. M., Thompson, W. L., & Ganis, G. (2006). *The case for mental imagery.* New York: Oxford University Press.

Kounios, J., & Holcomb, P. J. (1994). Concreteness effects in semantic processing: ERP evidence supporting dual-coding theory. *Journal of Experimental Psychology: Learning, Memory, and Cognition, 20,* 804–823.

Kroll, N. E. A., Schepeler, E. M., & Angin, K. T. (1986). Bizarre imagery: The misremembered mnemonic. *Journal of Experimental Psychology: Learning, Memory, and Cognition, 12,* 42–53.

Kuhl, P. K. (1991). Human adults and human infants show a "perceptual magnet effect" for the prototypes of speech categories, monkeys do not. *Perception & Psychophysics, 50,* 93–107.

Kuhl, P. K. (1993). Infant speech perception: A window on psycholinguistic development. *International Journal of Psycholinguistics, 9,* 33–56.

Kuhl, P. K., Williams, K. A., Lacerda, F., Stevens, K. N., & Lindblom, B. (1992). Linguistic experience alters phonetic perception in infants by 6 months of age. *Science, 225,* 606–608.

Kuhn, D. (1989). Children and adults as intuitive scientists. *Psychological Review, 96,* 674–689.

Kvavilashvili, L. K., & Mandler, G. (2004). Out on one's mind: A study of involuntary semantic memories. *Cognitive Psychology, 48,* 47–94.

LaBerge, D. L. (1990). Attention. *Psychological Science, 1,* 156–162.

LaBerge, D. L., & Samuels, S. J. (1974). Toward a theory of automatic information processing in reading. *Cognitive Psychology, 6,* 292–323.

Lachter, J., Forster, K. I., & Ruthruff, E. (2004). Forty-five years after Broadbent (1958): Still no identification without attention. *Psychological Review, 111,* 880–913.

Larkin, J. H., McDermott, J., Simon, D. P., & Simon, H. A. (1980). Expert and novice performance in solving physics problems. *Science, 208,* 1335–1342.

Lasnik, H. (2002). The minimalist program in syntax. *TRENDS in Cognitive Sciences, 6,* 432–437.

Laughery, K. R. (1969). Computer simulation of shortterm memory: A component decay model. In G. H. Bower & J. T. Spence (Eds.), *The psychology of learning and motivation* (Vol. 3). Orlando, FL: Academic Press.

LeBoeuf, R. A., & Shafir, E. B. (2005). Decision making. In K. J. Holyoak & R. G. Morrison (Eds.), *The Cambridge handbook of thinking and reasoning* (pp. 243–266). New York: Cambridge University Press.

Lesgold, A. M., Roth, S. F., & Curtis, M. E. (1979). Foregrounding effects in discourse comprehension. *Journal of Verbal Learning and Verbal Behavior, 18,* 291–308.

Levin, D. T. (Ed.). (2004). *Thinking and seeing: Visual metacognition in adults and children.* Cambridge, MA: MIT Press.

Levine, D. N., Warach, J., & Farah, M. J. (1985). Two visual systems in mental imagery: Dissociation of "what" and "where" in imagery disorders due to bilateral posterior cerebral lesions. *Neurology, 35,* 1010–1018.

Levine, M. (1966). Hypothesis behavior by humans during discrimination learning. *Journal of Experimental Psychology, 71,* 331–338.

Levy, B. A. (1978). Speech processing during reading. In A. M. Lesgold, J. W. Pellegrino, S. D. Fokkema, & R. Glaser (Eds.), *Cognitive psychology and instruction.* New York: Plenum.

Lindsay, D. S., & Read, J. D. (1994). Psychotherapy and memories of childhood sexual abuse: A cognitive perspective. *Applied Cognitive Psychology, 8,* 281–338.

Loftus, E. F. (1975). Leading questions and the eyewitness report. *Cognitive Psychology, 7,* 560–572.

Loftus, E. F. (1993). The reality of repressed memories. *American Psychologist, 48,* 518–537.

Loftus, E. F. (1997). Memory for a past that never was. *Current Directions in Psychological Science,* 60–65.

Loftus, G. R., Shimamura, A. P., & Johnson, C. A. (1985). How much is an icon worth? *Journal of Experimental Psychology: Human Perception and Performance, 11,* 1–13.

Long, D. L., & Lea, R. B. (2005). Have we been searching for meaning in all the wrong places? Defining the "search after meaning" principle in comprehension. *Discourse Processes, 39,* 279–298.

Long, G. M., & Toppino, T. C. (2004). Enduring interest in perceptual ambiguity: Alternating views of reversible figures. *Psychological Bulletin, 130,* 748–768.

Lorayne, H., & Lucas, J. (1974). *The memory book.* New York: Ballantine.

Lowenstein, G., & Issacharoff, S. (1994). Source dependence in the valuation of objects. *Journal of Behavioral Decision Making, 7,* 157–168.

Luchins, A. S. (1942). Mechanization in problem solving. *Psychological Monographs, 54* (Whole No. 248).

Lundeberg, M. A., & Fox, P. W. (1991). Do laboratory findings on test expectancy generalize to classroom outcomes? *Review of Educational Research, 61,* 94–106.

Lupyan, G. (2008). From chair to "chair": A representational shift account of object labeling effects on memory. *Journal of Experimental Psychology: General, 137,* 348–369.

Lutz, K. A., & Lutz, R. J. (1977). Effects of interactive imagery on learning: Applications to advertising. *Journal of Applied Psychology, 62,* 493–498.

Lyons, J. (1970). *Chomsky.* London: Collins.

MacDonald, M. C., Pearlmutter, N. J., & Seidenberg, M. S. (1994). Syntactic ambiguity resolution as lexical ambiguity resolution. In C. Clifton, K. Rayner, & L. Frazier (Eds.), *Perspectives in sentence processing* (pp. 123–153). Mahwah, NJ: Erlbaum.

MacKay, D. G. (1966). To end ambiguous sentences. *Perception & Psychophysics, 1,* 426–435.

Malpass, R. S., & Devine, P. G. (1981). Guided memory in eyewitness identification. *Journal of Applied Psychology, 66,* 343–350.

Malt, B. C. (1990). Features and beliefs in the mental representation of categories. *Journal of Memory and Language, 29,* 289–315.

Malt, B. C. (1994). Water is not H2O. *Cognitive Psychology, 27,* 41–70.

Mandler, G. (1967). Organization and memory. In K. W. Spence & J. T. Spence (Eds.), *The psychology of learning and motivation* (Vol. 1). Orlando, FL: Academic Press.

Mandler, G. (1980). Recognizing: The judgment of previous occurrence. *Psychological Review, 87,* 252–271.

Mandler, J. M., & Bauer, P. J. (1988). The cradle of categorization: Is the basic level basic? *Cognitive Development, 3,* 247–264.

Markman, A. B., & Dietrich, E. (2000). Extending the classical view of representation. *TRENDS in Cognitive Sciences, 4,* 470–475.

Markman, A. B., & Gentner, D. (2001). Thinking. *Annual Review of Psychology, 52,* 223–247.

Marschark, M., & Hunt, R. R. (1989). A reexamination of the role of imagery in learning and memory. *Journal of Experimental Psychology: Learning, Memory, and Cognition, 15,* 710–720.

Marsh, R. L., & Bower, G. H. (1993). Eliciting cryptomnesia: Unconscious plagiarism in a puzzle task. *Journal of Experimental Psychology: Learning, Memory, and Cognition, 19,* 673–688.

Marsh, R. L., Landau, J. D., & Hicks, J. L. (1996). How examples may (and may not) constrain creativity. *Memory & Cognition, 24,* 669–680.

Martindale, C. (1991). *Cognitive psychology: A neural network approach.* Belmont, CA: Wadsworth.

Massaro, D. W., & Cohen, M. M. (1991). Integration versus interactive activation: The joint influence of stimulus and context in perception. *Cognitive Psychology, 23,* 558–614.

Massaro, D. W., & Cowan, N. (1993). Information processing models: Microscopes of the mind. *Annual Review of Psychology, 44,* 383–425.

Mauro, R., & Kubovy, M. (1992). Caricature and face recognition. *Memory & Cognition, 20,* 433–440.

Mazzoni, G., & Nelson, T. O. (Eds.). (1998). *Metacognition and cognitive neuropsychology.* Mahwah, NJ: Erlbaum.

McClelland, J. L., & Rogers, T. T. (2003). The parallel distributed processing approach to semantic cognition. *Nature Reviews Neuroscience, 4,* 310–322.

McClelland, J. L., & Rumelhart, D. E. (1981). An interactive-activation model of context effects in letter perception: Part 1. An account of basic findings. *Psychological Review, 88,* 375–407.

McClelland, J. L., Rumelhart, D. E., & The PDP Research Group. (1986). *Parallel distributed processing: Explorations in the microstructure of cognition.* Cambridge, MA: MIT Press.

McCloskey, M. (1991). Networks and theories: The place of connectionism in cognitive science. *Psychological Science, 2,* 287–295.

McCloskey, M., & Glucksberg, S. (1979). Decision processes in verifying category membership statements: Implications for models of semantic memory. *Cognitive Psychology, 11,* 1–37.

McDaniel, M. A. (2007). Applying cognitive psychology to education. *Psychonomic Bulletin & Review, 14,* 185–186.

McDaniel, M. A., & Einstein, G. O. (1986). Bizarre imagery as an effective memory aid: The importance of distinctiveness. *Journal of Experimental Psychology: Learning, Memory, and Cognition, 12,* 54–65.

McKenzie, C. R. M. (2003). Rational models as theories – not standards – of behavior. *TRENDS in Cognitive Sciences, 7,* 403–406.

McKone, E., Kanwisher, N., & Duchaine, B. C. (2007). Can generic expertise explain special processing for faces? *TRENDS in the Cognitive Sciences, 11,* 8–15.

McKoon, G., & Ratcliff, R. (1990). Dimensions of inference. In A. C. Graesser & G. H. Bower (Eds.), *Inferences and text comprehension.* San Diego: Academic Press.

McKoon, G., & Ratcliff, R. (1992). Inference during reading. *Psychological Review, 99,* 440–466.

McKoon, G., & Ratcliff, R. (1998). Memory-based language processing: Psycholinguistic research in the 1990s. *Annual Review of Psychology, 49,* 25–42.

McKoon, G., Ratcliff, R., & Dell, G. S. (1986). A critical evaluation of the semantic-episodic distinction. *Journal of Experimental Psychology: Learning, Memory, and Cognition, 12,* 295–306.

McNamara, D. S. (Ed.) (2007). *Reading comprehension strategies: Theories, interventions, and technologies.* New York: Taylor & Francis.

McNamara, D. S., & Healy, A. F. (2000). A procedural explanation of the generation effect for simple and difficult multiplication problems and answers. *Journal of Memory and Language, 43,* 652–679.

McNamara, T. P. (1992). Priming and constraints it places on theories of memory and retrieval. *Psychological Review, 99,* 650–662.

McNamara, T. P., & Miller, D. L. (1989). Attributes of theories of meaning. *Psychological Bulletin, 106,* 355–376.

Medin, D. L. (1989). Concepts and conceptual structure. *American Psychologist, 44,* 1469–1481.

Medin, D. L., & Rips, L. J. (2005). Concepts and categories: memory, meaning, and metaphysics. In K. J. Holyoak & R. G. Morrison (Eds.), *The Cambridge handbook of thinking and reasoning* (pp. 37–72). New York: Cambridge University Press.

Medin, D. L., & Ross, B. H. (1992). *Cognitive psychology.* Orlando, FL: Harcourt Brace Jovanovich.

Medin, D. L., & Schaffer, M. M. (1978). Context theory of classification learning. *Psychological Review, 85,* 207–238.

Medin, D. L., Altom, M. W., Edelson, S. M., & Freko, D. (1982). Correlated symptoms and simulated medical classification. *Journal of Experimental Psychology: Learning, Memory, and Cognition, 8,* 37–50.

Medin, D. L., Lynch, E. B., & Solomon, K. O. (2000). Are there kinds of concepts? *Annual Review of Psychology, 51,* 121–147.

Mellers, B. A., Schwartz, A., & Cooke, A. D. J. (1998). Judgment and decision making. *Annual Review of Psychology, 49,* 447–477.

Metcalfe, J. (1986a). Feeling of knowing in memory and problem solving. *Journal of Experimental Psychology: Human Perception and Performance, 6,* 58–66.

Metcalfe, J. (1986b). Premonitions of insight predict impending error. *Journal of Experimental Psychology: Learning, Memory, and Cognition, 12,* 623–634.

Meyer, D. E., & Schvaneveldt, R. W. (1976). Meaning, memory structure, and mental processes. *Science, 192,* 27–33.

Mihal, W. L., & Barett, G. V. (1976). Individual differences in perceptual information processing and their relation to automobile accident involvement. *Journal of Applied Psychology, 61,* 229–233.

Milgram, S. (1970). The experience of living in cities. *Science, 167,* 1461–1468.

Milkman, K. L., Rogers, T., & Bazerman, M. H. (2008). Harnessing our inner angels and demons: What we have learned about want/should conflicts and how that knowledge can help us reduce short-sighted decision making. *Perspectives on Psychological Science, 3,* 324–338.

Miller, G. A. (1951). *Language and communication.* New York: McGraw-Hill.

Miller, G. A. (1956). The magical number seven, plus or minus two: Some limits on our capacity for processing information. *Psychological Review, 63,* 81–97.

Miller, G. A. (2003). The cognitive revolution: A historical perspective. *TRENDS in Cognitive Sciences, 7,* 141–144.

Miller, G. A., Galanter, E., & Pribram, K. (1960). *Plans and the structure of behavior.* New York: Holt, Rinehart & Winston.

Minda, J. P., & Smith, J. D. (2002). Comparing prototype-based and exemplar-based accounts of category learning and attentional allocation. *Journal of Experimental Psychology: Learning, Memory, & Cognition, 28,* 275–292.

Minsky, M. (1975). A framework for the representation of knowledge. In P. Winston (Ed.), *The psychology of computer vision.* New York: McGraw-Hill.

Mitchell, D. B., & Richman, C. L. (1980). Confirmed reservations: Mental travel. *Journal of Experimental Psychology: Human Perception and Performance, 6,* 58–66.

Miyake, A. (2001). Individual differences in working memory: Introduction to the special section. *Journal of Experimental Psychology: General, 130,* 163–168.

Miyake, A., Just, M. A., & Carpenter, P. A. (1994). Working memory constraints on the resolution of lexical ambiguity: Maintaining multiple interpretations in neutral contexts. *Journal of Memory and Language, 33,* 175–202.

Moray, N. (1959). Attention in dichotic listening: Affective cues and the influence of instructions. *Quarterly Journal of Experimental Psychology, 11,* 56–60.

Morris, P. E., Jones, S., & Hampson, P. (1978). An imagery mnemonic for the learning of people's names. *British Journal of Psychology, 69,* 335–336.

Moscovitch, M., & Craik, F. I. M. (1976). Depth of processing, retrieval cues, and uniqueness of encoding as factors in recall. *Journal of Verbal Learning and Verbal Behavior, 15,* 447–458.

Murphy, G. (2003). *The big book of concepts*. Cambridge, MA: MIT Press.

Murphy, G. L., & Medin, D. L. (1985). The role of theories in conceptual coherence. *Psychological Review, 92,* 289–316.

Musen, G., Shimamura, A. P., & Squire, L. R. (1990). Intact text-specific reading skill in amnesia. *Journal of Experimental Psychology: Learning, Memory, and Cognition, 6,* 1068–1076.

Myers, J. L., O'Brien, E. J., Balota, D. A., & Toyofuku, M. L. (1984). Memory search without interference: The role of integration. *Cognitive Psychology, 16,* 217–242.

Nairne, J. S. (2002). Remembering over the short-term: The case against the standard model. *Annual Review of Psychology, 53,* 53–81.

Nash-Webber, B. (1975). The role of semantics in automatic speech understanding. In D. G. Bobrow & A. Collins (Eds.), *Representation and understanding*. Orlando, FL: Academic Press.

Naveh-Benjamin, M. (1988). Recognition memory of spatial location information: Another failure to support automaticity. *Memory & Cognition, 16,* 437–445.

Nee, D. E., Berman, M. G., Moore, K. S., & Jonides, J. (2008). Neuroscientific evidence about the distinction between short- and long-term memory. *Current Directions in Psychological Science, 17,* 102–106.

Neely, J. H., & Keefe, D. E. (1989). Semantic context effects on visual word processing: A hybrid prospective-retrospective processing theory. In G. H. Bower (Ed.), *The psychology of learning and motivation* (Vol. 24). Orlando, FL: Academic Press.

Neisser, U. (1967). *Cognitive psychology*. New York: Appleton-Century-Crofts.

Nelson, T. O. (1977). Repetition and depth of processing. *Journal of Verbal Learning and Verbal Behavior, 16,* 151–171.

Nelson, T. O., & Narens, L. (1990). Metamemory: A theoretical framework and some new findings. In G. H. Bower (Ed.), *The psychology of learning and motivation* (Vol. 25). Orlando, FL: Academic Press.

Nelson, T. O., & Smith, E. E. (1972). Acquisition and forgetting of hierarchically organized information in long-term memory. *Journal of Experimental Psychology, 95,* 388–396.

Nelson, T. O., Dunlosky, J., Graf, A., & Narens, L. (1994). Utilization of metacognitive judgments in the allocation of study during multitrial learning. *Psychological Science, 5,* 207–213.

Newell, A., & Simon, H. A. (1972). *Human problem solving*. Englewood Cliffs, NJ: Prentice-Hall.

Newell, A., Shaw, J. C., & Simon, H. A. (1958a). Chess-playing problems and the problem of complexity. *IBM Journal of Research and Development, 2,* 320–335.

Newell, A., Shaw, J. C., & Simon, H. A. (1958b). Elements of a theory of human problem solving. *Psychological Review, 65,* 151–166.

Nickerson, R. S., & Adams, M. J. (1979). Long-term memory for a common object. *Cognitive Psychology, 11,* 287–307.

Nielsen, G. D., & Smith, E. E. (1973). Imaginal and verbal representations in short-term recognition of visual forms. *Journal of Experimental Psychology, 101,* 375–378.

Noice, H. (1991). The role of explanations and plan recognition in the learning of theatrical scripts. *Cognitive Science, 15,* 425–460.

Norman, D. A. (1968). Toward a theory of memory and attention. *Psychological Review, 75,* 522–536.

Nosofsky, R. M. (1991). Tests of an exemplar model for relating perceptual classification and recognition memory. *Journal of Experimental Psychology: Human Perception and Performance, 17,* 3–27.

Nosofsky, R. M., & Johansen, M. K. (2000). Exemplar based accounts of "multiple-system" phenomena in perceptual organization. *Psychological Bulletin & Review, 7,* 375–402.

Novick, L. R. (1990). Representational transfer in problem solving. *Psychological Science, 1,* 128–132.

Novick, L. R., & Bassok, M. (2005). Problem solving. In K. J. Holyoak & R. G. Morrison (Eds.), *The Cambridge handbook of thinking and reasoning* (pp. 321–350). New York: Cambridge University Press.

Novick, L. R., & Hmelo, C. E. (1994). Transferring symbolic representations across nonisomorphic problems. *Journal of Experimental Psychology: Learning, Memory, and Cognition, 20,* 1296–1321.

Novick, L. R., & Hurley, S. M. (2001). To matrix, network, or hierarchy: That is the question. *Cognitive Psychology, 42,* 158–216.

O'Donnell, A. M., Dansereau, D. G., & Hall, R. F. (2002). Knowledge maps as scaffolds for cognitive processing. *Educational Psychology Review, 14,* 71–86.

Olivers, C. N. L. (2007). The time course of attention: It is better than we thought. *Current Directions in Psychological Science, 16,* 11–15.

Orasanu, J., & Connolly, T. (1993). The reinvention of decision making. In G. A. Klein, J. Orasanu, R. Calderwood, & C. E. Zsambok (Eds.), *Decision making in action: Models and methods* (pp. 3–20). Norwood, NJ: Ablex.

O'Reilly, T., & McNamara, D. S. (2007). Reversing the reverse cohesion effect: good texts can be better for strategic, high-knowledge readers. *Discourse Processes, 43,* 121–152.

Osman, M. (2004). An evaluation of dual-process theories of reasoning. *Psychonomic Bulletin & Review, 11,* 988–1010.

Paivio, A. (1969). Mental imagery in associative learning and memory. *Psychological Review, 76,* 241–263.

Paivio, A. (1971). *Imagery and verbal processes*. New York: Holt, Rinehart & Winston.

Paivio, A. (1975). Coding distinctions and repetition effects in memory. In G. H. Bower (Ed.), *Psychology of learning and motivation* (Vol. 9). Orlando, FL: Academic Press.

Paivio, A. (2008). Looking at reading comprehension through the lens of neuroscience. In C. C. Block & S. R. Parris (Eds.), *Comprehension Instruction: Research-based best practices* (pp. 101–113). New York: Guilford Press.

Paivio, A., Smythe, P. E., & Yuille, J. C. (1968). Imagery versus meaningfulness of nouns in paired associate learning. *Canadian Journal of Psychology, 22,* 427–441.

Palermo, R., & Rhodes, G. (2007). Are you always on my mind? A review of how face perception and attention interact. *Neuropsychologia, 45,* 75–92.

Paquette, L., & Kida, T. (1988). Effect of decision strategy and task complexity on decision performance. *Organizational Behavior and Human Decision Processes, 41,* 128–142.

Pashler, H. (1994). Graded capacity-sharing in dual task interference? *Journal of Experimental Psychology: Human Perception and Performance, 20,* 1–13.

Pashler, H., Johnston, J. C., & Ruthruff, E. (2001). Attention and performance. *Annual Review of Psychology, 52,* 629–651.

Pashler, H., Rohrer, D., Cepeda, N. J., & Carpenter, S. K. (2007). Enhancing learning and retarding forgetting: Choices and consequences. *Psychonomic Bulletin & Review, 14*, 187–193.

Pashler, H. E. (1998). *The psychology of attention*. Cambridge, MA: MIT Press.

Payne, J. W. (1973). Alternative approaches to decision making under risk. *Psychological Bulletin, 80*, 439–453.

Payne, J. W. (1976). Task complexity and contingent processing in decision making: An information search and protocol analysis. *Organizational Behavior and Human Performance, 16*, 366–387.

Payne, J. W., Bettman, J. R., & Johnson, E. J. (1992). Behavioral decision research: A constructive processing perspective. *Annual Review of Psychology, 43*, 87–131.

Payne, J. W., Bettman, J. R., & Johnson, E. J. (1993). *The adaptive decision maker*. Cambridge, England: Cambridge University Press.

Pecher, D., Zeelenberg, R., & Barsalou, L. W. (2003). Verifying different-modality properties for concepts produces switching costs. *Psychological Science, 14*, 119–124.

Pellegrino, J. W., Chudowsky, N., & Glaser, R. (2001). *Knowing what students know*. Washington, DC: National Academy Press.

Pennington, N., & Hastie, R. (1988). Explanation based decision making: The effects of memory structure on judgment. *Journal of Experimental Psychology: Learning, Memory, and Cognition, 14*, 521–533.

Pennington, N., & Hastie, R. (1991). A cognitive theory of juror decision making: The story model. *Cardozo Law Review, 13*, 519–557.

Perfect, T. J., & Schwartz, B. L. (Eds.). (2002). *Applied metacognition*. Cambridge: Cambridge University Press.

Perfetti, C. A., Beverly, S., Bell, L., Rodgers, K., & Faux, R. (1987). Comprehending newspaper headlines. *Journal of Memory and Language, 26*, 692–713.

Perfetto, G. A., Bransford, J. D., & Franks, J. J. (1983). Constraints on access in a problem solving context. *Memory & Cognition, 11*, 24–31.

Peterson, L. R., & Peterson, M. J. (1959). Short-term retention of individual verbal items. *Journal of Experimental Psychology, 58*, 193–198.

Peterson, M. A., & Rhodes, G. (Eds.) (2003). *Perception of faces, objects, and scenes: Analytic and holistic processes*. Oxford: Oxford University Press.

Phelps, E. A., & Sharot, T. (2008). How (and why) emotion enhances the subjective sense of recollection. *Current Directions in Psychological Science, 17*, 147–152.

Phillips, W. A. (1974). On the distinction between sensory storage and short-term visual memory. *Perception & Psychophysics, 16*, 283–290.

Pickering, M. J., & Garrod, S. (2007). Do people use language production to make predictions during comprehension? *TRENDS in the Cognitive Sciences, 11*, 105–110.

Pinker, S. (1994). *The language instinct*. New York: William Morrow.

Pinker, S. (1997). *How the mind works*. New York: Norton.

Pinker, S. (1999). *Words and rules*. New York: Harper-Collins.

Plucker, J. A., Beghetto, R. A., & Dow, G. T. (2004). Why isn't creativity more important to educational psychologists? Potentials, pitfalls, and future directions for creativity research. *Educational Psychologist, 9*, 83–96.

Poeppel, D. & Monahan, P. J. (2008). Speech perception: cognitive foundations and cortical implementation. *Current Directions in Psychological Science, 17*, 80–85.

Pollatsek, A., & Rayner, K. (1989). Reading. In M. I. Posner (Ed.), *Foundations of cognitive science*. Cambridge, MA: MIT Press.

Pollatsek, A., Fisher, D. L., & Pradhan, A. (2006). Identifying and remedying failures of selective attention in younger drivers. *Current Directions in Psychological Science, 15*, 255–259.

Polson, P. G., & Jeffries, R. (1985). Instruction in general problem-solving skills: An analysis of four approaches. In J. W. Segal, S. F. Chipman, & R. Glaser (Eds.), *Thinking and learning skills* (Vol. 1). Hillsdale, NJ: Erlbaum.

Polya, G. (1962). *Mathematical discovery* (Vol. 1). New York: Wiley.

Posner, M. I. (Ed.). (1989). *Foundations of cognitive science*. Cambridge, MA: MIT Press.

Posner, M. I., & Keele, S. W. (1968). On the genesis of abstract ideas. *Journal of Experimental Psychology, 77*, 353–363.

Posner, M. I., & Rothbart, M. K. (1994). Constructing neuronal theories of the mind. In C. Koch & J. Davis (Eds.), *Large scale neuronal theories of the brain* (pp. 183–199). Cambridge, MA: MIT Press.

Posner, M. I., & Rothbart, M. K. (2005). Influencing brain networks: implications for education. *TRENDS in Cognitive Sciences, 9*, 99–103.

Posner, M. I., & Snyder, C. R. R. (1975). Attention and cognitive control. In R. L. Solso (Ed.), *Information processing and cognition: The Loyola Symposium* (pp. 58–85). Hillsdale, NJ: Erlbaum.

Postle, B. R. (2006). Working memory as an emergent property of the mind and brain. *Neuroscience, 139*, 23–38.

Postman, L., & Phillips, L. W. (1965). Short term temporal changes in free recall. *Quarterly Journal of Experimental Psychology, 17*, 132–138.

Pressley, M., Levin, J. R., Hall, J. W., Miller, G. E., & Berry, J. K. (1980). The key word method and foreign word acquisition. *Journal of Experimental Psychology: Human Learning and Memory, 6*, 163–173.

Pretz, J. E. (2008). Intuition versus analysis: Strategy and experience in complex everyday problem solving. *Memory & Cognition, 36*, 554–566.

Pylyshyn, Z. W. (1973). What the mind's eye tells the mind's brain: A critique of mental imagery. *Psychological Bulletin, 80*, 1–24.

Pylyshyn, Z. W. (1981). The imagery debate: Analogue media versus tacit knowledge. *Psychological Review, 88*, 16–45.

Pylyshyn, Z. (2003). Return of the mental image: Are there really pictures in the brain? *TRENDS in Cognitive Sciences, 7*, 113–118.

Radvansky, G. A., & Copeland, D. E. (2001). Working memory and situation model updating. *Memory & Cognition, 29*, 1073–1080.

Radvansky, G. A., & Zacks, R. T. (1991). Mental models and fact retrieval. *Journal of Experimental Psychology: Learning, Memory, and Cognition, 17*, 940–953.

Randel, J. M., Pugh, H. L., & Reed, S. K. (1996). Differences in expert and novice situation awareness in naturalistic decision making. *International Journal of Human-Computer Studies, 45*, 579–597.

Ratcliff, R., & McKoon, G. (1988). A retrieval theory of priming in memory. *Psychological Review, 95*, 385–408.

Raven, J. C. (1962). *Advanced progressive matrices, Set II*. London: H. K. Lewis. (Distributed in the United States by the Psychological Corporation, San Antonio, TX.)

Rayner, K., Foorman, B. R., Perfetti, C. A., Pesetsky, D., & Seidenberg, M. S. (2001). How psychological science informs the teaching of reading. *Psychological Science in the Public Interest, 2,* 31–74.

Read, J. D., & Bruce, D. (1982). Longitudinal tracking of difficult memory retrievals. *Cognitive Psychology, 14,* 280–300.

Redelmeier, D. A., & Tibshirani, R. J. (1997). Association between cellular-telephone calls and motor vehicle collisions. *The New England Journal of Medicine, 336,* 453–458.

Reder, L., & Kusbit, G. (1991). Locus of the Moses illusion: Imperfect encoding, retrieval, or match? *Journal of Memory and Language, 30,* 385–406.

Reder, L. M., & Anderson, J. R. (1980). Partial resolution of the paradox of interference: The role of integrating knowledge. *Cognitive Psychology, 12,* 447–472.

Reder, L. M., & Ross, B. H. (1983). Integrated knowledge in different tasks: The role of retrieval strategy on fan effects. *Journal of Experimental Psychology: Learning, Memory, and Cognition, 9,* 55–72.

Reed, S. K. (1972). Pattern recognition and categorization. *Cognitive Psychology, 3,* 382–407.

Reed, S. K. (2005). From research to practice and back: The Animation Tutor project. *Educational Psychology Review, 17,* 55–82.

Reed, S. K. (in press). *Thinking Visually.* New York: Taylor & Francis.

Reed, S. K., & Friedman, M. P. (1973). Perceptual vs. conceptual categorization. *Memory & Cognition, 1,* 157–163.

Reed, S. K., & Johnsen, J. A. (1975). Detection of parts in patterns and images. *Memory & Cognition, 3,* 569–575.

Reed, S. K., Hock, H., & Lockhead, G. R. (1983). Tacit knowledge and the effect of pattern configuration on mental scanning. *Memory & Cognition, 11,* 137–143.

Reed, S. K. (1993). A schema-based theory of transfer. In D. K. Detterman & R. J. Sternberg (Eds.), *Transfer on trial: Intelligence, cognition and instruction.* Norwood, NJ: Ablex.

Reeves, L. M., & Weisberg, R. W. (1994). The role of content and abstract information in analogical transfer. *Psychological Bulletin, 115,* 381–400.

Rehder, B., & Ross, B. H. (2001). Abstract coherent categories. *Journal of Experimental Psychology: Learning, Memory, and Cognition, 27,* 1261–1275.

Reicher, G. M. (1969). Perceptual recognition as a function of meaningfulness of stimulus material. *Journal of Experimental Psychology, 81,* 275–280.

Reitman, J. S. (1974). Without surreptitious rehearsal, information in short-term memory decays. *Journal of Verbal Learning and Verbal Behavior, 13,* 365–377.

Reitman, J. S., & Bower, G. H. (1973). Storage and later recognition of exemplars of concepts. *Cognitive Psychology, 4,* 194–206.

Rhodes, G., Brennan, S., & Carey, S. (1987). Identification and ratings of caricatures: Implications for mental representations of faces. *Cognitive Psychology, 19,* 473–497.

Richardson-Klavehn, A., & Bjork, R. A. (1988). Measures of memory. *Annual Review of Psychology, 39,* 475–543.

Rips, L. J. (2001). Necessity and natural categories. *Psychological Bulletin, 127,* 827–852.

Ritter, S., Anderson, J. R., Koedinger, K. K., & Corbett, A. (2007). Cognitive Tutor: Applied research to mathematics education. *Psychonomic Bulletin & Review, 14,* 249–255.

Robertson, S. I. (2001). *Problem solving.* Hove, England: Psychology Press.

Robins, R. W., Gosling, S. D., & Craik, K. H. (1999). An empirical analysis of trends in psychology. *American Psychologist, 54,* 117–128.

Roediger, H. L. (1980). Memory metaphors in cognitive psychology. *Memory & Cognition, 8,* 231–246.

Roediger, H. L. (1990). Implicit memory: Retention without remembering. *American Psychologist, 45,* 1043–1056.

Roediger, H. L. (2008). Relativity of remembering: Why the laws of memory vanished. *Annual Review of Psychology, 59,* 225–254.

Rogers, T. T., & Patterson, K. (2007). Object categorization: Reversals and explanations of the basic-level advantage. *Journal of Experimental Psychology: General, 136,* 451–469.

Rogers, T. T., & McClelland, J. L. (2004). *Semantic cognition: A parallel distributed processing approach.* Cambridge, MA: MIT Press.

Roland, P. E., & Friberg, L. (1985). Localization of cortical areas activated by thinking. *Journal of Neurophysiology, 53,* 1219–1243.

Rosch, E. (1973). Natural categories. *Cognitive Psychology, 4,* 328–350.

Rosch, E. (1975). Cognitive representations of semantic categories. *Journal of Experimental Psychology: General, 3,* 192–233.

Rosch, E., & Mervis, C. B. (1975). Family resemblances: Studies in the internal structure of categories. *Cognitive Psychology, 7,* 573–605.

Rosch, E., Mervis, C. B., Gray, W. D., Johnsen, D. M., & Boyes-Braem, P. (1976). Basic objects in natural categories. *Cognitive Psychology, 8,* 382–440.

Roskos-Ewoldsen, B., Intons-Peterson, M. J., & Anderson, R. E. (1993). *Imagery, creativity, and discovery.* Amsterdam: North Holland.

Ross, B. H. (1984). Remindings and their effects in learning a cognitive skill. *Cognitive Psychology, 16,* 371–416.

Ross, B. H. (1996). Category learning as problem solving. In D. L. Medin (Ed.), *The psychology of learning and motivation* (Vol. 35, pp. 165–192). San Diego: Academic Press.

Ross, B. H., & Kennedy, P. T. (1990). Generalizing from the use of earlier examples in problem solving. *Journal of Experimental Psychology: Learning, Memory, and Cognition, 16,* 42–55.

Rubin, D. C. (Ed.). (1996). *Remembering our past.* Cambridge, England: Cambridge University Press.

Rubin, D. C. (2006). The basic-systems model of episodic memory. *Perspectives in Psychological Science, 1,* 277–311.

Ruddell, R. B., & Unrau, N. J. (Eds.) (2004). *Theoretical models and processes of reading* (5th ed.). Newark, DE: International Reading Association.

Rumelhart, D. E. (1970). A multicomponent theory of perception of briefly exposed stimulus displays. *Journal of Mathematical Psychology, 7,* 191–218.

Rumelhart, D. E. (1977). Toward an interactive model of reading. In S. Dornic (Ed.), *Attention and performance* (Vol. 6). Hillsdale, NJ: Erlbaum.

Rumelhart, D. E. (1980). Schemata: The building blocks of cognition. In R. Spiro, B. Bruce, & W. Brewer (Eds.), *Theoretical issues in reading comprehension.* Hillsdale, NJ: Erlbaum.

Rumelhart, D. E., & McClelland, J. L. (1982). An interactive-activation model of context effects in letter perception: Part 2. The contextual enhancement and some tests and extensions of the model. *Psychological Review, 89,* 60–94.

Rumelhart, D. E., Hinton, G. E., & McClelland, J. L. (1986). A general framework for parallel distributed processing. In D. E. Rumelhart, J. L. McClelland, & the PDP Research Group (Eds.), *Parallel distributed processing: Explorations in the microstructure of cognition* (Vol. 1). Cambridge, MA: Bradford.

Runco, M. A. (2004). Creativity. *Annual Review of Psychology, 55,* 657–687.

Rundus, D. (1971). Analysis of rehearsal processes in free recall. *Journal of Experimental Psychology, 89,* 63–77.

Saariluoma, P. (1992). Visuospatial and articulatory interference in chess players' information intake. *Applied Cognitive Psychology, 6,* 77–89.

Sachs, J. S. (1967). Recognition memory for syntactic and semantic aspects of connected discourse. *Perception & Psychophysics, 2,* 437–442.

Sack, A. T., van de Ven, V. G., Etschenberg, S., & Linden, D. E. (2005). Enhanced vividness of imagery as a trait marker of schizophrenia. *Schizophrenia Bulletin, 31,* 1–8.

Sadoski, M. (2008). Dual coding theory: Reading comprehension and beyond. In C. C. Block & S. R. Parris (Eds.), *Comprehension Instruction: Research-based best practices* (pp. 38–49). New York: Guilford Press.

Sanders, A. F., & Schroots, J. J. F. (1969). Cognitive categories and memory span: III. Effects of similarity on recall. *Quarterly Journal of Experimental Psychology, 21,* 21–28.

Sawyer, R. K. (2006). *Explaining creativity: The science of human innovation.* New York: Oxford University Press.

Schacter, D. L. (1987). Implicit memory: History and current status. *Journal of Experimental Psychology: Learning, Memory, and Cognition, 13,* 501–518.

Schacter, D. L. (1989). Memory. In M. I. Posner (Ed.), *Foundations of cognitive science* (pp. 683–725). Cambridge, MA: MIT Press.

Schacter, D. L. (Ed.). (1995). *Memory distortion.* Cambridge, MA: Harvard University Press.

Schacter, D. L. (1996). *Searching for memory: The brain, the mind, and the past.* New York: Basic Books.

Schacter, D. L. (2001). *The seven sins of memory.* Boston: Houghton Mifflin.

Schank, R., & Abelson, R. (1977). *Scripts, goals, and understanding.* Hillsdale, NJ: Erlbaum.

Schmidt, S. R. (1991). Can we have a distinctive theory of memory? *Memory & Cognition, 19,* 523–542.

Schneider, S. L., & Shanteau, J. (2003). *Emerging Perspectives on Judgment and Decision Research.* Cambridge: Cambridge University Press.

Schneider, W., & Graham, D. J. (1992). Introduction to connectionist modeling in education. *Educational Psychologist, 27,* 513–530.

Schneider, W., & Shiffrin, R. M. (1977). Controlled and automatic human information processing: I. Detection, search, and attention. *Psychological Review, 84,* 1–66.

Schneider, V. I., Healy, A. F., & Gesi, A. T. (1991). The role of phonetic processes in letter detection: A reevaluation. *Journal of Memory and Language, 30,* 294–318.

Scholl, B. (2001). Objects and attention: the state of the art. *Cognition, 80,* 1–46.

Schooler, J. W., Fallshore, M., & Fiore, S. M. (1994). Epilogue: Putting insight into perspective. In R. J. Sternberg & J. E. Davidson (Eds.), *The nature of insight* (pp. 559–587). London: Bradford.

Schwanenflugel, P. J., & Shoben, E. J. (1985). The influence of sentence constraint on the scope of facilitation for upcoming words. *Journal of Memory and Language, 24,* 232–252.

Schwartz, B. L. (2002). *Tip-of-the-tongue states: Phenomenology, mechanism, and lexical retrieval.* Mahwah, NJ: Erlbaum.

Schweickert, R., Guentert, L., & Hersberger, L. (1990). Phonological similarity, pronunciation rate, and memory span. *Psychological Science, 1,* 74–77.

Sedlmeier, P., & Gigerenzer, G. (2001). Teaching Bayesian reasoning in less than two hours. *Journal of Experimental Psychology: General, 130,* 380–400.

Seidenberg, M. S. (1993). Connectionist models and cognitive theory. *Psychological Science, 4,* 228–235.

Seidenberg, M. S., Waters, G. S., Sanders, M., & Langer, P. (1984). Pre- and postlexical loci of contextual effects on word recognition. *Memory & Cognition, 12,* 315–328.

Sejnowski, T. J., & Rosenberg, C. R. (1987). Parallel networks that learn to pronounce English text. *Complex Systems, 1,* 145–168.

Semb, G. B., & Ellis, J. A. (1994). Knowledge taught in school: What is remembered? *Review of Educational Research, 64,* 253–286.

Shafir, E., & LeBoef, R. A. (2002). Rationality. *Annual Review of Psychology, 53,* 491–517.

Sharps, M. J., & Wertheimer, M. (2000). Gestalt perspectives on cognitive science and on experimental psychology. *Review of General Psychology, 4,* 315–336.

Shaughnessy, J, J. (1981). Memory monitoring accuracy and modification of rehearsal strategies. *Journal of Verbal Learning and Verbal Behavior, 20,* 216–230.

Shepard, R. N. (1967). Recognition memory for words, sentences, and pictures. *Journal of Verbal Learning and Verbal Behavior, 6,* 156–163.

Shepard, R. N. (1988). The imagination of the scientist. In K. Egan & D. Nadaner (Eds.), *Imagination and education* (pp. 153–185). New York: Teachers College Press.

Shepard, R. N., & Metzler, J. (1971). Mental rotation of three-dimensional objects. *Science, 171,* 701–703.

Shiffrin, R. M. (1988). Attention. In R. C. Atkinson, R. J. Hernstein, G. Lindzey, & R. D. Luce (Eds.), *Stevens' handbook of experimental psychology* (pp. 731–811). New York: Wiley.

Shiffrin, R. M., & Schneider, W. (1977). Controlled and automatic human information processing: II. Perceptual learning, automatic attending, and a general theory. *Psychological Review, 84,* 127–190.

Shulman, H. G. (1971). Similarity effects in short-term memory. *Psychological Bulletin, 75,* 399–415.

Silver, E. A. (1981). Recall of mathematical problem information: Solving related problems. *Journal for Research in Mathematics Education, 12,* 54–64.

Simon, H. A. (1957). *Models of man.* New York: Wiley.

Simon, H. A. (1974). How big is a chunk? *Science, 183,* 482–488.

Simon, H. A. (1983). Search and reasoning in problem solving. *Artificial Intelligence, 21,* 7–29.

Simon, H. A., & Gilmartin, K. (1973). A simulation of memory for chess positions. *Cognitive Psychology, 5,* 29–46.

Simon, H. A., & Newell, A. (1971). Human problem solving: The state of the theory in 1970. *American Psychologist, 26,* 145–159.

Simon, H. A., & Reed, S. K. (1976). Modeling strategy shifts in a problem-solving task. *Cognitive Psychology, 8,* 86–97.

Singer, J. L. (Ed.). (1990). *Repression and dissociation: Implications for personality theory, psychopathology, and health.* Chicago: University of Chicago Press.

Sloman, S. A. (1999). Rational versus Arational models of thought. In

R. J. Sternberg (Ed.), *The nature of cognition* (pp. 557–586). Cambridge, MA: MIT Press.

Sloman, S. A. (2002). Two systems of reasoning. In T. Gilovich, D. Griffin, & D. Kahneman (Eds.), *Heuristics and biases: The psychology of intuitive judgment* (pp. 379–396). Cambridge: Cambridge University Press.

Sloman, S. A., & Rips, L. J. (Eds). (1998). *Similarity and symbols in human thinking.* Cambridge, MA: MIT Press.

Sloutsky, V. M. (2003). The role of similarity in the development of categorization. *TRENDS in Cognitive Sciences, 7,* 246–251.

Slovic, P. (1997). Trust, emotion, sex, politics, and science: Surveying the risk assessment battlefield. *University of Chicago Legal Forum, 1997,* 59–99.

Slovic, P., & Lichtenstein, S. (1968). Relative importance of probabilities and payoffs in risk taking. *Journal of Experimental Psychology Monograph, 78* (3, Pt. 2).

Slovic, P., Finucane, M., Peters, E., & Gregor, D. G. (2002). The affect heuristic. In T. Gilovich, D. Griffin, & D. Kahneman (Eds.), *Heuristics and biases: The psychology of intuitive judgment* (pp. 397–420). Cambridge: Cambridge University Press.

Slovic, P., Fischhoff, B., & Lichtenstein, S. (1976). Cognitive processes and societal risk taking. In J. S. Carroll & J. W. Payne (Eds.), *Cognition and social behavior.* Hillsdale, NJ: Erlbaum.

Smith, E. E. (1978). Theories of semantic memory. In W. K. Estes (Ed.), *Handbook of learning and cognitive processes* (Vol. 6). Hillsdale, NJ: Erlbaum.

Smith, E. E. (1995). Concepts and categorization. In E. E. Smith & D. N. Osherson (Eds.) *An invitation to cognitive science* (Vol. 3, pp. 3–34). Cambridge, MA: MIT Press.

Smith, E. E., & Nielsen, G. D. (1970). Representation and retrieval processes in short-term memory: Recognition and recall of faces. *Journal of Experimental Psychology, 85,* 397–405.

Smith, E. E., Adams, N., & Schorr, D. (1978). Fact retrieval and the paradox of interference. *Cognitive Psychology, 10,* 438–464.

Smith, E. E., Shoben, E. J., & Rips, L. J. (1974). Structure and process in semantic memory: A featural model for semantic decision. *Psychological Review, 81,* 214–241.

Smith, E. R., & DeCoster, J. (2000). Dual–process models in social and cognitive psychology: Conceptual integration and links to underlying mechanisms. *Personality and Social Psychology Review, 4,* 108–131.

Smith, J. D., & Minda, J. P. (1998). Prototypes in the mist: The early epochs of category learning. *Journal of Experimental Psychology: Learning, Memory, and Cognition, 24,* 1411–1436.

Smith, M. E. (1983). Hypnotic memory enhancement of witnesses: Does it work? *Psychological Bulletin, 94,* 387–407.

Smith, S. M., Ward, T. B., & Schumacher, J. S. (1993). Constraining effects of examples in a creative generation task. *Memory & Cognition, 21,* 837–845.

Smyth, M. M., & Scholey, K. A. (1994). Interference in immediate spatial memory. *Memory & Cognition, 22,* 1–13.

Snyder, A. Z., Abdullaev, Y. G., Posner, M. I., & Raichle, M. E. (1995). Scalp electrical potentials reflect regional cerebral blood flow responses during processing of written words. *Proceedings of the National Academy of Sciences USA, 92,* 1689–1693.

Son, L. K., & Metcalfe, J. (2000). Metacognitive and control strategies in study-time allocation. *Journal of Experimental Psychology: Learning, Memory, and Cognition, 26,* 204–221.

Spence, C., Nicholls, M. E. R., & Driver, J. (2000). The cost of expecting events in the wrong sensory modality. *Perception & Psychophysics, 63,* 330–336.

Sperling, G. (1960). The information available in brief visual presentations. *Psychological Monographs, 74* (11, Whole No. 498).

Sperling, G. (1963). A model for visual memory tasks. *Human Factors, 5,* 19–31.

Sperling, G. (1967). Successive approximations to a model for short-term memory. *Acta Psychologica, 27,* 285–292.

Squire, L. R., & Knowlton, B. J. (1994). Memory, hippocampus, and brain systems. In M. Gazzaniga (Ed.), *The cognitive neurosciences.* Cambridge, MA: MIT Press.

Squire, L. R., & Zola, S. M. (1996). Structure and function of declarative and nondeclarative memory systems. *Proceedings of the National Academy of Science, 93,* 13515–13522.

Squire, L. R., & Zola, S. M. (1997). Amnesia, memory and brain systems. *Philosophical Transactions of the Royal Society of London B, 352,* 1663–1673.

Standing, L. (1973). Learning 10,000 pictures. *Quarterly Journal of Experimental Psychology, 25,* 207–222.

Stanfield, R. A., & Zwaan, R. A. (2001). The effect of implied orientation derived from verbal context on picture recognition. *Psychological Science, 12,* 153–156.

Stanovich, K. E. (1990). Concepts in developmental theories of reading skill: Cognitive resources, automaticity, and modularity. *Developmental Review, 10,* 72–100.

Stanovich, K. E., & West, R. F. (1983). On priming by a sentence context. *Journal of Experimental Psychology: General, 112,* 1–36.

Stanovich, K. E., & West, R. F. (2002). Individual differences in reasoning: Implications for the rationality debate? In T. Gilovich, D. Griffin, & D. Kahneman (Eds.), *Heuristics and biases: The psychology of intuitive judgment* (pp. 421–440). Cambridge: Cambridge University Press.

Stein, B. S., & Bransford, J. D. (1979). Constraints on effective elaboration: Effects of precision and subject generation. *Journal of Verbal Learning and Verbal Behavior, 18,* 769–777.

Sternberg, R. J. (1977). Component processes in analogical reasoning. *Psychological Review, 84,* 353–378.

Sternberg, R. J. (1998). Abilities are forms of developing expertise. *Educational Researcher, 27,* 11–20.

Sternberg, R. J. (Ed). (1999). *Handbook of creativity* (pp. 3–15). Cambridge, UK: Cambridge University Press.

Sternberg, R. J., & Davidson, J. E. (Eds.). (1994). *The nature of insight.* London: Bradford.

Sternberg, R. J., & Gardner, M. K. (1983). Unities in inductive reasoning. *Journal of Experimental Psychology: General, 112,* 80–116.

Sternberg, R. J., & Lubart, T. L. (1996). Investing in creativity. *American Psychologist, 51,* 677–688.

Sternberg, R. J., & Lubart, T. I. (1999). The concept of creativity: Prospects and paradigms. In R. J. Sternberg (Ed.), *Handbook of creativity* (pp. 3–15). Cambridge, UK: Cambridge University Press.

Sternberg, S. (1966). High-speed scanning in human memory. *Science, 153,* 652–654.

Sternberg, S. (1967a). Retrieval of contextual information from memory. *Psychonomic Science, 8,* 55–56.

Sternberg, S. (1967b). Two operations in character recognition: Some evidence from reaction time measurements. *Perception & Psychophysics, 2,* 45–53.

Stevenson, R. L. (1993). The strange case of Dr. Jekyll and Mr. Hyde. In I. Bell (Ed.), *Robert Louis Stevenson: The complete short stories* (Vol. 2, pp. 102–164). Edinburgh: Mainstream.

Stillings, N. A., Weisler, S. E., Chase, C. H., Feinstein, M. H., Garfield, J. L., & Rissland, E. L. (1995). *Cognitive science: An introduction.* Cambridge, MA: MIT Press.

Strayer, D. L., & Drews, F. A. (2007). Cell-phone-induced driver distraction. *Current Directions in Psychological Science, 16,* 128–131.

Strayer, D. L., & Johnston, W. A. (2001). Driven to distraction: Dual-task studies of simulated driving and conversing on a cellular telephone. *Psychological Science, 12,* 462–466.

Stroop, J. R. (1935). Studies of interferences in serial verbal reactions. *Journal of Experimental Psychology, 18,* 643–662.

Sulin, R. A., & Dooling, D. J. (1974). Intrusion of a thematic idea in retention of prose. *Journal of Experimental Psychology, 103,* 255–262.

Sutherland, N. S. (1968). Outlines of a theory of visual pattern recognition in animals and man. *Proceedings of the Royal Society, 171,* 297–317.

Sweller, J. (1988). Cognitive load during problem solving: Effects on learning. *Cognitive Science, 12,* 257–285.

Sweller, J. (2003). Evolution of human cognitive architecture. In B. Ross (Ed.), *The psychology of learning and motivation* (Vol. 43, pp. 215–266). San Diego: Academic Press.

Sweller, J., Mawer, R. F., & Ward, M. R. (1983). Development of expertise in mathematical problem solving. *Journal of Experimental Psychology: General, 112,* 639–661.

Swinney, D. A. (1979). Lexical access during sentence comprehension: Reconsideration of some context effects. *Journal of Verbal Learning and Verbal Behavior, 18,* 645–659.

Swinney, D. A., & Hakes, D. T. (1976). Effects of prior context upon lexical access during sentence comprehension. *Journal of Verbal Learning and Verbal Behavior, 15,* 681–689.

Swinney, D. A., & Osterhout, L. (1990). Inference generation during auditory language comprehension. In A. C. Graesser & G. H. Bower (Eds.), *Inferences and text comprehension.* San Diego: Academic Press.

Tanaka, J. W., & Taylor, M. (1991). Object categories and expertise: Is the basic level in the eye of the beholder? *Cognitive Psychology, 23,* 457–482.

Tarr, M. J., & Cheng, Y. D. (2003). Learning to see faces and objects. *TRENDS in Cognitive Sciences, 7,* 23–30.

Taylor, S. E., Pham, L. B., Rivkin, I. D., & Armor, D. A. (1998). Harnessing the imagination: Mental simulation, self-regulation, and coping. *American Psychologist, 53,* 429–439.

Technical Working Group for Eyewitness Evidence. (1999). *Eyewitness evidence: A guide for law enforcement* [Booklet]. Washington, DC: United States Department of Justice, Office of Justice Programs.

Thomas, A. K., & McDaniel, M. A. (2007). Metacomprehension for educationally relevant materials: Dramatic effects of encoding-retrieval interactions. *Psychonomic Bulletin & Review, 14,* 212–218.

Thompson, C. P., Skowronski, J. J., Larsen, S. F., & Betz, A. (1996). *Autobiographical memory: Remembering what and remembering when.* Mahwah, NJ: Erlbaum.

Thomas, N. J. T. (1999). Are theories of imagery theories of imagination? An active perception approach to conscious mental content. *Cognitive Science, 23,* 207–245.

Thorndyke, P. W. (1977). Cognitive structures in comprehension and memory of narrative discourse. *Cognitive Psychology, 9,* 77–110.

Thorndyke, P. W. (1984). Applications of schema theory in cognitive research. In J. R. Anderson & S. M. Kosslyn (Eds.), *Tutorials in learning and memory.* San Francisco: Freeman.

Toth, J. P., Reingold, E. M., & Jacoby, L. L. (1994). Toward a redefinition of implicit memory: Process dissociations following elaborative processing and self generation. *Journal of Experimental Psychology: Learning, Memory, and Cognition, 20,* 290–303.

Townsend, J. T. (1971). Theoretical analysis of an alphabetic confusion matrix. *Perception & Psychophysics, 9,* 40–50.

Trabasso, T., & Sperry, L. L. (1985). The causal basis for deciding importance of story events. *Journal of Memory and Language, 24,* 595–611.

Trabasso, T., & van den Broek, P. (1985). Causal thinking and the representation of narrative events. *Journal of Memory and Language, 24,* 612–630.

Trabasso, T., & Wiley, J. (2005). Goal plans of action and inferences during comprehension and narratives. *Discourse Processes, 39,* 129–164.

Treisman, A. M. (1960). Contextual cues in selective listening. *Quarterly Journal of Experimental Psychology, 12,* 242–248.

Treisman, A. M., & Geffen, G. (1967). Selective attention and cerebral dominance in responding to speech messages. *Quarterly Journal of Experimental Psychology, 19,* 1–17.

Treisman, A. M., & Gelade, G. (1980). A feature integration theory of attention. *Cognitive Psychology, 12,* 97–136.

Treisman, A. M., & Schmidt, H. (1982). Illusory conjunctions in the perception of objects. *Cognitive Psychology, 14,* 107–141.

Trueswell, J. C., & Tanenhaus, M. K. (1994). Toward a lexicalist framework for constraint-based syntactic-ambiguity resolution. In C. Clifton, K. Rayner, & L. Frazier (Eds.), *Perspectives in sentence processing* (pp. 155–179). Mahwah, NJ: Erlbaum.

Trueswell, J. C., Tanenhaus, M. K., & Kello, C. (1993). Verb-specific constraints in sentence processing: Separate effect of lexical preference from garden paths. *Journal of Experimental Psychology: Learning, Memory, and Cognition, 19,* 528–553.

Tulving, E. (1972). Episodic and semantic memory. In E. Tulving & W. Donaldson (Eds.), *Organization of memory* (pp. 381–403). New York: Academic Press.

Tulving, E. (1985). How many memory systems are there? *American Psychologist, 40,* 385–398.

Tulving, E. (2002). Episodic memory: From mind to brain. *Annual Review of Psychology, 53,* 1–25.

Tulving, E., & Thomson, D. M. (1973). Encoding specificity and retrieval processes in episodic memory. *Psychological Review, 80,* 352–373.

Tversky, A. (1972). Elimination by aspects: A theory of choice. *Psychological Review, 79,* 281–299.

Tversky, A., & Kahneman, D. (1973). Availability: A heuristic for judging frequency and probability. *Cognitive Psychology, 5,* 207–232.

Tversky, B. (1981). Distortions in memory for maps. *Cognitive Psychology, 13,* 407–433.

Tversky, B. (2005). Visuospatial reasoning. In K. J. Holyoak & R. G. Morrison (Eds.), *The Cambridge handbook of thinking and reasoning* (pp. 209–240). New York: Cambridge University Press.

Ullman, S. (2007). Object recognition and segmentation by a fragment-based hierarchy. *TRENDS in the Cognitive Sciences, 11*, 58–64.

Van Dantzig, S., Pecher, D., Zeelenberg, R., & Barsalou, L. W. (2008). Perceptual processing affects conceptual processing. *Cognitive Science, 32*, 579–590.

Van den Broek, P., Lorch, R. F., Linderholm, T., & Gusafson, M. (2001). The effect of readers' goals on inference generation and memory for texts. *Memory & Cognition, 29*, 1081–1087.

Van Dijk, T. A., & Kintsch, W. (1983). *Strategies of discourse comprehension.* Orlando, FL: Academic Press.

Vincente, K. J., & Wang, J. H. (1998). An ecological theory of expertise effects in memory recall. *Psychological Review, 105*, 33–57.

Vitali, M. R., & Romance, N. R. (2007). A knowledge-based framework for unifying content-area reading comprehension and reading comprehension strategies. In D. S. McNamara (Ed.). (2007). *Reading comprehension strategies: Theories, interventions and technologies.* New York: Taylor & Francis.

Vosniadou, S., & Ortony, A. (1989). *Similarity and analogical reasoning.* Cambridge, England: Cambridge University Press.

Wagner, S. M., Nusbaum, H., & Goldin-Meadow, S. (2004). Probing the mental representation of gesture: Is handwaving spatial? *Journal of Memory and Language, 50*, 395–407.

Walker, C. H., & Yekovich, F. R. (1987). Activation and use of script-based antecedents in anaphoric reference. *Journal of Memory and Language, 26*, 673–691.

Warrington, E. K., & Weiskrantz, L. (1968). New method of testing long-term retention with special reference to amnesic patients. *Nature, 217,* 972–974.

Warrington, E. K., & Weiskrantz, L. (1970). Amnesic syndrome: Consolidation or retrieval? *Nature, 228,* 628–630.

Wason, P. C., & Johnson-Laird, P. N. (1972). *Psychology of reasoning: Structure and content.* Cambridge, MA: Harvard University Press.

Wason, P. C., & Shapiro, D. (1971). Natural and contrived experience in a reasoning problem. *Quarterly Journal of Experimental Psychology, 23,* 63–71.

Watson, J. B. (1924). *Behaviorism.* New York: Norton.

Waugh, N. C., & Norman, D. A. (1965). Primary memory. *Psychological Review, 72,* 89–104.

Weaver, C. A., III (1993). Do you need a flash to form a flashbulb memory? *Journal of Experimental Psychology: General, 122,* 39–46.

Weber, E. U. (1998). Who's afraid of a little risk? New evidence for general risk aversion. In J. Shanteau, B. A. Mellers, & D. A. Schum (Eds.), *Decision research from Bayesian to normative systems: Reflections on the contributions of Ward Edwards.* Norwell, MA: Kluwer Academic.

Weber, E. U., & Hsee, C. (1998). Cross-cultural differences in risk perception, but cross-cultural similarities in attitudes towards perceived risk. *Management Science, 44,* 1205–1217.

Weisberg, R. W. (1993). *Creativity: Beyond the myth of genius.* New York: Freeman.

Weisberg, R. W., & Suls, J. M. (1973). An information processing model of Duncker's candle problem. *Cognitive Psychology, 4,* 255–276.

Wells, G. L., Malpass, R. S., Lindsay, R. C., Fisher, R. P., Turtle, J. W., & Fulero, S. M. (2000). From the lab to the police station: A successful application of eyewitness research. *American Psychologist, 55,* 581–598.

Wells, G. L., & Olson, E. A. (2003). Eyewitness testimony. *Annual Review of Psychology, 54,* 277–295.

Wernicke, C. (1874). *Der aphasische symptomencomplex.* Breslau, Germany: Franck U. Weigart.

Wickelgren, W. A. (1974). *How to solve problems.* New York: Freeman.

Wickens, C. D., & Kramer, A. (1985). Engineering psychology. *Annual Review of Psychology, 36,* 307–348.

Wickens, D. D. (1972). Characteristics of word encoding. In A. W. Melton & E. Martin (Eds.), *Coding processes in human memory.* Washington, DC: Winston.

Wickens, D. D., Born, D. G., & Allen, C. K. (1963). Proactive inhibition and item similarity in short-term memory. *Journal of Verbal Learning and Verbal Behavior, 2,* 440–445.

Widiger, T. A., & Clark, L. A. (2000). Toward *DSM-V* and the classification of psychopathology. *Psychological Bulletin, 126,* 946–963.

Widiger, T. A., & Trull, T. J. (1991). Diagnosis and clinical assessment. *Annual Review of Psychology, 42,* 109–133.

Wilson, M. (2002). Six views of embodied cognition. *Psychonomic Bulletin & Review, 9,* 625–636.

Winograd, E., & Neisser, U. (1992). *Affect and accuracy in recall: Studies of "flashbulb" memories.* New York: Cambridge University Press.

Wittgenstein, L. (1953). *Philosophical investigations.* (G. E. M. Anscombe, trans.). Oxford, England: Blackwell.

Wixted, J. T. (2004). The psychology and neuroscience of forgetting. *Annual Review of Psychology, 55,* 235–269.

Wright, W. F., & Bower, G. H. (1992). Mood effects on subjective probability assessment. *Organizational Behavior and Human Decision Processes, 52,* 276–291.

Wu, L. L. (1995). *Perceptual representation in conceptual combination.* Unpublished Dissertation, University of Chicago, Chicago.

Yerkes, R. M., & Dodson, J. D. (1908). The relation of strength of stimulus to rapidity of habit-formation. *Journal of Comparative Neurology and Psychology, 18,* 459–482.

Zacks, J. M. (2008). Neuroimaging studies of mental rotation: A meta-analysis and a review. *Journal of Cognitive Neuroscience, 20,* 1–19.

Zhao, Q., & Linderholm, T. L. (2008). Adult metacomprehension: judgment processes and accuracy constraints. *Educational Psychology Review, 20,* 191–206.

Zurif, E. B., Caramazza, A., Meyerson, R., & Galvin, J. (1974). Semantic feature representation for normal and aphasic language. *Brain and Language, 1,* 167–187.

Zwaan, R. A., & Radvansky, G. A. (1998). Situation models in language comprehension and memory. *Psychological Bulletin, 123,* 62–185.

Zwaan, R. A., & Yaxley, R. H. (2003). Spatial iconicity affects semantic relatedness judgments. *Psychonomic Bulletin & Review, 10,* 954–958.

NAME INDEX

A

Abdullaev, 11
Abelson, 230, 280
Adams, 151, 175–76
Adamson, 304
Adelson, 349
Ahn, 207
Alba, 297
Albrecht, 279
Alfonso-Reese, 206
Alibali, 265–66
Allen, 78
Altom, 205
Amador, 117
Anderson, 140, 227, 262–63, 275–76, 282, 289, 294, 332, 337–38, 349
Andrade, 95
Angin, 162
Anooshian, 148
Arguin, 28
Armor, 324
Armstrong, 189
Ashbrook, 148
Ashby, 205–6, 210
Ashcraft, 95, 99
Atkinson, 71, 75, 103–5, 110, 114, 134, 163–64
Atwood, 309, 335
Austin, 186–87
Awh, 92
Azur, 63

B

Baddeley, 91–97, 99, 107, 130–31, 139–40, 154, 172

Baer, 350
Bahrick, 102–3, 127, 177
Bain, 118, 127
Ball, 165, 167, 174
Ballie, 372
Balota, 282–83
Banerji, 330
Bar, 43, 112–13
Barbey, 233
Bargh, 59, 71
Barlett, 239
Barrett, 96, 98
Barsalou, 198–99, 232–35, 241
Bartlett, 5, 7, 228
Bassok, 324
Batterman, 224
Bauer, 210
Bazerman, 363
Beghetto, 350
Beilock, 62
Bell, 258
Bellezza, 183
Benjamin, 110
Bentall, 180–81
Bents, 66
Berkerian, 127
Berman, 99
Berry, 79, 183
Best, 183
Bettman, 374, 378
Beverly, 258
Biederman, 28–29, 343
Bjork, 108, 110, 112–13, 120, 122, 127
Black, 280
Blanchette, 332
Blaney, 360
Block, 293–94

Boden, 340
Bolger, 114
Boonthum, 295
Born, 78
Boucher, 177
Bourne, 188
Bower, 162, 213–14, 280, 360
Boyd, 375
Boyes-Braem, 190–92, 194
Boyle, 337
Brandimonte, 177
Bransford, 142, 151, 273–74, 276, 294, 327
Braun, 43
Brennan, 25–26, 145
Brewer, 228–29, 297
Britton, 292, 294
Broadbent, 5–6, 47 49, 51, 53, 57, 69
Broca, 247
Broekkamp, 108, 127
Brooks, 170–71
Brown, 114–15, 118, 143
Bruce, 114, 117
Bruner, 186–87
Bruner, J.S., 7
Buchanan, 349–50
Buckhout, 116, 118
Budiu, 262–63, 289
Burgess, 37
Burke, 114
Busey, 116, 118–19, 127

C

Cabeza, 236
Caccamise, 292, 294

SUBJECT INDEX

Note: Page numbers followed by "f" and "t" are figures and tables, respectively.